Sociomedia

Technical Communication and Information Systems
Edward Barrett, editor

The Nurnberg Funnel: Designing Minimalist Instruction for Practical Computer Skill, John M. Carroll, 1990

Hypermedia and Literary Studies, Paul Delany and George P. Landow, editors, 1991

Rhetoric, Innovation, Technology: Case Studies of Technical Communication in Technology Transfers, Stephen Doheny-Farina, 1992

Sociomedia: Multimedia, Hypermedia, and the Social Construction of Knowledge, edited by Edward Barrett, 1992.

Sociomedia

Multimedia, Hypermedia, and the Social Construction of Knowledge

edited by Edward Barrett

The MIT Press
Cambridge, Massachusetts
London, England

First MIT Press paperback edition, 1994

This book was set in Sabon by The MIT Press and was printed and bound in the United States of America.

Library of Congress Cataloging-in-Publication Data

Sociomedia : multimedia, hypermedia, and the social construction of
  knowledge / edited by Edward Barrett.
       p.   cm. — (Technical communication and information systems)
     "The majority of papers . . . were originally presented at the first
  conference on 'The Social Creation of Knowledge' . . . at MIT in
  Spring, 1991"—Acknowledgments.
    Includes bibliographic references and index.
    ISBN 0-262-02346-6 (HB), 0-262-52193-8 (PB)
    1. Hypermedia systems. 2. Knowledge, Sociology of.   I. Barrett,
  Edward.   II. Series.
  QA76.76.H92S63   1992
  378. 1'7346—dc20   92-16224
                                                                         CIP

Contents

Series Foreword

Technical Communication is one of the most rapidly expanding fields of study in the United States, Europe, and the Pacific rim, as witnessed by the growth of professional societies and degree-granting programs in colleges and universities as well as the evolving status of documentation specialists in industry. The writer, and writing, are no longer mere servants of science and engineering but rather partners in the complex matrix of forces that go into the construction of knowledge and information. And the audience is not a passive but an active player in this transaction. Furthermore, computational science has delivered a powerful tool for the creation, presentation, exchange, and annotation of text—so powerful that we speak not in terms of a text but rather of a hypertext, of seamless information environments that integrate a variety of media.

The MIT Press Series in Technical Communication and Information Systems will present advanced research in all aspects of this rapidly expanding field, including hypertext and hypermedia systems, online documentation, information architecture, interface design, graphics, collaborative writing in distributed networks, the role of the writer in industry, scientific and engineering writing, training and education in technical writing. Only in addressing such a wide range of topics do we begin to understand the complexity and power of this field of expertise.

Edward Barrett

Acknowledgments

Most of the of papers in this volume were originally presented at the first conference on "The Social Creation of Knowledge," which I directed at MIT in Spring 1991. The conference was funded by the Program in Writing and Humanistic Studies at MIT. Professor Kenneth R. Manning, Thomas Meloy Professor of Rhetoric and the History of Science at MIT, was head of the program then and he offered generous and enthusiastic support. In addition, I was fortunate to have my colleagues, Professor James Paradis (Program in Writing and Humanistic Studies, MIT), Professor Earll Murman (Head, Department of Aeronautics and Astronautics, MIT), Professor Tom Malone (Sloan School of Management and Head of the Center for Coordination Studies, MIT), and Professor Muriel Cooper (Director of the Visual Language Workshop at the Media Lab, MIT) serve on the advisory committee for this conference. I am also grateful to Teresa Ehling, Michael Sims, and Lorrie LeJeune of The MIT Press for their invaluable help in the production of this volume. I'd like to dedicate this collection to my students at MIT.

Sociomedia

Sociomedia: An Introduction

Edward Barrett

I am coining a new word, "sociomedia," to express what I believe is an important aspect of hypertext, hypermedia, and multimedia applications of computational technology in the university. These other terms stress attributes of the machine (hyper- or multi-media) or attributes of certain machinable functions calling on parts of a stored and retrievable database (hypertext, hypermedia). Either way, they make "machine" predominate in one's thinking rather than the ultimate worth of using the machine. "Sociomedia" calls attention to this ultimate value. "Sociomedia" suggests that computer media exist for "social" purposes: as means to objectify, exchange and collaborate, invoke, comment upon, modify, and remember thoughts and ideas (including "information"). "Sociomedia" implies that these social purposes obtain even when an individual sits in front of a computer and in essence talks to herself (Daiute 1984, Turkle 1984). The term also connotes that in bringing together various media to be manipulated through a display terminal we have a "society of texts" (shorthand for words, numbers, images, sounds) available to us (Barrett 1989). Computer media, in this perspective, present us with an "epistemological pluralism" (Turkle and Papert 1990). "Sociomedia," as a term, underscores the fact that computer media are ultimately social constructs themselves (Winograd and Flores 1986). In essence, then, "sociomedia" signifies that when we design computer media we are hardwiring a mechanism for the social construction of knowledge.

My notion of what paradigm best expresses the use of the computer in the university is not necessarily on the mind of any of the contributors to this volume. But I offer it here as a kind of subtext that I would like to have react with your reading of their contributions. Of course, many contributors to this volume knew something like this was in the works when they offered versions of these papers at an MIT conference I directed in April 1991. "The First MIT Conference on *The Social Creation of Knowledge*" presented exciting work in hypermedia/multimedia applications in the university. The conference subtitle contained the phrase "social construction" to highlight the value these new media brought to the highly human and social transactions that go on within a school environment.

Social construction in educational contexts has received much attention this past decade largely as a result of Kenneth Bruffee's writing on peer interaction in the classroom (Bruffee 1972, 1982, 1983, 1986). I use the phrase "social construction" in a very pragmatic fashion to remind us that the work we do in and outside the classroom involves people reading and talking and writing to each other in order to synthesize their thoughts about various topics using lots of information available to them. This process is a highly social one and computers can be used to support and enrich these social interactions resulting in the discovery of public and private knowledge. Hidden in this somewhat offhand statement of a complex philosophical issue is my distrust of theories of learning that equate knowledge with the accumulation of bits of information, or that equate thinking with purely associational acts of mind (Skinner 1961). The computer was Skinner's favorite teaching tool and hypertext systems are wonderful association machines, so it's not hard to see what direction one educational application of computers can take. In this introductory essay I'm just trying to remind us of another direction that parallels the associational one, but eventually peels off in another direction. I will use a Skinnerian reductionism later on in this essay, but only to isolate it and show how it can be used to get us somewhere else.

Perhaps the most concise statement of my use of "social construction" is Vygotsky's. In *Mind in Society*, he tries to demonstrate that "all the higher functions originate as actual relations between human individuals." These higher intellectual functions involve going beyond mere associational complexes of facts. Vygotsky, who is not writing about "the computer," terms this sort of associationalism "an object-oriented movement." For him, "object" was meant to be taken literally as things, facts, etc. Of course, I enjoy the new shade of meaning we can cast backward on to his phrase when we think of object-oriented programming as a metaphor for manipulations within and through the computer. For Vygotsky the higher functions of thought were movements (and notice the fluid metaphor he uses to characterize thought—moving, transformative, dynamic, changing, not fixed) "aimed at another person, a means of establishing relations," a synthesizing of "objects" and "complexes of objects" into something new, a thought embodied in the highly charged and fluid medium of language. For him, and for contemporary champions of social construction, thought is not necessarily a fixed, private, monolithic object; it is a complicated synthesis of facts, ideas, languages, "aimed at another person" and therefore subject to revision. That is, thought is an activity, a speaking of language, a communication which synthesizes anew familiar and unfamiliar objects into an inventive organic relationship. Thinking becomes a casting of a net (which is language), not merely a juggling of fixed objects—it is tentative (but testable), social both in the sense of grouping many things and of being articulated to an audience (and therefore responded to), "synthetic" or unifying (and therefore a personal possession—"original"—even in its social construction).

I like to quote from Vygotsky because his work calls to mind Coleridge's prose writings about faculties of mind in *The Friend* and *Aids to Reflection* (1971). In these works Coleridge tried to distinguish between the associative powers of the understanding and the unifying, synthesizing powers of the imagination. I think about Coleridge a lot when I think about hypermedia and multimedia because I believe Coleridge was the secret muse behind Nelson's visions of hypertext and his own hypertext system, Xanadu (Nelson 1980). I think these distinctions between associationalism and imagination aren't merely literary metaphors: they afflict Skinner and through him contemporary cognitive theory; they are present in the writing of Vannevar Bush on *memex* (Bush 1945) and Ted Nelson (and therefore on all developers of hypertext systems). Are we merely manipulating objects or supporting the synthesizing power of thinking in our applications of computational technologies in the university? This is, I believe, the central question we should be asking as developers and critics of these technologies.

The first conference on "The Social Creation of Knowledge" focused on applications of multimedia and information technologies to university research and teaching. MIT hosted a wide range of participants from across the United States, with many researchers from abroad. I mention this fact because we are in a recession and it is surprising to know that even though money is tight (and developments in this area require a lot of it) here was a large group of people voting with their feet, travelling considerable distances to hear and see what was happening in this field. Educational applications of computing technology, far from being a fad of the thick eighties, is an enduring concern in our schools. Educators know what this stuff can (and cannot) do, and they know the story is only just beginning. To cut back on research and development now would be tragic since we're just glimpsing some of the promise this work has for transforming education.

Of course, part of the problem with research in this area is the dependence of the university upon corporate sponsors. Not that the corporate world hasn't already been generous enough. But its realities are different from academic ones (at times) and cutbacks in industry choke off promising new research in the academy even when industry clearly knows how much of a return they get on their investment. Their "product" is a code, a text. Universities have always been the place to go to for training in textual strategies, it's what we—dare I say it?—what humanists—do best. The computer has textualized the workplace, says Shoshana Zuboff (1988). I say we must textualize the computer.

I chose to focus on university applications for several reasons. First, I wanted to see what my colleagues were up to so I could steal ideas and put them to work for me—for such is the real work of a conference. Second, universities are situated to support research into leading-edge technologies, so I assumed that this educational domain would be the right place to look first for important contributions. By saying this I don't mean to slight research efforts by faculty in elementary and secondary schools. A one-day conference, however, benefits from a tight focus, and I felt that broadening the scope to include all levels of education might diffuse our efforts. In general, I think applications and ideas discussed in this collection can have astonishing effects in elementary and secondary schools and that as a society we need to place much more value on those levels if we want to improve the overall educational performance of students in the university. Our current economy and social values, however, make it unlikely that educators in our elementary and secondary schools will get funding necessary to do much advanced research and development into computational support for education. Of course, these values can be changed: MIT, for example, has just launched a massive

K–12 educational initiative because faculty here (as elsewhere) know all too well how intimately connected all levels of schooling are.

Modeling the University in the Computer

A university can be viewed as a huge mechanism which supports various interactions. I mean nothing illiberal by this metaphor, only that a university can be defined "mechanically" for the purposes of modeling it in the computer. As I have discussed in Barrett and Paradis (1988) and Barrett (1988, 1989), it makes sense to use the protean power of the computer for simulation (Papert's phrase) in order to model observable phenomena in educational environments rather than programming for hypothetical mental activities whose supposed existence may dictate restrictive pedagogical practices. If we view the university as such a mechanism, then it can be defined (in no particular order of importance) by a specific geography, an infrastructure, an administration, groups of individuals who temporarily declare allegiances with one another, buildings, classrooms, walkways, loading zones, and of course libraries which perform a range of activities, including the preservation of hierarchies of knowledge, culture, truth, and information.

From a machine perspective, then, a university is like a *hypercontext*: a floating mass of different takes on what it is, any number of which may be invoked from time to time depending upon need. For the student or instructor during a scheduled class period, part of the hypercontext invoked is "classroom," defined as a certain physical setting and a set of particular activities. But submerged within this "real" momentary presence of the university are many other virtual presences: the registrar's office, campus security, the library and bookstores, the experiences that an individual brings into that room. Some of these virtual presences remain submerged—campus security, for example, generally has no role to play in a physics lecture except perhaps for checking on locked labs where the instructor conducts research which later informs her lectures. The library of course is a virtual presence—now and then invoked whenever a slide is shown or a reference to a text is made, or in the knowledgeable awareness of a student who has perhaps used the library for secondary reading, or as a place of repose to concentrate (or to sleep after pulling an all-nighter for an English class with a paper due). An effective lecturer tries to call up each necessary virtual presence in the classroom, as well as orchestrate other virtual presences students should invoke outside of class. This really is a balancing act: to get the right blend of information, sources, visuals, reading and writing assignments, trips to the library, rest time, peer interaction, and responsiveness within the momentary real georgraphy of the classroom; then to maintain some image of this presence once class is over, to keep students focused on course material, on development in a subject, on the larger conversation of knowledgeable peers which makes up a field of expertise and a culture (Bruffee 1982). Like all good hypertext systems, the university hyper-context is not ultimately a closed system; it is meant to leak all over the place as each virtual presence within the larger text of the place mixes with other parts of the ideal image.

It is not surprising, therefore, that we should go to computing technol-ogy to support these various calls on the hypercontext. "The computer" offers us an object to think with (Papert 1980), tools for embodying ideational realities before our eyes. Some of these "tools" are by-products of the computer's chief strengths: storing, classifying, compiling. It makes sense to use the power of a computational system to archive lots of information so that it can be more effectively ordered and retrieved. Since the chief window into the computer's storehouse of memory is the computer screen, it makes sense to have it communicate visually by means of pictures, animation, video. Since we still control that screen through a keyboard (and a mouse), it makes sense to use the computer to support other natural language operations. And since any number of computers can be linked together through distributed and local area networks, it makes sense to use the language processing capabilities of the computer to communicate our ideas to others.

Again, no surprises in anything said so far. But it is important to see how one machine can be used to model another one, and how "clean" that transcription from one to the other can be if we remain on the machine level. That is, if we can perceive a mechanical model working within what otherwise is said to be a highly intellectual enterprise—a mechanism which supports various observable processes that can be said to construct our sense or feeling of being in possession of knowledge—then we can map that machine to another machine without having to address mind itself. "Mind" can be deleted from the screen on which we design this transcription. And that is important because in a diverse culture such as ours we can not afford to adopt limiting definitions of human nature or human development. In essence, this is taking Skinner's notion of a teaching machine and turning it inside out.

I am perfectly aware of the reductionism implied in this description of a university. What about "learning" and "thought," "insight," "recognition of new ideas," "personal development," "cultural traditions," "history"? Where is education in this metaphor? Education remains where it should be—in the human domain (public and private) of sharing ideas and information through the medium of language. Education does not sit in a black box. Education is not hardwired in. Education is not algorithmic. Since each of you reading this paragraph has a different perspective on the meaning of "education" or "learning" and on the processes involved in "getting an education," think of the hybris in trying to capture education in a programmable function, in a displayable object, in a "teaching machine." Education is a virtual realm: a "being in essence or effect but not in fact" (from my on-line *Webster's Dictionary*), addressable, and only represented in part at any time, always a bigger conception than we can accomodate, yet because of its fullness, always enlarging whatever attempts we make to embody it in fact. Or, if this language is too fancy: education is like the biggest threat to a computer system—it is like a virus, combining with our codes, mutating, changing the individual's life in various ways, with uncertain results. So you see, I use reductionism in order to preserve value.

Experience and Presentation

On one point, however, I am not tempted to be reductionistic. Information is necessary but not sufficient to education. What do I mean? I have been developing the idea that "the computer" is best employed to model another machine, and that we can simplify our conception of something as complex as "education" by looking at the various contexts in which "it" "takes place" as if they were "mechanisms" that operate in various observable ways. And I think we best employ the computer in education to simulate and support those processes rather than in attempting to program the computer to program the student.

Then why am I so concerned about this word "information"? Because our words, hypertext, hypermedia, and multimedia focus attention on manipulation of information-objects or on descriptions of the media of transmission rather than on the goal of such manipulation. In this way they are terms that follow—not challenge—the early history of the word "book," frequently seen as the thing which computation will somehow kill off. For, at least in Greek and Latin and Germanic languages, the word "book" also, at root, refers to the means for preserving and displaying transcriptions upon it (beech trees or papyrus), and later to the actual messages or codes themselves which tended to be runic magical inscriptions or official, governmental notices, finally personal constructions. Alan Kay was following this tradition with his term "Dynabook." Computers chew up and spit out information in all kinds of fascinating ways. The temptation is to say that our students "know" something because they see a representation of "knowledge" on a computer screen, perhaps in color and 3-D, with video and sound accompaniment, or perhaps because an "expert system" has retrieved some pieces of information in a timely fashion. None of my colleagues would say students "know" or "have learned" anything simply by being able to access various chunks of information somewhere "out there" in a database. But everyone I know says that students should have access to those interesting chunks of information so that they can think and discuss topics in sophisticated ways.

Computational technology complicates this seemingly simple transaction between an individual and (for want of a better general term) texts (shorthand for words, numbers, images, sounds) because computers destroy textual integrity. The computer can compile a text every which way but up if you want it to. University scholars use texts to talk about many other things—or talk about the many other things that go into a single text (the word itself comes from a root meaning "to weave"). Either way, some sort of mapping out (or in) is being performed. "Information" about a text becomes as important as the primary text itself. The equation: power of the computer to dish out information in many different combinations + "traditional" approaches to textual scholarship + academic enthusiasm for the French school of thought which de-centers, deconstructs, and interleaves the text with other texts and readings = deep involvement with the concept of hypertext.

But is information processing education? Is it knowledge? Hypertext or hypermedia or multimedia are terms which describe machine (and machinable) operations, and, secondarily, performances of a "text" (and again that word is shorthand for words, numbers, images, sounds). Hypertext, hypermedia, and multimedia are unlike their cousin, the book, in that they are still too young, too close to their etymological root meanings to support the truth behind a book—that it is an address to an audience, an address which over time and space develops ideas out of information and (and this is easy to miss) sheds information from the development of an idea. A book is not a proto-hypertext.

But a hypertext is a proto-utterance.

Hypertext is an embodiment in a machine of the social construction of knowledge in the human domain of thought and language. Hypertext, hypermedia, multimedia support all of the functions that define social construction: the collection and classifying of texts, the review and deconstruction of these texts, the exchange of texts among peers, the empowerment of the individual through the ability to create marginalia (which may eventually take center stage). And computer media can do all these things quickly, with fine or coarse-grained thoroughness, and with complete documentation of every interaction with a text or another individual. In essence, applications discussed in this volume constitute a kind of extended conversation among knowledgeable peers, a conversation that can extend infinitely backward (through other recorded texts) and infinitely horizontally through a network of individuals currently making up a culture or subculture. "Sociomedia" denotes these social and meaning-making functions better than the self-referential terms, hypertext, hypermedia, and multimedia. "Sociomedia" forces us to look outward from the machine into the complex interaction of human relationships which define "university" and "education," human relationships that are the real content of all educational technology.

References

Barrett, Edward. 1988. "A New Paradigm for Writing with and for the Computer," in Barrett, E., ed. *Text, ConText, and HyperText: Writing with and for the Computer*. Cambridge, MA: MIT Press.

Barrett, Edward. 1989. "Thought and Language in a Virtual Environment," in Barrett, Edward, ed. *The Society of Text: Hypertext, Hypermedia, and the Social Construction of Information*. Cambridge, MA: MIT Press.

Barrett, Edward, and J. Paradis. 1988. "Teaching Writing in an On-line Classroom." *Harvard Educational Review* 58: 154–171.

Bruffee, Kenneth, A. 1972. "A New Emphasis in College Teaching: The Context of Learning." *Peabody Journal of Education* 50.

Bruffee, Kenneth, A. 1982. "Liberal Education and the Social Justification of Belief." *Liberal Education*. 68: 95–114.

Bruffee, Kenneth. A. 1983. "Writing and Reading as Collaborative or Social Acts: The Argument from Kuhn and Vygotsky," in *The Writer's Mind: Writing as a Mode of Thinking*, ed. Janice N. Hays et al. Urbana: NCTE.

Bruffee, Kenneth, A. 1986. "Social Construction, Language, and the Authority of Knowledge: A Bibliographic Essay." *College English* 48: 773–790.

Bush, V. 1945. "As We May Think." *Atlantic Monthly* 7: 101–108.

Coleridge, Samuel T. 1971. *The Friend*, in *The Collected Works of Samuel Taylor Coleridge*, ed. Kathleen Coburn. Princeton: Princeton UP.

Coleridge, Samuel T. 1971. *Aids to Reflection*, in *The Collected Works of Samuel Taylor Coleridge*, ed. Kathleen Coburn. Princeton: Princeton UP.

Daiute, Collette. 1983. "The Computer as Stylus and Audience." College Composition and Communication 34: 134–145.

Daiute, Collette. 1984. "Can the Computer Stimulate Writers' Inner Dialogues?" in Wresch, W. *The Computer in Composition: A Writer's Tool*. Urbana: NCTE.

Nelson, T. H. 1980. "Replacing the Printed Word: A Complete Literary System." IFIP Proceedings. pp. 1013–1023.

Papert, Seymour. 1980. *Mindstorms: Children, Computers, and Powerful Ideas*. New York: Basic Books.

Skinner, B. F. 1961. "Why We Need Teaching Machines." *Harvard Educational Review* 3: 377–398.

Turkle, Sherry R. 1984. *The Second Self: Computers and the Human Spirit*. New York: Simon and Schuster.

Turkle, Sherry, and Seymour Papert. 1990. "Epistemological Pluralism: Styles and Voices Within the Computer Culture." *SIGNS: Journal of Women in Culture and Society* 16: 128–157.

Vygotsky, L. S. 1978. *Mind in Society: The Development of Higher Psychological Processes*. Michael Cole, et al, ed. Cambridge, MA: Harvard UP.

Vygotsky, L. S. 1986. *Thought and Language*. Eugenia Hanfmann and Gertrude Vakar, ed. Cambridge, MA: MIT Press.

Wertsch, James V. *Vygotsky and the Social Formation of Mind*. Cambridge, MA: Harvard UP, 1986.

Winograd, Terry, and F. Flores. 1986. *Understanding Computers and Cognition: A New Foundation for Design*. Reading, MA: Addison-Wesley.

Zuboff, Shoshana. 1988. *In the Age of the Smart Machine: The Future of Work and Power*. New York: Basic Books.

I Perspectives . . .

1

Education by Engagement and Construction: A Strategic Education Initiative for a Multimedia Renewal of American Education

Ben Shneiderman

We can renew American education by offering students the opportunity to develop skills, experiences, and values they need to become successful individuals, workers, family members, and societal contributors. They can have fun while learning and gain satisfaction from meaningful accomplishments. The Strategic Education Initiative is a five year, $100 billion plan to help transform American education, provide powerful tools for teachers, promote advanced technology, and make schools more meaningful.

Dynamic multimedia, novel user interfaces, powerful computing facilities, and international networks can empower teachers and students in remarkable ways. These technologies can support teachers in fostering student engagement with peers and outsiders, and construction of projects that contribute to a better world. These approaches also promote each student's self-worth while learning the subject material. I believe that as teacher effectiveness increases and learning becomes interactive, creation generates satisfaction, process and product become entwined, and cooperation builds community.

Introduction

Government leaders, corporate executives, think-tank gurus, and academic social commentators have expressed their concerns over the decline of American education. This negative attention seems to engage journalists and media moguls, while corporate public relations staffers churn out the good news about how the business community is already doing its fair share. Cover stories in *Fortune*, *Newsweek*, and *Business Week* are helpful in focusing attention, but they are not the solution.

Renewing American education is a difficult job, but it must be done to preserve a productive and competitive economy, to enrich the life of each citizen; and to create a vital, safe, healthy, and meaningful society. This article is a call to action from two directions: a top-down, long-term national plan for a Strategic Education Initiative and a bottom-up local idea that each teacher can begin to apply immediately. There are many other directions, levels, and paths by which change can be pursued, but this article concentrates on the two stated directions.

These directions are oriented around the computing technologies of multimedia workstations, high-speed networks, and vast hypermedia databases of text, images, video, sound, music, maps, etc. There is always a danger of trying to solve social problems with technology, but I hope I have avoided the obvious pitfalls. The United States has a history of successfully blending social visions with technology. In the 19th century, immigration and western expansion were coupled with the development of canals and railroads, while the the 20th century highways and airports were the focus of major federal initiatives. It seems possible that computing technology and data highways might be the analogous paths for the 21st century.

Part I: My Star Wars Plan: A National Strategic Education Initiative

A major national commitment to education would engage the energy and enthusiasm of most Americans, just as the space program did during its glory days of the 1960s and 1970s. During that time science and engineering Ph.D. production soared while lower school children were entranced by manned travel to the moon, color photos of the whole earth, and pursuit of Martian life forms. The drop-off in support for spaceflight had a strong relationship to the corresponding drop-off in graduate science study. Further cuts in education programs and a failure to create compelling national goals in science and technology (the superconducting super-collider is too remote from most people's concerns or comprehension) have contributed to the decline.

Therefore I propose a bold national Strategic Education Initiative (SEI) (Shneiderman, 1989), patterned on the concept of the Strategic Defense Initiative (SDI) or the Strategic Computing Initiative (SCI). The

SDI was quickly labelled the Star Wars Plan because of the space-based battle station imagery reminiscent of the George Lucas movies. Mine is also a Star Wars Plan but it is linked to the image of Luke Skywalker's wise and gentle teacher Obi-Wan Kenobi (played by Alec Guinness) rather than to the terrifying Darth Vader. Instead of 1,000 space-based battle stations, I propose at least 10,000,000 school-based edu-stations, enough to have one for every five students, plus appropriate teacher training and software.

The focus of the Strategic Education Initiative would be on teacher-oriented tools for educational computing, including hardware, software, networks, teacher training, and research. The goal would be to invigorate education in a dramatic way by spending $100 billion over a five-year period. The impact would be to help teachers to empower students with a sense of their own capabilities in this emerging multimedia and networked world (Soloway, 1991). If the SEI is effective, students would be prepared with necessary skills for work and for responsible membership in multiple communities.

Beyond the benefits of training for millions of teachers, major spin-offs would include the stimulation of user interface research, refinement of educational evaluation, expansion of computer hardware manufacturing, development of software tools, and the growth of the whole computing industry. Improvements would be applicable to many fields beyond educational computing, such as home and office automation, medical informatics, image processing, tele-operation, scientific data analysis, engineering workstations, desktop publishing, and library information services.

Undoubtedly, the investment, impact, and ideas of the Strategic Education Initiative would lead to improving U.S. competitiveness internationally. At a time when the U.S. dominance of the computing industry is being vigorously challenged, these benefits to competitiveness could be helpful by stimulating user interface research and development (Shneiderman, 1987).

The draft budget in figure 1.1 is a rough estimate that would have to be refined and detailed, but the essential notion is to provide schools with funds to acquire and apply hardware, networks, software, training, etc. Leading universities would have larger amounts to conduct research,

20	Leading Universities	x $100,000,000	=	$ 2,000,000,000
200	Universities	x 20,000,000	=	4,000,000,000
2,000	Colleges	x 4,000,000	=	8,000,000,000
30,000	High Schools	x 800,000	=	24,000,000,000
80,000	Lower Schools	x 300,000	=	24,000,000,000
	National Data Highway			20,000,000,000
	Information Resource (Library of Congress)			10,000,000,000
10	Research Centers	x 800,000,000	=	8,000,000,000
			TOTAL	$100 billion

Figure 1.1
Draft budget for 5 years

evaluate projects, and develop advanced prototypes that could be applied by others. Regional partnerships among colleges of various sizes could share specialized resources (such as image databases or MIDI music synthesizers) and disseminate ideas, curricula, software, etc. High schools and lower schools would receive lesser amounts, but volume purchases would enable acquisition of adequate numbers of sufficiently powerful educational workstations. Collaboration with universities and regional research centers would provide access to emerging research results.

As a rough estimate, the price of a networked multimedia personal computer for high schools and lower schools should fall to under $1000 within five years, assuming high volume production runs. More powerful workstations at the university level might still be in the $5000 to $10,000 range, but the average cost per student workstation should be well below $5,000.

Construction of a high-speed National Data Highway to permit remote computing, communication, collaboration, and image access is a viable goal, although it will certainly take more than five years to complete (Carlitz, 1991). Allocation of $20 billion would get this project off to a fine start. The current High Performance Computing Initiative (Senate Bill 272, 102nd Congress) is a step in this direction, but it is likely to provide only about $1 billion. The construction of an online Library of Congress is another major goal that will take more than five years, but $10 billion should get this project going. The current Library of Congress public access online catalog could be made available nationally within five years; getting the texts and images online will take several decades. This goal may sound grand or even extreme, but it also seems inevitable and only a matter of our deciding when it should happen.

Such a utopian vision and such a large expenditure should be seriously questioned and challenged. There are complex and difficult administrative, legal, economic, and social hurdles that need to be overcome, but the benefits seem to be enormous. The cost may seem incredible in an age when school budgets are being trimmed and university salaries are declining, but $100 billion over five years would be much less than 1% of the GNP, about 2% of the federal budget, and less than 10% of the Defense Department budget. Strategies for business participation and state and local control to ensure diversity must be developed. However, if the SEI is successful the payoff might be several times the investment in terms of economic productivity and reduced unemployment costs.

A strong commitment to education is a vote of confidence in the future and a gift to our children. I say "let's do it!" But more than hardware or software we need to inspire teachers and children. For this I propose, in part II, a new vision of what education might become.

Part II: The Local Idea: Education by Engagement and Construction

Imagine that a national leader emerges who brings about the Strategic Education Initiative and sees to it that all the financial, legal, administrative, and technical problems are solved. Imagine that every school, college, and university has enough computing workstations to allow teachers and students essentially unlimited access to software, databases, networks, and electronic mail. Now the question becomes: How do we restructure education?

The old world of education often consisted of listening to lectures, memorizing facts, using drill and practice to acquire skills, and accessing information in books to complete worksheets. More facts meant higher grades and was somehow better. This theme was suggested by the Cultural Literacy movement of Hirsch (Hirsch, Kett, and Trefil, 1988), who claimed that there were 5,000 key concepts that every informed citizen should master. While there are undoubtedly facts, phrases, and names that are important to learn, the emphasis seems wrong. This approach may have been suited to the industrial age of assembly line productivity, but in the third wave (Toffler, 1980, 1990) electronic age of the global village (McLuhan, 1964) a new vision seems necessary. Content is certainly important, standards are vital, but current educational approaches are failing.

Businesses have learned, some more quickly than others, that mere numbers of workers is not a correlate of productivity and that fragmented assembly line thinking is archaic. A few well-trained workers who function as an effective team are more valuable than dozens or even hundreds of less competent and poorly organized individuals. Leaders of successful companies understand that creative solutions, flexible plans, and competent relationship skills are key ingredients for modern organizations. When corporate placement officers call me for a reference on a student they ask whether the candidate works well with others, handles responsibilities, accepts guidance, and is a self-starter. They want to know about process and whether the candidate has been a producer.

To educate students for the modern world of rapid change and teamwork we need to give teachers appropriate tools to increase their effectiveness (Shackelford, 1990) and related tools for students to exercise their creative powers. Computing a correlation coefficient is an archaic skill when computers do that task, but understanding how to present a statistical report on cancer causes to a teenage smoker is a modern challenge. Teachers can make a difference by restructuring the school experience away from individual fact acquisition towards team-building experiences with project-oriented processes that address the stated educational goals of school districts and university curriculum committees.

Defining Engagement

The theme I have chosen to represent this new environment is "Education by Engagement and Construction." By engagement, I mean to convey *interaction with people*. Engagement has two complementary components: students use the world as a rich resource for learning experiences, and students attempt to produce some positive impact on the world. The purpose of learning is not to store facts in the student's head, but to *engage with people*. So instead of the isolationist goal of learning Spanish grammar, the engagement goal is *to give a guided tour of your school to someone in Spanish*. Instead of memorizing the order of succession of the kings and queens of France prior to the revolution, the goal is *to explain to classmates* the background of Charles Dickens's *Tale of Two Cities*.

An important part of engagement is information gathering from people outside of the school environment. Instead of limiting research to books in a library, students should interview, in person or by phone, appropriate peronalities. Imagine how a report on World War II would be enriched by *an interview with a D-day participant in a retirement home*. An economics report becomes more real after *a discussion with a local banker*, a political science project becomes livelier after *an interview with a local or state politician*, and biology becomes more meaningful after *a visit with a hospital lab technician*. The experience of speaking to adults at work should be educational, the process can improve social and communication skills, and the discussions are potentially illuminating for everyone involved.

The second aspect of engagement is the cooperation among students to complete projects. By working in teams, students can take on more ambitious projects and they must make their plans explicit in order to collaborate. Engagement with fellow students can help make learning more lively and more effective as a model for the future world of work, family, and community.

Now imagine the rich environment of computers and networks created by the Strategic Education Initiative. The engagement can transpire over the networks. Bulletin boards can provide sources of information and contacts for personal encounters. Networks can enable students working on similar projects at different schools to collaborate. For example, approximately 10,000 elementary school children were involved in a project to collect and exchange acid rain data. High school students in the U.S. were paired with Russian students for e-mail exchanges. Hundreds of sixth graders simultaneously measured the length of a shadow and exchanged data in an attempt to measure the diameter of the earth.

Electronic mail enables contact with key figures in many fields. For example, students in my graduate seminar on user interface design did the common task of reading research journal papers and critiquing them, but the task took on heightened interest when they were required to send their critiques to the authors by e-mail. The discussions seemed deeper, the usual offhand attacks became softened in tone but sharpened in insight. The replies and contact with leading professionals gave my students a sense of importance and maturity. Similarly, I offered my e-mail address to Prof. Chris Borgman at UCLA who was using one of my books for her user interface course. When her students sent me comments on my book, I replied with my reactions, and saved their insights as input for my current revision. My undergraduates were delighted that they could contact students and professors at other universities for a comparison of university computing policies and for a study of uses of computer supported classrooms.

Defining Construction

The second part of my theme is construction, by which I mean that *students create a product from their collaboration.* This may not seem so different from current expectations of writing a computer program or a term paper. But when coupled with the engagement theme, I mean *constructing something of importance to someone else.* Instead of having database management students write the same safe class project, I have had students prepare database management programs for the University's bus service, generate a scheduling program for a local TV station, prepare an online information retrieval program for a nearby suicide hotline, or develop record keeping software for a student Scuba Club.

Instead of writing a term paper on uses of computers by the elderly, two of my students in a Computers and Society course conducted computing classes for elderly residents of a local apartment complex. Then the students prepared a report for the director of the complex, with a copy for me to grade. Several teams of students worked with their high schools or elementary schools to suggest ways to improve the use of computers. Another student wrote computer programs to manage lists of volunteers and contributors for a local soup kitchen that serves homeless people. One student challenged the University's legal policy about student access and privacy rights with respect to their accounts. Another student wrote a handbook about educational software for parents of deaf children, while another pair of students prepared a hypertext guide to coping with computer software viruses. Computer tools enable construction of ambitious projects; there is a special sense of pride when students produce an animated hypertext, laser-printed report, or collect/disseminate data through networks.

In addition to these semester-long projects, there are many opportunities for short-term construction projects ranging from the traditional programming exercise done as a team project to class presentations by students on normal lecture material. Requiring a team of two students to present a topic to the entire class can make it appealing for the whole class, and the designated students will be likely to take their responsibility seriously. In programming classes, it is possible to require students to read each other's computer programs and to share the grade 80% to the author and 20% to the reviewer. Code reading has been shown to be effective in professional and student environments. Having students read each other's written reports is a key technique in the emerging collaborative education movement and a well-established idea for professionals. Turning work into a communal experience is made more practical by the presence of word processors/text editors because making suggested revisions has become easy.

Cooperative Groups in General Studies

College-level computer science has been my academic domain, so it might seem that these notions are only suitable for that age group and subject. However, I feel that Engagement and Construction are appropriate at most ages and in most fields. In fact, related ideas have been proposed by many reports on education during the past decade. The Final Report of the Study Group on the Conditions of Excellence in American Higher Education, National Institute of Education wrote that "active modes of teaching require that students be inquirers—creators, as well as receivers of knowledge." That report also stressed projects, internships, discussion groups, collaborations, simulations, and presentations (figure 1.2). Similarly, the Principles for Good Practice in Undergraduate Education presented by the American Association for Higher Education (figure 1.3) pushed for cooperation among students and active learning projects. Multiple strategies for cooperative learning groups have been carefully developed and evaluated (Millis, 1990) and software to support cooperation has become a hot topic (Ellis, Gibbs, and Rein, 1991).

1) Student Involvement
- involving students in faculty research projects
- encouraging internships
- organizing small discussion groups
- requiring in-class presentations and debates
- developing simulations
- creating opportunities for individual learning projects
2) High Expectations
3) Assessment and Feedback
Involvement in Learning: Realizing the Potential of American Higher Education
Final Report of the Study Group on the Conditions of Excellence in American
Higher Education, National Institute of Education, 1984

Figure 1.2
Conditions for excellence in undergraduate education

Encourage Student-Faculty Contact
Encourage Cooperation Among Students
Encourage Active Learning
Give Prompt Feedback
Emphasize Time on Task
Communicate High Expectations
Respect Diverse Talents and Ways of Learning
American Association for Higher Education, 1987

Figure 1.3
Principles for good practice in undergraduate education

Exploration and Creation

Part of the engagement concept is to provide students with the chance to experience the challenge of exploratory research and the satisfaction of accomplishment. I believe that imaginative teachers can find ways in every discipline and at every grade to create an atmosphere of exploration and challenge. Whether collecting scientific data or studying Greek theater, there are open questions that students can attempt to answer. My undergraduate students regularly conduct empirical studies related to my research in user interface design and their work is published in scientific journals. It is true that only one in ten projects leads to a publishable result and that I or others must participate in a final revision, but the atmosphere of exploration at the frontier of research produces a high level of engagement even for introverted and blasé computer science students at my state university.

The concepts of exploration and creation are also well-established in the education literature from John Dewey to Seymour Papert (1980). Piaget wrote that "knowledge is not a copy of reality. To know an object, to know an event is not simply to look at it and make a mental copy, or image, of it. To know an object is to act on it. To know is to modify, to transform the object, and to understand the process of transformation, and as a consequence to understand the way the object is constructed" (1964). The phrase "discovery learning" conveys the key notion that "whatever knowledge children gain they create themselves; whatever character they develop they create themselves," as Wees wrote in his aptly titled book *Nobody Can Teach Anybody Anything* (1971).

The pleasure of learning can be a powerful attraction, if teachers and students arrive with positive expectations. Furthermore, education can provide a constructive sense of community where respect for individual differences and diversity fluorishes. To promote the experience of cooperation, facilitated by computer networks, rather than competition (Eisler, 1987; Cohn, 1986), partnerships, team projects, class workshops are recommended.

Summary

I believe that renewing American education can be a positive experience for teachers, students, and parents. Much creativity is needed to implement Education by Engagement and Construction (figure 1.4), but my explorations and reports from colleagues are encouraging. There are many problems such as how to scale up small class projects to lecture sections with hundreds of students, how to preserve the breadth of content coverage that is currently required by many school districts, and how to evaluate and grade students.

More problems await us, but the process of change is engaging, and the chance to construct a vigorous educational environment is alluring. As George Leonard (1968) wrote, "Ways can be worked out to provide a new apprenticeship for living, appropriate to a technological age of constant change . . . What then is the purpose, the goal of education? A large part of the answer may well be what men of this civilization have longest feared and most desired: the achievement of moments of ecstasy."

1) Students want to:

Create	Communicate
Engage	Help
Explore	Build
Discover	Participate

2) And construct products by:

Writing	(poems, plays, essay, novels, newspapers)
Drawing	(pictures, logos, portraits, birthday cards)
Composing	(music, songs, operas, hypermedias)
Designing	(buildings, maps, games, animations, family tree)
Planning (class trips, vacations, parties, elections)	

3) Teachers should promote:

Engaging in the world	(lobbying a Senator)
Helping where needed	(teaching computing to the elderly)
Caring for others	(raising funds for the homeless)
Communicating ideas	(writing to a newspaper editor)
Organizing events	(preparing a bake sale)

4) Multimedia technologies can empower students:

Enable students to create multimedia reports
Encourage media supported class presentations
Develop communication through electronic mail
Provide experience in searching databases
Explore information networks
Promote use of word processing, drawing, spreadsheets, . . .

5) Project orientation enhances engagement:

Help an elementary school to improve computer use
Teach elderly word processing
Find or develop aids for a handicapped person
Revise university policy on information protection
Improve university administration, registration, . . .
Evaluate and suggest improvement to ATMs,
library systems, voicemail, . . .
Write guide for parents about kids' software
Review workplace practices for computer users

Figure 1.4
Outline of education by engagement and construction

Acknowledgments

I appreciate the thoughtful comments made on drafts of this paper by Jim Greenberg, John Kohl, Delia Neuman, Anthony Norcio, Kent Norman, Catherine Plaisant, and Sherry Turkle. I am also grateful to Teresa Ehling, Michael Sims, and Lorrie LeJeune of the MIT Press for their invaluable help in the production of this volume. My thanks also go to Ed Barrett who had the courage to organize this innovative conference.

References

American Association for Higher Education, 1987. *Principles for Good Practice in Undergraduate Education.*

Carlitz, Robert D., 1991. Common knowledge: Networks for kindergarten through college, *EDUCOM Review* 26, 2, (Summer 1991), 25-28.

Cohn, Alfie, 1986. *No Contest*, Houghton Miflin Company, Boston, MA.

Eisler, Riane, 1987. *The Chalice and the Blade: Our History, Our Future*, Harper and Row Publishers, San Francisco, CA.

Ellis, C. A., Gibbs, S. J., and Rein , G. L., 1991. Groupware: Some issues and experiences, *Communications of the ACM* 34, 1, (January 1991), 39-58.

Fortune Special Issue, 1990. Saving Our Schools, Spring 1990, New York, NY.

Hirsch, Jr., E. D., Kett, Joseph F., and Trefil, James, 1988. *The Dictionary of Cultural Literacy*, Houghton Mifflin Company, Boston, MA.

Leonard, George B., 1968. *Education and Ecstasy*, Dell Publishing Co., New York, NY.

McLuhan, Marshall, 1964. *Understanding Media: The Extensions of Man*, McGraw-Hill Book Company, New York, NY.

Millis, Barbara J., 1990. Helping faculty build learning communities through cooperative groups. In Hilsen, L. (Editor), *To Improve the Academy: Resources for Student Faculty and Institutional Development*, 10, New Forums Press, Stillwater, OK, pp. 43-58.

National Institute of Education, 1984. *Involvement in Learning: Realizing the Potential of American Higher Education*, Final Report of the Study Group on the Conditions of Excellence in American Higher Education.

Papert, Seymour, 1980. *Mindstorms: Children, Computers, and Powerful Ideas*, Basic Books, Inc., New York, NY.

Piaget, Jean, 1964. Cognitive development in children: The Piaget papers. In R. E. Ripple and V. N. Rockcastle (Editors), *Piaget rediscovered: A report of the conference on cognitive studies and curriculum development*, Ithaca School of Education, Cornell University, pp. 6-48.

Shackelford, Russell L., Educational computing: Myths versus method: Why computers haven't helped and what we can do about it, *Proc. Conference on Computers and the Quality of Life*, SIGCAS, ACM, New York, NY (1990), 139-146.

Shneiderman, Ben, 1987. *Designing the User Interface: Strategies for Effective Human-Computer Interaction*, Addison-Wesley Publ. Co., Reading, MA.

Shneiderman, Ben, 1989. My Star Wars Plan: A Strategic Education Initiative, *The Computing Teacher 16*, (7), p 5.

Soloway, Elliot, 1991. Quick, Where do the Computers Go?, *Communications of the ACM 34*, (2), 29-33.

Toffler, Alvin, 1980. *The Third Wave*, William Morrow and Company, New York, NY.

Toffler, Alvin, 1990. *Powershift*, William Morrow and Company, New York, NY.

Wees, W. R., 1971. *Nobody Can Teach Anybody Anything*, Doubleday Canada, Toronto, Ontario.

2

Is There a Class in This Text? Creating Knowledge in the Electronic Classroom

John M. Slatin

Introduction

My purpose in this chapter is to explore the role of technology in the social construction of knowledge in the humanities generally and English in particular. More specifically, I shall be trying to map Shoshana Zuboff's (1988) findings about the way computers transform the content and nature of work, and the workplace itself, onto the English classroom.

For my illustrative case, I shall take my own upper division course in 20th-century American poetry, which I taught during the Spring 1991 semester,. Fifteen students were enrolled in the course, which met twice a week in the English Department's networked computer classroom, a total of 30 meetings. Course materials consisted of poems drawn from the widely-used *Norton Anthology of Modern Poetry*, a volume of critical essays, and a body of short documents contributed by students carrying out a weekly research assignment.

Our interactions with these materials and with one another were heavily computer-mediated. At the heart of the course were interactive written discussions (Ferrara, Brunner, and Whittemore, 1991), conducted twice weekly in real time over the network, using the InterChange module of the Daedalus Instructional System. Between sessions, we used the asynchronous e-mail module, Contact, as a kind of bulletin board where, each week, students posted documentary material they'd collected about the poet under discussion, and read material posted by their classmates. Finally, at two points in the semester we used the hypertext program StorySpace in an effort to integrate and synthesize what we had done. The StorySpace hypertexts contained the poems we had discussed in class, plus full transcripts of all InterChange sessions and all the documentary materials the students had posted in their Contact messages.

In tracing the intersection of two different types of knowledge—knowledge of subject matter-on the one hand, and on the other what I call meta-knowledge about the class and its workings—I shall be concentrating for the most part on InterChange, that is, on the transcripts of our interactive written discussions. These transcripts reveal important aspects of knowledge making; they also reveal transformations in classroom relationships very similar to those Zuboff has described as taking place in corporate environments undergoing computerization.

Computers and the Transformation of the Workplace

Zuboff argues that introducing computers into the workplace forces a new understanding of work as well as a new set of relationships—between workers and their work, among workers themselves, and between workers and managers. Computers do not create these new understandings and new relationships, however. Rather, they arise because, in order to use the computer, the organization has to cast its vital information—whether about personnel or inventory or purchasing procedures or manufacturing processes or pedagogy—into new forms. System designers and end users must decide how to display processes and transactions as well as other data in textual or graphical form on the computer screen. That is, the organization has to make its knowledge explicit, and must render it textually. This is especially difficult, Zuboff says, because such knowledge usually involves a great deal of tacit "know-how" that has been acquired through experience and apprenticeship rather than formal instruction. (Winograd and Flores [1986] make a similar point in *Understanding Computers and Cognition* when they speak of knowledge as lying ready-to-hand.) According to Zuboff, such knowledge has many of the characteristics of oral rather than literature cultures.

Once textualized and abstracted, the organization's knowledge is no longer so readily available to action and becomes accessible only through what Zuboff calls "intellective" processes. Workers who had relied on tacit knowledge acquired and expressed through action must now gain and express knowledge by looking at and manipulating complex symbolic representations of the processes involved, and must learn to intervene in those processes not directly, not bodily, but (as Emerson put it more than a century ago) "mediately," that is, through the mediation of the computer. And they must do so collaboratively.

Textualization and Literary Studies

There is a sharp difference between the way people in literary studies think about the nature of their work and what we actually do in practice. People in literary studies have been accustomed since at least the early 1970s to thinking of virtually everything as having been always already textualized. We study texts, of course, and the principal expression of our interest in them is the production of new texts that propose our understanding of the "primary" texts themselves. By the same token, much of our pedagogical energy is also organized around and directed toward the production of written texts. Instructors write syllabuses, course outlines, essay topics, study questions, exam questions, quizzes, and the like; students dutifully produce the written responses most of these things require, and instructors respond in kind. So it might seem reasonable to suppose that English professors are largely immune to the impact of the computer, or at lest to the kind of impact that Zuboff describes so eloquently.

But we are not immune. Blue- and pink-collar workers are not the only people who rely on action-centered skills which computerization renders largely irrelevant. Zuboff shows that middle managers and executives spend much of their time in talk—everything from hallway chat and telephone schmoozing to formal presentations and meetings. Success depends heavily upon "people skills" used in transactions which are oral and transitory—action-centered rather than intellective. Computerization transforms these activities, as it transforms other kinds of work, into text—electronic mail, computer conferencing, electronic calendars, and the like. As many of us know all too well, conversations and meetings take up a great deal of academics' time, too. For all our emphasis on publishing and perishing, we spend a great deal of our time talking, both in and out of the classroom. And that makes the classroom one of the best places to watch the interface—or collision—between orality and literacy.

From the vantage point of the computer classroom, it now appears that much of our teaching and learning has involved what Zuboff calls action-centered rather than intellective skills. What happens in English classes is that people talk about written and printed texts. The instructor sets out a reading or a writing assignment (or both) which the students carry out on their own, usually in the kind of privacy which is associated with reading (and, in the West, with the emergence of the middle class). Then, at an appointed time, everyone meets in a room to talk about what they have read. This happens in the electronic classroom, too. I shall argue, however, that introducing information technology into the classroom yields transformations and new relationships and new forms of knowledge that are closely analogous if not precisely identical to those Zuboff has observed in various corporate settings. As we see below, it does so by textualizing those aspects of classroom interaction that have always been primarily action-centered.

Creating the Traditional Classroom

Perhaps the first consequence of introducing computers into the classroom is to create a difference that wasn't there a minute ago, a difference whereby the classroom we've always known is transformed into the "traditional" or "proscenium" classroom (Barker and Kemp, 1990). By this I mean that in the light of the computer screens, the traditional classroom becomes suddenly visible as a technological construct, constituted by a matrix of power relations and a supporting technology—the printed book—which installs the Professor in an exalted and often literally elevated position at the "head" of the room. Meanwhile, as if burlesquing Plato's Allegory of the Cave, the students sit quietly in rows with their attention fixed on the front of the room. (Indeed, in some English Department classrooms at the University of Texas, the chairs are literally bolted to the floor.) The professor's status in this medieval arrangement is conferred by a privileged relation to that once rare commodity, the book. If the primary concern of Western scholarship since the Renaissance has been to "fix" the text forever, as Richard Lanham (1987) has said, then the teacher's job has been to transmit the rare knowledge embodied in the rare book to the assembled students.

The Electronic Classroom

The electronic classroom in which we met last Spring was a room containing 23 IBM PC's in a Local Area Network, running NetWare 286 v 2.15 over an IBM Token Ring. The computers themselves are arranged in a ring around the outer walls; when students sit facing their screens they are facing away from the center of the room and away from one another; to compensate for this, and to permit more traditional face-to-face interactions, there is a large, seminar-style table in the center of the room. Our classroom software was the Daedalus Instructional System v. 3.10, an integrated environment designed specifically for the electronic English classroom. (Both the equipment and the software have since been upgraded, though the layout of the room remains unchanged.) For the StorySpace project, we also made use of a new and, at the time, still incomplete Macintosh-based classroom across the hall.

While the layout of a particular classroom can have a significant impact on the interactions that take place inside (see Boiarsky 1990; Selfe 1990), and while concern about classroom design is itself evidence of the extent to which computerization forces us to rethink the most fundamental aspects of our work, there is another sense in which physical configuration is nearly irrelevant. Although all our class meetings took place in the computer classroom itself, the electronic classroom need not occupy physical space at all. It may be a kind of virtual classroom, constituted entirely by the network, with terminals in a number of different locations. It may involve real-time interactions among people who log in at a specific time just as everyone comes to the traditional classroom at a set time; or it may be completely asynchronous, with participants logging in at their own convenience and discretion.

Creating Knowledge in the Electronic Classroom

The electronic classroom I am interested in is not about one-way transmissions. Creating knowledge in the electronic classroom is a process whereby students and instructors interact with one another and with the course materials through the medium of interactive written discourse. These interactions lead to an understanding, which did not exist prior to the interactions and which persists after them, both of the course materials and of the participants' relation to the materials and to one another. The work of the course is to build the relationships that, in my view, constitute not only the meaning of individual poems but poetry itself. The class carries out its work in the continual and usually interactive production of text.

Classroom Talk and Interactive Written Discourse

When students in the traditional classroom talk about poetry (or anything else), their talk necessarily occupies a different plane from the texts of the poets or of "professional" readers like me, who have access to scholarly journals and other print media. The electronic classroom changes that situation by textualizing classroom discourse. It puts students' remarks more nearly on a par with those of other readers, including the instructor as well as the poets themselves. The transformation of traditionally ephemeral classroom talk into text by means of interactive written discourse does not simply re-organize knowledge of subject matter, then. It changes relationships among people by changing their relationship to knowledge.

From the student's standpoint, interactive written discourse offers unprecedented access to the "floor"—that is, the screen—during class discussion, without depriving any other student of his or her access rights (see Bump, 1990). From the instructor's standpoint, interactive written discourse offers unprecedented access to what's going on in the minds of students, and to their understanding of the course material. It also provides unprecedented access to the processes by which, individually and collectively, the class members reach that understanding.

It thus makes meta-knowledge both possible and necessary. Meta-knowledge, as I said earlier, is the knowledge participants have of what is going on in the class and of how the class is operating. It is knowledge of themselves as participants in an evolving, ongoing conversation, participants who can intervene in that conversation and affect both its content and its direction (spelling errors are reproduced as in the original):

Pardon wy absense on Tuesday- I've been a little under the weather. Commenting on Lisa Grant's statement- in reading Hughes' work I not only was aware of the individual statement he was making on his own personal life, but I was also aware of the statement he was making for the greater mass of people who shared his experiences. I think it is interesting that he could be successful at both simultaneously. (InterChange 3/28/91, message 11)

Here the student (1) joins the discussion, (2) apologizes for missing the previous class, thereby acknowledging her status as a member of a community whose members have expectations of one another, and (3) responds to a point made by another student.

Just as students gain knowledge of themselves as participants in the ongoing conversation, so instructors come to see their role in a different light as their words join the others in the screen. For both instructors and students, it is the existence of their remarks as text that makes meta-knowledge possible. And it is the sheer volume of the class as text—the printed transcripts of our interactive written discussions ran to some 600 pages—that may necessitate such metaknowledge.

Transforming the Instructor's Perspective

Nor is it only student knowledge that is constructed in this process: the instructor, too, comes into a newly constituted and evolving understanding in the course of the classroom interactions. My own view of poetry, for example, has been profoundly re-shaped. While I owe to hypertext my increasing emphasis on building up webs of links among poems (Slatin 1988, 1990a, 1990b), I owe to my many interactive written conversations with students over the past four years my evolving conception of the dynamic nature of the linking process and my sense of poetry itself as an ongoing conversation among poets living and dead, between poets and readers, and among readers. The conversation may cover many topics, but it is always in one way or another about poetry itself, and it always has as its goal to perpetuate the conversation, and thus poetry. Individual poems might be understood—heuristically, at least—as "turns" within this ongoing conversation, with the poet speaking not only to the reader (as we commonly say s/he does) but also to other poets, both predecessors and contemporaries.

At the same time, I want my students to understand that the conversation is not limited only to poems, but also goes on in the poets' other writings—in letters, essays, and reviews as well as face-to-face conversations of which we generally know little or nothing. I have wanted them to understand, too, that the conversation goes on among readers like them, and that one goal—or at least one consequence—of that conversation is the perpetuation of poetry. In other words, I regard poetry as socially constructed.

The electronic classroom forces a new set of relations between instructors and students, among students, and between all members of the group and the body of material whose meaning, it now becomes apparent, we are all there to construct. Knowledge ceases to be an artifact (or to be embodied in artifacts) and becomes instead a process; it is dynamic rather than static, not to be confused with mere information. If information is news of difference (Bateson, 1980), then knowledge has to do with recognizing the implications of the news, with creating the patterns that connect the differences but do not resolve or dissolve them. These patterns do not inhere to the material itself; they belong to the mind of the reader.

InterChange

I turn now to InterChange and a discussion of what we might hope to learn from the printed transcripts of class discussions. I will present a breakdown of student-instructor interactions in the transcripts of four InterChanges which occurred at two-week intervals during the first half of the course, plus an overview of these patterns for the entire semester. In addition, I will examine the ways in which students are able to generate and sustain topics for discussion. I begin, however, with a brief explanation of classroom procedures and an excerpt from an InterChange transcript.

At the beginning of class, each student sits at a computer and logs on to the network. After consulting the read-only Class Assignment file, s/he selects InterChange from the menu. As the program loads, current messages—those that have already been sent, for example, by the instructor prior to the official beginning of class—appear on the screen in the order in which they were composed and sent out over the network. Students then join in as they are ready to do so.

The result is an especially intense variety of interactive written discourse. As Ferrara, Brunner, and Whittemore (1991) have noted, interactive written discourse is a "hybrid" form. Neither speech nor writing, it combines the informality and spontaneity of oral communication with the permanence of written discourse. It is thus an ideal medium for conducting computer-mediated discussions in the English classroom (Bump 1990). What follows is the opening sequence from the session of 5 February 1991, on the poet Wallace Stevens:

John Slatin:
Hi. I've just been reading through the transcript from Thursday's InterChange—pretty intense, wasn't it? But still a good discussion. I know I enjoyed it, and I know I learned from it. I learned from it because we were discussing tough problems for which there is no ready solution: what IS the relationship between the poet (any poet) and his or her work? how do we describe that relationship? to what extent should our judgment of the work, the poems, be influenced by our judgment of the poet's life, of the way s/he lives out or fails to live out in his or her relationships the values and ideals s/he seems to hold up in her or his work?

These are real and important questions, but in our eagerness to address them we spent far more time looking at the life (or at aspects of the life) outside the work than we spent looking at the work itself. As a result, I think we lost track to a certain extent of the "conversation" in which Eliot was involved, the conversation with other poets living and dead, the conversation with readers.

I'd like to think about that conversation today as we begin our discussion of Stevens. Let's start with a poem—I'll leave it up to you to decide which one—and try to get a handle on the way Stevens is defining the poetic conversation.

Jeannie Williams:
It seems to me that Stevens' main point is the way that imagination and reality come together. For him, it seems that that particular line between the two is often blurred, and his poetry speaks to the gray area where they overlap. I also get the feeling that he doesn't expect other people to share his ideas about imagination and reality, that this is essentially what his poetry is about: how he sees the world, his subjective reality.

Lisa Gipson:
I enjoyed "Thirteen Ways of Looking at a Blackbird." As Jeannie said, he blends together imagination and reality. He describes different things, things that are not blackbirds, but then, in the imagination, they are. He compares blackbirds to different things, and in my minds eye, I was able to see them as one.

Jennifer Godfrey:
I really enjoyed Stevens. He seemed to deal more with tangible messages than did Eliot or Pound. Stevens uses interesting analagies to express opinions and thoughts on the interaction if things in the world (I'm thinking of Thirteen Ways of Looking at a Blackbird). Stevens seems to be more concerned with his audience than did Eliot or Pound.

Ronda Northen:
The Snow Man impressed upon me a real sense of having to know about things before you can effectively tell others about it. The first two stanzas state "One must have a mind of winter to regard the frost and the boughs of the pine-trees crusted with snow; And have been cold a long time . . . I think that Stevens was saying that one must spend time with nature (or anything else) in order to understand and explain it. He might also be referring to his poetry . . ?

. . . .

Deanne Metz:
Jeannie: What you said about Stevens portraying the interrelationship between imagination and reality is a great observation. I "read up" on Stevens before reading his poems and found that he believes that we can be rescued from the confusion of reality through our imagination. Our imagination gives meaning to reality. I would love to talk about "The Man with the Blue Guitar" because he addresses this idea in a pretty cool way. I would like to know how everyone perceives the guitar; as reality or fantasy. When he says, " Things as they are are changed upon the blue guitar," is he referring to changing reality through imagination?

Lisa Hagy:
I think that Stevens poem "Of Modern Poetry" is a great example of the way he views poetic conversation. I felt like Stevens was saying that poetry had to be more than just flowery words and classical allusions. According to Stevens good poetry must touch the soul of the "invisible audience," presumably the reader. I just love that passage that talks about the audience. "Of which an invisible audience listens,/Not to the play,but to itself, expressed/In an emotion as of two people, as of two/Emotions becoming one. . . .

Paul McCann:
Deanne: I think your right about the guitar and to some extent I believe Stevens believes that a poem also changes reality through imagination.

Jeannie Williams:
Deanne: I was thinking about "The Man with the Blue Guitar" in particular when I said what I did about Stevens. . . . I think your interpretation of the blue guitar as imagination is very interesting. When I read this poem I was thinking more along the lines of poetry—or music—altering reality in telling a story in which the facts are altered to make the story more interesting. But that's imagination, isn't it?
    The blue guitar seems to me to be like a magic wand . . . sort of how one can transform something which is rather ordinary into something very beautiful.
(InterChange 2/5/91, messages 1–11)

The sequence above is typical in certain respects but atypical in other ways. It is typical in that it begins with a relatively long statement by the instructor pointing out salient features in the previous InterChange session and suggesting a broadly defined goal for the current session; it is also typical in that the long opening message is followed by a series of student-authored messages, and that the students begin rather quickly to engage one another's remarks. It is typical, too, in the way that thematically connected messages are interspersed among messages concerning quite different topics. And, finally, the sequence is typical in that seven of the eight student messages represent contributions from women. What is most atypical is that the stream of student messages continues uninterrupted until message 46, when the instructor again intervenes. (An interval of eight or nine messages is more common.)

As the foregoing excerpt indicates, InterChange differs in important respects from the electronic messaging studied by Ferrara and her colleagues and from the highly restricted on-line messaging permitted in the computer conversations examined by Wilkins (1991). Practically speaking, InterChange imposes no limit on message-length. Participants compose in a private, pull-down editing window; they may edit as much as they like (the editor supports cut-&-paste and other major word processing functions), and they need not send their messages until they are satisfied with them; they may take as much time and as much space on screen as they need. (In practice, however, most messages are relatively short, averaging some 5–6 lines of text and taking up less than half the screen.)

InterChange messages have considerably more permanence than those studied by Wilkins (1991). In the system Wilkins examined, messages disappeared forever once they had scrolled off the screen, and they could be interrupted and wiped out by incoming messages. By contrast, InterChange messages remain available for the duration of the session. Thus a message that has scrolled off the screen is easily retrieved rather than being consigned to oblivion.

The messages are endowed with additional permanence by the utility program that produces a transcript of the entire session; the transcript may be archived in electronic form, or printed for distribution to all members of the class for review and later use. The continuing presence and availability of individual messages during class time, and of the entire transcript throughout the semester, is a crucial factor in "textualizing" the work of the classroom. The results of this textualizing process will become more evident through a review of data obtained from the transcripts of representative sessions.

Week 2: Transcript of 22 January 1991

The difference between traditional and electronic classrooms is already visible in the second electronic InterChange of the semester, which took place on 22 January. The typical undergraduate class involves approximately 26 verbal exchanges in 50 minutes (Karp and Yoels, 1983). In most cases, some 75 percent of the interaction takes place among four or five students and the instructor, with 75 percent of those interactions amounting to short, dyadic exchanges between the instructor and a single student (Karp and Yoels, 1983). This 75-minute InterChange session, however, involved a total of 87 messages (including only three "spoiled" ones without content—a very low number for a session so early in the semester). There were 12 participants, including the instructor.

What we see here is more than just an increase in student involvement. There is also a qualitative shift in the nature of the student-teacher relationship. Not only do students initiate just over 80 percent of the message traffic, but fewer than 20 percent of student messages are addressed specifically to the instructor; the remainder are addressed either to individual students or to the class generally.

Week 4: Transcript of 5 February 1991

This shift becomes more pronounced as time goes on. The sixth InterChange session occurred two weeks later, at the beginning of the fourth week of classes. The poet under discussion was Wallace Stevens, who proved far more popular with the students than Ezra Pound had been two weeks earlier. Both message traffic and participation were up: 16 participants, including the instructor, sent 114 messages for an average of 7.6 messages each. The highest number of messages sent by any one participant was 14

Table 2.1
InterChange Session, 22 January 1991

Participants	12
Total messages	87
Spoiled messages	3
Avg per participant	7
Total instructor messages	16
Instructor-to-all	12
Instructor-to-student	4
Total student messages	68
Student-to-all	35
Student-to-student	24
Student-to-instructor	12

(one participant); the lowest was four (three participants). As I noted in discussing the long excerpt from this transcript quoted above, the instructor participated very little in this session, sending only nine messages—substantially less than 10 percent of the total—during the entire class.

The most impressive statistic here is that over 96 percent of the messages initiated by students are addressed either to individual students or to the class generally—a figure that clearly demonstrates the extraordinary shift that has occurred in the student-teacher relationship. Indeed, the shift is so extraordinary that it raises questions of its own, both about the instructor's role and about the claim that learning is taking place.

Zuboff contends that translating operational knowledge into textual form on the computer screen poses interpretive problems which, in turn, demand that employees work together to construct an interpretation of what they see on the screen. This involves a shift in relationships among workers.

I would love to talk about "The Man with the Blue Guitar" because he addresses this idea in a pretty cool way. I would like to know how everyone perceives the guitar; as reality or fantasy. When he says, " Things as they are are changed upon the blue guitar," is he referring to changing reality through imagination?

Addressed to the class at large, and thus showing considerable meta-knowledge on the student's part of her situation in a community of poetry-readers, this message (#8) initiates a series of comments on "The Man with the Blue Guitar" that extends through 9 different messages (the last is #70). What we see in this series is an analogue to the scenes Zuboff describes, in which plant operators huddle around a screen, trying to negotiate understanding of a problem one of them has noticed. While the instructor participates in the discussion, his is not the final word.

Table 2.2
InterChange Session, 5 February 1991

Total messages	114
Participants	16
Avg messages per participant	7.6
Total instructor messages	9
Instructor-to-all	4
Instructor-to-student	5
Total student messages	105
Student-to-all	47
Student-to-student	54
Student-to-instructor	4

Week 6: Transcript of 19 February 1991

The most controversial InterChange during the first half of the semester—
that is, the one in which there was most intense dislike of the poet we were
discussing at the time (Gertrude Stein) and the most disagreement among
the participants—took place at the beginning of week 6, on 19 February.

James Ellis:
I agree agree agree meanith. agree there's
no
direction direction direction
I like it.

Paul McCann:
Stein's poetry is alto more like repetitive prose. George Hugnet" makes "The Red
Wheelbarrow" look like Jonathan Edward's "Sinners in the Hands of an Angry
God." Her petry I found almost completey lacking in emotion or any artistic
merit.

Jennifer Godfrey:
Wallace Stevens made good use of imagination. His poems were structured in
such a way that the use of the imagination was vital to the comprehension of the
poem. I think that Stein was going somewhat along the same lines except she went
too far. Stein thought our imaginations could dream up what she flat out left from
her poems.

Lisa Grant:
Dr. Slatin, I remember being a little lost in that particular part of the conversation
on Stevens, however I have much more respect for Stevens' work than Stein's.
There seems to be at least some conceptual significance. Something which people
of varied opinion can intelligently discuss without feeling like total dimwits. I fail
to grasp any significant theme in Stein's work except for an infatuation with the
versatility of words, something we learn about in grade school and ponder on in
PRIVATE!!

(InterChange 2/19/91, messages 35–38)

The number of participants is down (to 13), but message traffic is up
dramatically—to 137, a 57.5 percent increase over 22 January. Students
initiate over 85 percent of the messages, the instructor just over 13
percent; only 11 percent of the student messages are directed to the
instructor. The instructor is more actively involved in this discussion than
in the InterChange on Stevens (5 February), but the trend toward
heightened student involvement remains strong, and it is evident that a
strong, good-humored sense of community has developed. In the first

Table 2.3
InterChange Session, 19 February 1991

Participants	13
Total messages	137
Avg messages per participant	10.54
Total instructor messages	18
Instructor-to-all	4
Instructor-to-student	14
Total student messages	119
Student-to-all	56
Student-to-student	49
Student-to-instructor	14

message quoted above, James Ellis takes issue with another students evaluation of Gertrude Stein in a message whose Stein-like style acknowledges the other student's point without accepting its judgment. The student-instructor relationship has continued to evolve as well. As the last message quoted above indicates, by this point in the semester students have come to feel increasingly free to challenge the instructor.

Week 8: Transcript of 5 March 1991

The fourteenth InterChange discussion was held on Tuesday, 5 March, at the beginning of the eighth week of classes. The poet under discussion was Marianne Moore. The number of messages is down slightly, to 119, and the number the number of participants (including one visitor) is up to 17. Instructor involvement is up to almost 16 percent. The latter increase may be partly accounted for by the fact that much of his scholarly work, including an essay assigned for the course, is on Marianne Moore. Nevertheless, students were responsible for more than 80 percent of all traffic, and more than 80 percent of their messages are addressed to other students.

Patterns of Interaction, 22 January–25 April 1991

The patterns examined so far hold throughout the semester. The graph below shows the typical pattern of student-instructor and student-student interactions for the period from 22 January–25 April, that is, until the second-to-last week of the semester.

Table 2.4
InterChange Session, 5 March 1991

Total messages	119
Participants	17
Avg messages per participant	7
Total instructor messages	19
Instructor-to-all	3
Instructor-to-student	15
Instructor-to-visitor	1
Total student messages	97
Student-to-all	49
Student-to-student	33
Student-to-instructor	12
Student-to-visitor	3
Total visitor messages	3

These data suggest that interactive written discourse may bring about a striking shift in the sociopolitical balance of the classroom, just as Zuboff might predict. We see a shift away from the standard pattern of initiation-response-evaluation that dominates traditional classroom talk, toward a pattern of interaction in which students speak mostly to one another: student messages make up more than 85 percent of the total, with student-to-student messages and messages addressed to the entire class accounting for just over three-fourths of all message traffic. The instructor, joining in as participant and facilitator, is responsible for only 14 percent of all messages.

This is not to say, however, that the instructor has neither power nor authority (which Zuboff calls the spiritual dimension of power). The instructor sets the main agenda for the course with the design of the syllabus, and maintains a measure of control with read-only class assignment files posted each day. Further, he sets the agenda for each individual session and links it to the larger course objectives in his initial InterChange messages. Subsequent messages provide information, synthesize student comments, or refocus the discussion. Moreover, although messages from the instructor make up less than 15 percent of the total, this figure consistently represents the largest contribution by any individual participant. At the same time, however, the electronic classroom is student-centered to the extent not only that most message traffic is initiated by and directed to students, but also that students easily and frequently generate the local topics within each InterChange, and indeed across sessions.

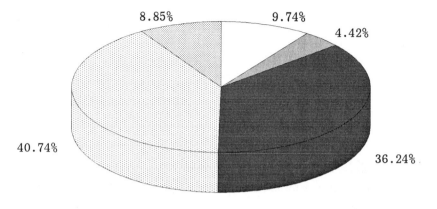

Figure 2.1
Patterns of interaction in InterChange

Generating Topics in InterChange

The 5 February InterChange on Wallace Stevens is a case in point. The long opening message from the instructor (see above) is mostly retrospective: it says much more about the previous InterChange on T. S. Eliot than it does about Stevens, and the questions it poses are primarily about issues that came up in the Eliot discussion, such as the problematic relationship between the poet's biography and the poetry itself—a student-generated topic that was of persistent interest in different contexts throughout the semester. If the class had talked about Stevens in a traditional classroom setting, one could have expected early student remarks to respond fairly directly to the instructor's opening comments. But as the excerpt quoted above indicates, the second message is a student comment on the way Stevens represents the interplay of imagination and reality—two terms which had not appeared in the instructor's opening message at all. Far from being a distractor, the imagination/reality dichotomy becomes the primary topic of discussion for the day. The word *imagination* occurs 159 times in this single InterChange; of those 159 occurrences, 139, or 87.42 percent, are in student messages.

Something similar happens with the idea of color during the same discussion. Words having to do with color—*color, colorful, colorless, colors, red, yellow, blue, green, white, black*—occur 78 times in 28 student messages (as against eight times in four messages from the instructor) on 5 February, beginning in message 7 and continuing through message 111. *Imagination*, then, is the dominant concern throughout the InterChange, with *color* as a strong sub-theme. These topics intertwine with discussion-threads pertaining to specific poems ("The Man with the Blue Guitar," "Postcard from the Volcano," "The Plain Sense of Things," "A Quiet Normal Life") and with other issues as well.

Imagination and color are topics of local concern during the discussion of Stevens. The word *imagination* had occurred only twice—both times in student messages—during the four previous InterChanges on Ezra Pound and T. S. Eliot; it occurs a total of only seven times—again, all in student messages—in three subsequent sessions on H.D. and Marianne Moore (26 and 28 February, 5 March). But as I have said, there were many other topics besides these local ones: I have already mentioned the issue of biographical relevance, for instance, which comes up in muted form late in the Stevens discussion after having been a subject of intense concern during the previous discussion of Eliot; it comes up again later, in discussions of Gertrude Stein and H.D., and again in talking about Langston Hughes and Amiri Baraka.

Links to Knowledge: Contact and StorySpace

While the intense interest in imagination and color was almost exclusively confined to the 5 February InterChange on Stevens, the InterChange itself had an important effect on the students' approach to the research component of the course. Students were assigned each week to locate one piece of documentary material pertaining to the poet under discussion. They transcribed that material into a text file, and then imported the file into Contact and sent it as a message addressed to their classmates. Each student would then read two or more messages containing transcribed materials, thereby adding to his or her store of information about the poet and what others had found interesting about that poet. Equipped with a new store of information about the poet, all students would then join InterChange for a renewed discussion.

Students seemed to be carrying out almost random searches in the library prior to the discussion of Stevens. On 7 February, however, every student came to class with material about Stevens's views on the relationship between imagination and reality. Clearly, the discussion had stimulated them to learn more. Although the relationship between InterChange and Contact would never again be so dramatic, from that point on students' research was generally guided by the topics that had most interested them during InterChange.

Students were also eager to establish connections between the materials they discovered in the library and posted in Contact, and other elements of the course. They frequently referred to these materials during InterChange. Moreover, in the first hypertext project, midway through the semester, most students concentrated on linking the Contact material to InterChange messages and poetic texts. This was no small matter: the project posed major logistical difficulties for me and for them, and it is a testament to their enthusiasm and commitment that they persisted despite buggy beta software, lack of adequate documentation, and the necessity of learning both a new operating system (we had been using DOS machines, but StorySpace runs only on the Macintosh) and an entirely new kind of application. Nonetheless, the students persevered, and, despite occasional bursts of quite legitimate frustration, worked hard to create for themselves the connecting patterns that reveal significant relationships.

Temporal Dynamics in InterChange

In order to understand more clearly how topics emerge and persist and decay, we need to consider the temporal dimension of InterChange. We may get a crude sense of this by looking at what Paul Taylor, the author of InterChange, calls the "velocity" of InterChange sessions. The InterChange of 2 April was a typically lively session. Eighty-three minutes elapsed from the time the instructor sent the first message to the time the last message was sent; in that time participants sent 125 messages totaling just under 60 kilobytes—about 30 pages of text. This averages out to about 722 bytes per minute, or roughly 120 words if we allow an average of 6 bytes per word. If we slice it a different way, we're averaging just over 1.5 messages per minute. But of course it doesn't actually work that way in practice.

It is not precisely accurate to describe InterChange as a synchronous medium. Each participant reads, writes, and sends messages at his or her own pace. Some compose fluently and type quickly; others are less fluent or perhaps just less adept on the keyboard, or perhaps they're simply more

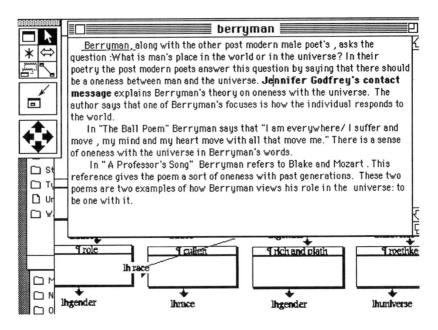

Figure 2.2
StorySpace screen from second hypertext project shows a student comment on
the poet John Berryman. The boldfaced phrase indicates the presence of a link
to a Contact message in another portion of the hypertext.

thoughtful and compose more slowly. A message sent at the beginning of
class may be the subject of intense discussion for a while, until interest and
momentum shift to another topic which occupies most participants'
attention for a time. But there may be a student still mulling over a
response to that earlier message, and that participant will in due course
finish composing his or her response and send it out over the network. At
that moment, the seemingly dead topic may be revived, and participants
who have been discussing other matters return to the earlier topic with
renewed interest and an expanded context for it.

Not only do topics and messages remain available: whole InterChanges
remain available as well, although in different form. InterChange transcripts were distributed to students either electronically or in hard copy
and assigned as part of the reading for the next class meeting. This had the
effect of keeping the whole InterChange live, and introduces a kind of
large-scale recursion into the process.

Persistence of Topics in InterChange

Such recursiveness is vital to the project of creating knowledge in the electronic classroom. Among the topics that persist from one InterChange to the next are the poets whose work formed the subject of previous InterChanges. As I have argued elsewhere (Slatin, 1990a), poems are defined by their "conversational" relationships with other poems (and other texts as well). In reading a new poem, students must learn to link it with other things they have read—to hear, as it were, whom the poem is addressing. This has posed real problems in the traditional classroom, where it has proved extremely difficult to keep early topics alive throughout the semester. By mid-semester, for instance, Pound and Eliot—the first two poets on the syllabus—normally go a bit dim in students' memories. InterChange, however, seems to keep them alive. The graph below (figure 2.3) shows the distribution of references to Ezra Pound after we had completed formal discussion of him and his work.

We discussed Pound in two InterChanges on 22 and 24 January. The students disliked him and his work intensely, as students usually do—one reason, perhaps, why they might tend to let his memory fade. But the following week, when the focus was on T. S. Eliot, Pound's name was mentioned 116 times—105 times by students, and 11 times by the instructor. In sharp contrast, Pound's name came up only 21 times (17 times in student messages) during the discussion of Stevens. This might seem to confirm the tendency for early topics to disappear. But Pound was mentioned 45 times (32 in student messages) in the discussion of Williams on 12 and 14 February, and no fewer than 183 times—131 by students—in three InterChanges that took place between 26 February and 5 March, when the poets under discussion were H.D. and Marianne Moore, respectively. From this perspective the scarcity of references to Pound during the Stevens discussion appears to be the anomaly—and in fact the anomaly may be explained by saying that, indeed, Pound is a less important figure for Stevens than T. S. Eliot, who is in fact mentioned 30 times during the same discussion, while Pound and his work were central to both H.D. and Marianne Moore. This is not an isolated phenomenon, limited only to Pound. During the same period (26 February–5 March) Eliot is mentioned 66 times (41 in student messages); Stevens 37 (23 in

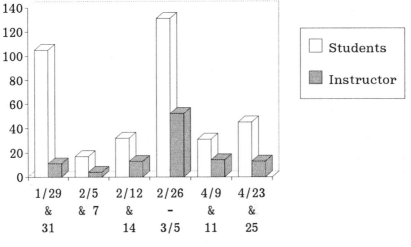

Figure 2.3
References to Pound, 29 January–25 April

student messages); Williams is named 40 times (19 times by students); and Gertrude Stein is also mentioned 40 times (23 times by students).

The point is that these poets and their work remained in play as the semester went on, figuring actively into the evolving perception of new work as we encountered it and into the understanding we continually constructed and reconstructed. Allusions to Pound are especially important, because they confirm that Pound remained a reference point throughout the semester—indeed, his function as a reference point seemed to grow stronger with the passage of time. I shared the findings reported above with my students, suggesting that their continuing reference to Pound had its counterpart in the response to Pound in the larger community of readers over the years. These readers, too, have often been exasperated, even driven to fury by Pound—and yet he remains a pivotal figure, one who must be dealt with in any serious discussion of 20th-century poetry in English. The students rejected my argument:

Lisa Gipson:
SLATIN—I know we do talk a lot about Pound, and he is a major reference point for many of us. But I kindof wonder if we would use him as such a reference point if that had not already been marked before by our anthology and by our past teachers. It has always been stressed that Pound in so important, (and I don't necessarily disagree) but I wonder if I had never been told about Pound and just read a few of his poems along with a few of others' poem if I would find him to

be such an important figure. I might have just disregarded him. (InterChange 4/4/91, message 38)

Another student seconded the argument a few messages later:

Ronda Northen:
Slatin—Also I think one rason why the class uses Pound as a sort of reference point is because we were introduced to him early in the semester. I realize that I am oversimplifying , but it is one possible reason. (InterChange 4/4/91, message 42)

That both students address me as "Slatin" is further evidence that the sociopolitical balance in the class has continued to shift. More importantly, their counterarguments evince a high degree of metaknowledge. These students and their classmates are well aware, not only of their position as members of a community of readers, but of their role in constructing that community: the InterChange as a whole was concerned with the question of how anthologies are constructed (in fact, one student proposed that the class should put together its own anthology to redress what she saw as the imbalances of the Norton anthology).

Conclusions

The class I have described at such length was, I think, the single best experience I have had in 15 years of teaching; but I want to stress that it is representative of my experience in the computer classroom since 1987. In my view, the class offers a clear demonstration (and vindication) of what the transformations Zuboff describes as taking place in the corporate world might look like in an academic setting. I want to end on a cautionary note, however. The Computer Research Lab is only a few years old, but we have a growing body of folklore, and one story seems particularly germane here. It's about the visitor who comes into the computer classroom while an InterChange is in progress. He watches for a while, in fascination and mounting bewilderment. And finally he says, just before he walks out the door, "But when will you begin to *teach*?"

There seems little doubt that the coming years will see a proliferation of computers in the university. This proliferation is likely to be especially evident in the humanities, for the simple reason that computers have been so scarce in these fields up till now. It behooves us to be careful. As my little anecdote was meant to illustrate, there will be people—colleagues, administrators, legislators, alumni—who fail to see anything remotely resembling education as they understand it when they look at what we do in the electronic classroom, nor do they see the computer as anything but hostile to the humanities. We would do well, I think, to understand their antipathy as responding at least in part to the phenomena Zuboff has defined, to the necessity for developing new kinds of knowledge and a new relation to their life's work.

We would do well, also, to bear in mind one of Zuboff's most important points. Computerization can go either way, she reminds us. Universities, like other organizations, can use the technology in an effort to increase regimentation and control, with a resulting estrangement between workers and management—between students and faculty on the one hand and faculty and administrators on the other. Or the universities can use the technology to distribute authority and power more widely, to bring students and faculty and administrators actively into collaboration in an educational process which is explicitly understood as extending beyond the limits of time and space imposed by classrooms and course schedules and departmental boundaries. There's a choice, and it's easy to make the wrong one.

Works Cited

Bateson, G. (1980). *Mind and nature: A necessary unity.* New York: Bantam.

Boiarsky, C. (1990). Computers in the classroom: The instruction, the mess, the noise, the writing. In C. Handa (Ed.), *Computers and community: Teaching composition in the twenty-first century* (pp. 47–67). Portsmouth, N.H.: Boynton/ Cook.

Bump, J. (1990). Radical changes in class discussion using networked computers. *Computers and the Humanities,* 24, 49–65.

Ferrara, K., Brunner, H., and Whittemore, G. (1991). Interactive written discourse as an emergent register. *Written Communication,* 8(1), 8–34.

Karp, D.A. and Yoels, W.C. (1983). The college classroom: Some observations on the meanings of student participation. 2d ed. In H. Hobboy and C. Clark (Eds.) *Social interaction: Readings in sociology* (pp. 195–209). New York: St. Martin's.

Lanham, R. A. (1987). Convergent pressures: Social, technological, theoretical. Wayzata, Minnesota.

Slatin, J. M. (1988). Hypertext and the teaching of writing. In E. Barrett (Ed.), *Text, context, and hypertext: Writing with and for the computer* (pp. 111–129). Cambridge, Mass.: MIT Press.

———. (1990a). Reading hypertext: Order and coherence in a new medium. *College English*, 52, 870–883.

———. (1990b). Text and hypertext: Reflections on the role of the computer in teaching 20th-century American poetry. In D. S. Miall (Ed.), *Computers and the humanities: New directions* (pp. 123–135). Oxford: Oxford University Press.

Taylor, Paul. Personal communication.

Wilkins, H. (1991). Computer talk: Long-distance communication by computer. *Written communication*, 8(1), 56–78.

Winograd, T., and Flores, F. (1986). *Understanding computers and cognition: A new foundation for design.* Norwood, New Jersey: Ablex.

Zuboff, S. (1988). *In the Age of the Smart Machine: The future of work and power.* New York: Basic Books.

3

Varieties of Virtual: Expanded Metaphors for Computer-Mediated Learning

Patricia Ann Carlson

Introduction

Virtual—Being such in essence or effect though not formally recognized or admitted . . . the definition seems clear enough. Yet it's one of those words that slip their moorings and run loose on the swirling waters of fad. We sometimes call them buzzwords, but this attempt to demean them disregards their real power. They should be called shibboleths, for pronouncing them correctly in context may secure passage into the fellowship of an enclosed group.

In effect, the variety of meanings for the term *virtual* constitutes a miniature case study for the social making of meaning. In the educational community, technology has driven the definition of *virtual*. So far the emphasis has been on networking, spawning phrases like *virtual classroom* and *computer-supported collaborative work* (CSCW). In this chapter, I suggest that emphasizing other technologies will create new meanings for *virtual*. (And—though not covered in the chapter—these variants of virtual will trigger concomitant re-examination of existing and past pedagogical theory and educational philosophy.) The three technologies I see as having a major impact on education in the 1990s are (1) hypermedia, (2) artificial neural networks, and (3) artificial realities.

To better explain my point, I have devised a simplified diagram of the components of a learning community engaged in the social creation of knowledge (see figure 3.1).

Interaction among the elements of *content, context, teacher,* and *student* generates the zone where knowledge is formed. Additionally, I've associated technologies with each element: *context* with networking; *teacher* (or expert) with hypermedia; *student* with neural networks; and

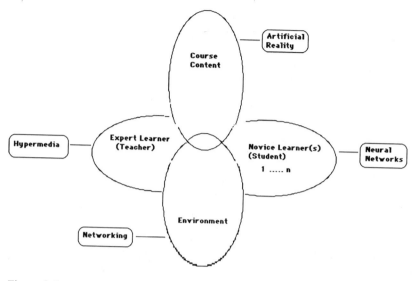

Figure 3.1
Conceptualized overview of a learning community

content with artificial realities. Admittedly, these linkages are something of a convenience for my argument. Just as networking gave us the *virtual* classroom, I'm proposing that new technologies will allow us to "virtualize" other elements of the system. I'll start with a brief description of computer-supported collaborative work (CSCW) as the foundation for my imaginings.

Networks and Electronic Communes

That each computer creates its own "society" has long been of concern, one way or another. In the beginning, when computers were little more than large CPUs, time sharing came into being because an individual could not input information quickly enough to occupy the entire processing capacity of the computer. Resources were being wasted: the single-machine/single-user model was just too expensive. With the advent of time sharing, many people occupy the system simultaneously, but they only know of one another's existence when response time degrades because of too many user connects or too much process-intensive work going on. In this context, "social awareness" takes on the meaning of "malfunction."

With the advent of the desk-top computer in the early 1980s, stand-alone, single-user machines became the norm for certain types of work.

Now a different kind of waste took place and a different kind of inconvenience resulted. Some resources need to be shared: large databases, software applications, and hardware peripherals, to name just a few. Another concern entered the minds of parents: the realization that for an increasing number of young people, the phrase "window on the world" was limited to three types of CRTs—the T.V., the electronic arcade game, and the home computer. As a third constituency of concern, teachers couldn't help but notice that the process of learning with a computer (intensively individual and requiring long, silent sessions at the keyboard) wasn't meshing very well with a social constructionist theory of the making of meaning. Networking—the sharing of resources and of ideas over an electronic highway—helped to alleviate some of these concerns.

While today this software is variously called online conferencing, collaborative environments, or groupware, adaptations of LAN technology to teaching or to work have been around for a number of years. Some of the earliest took advantage of e-mail's ability to facilitate communication (Quinn et al., 1983; Welsch, 1982). Others were modeled on electronic bulletin boards and were some of the first exploitations of the medium's ability to foster a kind of bonding in an amorphous and anonymous social grouping.

Certainly, the "communication" model of the virtual classroom has its pragmatic benefits. Networking makes the dissemination of information quick, convenient, and uniform. Indeed, a whole discipline of "distance education" has grown up around the need for a course delivery mechanism that overcomes spatial or temporal difficulties. On the other hand, the "conference" model of the networked classroom provides a mechanism for peer evaluation, a proven approach to learning.

As experience with network classrooms grows, other types of benefits become apparent. For example, the electronic environment becomes an instrument of enpowerment. Students who may have felt themselves "disenfranchised" in the traditional setting of the classroom speak out more often in a virtual classroom. Additionally, the freedom from social constraints and the verbal formality of a more traditional environment promotes spontaneity, resulting in more committed participation and "authentic" commentary in the learning exchange.

Michael Shrage's book *Shared Minds: The New Technologies of Collaboration* (1990) examines the idea that electronic media not only facilitate but also enhance the nature of human interchange. Shrage makes a distinction between the quality of communication and collaboration, and by extension, the nature of computer support for each activity. Basically, communication is the transmittal of information and the electronics used in this activity are relatively static. In other words, data is passed from a sending node to a receiving node. The human intelligence that either sends or receives the packet makes decisions on the relevance of the transmission, how it should be altered in form or substance, and whether it should be retransmitted. Though communication implies a relationship between sender and receiver, this is often tenuous and transient at best. (The mass of unassimilated "for your information" type of communication that works its way though organizations is an example of how inane electronic communication systems can be.) Though it is possible for the channel to dynamically direct the communication—as in sorting or filtering—it is atypical for the system to be assigned such a role. While electronic communication is lauded for its convenience, it might equally well be charged with precipitating much of the debris in the information explosion.

Collaboration, on the other hand, requires a different conceptualization of the elements of communication just mentioned. First, the purpose of the transaction is primary, so most interchanges are charged with goal-oriented energy. Second, the participants must build and sustain a complex relationship that fosters mutual respect and that nurtures complementary mixes of talents and expertise. Third, what is transmitted from one participant to another is not just information but proto-knowledge. In other words, it is expected that the participants will "... work cooperatively to elaborated and upgrade information ..." using some communally agreed to conventions of knowledge development (Scardamalia, 1991). Fourth, the electronic medium (groupware) has been designed both to enable and to empower all parties to meaningfully participate in the intellectual exchange.

Opponents might argue that computer-mediated collaborative environments are a complex and expensive redundancy—a needless replication of what goes on naturally in the boardroom, the design room, or the classroom. Proponents counter by pointing out that even the best of these collective environments are dysfunctional. For example, despite compelling evidence of group learning's effectiveness, most classroom dynamics are characterized by teacher-led situations, "seatwork," and individual problem-solving activities. Overcoming traditional models of student-teacher interaction takes tremendous energy and commitment; therefore, mediating software makes it less likely that either party will slip back into old patterns of behaviors. Additionally, cognitively oriented groupware encourages learning activities that would not necessarily evolve in the traditional classroom. As a simple case example, participants are able to converse in dyads or triads with classmates not in close physical proximity; whereas, in the real classroom multiple, simultaneous discussions quickly degenerate into a cacophony of voices.

On a more sophisticated level, software can mediate both in the social exchange and in the cognitive activities to suggest patterns of meaning or problem-solving strategies that would be hidden to the novice learner. When networks are enhanced with computerized facilitators, a qualitative change takes place—a transition from aggregate to commune begins. Consider Marlene Scardamalia's description of a software-enriched learning environment:

CSILE (Computer-Supported Intentional Learning Environments) is a hypermedia system built around a student-generated database. In CSILE, the basic knowledge object is a note/idea. Notes are the objects of inquiry and are compiled into note complexes within knowledge-building environments. Students work cooperatively to elaborate and upgrade information in line with the support systems within different knowledge-building environments—including data explorations, explanatory coherence, "how-it-works," analogy, and publication environments. *The idea of a knowledge-building environment is that knowledge is brought into the environment and something is done to it that enhances its value. Tools available in the environment are means by which the value-adding work is done.* Consequently, the design of environments and tools is guided by the goal of maximizing the value added to knowledge—either the public knowledge represented in the community database or the private knowledge and skill of the user. (Scardamalia, 1991; emphasis mine)

CSILE harbingers the future of collaborate software as a knowledge habitat where cognition enhancers (or mind tools) leverage old skills and teach new ones; where mental abstractions are reified into concrete, manipulable objects; and where "intelligent" others mentor the user. To better explain this notion of knowledge as environment, I turn to hypertext/hypermedia.

Hypermedia: AI in Reverse

Individualized teaching is not a new concept. A formalized master/apprentice model of instruction goes back to the medieval guilds, and this mode of teacher/pupil interaction is certainly the form of instruction used for passing along survival skills in pre-literate cultures. However, because of the high costs of such labor-intensive instruction, today the model is enacted only in cases where the skill/knowledge to be imparted is regarded as highly valuable or exceptionally intimate. For the most part, instruction in industrialized societies has been patterned on an economy-of-scale, with a heavy dependency on textbooks and other printed materials.

Computer-supported Instruction

Educational institutions face enormous challenges in designing curricula which match students' levels of preparedness. Demographic projections for the coming years indicate that these problems will not lessen as a wider diversity of students enter the educational stream. The combination of increasing need for individualized attention in the student population and increasing labor-costs for individualized instruction has encouraged educational technologists to find ways to automate the talents of a good teacher. Computer-based training (CBT) seems to have proven too static, so research has turned to a variety of intelligent computer-aided instruction (ICAI) forms.

These systems extend the computer-aided instruction paradigm by adding artificial intelligence capabilities. The goal is a complete "teacher-in-a-box," a comprehensive software program that knows who is being taught (the student model), what is being taught (the knowledgebase), and how to teach (the expert domain). The result is a patient instructor, available 24 hours a day, always able to assess the student's level and correctly adjust instruction, and never tiring, even in the face of seemingly infinite repetitions.

Though the theory of ICAI looks good, in reality, the technology shares many of the problems of AI in general. John Carroll, an advocate of "minimalism" in user documentation for computer systems, also articulates some of the difficulties associated with intelligent tutoring systems (ITS). The architecture of an ITS is computation-intensive; in other words, the system is ". . . heavily invested in developing and maintaining an explicit, symbolic model for each particular learner" (Carroll, 1990). Because of the difficulties of capturing and representing "knowledge" in symbolic representation, subject domains are usually limited and highly procedural in nature. Additionally, though the "teacher" segment of the tutor sometimes does have a semblance of adapting the content of the instructional statements based on the situation and of having a rudimentary tone and style, no working model actually comes anywhere close to duplicating the flexibility or insight of a human teacher. However, these observations are a commentary on the limitations of expert systems in general: as the best understood of traditional AI formalisms, they are still expensive to build and are often too "brittle" to be of real value for tutoring in most domains.

A Teacher in Every Text

The case for hypertext—and its extension, hypermedia—is frequently made in terms of freeing text from the confines of print. In a hypertext environment, information is liberated from its static presentation on the page. Modules are stored as a textbase and can be accessed in a sequence determined solely by the reader. Thus, learners can individualize their exposure to course content by constructing their own paths through an information space, can visit or revisit units of meaning based on their own learning needs, and can use strategies of information processing which accommodate their specific cognitive style.

The first wave of hypertext concentrated on the nodes and envisioned hypertext as an enhancement to online information delivery systems. The next generation of implementation—still in the making—focuses on the linkages and exploits the enormous diagnostic and tutoring potential of the web (which is a form of knowledge representation as powerful as the if-then rules of an expert system, and certainly more flexible and synoptic than production rules).

Text (connected discourse) is a primary form of knowledge representation for literate cultures. While the means of recording and storing text has changed with time (stone tablets, papyrus, vellum, paper, film, and magnetic tape or disk), the overall conventions of this symbol system have remained relatively stable (Bolter, 1991). A collection of wisdom or body of knowledge is encoded into a set of language statements. A learner, skilled in the art of reading, deconstructs the patterns of meaning represented in the text and reconstructs the knowledge configuration within the mental landscape of her own understanding.

There's a teacher in every textbook. However, only experienced readers are proficient at finding the instructor by decomposing the monolithic structure of text. For example, expert readers can vary speeds (skim, scan, thumb) to extract meaning. They also have a wider repertoire for manipulating the design features of the artifact (as in estimating a knowledge "footprint" from format and layout cues, fast lookup routines, integration of text and graphics, and the like). In a hypertext system, a good portion of this expert behavior either has been automated or the need for it has been eliminated. (See figure 3.2.) In short, an intelligent hypertext turns virtual text into a knowledgebase powerful enough to drive an abridged version of an intelligent tutoring system. An extended example explains how this happens.

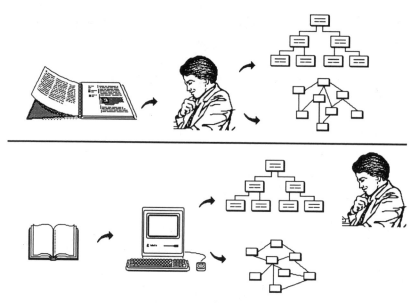

Figure 3.2
In the traditional process, the reader decomposes the text structure and stores knowledge representations in memory. In a mediated hypertext environment, these knowledge structures are prefabricated, automated, and accessible.

Knowledge in the Web

Thanks to advanced information technologies (such as CD-ROM), organizations can now store huge quantities of data. However, if these "organizational memories" are to live up to the metaphor, retrieval mechanisms as fast and as flexible as those used by the human brain must be available. One widely-accepted model for human memory posits that entities ("chunks" of information) are stored as items linked in a pattern of associations. Like a *gestalt*, this rich pattern of nodes and links becomes more than the sum of its parts. Therefore, unlike flat database access, search in the human mind addresses the clusters and relationships formed by these associations. Furthermore, humans are capable of forming categories from observed instances; therefore, the landscape of our minds is not a jumble of discrete properties. The ability to perform feature-extraction analysis (through a mechanism similar to comparison/contrast) produces higher-order representations.

The virtual aspects of hypertext mimic some features of the brain, particularly the associative quality of memory. Additionally, because information in hypertext can be filtered based on layered criteria (such as general to specific, density or complexity, and levels of detail) the system models the cognitive process of abstraction, or the ability to place entities in increasingly higher levels of categorization based on relationships.

Concentrating on nodes and content in a hypertext system creates an enhanced online information delivery system. Focusing on the links and relationships creates a web of associations, not unlike a semantic net—an accepted AI formalism for representing knowledge (Rada, 1991). Like many aspects of computer architecture, the notion of semantic nets was not a direct product of computer research. Rather, the idea was derived from research by cognitive psychologists to explain how overt patterns of reasoning might indicate the covert organization of human memory (Quillian, 1966). A semantic net starts with nodes (facts) and links (relationships). It's the second part that is important. The links can be tagged to indicate attributes and types. This information constitutes the "semantics" of the web; if you don't have typed links, you have a net but not a semantic net.

The resulting conceptual graph (see figure 3.3) can be "read" in ways that a simple net (such as the set of pointers used in crude hypertext) cannot. Obviously, a semantic net is not a tangle of random associations;

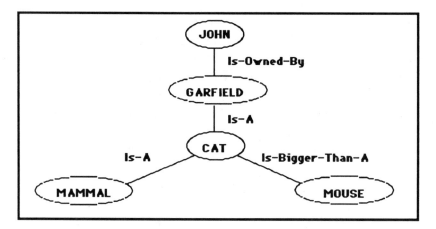

Figure 3.3
Semantic net with property inheritance, adapted from Mishkoff (1988)

therefore, the interrelationships can be sorted and filtered for specific combinations. Other characteristics may yield useful information, such as the distance between related nodes as determined by the number of intervening nodes. Like all artificial intelligence, how you use a semantic net depends on what you want the machine to know. Some computerized semantic nets are designed to have a more rigorous logical structure through a feature called property inheritance, which means that the net has deductive reasoning features. For example, the syllogism "A cat is a mammal and is bigger than a mouse; Garfield is a cat; therefore, Garfield is a mammal and is bigger than a mouse" is contained in the sample network (Mishkoff, 1988).

The graphical browsers in a hypertext system can visually represent the "semantics" (the relationships) of the knowledge web. These maps are essential in overcoming the cognitive load of navigating through a body of text because the web becomes a higher-order abstraction of knowledge. Perhaps more important, such "meta-views" of data help the user to see patterns in a body of information and thus more easily assimilate meaning. Hypertext not only models external reality, it also can shape the interior of our minds by giving us new ways to "see" and to "feel" our information environment. To *reify* a concept is to transform the unobservable into objects that can be examined and inspected. This potential to make implicit knowledge structures explicit is one of the most exciting aspects of hypertext.

Semantic Navigation in Hypertext

Many of our current knowledgebases have limited access points and relatively few ways of searching for concept clusters rather than simple string searches. Traditional organizational conventions—such as the pervasive alphabetical order—have only limited ways of indicating associational trails (the "see also" reference in dictionaries is an indication of how rudimentary our ability is in this area). Users, on the other hand, have a task orientation and need conventions which integrate information from a perspective that reflects the job they are doing. Figure 3.4 demonstrates how a hypertext semantic browser serves an integrative function for a user trying to accomplish a task.

The topic is orbital mechanics. Panel A is a microworld or constrained work space, where the learner tries out the various features of the simulation. Panel D is a textbook representation of the theory associated with the example presented in panel A. Panel C indicates where this topic

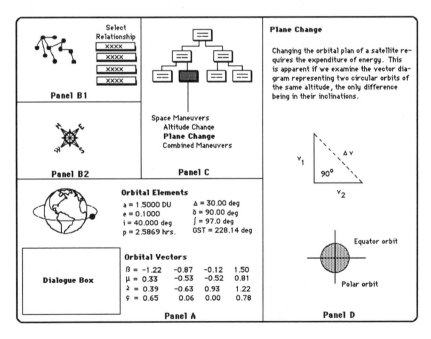

Figure 3.4
Reconfigurable, task-oriented interface for orbital mechanics system. (For more elaborate ideas on how semantic nets — represented as visual constructs — can foster three-dimensional thinking, see Fairchild, Poltrock, and Furnas, 1988; Shum, 1990).

falls in a hierarchical organization of the material. The B panels show two different "knowledge" browsers. For B1, the learner selects a relationship for the keyword and the conceptual map shows nodes connected by the appropriately typed link. B2 treats the text as landscape and uses algorithms to calculate proximity of ideas. Thus, the user can systematically explore the terrain of the knowledge space.

Menu-driven interfaces facilitate a task-orientation by presenting system options at appropriate times in the user's session. However, even embedded menus tend to be too brittle in that they presume a specific procedure is being followed. With a "semantic" interface, conceptually or associationally related parts are integrated on the screen (Fairchild, Poltrock, and Furnas, 1988). My example is fairly straightforward: several different treatments or representations of the same concept are presented simultaneously. Another example, from a high-tech maintenance manual, might integrate a three-dimensional graphic of a particular electronic device, a schematic of the same part, text instruction for test and repair procedures, and a presentation of the theory of operation. Other types of implementations could be more "meta-cognitive" in presenting associational webs, as for example in simulating the "belief" structure of a complex argument. Such hypertext integrations encourage the user to see elements as causally interconnected and consider issues from multiple points of view.

Modeling Expert Behaviors

Chunks and links—a simple idea. Yet how often this connectionist paradigm comes up in modern computing. Once we start thinking of electronic text as a web of knowledge—rather than a collection of bits and bytes—all kinds of symbiotic relationships between words and reader(s) are possible. As a much softer, more tractable form of knowledge representation, hypertext can expand intelligent tutoring systems (ITS) technology by making possible new, more flexible paradigms.

Specifically, mediated, intelligent hypertext provides an exploratory world where the learner is helped to discover the empowering strategies of a domain expert. Like an elaborate form of storyboarding, these systems encourage the "problem-solver" to emulate the heuristics of an expert by providing "templates" which encourage guided-inductive exploration of the problem space. Like a set of "training wheels for the mind" (Carroll, 1990), the embedded semantics in an integrated learning environment provide balance and confidence.

Additionally, hypertext as a platform for teaching exploration strategies in a body of knowledge constitutes a bold reversal of the AI tradition in tutoring, where a machine simulates human cognitive processes and ". . . one expects to save the learners . . . unnecessary cognitive transformations and operations" (Solomon, 1988). In tutoring higher-order cognitive skills, internalizing a large repertoire of such "cognitive transformations and operations" and developing judgment about the situational efficacy of each *may be exactly what is being taught.*

In a traditional classroom, the teacher performs as a "knowledge guide": one who is familiar with the terrain of the discipline and encourages students—through guided-inductive teaching methodology—to explore the many paths of the knowledge space. Well-designed hyperenvironments, because they mediate exploration, can "virtualize" this role of the teacher.

Artificial Neural Networks: The Simulated "Other"

Once dismissed as capable of only trivial results, neural networks now offer exciting new alternatives to traditional AI formalisms. The first wave of interest in the revitalized field of neural networks emphasized tasks naturally amenable to "threshold" representations: visual pattern recognition, electronic circuitry diagnostics, and filtering noise from signal in such applications as sonar devices are just a few examples.

Recently, significant research has focused on making use of the technology's ability to perform feature extractions in large bodies of information, to provide a "mapping" of variables and their interaction in a complex system, and to work with fuzzy logic (Caudill and Butler, 1990). Tasks under investigation are drawn from domains requiring such higher-order cognition as judgment, intuition, and decision analysis. Included in this category are attempts to model learner behavior in specific domains. For example, the Air Force Human Resources Directorate is working to categorize powerful and weak patterns of behavior in learning to play a computer game requiring visuo-spatial motor skills. And a researcher at Duke University is using neural networks to model student errors in learning German grammar via computer-aided instruction. (Let me be clear that the network, by acting as an adaptive filter, models the student's behavior at a very high level of abstraction; it does not duplicate the subsymbolic processing that takes place in neurophysiology.)

How a Neural Network Learns

Artificial neural networks are modeled on the micro-physiology of the brain. The *neural* part is the processing element, a device which "sums" incoming data, records the current state, and passes data on to processing elements in an adjacent layer of the web. The *network* part indicates the rich interconnections linking the layers of processing elements. These links, like axons in brain tissue, interface with other processing elements. This interconnection is analogous to the synapse-neuron juncture in neurophysiology.

The diagram below (figure 3.5) shows how the pieces work together. The particular architecture depicted has three layers of neurons: an input, a throughput, and an output. The internal layer is sometimes called the hidden layer, and sophisticated applications may have several. In this example, the input data is a pattern of two elements. Each input neuron

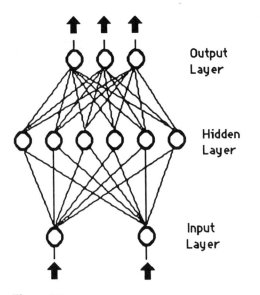

Figure 3.5
Basic artificial neural network (ANN) structure

is connected to all of the processing elements in the hidden layer, producing 12 interconnections between the input and the hidden layer.

Each hidden layer neuron "sums" and stores the total of all values in the input vector. However, after this operation, each middle layer neuron contains a different value because the synapse junctures are weighted; that is, they each multiply the input by a different factor. (Typically, these weights are randomly set somewhere between –1 and 1 upon initializing an untrained network.) Additionally, each neuron has an individual firing threshold. If the sum of the weighted incoming data does not reach this minimum level, no output is sent by that particular neuron to the next layer of processing elements.

Networks *learn* by changing the weights for each processing element in the various layers of the web. How this happens is determined by a *learning rule*, a part of the network's architecture established during its design. Choices in design determine—among other things—if neurons in the same layer are interconnected, how feedback is accomplished, and the sequence and timing of the summation function for each processing element.

To learn, the network must be presented with a set of examples drawn from the target domain. Learning is either supervised or unsupervised. In supervised learning—the more commonly used convention—each element in the training set is paired with an acceptable response. The system makes multiple passes through the examples and the weights adjust in a series of successive approximations toward the goal state. When the weights can represent the examples in the training set without error, the network has learned to associate a class of input patterns with a specific output. In unsupervised learning, the net is not given an indication of correct or incorrect answers. After what could be a lengthy session of running the data sets, the net reaches a kind of equilibrium, or self-organizes. This kind of learning is useful for feature extraction or for finding hidden patterns in large, seemingly chaotic bodies of data.

The training set should contain variations of a specific case. (For example, if we are teaching the net to identify handwritten numbers 1 through 9, we would need a sample drawn from a range of people.) Without this variation, the associational memory is simply a one-to-one matching, and the net cannot be said to have truly learned. Because the designer purposefully introduces "noise" into the data, a trained net can generalize. In other words, portions of the input data may be missing, garbled, or different from what the net has seen before, and the net can still function with a high probability of a correct outcome. The ability to deal with "fuzzy logic" makes this technology especially useful in human systems applications.

Distributed Intelligence: Pseudo-Students, "Knowbots," and Other Simulacra

Including a "student model" has long been recognized as a crucial part of an intelligent tutoring system's architecture. In order for the tutor to adapt to the individual, some mechanism must interpret student response and adjust the treatment accordingly. One approach is simply to contrast the learner's responses with a map of an expert's behavior and to provide more exercise on portions of the knowledge space where the student is weak. A more sophisticated mechanism requires the designer to build catalogs of errors ("bug libraries") students can make in the domain and adjusts treatment whenever misconceptions are detected in the student's responses.

A "virtual student" is similar to a student model but different enough that it needs additional explanation. The idea has utility in a number of areas; diagnosis and peer review come readily to mind. A third use—that of a simulated knowledge "agent" or "knowbot"—has not been fully explored. As practitioners, we all know that the "mixture" in a room of students is a factor in determining the nature of the learning community. An overly aggressive student may be met with hostility; on the other hand, an "off-the-wall" thinker may challenge the creativity of others. Being able to "insert" a specific type of "pseudo-student" into a networked class dialogue as an agent provocateur might provide the teacher with interesting ways to modulate the group dynamics. Or, using a more futuristic scenario, one can imagine a teacher designing a whole spectrum of virtual students embedded in the knowledge landscape, awaiting—like the daemons of frame AI formalism—a particular set of conversational circumstances to awaken them.

Imagine, for example, how a simulacrum might be positioned in a computer-supported collaborative work environment such as MCC's gIBIS (Conklin and Begeman, 1988). In this automated conferencing environment, a conferee starts things off by posting a central issue (see figure 3.6). Other participants respond with positions (a statement or assertion addressing the issue). Arguments pertain to a position. The nodes are linked by using one of nine different relational connections (e.g., responds-to, questions, supports, objects-to, specializes, generalizes, replaces, refers-to). The software more rigorously enforces the agreed-upon conventions of collaboration than typically happens in face-to-face discussion. Thus, nonproductive forms of interaction are minimized. However, a "pseudo-player" could be place in the conference. This artificial neural network (ANN) has been trained to recognize "state transitions" in the web structure and react accordingly. For example, the ANN might detect the emergence of "group-think" abnormalities through overlapping ideas and complementary relationships that are out of tolerance with a norm. The ANN might then intervene as a persona intent upon challenging the clique by intruding directly opposed positions and arguments.

The above example suggests that the simulacrum mimics a human and achieves a kind of full partnership in the knowledge habitat. Other forms of distributed intelligence are possible. For example, a neural network—through its property of spreading association could serve as an adaptable memory for an entity (or entities) in an information environment. In other

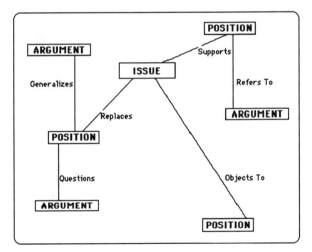

Figure 3.6
Simulation of a gIBIS conceptual map

words, the simulacrum could learn from use. Such is the case of a "knowbot" or intelligent agent. Over time, the "knowbot" learns the interests, life-style, and habits-of-mind of its mentor. As illustrated by Apple Computer's concept of the "knowledge navigator," this agent becomes a kind of personified filter which acts as a guide, an alter ego, a counselor, an associate for the human user.

Marvin Minsky and Seymour Papert's *Perceptrons* (1969) damped enthusiasm for ANN research by saying that the approach could never produce anything other than sophisticated pattern matchers; that similar results could be achieved through symbolic representations (which would then have more generalizable applications); and that whole classes of really "interesting" cases in problem solving could not be addressed by neural networks. This debate about the relative merits of symbolic formalisms over distributed or parallel processing still goes on in AI. Certainly ANNs are only one way of distributing intelligence in a computer system. However, the fluid and associational quality of ANNs over symbolic representation make this an intriguing technology for creating a "virtual" student.

Artificial Reality: The Mad-Hatter's Tea Party

Known limitations loom on the horizon for computer development. For example, the very basics of computing—silicon and electric current—preclude calculations taking place faster than the speed of light. Either a radically new physical medium must be found or software engineers must consider new architectures (such as parallel processing) to improve performance. A similar situation exists for the human-machine interface. There are limitations to how much information a human can process at a given time. Though progress has been made (cryptic command languages became menu selection, which in turn became icons embedded in extended metaphors), physical limitations do exist. One approach for increasing the bandwidth of human information processing is to collapse the *metaphor* of reality most interfaces now use and to replace it with a *simulation* of reality (called a virtual world), thereby eliminating a layer of translation. We have all grown up in a highly visual, auditory, tactile, three-dimensional world and have amazing skills for processing billions of bits of information per second when encompassed in these environmental cues.

Dynamic, real-time, computer generation of complex imagery already exists. Well-financed disciplines, such as medicine and the military, have had these capabilities for some time now—as evidenced by various non-invasive diagnostics scanners and flight simulators or war-game platforms. While the user can directly manipulate objects on the screen, the sensation is one of sitting at a window or a drawing board rather than being in the picture itself. Virtual world technology changes this by adding more realistic sensory cues. Stereo vision (binocular disparity) displays a different image perspective for each eye and produces 3-D representations. The Air Force uses two miniature CRTs mounted in a pilot's helmet to display a 3-D representation of the cockpit and external landscape. A device on the helmet detects head motion and dynamically updates the field of vision. Add a "data glove" or "data suit"—devices which translate hand or body movements into mathematical coordinates that update a graphical screen in real time—and the inhabitant of this artificial reality can directly manipulate objects in the visual field. Though these devices are still experimental, many practical applications are being planned. NASA, for instance, expects to use virtual worlds to expand the confines of the space station. Banks of electro-mechanical control panels can be computerized and literally done away with, yet their image can be represented as a virtual world.

The Desktop Prefrontal Lobe

Perhaps the richest description of virtual reality can be found in the science fiction novels of William Gibson where the author creates the notion of *cyberspace*, an electronically induced, hallucinogenic melding of mind and information structures (1984, 1986, 1989). Experiencing cyberspace for the heroes of Gibson's phantasmagoric adventures is similar to an "out of body" experience.

Though Gibson's version of virtual reality is far beyond what we're able to do now, his image of futuristic information processing depicts two fundamental and defining characteristics of VR technology, no matter what its level of implementation. First, the human no longer sits before the screen display, entering commands through keyboard, mouse, or joystick. Input is through a dataglove or datasuit, which tracks the gestures of the user and maps them onto a user surrogate (perhaps a cartoon-like hand or a mannequin) visible within the display. The situation is much like a puppet and a puppeteer—powerful terms for describing the qualities and nature of the user control.

A second important feature of VR is the changed role of the human in the loop. In traditional computing, the human "controls" the system; she enters a command and the computer responds by carrying out some function. In a virtual environment, the human is just one of possibly many active (even intelligent) elements in the landscape. Something like animate icons, each object in the scene has characteristics and behaviors programmed into it. A controlling program, running in background monitors all the interactions on the landscape and keeps track of the system state. The human does not enter commands per se, but rather performs functions by interacting with other elements in the scene. Input from the human is but one source of control, and, depending up the situation, may be bypassed by the computer in favor of other events or combinations of events taking place in the "frame."

Right now, the "education" industry's major interest in VR technologies is in computer-generated environments that simulate real-work situations. Additionally, most fielded systems focus on training tasks where actual hands-on experience would be either too expensive or too dangerous. These tasks are clearly more skills oriented than they are intended for teaching higher-order cognitive processes. However, the door is open to more creative applications; we need only walk through.

Imagine, for example, the potential for a knowledge domain or "library land" (say late eighteenth-century European history) to be represented in 3-D space. As a learner, you walk through the information environment—or better yet, fly over the landscape—looking for a particular subject. Since your assignment is to write a research paper on some aspect of the French Revolution, you land in Paris, zoom in on the knowledge shop in the Rue de Calais, and walk in.

The friendly proprietor asks you a series of questions to determine your needs and then decides that, since you're just getting started on your project, it would be best for you to visit the Sculpture Gallery. Entering the majestic salon, you are amazed to see life-size figures of the major names associated with the period, clustered in order of importance. (Were you to find this grouping unsuitable for your purposes, you could select another arrangement—alphabetical, let's say—enter your request, and watch the clusters dynamically reconfigure.) As you stroll through the hall, you stop occasionally to activate a button at the base of each figure. The statute dissolves into a collection of icons representing the major subsets of information about this person. You place some of these icons on the automated notepad you are carrying.

After getting a feel for the period, you return to the shopkeeper and show her the items you have gathered. She helps you to refine and focus your collection of topics, and gives advice on gathering further information. Since you've now narrowed your focus sufficiently to make more detailed reading profitable, she directs you to the Hall of Records. This room reminds you of a well-stocked library, except that the items on the shelves are topic modules rather than titles of specific publications. The aisle on the French Revolution is organized alphabetically. However, as in the statue gallery, you can ask for a different configuration. You've decided to write on Danton and the Reign of Terror, and ask that only those items containing a set of keywords be visible. You've further requested that these items be rank-ordered based on a sophisticated algorithm that calculates the number of times the keywords appear and the size of the segment where the word appears.

Starting with the module that appears to be the best choice for finding quality information, you read an initial summary and begin to follow the links indicated by highlighted terms. Some nodes are visual—for example, a four-minute video on Robespierre or a detailed genealogical chart on the French monarchy. An account of Danton's childhood is more comprehensive than you need, so you take the module in your hand and squeeze slightly. On reopening, you find that the text now presents information on a higher level of abstraction. Yet you still have the option of seeing the detail by selecting highlighted terms which then explode into a more fine-grained presentation. You've repositioned the content of your notepad onto a large, interactive workspace, and your icons now serve as a visual outline of the project. As you wind your way through the subject-matter modules, you can select segments and make links to your storyboard outline. You can also tag these links so as to indicate the nature of the relationship. This allows you to "view" your web from multiple perspectives. In other words, you might construct a web which links the materials chronologically, and you might—using the same set of nodes—construct a web that more clearly reflects an argumentative/analytical focus.

Since this is a labor-intensive project, you will spend several sessions at the terminal, each time returning to your workspace and further refining your paper as you continue to "experience" the research material. As you become comfortable with the subject—and in fact become something of an expert in the content area—you develop enough background to appreciate the major scholarly works. So at this point, you may want to read in their entirety relevant masterpieces such as Thomas Carlyle's multi-volume history, *The French Revolution,* or Georg Buchner's play, *Danton's Death.*

The above example demonstrates an important cognitive feature of virtual reality: though the "knowledgescape" may have familiar features, neither the scene nor "puppet" shares 100 percent fidelity with reality. They are symbolic, and hence amenable to all sorts of purposeful manipulations and distortions. In other words, virtual realities may more aptly be described as "alternative realities," and their most powerful features may stem from making the familiar strange, from combining fantasy with fact, and from engaging the imagination with the purely rational. One of the key vendors of virtual world technologies uses simulated participation in a non-Newtonian Mad-Hatter's Tea Party where nothing behaves according to the laws of gravity to demonstrate the features of the system—and, of course, to suggest the power of serious parody, placed literally in our hands by artificial reality.

This technology will become the vehicle for liberating domain knowledge from sequentialism. Right now, the requisites for defining course content are rigorous. Instigated by textbook publishers, enforced by legalism, and rationalized by the responsibilities of professionalism in teaching, most course content is ossified. I'm not advocating that all course content be "virtual," but I am saying that the ability to appropriately introduce the "divine madness" of a virtual environment has benefits.

Tools that Teach

Two almost diametrically opposed scenarios seem to be unfolding around the expectation and effects of computers in the workplace. One is a tale of displacement and "dumbing down" of jobs by machines that all but take the employee out of the loop. In the service industries, point-of-sale-job-aids handle everything except the face-to-face exchange between the customer and the salesperson. In the professions, expert systems involve the human in the decision-making process only as an observer of symptoms (for example, in medicine) or as a collector of parameter data (for example, in prospecting and mining).

The second scenario is one in which a high-tech workplace makes greater and greater demands on the cognitive skills of the work force. However, in this future world, the notion of computer applications has been "enriched" so that they are now both teaching devices as well as tools of production. As a kind of AI in reverse, the software diagnoses the user's ability and accommodates both strengths and weaknesses, all the while nurturing, coaching, and challenging the user on to ever-higher levels of achievement.

Such a partnership between human and machine is not as futuristic as it may sound. It's a relationship that has been enacted throughout the development of our species. The argument that intelligence is not an indigenous quality of the mind but a product of structures of the brain and "technologies of the intellect" (Goody, 1977, 1986) has been made many times (Olson, 1985; Solomon, 1988). And, anthropologists studying even prehistoric societies can point to "cognitive tools"—cultural artifacts which by their very use shape and enrich mental operations (Boas, 1983; Levi-Strauss, 1968). "Tools that teach" is not a new concept, just an underexploited one.

The computer may be the most complex of tools created by humankind. Though no one can forecast the future of the computer, the growth of educational technologies would indicate that the computer may also be the most compelling of teaching media. My somewhat sportive virtualization of *content, context, teacher,* and *student* mirrors the convergence of three general trends in computer-mediated advanced media: (1) computer-supported collaborative work, (2) knowledge as environment, and (3) scientific visualization (McCormick, DeFanti, and Brown, 1989; Defanti and Brown, 1989). The convergence of these trends should bring us intelligent, communal learning environments that emphasize synergy over isolated skills, productive interaction over radical individualism, and cooperation over competition.

Acknowledgments

This paper was written during the author's tenure as a University Resident Researcher at the Air Force Armstrong Laboratory, Human Resources Directorate, Intelligent Systems Branch, Brooks Air Force Base, Texas. The findings and opinions of the paper are those of the author and should not be construed as an official Air Force position or policy.

References

Boas, F. (1983). *The Mind of Primitive Man.* Westport, CT: Greenwood Publishing Company, 1983 reprint of the 1963 revised edition.

Bolter, D. J. (1991). *Writing Space: The Computer, Hypertext, and the History of Writing.* Hillsdale, NJ: Lawrence Erlbaum.

Carroll, J. M. (1990). *The Nurnberg Funnel: Designing Minimalist Instruction for Practical Computer Skill.* Cambridge, MA: MIT Press.

Caudill, M. and Butler, C. (1990). *Naturally Intelligent Systems.* Cambridge, MA: MIT Press.

Conklin, J. and Begeman, M. L. (1988). "gIBIS: A Hypertext Tool for Exploratory Policy Discussion." *ACM Transactions on Office Information Systems,* 6(4), 303–331.

Defanti, Thomas A. and Brown, M. D. (1989). "Insight through Images," *Unix Review,* 7(3), 42–50.

Fairchild, K. M, Poltrock, S. E., and Furnas, G. W. (1988). "SemNet: Three-dimensional Graphic 'Representations' of Large Knowledgebases." In R. Guindon (Ed). *Cognitive Science and Its Applications for Human-Computer Interaction.* Hillsdale, NJ: Lawrence Erlbaum.

Gibson, W. (1984). *Neuromancer.* New York: Ace Books.

Gibson, W. (1986). *Count Zero.* New York: Ace Books.

Gibson, W. (1989). *Mona Lisa Overdrive.* New York: Bantam Books.

Goody, J. (1977). *The Domestication of the Savage Mind.* Cambridge, England: Cambridge University Press.

Goody, J. (1986). *The Logic of Writing and the Organization of Culture.* Cambridge, England: Cambridge University Press.

Levi-Strauss, C. (1968). *The Savage Mind.* Chicago: University of Chicago Press.

McCormick, B. H., DeFanti, T. A., and Brown, M. D. (1989). "Visualization in Scientific Computing," *Computer Graphics,* 21 (6), 1–14.

Minsky, M. and Papert, S. (1969). *Perceptrons.* Cambridge, MA: MIT Press.

Mishkoff, H. C. (1988). *Understanding Artificial Intelligence.* Second Edition. Indianapolis, IN: Howard W. Sams.

Olson, D. R. (1985) "Computers as Tools of the Intellect," *Educational Researcher,* 5–8.

Quillian, M. R. (1966). *Semantic Memory*. Cambridge, MA: Bolt, Beranak and Newman.

Quinn, C. N., Mehan, H., Levin, J. A., and Black, S. D. (1983). "Real Education in Non-real Time: The Use of Electronic Messaging Systems for Instruction," *Instructional Science*, 11, 313–327.

Rada, R. (1991). *Hypertext: From Text to Expertext*. London, England: McGraw-Hill Book Company.

Scardamalia, M. (1991). "An Architecture for the Social Construction of Knowledge." In Lawrence Birnbaum (Ed). *Proceedings of the International Conference on the Learning Sciences*. Charlottesville, VA: Association for the Advancement of Computing in Education, 397.

Schrage, M. (1990). *Shared Minds: The New Technologies of Collaboration*. New York: Random House.

Shum, S. (1990). "Real and Virtual Spaces: Mapping from Spatial Cognition to Hypertext," *Hypermedia*, 2(2), 133–158.

Solomon, G. (1988). "AI in Reverse: Computer Tools that Turn Cognitive," *Journal of Educational Computing Research* 4(2), 123–139.

Welsch, L. A. (1982). "Using Electronic Mail as a Teaching Tool," *Communications of the ACM*, 25(2), 105–108.

4

Cognitive Architecture in Hypermedia Instruction

Henrietta Nickels Shirk

Introduction

Since the availability of hypertext authoring tools for the general public, beginning with Apple Computer's release of "HyperCard" in 1987, this relatively new communication medium has been heralded as ideal for providing instruction (see, for example, Landow, 1989; Marchionini, 1988; and Jonassen & Mandl, 1990). Although the initial term "hypertext" has now given way to its successor "hypermedia," we are still dealing with text, or at least textual concepts. As David Jay Bolter (1991) assures us, "A hypermedia display is still a text, a weaving together of elements treated symbolically. Hypermedia simply extends the principles of electronic writing into the domain of sound and image." In this analysis, the term hypermedia is used inclusively to represent all forms of electronically linked symbolic elements which are employed for instructional purposes. Likewise, information from sources referring to hypertext applies equally to hypermedia, so the terms are often used interchangeably.

Hypermedia may be defined as information which is presented via computer-controlled displays so that readers can jump easily and quickly between different items. The question which is important for hypermedia instruction is, after all, not so much the terminology, but rather the implications of hypermedia for audiences (users and learners) of this instruction, and specifically, how one should organize and structure instructional information in this relatively new medium. This analysis presents an examination of hypermedia designed for instructional purposes from the perspective of the different categories of cognitive architectures (or maps) which it makes possible and which differentiate it from traditional oral and paper-based instruction. While the discourse structures inherent in the content of hypermedia materials influence to a certain degree the design options available to their creators (instructional technologists or information designers), these structures likewise project their creators' differing views of human cognition through the mental maps they select for presenting their material.

Similarly, those learning about a particular subject through the technology of hypermedia often assimilate from its cognitive architectures various assumptions about the material they are learning, as well as the creator's implied guidelines about how best to learn a particular body of discourse. The dangers inherent in using the medium of hypermedia are in keeping with Marshall McLuhan's warning that the use of any medium entails the danger of "imposing its own assumptions on the unwary" (1964). Perhaps by understanding some of the assumptions becoming evident in hypermedia construction, users of instructional hypermedia can become more aware about the issues surrounding how learning takes place in this medium, and authors of instructional hypermedia can become more aware of the impact of their organizational choices upon the recipients of their instruction. An examination of some of the organizational problems in hypermedia instruction, as well as their suggested solutions, is followed by an analysis of why many of the current solutions are inadquate. Finally, some recommendations are made for establishing a structure and rationale for developing guidelines to be applied to instructional information presented via hypermedia.

The Problems Inherent in Creating Hypermedia for Instructional Purposes

The problems which surface when creating hypermedia for instructional purposes revolve around issues of control and responsibility. As Bolter (1991) explains, "In general, the reader of an electronic text is made aware of the author's simultaneous presence in and absence from the text, because the reader is constantly confronting structural choices established by the author." Because of these built-in choices, there is a randomness and therefore an unstable quality inherent in hypermedia, especially in those programs in which the reader (learner) is allowed by the software to make choices about what to study, and even to make changes to the text or to add new links among the text's various symbolic components and structures.

Jakob Nielsen (1990) expresses the essence of the issues surrounding instructional hypermedia. As he explains, "hypertext is well suited for open learning applications where the student is allowed freedom of action and encouraged to take the initiative. . . . On the other hand, hypertext may be less well suited for the drill-and-practice type learning that is still necessary in some situations." A medium which allows the learner to "wander" through information, determining individual learning paths and (by implication) even learning objectives is certainly discomfiting to many professionals involved in instructional design. The assumptions behind instructional design imply the structuring of learning experiences. Several unsettling questions are inherent in hypermedia: How do learners know what they don't know? How will learners be encouraged to discover what they don't know, and should this discovery be allowed to occur purely by chance? And finally, how much structure, or how many structures should be included in a effective hypermedia instruction, and what should be the characteristics of these structures?

There are no easy answers to these questions. As Shneiderman and Kearsley (1989) advise, "The authoring challenge is to design the *structure* of the hypertext database to match the ways that a user might want to think about the topics. . . . Knowledge must be *structured* in a way that supports the mental models that readers may create when they use the hypertext system" [italics added]. But how does one accomplish this task of creating multiple structures of information for learning purposes? Responding to this challenge requires that one have considerable experience in teaching a particular subject and that one have an excellent understanding of the various ways in which the content of a subject area can be structured and its various parts interrelated. Knowing about some of the cognitive architectures which the medium itself makes possible provides a useful starting point for applying hypermedia to instructional requirements.

Some Solutions to Problems in Creating Instructional Hypermedia and Their Limitations

There are two categories of solutions to the problems of creating hypermedia for instructional purposes—those which are product-oriented, and those which are process-oriented. The former deal with structural patterns for organization, and many of these approaches tend to catalog possibilities for organizing materials. The latter deal with how-to information and suggest activities and methods for ascertaining effective techniques for organizing hypermedia instruction by examining its users' (learners') needs and actions. Both approaches contribute different facets to the ongoing discussion about appropriate structures for instructional hypermedia, and both approaches have their limitations.

Product-Oriented Organization

Among the product-oriented approaches to hypermedia organization are those expressed by Jonassen (1989), Horn (1989), and Horton (1990). All three of these authors view hypertext/hypermedia/online documentation as but alternative media (or containers) for cognitive and organizational structures with which are familiar existing thought-patterns for presenting information. These commentators look at products rather than processes.

On a fundamental level, one can envision hypermedia as a system of relationships (links) between information units (nodes), which many commentators believe is similar to the way the human brain works. As Jonassen (1989) observes about hypertext, "It is this organizational structure that mimics the organizational structure of memory. It also provides a structure for the information model for storing information in the hypertext. That is, the organizational structure of the hypertext may reflect the organizational structure of the subject matter or the semantic network of an expert." Information stored in an organized way is easier for learners to find when they are searching for it, and it provides the learner with structural models of the preferred ways in which a particular knowledge domain should be organized. Jonassen further describes the advantages the hypermedia in presenting information in multi-dimensional ways: "Because of its ability to explicitly convey the organized structure of information, hypertext is able to externalize the structure of the subject matter. It represents the information as it should be stored in memory. The semantic network of ideas provides a representation scheme." But how does one "externalize" a semantic network, or the organization of knowledge in memory?

Jonassen suggests that we use concepts from the study of reading and rhetoric, and consider employing several possible structures found there, such as problem-solution, chronological or sequential, parts-whole, cause-effect or antecedent-consequent, and others. While Jonassen does not prescribe when to apply these paper-based rhetorical structures to hypermedia, he does suggest some processes for designing information models, which will be summarized in the next section. Jonassen's reliance on paper-based organizational structures is understandable in view of the relative newness of hypermedia as an instructional medium. It is difficult to relinquish communication structures with which we are already familiar to create new structures for a new medium.

Others suggest that known cognitive architectures should be the bases for structuring hypermedia. Robert Horn, in *Mapping Hypertext* (1989), recommends that hypertext be structured according to its linkages, which can be based on either paper or computer metaphors. He suggests that the associative links writers try to get onto paper integrate quite easily into the link and node structure of hypertext. The paper-based structures espoused by Horn are: library card catalogs, footnotes, cross-references, sticky notes, commentaries (extended discussion of one text in another text), indexes, quotes, and anthologies. Horn further suggests that, as an alternative, we can use computer metaphors to conceptualize hypertext systems. The computer-based structures he identifies for this purpose are: linked note cards, popup notes, linked screens or windows, stretch notes (outline), semantic nets (knowledge representations consisting of networks of concepts and their relationships), branching stories, relational databases, and simulations. Horn does not indicate, however, when one should use a particular metaphor, or whether and how metaphors should be combined, if at all.

William Horton, in *Designing and Writing Online Documentation* (1990), has also used paper and computer metaphors in suggesting ways to structure online information in general. Horton maintains that "throughout all disciplines, all cultures, and all ages, certain ways of organizing and presenting information have been popular. . . . They are popular because they are conceptually simple and hence easily learned and remembered." According to Horton, these patterns include: sequences, grids, hierarchies, and webs. His descriptions of the characteristics and uses of these patterns provide starting points for making decisions about applying them. Briefly, these organizational structures may be summarized as follows:

(1) *Sequence*—a linear organization in which the user has the choice of moving either forward or backward, while being directred down a prescribed path. It is appropriate for fixed training sequences and step-by-step instructions.

(2) *Grid*—an orthogonal structure which organizes and presents information in two logical dimensions, as in a table. Users look up information by scanning the row and column heads and then zeroing in on the intersection of the selected row and column. It is appropriate for presenting information which has two logical dimensions.

(3) *Hierarchy*—a topic and subtopic structure which emphasizes top-level generalities and overviews, from which one can move to ever more specific information. In all types of hierarchies, users are given previews of what lies below each topic. The "star" hierarchy (which moves from a central topic out in all directions) is appropriate for online help systems, where users need to return to a central list of topics. The cross-referenced hierarchy makes scattered information rapidly accessible without duplicating it everywhere it is needed.

(4) *Web*—a network structure in which any topic can refer to any other topic. Webs can join topics together in vast networks of related information, much like associational thought. In fact, this structure is most appropriate for promoting the kind of exploration that occurs during development of new ideas.

Horton's four structures for online information are familiar thought patterns which are usually expressed on paper or within computer programs. Like the descriptions of Jonassen and Horn, Horton's structures are based on what we already know about human thought patterns. However, Horton does ask a question crucial for hypermedia instructional designers: "What structure is best?" According to Horton, "picking the right structure for an online document involves trading expressive power for predictability. . . . [It] also requires matching the organization to the purpose of the system. In general, for learning, provide a strong sequential path with possible side excursions; for browsing, organize information in a cross-referenced hierarchy; for fact-finding, organization does not matter. Just make it quick." Instructional designers may argue that true learning involves not only the study of sequences, but also browsing, and fact-finding, and even fact-creation.

A common characteristic of all these product-oriented approaches to hypermedia architecture is that they rely on existing, paper-based, and computer-based cognitive structures. Designers of hypermedia are selecting structures they already know. These structures assume somewhat static models, which are suitable for existing paper and computer applications, but which may not always be directly transferable to the multidimensional and dynamic structures made possible in hypermedia. It might also be questionable whether these existing structures, recast in their new electronic "clothing" as instructional hypermedia, are currently contributing to a new art form in the sense that Marshall McLuhan (1964) intended when he observed that "each new technology creates an environment that is itself regarded as corrupt and degrading. Yet the new one turns its predecessor into an art form." On the othe hand, if (according to McLuhan) the "content" of any medium is always another medium, then perhaps these product-based approaches to designing hypermedia are a necessary step in its evolution.

Whatever one's perspective on learning requirements, the question still remains as to how one goes about deciding upon a structure for hypermedia instruction. Other authors have addressed this issue not in terms of what is available from our past experiences of structural organization, but rather in terms of how we should go about analyzing the needs of hypermedia learners and use the results to build our structures, and in terms of how some of these structures function. These commentators look at processes rather than products.

Process-Oriented Organization

Among the process-oriented approaches to hypermedia organization are those expressed by Jonassen (1989), Wright and Lickorish (1989), and McKnight, Richardson, and Dillon (1989). All three of these authors view hypertext/hypermedia/online documentation as the result of processes that they recommend or observe in its creation. Their views are similar in that they perceive appropriate cognitive and organizational structures for hypermedia emerging from these processes.

Jonassen recommends that information models can be either deductively or inductively developed. His two approaches may be summarized as follows:

(1) *Deductively Developed Model.* This top-down approach to designing the information model requires starting with a content structure or expert's knowledge structure. According to Jonassen, "if we assume that learning is the process of replicating the expert's knowledge structure in

the learner's knowledge structure, then learning should be facilitated by a hypertext that replicates the expert's knowledge in the structure of the hypertext and explicitly conveys that structure." He further suggests that one can define that ideal knowledge structure by using quantitative methods to develop a cognitive or semantic map of the expert's knowledge, statistically analyzing word associations of all of the related concepts in the content domain. Semantic networking software can also be used to assist in identifying all the nodes and their relationships, resulting in a map of the subject matter domain.

(2) *Inductively Developed Model.* This bottom-up approach to hypertext design is based on observations of how users navigate through unstructured hypertext and how they assimilate information from hypertext. When looking for patterns of access and their relationship to individual differences in orer to use this information as predictor variables, Jonassen suggests starting by providing learners with access to unstructured hypertext, and then auditing the paths which these users take, classifying the prominent paths or routes. Next one can develop guided tours of the hypertext based upon these path analyses, evaluate the user's preferred learning styles, and finally assign a guided tour of the hypertext that is consistent with the user's style.

Jonassen's two developmental approaches are opposites—the deductive model is focused on the knowledge expert, and the inductive model is focused on the learner. Jonassen does not explain how to reconcile the potentially different cognitive maps of knowledge experts working in the same subject areas. One also wonders how the two developmental approaches are related, or even if they should be related. By employing one model in designing a hypermedia structure, one may be omitting important contributions from the other perspective. Suppose, for example, that a learner's typical paths through information and preferred learning style do not match those of a knowledge expert? Whose view is to be assumed as the correct one? These concerns finally cohere around the question of what are to be the most appropriate sources for hypermedia structures.

McKnight, Richardson, and Dillon (1989) provide a slightly different perspective on these sources. Somewhat like Jonassen's inductive model, they prefer to approach the question of structural design from the perspective of observing learners. But rather than work with hypermedia itself, these authors suggest that, when a paper document is being converted to hypermedia format, one possible approach to structure is to study a group of users interacting with the paper document, not a hypermedia system. They further suggest that this kind of observation and analysis enables the electronic version of the document to be structured in a manner best suited to the way in which it is likely to be used. Their assumptions, of course, are that there is a paper document to work with at the beginning of the process and that the paper-based habits of users are directly translatable to electronic equivalents. In fact, Horton (1990) carries this translation viewpoint to the extreme, when he summarily advises, "Don't put documents online until you have good paper documents." The implication appears to be that hypermedia should not be created until one first creates the same information in a paper medium.

Perhaps the most comprehensive process-oriented solution to the problem of creating instructional hypermedia structures is that espoused by Patricia Wright and Ann Lickorish (1989). Unlike the previous authors, Wright and Lickorish show that the discourse structures inherent in the content of a hypertext influences design options in terms of selecting content (including its quantity and representational form), creating links which define the routes through text which readers can take, offering users signposting and navigational techniques in moving through the content, and providing assistance to users in manipulating information and accomplishing the tasks which have led them to study the hypertext materials. It is particularly useful to analyze these structures in terms of their linkage styles, because the links provide the methods for more static structures to become dynamic. While there is not space to present all of these authors' conclusions about hypertext design decisions here, the following summary of the four discourse structures which they identify are useful in thinking about instructional hypermedia as a medium capable of contributing to the creation of knowledge.

(1) *Highly Cohesive Text Structures*. These linear text structures assume that the learner will start at the beginning and read through to the end, and they therefore often use book-like mental metaphors. Typically, such structures communicate procedural instructions and tutorial materials where it is important to learn basic skills and knowledge before proceeding further. A typical linking mechanism in thse structures is the "loop," which takes learners out into related materials but always returns them to the exact points where they began searching for additional information. This kind of hypermedia structure automates the footnoting and referencing mechanisms typical of paper-based learning, and it provides a linear view of human cognition.

(2) *Modular Text Structures.* These discourse structures are composed mainly of independent modules of information. They typically communicate many kinds of encyclopedic and reference information, and they therefore often employ notecard or file metaphors. The linkage is usually to other modules, and it may be either reader or text initiated. Reader-initiated links are open-ended with no requirement to return to the point of departure, while text-initiated links require a return to the original place. In tests where the modules of information are independent from each other, labeling the links is not important. However, hierarchic or multi-theme texts do require precise labeling for their links. Modular text structures are common in instructional hypermedia, and its conventions are only beginning to emerge. These structures view the human mind as working with "chunks" of information.

(3) *Hierarchical Text Structures.* These discourse structures offer no symmetry either in format or content across the information in the different branches of the hierarchy. Most technical texts are probably of this kind, where a series of topics is discussed, each having its own internal structure. When the structure of a hierarchy is highly symmetrical, it can also be presented as a matrix. Typical mental metaphors for presenting this kind of information are tours through buildings, following roads and streets to certain goals, and various other game models involving quests. Linkage to such structures is either up or down within a branch of the hierarchy or across to another branch. This cognitive architecture encourages the establishment of relationships among different meanings and pieces of information in a web-like configuration.

(4) *Multi-Theme Text Structures.* These discourse structures present a wide variety of options for ordering information. They can be used for cross-referencing verbal and visual information, and they might be thought of as being multidimensional (the metaphor of the "electronic book"). Their links are created by the individual learner to meet specific needs and interests. These linkages are usually a wide variety of semantic links, and it becomes important that the discourse structure itself influence the learner's information retrieval strategies, perhaps even leading the learner to asking the appropriate questions at various points in the learning process so that movement can occur to the next several possibilities. Unless learners are provided with ways of identifying different categories of links and of perceiving the material from some particular viewpoint, the result may be great confusion (discourse anarchy) rather than meaningful learning. This structure encourages multiple cognitive views of material.

While Wright and Lickorish's descriptions of discourse structures covers some of the same categories as those presented by Horton, they differ in the emphasis these authors give to the dynamic processes involved. They aptly point out how the discourse structures inherent in the content of hypermedia influence the design options available. They are not only applying structures already known, but reinterpreting them within the expanded boundaries of the new medium. It appears that they are much closer to McLuhan's "new art forms" than many of the views previously presented.

However, all of the process-oriented approaches to hypermedia cognitive structures entail the assumptions of their creators. Jonassen's deductive and inductive models might be effective, if they could be combined, but he does not tell us how to accomplish this feat. He may be assuming that a hypermedia designer would know when to use one or the other approach, or even how to merge them. McKnight, Richardson, and Dillon (1989) assume that paper-based user habits and practices are directly transferable to the online realm. Their approach does not consider the different possibilities available through the new medium, nor the fact that adaptations and changes to old mental patterns will need to be made. Wright and Lickorish's concentration on the display and navigation aspects of hypermedia discourse structures is useful in examining the processes involved in designing. However, like the product-oriented approaches, one may wonder whether all the possible structures have been identified, and whether the current perspectives are still too bound to our paper-based perceptions.

Recommendations for Developing a Rhetoric for Instructional Hypermedia

While both the product and process approaches to structuring hypermedia for instructional purposes contribute to defining the cognitive architectures for this medium, as we have seen, each approach has its limitations. One is left with questions about the best ways to replicate and create cognitive architectures within hypermedia instruction.

How does one identify a cognitive architecture? And is it possible that knowledge domains have more than one such structure? How is the designer of hypermedia to know which thought patterns to present? Should users of instructional hypermedia be able to select those structures which are most congenial with their learning styles? Finally, how does one know when a particular hypermedia system is effective as a learning tool? While not all these questions can be answered here, we can learn from the trends described in the current commentary and research, as well as identify several potential directions for further work in this area. There is much to be accomplished as the medium of hypermedia is given meaning within the context of instructional design, and as knowledge is constructed through it by both instructional designers and learners.

As the research which is summarized here indicates, there are four categories of cognitive architectures operative in a hypermedia learning situation. One needs to consider the presence of:

(1) *Cognitive architectures inherent in the subject matter itself.* One can assume that there is more than one cognitive architecture available within most subject matter areas and disciplines. Robert Horn (1989) hints at this possibility, when speaking of paper metaphors for hypertext linkages: "Usually, a specific hypertext system has a dominant metaphor and may have facilities for other metaphors." And Wright and Lickorish (1989) emphasize the importance of multiple cognitive architectures in their description of multi-theme texts, in which "there are likely to be a rich diversity of text structures" and for which there is the need for hypermedia authors to consider all design options available. Identifying all these structures may never be entirely possible, but assuming that there is only one suitable one is a narrow vision of the social construction of knowledge within this medium. Of course, there are no precise rules for deciding which knowledge experts to rely upon, and even how many knowledge experts should be consulted when designing instructional hypermedia.

(2) *Cognitive architectures which are imposed on the hypermedia instruction by the designer.* These are structures based on the designer's own assumptions about the subject matter, the learners, and the medium itself. For example, if one assumes that the subject matter in a particular discipline is best presented only through drill-and-practice, then the sequenced, linear structures described by Horton and Wright and Lickorish become the only possibilities for presenting the material, even though the medium allows for other possibilities. On the other hand, if one assumes that any learner presented with a hypermedia system is going to expect that self-directed, randomly generated pathways through the information are available, then one would naturally always present instructional information in a web-like structure. Like the media to which McLuhan refers, humans too need to be careful about imposing their own assumptions on the "unwary" learner. The range of possibilities available in hypermedia make the decision to use it more complex than the decisions

to use more conventional media with which we usually have more predictable results.

(3) *Cognitive architectures brought to the hypermedia instruction by the learner.* Perhaps, in their planning during this early stage of development, instructional designers of hypermedia should be a bit less concerned about selecting the mental models for the information they present for instructional purposes based on content and their own predilections, and more concerned about the mental models readers bring to a particular subject matter or body of knowledge. Regardless of what design selections are made, learners will impose their own assumptions on them, and hypermedia provides a wide variety of options for such assumptions. For example, if certain learners always learn more effectively through highly structured material, the most creative multi-theme hypermedia text will not impress them, and they may even be inclined to skip parts of it. Little research has been accomplished in the area of learning styles and their design assumptions as applied to hypermedia instruction, so we know virtually nothing about how effective certain hypermedia discourse structures are upon the learning process or on different learning styles. There is much work to be done in observing learners using hypermedia systems of all sizes and in a wide variety of subject areas. Perhaps, then we can make more accurate predictions about what is effective and what is not.

(4) *Cognitive architectures which are made possible by the medium of hypermedia itself.* While text, graphics, audio, animation, and video can now be combined through hypermedia, we do not yet know the best combinations of these techniques for particular learning purposes. Perhaps it is too early to list discourse structures for hypermedia, because, as we have seen from the research summarized here, one tends to view it from the perspective of the existing technologies of which it is composed. We have not yet evaluated hypermedia *as a medium* in itself, but rather efforts to date have attempted to describe how existing cognitive architectures can be reflected in its design. We know that, through its ability to incorporate other media, hypermedia becomes multi-dimensional. But we do not know for sure what this multidimensionality means for instructional design. Hypermedia requires more observation and testing within actual learning environments before reliable lists of rhetorical options (both product-based and process-based) and their implied cognitive architectures can be composed with any degree of accuracy and reliability for implementation.

McLuhan (1964) reminded us that within any medium or structure there is something called a "break boundary," a point at which a particular system suddenly changes into another or passes some point of no return in its dynamic processes. He viewed these break boundaries as resulting from the cross-fertilization of one system with another, which creates huge reversals, as well as paradoxes, in society. Hypermedia is a cross-fertilized medium, which incorporates all the communication media we have experienced to the present time, and which is in the process of turning these media into something else. According to McLuhan, the "message" of any medium or technology is "the change of scale or pace or pattern that it introduces into human affairs." That is, the medium shapes and controls the scale and form of human association and action, frequently speeding it up, moving from stasis to motion, or from mechanical to organic. It seems that some of the difficulties in defining hypermedia and some of the discomfort in applying it (especially to instructional design) that we are currently experiencing result from the fact that it is a potential break boundary medium which has not yet entirely emerged from the boundaries it has assumed from our "old" technologies.

The information structures of hypermedia have no simple counterparts in printed media, although they often borrow mental metaphors from print in order to enhance learner understanding. The new flexibility made possible by the differing cognitive architectures possible in hypermedia demand that we eventually create a new rhetoric which will serve as a set of guidelines for those creating as well as evaluating hypermedia in instructional environments. It may be too soon to articulate all the details of that rhetoric, but it is not too soon to recognize the limitations of our current perspectives on hypermedia. Such recognition should help to clarify our goals as we move toward defining the "break boundary" of this new rhetoric.

References

Bolter, Jay David. 1991. *Writing Space: The Computer, Hypertext, and the History of Writing.* Hillsdale, New Jersey: Lawrence Erlbaum.

Horn, Robert E. 1989. *Mapping Hypertext: The Analysis, Organization, and Display of Knowledge for the Next Generation of On-Line Text and Graphics.* Lexington, Massachusetts: The Lexington Institute.

Horton, William K. 1990. *Designing and Writing Online Documentation: Help Files to Hypertext.* New York: John Wiley.

Jonassen, David H. 1989. *Hypertext/Hypermedia.* Englewood Cliffs, New Jersey: Educational Technology Publications.

Jonassen, David H., and Heinz Mandl, eds. 1990. *Designing Hypermedia for Learning.* New York: Springer-Verlag.

Landow, George P. 1989. The Rhetoric of Hypertext: Some Rules for Authors. *Journal of Computing in Higher Education* 1:1, 39–64.

McKnight, Cliff, John Richardson, and Andrew Dillon. 1989. The Authoring of HyperText Documents. In *HyperText: Theory into Practice*, edited by Ray McAleese. Norwood, New Jersey: Ablex.

McLuhan, Marshall. 1964. *Understanding Media: The Extensions of Man*. New York: McGraw-Hill.

Marchionini, George. 1988. Hypermedia and Learning: Freedom and Chaos. *Educational Technology* 18:11, 8–12.

Nielsen, Jakob. 1990. *Hypertext and Hypermedia*. New York: Academic Press.

Shneiderman, Ben, and Greg Kearsley. 1989. *Hypertext Hands-On!: An Introduction to a New Way of Organizing and Accessing Information*. Reading, Massachusetts: Addison-Wesley.

Wright, Patricia, and Ann Lickorish. 1989. The Influence of Discourse Structure on Display and Navigation in Hypertexts. In *Computers and Writing: Models and Tools*, edited by Noel Williams and Patrik Holt. Norwood, New Jersey: Ablex.

5

Multimedia: Informational Alchemy or Conceptual Typography?

Evelyn Schlusselberg and V. Judson Harward

Articles on multimedia are appearing faster than the tulips this spring.[1] And not just in the trade journals and technical magazines. Scarcely a week goes by now without a reference to multimedia in those telltales to mainstream currents, the *Wall Street Journal* and the *New York Times*. If you have worked in multimedia for a while, either in a university research laboratory like us, or in industry, it's hard to avoid feeling a heady excitement. We all believed that this day was coming, but like a sunny harbinger of June in a New England March, commercially viable multimedia may have arrived sooner than any of us expected.

And now a confession—our feeling of enthusiasm and excitement is followed almost immediately by an embarrassing nervousness. For several years, we have developed prototypes and some full-scale applications while experimenting with multimedia design. We have been able to write off our less successful efforts as the result of hardware limitations or inadequate funding or simply as bold experiments that failed. If manufacturers really have generated the silicon to make multimedia affordable, then we can expect a production-oriented market that will expect far more of the multimedia software community. Multimedia application design is a field that we expect to mature quickly but with some pain.

The simple truth is that multimedia application design is hard. Today's students and even their parents have grown up appreciating the increasingly visual sophistication of modern advertising and television. MTV presents a more sophisticated visual environment than the magazines and television shows of the fifties. Today's students lose patience with visual juxtapositions they consider to be bland, trite, or insincere. So, if we are assembling a multimedia document, contemporary culture challenges us with the richness of everyday media and the ingenuity with which magazine editors and television producers compete for our attention. Obviously we can not nor do we want to compete with television on its own terms, but the novelty of multimedia will wear off very quickly unless we can fuse meaningful content with rich visuals in a sophisticated design.

There are a number of problems here. Attractive video or complex graphics cost money. It takes talented people to produce them, people that we can expect to be in increasingly short supply now that a new market for their talents has opened. The expectations of today's school and college audience are such that an attractively produced textbook may well be more acceptable than a modestly produced but more expensive multimedia application. How can we select those instances where multimedia has something to contribute?

What Makes a Good Application?

We have come to look for five characteristics in the applications we tackle. We think of these characteristics as points of leverage for the new technology, a fulcrum that justifies the use of multimedia.

• We look for subjects that are more immediately understandable through video or animation than through text or diagrams. Frequently, these subjects involves understanding a process, even one as simple as tying a knot. It is much easier to learn how to tie a bowline by watching someone, even on video, than it is by reading a book, no matter how many diagrams it contains.

• We look for subjects that are complex in a way that visual reference can simplify. Marcel Ophuls' film, *The Sorrow and The Pity*, explores the Nazi occupation of France in a series of interlocking interviews that both inform and contradict each other. The settings and faces of the interviewees are crucial in helping the viewer start to find his or her way through the historical and moral ambiguity of those years in Clermont-Ferrant. The documentary is held together by visual and audio cues that help us come to recognize the witnesses whose testimony we must judge. The film and any multimedia application built from the reedited interview footage will be more complex and at the same time more comprehensible than any plain text transcript because the viewer can associate face with voice with content.

• We look for applications that present an experience that the student is unlikely to have had but which we can simulate. If we can adequately recreate the experience of walking though a Parisian neighborhood, then we can immerse the student in the sounds and gestures and manners of the French streets. And more importantly, we can help the student appropriate that experience as her own. We can allow the student to explore the streets and shops in a very real sense, one that allows for simple curiosity and dead ends.

• We cherish applications that make the abstract real and the distant immediate. We admire the courage of Preston Covey's videodisc and application, *A Right to Die? The Case of Dax Cowart* or Orson Welles' film, *F for Fake*, in which you can watch Elmyr de Hory forge a Picasso sketch and then pitch it into the fire.

• We look for applications where multimedia techniques can make the student or scholar more efficient at a task. Often these applications involve the organization and comparison of large numbers of images or video segments. The application fits the hand and mind of the user better than more traditional tools.

If multimedia were a science, then we should be able to use multimedia to enhance any document or presentation. Instead, we are opportunists, looking for an angle, "a hook to hang the story on" as journalists say. We shall have more to say about the kind of hook we look for in a minute. On the other hand, we want to emphasize that multimedia is most certainly NOT informational alchemy. An ugly or poorly structured application can destroy a student's interest just as quickly as a dull textbook. We think of multimedia design today as a craft or art, but one with many apprentices and few if any masters.

We recall the populist enthusiasm that greeted desktop publishing a few years ago. Many expected that the new technology would liberate them from the tyranny of book and graphic designers. Our colleagues in publishing describe one result as "ransom notes," books or handbills printed in such a plethora of fonts and point sizes that it looks as if each heading and caption had been cut from a separate newspaper like the ransom notes in a Victorian mystery. And the desktop publishers had mentors available, the typographers, printers, and designers who had served them so well for years. Recently we hear that desktop publishers have either availed themselves of a subset of the old services that they required or they have schooled themselves to become typographers and designers themselves. The problem for us in multimedia is that we lack these mentors. We are producing what will probably be considered multimedia "ransom notes" in years to come, but we have no sure models with which to improve our design. We feel certain that evolution will triumph in the end—good design will prevail over bad. We believe the process is already underway.

Multimedia Design

The rest of this chapter will suggest some of the design principles that we have arrived at empirically. In part, we would like to share some of our ideas about what constitutes good design and how to achieve it, but for us, these ideas also go to suggest what multimedia IS and what it IS NOT.

The Importance of Metaphor

We have found in the first place that multimedia design proceeds in a different way from the other kinds of design with which we are familiar. Such projects begin normally enough with conversations between the designers in our group and the content experts we are working with, often faculty members or museum curators. The content experts define the goal. If they are teachers, then they know what they want their students to learn. If they are scholars or engineers, then they have a task they habitually perform and want to expedite. I have already mentioned that as opportunists we look for a hook, a point of leverage before commencing a multimedia project. Often while talking among ourselves or with the content experts, there comes a moment when a way to present the material in the multimedia application emerges that seems both natural and at the same time unexpectedly right. Our enthusiasm for the concept is the best indicator that we are on the right track. Significantly, in every case that we can remember that hook has involved an analogy or metaphor.

We would like to describe you a very simple example and one which required little invention on our part. The French film director, François Truffaut, idolized Alfred Hitchcock, and in 1962 he conducted a series of interviews with the British director. These interviews eventually appeared in an attractive coffee table book.[2] The book was structured to present the two directors comments on Hitchcock's work, film by film. Truffaut was particularly fascinated by Hitchcock's visual technique, and the book included plentiful black and white illustrations to remind the reader of the scene under discussion. If the discussion dealt with editing or, say, a tracking shot, the book would offer a sequence of small pictures to recall the whole sequence.

It occurred to us that this book in a very immediate way WANTS to be multimedia. In a sense, the book is a metaphor for a multimedia application, so we decided to pay it the reverse compliment of creating a prototype multimedia application that resembles both the book and a VCR through which so many of us have come to know or reknow old movies. Using an X toolkit widget designed by Mark Ackerman, we can page through the text of the interview using multiple fonts and point sizes for typographical emphasis. This chapter deals with the film *Suspicion*, and the famous scene in which Joan Fontaine comes to believe that her husband, played by Cary Grant, is out to poison her through a bedtime glass of milk. Hitchcock explains with glee that the scene is so riveting because he inserted a light in the milk glass. Truffaut initially misunderstands and asks if Hitchcock means he directed a spotlight on the glass. No, Hitchcock insists, he actually put a small light in the glass so that it would appear luminous as Cary Grant ascends the spiral stair to Fontaine's bedroom. In the coffee table book this exchange appears on a page with a single illustration of the scene. Figure 5.1 shows it as it appears in our prototype application.

The screen is book-like until the user clicks on the illustration, but then a second screen appears to play the entire scene. This screen suggests a combination television and VCR because the user can play the scene under his own control, even frame by frame if he wishes. The application depends on the realization of two metaphors, the book and the video player. The original book instantiated the first but couldn't suggest the second. We hope neither director would object to what we have done here. In fact, we wish we could show them. We suspect that they would be enthusiastic about the possibilities of this new way of conducting film criticism. For us, one of the interesting things about the prototype is that the very bookishness of the first part of the interface reinforces the flow of the interview.

The Stages of Design

The identification of appropriate metaphors or "hooks" is only the start of the design process. In fact, we feel that the design of multimedia applications typically proceeds on three interdependent levels:

• *Conceptual design* specifies the goals, the content and the structure of the application. The conceptual design must also identify the metaphors

Figure 5.1
In this prototype application the upper right window is booklike while the
lower left window uses the VCR metaphor.

or analogies that will guide the user through the process of using the
application.

• *Interactive design* specifies how the user will affect and be affected by
the application, and how this interaction will support the underlying
application metaphors.

• *Visual design* specifies the actual appearence of the application. It
should lead to the fusion of complementary media and the efficient
manipulation of visual elements for communicating information in a clear
and attractive manner.

Conceptual Design   The conceptual design must depend somewhat on
one's multimedia authoring environment. If one is using Hypercard,
which possesses a base underlying metaphor, the index card, the units
upon which the application is built are cards, backgrounds, and stacks.
Muse, the authoring environment that we have developed in Project
Athena's Visual Computing Group possesses no single underlying
metaphor, and uses a completely flexible visual scheme. We structure

an application into packages, which inhabit screensets. A screenset is any group of windows (technically a window tree) that can be moved as a group across the screen. In the Hitchcock application, the book pages and the video player are both separate packages supporting distinct metaphors.

Thus, the first stage of conceptual design involves the specification of the application's goals, content, and metaphors. The second stage can then be thought of as the process of partitioning the application's content into segments which map onto the metaphors as they are expressed through the structure of the authoring environment.

Let us discuss a much more complicated example. We have worked for a number of years with Gilberte Furstenburg and Janet Murray of MIT's Modern Language Department on an interactive application that allows a student to explore a French neighborhood, the Quartier St. Gervais in Paris. This district has undergone the sort of economic change that we are all too familiar with here in America—the quartier has gentrified bringing in a young affluent set of new residents and shop owners at the same time that it has forced many older long time residents to move elsewhere. Professor Furstenburg wanted to use the quartier's setting and this social question as a vehicle to expose students to the vocabulary, accents, gestures, and points of view of the many different subcommunties of the quartier. She wanted her students to come away with a sense of the range of French language and culture possible within the bounds of a few city blocks.

She also wanted the student to find her own way in this environment and to have the freedom to savor this linguistic and cultural diversity. This goal of exploration and the inspiration of the Aspen Moviemap Project[3] led to the first application metaphor, the walking tour. The student can walk the streets of the quartier and can choose which direction to take at the corners. The walking tour suggested the usefulness of a map, and we, therefore, included an intelligent street map that always marks the students's current position.

The quartier is also one of the oldest parts of Paris, and possesses many attractive buildings with long histories. Professor Furstenburg assembled a collection of historical views that suggested a further guidebook metaphor to supplement the walking tour. At important monuments, video segments record interviews that explain the building's history and significance. French subtitles help the student disentangle what may be an unfamiliar accent, and if she does not recognize a word she may look it up in an illustrated interactive dictionary. A second set of interviews addresses the neighborhood changes already mentioned, and the student can pose the same question to a cross section of the quartier's residents and shop keepers. Since the student chooses the question and the respondent, she assumes the role of researcher and interviewer. This application then is carefully built up from a series of interrelated metaphors and analogies that range from the simulated walking tour to the tool-like illustrated dictionary. Figure 5.2 shows some of the application's features.

Interactive Design   Conceptual design leads smoothly into a consideration of interactive design. Having settled on the application metaphors

Figure 5.2
In this application the student's current location, the St. Gervais Church, is marked on the map (upper left corner). Students learn about the church by browsing through the "historical guidebook" (bottom left corner), listening to the monk (center), and visiting the church (by pressing right side icons). The online dictionary (bottom right corner) is always available as well as subtitles when there is a speaker.

with the content expert, the multimedia designer has the challenge of making it real to the user given the capabilities of computer and authoring environment. The art lies in the adaptation. How elaborate a realization of the metaphor is useful? What can the designer omit? What additional elements might the designer want to include that extend the real world capabilites the analogy mimics? No tourist map that you can carry in your pocket will point out your changing position as you stroll the streets.

Each metaphor or set of metaphors suggests a separate reality. How do you ease the user gently from one to the other? In the Quartier St. Gervais we extended the walking metaphor to provide a transition to the interview segment. One steps into a shop to interview the shopkeeper. Once the student listens to the shopkeeper's interview, she can then move to a matrix of questions and respondents to become the interviewer herself. As the user becomes more familiar with the application, these metaphors become less important, and she may favor buttons which trigger direct transitions to other application segments. The interface should accommodate both the novice and the expert user. While the expert needs access to options, the novice is all to often confused by them. A consistent look and feel is important. Each application screen should behave in a predictable way while not sacrificing visual interest. The application may present the same content at different levels of sophistication to support students with different skills and interests. In the Quartier St. Gervais, the student can select one of two levels of subtitles. The first records every word, every pause, every slur and stutter, for those students getting used to a particular accent. The second presents only the keywords of the conversation to aid in vocabulary recognition.

Through all this, the designer should remember that the student experiences the application through time, not as a series of static screens. Using a multimedia application is a little like sitting in a theatre audience watching a drawing room comedy except that the user, not the play's director, is signalling the actors' entrances and exits.

Visual Design   For some media designers, particularly those most comfortable with paper, we have been skirting the fundamental issue of screen design. Visual presentation is a critical issue, but we feel that it should reinforce and, therefore, derives from the application model specified by the conceptual and interactive design. An application designer lays out a screen, positions buttons, and selects fonts and colors to enhance the application metaphors and the underlying logic of the interface. The visual design shouldn't drive the concept or the interaction but rather the reverse. Visual design both directs the user's attention and reduces competition for it. A hierarchy of font sizes may emphasize the structure of a table of contents. This principle is drawn directly from conventional typography. But multimedia possesses problems that are peculiarly its own. Our daily lives are so media-saturated that we filter everything that we see or hear. Different types of media preempt our attention at their own level. If a screen presents a still image and a motion video segment in separate windows, most of us will watch the motion video and ignore the still image. After all we can return to the still once the video has stopped. But if we change the still image, almost everyone will momentarily turn from the video to examine the new still. The spoken human voice preempts silent video while silent video preempts most other types of sound. Note that we have moved beyond purely visual design. So perhaps we should term this third category sensory design. In any case, we propose that a hierarchy of media priorities exists. Successful applications should respect this hierarchy and should not allow a less important part of an application to preempt a more important one through an ill-timed or poorly selected presentation of a media element.

Conceptual Typography

The multimedia designer should look to the fields of typography and graphic design for inspiration and critical judgment, but multimedia design goes far beyond electron typography. We feel the true unit of multimedia design is not the pixel or the window or the screen, but rather the concepts and metaphors represented by these screen elements. The success of a multimedia application depends in large part on the designer's skill in assembling a symphony of metaphors that advances the goals of the application at the same time they complement each other.

We have collaborated with Lois Craig of MIT's Department of Architecture and Merrill Smith of the Rotch Visual Collection in building an interface for their videodisc on the Boston suburbs. Our goal in this case was to build an interface that incorporated but improved upon the tools an architectural historian normally calls upon in a slide library. The suburbs application possesses a browser, a light table, and a four-part slide viewer for lectures that all draw upon a slide collection recorded on videodisc. Unlike the slide collections in libraries the slides in this application are never in use, or misfiled, or smeared with finger prints. Each scholar can have a copy of the whole collection in his office. The light table, as shown in figure 5.3, allows one to magnify the slides as well as to position them freely. What makes the application particularly seductive, however, is that the architect or scholar is already familiar with all these functions because they are a normal part of his everyday work. The application simply integrates them more closely than they appear in a normal library. Our conceptual design began with a consideration of how people currently use visual resources in a library and then transferred that model into the workstation environment while improving its functionality.

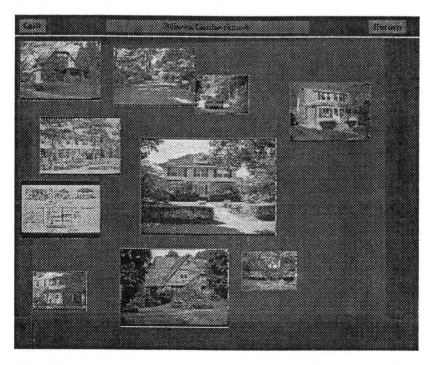

Figure 5.3
The online light table displays user-selected images that can be easily repositioned and resized.

At this point you might ask, as we have, why multimedia must be LIKE something else. Why does multimedia need metaphors and analogies? After all, books and films have their own aesthetics; they usually don't borrow them from other media. Or is it that they quickly diverged from their design inspirations. The earliest printed books owed a great deal in form and design to the preceding manuscript codex and the codex owed a great deal to the scroll. We expect that over the next several generations multimedia design will depend less and less on models from other media and will discover its own design principles. But is it surprising that in coming to grips with a radically new technology, we turn to models with which we are familiar and use them to master a new way of seeing, of composing, and eventually we believe, of thinking?

Notes

1. For instance, the February 1991 issue of *MacUser* featured multimedia through a series of keynote articles targeted at the average Macintosh user, and the April 1991 issue of the *Communications of the ACM* focused on the issue of digital multimedia for a more technical audience.

2. François Truffaut, *Hitchcock*, 2nd edition (New York: 1985).

3. Robert Mohl, "Cognitive Space in the Interactive Movie Map: an Investigation of Spatial Learning in Virtual Environments," Ph.D. Dissertation, Department of Architecture, M. I. T., (1982); Andrew Lippman, "Movie-Maps: An Application of the Optical Videodisc to Computer Graphics," *Computer Graphics*, Vol. 14, no. 3 (1980): 32-42.

6

Dimensions, Context, and Freedom: The Library in the Social Creation of Knowledge

Gregory T. Anderson

Introduction

This chapter will look at the use of multimedia information technologies and libraries in the social creation of knowledge. Multimedia are the technological analog of the social construct of libraries. For centuries libraries have held the physical collections and provided the social space for interactions between readers and knowledge. Now multimedia technology and libraries enable new relationships between knowledge and individuals. In the world of networked information these two mechanisms for creating knowledge free that social process from the constraints of media format, time, and geographical proximity. Through use of multimedia information technologies, libraries can fully support the organizational and personal freedom in the pursuit of knowledge creation. Dertouzos (1991) describes the potential of freedom of choice, relationships and communication:

Philosophically, the NII [National Information Infrastructure] should be viewed as a new means of controlling our personal locality—choosing our working associates, vendors, entertainers, and perhaps even friends—without being limited to those that happen to be physically near. With the importance of physical proximity diminished, every person on the national information infrastructure could assemble his or her own electronic "neighborhood." (p. 40)

In the creation of his or her own electronic "neighborhood," the individual is making social decisions, linkages, and constructs about the communication of knowledge and about those relationships which are most rewarding. These are choices of freedom. As in any good neighborhood, the library is a cornerstone which provides the social space for interactions and the knowledge which informs the content and value of the relationship. Libraries today present themselves as pivotal transition points and models for information technology development because they are an active agent where freedom and dimensions for knowledge creation occur. By providing the shared space, either physically or virtually, for the relationship between readers and knowledge, libraries are knowledge creation organizations. Multimedia technologies now seek to emulate and improve this environment without regard to physical proximity and time.

The creation and communication of knowledge and the role of libraries as active agents in that process encompass many issues and perspectives that involve the interaction between libraries, readers, and information technology in the sociological process to construct new knowledge. As universities articulate and consider the questions about the interaction of learning, society, and technology, libraries offer themselves as models, and laboratories to help answer those questions. As a forum for techno-logical solutions, libraries symbolize the past and provide a prologue to answer these complex, social issues. As established components of the knowledge process, libraries are currently in a great period of transforma-tion, so they become good testbeds for what has worked, what hasn't worked, and what we envision in the world of multimedia information technology.

Through the use of multimedia technologies and communications, libraries begin to fulfill the promise to support the authorship, collection, management, and delivery of linked information and media. The focus on the authorship of knowledge speaks to the core value of librarianship–service to the reader/author. The promise of multimedia technology frees knowledge creation from the structure of the library and empowers the author to create his or her own frame of knowledge. Creation of new knowledge is barren without communication, and communication is the social interaction in the creation process. Garvey (1979) describes science as a social system:

Science is a social system in which interactive communication is the salient feature. In effect, this view proposes that what any innovation in scientific communication must do is *change the information exchange behaviour* of scientists. Innovator's should take cognizance of the fact that alterations of the system may not always effect the desired changes in scientists' behavior unless the goals of the innovation are compatible with the individual and aggregate goals of the scientific community. (p. 125)

The individual and aggregate goals for the social creation of knowledge hinge on the individual's freedom to pursue knowledge in a personalized, meaningful way, and to communicate that knowledge with context and multiple dimensions but without the constraints of time and distance.

Context and Dimensions

The creation of knowledge happens in a context of other knowledge. Knowledge inevitably springs from the varied worlds surrounding us, and we incorporate these various natures into our creative process. Through the library, the reader is aware of the context of the knowledge in hand— that is, how knowledge relates and interrelates to the other knowledge surrounding it.

The evolution of library services can be viewed as expanding, inclusive concentric circles. Originally libraries stood as separate buildings housing collections, and their activities were concentrated within this physically bound structure. The next circle encompassed cooperative arrangements between libraries. The process of interlibrary lending and borrowing remains with us today as a basic service which enlarges the sphere of materials available to researchers. Another aspect of that circle is the development of consortial arrangements and agreements between libraries for cooperation or among a set of libraries with shared features.

In both of these circles, library procedures provide a context for the knowledge collected. Through the physical and intellectual control of books and journals, libraries have arranged their knowledge coherently together with other materials. A book on the shelf is surrounded by other books which speak to the same (or similar) topic. This context supports the serendipitous activity known as browsing, where the reader can review items in the stacks and perchance discover materials previously unknown. This highly personal and invididualized method of knowledge creation is an important service and social value to maintain in the world of technology. It is all about linking knowledge—either author-to-knowledge or knowledge-to-knowledge linking.

Today, the development of high speed network communications challenges libraries with a quantum leap in communications capabilities and a challenge to the definition of "library." In essence, the network becomes the library through the provision of access to a dizzying array of resources.

Now libraries must grapple with the actual delivery of documents to the reader, with the development of intelligent, evaluative directories to point readers to productive resources, and with the management issues related to providing links among knowledge in a variety of formats.

Clearly, libraries have been most comfortable providing the context for printed and textual knowledge. This class of information has been managed by libraries and an array of procedures have been established to handle these formats in an effective manner. Non-textual knowledge, however, such as visual information—slides, maps, videos, etc. have been treated as second-class elements of knowledge. Libraries have not done a good job of organization and context setting for these key forms of knowledge. As society becomes more visually literate, supporting these knowledge media becomes increasingly important.

Multimedia information technologies support the electronic creation of contexts for all forms of knowledge, and offers the potential for handling visual materials especially well. In this multimedia world, information systems and libraries must improve their understanding of the relationships and context of knowledge. Negroponte (1992) responded to the question: "What is the biggest challenge you see to realizing the Media Lab's visions?" by stating:

Making computers with common sense and understanding. And to do that, we need to understand understanding itself. Today, computers push bits and pixels around with no knowledge of what they are. But as soon as signals have a sense of themselves and communication channels can recognize content, we can begin to build truly personalized systems that filter and fashion information for an audience of one. (p. 40)

Libraries already have a sense of "what they are." The signals, namely, the printed materials that libraries receive and collect, are understood as communication channels and containers of knowledge. Their format and organization give an awareness of the knowledge they contain. Textual materials exist to be a communication channel. Libraries are experts at recognizing the value and content of these "communication signals." Even with this expertise, however, librarians are now under the transforming influence of information technology, and they are re-assessing their role and skills in providing services to readers. The value of context which libraries contribute to the creation of knowledge will continue to be valid; in fact, it becomes more important than ever in the world of information technologies. Building systems—physical, human, and technological, to provide this context is the challenge for the academic library. In Negroponte's terms, libraries recognize the knowledge signals that they collect, and as a communication channel, libraries are expert and efficient in recognizing both content and value to knowledge. A task for libraries is to leverage technology for gathering and communicating information in a variety of forms so that personalized systems can manipulate and present the information rather than attempting to make the presentation themselves.

Knowledge is multi-dimensional and flexible. Until now, libraries and information technology have presented knowledge as two-dimensional. This presentation has not been very deep; we describe objects well, but we do not provide the deep access to knowledge content. The potential of multimedia technologies is to offer knowledge in its natural setting: a multi-dimensional frame which lends itself to an infinite variety of permutations. Tufte (1990) describes our present knowledge environment as a two-dimensional "flatland" and urges us toward a more interesting world:

Even though we navigate daily through a perceptual world of three spatial dimensions and reason occasionally about higher dimensional arenas with mathematical ease, the world portrayed on our information displays is caught up in the two-dimensionality of the endless flatlands of paper and video screen. All communication between the readers of an image and the makers of an image must now take place on a two-dimensional surface. Escaping this flatland is the essential task of envisioning information—for all the interesting worlds (physical, biological, imaginary, human) that we seek to understand are inevitably and happily multivariate in nature. Not flatlands. (p. 12)

Context and Dimensions for the Library

It is critical for libraries to understand knowledge and communication in order to transform their services and to assume a more balanced, collaborative role in the process of knowledge creation.

Tufte (1990) says that information consists of "differences that make a difference" (p. 65). The measure of this description is: "different from what?" Libraries traditionally provide the setting and structures to answer this question by providing the context for knowledge pursuit. Libraries are the home of the society of text: text, context, and, now, technological hypertext. Hypertext is an exciting concept only because it is now crudely possible in present technology. The human, social process of knowledge creation is hypermedia in its most elegant form. The cognitive linkages, relationships, and context of information where new knowledge is created is a social, collaborative process which libraries have always nurtured.

In providing the context for knowledge, several interwoven relationships exist in libraries: the creation and management of relationships among information objects, the creation of context to enable the interaction and discussion of information between the user and that knowledge, and the communication and promulgation of the resulting new knowledge creations.

Context and relationships are the social part of the equation in creating knowledge. As raw material that is fungible and extensible, information lends itself to dramatically new experiments. Multimedia technologies exploit these characteristics of information and begin to emphasize the fact that information has many forms and a variety of depth and breadth. The use of technology to support the libraries traditional function of linkage and coherence confirms that knowledge is both deep and must be presented in context. Knowledge is not linear and sequential. The promise of multimedia is that it can emulate the society of the library's relationships by enabling the use of a wide range of information by people who are using it in different ways.

The knowledge which the author shares with the reader should dynamically communicate the coherence, the simultaneity, and the author's interactions and relationship with the knowledge. This ability cannot happen in the static, two-dimensional world of paper. The richness of knowledge is the linking and contextual presentation of the variety of related information created by the author and shared in a cognitive, social relationship with the reader.

Librarians must engage in a more active dialogue with their users in order to understand the essence of knowledge creation: communication. Garvey (1979) says:

When scientists are convinced that librarians understand *why* communication is the essence of science, then librarians will find that they will have some enthusiastic, collaborating scientists on their hands. (p. 126)

Given the librarian's understanding of the critical importance of communication to researchers, one of the collaborations which librarians and scientists can pursue is information systems design. Librarians need to hear from the users how information is used and how information technology is changing those information behaviors. There is a tendency to attribute confusion and cognitive overhead to the amount of information now available. "The information glut" is a real condition because of the immediacy of communications and the infinite expansion of knowledge. Tufte (1990), however, identifies information delivery design as the culprit, not information itself:

Confusion and clutter are failures of design, not attributes of information. And so the point is to find design strategies that reveal detail and complexity—rather than to fault the data for an excess of complication. Or, worse, to fault viewers for a lack of understanding. Among the most powerful devices for reducing noise and enriching the content of displays is the technique of layering and separation, visually stratifying various aspects of the data. (p. 53)

The partnership of librarians and users understanding this complexity and designing systems together is a shared effort toward attaining the improved communication and knowledge creation.

Context and Dimensions for Multimedia Technologies

Multimedia information technologies offer approaches to stratify information in a visually effective manner and to offer a promising answer to the continuing question: what benefits can we really expect to achieve from these new technologies? Computers and communications are moving toward the environment where the knowledge compact among authors, readers, and libraries can become reality. The technological requirements remain formidable, but understanding the quality and relationship of knowledge creation is yet more fundamental to the process.

As Tufte points out, layering and separation of information are powerful tools to address detail and complexity. These strata also point out the need to go beyond the "flatland" of the video screen and to present the reader with a multi-dimensional display that is rich in knowledge content and has minimal confusion because the reader is free from the two-dimensional constraint of presentation. Tufte (1990) believes that multimedia visualization offers promise for productive support of the knowledge creation process:

. . . the essential dilemma of narrative designs—how to reduce the magnificent four-dimensional reality of time and three-space into little marks on paper flatlands. Perhaps one day high-resolution computer visualizations, which combine slightly abstracted representations along with a dynamic and animated flatland, will lighten the laborious complexity of encodings—and yet still capture some worthwhile part of the subtlety of the human itinerary. (p. 119)

This human itinerary has always been highly personalized and has not been fettered by any restriction to a single medium. While the need to create a more dynamic presentation of information is readily acknowledged by librarians and technologists alike, the technological progress to move us toward this new sphere is an ongoing process. The process now appears to be in an early stage of evolution—somewhat fractured, many possibilities, few standards, and lack of a common focus. As a social organization, libraries should accept the shared responsibilities of invigorating their efforts to understand communication as Garvey advises, and making known to system developers the needs of authors. In such a world, the linkage between development and application can be immediate and immediately effective. Libraries become the perfect testbed for multimedia development efforts because they are the social space where the creation of knowledge is most common. The greater the continuity and the more the application of research efforts in multimedia to the application in real settings, then the greater is the substantive progress and the ability to build more powerful systems with each cycle. Libraries provide the content, the relationship space, and the human itinerary for knowledge creation. Libraries and readers/authors need the multimedia technologies as the spark for new, more productive forms of knowledge.

Freedom

The goal of libraries and technology is freedom; to enable the reader or author to frame knowledge without constraints, and focus energy toward the creation of knowledge rather than on understanding an imposed, external organization of that knowledge. Freedom exists when the author/ reader can build upon the linkages and paths of knowledge in a flexible, multi-faceted world. In describing the goal of aesthetic education, Friedrich Schiller (1967) describes a force or drive which is playful and free, *Spieltrieb*:

Spieltrieb, the drive to play, is a power or force . . . where the individual becomes self-sufficient and creative and truly free. It is a confluence of two opposing drives: the sensuous drive and the formal or rational drive. The balance and perfect melding of this results in a whole, free individual. Spieltrieb exists where, then, the formal drive holds sway, and the pure object acts within us, we experience the greatest enlargement of being: all limitations disappear, and . . . man has raised himself to a unity of ideas embracing the whole realm of phenomena. During this operation we are no longer in time; time, with its whole never-ending succession is in us. The judgement of all minds is expressed through our own." (Letter XII)

Freedom and Libraries

The role of the library and of multimedia technology is to endow the individual with freedom in the pursuit and creation of knowledge. To free the individual from the existing organizational and physical constraints of the library, we should understand the future roles of libraries and how those new visions can free the individual.

If libraries are to remain pivotal in the social creation of knowledge, how must their relationship with the reader and the author change? What is the role of the library in this knowledge space that is virtual, bountiful, multi-dimensional, fungible, and social?

The role of the library in an information rich society is capturing, creating, and nurturing the linkages, pathways, and management of nodes of information. This role requires a broad, encompassing perspective to understand the relationships among knowledge and the linkages an author has used to create knowledge. Within that web of connections, a reader is free to pursue the author's linkages captured and created by the library and to create an infinite variety of new linkages which speak specifically to the new reader's personal needs.

In addition to establishing the intellectual relationships among separate knowledge items, libraries should also look deeper to support and mirror the authorial imperative of the process of knowledge creation. Into this vacuum comes then the variety of multimedia links which bear the authorship of the creator, and the library provides the technology and the society to support those links and to provide the connections to the information as requested by the reader. It is here that libraries and technology begin to understand and support understanding. In the process of research, the reader follows the linking paths back to primary materials in order to understand how an author came to the conclusions.

By preserving and making these linkages in hypermedia, the library represents to readers the official publication. The reader is then free to create personal linkages which express the reader's social interaction with that published knowledge.

Libraries must become a vacuum into which the kernels of knowledge creation can freely enter. This metaphor by Kakuzo (1977) illustrates why a vacuum is essential:

This Laotse illustrates by his favourite metaphor of the Vacuum. He claimed that only in vacuum lay the truly essential. The usefulness of a water pitcher dwelt in the emptiness where water might be put, not in the form of the pitcher or the material of which it was made. Vacuum is all potent because it is all containing. One who could make of himself a vacuum into which others might freely enter would become master of all situations. (p. 45)

As a vacuum, the library redefines its concept of collection and space. This new definition is an active collaboration with the reader and the author who are in the process of creating knowledge, and not the old, passive definition of the library as collector after the fact. The concept of collection has an important historical and future meaning for libraries. Previously, the care and selection in the collections process described the intellectual pursuits and academic priorities for an institution. The text-oriented constructs used in this two-dimensional "flatland" were oriented toward a large coherence of locally assembled knowledge that became greater than the mere sum of its volumes. In other words, the library built linkages and context into the library collection based upon those completed creations of knowledge. Today, libraries are capitalizing upon the communications capabilities of computer networks and nurturing the creation of linkages, pathways, and management of information nodes without regard to physical location. Understanding the coherence of this new, networked information society may help respond to Garvey's counsel that librarians understand that the essence of science is communication. Communication is an active entity, and as knowledge is communicated, it is changed by that action. Similarly, libraries are changed by the action and communication between reader/author and the information supplied by the library.

The new definition of "collection" for the library may become the dynamic management of linkages, both across the network of information as well as the preservation of the multimedia knowledge links that authors/readers determine. Libraries must balance and nurture both perspectives: the large, outward-looking view of communicating knowledge via computer networks, and the inward-looking view to support the links and tools that an author has used in the process of creating a new knowledge object. In both views, libraries begin to achieve the goal of empowering authors and readers to define their own virtual collections by establishing links that speak to their knowledge needs.

The library's understanding of its space is further advanced because of the impact of computer networks and remote access to information resources. Still, the library can and should fulfil its societal role of a neutral, information-rich environment where knowledge is created and sought. This environment will be both physical and virtual. The physical space will continue to be that sphere where the drive for learning can be expressed, and the personal journey of the intellect can be charted. This will remain true especially for the interaction between the reader and the materials that remain in the "flatland." Through powerful computing power and liberating computer tools, the reader can experience that same freedom of linkage to knowledge in the virtual computing sphere as in the physical. The librarian's skill in linking, managing, and facilitating connections becomes yet more important in this technological world.

The professional librarian becomes the facilitator and the expert in making the linkages for the authorial work, and from that supported base, the reader is then freed to explore those links as well as adding their own linkages to other information. This personalized system includes linking, manipulating tools that are flexible to work with any media and to inform the creation process in a meaningful way. Based upon the experience and collaborative development by the professional librarian, these tools are freely available to the reader. The reader is then free to dwell on the reason for the creation of knowledge rather than trying to fathom the superstructure of the collection of knowledge available.

In order for the library and librarian to become a vacuum, they must acquire the fundamental skill of "understanding understanding." By actively becoming the vessel of context and dimension into whose emptiness the reader can freely enter and pour knowledge, the library becomes the collection of the creation process as well as the social collection of knowledge and relationships. As a physical and virtual space, the library nurtures the *Spieltrieb* of the individual's drive for knowledge.

Freedom and Multimedia Technologies

As it is for libraries, the goal of multimedia technologies is to free the individual from the constraints of system design and media focus, and permit instead the focus on knowledge content and relationship. As noted above, the technological need to provide more dimensions is critical to the success of multimedia technologies. Multimedia technologies can provide the three-dimensional landscape of mountains instead of the two-dimensional flatland of current presentations. Multimedia technologies can progressively disclose layers of separated information and reduce the noise and clutter of the perception of "information overload." The continuous curve of computational power holds promise to meet these technological obstacles. As the power of computing increases, the empowerment of the individual increases as well. When plugged into a high-speed communications network, the social potential of computing expands dramatically; the relationships that are established electronically between individuals and between knowledge and the individual already constitute a new era in learning. The application of multimedia technology in a networked environment further enhances the degree of freedom available to the knowledge creator. As computers and networks shrink time and space by providing context, dimensions, and freedom, they too become a vessel which is a vacuum. The ability to create within a networked, multimedia technology environment is a powerful and liberating force.

Structures

Today, libraries must transform themselves and their services to encompass a new world of network communications and the promise of scalable, operational information systems that support a multimedia environment. This transformation has three basic components:

1. Collaborative relationships
2. Technology
3. Organization

In moving from the historical physical setting with "flatland" collections, libraries have advanced through a modernization phase of automating manual procedures and through an innovation phase of creative use of existing technologies. Libraries must now engage the philosophical and ethical questions of how they wish to re-create themselves in this new era where physical proximity and time constraints can be overcome.

Collaborative Relationships

Libraries have always had a role in the support of academic programs and research in higher education. In this world of networked information when libraries can determine their own destiny and craft their own future, they must forge an active, collaborative relationship with the community they serve.

The relationships formed will enable libraries to understand better the research process and the fact that communication is everything in the creation of knowledge. The outcome of this relationship is a better balance for libraries and researchers that offers a fluid, active environment for efficient scholarship, cooperation, and improved services. Garvey (1979) states:

> The ultimate information service for science will probably come about through some collaborative effort among librarians (information specialist) and scientists active on the research front, since it will be the libraries who provide the service and the scientists who determine its value (by using it). (p. 126)

In addition to more active social relationships built with researchers, libraries must also build more creative relationships with the knowledge they collect. The context and linkages must become format independent, and we must be able to control and manage this electronic world more effectively. More information that is better managed and more flexible needed to provide a better sphere for the reader. The ability to create these new relationships is enabled by technology and organization. The results of this new environment is a new set of services which are valuable because they free the researcher in the pursuit of knowledge.

Technology Structures

As the medium for more productive processes to create knowledge, multimedia technologies must be informed by intelligent analysis and by the collective, cooperative determination of needs by librarians and researchers. Presently there are successful examples of multimedia technologies that illustrate the potential of this new form of knowledge management. Libraries, however, are production environments where a technology must be stable and scalable. With researchers, librarians must engage in a research process to move these systems towards production applications that function across a powerful networked structure. The motto of MIT, *MENS et MANUS*, captures the essence of this critical requirement to move from analytical thought and goal determination to the hands-on application of the fruits of that research.

The technological base available today is both extensive and promising for multimedia. Scott Morton (1991) describes the current environment:

The technical realities of today and tomorrow are extensive. Of these, four seem to be most important.

1. Shared data and information.
2. The availability of a wideband (satellite andfiber optics) communications infrastructure on a global basis.
3. The emergence of a totally new computer architecture, parallel processing.
4. Developments in the field of Heuristics. These have begun to allow us to capture the human judgements central to so many business actions.

This mix of available conceptual and physical technologies affects information, both qualitative and quantitative, verbal pictorial, and numeric. When this happens, there is an impact on production work, coordination work, and certain aspects of management.

These technical realities exist to support the larger, national agenda of computing, communications, and information flow. In *Grand Challenges: High Performance Computing and Communications, a report by the Committee on Physical, Mathematical, and Engineering Sciences, Federal Coordinating Council for Science, and Office of Science and Technology Policy to supplement the President's Fiscal year 1992 Budget,* figure 6.1 charts the NREN (National Research and Education Network) Applications by Bandwidth and Traffic Characteristics.

At the high end of the chart, that is, at or near the gigabit bandwidth requirement and "bursty"—high human-computer interaction, these applications are clustered together: "multimedia database access," "collaboration technology," "image transfer," and " distributed computing." Each of these applications speak to the social creation of knowledge that is integral to the new world of libraries. This clustering at the upper reaches of the NREN applications is surprising because most present library applications are considered at the low end of the network scale because these present applications are relegated to the "flatlands." The technological realities call for context, dimensions, and the provision of free interactions between the researcher and knowledge.

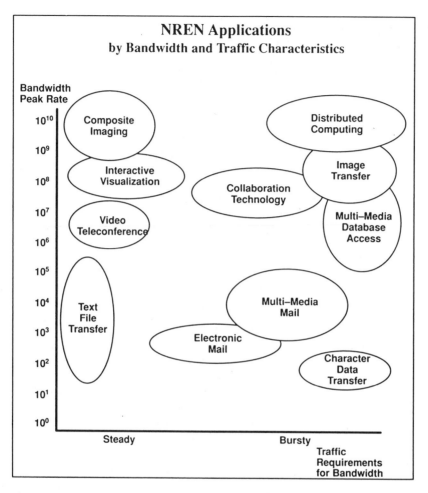

Figure 6.1
NREN applications by bandwidth and traffic characteristics

The system designs for multimedia technologies must support coherent linking systems which are infinitely flexible for the library and for the author. These system designs must be based upon a client/server architecture. This means that the data contents are stored on network-based servers (libraries), and the workstation used by the client retrieves and manipulates the data. Again, libraries become the vacuum into which the content of knowledge is poured. The workstation enables the reader to utilize software for manipulating the information in the manner which speaks to the reader. This disaggregation, locating knowledge content in the server and the tools to manipulate knowledge in the client, is important for multimedia because the architecture supports the ability to pull together data from a variety of sources and to make intelligent linkages at the workstation.

Organizational Structures

To support the provision of new services and collaborations, libraries must also address their internal, organizational structures and adjust them to improved delivery of information services.

Collaboration means both outreach and inclusion; that is, the library organization must be willing to accept others outside the library into the library structure. The essence of collaboration is contact with a broad range of potential researchers, and the library must maximize the opportunities for this contact.

Scott Morton (1991) describes this organization which offers maximum opportunities for outside contact and establishes a modular arrangement which permits multiple and flexible associations:

The flexible organization will be flatter, more horizontal. This maximizes the contact points with the outside work and reduces the time delay for vertical communication. Such a flatter organization assumes effective use of I.T. [Information Technology] to permit the shrinkage of time and distance, and installation of powerful new co-ordination mechanisms.

Because organizational boundaries are permeable to I.T., it becomes possible to link any segment of one's "value added chain" to any segment of any other organization. This dis-aggregation and re-combination permits the creation of whole new entities put together to achieve new value for the customer. . . . People are working together to create and deliver a product or service, and yet they are not legally part of the same corporation. (p. 9)

Clearly, multimedia technologies become one of the "powerful new coordination mechanisms." The "value added chain" of libraries and knowledge exists in the construction and preservation of the many links between information regardless of the format. The flatter organization with its ability to disaggregate and recombine information offers the potential to address specific knowledge needs of researchers and tailor services. This organization frees the individual for greatest productivity by focusing and tailoring services that have the greatest value. The organization becomes less fixated upon its own structure and more focused upon its mission—the delivery of knowledge services.

In this collaborative world the dimensions of the organization and of knowledge are reversed. We need knowledge in "the four-space of three dimensions and time" to move us beyond the information "flatland," and the better organizational structure for this delivery is flat and horizontal. This reversal, information no longer flat, and organizations no longer deep, is at the core of the transformational process for libraries.

Conclusion

Knowledge creators, librarians, and technologists need to establish the organizational and technological infrastructures to play with the possibilities for the creation of knowledge. We need to build libraries that are transformed into the networked information environment, and we need to propagate them with a variety of electronic data upon which systems can be designed and prototyped. We must find data and work with them in order to learn about delivering knowledge and about multimedia system design.

We need to play, to fulfill our drive to play, our *spieltrieb*. Let's strive for greater continuity between research and application. Let's be prepared to fail and be prepared to succeed. As we succeed we must prepare ourselves for a very different and exciting world where the social creation of knowledge is nurtured by the services of libraries and of multimedia.

References

Dertouzos, Michael L. 1991. "Building the Information Marketplace," *Technology Review*, v. 94, no. 1:28–40.

Garvey, William D. 1979. *Communication: The essence of Science, facilitating information exchange among librarians, scientists, engineers and students.* Oxford: Pergamon Press.

Grand Challenges: High Performance Computing and Communications: The FY 1992 U.S. Research and Development Program, a report by the Committee on Physical, Mathematical, and Engineering Sciences, Federal Coordinating Council for Science, and Office of Science and Technology Policy to supplement the President's Fiscal Year 1992 Budget, Washington, D.C.: Office of Science and Technology Policy.

Kakuzo, Okakura. 1977. *The Book of Tea*. Rutland, Vermont: Charles R. Tuttle.

Negroponte, Nicholas. 1992. "Machine Dreams: an Interview with Nicholas Negroponte," *Technology Review*, v. 95, no. 1:33–40.

Schiller, Friedrich. 1967. *On the Aesthetic Education of Man: In a series of letters*. Translated by Elizabeth M. Wilkinson and L. A. Willoughby. Oxford: Clarendon Press.

Scott Morton, Michael S. 1991. "The Information-Driven Corporation," presented at the MIT Industrial Liaison Program Symposium: *Building the Information Marketplace*, October 11, 1991.

Tufte, Edward R. 1990. *Envisioning Information*. Cheshire, Connecticut: Graphics Press.

7

Multimedia and the Library and Information Studies Curriculum

Kathleen Burnett

Introduction

The past twenty-five years have brought enormous changes to the types of employment graduates of master's programs in library studies seek. Today's graduates are much more likely to be employed outside libraries than their counterparts of the past, and even those who do pursue careers in traditional settings are expected to perform very different duties. The purview of master's programs has expanded tremendously as well. Even the traditional epithet *library studies* has undergone expansion to *library and information studies*. I do not, however, mean to imply that the change is a cosmetic one. It is not—library and information studies educators have had to search long and hard for new organizing principles to provide coherence and continuity in a diverse and sometimes eclectic program.

Twenty-five years ago most graduates of master's of library studies programs in the United States expected to find employment in one of several traditional library settings as professional librarians. Although a sense of fellowship united the profession as a whole, the raison d'etre of each setting, be it academic, public, corporate, special, or school was perceived as being so unique as to require separate courses of study. The typical MLS curriculum (figure 7.1) consisted of a few core courses designed to provide cross-disciplinary training for the "generic library," followed by advanced courses which focused either on the specific library types—such as those illustrated in figure 7.1—or on cross-typical library functions—such as technical services, public services, circulation, collection development and management (figure 7.2). The curriculum which supported this kind of vision might be illustrated as in figure 7.3. The "core" typically consisted of three or more introductory courses, includ-

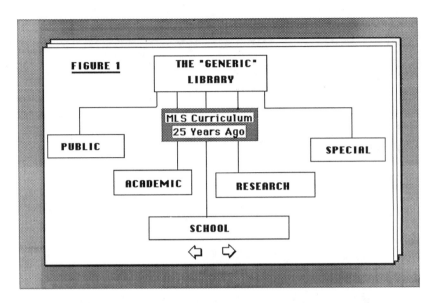

Figure 7.1

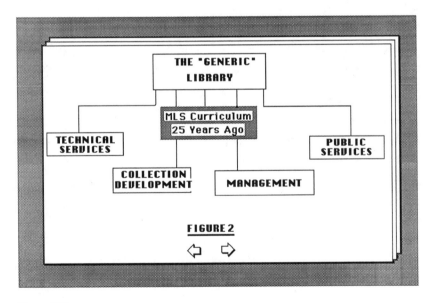

Figure 7.2

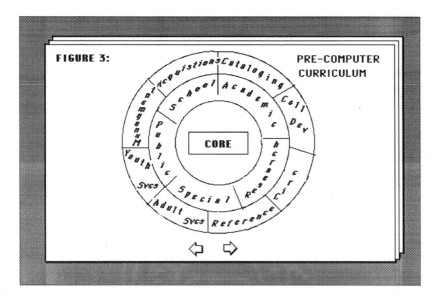

Figure 7.3

ing a general introduction to the profession, an introduction to library management, and one or more courses falling under the general rubric of "bibliography." An MLS candidate wishing to pursue a career in cataloging in an academic library might be expected to follow a path similar to the one outlined in figure 7.4, while one considering a career in reference in a public library setting might follow the path outlined in figure 7.5.

Computers and the MLS Curriculum

The introduction of computers in libraries—both in terms of automating library functions and as tools for the end-user—has rendered this curriculum obsolete for reasons which appear, at least on the surface, to be contradictory. On the one hand, with the introduction of automation, it became apparent that the organizational structures of the various types of libraries were *not* dissimilar—a fact which belies the rationale of the precomputer curriculum organized according to library types. Figure 7.6 illustrates one possible, and fairly typical, organizational structure for a medium to large public library, while figure 7.7 illustrates a similarly typical configuration for an academic library, the only significant difference between the two being the focus on services to populations (Youth

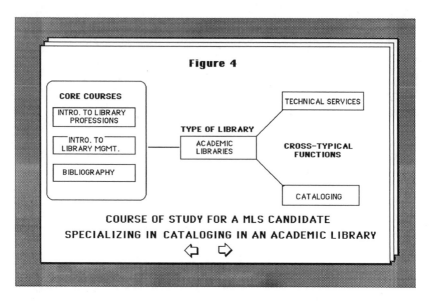

Figure 7.4

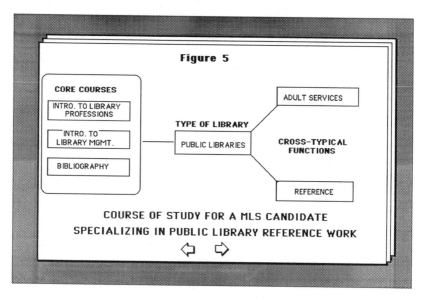

Figure 7.5

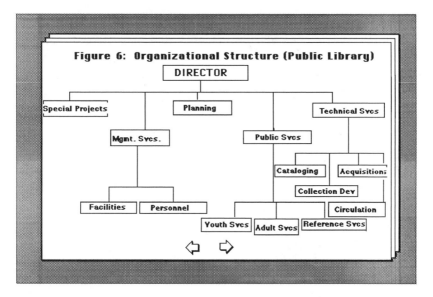

Figure 7.6

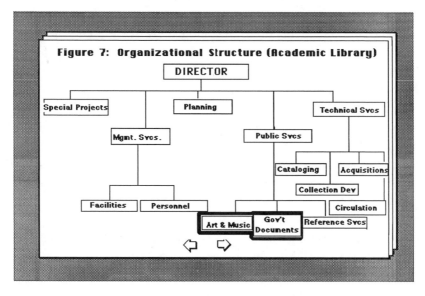

Figure 7.7

Services and Adult Services) in the former, as opposed to organization by discipline (Art & Music and Government Documents) in the latter. Public libraries serve divers populations; academic libraries support academic programs—in both contexts the organizational structure reflects the goals and mission of the library itself. Despite this slight variation, the majority of functions performed in all types of libraries remain undifferentiated. All libraries require professionals who can perform technical services, public services, circulation, collection development and management functions.

On the other hand, the integration of computers into libraries has engendered an increased need for specialized technical knowledge—systems analysis is required to ensure the smooth operation of automated functions, many libraries have added database searching to their public services, and reference staffs are now required to have enough technical competence to assist patrons requiring online and CD-ROM database searches. Twenty-five years ago it was sufficient to teach technology, if it was taught at all, in the library functions courses, so that our hypothetical student following the course of study to prepare for cataloging in an academic library (figure 7.4), would probably not be exposed to any technology—computer or otherwise—until the end of his or her program. In 1968 the technologies covered in the technical services and cataloging courses would have included the card catalog, typewriter and copying machine, and the approach taken toward them in course work would have been strictly an applications one.

Yet, by 1968 libraries had already begun to discuss the possibilities of automating the card catalog, and that very year the Library of Congress and the American Library Association began a cooperative effort which resulted in the development of a machine-readable cataloging format known as US MARC. The need to incorporate technologies into the MLS curriculum became increasingly apparent from this point on. While the initial reaction of many MLS programs (and, indeed, many libraries) was to ignore technological change as (1) cosmetic, and (2) of significance only to the non-professionals (who, it was assumed, would operate the machinery and perform the clerical record-maintenance tasks), and computer scientists who would design and maintain the hardware and software. School libraries—which had already begun to make a rhetorical shift from "libraries" to "media centers" in order to accommodate the various nonbook materials that were rapidly becoming part of their collections—were among the first libraries to break with this conservative approach. Meanwhile, the more innovative MLS programs began to recognize the significance of technology with the addition of a class or two devoted to topics such as "library automation," "database management," and "database searching." While there is no evidence that any alteration of the discipline's self-perception accompanied this "band-aid" approach to the inclusion of technology in the curriculum during the late sixties and early to mid-seventies, I think it is fair to say that it was precisely these additions which sounded the death knell for the MLS as an applied professional program designed solely to prepare candidates for the pursuit of careers in predetermined settings performing specified functions.

Today's MLS curriculum has evolved into something quite different largely because of the changes which accompanied the introduction of computer technologies. The single profession of "librarianship" has exploded into a myriad of allied "information professions" sharing a common theoretical infrastructure, as illustrated in figure 7.8. This diagram, taken from Michael Buckland's *Library Service in Theory and Context*, illustrates the two most important objectives of the contemporary MLS curriculum: (1) it must recognize and include information

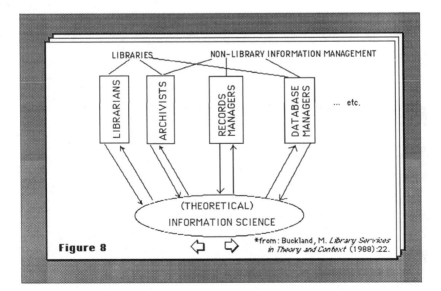

Figure 7.8

service functions outside the traditional library context, and (2) its foundations must be in theoretical information science.

The MLS curriculum conceptualized in figure 7.9 is one recently developed by the Department of Library and Information Studies at Rutgers University.[1] While other programs will conceptualize their curricula differently, most will agree that the infrastructure must be a theoretical one.

Foundation Courses

At Rutgers, this infrastructure is built on three "foundation courses"— Human Information Behavior, Information Structures, and Technology for Libraries and Information Agencies.[2] Each of these courses introduces one of the four areas of knowledge which inform the curriculum: human information behavior, information structures, information technologies, and organizational behavior.[3] The Human Information Behavior and Information Structures courses, which serve as introductions to the areas of the same name, are purely theoretical in their conception and orientation. This in itself represents a major shift from the old "generic-to-special library studies" curriculum which emphasized application—though not

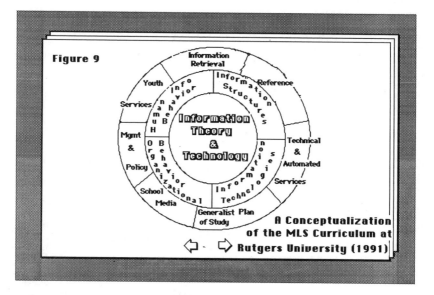

Figure 7.9

technology—even at its most introductory stage. A second shift—and a more important one to this discussion—has also taken place with the introduction of an entire area of study "information technologies," and the lecture/laboratory course which is designed to introduce technology on both theoretical and applied levels, thus making it the only introductory applications course. Currently, laboratory sessions include introductions to online database searching, CD-ROM searching, word processing, spreadsheet applications, and electronic mail functions. Clearly, this is the foundation course in which multimedia ought to be introduced. According to the course description (figure 7.10), "basic media technology" are supposed to be covered in the course, and, if we are to be assured that all graduates will have at least some exposure to multimedia technologies, they must be.

Do all graduates of MLS programs need to know something about multimedia? In the late seventies libraries were concerned with incorporating library automation systems and online searching. In the eighties, the focus shifted to end-user technology—online public access catalogs (OPACS), and CD-ROM searching. Library and information studies programs struggled to provide the basic applied knowledge their graduates would need to have in an ever-changing technological environment

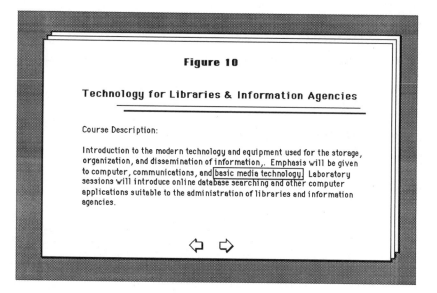

Figure 7.10

through what I earlier designated as a band-aid approach. The fallacy of such an approach is precisely its emphasis on application. Each application requires a full course of training since each is apparently unique. But a re-examination of the categorization I have used in discussing the technologies of the seventies and eighties will reveal that this apparent uniqueness is only superficial. Library automation and online bibliographic databases can be approached as systems, while OPACs, CD-ROM databases, and related personal computer applications can be approached as end-user technologies. Where does multimedia fit into this categorization?

Currently, most library multimedia applications, including library tours, multimedia reference databases and hypermedia stacks, fall into the end-user category. On the other hand, the Image Database Project at the University of California at Berkeley, Libernet, and related projects across the country fall into the systems category. Is multimedia simply a hybrid—a conglomeration of existing technologies falling in both categories—or is a new theoretical infrastructure at work here? I would maintain the latter. If I am correct, then the band-aid approach to incorporating multimedia into the MLS curriculum today will not be anymore successful than it was to incorporating earlier computer technologies in the sixties and seventies.

Clearly, then, the most comfortable home for multimedia within the foundation course structure, is the Technology for Library and Information Agencies course, But, just as clearly, the theoretical infrastructure of the course. itself will have to be revised in order to accommodate this new technology.

Reference Specialization

The rapid introduction of technologies in the late seventies through the eighties was accompanied by the development of new specializations designed to ease their incorporation into library settings. Many of these new specializations were technical and managerial; that is, the new specialists were rarely involved in public services. The exception was the bibliographic instructor. Despite its rather archaic title, bibliographic instruction (BI) is a true stepchild of the computer age. Historically, BI has been perceived as a task assigned to Reference Services, and has generally been conceived of in terms of librarian-led tours and instructional seminars. Increasingly in the nineties, BI will be handled through the aegis of end-user-directed multimedia presentations, such as Hypercard stacks—in other words, multimedia will perform the explanation function which necessitated the development of the specialization in the first place. However, because the normal interaction in such presentations is human-computer, and librarian intervention is generally not sought, it is absolutely essential that the presentations be well designed and extremely user-friendly. Who will design these presentations? This is a question which remains as yet unanswered, but if we look back again to the patterns established with the introduction of earlier computer technologies, we can perhaps make some reasonable predictions.

Library automation systems have been largely designed by computer scientists working outside the library context, and it is not unreasonable to expect that the same will hold true for multimedia systems, especially given their greater complexity. However, hindsight would indicate that if libraries want systems that do what librarians want them to do, they will need to be actively involved in the development process from its inception. Bibliographic instruction presentations, on the other hand, will have to be almost entirely library specific; therefore, either libraries will create yet another specialization to fulfill this function, or bibliographic instruction and other reference librarians will find themselves with a new duty added to their job descriptions. Given the fact that good, user-friendly multimedia presentation software is already under development, I suspect the latter will be the more usual scenario.

Returning, then, to the MLS curriculum illustrated in figure 7.9, we can see that some course work in multimedia production is required for the reference specialization. Currently at Rutgers, however, the course of study for reference specialists beyond the foundation courses mentioned earlier includes a "Basic Information Resources" course followed by several information resources courses in particular subject areas, such as the humanities, business, and science and technology. There is no advanced technology course within this area; rather technologies are integrated into the various subject courses. Thus, students taking the "Information Resources in the Humanities" course will have the opportunity to search the various CD-ROM and online database services in that field. Notice that the emphasis is on searching *existing* databases, not on creating new ones. In fact, most courses in the current curriculum offer this same passive approach to technology, although those interested in the creation and structure of traditional databases are encourage to take a course entitled "Knowledge Representation for Information Retrieval," and a course in "Database Management" is also offered. A multimedia production course might be offered according to this same model—we might design a single course to be offered within the technologies area and encourage, among others, interested reference specialists to take it. But the fact of the matter is that the course of study in this specialization is already so full that little opportunity for elective course work is afforded within the 36-credit structure. Such an approach, therefore would do little to ensure that all candidates in this area have some exposure to multimedia production work.

The best alternative within the current curriculum, then, would be to incorporate multimedia production into the "Basic Information Resources" course required of all reference specialists. The current course description at first glance offers no home for a production orientation; it reads, "the full range of information resources will be studied and used in applied contexts. Access to information through reference tools and uses of information by learners will be emphasized. Students will explore strategies for searching and evaluating these works, with special emphasis on comparisons between printed and electronic media." This could easily be expanded by adding "and extensions into the use of multimedia to produce guides for the end-user" to the end of the description.

Other Specializations

I mentioned earlier that school libraries were among the first to adopt multimedia, the attractions of which for work with children should be obvious. Currently, all school media specialists and youth services specialists are required to take a course in the technology area which has been recently revised from "Information Technology and Media Services" to "Multimedia Structure, Organization, Access, and Production." The course, which will be taught for the first time in Spring 1992, will consist of an introduction to *theory and practice* in the design, development, structure, organization and use of multimedia, including issues of access and copyright. The intent is to design the course in such a way that it will attract not only school media specialists, who were the primary audience for the course it replaces, but students in other concentrations as well who are interested in obtaining a strong theoretical grounding, supplemented with practical exercises, in the technology of the future. Such a redefinition—from a course that focused on a library type (the school media center) to a course which discusses and demonstrates particular applications within a broader, more generally applicable, theoretical context—fits comfortably within the current curricular structure, and would ensure that most—though not quite all—of the students leaving the program would have the opportunity to pursue course work in multimedia beyond the basic rudiments that can be introduced in the Technology for Library and Information Agencies course.

Of the three remaining specializations, Technical and Automated Services would be sufficiently served by the introduction of the "Multimedia Structure, Organization, Access and Production" course, and Information Retrieval, by either that course or the expansion of the advanced reference courses to cover multimedia. Management would be the sole area in which exposure to multimedia at something more than the rudimentary level would be entirely at the student's (in consultation with an advisor, of course) discretion.

The Multimedia Library

Five years ago, librarians and information service professionals could argue that "multimedia" was a lot of talk but little-to-no substance, and therefore could be ignored. This is no longer the case. Recently, two or three articles discussing multimedia technology have appeared every week in the Business and Science sections of the *New York Times*. In October *Time Magazine* ran a feature story on multimedia and *PC Weekly* stated that within five years the personal computer (as we know it) will be obsolete. Multimedia technologies will enter the library and information professions, both at the end-user and at the systems level.

How will this entree change our libraries? What will a multimedia library look like? Early applications of multimedia technology in libraries have included library tours and multimedia reference files in the form of HyperCard® stacks running on Macintosh® platforms. In several academic and special libraries, digitized images are being added to the now-familiar online public access catalog. Five years from now, a patron entering the library will be able to walk up to a terminal and use any one of these tools and others like them. Ten years from now, our old card catalog may well have metamorphosed into a "virtual library" of its own. It should be possible to "browse" the stacks without leaving the terminal; to "open" a book and view its table of contents; perhaps even, to flip through the pages of two books, physically located on different levels of the stacks, and compare them. "Virtual browsing" may allow libraries to prohibit patron access to the stacks, which in turn would permit the reconfiguration and consolidation of shelving layouts. While libraries would still be repositories of information—in fact, would still contain information in the comfortingly familiar packages we know as books— a patron might conceivably complete an entire research project without ever consulting anything more than the catalog. Given recent developments in networking, and accessibility to many academic library catalogs via networks such as the Internet, it is entirely conceivable that many functions which have previously required a trip to the library might someday soon be carried out from the home, via the "virtual library."

Multimedia and the Library and Information Professions

What does this mean to the profession? Clearly, future librarians and information professionals will need to have a solid grounding in multimedia theory and practice in order to function well in the library and information service environment of the future. Our librarians will need to be advocates for the freedom of information, while understanding the complex interrelationship of issues such as the individual's right to privacy and the role of copyright in a capitalist society. In addition, they will need to have a high level of technical competence. While it is reasonable to expect that the development of better human-computer interfaces will accompany the growth of multimedia, it is also true that the systems themselves will be more complex than any technology currently available for patron use in the library today. Librarians will be expected to understand and explain the implications of compression and the importance of standards. They will need to act as guides through a technology which prides itself on being nonlinear. They will have to assist patrons in developing alternative strategies to negotiate hyperspace.

Librarians have traditionally been engaged in the function of interpretation. Yesterday's librarian's were called upon to interpret the library's card catalog, the particular classification system used by the library, and the various reference tools found within the walls of that library. Tomorrow's librarian's will be called upon to interpret all sorts of information, much of which will reside physically outside of those four walls. The ramifications of the introduction of multimedia technology in libraries will undoubtedly be at least as profound as those resulting from the incorporation of computers.

Multimedia and the Curriculum

As the theoretical infrastructure of multimedia develops, and its impact on the library and information service professions becomes more apparent, a curricular redefinition of similar scope to that which occurred with the introduction of computers in libraries will become necessary. In the meantime, it is essential that we not allow ourselves to take the "band-aid" approach to integrating this new technology. Any integration must be on the theoretical, as well as applied, level. Most, if not all courses must include this new technology and its impact in their designs. Otherwise, we will not be educating library and information professionals for future positions of leadership, but rather preparing them for the past.

References

1. This conceptualization is my own. Some of my colleagues would probably argue that I have implied a "core" which they would insist does not exist within our program. In fact, there are currently only three course which *every student* in *every specialization* must take: Human Information Behavior, Information Structures, and Technology for the Information Professions. One might argue that these courses constitute a de facto core, although I prefer to think of them as "foundation courses"—as the theoretical underpinning which informs the curriculum as a whole, and it is this conception that I intend in my representation.

2. In addition, the program is framed by an orientation and introduction to the basics of library and information studies, which begins the program, and colloquia, which are usually taken the last semester and offer an advanced look at particular issues and problems.

3. Originally, a foundation course in management provided an introduction to the fourth area of knowledge, organizational behavior, as well, but the constraints of a 36-credit program have resulted in its dismissal as a requirement in some specializations. Each of the remaining foundation courses provides some introduction to this area.

8

The Virtual Museum and Related Epistemological Concerns

Glen Hoptman

A Brief History

The concept of the *Virtual Museum* evolved out of my consulting for museums, cultural, and educational organizations.[1] I found the need for an organizing concept that would suggest what I regard as true interactivity,[2] as opposed to the dronelike programming whose structural metaphors continue to dominate the electronic media.[3] The idea came into *being*, so to speak, around 1983 during the planning for reinstallation of the "Eighteenth Century Life in America" exhibition in the National Museum of American History when I suggested that the exhibition be planned to allow the visitor to compare and contrast the artifacts from each of the communities depicted in the displays with information not on display. The additional information would have been drawn from other elements of the Smithsonian's collections together with those from other Americana collections and libraries. The concept was never incorporated within the exhibit for some of the problematic reasons discussed in this article.

Basic to the *Virtual Museum* is the term *connectedness*.[4] *Connectedness* enriches information searches and publications as educational learning resources. *Connectedness* is a basic manner of referring to the interrelated or interdisciplinary as well as the integrated media nature of information. Human perception and understanding of the meaning of a concept, and the way in which we study that concept, depend largely on how the concept has been defined by information providers. In determining what information is integral to a concept and how that (and related) information should be conveyed, information providers are, in essence, exercising significant influence in terms of highly personal editorial opinions and judgments.

Given the limitations of traditional (primarily print) media, these editorial judgments have resulted in the use of very narrow terms to express the meaning of a concept and to suggest what other information is related to that concept. In order to have access to information provided through this traditional media, information about various concepts has to be categorized and grouped into fairly rigid "disciplines" and systematic indexes. Generally, we are then limited in our understanding of a concept to that reduced amount of information which has been captured and conveyed in this manner. The use of digital integrated mixed media enables us to break through some of these limitations in conveying information. By applying the concept of *connectedness* throughout the editorial and production process, digital integrated mixed media publications can better represent the broad *contexts* from which information is *reduced* as a natural part of its capture and in all forms of its being "told." Thus, the user of these publications will have available information that has not, by necessity or habit, been filtered through the narrow funnels of traditional media.

The concept of the *Virtual Museum* was continually refined over the course of my work in the founding of what was the National Demonstration Laboratory for Interactive Educational Technologies, the research Consortium, and subsequently as Consulting Coordinator for Technology Initiatives and Experimental Publishing at the Smithsonian Institution.

Background and Description

The purpose of this chapter is to provide a preliminary characterization of the concept of a *Virtual Museum*.[5] Additionally, this chapter identifies the need for development of *intelligent tutors* and or *agents*, along with additional artificial intelligence research, in order to develop alternative systems for organizing and retrieving complex data structures in interdisciplinary and integrated media formats.[6]

Models utilized for organizing educational activities are principally drawn from traditional frameworks used to assemble information. For example, a geology lesson will be organized according to the logic of earth science and that of a science curriculum. While we recognize that it would be foolish to arrange the instruction based on medieval styles of printing, we have yet to recognize that similar limitations on our understanding are imposed by traditional, print-driven methods of organizing information.

Because we have primarily communicated in a two-dimensional, print environment, we have developed methods of organizing information to facilitate its storage and retrieval within this environment. For example, a series of subject headings and subheadings, which can be easily recognized by researchers, enables us to retrieve information relevant to virtually any topic. Through the use of indexes, based on fairly consistent subject headings, large amounts of information can be assembled and disseminated to diverse researchers and readers. In many ways, these subject headings correspond to the fields of study or "disciplines" we might find in academic institutions or museums.

While these methods of organizing information have proved invaluable in the management of printed information, they also have imposed limitations on the kind of information we receive. These limitations are imposed by those information providers who determine what information is "relevant" to a particular topic. For example, when a reader looks up "frogs" in a traditional print reference resource, he or she will find a particular kind of information. The information providers have determined that primarily natural science information is relevant to the topic of frogs, with perhaps a bit of geographical or maybe environmental information about frog habitats. However, there is a wealth of other information "relevant" to the topic of frogs—cultural, literary, folk tales and folk music, and medicinal uses of the frog—that never make it into the traditional subject heading "frog."

To date, the newer technologies (such as improved video, audio, or computers) have been used primarily to upgrade the traditional, two-dimensional methods described above. For example, computers have made it possible for us to store more information, and to do "faster" index (or comparable) searches for retrieving relevant information within a particular subject heading. In other words we can now get to more of the same information faster. Similarly, videos and/or animation enable us to "see" action in an environment, instead of exclusively viewing still photographs or illustrations. We still are limited to receiving primarily that material which the information providers in traditional print environments have deemed "relevant" to a specific subject.

Current technologies enable us to break through some of the limitations imposed by the two-dimensional print environment on the storage, retrieval, and dissemination of information. As we make this breakthrough, questions that need to be asked are: (1) whether the traditional approach to the presentation of information for purposes of education, interpretation, or other acts of communication necessarily provides the maximum beneficial response; and (2) how do individual and collective minds act to aggregate and compile information? Only by asking and experimenting with answers to these questions among many others will we realize the true potential that is provided by the new interactive integrated media technologies. It will be essential to avoid organizational and representational metaphors common to less robust media.

Current research in cognitive development[7] and philosophic speculation on the nature of understanding and the structures within classifications of knowledge[8] suggest that extant models of organization can limit the contextual understanding and appreciation of significance identified with the subject. Examples of inventions or scientific "discoveries" made possible as a result of the utilization of integrated digital syntheses and integration of information, and otherwise impossible visual representations of information, show that our traditional organization of information can serve to inhibit knowledge. An example of thinking otherwise inhibited by traditional patterns of thought and research includes the use of massively parallel computational systems in the design of functional chip specifications that can only be modeled. Additionally, use in medical research of three-dimensional visualizations of sections of the human body provide opportunities for understanding complex biochemical and other relationships that only can be accomplished by *seeing* these processes.

Moreover, research in the fields of mental imagery and neurophilosophy is providing insights and information that has value in guiding the restructuring of knowledge definitions and architectures, building adaptable search and retrieval agents, and in creating flexible models for experimenting with meaning and its categorization.[9] It is peculiar that so little attention has been given to the relevance of these fields in organizing information fields for data management in information-rich, cultural institutions such as museums. Neil Harris (1990) provides an excellent discussion of the need for examining the role of the museum. In the context of this discussion he raises the following important aspect of the word to object relationship: ". . . [W]hen words are eclipsed, diluted, abandoned, transcended, or denigrated as instruments of communication and description, in favor of direct visual representation or reporting, then many museum visitors are literally abandoned to the objects. And, ironically enough, in their abandonment they can rely only upon label-reading or picture-taking as structuring devices."[10]

In contemplating how we might experiment with challenging the order of things as practiced and believed within society and research environments, and as exhibited in museum display cases, and textbooks, the traditional organization of education and media and their associated economic logic makes change almost inconceivable. This difficulty arises not so much from any lack of technological capacity or of respected research in psychology or philosophy. Instead, it arises primarily from inertia: we have "always" organized and presented information in "this way," and many "institutions," whether they are buildings, academic departments, or other groups of people, have their identities and job descriptions based on this method of organizing and presenting information. Change of the order discussed here is very threatening.

Perhaps for these reasons, there are far too few efforts unfolding within professional communities and university research centers to provide the requisite new definitions of descriptive norms for data design and management in research, education, curatorial, and library milieus. Tools that can be used to organize and access information in databases allowing for management of interdisciplinary multimedia research processes are limited to either a specific circumscribed set of data or a single disc of information. While there are examples of "smart corporations,"[11] applications of expert systems tools are principally for management analysis of routine administrative or fiscal functions of proscribed individual or manufacturing systems behaviors. The museum community desperately needs a broadly defined research and development program that will have as one of its principal goals the development of expert systems tools, specifically, very sophisticated pattern-recognition algorithms. These tools, agents, and or tutors should be able to retrieve information despite the nature of the limiting characteristics of associated captions. For example, we need retrieval tools that can locate all visual images from photographs, line drawings video, all lyrics, and all text, etc., associated with, for example, cloven-hooved animals, without regard to the traditional subject headings under which this information has been "filed," or "categorized."

Consideration of the linguistic and aesthetic styles of individual researchers, curators, and the like should not become limiting factors in the automated search and retrieval of the files which have been created. With the aid of such expert tools, while nonetheless remaining subject to the eventual professional scrutiny of researchers and cultural historians, objects, etc., can be made accessible even if only in a tacit sense for initial study. Nonetheless, expert tools must not become indiscriminate filters which impede appreciation of personal style, the variety of opinions and schools of thought.

In the case of the Smithsonian the information search would include datasets from such ostensibly distinct collections as those of the National Zoological Park, Museum of American Art, Museum of the American Indian, Air and Space Museum, among other ethnic, art, and scientific collections. At this point in time such a search is virtually impossible not only with the Smithsonian museums, but also in most cultural and scientific collections around the world.

The concept of the *Virtual Museum* demonstrates how limitations imposed by the traditional methods of organizing and presenting information can be overcome in the context of museum "visits." In a nutshell, the *Virtual Museum* provides multiple levels, perspectives, and dimensions of information about a particular topic: it provides not only multimedia (print, visual images through photographs, illustrations or video, and audio), but, more important, it provides information that has not been filtered out through these traditional methods. All elements of collections information from the full array of media forms will be stored at the highest possible digital resolution so as to provide for use in varied presentations including three-dimensional holograms, and all forms of high resolution display and printing.

A "visitor" to the *Virtual Museum* will not only find artifacts and other materials that may rarely, if ever, have actual museum exhibition display space; he or she will also have easy access to information that would be found under very diverse "subject headings" in traditional print indexes, or in disparate museums representing different fields of study, and therefore not ever be seen or put together for that "visitor" in that particular way. Each museum visitor has his or her own interests and concerns. It is impossible to anticipate them in a physical or spatial sense within the museum. In a digitally represented virtual world the absence of a specific exhibit is not an obstacle to finding the information one requests. This information can be found as it is represented in all available media in extensive digital data resource files and assembled in individually tailored formats bringing together even the most disparate sets of information.

For example, a visitor to the Smithsonian Institution who wishes to explore a particular object or event first must ascertain where the information related to this object or event is located. It is easy to speculate that information about social conventions of dress in eighteenth-century America would be found in the National Museum of American History. The visitor to that museum would not necessarily know nor be directed to the National Portrait Gallery, Museum of American Art, or to the other collections within the Institution which hold relevant collections and or research. And, if indeed the area of interest was the "social conventions of dress," the museums of Asian and African Art, and the Museum of Natural History would contribute greatly to one's information pool. If one could *listen* to the music collections from the Smithsonian's extensive ethno-musicological holdings this could add even more to their understanding.

A "virtual" representational museum is really the only way to assemble all of the information related to each individual "visitor's" interests that are spread across the diverse collections and research of the Smithsonian Institution. It is not practical to move the collections between museums nor can the entirety of most museums be publicly displayed.[12] Also, other factors limit the "visitor's" capacity to discover in any detail information related to collections located in other buildings. Additionally, as is the case in numerous major museum situations, most of the collections are never seen by the public and it is difficult even for the researcher to know of their existence.

In its initial digital form *The Virtual Smithsonian Institution* will have to be a series of experimental integrated digital multimedia publishing efforts and data resources which will represent the collections of the Smithsonian Institution. This project does not exist as a formal priority of the Smithsonian Institution, but is a research and development initiative linked to defining the information resource requirements of the SI in the future. This effort has been given the name *Mosaic* by the corporate group working on defining comprehensive systems requirements. Key factors at play in the determination of whether the project will move forward are financial and re-education of the personnel as to the scope of change and opportunities before them. Theoretically, the *Virtual Museum* is a means to create a flexible envelope for design of the SI's long-range information management requirements. This will best be done by understanding the benefits of using new information technologies and communications capacities[13] and the possible impact they will have on information systems not anticipated in current planning cycles and methods. In a real sense at this point in administrative time and intellectual history the *Virtual Museum* is as much a gadfly as it is a means to an end.

Various technical issues will also have to be considered as part of the initial planning. For example, configuring the infrastructure for the *Virtual Museum* will need to address the networking of many disparate media-data resources through the use of mainframe architectures and *new* digital-multimedia PCs. In addition, various issues will arise in connection with the distribution of the *Virtual Museum* and the requirements and benefits of very broad-bandwidth Integrated Service Digital Network (ISDN) implementation. Fiber optic and satellite-based communications, among others, will also demand careful study. Because of the rapid rate of technological advances, distribution issues must be considered on an ongoing basis. We should therefore anticipate the allocation of considerable human, capital, and technical resources to address this dimension of *Virtual Museum* operations.

Most of the critical factors that will help establish the credibility of a *Virtual Museum* will not reside in the domain of hardware systems. Instead, our biggest challenge will be to reexamine current paradigms and emerging theories of knowledge. This is an essential element in developing new information systems which, unfortunately, is routinely ignored by most managers of information systems and designers of educational programs.[14] An even greater challenge will be informing the governmental bodies responsible for managing our information-distribution channels and formulating broad-based educational policy of the relevance of these epistemological concerns.

Existing paradigms, or the organizing metaphors we use to aid in understanding information, are by-products of millennia of reporting information, which originated from multisensory and multidimensional cognitive archetypes and processes, with one or two dimensional methods or perhaps only through oral traditions exclusively.[15] To suggest how to properly manage, display, and, most important, how to organize information to encourage its exploration and synthesis based on unanticipated cross-disciplinary methodologies is not yet possible. Therefore, a crucial aspect of the initial planning of the *Virtual Museum* will be to call upon experts in the fields of epistemology and cognitive sciences.[16]

Applications of the *Virtual Museum*

To suggest all of the specific applications of a *Virtual Museum* is well beyond the scope of this paper; indeed it is not too bold to state that an entire industry could be built around the *Virtual Museum*. In the *Virtual Museum*, a desktop information management device, assisted by advanced expert knowledge systems, could access all elements of the Smithsonian collections in all media. This will allow the user to integrate information from across the diversity of the Smithsonian collections whether or not the data was designed as an interdisciplinary file. This paper will focus on three kinds of applications of the *Virtual Museum* at the Smithsonian Institution: the *Virtual Museum* as a storage bank of high-resolution digital images; the *Virtual Museum* as the basis for museum-based programming; and the *Virtual Museum* as the basis for multilevel publications. I would like the opportunity to spend considerable time musing on the social, economic, intellectual, psychological, among other issues that will arise from the creation of all forms of virtual institutions (Wheeler 1987). In particular we will need to comprehend how to reasonably and individually assess the learner in all possible educational contexts. Multitudinous contexts might also be considered educational, given progress in communications and networking technologies. In any event, for the time being, these and related matters will need to be thought through within conceptual frameworks as yet not developed, which of course represents other conceptual and behavioral challenges.

As a storage bank of high-resolution digital images, the *Virtual Museum* has many applications. For example, in the Smithsonian *Virtual Museum*, an in-house curator or researcher can call up and view high-resolution digital images of objects that are stored "off-site" (either in another Smithsonian museum or at a storage facility. The curator or researcher can then comment on, or add to, the information associated with the article in a special electronic notebook.[17] Similarly, outside researchers could access the storage bank of images in the *Virtual Museum* and utilize the high-resolution images (as well as accompanying information) as part of their research study. In addition, as a storage bank of images the *Virtual Museum* could greatly augment the value and meaning of the various exhibitions throughout the museum, providing a "visual-vertical file cabinet" adjacent to each exhibition, at each research carrel, or at any other local or remote point-of-inquiry. By accessing this "file cabinet," a museum visitor can view, perhaps in three dimensions, high resolution digital images of objects or events that are related in some way to the objects on display in the exhibition. At the very least, the ability to provide conceptual tools to visualize relationships among the diverse and dispersed collections of the Smithsonian and to develop interdisciplinary resource aids would be extremely valuable.

In this format the Smithsonian Institution's collections could be the basis for developing a series of distributed networks located *anywhere*. The Smithsonian could be "found" in a classroom in Chillacothe and with identical ease in a research lab in Kuala Lumpur. With the continued growth in technical capacities offered by the Regional Bell Operating Companies (RBOCs) and television cable systems, distribution to schools and research institutions could be complemented by distribution of museum-based programming on the arts, sciences, and humanities specifically linked to the *Virtual Museum*.[18] The *Virtual Museum* could also be used as a "file" for generation of virtual textbooks in association with locally developed lesson plans or other software developed to manipulate its data.

Finally, the *Virtual Museum* can be the basis for multilevel publications. These publications are "multilevel" in the sense that they convey information about a topic not only in several media, but also in ways that cut across the traditional methods of organizing and presenting information. The Smithsonian bureaus or separate museums seldom cooperate in the presentation of information to the public. The Institution's anachronistic means and methods of information categorization and storage, and the separate non-communicating systems for each bureau, prevent the diffusion of its resources in the realm of current technologies. The frustration of not being able to readily access information will increase in exponential terms with the advent of broadband networks coming online for research, commercial, and consumer purposes.

There is currently under development a series of integrated media publications, which are tentatively entitled *The Smithsonian Institution Interdisciplinary Series on Animals and Culture*. The first project scheduled for release within this series in both integrated and separate standalone media formats is *Frogginess*. Although this is only one concept drawn from across the collections and research of the Smithsonian Institution, it demonstrates that the work for these publications would be greatly simplified through existence of a fully operational *Virtual Museum*. Among the many and varied goals associated with *Frogginess* is the value of a broadly defined and interdisciplinary understanding of the environments in which human and animal worlds both exist and compete; preservation of the environment; animals and their multidimensional influences on culture; and role of anthropomorphisms in the development of human psychology, mythology, and religions. No one specific museum collection within the Smithsonian could possibly reveal the information called for above. Nor is any one scholar adept in all of these "disciplines." It is through the use of the term *frogginess* that I began to develop an understanding within curatorial and research circles of the suggested value of a *Virtual Museum*.[19]

In many ways the Smithsonian is not unlike any college, university, or research center. General and specialized research information, objects, and stylistic and aesthetic analyses are classified in a manner that distinguishes the information, and at the same time, de-contextualizes and isolates the object or concept.

Whether in its purest form as a high-resolution digital image storage bank, or as part of museum-based programming or multilevel publications, the *Virtual Museum* expands incredibly the ability of a museum to disseminate and study information. The forms of information manipulation that will be possible in the future now reside exclusively in the province of laborious searching of trays, shelves, boxes, notebooks, and vaults. Many objects located in museum collections are fragile, if not totally inaccessible, due to their condition. The absence of comprehensive image inventories in even traditional photographs, let alone in very high-resolution digital and or holographic images (for interior and exterior three-dimensional representations), is a hindrance that will have to be overcome at the cost of considerable time and financial expense.

Multiple Cultures Triumph over Multiculturalism

Most curators and researchers attempting to identify the historical, aesthetic, and or scientific facts associated with an *object* are compelled by tradition, administration, and finance to develop their studies in a manner consistent with their sponsor. The department in which a person is employed, unless by definition a joint or interdisciplinary effort, requires the individual to represent and promote the interests of that unit. In this respect, they are not any different from teachers, nor for that matter from editors and publishers, in qualifying information for a particular purpose. There are established benefits to this manner of traditional representation of scholarship. There are also significant drawbacks.[20]

There are a series of codified concerns in the field of education referred to in contemporary nomenclature as *Multi-cultural, Cultural Diversity, The Canon, Afro-Centrist, Euro-Centrist,* and *Political Correctness* among others, that now serve to wreak, in many cases well deserved, havoc on the learning process and educational institutions. There have been many occasions in which it has been very hard for me to learn how to understand and work with points of view that are derived from historical circumstances foreign to my view of the world. It is easy in these circumstances to impose a point of view, though correct to a particular community, which represents either benign (intent) or overtly prejudicial behavior to others. Similarly, the "politically correct" multiculturalists, although well-intentioned, run the risk of unnecessarily censoring works and viewpoints, and of presenting a multicultural approach that is reflective of no one's culture. It is a benign form of politically correct intellectual authority that the curator exercises within a specific bureau to restrict contextual understanding.

The *Virtual Museum*, by its nature, can present contrasting or complementary information on a particular subject or time period in a way that a book or a single museum exhibition really cannot. Thus the *Virtual Museum* user can experience more of the "context" from which a print author/editor or a museum curator might draw his or her conclusions. Multiple cultures or multiple viewpoints can be presented to the *Virtual Museum* user, instead of presenting merely one person's (or one group's) perception of what a politically correct, multicultural viewpoint should look like. As a result, in a realm of the virtual representation of information afforded through massive integrated media databases, concerns such as those expressed by groups with particularistic convictions can be addressed without establishing a "politically correct" view.

A recent example of some of these problems can be found in the noting of the five-hundredth anniversary of the Columbus expedition. The appropriate manner of celebrating (or lamenting) this event has already caused significant paroxysm in numerous ethnic and scholarly circles. Many Native Americans have focused attention on the decimation of their cultures and the destruction of whole tribes of peoples that resulted from Columbus' landing on the shores of the "New World." While many of European decent look at the marvelous contributions the nation which eventually came to be has made.

It is impossible to assume that any one individual can represent or instruct in any educational setting and satisfy the historical-religious-social-economic concerns of all possible audiences. Belief systems that validate particular interpretations of events can always be directly challenged by other patterns of belief which are as well founded and distinct. Witness the reaction to the proposed beatification of Queen Isabella of Spain. Not only have Native American groups challenged this proposal, but also representatives from Jewish communities worldwide, and in particular those who are descendants of Jews exiled from Spain during the Spanish Inquisition which began the same year as Columbus's voyage, 1492, are challenging the wisdom of granting sainthood to Queen Isabella.

In a practical sense to accommodate all opinions and to reconcile them with history is an almost impossible task and in a philosophical perspective probably impossible. The development of the expert systems tools for finding and representing will not resolve for all time issues of inadequate representation. But they can serve to call attention to the pluralistic accounts of history and interpretation in a manner economically and or practically impossible in traditional classroom, movie, library, or home settings can accommodate.

Another example of how the *Virtual Museum* concept can facilitate understanding by presenting several viewpoints on the same series of historical events can be found in the recent celebrations of the bicentennials of the United States and the variety of unique institutions which were created by the founders of this nation. Each of the departments of government (executive, legislative, and judicial branches) focused the attention of the programs it sponsored on the history and evolution of itself. Without criticizing either the individuals responsible for the records and interpretation of these bodies, or the individuals who have and do now constitute these bodies, it was hard to discern the thread of continuity in the creation and evolution of the various branches. In other words, it was extraordinarily difficult to comprehend the interrelationships of events, and the evolution of American governmental process, through the events sponsored for the bicentennial period due to the particular and piecemeal manner of each sponsored project. Here, too, the opportunities for the integration of information, which presented from a particularistic point of view can be extended to, indicated the direct relationship between elements of a complex system in operation.

Once extensive integrated media databases are in place in several countries spanning several continents the development of an *international Virtual Museum* should be attempted for numerous reasons. The author, in planning for such an eventuality, is principally concerned with the support in multicultural understanding that the searching of concepts such as *discovery, encounter, shelter, home, nature,* across different cultures could offer.

By this time in history intellectual diversity should have become a more respected essential element of a healthy society. Perhaps the flexibilities afforded in presenting multiple representations of events and objects, along with enhanced information and communications technologies, will expand individual capacity for understanding or tolerance. So that these contemplated advances in individual capacities to comprehend, better appreciate, if not to reconcile, can be realized in systems design there remains a great deal of epistemological, cognitive, and social research to be done.

Broad Impact of the *Virtual Museum*

Trends in current and emerging technologies clearly indicate that the technical capacity to capture, store, display, and distribute a database such as the *Virtual Museum* will be available within the next decade if not sooner.[21] The work of the Corporation for National Research Initiatives, directed by Robert Kahn, creator of DARPANET, has been promoting the concept of a gigabit network for several years. In the October 7, 1991, edition of *Business Week*, there is extensive discussion of the super phone and the service, including on-demand video programming, that could be made available shortly. Appearing on the newsstands during the same week was a cover story in *Forbes*, "*Smart TV*" (referring to machine assisted intelligence). Several weeks earlier an article in the trade journal, *Publishers Weekly*, discussed a technology which will allow for the capture of several thousand books on one *smart*card. The possible benefits associated with such endeavors were anticipated and discussed in depth in the now legendary article by Vanevar Bush, *As We May Think,*[22] and referred to in the writings of Ted Nelson[23] and associated with his work on "Project Xanadu."

What is not clear is how the retrieval of various data resources will be affected. These changes will ultimately result in a modification of numerous normative patterns of social organization and function. Particularly, and of considerable significance, we must reconsider how we define education and organize the process of formal education. Whether, and how well, we are prepared to accept the social, economic, philosophic, and perceptual changes associated with large-scale virtual representations will in part determine the success of the opportunities that future information utilities can dispense.[24]

An example of social change associated with the development of the new information technologies and information resources can be seen in the current controversy about the organization of our educational system. Policies that once seemed axiomatic are now being questioned. These policies include structuring schools based on age levels, the redundant nature of the curriculum, the limited use of physical plant, the fluctuations in the teacher/student and student/dollar ratios, and the lack of qualified personnel to teach. A *radical* reconstruction of the nature of information and the definitions of knowledge can have an equally *radical* impact on social and economic areas.

Designing and developing the *Virtual Museum* will provide an opportunity for exploring the technical, intellectual, and broad policy-related issues associated with building virtual representations of large-scale information resources.

Notes

1. I was fortunate to find the support for my work in the Office of the Secretary of the Smithsonian Institution and select members of the Secretary's Management Committee. I am particularly indebted to Ms. Marie Mattson, who was then the Secretary's Special Assistant, for seeing the importance of a theoretical presentation in helping to attract much needed corporate support in areas of information sciences to the Smithsonian. Another individual, Richard Rockwell, of the IBM Corporation, forcefully encouraged me to consolidate my thoughts and various extended memos into a single work. A good friend and current business partner, Jonathan Latimer, helped me to make a sensible presentation of many of the previous textual incarnations associated with this paper. Without the emotional, editorial and intellectual scrutiny, concern, and support of Virginia Whitner Hoptman, many of the detractors of the *Virtual Museum* would have bested me long ago.

At present the *Virtual Museum* is a series of products and projects under development by Lightbeam Communications. All rights related to use of the term or development of the projects discussed in this paper belong to Lightbeam Communications, Washington, D.C.

2. I regard as more realistic form of interactivity the technically assisted individual capacity to browse allusions across all disciplines and in all media in which such information might be represented. The datasets in which the information is kept need not be adjacent to the point of inquiry. Ultimately cooperation of educational, research, and cultural institutions on an international basis will be required.

3. Analyses of the deficiencies associated with computer assisted instruction (CAI) are plentiful. I have found Brenda Laurel's (1991) *Computer As Theatre* to be one of the more informed and informative presentations. Though not written as an analysis of CAI her discussion of the human-computer interface is broadly defined so as to adequately deal with associated issues.

4. Use the term is a refinement of the definition of *interdisciplinarity*. See the discussion of various definitions of and associated academic politics related to the term *interdisciplinarity* in Mayville (1978) and Pemberton and Prentice (1990).

5. Harvey Wheeler (1987) discusses the concept of a *Virtual Library*. Wheeler considers such follow-on concepts to the *Virtual Library* as The Virtual University among other "virtual social institutions."

A *Virtual Library of Congress* would be an example of a source, complementary to the collections of the Smithsonian Institution, for creation of principally literary or textual data base structures. Additionally, the vision related to this initiative includes the linkage of the *British Museum*, the *Canadian Museum of Civilization* in Toronto, and other major institutions and organizations, to build an international network for object- and image-based research and publishing; education; curatorial support; and information distribution. An experimental design for a trial international *Virtual Museum* is being developed by the author. See the discussion Multiple Cultures Triumph over Multiculturalism in this chapter.

6. The following topics are among those chapters under development for inclusion in the *Virtual Museum Working Papers*: "The Shape of Content Revisited; or the Influence of Ben Shahn on Conceptual Development of the *Virtual Museum*;" "Virtual Publications: The Air and Space Magazine as a Proposed Example;" "Not A Virtual Anything: A Curatorial Demurral;" "Culture and Nationalism: Towards A Global Consciousness;" "Advanced Expert Systems Requirements and N^{th} Dimensional Databases in the *Virtual Museum*."

7. Stephen Michael Kosslyn (1983); Patricia Churchland (1986); Michael Arbib and Mary Hesse (1986); and George Lakoff (1987).

8. George von Furstenberg (1989); J. Michael Pemberton and Ann Prentice (1990); and Irving Louis Horowitz (1991).

9. Paul Churchland (1989), pp. 281–282.

10. Neil Harris (1990), p. 146.

11. The placement of robots in storage and retrieval (the story of the original Macintosh computer factory) together with robotic manufacturing, and grocery store checkout-inventory-ordering systems are several examples of change to major elements of the traditional workplace in to automated, smarter environments. Also, see Shoshana Zuboff's (1988) discussion of related issues.

12. It is unclear as to the actual number of objects held within the collections of the Smithsonian Institution. The Office of the Registrar places the official size of the collections at over 134,000,000 objects. In reality some of these objects are collections within collections. One unofficial and conservative estimate regarding the time period required to undertake a comprehensive capture of visual information for each object was over seventy-five years . . . cost, technical, and human resources not withstanding. This *estimate* did not include capture of text, graphic, audio, or other information in the Smithsonian's collections. Also the information capture was assuming the use of 35mm equipment which would not allow for three-dimensional holographic or other multi-dimensional representation.

13. Glen Hoptman (1991). A series of articles from news reports in magazines along with annotative remarks by the editor.

14. Rexford Brown (1991); Irving Horowitz (1991); and Steve Fuller (1988) each provide excellent discussion of highly relevant issues.

15. Henry Petroski (1990) provides an excellent discussion of the history of the design and use of the pencil with elaboration on its cultural and intellectual consequences. Also, Derek Leebaert (1991) provides us with a selection of articles that in looking to the future of computing and communications provides the reader with engaging accounts of previous communications contexts. In particu-

lar see Leebaert's introductory chapter and Roger Levien's chapter "The Civilizing Currency: Documents and Their Revolutionary Technologies."

16. Recent publications, including: A. Kohn, *Fortune or Failure; Missed Opportunities and Chance Discoveries in Science*, Blackwell, Oxford (1989) and, *The Second Computer Revolution*, Visualization, Richard Mark Friedhoff and William Benzon. Abrams, New York (1989).

17. These special "notebooks" would be created and become part of the overall *Virtual Museum* file so others can see the comments or additions made by Smithsonian scholars from various museums. These special notebooks would not alter the "history" of the object, but would be additions or commentary on the object and its "history."

18. This concept was originally suggested to the SI in 1984 in a working paper titled *The Museum Channel*, prepared by Glen H. Hoptman and Jim Dellon. The concept was to link an internal network of visual information services to a cable system that was then being planned for the District of Columbia. More recently (1988 & 1990 revisions), I incorporated within the original paper a formal proposal to develop the *Museum Channel*. The idea was discussed with representatives from several cable systems operators (MSOs) and national television programming and distribution associations. Modeled on C-SPAN, this channel could provide a national/local/regional museum-based education network. Programming from museum and cultural institutions on a local cable system basis would supplement national programming.

19. William G. Conway (1968) presented an idea for an exhibition that he very much wanted to build exhibiting the world of a bullfrog. He presented the concept as a bed-time story because of the considerable difficulties associated with its production.

20. Neil Harris discusses some of the limitations which traditional museum exhibition represents. He poses several key questions regarding the information conveyed to the visitor which he leaves for curators to answer for themselves. Also refer to George von Furstenberg (1989).

21. Glen Hoptman (1991).

22. Vanevar Bush (1945).

23. Creation of very large-scale data resources for the exchange and augmentation of data (also part of the valuable work of Doug Englebart . . . video tape: Source unknown. New concepts of compensation to "authors" for publishing, and other differences in styles of information display are discussed in Nelson's works.

24. There are significant regulatory issues associated with this area of discussion. The most recent publications of the Office of Technology Assessment related to Communications and Information Technologies, and Supercomputing Networks are of particular relevance.

References

Allman, William. F. 1989. *Apprentices of Wonder. Inside the Neural Network Revolution.* New York: Bantam Books.

Arbib, Michael, and Mary Hesse. 1986. *The Construction of Reality.* Cambridge, England: Cambridge University Press.

Brown, Rexford G. 1991. *Schools of Thought. How the Politics of Literacy Shape Thinking in the Classroom.* San Francisco: Jossey-Bass.

Churchland, Patricia Smith. 1986. *Neurophilosophy. Toward A Unified Science of the Mind/Brain.* Cambridge: The MIT Press.

Churchland, Paul. 1989. *A Neurocomputational Perspective. The Nature of the Mind and the Structure of Science.* Cambridge: The MIT Press.

Conway, William. 1968. "How to Exhibit a Bullfrog; A Bed-Time Story for Zoo Men." *Curator,* 310-318.

Fuller, Steve. 1988. *Social Epistemology.* Bloomington: Indiana University Press.

Hardison, O.B. 1989. *Disappearing Through the Skylight. Culture and Technology in the Twentieth Century.* New York: Viking Penguin.

Harris, Neil. 1990. *Cultural Excursions.* Chicago: University of Chicago Press.

Hayles, N. Katherine, ed. 1991. *Chaos and Order.* Chicago: University of Chicago Press.

Hoptman, Glen H., ed. Forthcoming (available in photocopy from the editor). *The Virtual Museum: Annotated Background Information as Reported in Recent Newspapers and Magazines.* Washington, D.C.: Lightbeam Communications.

Horowitz, Irving Louis. 1991. *Communicating Ideas. The Politics of Scholarly Publishing.* 2nd Expanded Edition. New Brunswick: Transaction Publishers.

Kosslyn, Stephen Michael. 1983. *Ghosts in the Mind's Machine. Creating and Using Images in the Brain.* New York: W. W. Norton.

Lakoff, George. 1987. *Women, Fire, and Dangerous Things.* Chicago: University of Chicago Press.

Laurel, Brenda. 1991. *Computers as Theatre.* Reading: Addison-Wesley.

Leebaert, Derek. 1991. "Later Than We Think." *Technology 2001. The Future of Computing and Communications,* edited by Derek Leebaert. Cambridge: The MIT Press.

Levien, Roger. 1991. "The Civilizing Currency: Documents and Their Revolutionary Technologies." In *Technology 2001. The Future of Computing and Communications,* edited by Derek Leebaert. Cambridge: The MIT Press.

Mayville, William. 1978. *Interdisciplinarity: The Mutable Paradigm.* AAHE-ERIC/Higher Education Research Report No. 9. Washington, D.C.: AAHE

Mellor, D.H., ed. 1990. *Ways of Communicating.* Cambridge, England: Cambridge University Press.

Pemberton, J. Michael, and Ann E. Prentice. 1990. *Information Science. The Interdisciplinary Context.* New York: Neal-Schuman Publishers

Petroski, Henry. 1990. *The Pencil. A History of Design and Circumstance.* New York: Alfred A. Knopf.

Rheingold, Howard. 1991. *Virtual Reality. The Revolutionary Technology of Computer-Generated Artificial Worlds—and how It Promises and Threatens to Transform Business and Society.* New York: Summit Books.

von Furstenberg, George. 1989. *Acting Under Uncertainty: Multidisciplinary Conceptions.* Boston: Klumer Academic Publishers.

Zuboff, Shoshana. 1988. *In the Age of the Smart Machine.* New York: Basic Books.

9

An Epistemic Analysis of the Interaction between Knowledge, Education, and Technology

David Chen

Introduction

New information technologies present an enormous challenge for the educational system. For more than forty years a whole array of electronic information technologies beginning with mass media such as radio and television and ending with computers and telecommunications has transformed the entire social infrastructure (Forester 1987). Industry, business, bureaucracy, employment, international relationships, the distribution of wealth, the nature of conflict and warfare have changed and transformed to the extent that sociologists call this era the Information Society or the Knowledge Society (Noza and Minc 1980). However, the impact of information technologies on the social institutions responsible for knowledge production and distribution such as universities and schools is far less significant.

In surveying the literature concerned with the integration of information technologies in schools and universities it is very difficult to find an explicit articulation of the role these technologies should assume in the educational setting. Many theories have been invoked to provide a rationale for linking information technologies and schooling. Behaviorism provided the ground for computer aided instruction by Skinner (1968) and Suppes (1981), among others. Cognitive sciences laid the foundation for intelligent tutoring systems by Newell (1990), Brown (1982), Anderson (1983), and many others. Developmental psychology was mobilized by Papert (1988) to formulate the constructionist learning environment in the so-called "microworlds" style. Computer science provided theoretical models for Minsky (1986), Soloway (1988), Clancey

(1987), and others. Education psychology gave rise to individualized and adaptive systems proposed by B. Glazer (1984) and others.

It would be almost futile to search for a common ground for the host theories mentioned, except for one aspect, and that is that almost all of the theories that are concerned with the interaction of technology and learning focus on the same unit of analysis—individual cognitive development. In other words, closer examination of this set of theories reveals an implicit paradigm: Information technologies somehow have the potential to extend the cognitive faculties[1] of the individual learner. Nickerson (1988) uses the term "cognitive tools" when referring to the application of information technology in the schools, and indicates that "the term has interesting and useful ambiguity connoting either tools that have some cognitive properties or tools that are usefully employed in the performance of cognitive tasks." Perhaps the definition offered by Resnic (1988) provides the clearest articulation of the cognitive paradigm:

The goal of both computer aided instruction and intelligent tutoring system will be extending human intelligence, to make humans more powerful thinkers and therefore actors. . . . The goal of bringing students to a point where they can perform complex tasks without the computer.

The notion of information technology as a long-range intelligence extender or amplifier is a very powerful one, and despite the differences in the mechanisms offered by the different theories, it is this cognitive paradigm that is the major driving force that has built the high expectations for the technology in a society that is so frustrated with the performance of its schools. If the "cognitive paradigm" managed to dominate both research and educational practices for the last 30–40 years, there must be some evidence to support it.

In a recent extensive and meticulous study of the impact of computer-based instruction, Roblyer, Casting, and King (1988) analyzed approximately 200 studies using meta-analysis techniques (Glass 1976). The results showed positive effects across the board, which were significantly different from zero. The enhancement of achievement in cognitive skills, science, math, reading, problem solving with logo, creativity, and word processing were found indeed at all educational levels (elementary school to college) and for all student populations.

This trend was further supported by the findings in the Office of Technology Assessment report *Power On* (1988). These findings seem to substantiate the claims made by the cognitive paradigm. However, in all the studies surveyed so far, the effect size of technology on the cognitive variable did not exceed about .3 standard deviations. Even in those cases where highly intensive technology programs were studied by McDermott (1985), Ferrell (1986), and Morehouse, Hoagland, and Schmidt (1987) the overall results did not surpass the effect size reported in the meta-analysis of Roblyer, Casting, and King (1988).

It seems that while the basic premises of the cognitive paradigm can probably be substantiated by the empirical findings, it is the scope and the magnitude of the paradigm that have to be questioned. I would like to suggest a different paradigm, based on an extended unit of analysis consisting of the social context pertinent to knowledge. The two paradigms are not mutually exclusive as the individual learner is unequivocally part and parcel of the larger knowledge system.

In order to be able to draw an extended epistemic analysis of the relationship between knowledge, technology, and schooling we need to define several constructs which we will have to use. The first construct is that of Ontogenic knowledge, namely the knowledge that grows in the individual. The notion of Ontogenesis is used to conjure up the biological, dynamic nature of the growth and development of the individual. Ontogenic knowledge, (K_O), can thus be defined as a result of the complex process interrelating the innate knowledge (K_P) emanating from the unfolding expression of the genetic pool, and knowledge acquired by learning through the environment (K_E). We can use the following notation to describe the knowledge system of the individual as follows:

$K_O = K_P + K_E$ (Ontogenic Knowledge = Innate Knowledge + Learned Knowledge)

In so defining Ontogenic knowledge we allow for the complexity of the internal, endogenous dynamic processes without the necessity of getting involved in the details pertaining to the nature/nurture issue.

In using the term "Ontogenic knowledge" we define the unit of analysis as the individual person. All knowledge and the processes concerned with it are endogenous whether they be in the central nervous system, the lymbic, or the genetic system. The time scale of the Ontogenic knowledge development is equivalent to the life span of the individual, namely up to 100 years. It would be interesting to estimate the individual information capacity, and after exploring several aproaches we have chosen a somewhat naive, yet simple and practical measure. We can use the number of books read by the individual as an equivalent to the amount of his acquired information, and therefore, a rough quantitative estimation of the individual ontogenic knowledge.

An average individual acquires information at the rate of about one to four books a month; that is twelve to forty books a year, or about 600–2400 books per active life span of fifty years. If we add to this number the information equivalent of 300–600 books acquired indirectly through the mass media, we will end up with an estimate of an average Ontogenetic knowledge capacity in the vicinity of 1×10^3–3×10^3 Book Equivalents. This estimate is important not in its absolute value but because it can serve for comparative analysis of changes in the relative capacities of information at different levels.

The second construct we would like to introduce is that of Exogenic public knowledge (the term "exogenic" is used to define knowledge external to the body). The notion of public knowledge was introduced first by McLlup (1972) and we have expanded McLlup's definition by stressing the epigenetic (outside of genetic control) nature of this type of knowledge. It was very tempting to use the term "phylogenetic knowledge"; however, the use of this term would have evolutionary implications, which we are not yet ready to examine.

By Exogenic knowledge we mean all public knowledge accumulated by mankind since the beginning of civilization by complex social processes. What distinguishes Exogenic from Ontogenic knowledge is the fact that Exogenic knowledge is born by means which are not biological. Social institutions and information technologies are the major carriers of this knowledge. The unit of analysis for examining Exogenous knowledge is therefore the global social system including the scientific enterprise, the educational systems, the mass media, religious and other ideological institutions, etc. The time scale for that type of knowledge is in the order of magnitude of 3 million years for the existence of mankind, 100,000 years for homo sapiens, or 10,000 years for contemporary civilization.

It is difficult to try to estimate the total amount of information in the public domain although some figures are available in the literature (Forester 1987, McLlup 1972). The very fact that much of the phenomenon of the information explosion in the modern era is due to a high degree of information redundancy mechanisms embedded both in the language and in the social knowledge system makes this task very complicated. However, what can be done is to estimate the actual growth of knowledge in the public domain by figuring out the number of new (not translated) book titles published every year all over the world.[2] This number is about 775,000 books per year during the late eighties. If we ignore changes in the growth rate, this figure would yield 38.5 million new books over the above mentioned period of 50 years. This figure is a minimal estimate as no effort was done here to account for the enormous information output in media such as newspapers, magazines, or electronic publishing (the number of newspapers in the USA alone is over five thousand). On the other hand, the extent to which new book titles stand for a net increase in totally new public knowledge is probably somewhat smaller due to a certain degree of redundancy. Nevertheless, this estimate provides a baseline sufficient for further analysis.

Table 9.1 summarizes the differences between the two types of knowledge.

Dynamics of Exogenic Knowledge and Technology Interactions

It is the Exogenic knowledge that is interwoven intimately with technology. Historically relationships between Exogenic knowledge and technology have gone through three stages:

Stage 1: At about 3000 B.C. writing systems emerged. Number systems appeared at about 1000 years B.C. Writing technologies have enabled man to preserve representations of knowledge by transferring the ephemeral language from an acoustical entity into a physical artifact that could last for a very long period. Representing knowledge (to be exact—

Table 9.1
Comparison between ontogenic and exogenic knowledge

	Ontogenic Knowledge	Exogenic Knowledge
Unit of Analysis	The Individual	Global Social System
Locus	Endogenous	Exogenous
Time Scale	<300 years	2×10^3 years– 1×10^6 years
Estimated Information Capacity	$1–3 \times 10^3$ Book Equivalent	3.85×10^7 Book Equivalent

language) exogenously enabled civilization for the first time to accumulate knowledge outside the individual brain, and social mechanisms and institutions were created laying down the foundation of our culture. Writing technology provided Exogenous knowledge with two new dimensions: the transfer of knowledge was not limited any more to the constraints of time or place. Knowledge could be communicated horizontally to any place where people needed it, or vertically across generations in time.

Stage 2 started in the 15th century when print technology became available. Print technology enabled the massive replication of Exogenous knowledge from a single to multiple copies of the same representation, therefore allowing the distribution of knowledge among the members of society.

Stage 3 has to do with the emergence of the new electronic information technology. The unique characteristic of this technology is that it enabled for the first time the Exogenous processing of knowledge outside the human brain. At the same time the electronic information technology has managed to improve immensely the preservation and accumulation functions of stage 1, and the replication function of stage 2. Thus, it is very clear that the primary role of information technology was to provide Exogenous knowledge with an infrastructure analogous only to that provided by the body to Ontogenic knowledge. Thus we can conclude that information technology is mainly involved in the social fabric concerned with the creation, accumulation, preservation, and distribution of Exogenic (public) knowledge, and we must bear this in mind when we want to understand the relationships between knowledge technology and education.

Redefining the Problem

Extending the unit of analysis from the individual to the social realm enables us to redefine the problem concerning the relationships between knowledge technology and education. First we would like to examine the dynamic aspects of both Ontogenic and Exogenic knowledge. The development of Ontogenic knowledge during ontogeny is known to assume the shape represented either by the long range intelligence studies or short-range learning curves (figure 9.1).

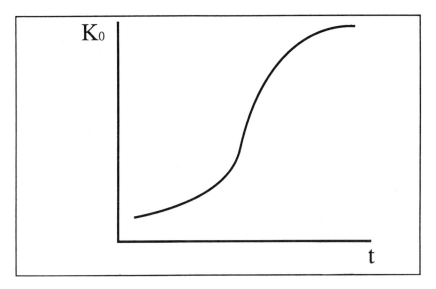

Figure 9.1
Development of Ontogenic knowledge (K_o) in time (t)

Exogenous knowledge growth is best represented by the scientometric studies by Weiss (1960) and De Solla Price (1963) in the early sixties (figure 9.2). This model is based on measurement of several indicators such as number of publications, books, and number of researchers, over a time scale of several hundred years. The model displays a three-phase process starting with a lag phase, followed by rapid exponential growth and a prediction of a stationary phase based on what happens to traditional growth curves.

In order to compare and analyze the dynamics of the two types of knowledge we can use qualitative estimation of the relative changes over time for the two of them or the total amount of information, looking at changes in the overall potential for Ontogenic growth (figure 9.3). There seems to be no evidence that any meaningful changes have occurred whether in memory capacity, learning rate, or high-order thinking skills. A child from Athens in 200 B.C. would probably do at school as well as a child from Boston in 1991 A.D.

At the same time Exogenous public knowledge continues to expand at an exponential rate. The gap between the curves is growing rapidly, exerting tremendous pressure on the individual who aspires to have a share in the Exogenic (public) knowledge pool. We can have a rough idea

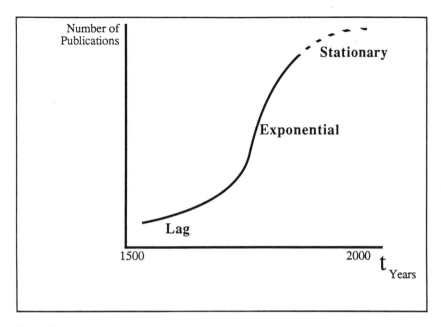

Figure 9.2
Development of Exogenic knowledge

about the extent of the gap between the overall Ontogenic knowledge capacity in the individual and the knowledge in the public domain by just comparing the figures concerning newly accumulated information with those esitmating the limits of the individual information load. This gap corresponds to at least four orders of magnitude in terms of book equivalents (1–3×10^3 and 3.8×10^7) and possibly much more. If there is no way an individual can cope with the vast scope of new information accumulated during his own lifespan, how can we possibly conceive the idea that he can follow a renaissance model of being able to reach the full scope of knowledge resources which are at the disposal of the entire human race?

The extent to which technology can extend K_0 has been shown to be in the order of magnitude of .3 standard deviations. Even if we could improve the efficiency of information technology for learning by making it more sophisticated, by introducing expert systems, intelligent programs, effective feedback or adaptive interfaces, there is no reason to believe that we could surpass the limitations to K_0 given by the biological constraints.

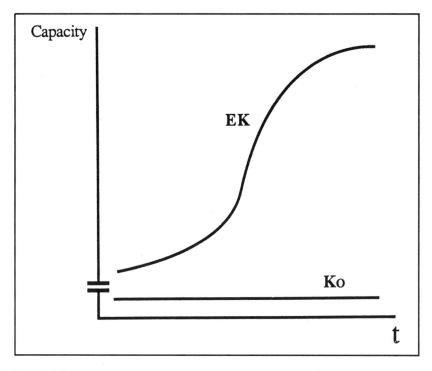

Figure 9.3
Changes in information capacity over time (EK—Exogenic Knowledge, K_o—Ontogenic Knowledge

The cognitive paradigm requires a thorough examination as Eugenic ingredients and to some extent even implicit Larmarckian elements underline the expectations that intelligence can be improved and extended and cognitive faculties can grow and persist during the life cycle of the individual.

To summarize this analysis we can say: The distinction between Ontogenic and Exogenic knowledge allows us to analyze the different roles of technology with regard to these two entities. It can be concluded that the primary role technology plays is in providing the backbone for Exogenic knowledge. Exogenic and Ontogenic knowledge differ on several dimensions by several orders of magnitude. It is the Exogenic knowledge scene that we should concern ourselves with if we want to understand the interaction between knowledge technology and education.

Starting from the theory of knowledge we have reached the conclusion that in order to understand the role of information technology in learning and education we must extend our search to the wider social system rather than the individual. The epistemic analysis of the extended framework leads us to conclude that the prevailing cognitive paradigm has by definition several constraints in terms of its possible impact on the relationship between Ontogenic (individual) and Exogenic (public) knowledge. In order to gain both a better insight and develop sound and realistic strategies toward the future application of technology for knowledge distribution (in other words: education) we have to shift our focus from the cognitive paradigm of technology to an agenda that will concentrate on the interaction between technology and knowledge in the social domain, namely Exogenic knowledge. Such an agenda can attract our efforts in order to understand the relationships between Exogenic knowledge, education, and technology at three different levels: (1) the level of public, Exogenic knowledge where questions should be asked concerning relationships between the dynamics of knowledge growth and change, and the curriculum, namely that segment of public knowledge specifically serving education; (2) the level of the curriculum where the very nature of educational knowledge representation should be studied and designed; and (3) the level of the interactive interface where Exogenic knowledge is transformed to Ontogenic knowledge.

At the first level the R & D efforts should aim at questions concerning the ways and means by which technology can facilitate processes in which new knowledge in the public domain must flow into the "curriculum" segment efficiently and effectively. Curriculum theory does not provide us today with a model explaining the relationship between disciplinary knowledge and curriculum knowledge, nor does it provide us with the rules and criteria explaining the dynamics of the reduction process underlying such transition. Electronic publishing, knowledge bases, and network communications are some of the technologies that transform the nature of knowledge growth and dissemination. However, educational applications require their special R & D, with specific answers tailored for educational needs.

At the second level many more questions await an answer. Should learners have a direct access to the public knowledge? Do we need educational databases that would serve as a buffer between the learner and the immediate knowledge?

If we do need intermediary knowledge pools at the curriculum level, do we need accessories that would channel and help the selection and reduction of public knowledge to manageable entities (i.e., the contemporary textbook). Will expert systems or decision support systems help to that effect? What is the organizational framework necessary for the development of learning networks? Will they be more effective than contemporary schools and thus replace them? What would be the nature of control that society would like to maintain over the learning process? If independent learning over distance becomes practical, what about the social outcomes of massive learning? What about accreditation? What about the "standards" of learning and achievement? How much structure and what type should be given to educational knowledge bases? Should the linearity principle be maintained or hypertext flexibility enacted? What would happen to equal opportunity to learn? Would there be any means to monitor it? Would it have the same meaning in a traditional school and in a knowledge-based school?

At the third level the agenda changes again and the main question will have to deal with the interface that transforms Exogenic to Ontogenic knowledge. Evidently a cognitive paradigm is at work here; however, there is much more to it than meets the eye. What are the knowledge "atoms" or frames from the learner perspective? Who is in charge of learning? Is it controlled by the learner or is it mediated by the system? How can we individualize learning? Can we use the adaptive instruction paradigm in conjunction with artificial intelligence techniques? Would intelligent tutoring systems converge with the prevailing CAI approach? How can we bridge motivation and knowledge technology? These and many other questions demonstrate the complexity of the interaction between knowledge technology and education.

This agenda reflects our belief that it is the interaction between sociocultural institutions and technology that will lead to comprehensive and far-reaching changes in the social arrangements of knowledge distribution. However, we also believe that most of the individual gains from these changes would be qualitative rather than quantitative, and therefore our agenda must change in accordance with the extended theoretical framework.

References

Anderson, John R. 1983. *The Architecture of Cognition.* Harvard University Press. Cambridge.

Brown , J. S., and D. Sherman. 1982. *Intelligent Tutoring Systems.* Academic Press. New York.

Clancey, W. J. 1987. *Knowledge Based Tutoring.* MIT Press. Cambridge.

De Solla Price, Derek J. 1963. *Little Science, Big Science.* Columbia University Press. New York.

Ferrell, B. G. 1986. "Evaluating the Impact of CAI on Mathematics Learning, Computer Immersion Project." *Journal of Education Research* 2 (3) 327–336.

Forester, Tom. 1987. *High-Tech Society.* The MIT Press. Cambridge.

Glass, G. V. 1976. "Primary, Secondary, and Meta Analysis of Research." *Educational Research* (5) 3–8.

Glazer, Robert. 1984. "Education and Thinking: The Role of Knowledge." *American Psychologist* 29 (2) 92–104.

McDermott, C. W. 1985. *Affecting Basic Skills Achievement Through Technology: Research Report.* Little Rock, Ark. State Department of Education.

McLlup, F. 1972. *Knowledge and Knowledge Production.* Vol 1. Princeton University Press. Princeton, N.J.

Minsky, Marvin. 1986. *Society of Minds.* MIT Press. Cambridge.

Morehouse, D. L., M. L. Hoagland, and R. H. Schmidt. 1987. *Technology Demonstration Program Final Evaluation Report.* Menomonie, Wisconsin. Quality Evaluation and Development.

Newell, Allen. 1990. *Unified Theory of Cognition.* Harvard University Press. Cambridge.

Nickerson, Raymond S. 1988. *Technology in Education: Possible Influences on Context, Purposes, Context and Methods.* Lawrence Erlbaum Associates. N.J.

Noza, Simon and Alain Minc. 1980. *The Computerization of Society.* The MIT Press. Cambridge.

Papert, Seymour. 1988. "The Conservation of Piaget: The Computer as Grist to the Constructivist Mill." In *Constructivism in the Computer Age.* G. Forman and P. B. Pufall, eds. Lawrence Erlbaum Associates. N.J.

Power On: New Tools for Teaching and Learning. 1988. Office of Technology Assessment. U.S. Government.

Resnic, Laurence B., and Ann Johnson. 1988. "Intelligent Machines for Intelligent People: Cognitive Theory and the Future of Computer Assisted Learning." In *Technology in Education.* R. S. Nickerson and P. P. Zodihiates, eds.

Roblyer, M. D., W. H. Casting, and F. J. King, eds. 1988. *Assessing the Impact of Computer-Based Instruction.* Haworth Press, Inc. New York.

Skinner, B. F. 1968. *The Technology of Teaching.* Prentice Hall, Inc.

Soloway, Elliot. 1988. "It's 2020: Do you know what your children are learning in programming class?" In *Technology in Education.* R. S. Nickerson and P. P. Zodihiates, ed. Lawrence Erlbaum Associates.

Suppes, P. 1981. *University-Level Computer-Assisted Instruction at Stanford: 1968–1980.* IMSSS. Stanford University.

Weiss, Paul. 1960. "Knowledge and Growth Process." *Science* 131 1716–1719.

10

The Many Faces of Multimedia: How New Technologies Might Change the Nature of the Academic Endeavor

Alison Hartman, John E. Diem, and Matthew Quagliana

Introduction

Instructional technologies, loosely defined as technology-based tools used for purposes of education, have long held interest as means of improving teaching and learning. In the 1980s, computers and videotape joined filmstrip, slide show, and microfiche systems to teach students from kindergarten to graduate school about English, history, mathematics, and science. The 1980s also produced a burst of interest in "interactive video" and "computer-aided instruction," and many institutions began to use and develop computer-based instructional materials as their resources allowed.

The step from the early, largely linear and highly-structured computer-based instructional systems to today's concept of interactive multimedia is a giant one in the evolutionary development of instructional technologies. The convergence of the television, computer, and publishing industries has created desktop systems that combine images, sound, and text, and the relative cost of these systems has decreased significantly (Ambron and Hooper, 1988). Software development tools such as HyperCard and Toolbook, which are easy to use and widely available, enable non-programmers to create cohesive applications that link various sources and types of information. Videodisk formats have become standardized, and desktop video systems such as Video F/X enable video professionals (and would-be professionals) to perform non-linear editing at a fraction of the cost of high-end digital broadcast systems. The availability of off-the-shelf applications has grown as videodisk and CD-ROM players have become increasingly commonplace and companies such as Voyager and ABC

News Interactive have recognized the added value to their videotapes of world events.

Interactive multimedia is a synthesis of computers, video, text, and sound. Using a computer as the primary control center, an individual might read text and view images on the computer screen, watch still or moving video, hear digital-quality sound, respond to questions and receive feedback, and, in response to each of these stimuli, choose the next step in the process. Interactive multimedia combines the best parts of *multimedia*—the integration of various forms of information—and *hypermedia*—the non-linear linking of information—to create applications that both stimulate and respond to the individual. Multimedia applications may include hypertext, graphics, sound, animation, and video, all of which create an information-rich environment that enables an individual to delve deeply into areas of particular interest and skim the surface of others.

A typical multimedia delivery system might consist of a computer with a large hard disk, a color monitor, a keyboard (if the monitor is not touch-sensitive), a mouse, and one or more of the following items: a videodisk player, a video monitor or an adapter board that will display full-motion video on the computer monitor), audio speakers or headphones, and a CD-ROM drive. The system may be connected to a local area network, which may in turn be connected to a high-speed building or campus network. For purposes of developing multimedia applications, one might add a graphics scanner, video acquisition and editing equipment, microphones, a 35-millimeter slide scanner, musical interface (MIDI) equipment, and appropriate software tools (Hooper, 1988).

In this paper, we explore the many faces of multimedia, describing ways that a diverse group of individuals at one private research university views and uses these new and powerful tools. We present background about how multimedia fits into current theoretical models of teaching and learning, and describe Tulane University's efforts to promote the development and use of multimedia by faculty and students. We also explore some of the ways that new technologies may change the nature of education and research in the next decade and century.

Background

While a few Tulane faculty had developed an interest in exploring the potential of educational technologies to improve teaching and learning, never had the University put forth a systematic effort to encourage and support such activities. Some two years ago, however, a number of factors compelled us to establish a program to integrate technology into the curriculum. First, students began to look more critically at the cost and quality of their education, and, as a result, institutions at the soundness of their educational programs (Grassmuck, 1990). Second, there is growing evidence that the use of multimedia has a positive effect on students' perception and enjoyment of the subject material. Perhaps because of their exposure to MTV and Nintendo, books and lectures alone seem unable to capture students' attention the way a video clip can. Heightened interest in the material may also improve student retention, maintaining enrollment better than a lecture-only class might be able to do (The Joe Wyatt Challenge, 1991). Finally, high-speed networks and distributed computing environments are laying the foundation for the delivery of multimedia materials to every desktop in every laboratory, residence hall, and classroom. This, perhaps, is the most compelling argument: networks make it possible to deliver interactive multimedia materials across campus or across the country, ultimately providing every student with access to information on any subject.

Despite these exciting advances, faculty encounter no small number of obstacles in the pursuit of instructional software development. The context of a research university offers little incentive for faculty—particularly junior faculty—to engage in activities directly related to instruction. In some cases, faculty may suffer during tenure, promotion, and salary reviews, especially if the development of instructional software took time from research activities, which it almost inevitably must. Inertia is another potential obstacle to the development and use of instructional software by faculty, particularly for those who have taught the same course for a number of years. It is usually easier to continue in the same manner than to engage in the time- and energy-consuming activities involved in the adoption of new technologies. Support is yet another obstacle: most faculty don't want to be programmers, and even those who can master the relative intricacies of HyperCard or ToolBook need someone to whom they can turn for answers to specific questions. Academic computing centers are so often overwhelmed with the day-to-day aspects of routine technical support that they are unprepared to provide the level and range of support required for development projects. The use of technology also raises some important pedagogic issues. Effective applications should incorporate the fundamental tenets of effective teaching and learning. And finally, the end result must not only be esthetically pleasing, but its interface must be intuitive and easy to use.

Multimedia and Learning

Multimedia holds considerable promise as a way to enhance learning. Wingfield (1979) defines learning as "a relatively permanent change in behavior or knowledge brought about by practice or experience" (p. 3). However, psychologists recognize many varieties of learning, including classical conditioning, sensorimotor learning, and verbal learning. In fact, "there is no single 'theory of learning,' so much as attempts to understand the many varieties of learning" (Wingfield, 1979, p. 7). To compound the difficulty, we cannot usually measure learning directly; we measure the products of learning. "Learning itself is an internal event, which, like the wind, is invisible to the eye and can only be judged by its effects" (Wingfield, 1979, p. 13).

Most cognitive theories of learning describe at least three functions of the process: (1) the new information must be collected and filtered from spurious environmental stimuli, (2) the disparate pieces of new information must be combined and organized, and (3) the new information must be related in some way to old information. Several other functions may also be involved (Sternberg, 1984).

Current conceptions of learning from the viewpoint of modern-day cognitive and educational psychology are concerned with thought processes and mental activities, rather than behavior alone. Cognitive approaches to learning stress that learning is an active process, and research has revealed a number of factors that affect one's ability to learn (Shuell, 1986). The amount of related knowledge that a learner possesses has a substantial impact on the learning process, and the information's organization also impacts the retention and accessibility of that information. (Learners attempt to organize material they are learning, even when no obvious basis of organization exists.) Metacognitive processes such as planning and goal setting also influence learning. Finally, individuals learn in many different ways. Kinesthetic or tactile experiences may promote optimum learning for some individuals, while others learn best through visual or auditory stimuli (Wingfield, 1979).

If students are to learn effectively, they must engage in learning activities that are likely to result in their achieving the desired outcomes. These activities should take into account factors such as prior knowledge, the context in which the material is presented and organized, and the availability of appropriate schemata, or framework with which to integrate the information. Multimedia technology offers the ability to perform these tasks in such a way that the students are in control, actively guiding the learning process and tailoring it to their individual needs.

Multimedia and Teaching

Effective instruction should take advantage of the general principles of learning described above. For example, effective teaching usually incorporates the following activities:

• review of previous material
• clear statement of goals
• high levels of student practice
• periodic checks for understanding
• relevant examples
• provide systematic feedback and corrections.

Thus, a general model of effective instruction would include a number of factors related to effective learning (Rosenshine & Stevens, 1986). Effectively designed multimedia applications will take these factors into account (as appropriate to the subject matter), thus, potentially offering advantages to both instructors and students.

For faculty, the use of interactive multimedia in the classroom can have a number of significant advantages. The technology provides the faculty member with the ability to access information at random, regardless of the nature of that information. Multimedia also provides the ability to link information non-linearly and to demonstrate events in a way not possible with blackboard and chalk. It also enables an instructor to share research findings with students—even at the undergraduate level.

Interactive multimedia offers a number of significant benefits to teaching and learning. Multimedia ensures that learning is an active process and that ancillary information is readily available. The individual learner is in control of the application, performing actions that move through the learning process and tailoring it to his or her individual needs. Technology also offers the opportunity to store enormous quantities of information and to retrieve that information readily. It provides a framework by which this information is organized and the capability for students to further organize the information to facilitate learning. Multimedia combines the interest, entertainment, and familiarity of video with the ability to explore different directions independently. It also enables one to present the best in a class, as admirably demonstrated in IBM's Illuminated Books and Manuscripts project, which includes the recitation of poetry by the best of today's performers—be they Shakespearean actors or rap singers.

Evaluation of Multimedia

Just as other teaching methods are subject to evaluation, determining the effectiveness of instructional technology, especially in light of its cost, should be part of its use. However, irrefutable "proof" that information technology improves learning has been elusive when studied using traditional methods of measuring teaching and learning effectiveness. Costs and benefits must be weighed in tandem; for example, while it may be expensive to establish a multimedia chemistry lab, if the students learn as well or better using the computer, the benefits of reallocating space otherwise used for introductory laboratory paraphernalia may outweigh the costs. The ability to perform experiments on the computer that would be too costly or dangerous in the lab is another potential benefit.

Early studies emphasized behavioral approaches and focused on external events in instruction. Often, researchers performed undifferentiated comparisons of the learning impact of "new" media such as television with more "traditional" media such as classroom instruction. Recent studies have replaced the behaviorally-based comparison between media with more cognitively oriented questions. "We moved from asking which medium was a better teacher to a concern with which 'attributes' of media might combine with learner traits under different task conditions and performance demands to produce different kinds of learning" (Clark & Salomon, 1986, p. 473).

Multimedia applications should be evaluated within the framework of effective teaching and learning. Shuell and Schueckler (1989) conducted an interesting study in which they evaluated 16 randomly-selected educational software packages according to principles of learning and teaching. They found that in general, the software rated high with regard to presenting material in appropriate steps or blocks, consistency between program and stated objectives, providing appropriate examples, and opportunities for independent practice. Generally the programs were rated low with regard to informing students of instructional goal, reviewing prerequisite knowledge, and several other areas.

Approach

The growing acceptance and adoption of multimedia technology by faculty and students at institutions across the country are precursors to true integration. In 1989, Tulane Computing Services (TCS), Tulane's central computing agency, launched an initiative to heighten faculty's interest in and awareness of instructional technologies and to encourage Tulane faculty to use and develop applications in Tulane's graduate and undergraduate instructional programs. The goal was to provide both *incentive* and *support* to stimulate the development and use of instructional software. A concomitant goal was to establish methods by which to evaluate the effect of instructional technologies on teaching and learning. By encouraging faculty to develop and use instructional applications, we could create an environment rich with opportunities for studying both the advantages and disadvantages of technology on education.

The initiative began with an invitation to all (approximately 600) full-time members of the Tulane faculty to submit to an advisory committee a proposal presenting their interest in attending an intensive four-day workshop on multimedia tools and applications. Some 40 faculty responded to the invitation, and the faculty advisory committee selected ten faculty members to attend the workshop. Attendees to the workshop came from a broad spectrum of disciplines: humanities, arts, engineering, business, social sciences, and medicine. Two of the attendees were women and eight were men. Four of the attendees held the rank of associate professor; the remaining attendees were assistant professors.

The hands-on workshop, which was supported in part by Apple Computer, Inc., included a variety of information, from HyperCard programming, to pedagogical considerations in software development, to mastering a CD-ROM disk. At the conclusion of the workshop, each participant submitted a more fully developed proposal describing his or her vision for an instructional multimedia project. On the basis of these proposals, three of the ten faculty members were awarded multimedia development systems that included a Macintosh IIcx computer, laserdisk player and monitor (in addition to the computer monitor), and a variety of software appropriate to their proposed projects. Each of the seven other attendees received a Macintosh SE/30 computer and software. All workshop attendees then began the task of developing their envisioned projects.

To address the issues of support, TCS established the division of Information Technology Development. As part of Academic Computing, Information Technology Development staff collaborate with faculty and students to encourage excellence in scholarship and education through the effective and innovative use of computers and information technology. In addition to several professional staff members who support research computing and some exceptionally talented students, this group includes a courseware development specialist, an individual with expertise in computer interface design and educational software development. The courseware development specialist works closely with faculty members who are interested in developing information technology applications, and interactive multimedia applications in particular, for use by their students. In addition, the staff includes a full-time video production and editing professional who is involved in all aspects of producing non-commercially available video for multimedia projects.

TCS also established a Multimedia Development Studio equipped with several multimedia development systems and a large collection of software and peripheral devices. The studio provides an environment in which faculty and student assistants can use specialized equipment and software to develop interactive teaching applications. Here, faculty can examine for themselves other applications that are available commercially or through educational outlets. They (or their students) can use a scanner, CD-ROM drive, or other devices not yet commonly available at each desktop.

An additional component of support for instructional computing is the classroom of color workstations, established in part through a barter agreement with Apple Computer, Inc. Each machine in this facility is connected to Tulane's fiberoptic backbone through a local area network. A projection device enables computer and video images to be displayed on an overhead screen. Faculty are able to use this facility for both hands-on classwork and for laboratory assignments. We have also recently upgraded the student laboratory facilities, installing new Macintosh and IBM PS/2 computers that are capable of running interactive multimedia applications.

In 1991, the Board of Regents of the State of Louisiana, through its Louisiana Educational Quality Support Fund, awarded a grant for the project "Interactive Multimedia in the Humanities," an interdisciplinary effort to bring state-of-the-art technology to the teaching of classical languages, Russian, and history. The goal of the project is to develop three interactive multimedia applications that can be used to improve undergraduate education. This grant has enabled us to hire the professional video specialist and to purchase a complete video production and post-production system. The video production equipment includes a camcorder, tripod, microphones, and lighting equipment. The post-production system reflects the leading edge in desktop video technology, with the Video F/X editing system to do non-linear offline editing, which greatly decreases editing time and expands creative decision making in a way that is not possible on a standard (non-computer-based) editing system.

Assessing the effect of interactive multimedia on teaching and learning is of great importance, especially under increasingly constrained financial conditions. Attitudinal measures appear to show that students are motivated and interested by subjects that are presented using technology, and anecdotal evidence demonstrates that both faculty and students feel that the appropriate use of technology can significantly improve both teaching and learning. Faculty report that they are able to teach certain concepts much more readily, thereby allowing increased time for the interesting and important work that assumes mastery of the fundamentals. Traditional comparisons of examination scores, grades, and the like may have failed to demonstrate a compelling argument in favor of instructional technologies. However, both qualitative and quantitative measures will be required to determine the real value.

Results

The initiative to integrate interactive multimedia into Tulane's educational programs has been successful so far. A number of development efforts are currently underway by faculty in various disciplines. Faculty awareness of and interest in instructional technologies is heightened. We have also begun to evaluate those projects that are being used in the classroom and laboratory. Each faculty member has a unique perception of the computer medium and its ability to meet the challenges of his or her profession. Although each received the same initial indoctrination, each has developed a different vision of interactive multimedia.

Education

A professor of education uses interactive multimedia to bring together a large body of information for one segment of his Educational Psychology class. His project, entitled "Cognitive Psychology in the Classroom," includes class lecture notes, online experiments that reinforce cognitive learning theory, the full text of journal articles (used with permission), and a large database that drives a videodisk of teaching episodes (purchased from the Minnesota Educational Computing Consortium). This program can be used by students to review material previously covered in class; it also provides the instructor with a central repository of information that he uses to reinforce classroom presentation and stimulate discussion. At any moment he may play a video clip that demonstrates the topic at hand or present the class with a brief exercise to clarify an abstract concept.

As a replacement for on-site classroom observation, this approach can have a number of advantages. At this introductory level, students have yet to learn to observe the activities in a typical busy elementary or secondary school classroom. Often, observers reach a school to find students engaged in some non-learning activity. The videodisk segments allows the faculty member to highlight important points, while knowing exactly what the students observed.

Medicine

A gastroenterologist and professor at Tulane Medical School is building an ambitious project to teach both students and medical professionals how cirrhosis of the liver develops and how it might be countered or reversed. The initial stage of the project is a hypertext that links text, diagrams, and high-quality images of cell structures taken under both light and electron microscopes. On this foundation, we plan two additional features. First, using the Inter-Application Communication feature of Apple's System 7, will be the ability to perform Medline database searches in the background. In this manner, the software can be viewed as a high-level front end for a remote database, acting, in a limited sense, as an "agent" for the student. The second module will be an interactive model of the liver. The student will be able to adjust different variables, such as alcohol consumption, over a period of time and watch the advance of the disease on microscopic and electron microscopic levels. Since the model will be based to some extent on theoretical material, one will be able to selectively turn on and off various relationships, thus accepting or rejecting some of the author's premises. In this light, the project may be viewed as a new form of academic publication.

Library

A reference librarian has developed a hypertext "interactive tour" of the Tulane University Libraries. The tour delivers extensive information about the libraries' services, facilities, history, holdings, and collections. The information is linked in such a way as to allow an individual to explore as much or as little information as desired along a variety of paths. The computer-based tour overcomes some of the disadvantages of traditional methods of bibliographic instruction. Moreover, libraries of the future will not necessarily be physical entities; they may be vast data banks accessed through national and international computer networks. Although searching such libraries will be significantly easier than is possible today, their lack of physical presence will make them more difficult to browse casually. This project is an effort to overcome some of those challenges.

Civil Engineering

A professor of civil engineering is creating a highly interactive replacement for a printed lab manual that for years has inundated engineering students with a massive volume of data and information. It is his goal to convert much of this textual information into video, allowing students to prepare for lab work by watching the lab procedure being performed and making decisions that directly affect the on-screen results. Thus, students enter the hands-on laboratory with experience, prepared for the challenges ahead of them. For this professor, multimedia provides a way to improve the quality of the laboratory experience.

Russian

For the past 18 months, a member of the Russian faculty has been working to develop an Interactive Language Teaching Model that combines all four language learning skills: aural comprehension, oral facility, reading, and writing. Intended for use in a Russian Poetry course, the project will familiarize intermediate and advanced Russian students with Pushkin's classic masterpiece *The Bronze Horseman,* and through this, with in-depth insight into the Russian language and culture. The project currently includes digitized sound and text, and the Board of Regents grant will enable us to add a videodisk component that ties historical information with current events in Russia, and particularly, in St. Petersburg (formerly Leningrad), where the statue of the Bronze Horseman stands.

With material presented interactively though various media (sound, video, text), the student who wants to learn Pushkin is lured into exploring the text extensively and then has the ability to gain a clear conception of its pronunciation, rhythmic flow, and composition in a way that could not be duplicated by any other collateral teaching method. This project presents an opportunity for students to explore in-depth a classic literary masterpiece while refreshing and updating knowledge of the many levels of linguistics and culture that this masterpiece represents.

Classics

The Classics project focuses on the development of a HyperCard template and videodisk for use by students in the Introduction to Classical Civilization course, as well as in other classics courses. Using the template, the faculty member will be able to add textual or image information, link text or images with other text, images, or with the videodisk, create a bibliography and glossary, and select a pre-determined series of images to display from the computer and/or videodisk. The template will focus on making these tasks extremely easy for the non-programmer/faculty member. The primary use of the application will be by students outside the classroom to prepare for examinations and to complete written assignments. The instructor will also be able to use the program during class sessions, although the quality of the projected images and the present inability to display two video images simultaneously suggest that initially, use of the project in-class will not be as great as that in the laboratory.

The HyperCard template will provide the framework for organizing the information. The videodisk will contain still images of maps, people (and gods), architecture, artwork, and expert interpretation of various issues surrounding ancient Greek and Roman civilization. In addition, we may include clips from relevant films, for example, theatrical productions of ancient Greek and Roman plays, some in the original language.

History

The History project will cover the six-week period preceding the firing on Fort Sumter and the onset of the Civil War, specifically, March and April of 1861. This project is based on a simulation that places the student in the role of one or more "characters" involved in the Ft. Sumter incident and other critical events of the time. The program will place the student in a simulated situation, and, providing information about each situation, require the student to make decisions. Feedback on the results of each decision will be included, as will information about decisions made at the time and their outcomes. To further organize the information, students will have access to an electronic notebook in which they can write and prepare notes for written assignments and class discussion.

The video component of this project will include images of maps, people, newspaper headlines (with corresponding full-text from newspaper accounts on the computer, where appropriate), archival materials (letters, diaries, etc.), excerpts from public speeches made around the time, and stock footage of the events that preceded the firing on Fort Sumter and the subsequent onset of the Civil War. In addition, interviews with subject matter experts will provide students with information about the controversies that surround any such historical event, and thus, with an insight into the study of history.

Multimedia Toolkit

A concomitant goal of all of these projects is to develop a multimedia toolkit—a set of basic software tools that might be useful in a variety of applications. Two examples of such tools are the "Slide Show" and the

"Link Manager." The Slide Show, developed as part of the Educational Psychology project, enables a faculty member to piece together a series of screens and then to "replay" those screens easily, either for review or for use during class. The Link Manager, which was developed for the Liver project, provides a simple way to connect single words and phrases to images or other pieces of information. In this way, even those unfamiliar with HyperTalk are able to create meaningful connections among information.

Evaluation

We have also begun work with several of the faculty on ways by which to assess the impact of interactive multimedia on themselves and on their students. In one civil engineering lab, a required course on soil analysis, we videotaped students at work in their laboratory session using the worn laboratory manual. Next year, when the computer application is used for the first time, we will record comparative information for the two groups of students. We also collected information on the students' perception of the difficulty of the lab material, how much time they spent on the lab, the grade they expected to receive, and other motivational and attitudinal factors. By collecting the same type of information next semester, we may be able to detect both qualitative and quantitative differences in the students' work. In an educational psychology course, where the students used an interactive multimedia application the professor had developed to prepare their term papers, we are comparing these students' papers to those done in previous years. The papers will be rated according to certain criteria by independent readers to determine how the use of multimedia may have influenced students' comprehension and integration of the material.

Discussion

Interactive multimedia clearly has the potential to take advantage of principles of effective learning and teaching. It is active rather than passive. The learner has the opportunity to access a great deal of varied information that is linked to a great deal of other information. The well-designed interactive multimedia application provides a schemata, or framework, with which the learner can organize the information, and additional tools that enable the learner to further organize it. The computer can review a learner's understanding of prerequisite material and provide feedback to the learner about that understanding.

A number of obstacles hinder the ability of faculty to enter the arena of interactive multimedia development. First, although development tools such as Authorware and Guide have come a long way toward becoming easy for non-programmers to use, the effective use of such tools still requires time and dedication. Interactive multimedia is costly. High-quality video production and editing requires a substantial investment, not only in equipment, but in professional production and post-production staff to use the equipment. The human resources required for interactive multimedia development are significant. All of these projects are team efforts, the result of collaboration of a number of individuals with unique abilities. Finding the appropriate people for this type of work is difficult; individuals with the broad set of requisite skills in programming, interface design, and pedagogy are rare. Finally, solid assessment of instructional technologies is still in its infancy, making it difficult to demonstrate the true value of interactive multimedia in education.

Despite these obstacles, the development and use of interactive multimedia by Tulane faculty is important, and Tulane's initiative to integrate interactive multimedia into the educational programs has been successful so far in many respects. Some 20 faculty are interested in and actively working on projects that use technology to broaden the teaching and learning experience. A few faculty have already taught classes using interactive multimedia; both they and their students seem to be pleased with the results. Several departments are considering the development of instructional software as a scholarly activity, worthy—as part of a well-rounded professional life—of reward through promotion, tenure, and salary reviews. The University network is nearing completion, and has been developed with the intent of delivering all types of information to the desktop workstation. The establishment of a truly distributed computing environment will facilitate the delivery of a variety of applications to the classroom, laboratory, office, or residence hall. In the future, such technologies will be commonplace in education, just as the blackboard and textbook are today.

Multimedia has and will continue to create change in the nature of education. Each of the faculty members described above views interactive multimedia differently, but all view it as an important tool for education. These projects and the others like them will have a significant affect on education in the next decade and beyond, and these changes will affect all of the individuals involved: students, faculty, staff—even the institutions themselves.

Among the most marked changes to take place will be the transition of students—from passive learners to information travellers. Using interactive multimedia, students proceed at their own pace, perhaps reviewing and exploring supporting materials (glossaries, images, sounds) to suit their specific learning styles. Far from the passive response required of television or videotape viewers, interactive multimedia involves the student integrally in the learning process. In contrast to traditional "computer-aided instruction," where the student proceeds in a pre-determined fashion through a set of pre-defined materials, with interactive multimedia the student is free to—indeed, must—control the system's operation.

Technology is also likely to change the process of teaching at both undergraduate and graduate levels. Already we have seen that the role of the faculty member often changes with the integration of computers— from lecturer/teacher/ultimate authority to coach and facilitator or guide. Technology will provide faculty with the ability to draw upon vast information resources in preparing for class and during lectures. Lectures may incorporate information and examples that were previously unavailable and better demonstrate concepts that are abstract and difficult to explain. Perhaps more efficient ways to teach certain basic foundations will allow additional time for important, more advanced material.

The nature of research publications will also change as a result of multimedia and digital technologies. The ability for faculty to expose students to research findings at the undergraduate level will enable students to learn that disciplines are evolving entities subject to disagreement and discussion. Digital technologies are already decreasing the time between an idea and the dissemination of that idea so that research results can be transmitted in a more timely manner. Digital publications will also enable scientists and researchers to display information in manners other than textual—for example, using graphics, animation, and video—enabling scientists to convey complex findings to peers and to students.

At the present time, because this is so new, most of the time and effort in developing interactive multimedia is spent on translating existing information into digital form. In other words, we must focus on the process as much as or more than on the content. With time, as information becomes more widely available in digital form and as the tools to organize that information improve, the focus will shift to the content. At this point, interactive multimedia will be the electronic equivalent of blackboard and chalk.

Institutions will also be transformed as a result of technology. At Tulane, if a faculty member writes a textbook, that person keeps all of the royalties from that publication. However, since the development of instructional software consumes far more of the university's resources, the institution may feel entitled to a portion of the royalties from the "textbooks of the future." When networks connect our homes and offices, the definition of a college or university changes, as well. What is a classroom if we can connect to a network backbone and vast data resources without leaving home? What is a university if we can interact from our living rooms—face-to-face (through two- or more-way video) with peers and professors around the world?

We envision the delivery of full-motion video, digital sound, high-quality color graphics, and hypermedia links from everything to everything else to the desktop workstation. Admittedly this vision may be realized only some 10 years hence, but the technological capabilities exist today. The widespread distribution and integration of technology into academic life will enable us to overcome barriers to education caused by geographical distance or individual disability. Technology will also continue to enhance the accessibility of information. If the relevant sources of information are literally a mouse-click away, students are more likely to use them to explore than they might if they had to walk across campus each time they came upon a word or reference with which they were unfamiliar.

Interactive multimedia is far from being all things to all people. This technology must find its niche in higher education—where it best fits into traditional teaching methods and augments traditional learning. The changes we describe will not take place overnight, but many are already underway. And with the changes will come many challenges. Technical issues of standards, tools, networks, and cross-platform development are only part of the puzzle. Sociological, legal, and ethical questions are often far more difficult to address. Interactive multimedia can be a valuable teaching tool: effective, non-judgmental, and ever-patient. But just as development of interactive multimedia is a team effort, collaboration within and among institutions will be necessary to meet these challenges. We hope the rewards will be gratifying.

Note

HyperCard is a trademark of Apple Computer, Inc. ToolBook is a registered trademark of Asymetrix Corporation. Video F/X is a trademark of Digital F/X. Authorware is a registered trademark of Authorware, Inc. Guide is a trademark of Owl International, Inc.

References

Ambron, S., & Hooper, K. (1988). *Interactive Multimedia.* Redmond, WA: Microsoft Press.

Clark, R. E., & Salomon, G. (1986). Media in teaching. In *Handbook of Research on Teaching 3rd Edition* (Merlin C. Wittrock, Ed.) New York: MacMillan Publishing Company, 464–478.

Grassmuck, K. (1990, September 12). Some research universities contemplate sweeping changes, ranging from management and tenure to teaching methods. *The Chronicle of Higher Education,* 1, A29–A31.

Hooper, K. (1988). *Interactive Multimedia Design 1988.* Technical Report #13, The Multimedia Lab: Apple Computer, Inc.

Hooper, K., & Ambron, S. (1988). *Multimedia Production: A Set of Three Reports.* Technical Report #14, The Multimedia Lab: Apple Computer, Inc.

The Joe Wyatt Challenge: 101 Success Stories of Information Technologies in Higher Education (1991). Washington, DC: EDUCOM.

Rosenshine, B., & Stevens, R. (1986). *Teaching Functions.* In *Handbook of Research on Teaching 3rd Edition* (Merlin C. Wittrock, Ed.) New York: MacMillan Publishing Company, 376–391.

Shuell, T. J. (1986). Cognitive conceptions of learning. *Review of Educational Research, 56(4),* pp 411–436.

Shuell, T. J., & Schueckler, L. M. (1989). Toward evaluating software according to principles of learning and teaching. *Journal of Educational Computing Research, 5(2),* 135-149.

Sternberg, R.J. (1984). A theory of knowledge acquisition in the development of verbal concepts. *Developmental Review, 4,* 113-138.

Wingfield, A. (1979). Human Learning and Memory: An Introduction. New York: Harper & Row, Publishers.

II ... and Practices

11

Bootstrapping Hypertext: Student-created Documents, Intermedia, and the Social Construction of Knowledge

George P. Landow

Introduction

Initially developing the first set of humanities materials for the Brown IRIS Intermedia project required year-long support for three and a half advanced doctoral and postdoctoral students and partial support for a faculty member who served as designer, editor, and coordinator of the resulting corpus and who himself also contributed some of the materials.[1] Few projects and few institutions can afford such resources. Fortunately, recent experience with Intermedia has shown that one can use hypertext's defining characteristics as a collaborative writing environment to bootstrap educational materials at vastly lower costs than our original project demanded.[2] Student-created metatexts (that is, hypertext corpora or bodies of electronically linked materials) offer a workable, efficient solution to the problem of creating materials for electronic educational environments.

Benefits and Costs of Educational Hypertext

Classes using the hypermedia materials created for Intermedia at Brown and other institutions demonstrate that hypertext, as promised, offers many educational benefits. In the first place, connectivity, which is the essential, defining characteristic of hypertext, easily accustoms those who use it to make connections, and students can benefit from this characteristic of this information medium in many ways. Hypertext materials can, for example, both teach students the context of materials they study and accustom them to ask questions about contextualization as well. In other words, working with hypertext gives learners both factual information and sophisticated ways of dealing with it. In literature courses at Brown, for example, working with bodies of hypertext materials permits students to follow links between words and images, between essays about a single author's life and specific works by that author, and between specific works by that author and a wide range of contextual information, including other authors, history, religion, philosophy, economics, and the arts; the components of this linked information can take the form of collections of essays, timelines, images, and graphic directories.

Because bodies of linked texts and images contain such a rich abundance of connections, using them can develop beginning students' habits of linking ideas and contexts. Furthermore, because hypertext can link so many subjects, disciplines, and approaches, it encourages its users to discover and practice sophisticated interdisciplinary thought, which requires finding or making connections among these various disciplines and approaches. Nonetheless, all these features of the medium can appear a mixed blessing, since they require that someone somehow provide potentially enormous bodies of linked materials. *Context32,* the web first begun, contains almost 1600 documents and more than 3000 bi-directional links, which are equivalent to double that number of Hypercard-style unidirectional ones; *Context34,* a large proportion of which students created, contains 570 documents and more than a thousand bi-directional links, and the *Chinese Literature Web* created by Paul Kahn and used in a Comparative Literature course at Brown contains 200 documents and more than 1700 bidirectional links.[3]

Three Methods of Creating Educational Metatexts

Educational hypertext can certainly encourage students to think in more sophisticated ways. In particular, it can accustom them to formulate problems in terms of multicausal and multidisciplinary approaches, and to put this last point in a slightly different way, it can encourage them to contextualize whatever phenomenon they study—whether it be a literary text, scientific discovery, or other historical event. Nonetheless, even though there is a useful educational message in the medium, this message of connectivity still requires things to connect to one another. Ultimately, in other words, the success of hypertext in higher education depends not only on intrinsic connectivity, effective screen design, and such crucial factors but also on the materials that teachers and students encounter in that hypertext environment. Such bodies of electronically linked materials, like printed text books, anthologies, and any other bodies of information created as an educational resource, demand time and energy—often far more time and energy than individual instructors have available. In fact, one of the most common responses to presentations of my experiences teaching with the Intermedia, the hypertext system developed at Brown University's Institute for Research in Information and Scholarship, takes the form of a statement to the effect that the listeners would love to have such a system but simply don't have time or resources to develop appropriate materials.

During the course of the Intermedia project and its subsequent educational applications at Brown (1985–92), we have tried a number of different ways of creating these necessary educational materials. During the first phase, which was funded chiefly by IBM and the Annenberg/CPB Project, an Annenberg contract paid for three and a half doctoral or postdoctoral students in English to write the documents that became the kernel of *Context32,* the hypermedia corpus that supported the teaching of English 32, the *Survey of English Literature, 1700 to the Present.* During these first two years (1986–87), I served as designer, author, and editor of the documents, and I later began to write an increasing number of documents myself. Most of the documents I have created for this original Intermedia web and for later ones, including *Context34,* take the form of quotations of one or two paragraphs in length from a primary text to which I append a series of questions. I have elsewhere described *Context32* and the educational use of Intermedia in detail.[4] I shall here point out only that by the close of the Annenberg project this hypertext corpus contained approximately 500 documents—a combination of overview or graphic directory documents for 60 British writers, timelines, digitized images, and essays containing information on matters of literary technique and contextual information, including religion, philosophy, history, science, technology, and the arts. This method of producing educational materials, which requires several developers working near full time, was necessary to get us started during this first stage, but it demands time and money not often available to most instructors, and therefore it does not seem to be a particularly useful model of developing educational materials in a hypertext environment.

This approach has other problems as well: Since the development team began to create materials at the same time that the IRIS software engineers were creating the system on which they were to appear (and this was in the days before Hypercard), none of us had yet used a hypertext environment, and we inevitably created essays or took design approaches that experience subsequently showed to be less effective than we had hoped. Fortunately, these minor problems proved easy to remedy. Since Intermedia is a hypertext (or hypermedia) environment in which reader and writer or teacher and student share the same interface, one does not relate to it the way one relates to write-only media like printed books or hypermedia corpora based on videodisks. In other words, bodies of material on the Intermedia system remain unfinished, unfixed, and adaptable because the original author can easily modify his work and because others, including students, can add materials, including skeptical comments, by writing and then linking them to original author's materials.

The way we easily remedied some of the limitations of the original Intermedia documents suggests one of the educational strengths of hypermedia: they remain adaptable, and they permit student feedback. They permit, in other words, the continual development of the materials students encounter and do not demand that everything be set in advance, as obviously is the case with a textbook.

This flexibility permits a second means of developing hypertext materials, one that took the form of various kinds of collaboration among members of the same institution and members of different institutions. Realizing that, at least at the beginning of such educational experimentation, few people at any one department or even college or university would likely make the commitment to working in an experimental media, IRIS conceived an extension of the Intermedia Project to be called "The Continents of Knowledge" that would bring together faculty from several dozen institutions and a wide range of disciplines. The Annenberg/CPB Project, which funded the planning stage of Continents, ultimately decided not to support its implementation, but several faculty members from other institutions who had wanted to take part in the project created and shared hypertext materials with each other and with us. Furthermore, other scholars who had no access to a hypertext system generously provided materials, such as bibliographies or brief essays, that were entered on Intermedia.[5]

The third form of creating a body of electronically linked educational materials consists of having faculty and students work collaboratively to create them. The most important part of such a manner of proceeding takes the form of students bootstrapping the materials that they use. Such bootstrapping, which obviously has practical advantages for the instructor, also fulfills hypertext's implicitly student-directed, constructionist theory of education. In an important sense, therefore, such bootstrapping represents the obvious end point of both of the educational applications of the Intermedia project and of any hypertext system, since they are inevitably collaborative in conception and application. At its most basic level, hypertext, which demands an active reader, also demands the collaboration of readers (or students) by making them choose their way through a body of materials. Furthermore, hypertext used educationally as a writing medium inevitably demands additional collaborative work from the student—collaborative between student and teacher and between student and student—because the student writer (or rather, reader-writer) always writes in the electronic or virtual presence of other documents by other students and faculty and hence is always writing collaboratively with them in a way not possible in the world of print technology.

History

I have elsewhere reported upon the changing use of Intermedia in my teaching, and this discussion of using student work to create educational materials represents a kind of final report on the Intermedia project, the software portion of which saw completion in 1990.[6] The hypertext component of the English survey course originally served chiefly to promote critical thinking. It attempted to do so by encouraging students to develop a knowledge of the cultural, ideological, and historical context of individual literary works.[7] Although Intermedia has continued to serve as an efficient means of teaching students to ask questions and formulate research problems, my own interest in its application has extended to using it for experiments in collaborative learning and the creation of knowledge and knowledge bases. From the very first, however, Intermedia has supported various kinds of collaborative work, and the first Intermedia assignment, which acts as a kind of user's manual, requests students to make suggestions about links and asks them to contribute brief texts, which are then linked to preexisting essays, graphic materials, timelines, and overviews.[8]

When such course assignments, which had originally developed primarily as a means of evaluation, produced useful materials, the resulting student work was placed on Intermedia. Having seen how effective such student contributions were, I then discovered that subsequent assignments that requested students to compare two works in terms of theme, technique, and context produced essays that valuably supplemented materials created by original faculty-graduate student team. The following year I extended my use of Intermedia to include other classes I taught, including graduate and undergraduate seminars in Victorian poetry and fiction. The next stage of Intermedia use arrived when I asked students in the survey class to create a body of hypertext materials on a single author, the Nigerian Nobel-prize winning poet, novelist, and dramatist Wole Soyinka.[9] I did so by providing the following final exercise for the course:

Since the purpose of this final exercise involves both creating some sort of synthesis of the course and creating the beginnings of electronically linked materials on this African poet, the assignment requires two parts: (a) a discussion of one poem from *A Shuttle in the Crypt* and (b) an essay discussing Soyinka and one of the following topics:

1. The history or contemporary politics of Nigeria
2. The tribes of Nigeria (Soyinka is a Yoruba)
3. Yoruba myth
4. The Biafran War
5. Soyinka's prison experiences in the poetry and in *The Man Died*
6. Jonathan Swift
7. James Joyce
8. His essays "The Writer in a Modern African State" and "Between Self and System: The Artist in Search of Liberation"
9. His essay "The Critic and Society: Barthes, Leftocracy and Other Mythologies"
10 Négritude (in relation to his poetry and his criticism, especially "Cross-Currents: The 'New African' After Cultural Encounters")
11. Yoruba art (see recent *N.Y. Times*)
12. Dylan Thomas (see essay on this topic)
13. His drama
14. European drama
15. The literary canon, or what an African poet adds to the body of literature in English

In contrast to their experience of working with Intermedia earlier in the term, students now encountered virtually no literary or contextual information. To get them started I created only the standard graphic overview for an author, a list of his works, and a chronology of his career (figure 11.1), and I also added two maps of Nigeria and images of Yoruba and Hausa dwellings. Later, after the first class of students to undertake this assignment had finished their essays, I added several examples of Yoruba art, a concept map of Soyinka's literary relations (figure 11.2), and the Nigeria overview (figure 11.3).

I had hoped that after students had worked for several months with bodies of linked materials on canonical authors like Jane Austen, Robert Browning, and James Joyce, I could leave them to their own devices and they would come up with relevant information. As it turned out, they headed to the library, discovered all kinds of resources (from which we later compiled a useful bibliography), and produced a wide range of valuable essays. The first two classes to carry out this assignment produced some sixty documents ranging from discussions of a dozen and a half poems to Hal Horton's "Effects of Colonialism on Yoruba Religion" and Minna Song's "Effects of the Biafran War on Wole

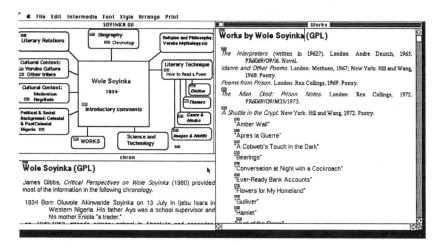

Figure 11.1
The Intermedia documents furnished by the instructor to begin the *Soyinka Web:* a standard graphic overview for an author, a list of Wole Soyinka's works, and a chronology of his life and career.

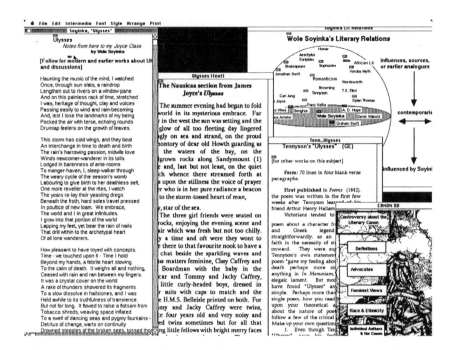

Figure 11.2

"Wole Soyinka's Literary Relations." In the upper-right corner of the screen appears this concept map, which is based on a paradigm created by Paul Kahn for *The Dickens Web*. It organizes student essays on Soyinka's relations to other writers, and in this screen shot it appears surrounded by the texts of Soyinka's poem "Ulysses" and a passage from Joyce's novel of the same name as well as by comments about Tennyson's "Ulysses" and an overview for discussions of the literary canon.

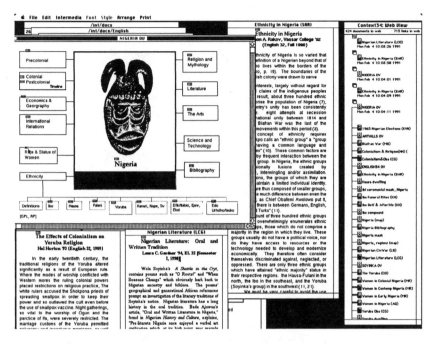

Figure 11.3

"The Nigeria Overview." At the upper left of the Intermedia screen appears a graphic directory indicating the kind of documents related to Nigeria. This concept map derives from the overviews *Context32* employs for authors and individual works. It replaces the "Literary techniques" category with one for various ethnic and tribal groupings (see figure 11.5). Below it appears "The Effects of Colonialism on Yoruba Religion," by Hal Horton '93, and "Nigerian Literature: Oral and Written Tradition," by Laura C. Gardner '94. To the right of the Nigeria Overview appears "Ethnicity in Nigeria," by Simon Rakov, Vassar College '92. At screen right appears Intermedia's Web View, which (a) provides a retraceable reading history, (b) a dynamic indication of the documents linked to the currently active document (in this case the Nigeria Overview), and (c) active icons that permit the reader to open documents by double-clicking rather than by clicking upon the link markers in the active document.

Soyinka's Works." Other students concentrated on the poet's literary relations: Amelia Warren, for example, contributed "Soyinka's 'Gulliver' and *Gulliver's Travels,*" and Anne Pycha wrote "Wole Soyinka and Dylan Thomas: Time and Mystery."

The assignment proved so successful that I made plans to use it a third time, at which point I realized that the materials it produced would provide the basis of the hypermedia component for English 34, a new course on recent postcolonial fiction I was about to begin teaching (see appendix 1 for reading list). On learning that students in this other course would read their documents, several students in the survey decided to work on additional works by Soyinka and on several other African authors who did not appear on the reading list, including Chinua Achebe and Ken SaroWiwa. Meanwhile, having realized that students in one course could provide materials for another, I asked members of my upperclass nonfiction course, which read three works also read in the planned postcolonial literature course—Sara Suleri's *Meatless Days,* Bruce Chatwin's *In Patagonia,* and Wole Soyinka's *Aké: The Years of Childhood*—if they would like to share their documents by placing them on Intermedia. Then, after having students who were willing to place documents on Intermedia sign a permission form (see appendix 2), I began to build *Context34,* the hypermedia corpus that supported the new course.

The creation of *Context34,* which continued throughout the semester it was used (semester II, 1990–1991), involved creating a course overview (figure 11.4), and overviews for individual texts (figure 11.5) as well as concept maps for the literary relations of each author. I then assigned a series of comparative essays, which turned out, as expected, to produce ample materials for *Context34.* Like most Intermedia assignments I devise, those for English 34 invited students to consider matters of political and historical context: "The books read in English 34 continually raise the question of how contemporary political and historical contexts relate to the individual text. Drawing upon the fact that the works by Soyinka, Suleri, Lively, and Chatwin all in some way mention World War II, Nazism, and genocide, explain how context enters each work's themes *and* techniques. Finally, ask yourself what, if anything, this concern with the World War II era has to do with Postcolonialism."[10] This assignment produced Intermedia documents such as Caleb Paull's "Narrative and the

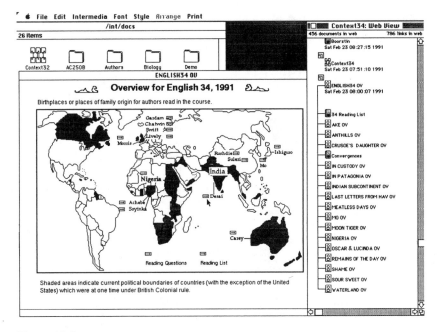

Figure 11.4
"The English 34 Overview"

Interaction of Subjectivity and Context in [Lively's] *Moon Tiger*," Jason Roach's "World War II and Personal History in *Moon Tiger,*" and Elizabeth Soucar's "War as Setting in *Moon Tiger.*"

The final assignment for English 34 seems much like that for the usual term paper for an orthodox, print-based English course:

Using passages that you choose yourself, answer *two* of the following:

1. Quoting from at least three discussions on Intermedia about the literary canon, argue either (a) that Suleri, Soyinka, Mo, and one other author read in the course add to the canon or (b) that they call into question the notion of a literary canon.

2. Explain how (and why) so many of the books read in this course make extensive use of grotesque set pieces and grotesque stories. Does the "why" have anything to do with Postcolonialism?

3. Explain the relations among women, power, and colonialism in any five books read during the course.

Remember, since your responses to this exercise will demonstrate your knowledge and understanding of the works read, use as many works as possible and try not to repeat detailed discussions of works. Include within parentheses the author and title of all documents quoted or cited from Intermedia, e.g., Julie Cohen '91, "The Good Stuff," Intermedia.

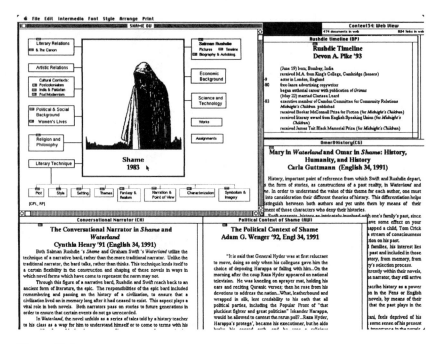

Figure 11.5
Overview for an Individual Work—Salman Rushdie's *Shame*. At upper right appears a box containing the author's name and link markers indicating that one can follow links to a timeline of events in Rushdie's life and to other biographical information. Continuing clockwise, one encounters categories labeled "Economic Background," "Science and Technology," "Works," and "Assignments," none of which yet have materials linked to them. Starting at the upper left and moving counterclockwise, one encounters categories labeled "Literary Relations," "& the Canon," "Artistic Relations," "Cultural Contexts" ("Postcolonialism," "India and & Pakistan," and "Postmodernism"), "Political and Social Background," "Women's Lives," "Religion and Philosophy," and, finally, "Literary Techniques," which divides into the following subcategories: "Plot," "Style (grotesque)," "Setting," "Themes," "Fantasy and Realism," "Narration and Point of View," "Characterization," and "Symbolism and Imagery."

This assignment and the earlier one produced a large number of useful contributions to *Context34*. Moreover, since it encouraged students to refer to authors read throughout the course, students writing the final term paper read and commented on essays written earlier by their own classmates. Student essays on Salman Rushdie, whose novel *Shame* was assigned reading, present a fair indication of the range of materials this exercise created:

"Contrasting Uses of the Narrator: An Analysis of Rushdie and Ishiguro." Joshua Newell.

"Dueling Stories in Rushdie and Ishiguro." Jason Roach.

"Explanation as Fiction: Interpretation and Role-Playing in *Waterland* and *Shame*," Caleb Paull "Mary in *Waterland* and Omar in *Shame*: Stories, Humanity and History." Carla Gutman.

"The Political Context of *Shame*." Adam G. Wenger.

"*Shame* and the Beginnings of Stories." Mathew Meschery.

"Uses of the Grotesque in *Shame* and *In Patagonia*." Beth Soucar.

These, like other student essays on Intermedia, range in length from 300 to 1000 words. Some student contributors wrote their essays directly on Intermedia, and others divided the essays they wrote in Microsoft Word into separate Intermedia-style documents. Others wrote normal essays, all of which nonetheless turned out to divide easily into hypertext documents on separate authors or paired comparisons of them.

Results

Comments on teaching evaluations filled in by the students in English 34 suggest that the Intermedia component had been a success. I asked students not to pull any punches and provide their reactions to using the hypertext component on the unsigned forms that I did not read until after grades were turned in. Unfortunately, several of the students who most used the system were ill with flu or some other illness that swept our campus last spring, and they did not have an opportunity to describe their reactions. None of the students completing the form stated any dislike for the system or resentment at its use, and, to my surprise, all the comments were positive. In response to the standard question on the course evaluation if the course has labs, one student wrote: "We had 'labs' where we were supposed to use Intermedia. I didn't go too often, but when I did, it was very helpful," and another commented: "The Intermedia labs took up much time but were very helpful." A third similarly responded that "labs were helpful and fun—made doing research interesting."

One of the comments proved particularly interesting because it gave an idea how the student actually employed the hypertext component. In response to the question if the course had a lab, this person answered, "There were very useful Intermedia sessions which allowed me to catch up on books I fell behind in reading as well as to see what other students in the course were thinking." This response confirms earlier observations that hypertext doubly individualizes the time of learning, for students can draw upon secondary materials when they become particularly useful and relevant, not when the course schedule demands consulting them, and students can similarly work in the continual virtual presence of their fellow students when they are not present in the Intermedia lab.[11]

Yet another student found the course "definitely satisfying, especially the computer system, which encouraged cohesive understanding. My fear of the computer was completely unnecessary." To the instruction "Describe possible ways for improving this course in the future," this same student wrote: "This course is *excellent*. The best way to help it would be to have other classes, both in and out of the English department, start adding *Intermedia* materials."

In addition to these encouraging, generally favorable comments, one can also point to five observed effects of this attempt to create and then employ a body of hypermedia materials largely created by students student. First, this approach turned out to produce materials generally more suited to student needs than did the original materials produced for *Context32* by talented group of graduate students who had not yet experienced working with hypertext. The original *Soyinka Web,* which provided the basis for *Context34,* contained dozens of student-created discussions of individual poems as well as work read outside of class, including plays, novels, and Soyinka's autobiography. Furthermore, students created many discussions of the contexts of individual poems, ranging from sources and analogues (Jung, Thomas, Swift, Joyce) and explorations of the African background, about which most students were completely ignorant when they began this assignment; these explorations included discussions of the Biafran war and its aftermath, ethnicity in

Nigeria, Yoruba myth, religion, burial customs, political organization, and art, and the role and status of women in pre-colonial, colonial, and post-colonial times,

Second, contributing to a body of hypertext documents created an ongoing relation of the student-author both to the course for which the materials were created and other courses that make use of them. These student-created documents turned the student-author into a continuing virtual presence on the system with which later students interact.[12] Hypertext, in other words, simultaneously produces an institutional or course memory.

Third, students tended to write better and certainly more carefully when they knew they had an audience. Students more willingly revised when they knew that they had to do so in order to remain on the system and when they knew that others would read and discuss their work.

Fourth, students in one course created materials for those in other ones. At Brown, students in English 32, created documents on Soyinka, related authors (Achebe, SaroWiwa), and Nigeria, for English 34, *Recent Postcolonial Fiction in English,* as did members of English 137, who created essays about Chatwin and Suleri, travel writing, and autobiography. Finally, as the comment above by a student in English 34 demonstrates, members of the class found materials created by their classmates of interest.

Finally, one of the most promising effects of thus bootstrapping a hypertext corpus lies in the fact that such a procedure encouraged students to take a more active role in their own education. In fact, they begin to suggest assignments or subjects. Whereas students in earlier courses to use Intermedia components had suggested or requested new materials by pointing out that "we need materials on labor conditions in the nineteenth century," or "I like documents like those on Swift [which contained discussions of specific passages] better than those on Austen [which at first did not]"—both actual examples of earlier student reaction—in this course, the first to emphasize that students had created and were creating the large majority of materials, they suggested their own projects. For example, reading ahead and noticing that *Context34* contained comparatively few materials on Australia, one student suggested, "Why don't we each bring in a few paragraphs on Australia." After the rest of the class concurred, I devised the following assignment, which I distributed at the next class meeting: "Bring in one paragraph of factual information about Australia on the Friday before we discuss Peter Carey's *Oscar and Lucinda*. I shall then put your information in an Australia folder on Intermedia. Hand in a printout of your paragraph and either put it on Intermedia in your own folder or submit a disk with the paragraph in MS Word with your printout. (Because this assignment produces a small example of collaborative work that we shall all draw upon, no late assignments will be accepted without deductions from grades.)"

Here, then, are the documents the Australia assignment produced:

Atchison, Gabriél J. "Post-World War II Australian Immigration"

Chapin, Jen. "Effect of Colonization upon Aborigines"

Chisolm, Adrienne T. "Government-Sanctioned Religious Tolerance in Early Australia"

Garcia, Elizabeth. "Value of Women's Labor in Australia"

Henderson, Joel. "Australian Colonies Government Act," Australia History Timeline, "British Motives for Australia's Settlement"

Henry, Cynthia M. "Australian Aboriginals"

Joo, Heidie Y. "The Spiritual Beliefs of Australia's Indigenous Peoples"

Kane, Erika N. "Australia's Original Settlers"

Khabie, Nissim. "Religion and the Development of the Australian Educational System"

Meschery, Matthew. "Convict Women" and "Aboriginal Women"

Nelson, Erik H. "Australia Fauna," "Australian Animals: Convergences between Placental and Marsupial Mammals" (image)

Newell, Joshua P. "Anglicanism in Nineteenth-Century Australia"

Paull, Caleb. "The Anglican Church of Australia"

Pittet, Diana. "The History of [the Repression] of Australia's Convict History"

Roach, Jason E. "Windeyer, Taylor, and Nineteenth-Century Sydney"

Singh, Anjali B. "Australia—the First Settlement"

Soucar, Elizabeth A. Map of Australia, "Governor-General Anthony van Dieman" (image), "The Origins of Aborigines: Anthropologist's Speculations"

Tracy, Matthew. "Australia's Political Organization"

Wenger, Adam. "Aggressive Masculinity in Australia"

Problems and Solutions

This approach to creating hypertext document sets requires some planning. First of all, the instructors must make sure that someone, either they or the original student authors, fully integrates new materials into previously extant ones by means of both appropriate links and commentary within individual documents. If, for example, students create essays on the role of women in colonial Australia, one begins by checking that obvious links have been made to, say, an overview for Australia and to essays on novels set in that country. One might also consider linking this student essay on women in Australia to parallel ones on the role of women in, say, South Asia or Africa. Such links, one realizes, will probably require minor changes in the older documents or even the creation of a new one, suggesting that readers might wish to compare the situations of women in different countries. Thus, instructors, who almost automatically become coordinating editors, might have to add to an existing essay or overview a brief phrase or question something like the following: "Follow for material on women in other colonies" or "How did the position of female colonists in Africa and India differ from those in Australia?" Similarly, if an essay introduces an entirely new vantage point, one might wish to link it to materials it doesn't mention. For example, an essay on a particular literary technique (characterization, word-painting, dialogue) in one novel might be linked to an essay on another, possibly related work, and the reason for a link might be suggested by a query or other lead-in.

Second, instructors wishing to insure that students make use of work created by members of their own course will have to assign exercises that encourage students to return to works read earlier in the course during later weeks. Hypertext, which permits the simultaneous existence of multiple organizations of information, demands that the instructor using it remain flexible and on the lookout for ways to connect older to new information.

Following such procedures permits hypertext to serve as an efficient means of using the work that one class produces to support later iterations of the same course. In essence, the instructor who wishes to use students to create part of either their own educational materials or those for other classes encourages them to create something like an electronic version of

T. S. Eliot's notion of tradition and the individual talent. Whenever a great writers appear, Eliot argues, they immediately become the contemporaries of all chronologically earlier authors. According to Eliot, in literature, "the existing monuments form an ideal order among themselves, which is modified by the introduction of the new (the really new) work of art among them. The existing order is complete before the new work arrives; for order to persist after the supervention of novelty, the *whole* existing order must be, if ever so slightly, altered; and so the relations, proportions, values of each work of art toward the whole are readjusted; and this is conformity between the old and the new." Conceived as a system, literature rearranges itself in the manner, one observes, of a giant hypertext corpus or docuverse to allow for new relations among individual works.

Using Low-End Systems

My approach to teaching with Intermedia gradually changed as the system became increasingly stable, fast, and more convenient to use in other ways. Originally, my educational uses of hypertext chiefly emphasized the student as reader and explorer. Only later did the student's role as writer and linker become important. In essence, this later emphasis upon collaboration—upon the social construction of knowledge—to some extent comes close to fulfilling the vision of Intermedia's designers, who conceived true hypertext as an environment in which the roles of reader and writer merge.[13] Nonetheless, even though students now create many of the materials present on Intermedia, the majority of them still do not write their essays directly on the system. Our experience confirms the not very surprising fact that system stability, accessibility, security of documents, and the cost or even just the convenience of printing effect the degree to which students create their documents directly on a hypertext system.

At Brown University, documents written by students, *Context32*, *Context34*, and other webs, such as the *In Memoriam* and *Dickens* webs, have been placed on Intermedia in various ways. Every year since the system's introduction, a small number of students do all their work from the initial notes and outlines to finished essays directly on Intermedia. A much greater number of students, probably at least half of every class, do their reading and research using Intermedia but write their essays in their rooms or in campus computer clusters on Macintoshes using Microsoft Word, which transfers easily to Intermedia. Some students transfer their own documents to the system, others ask classmates to do so, and yet others hand in a disk and ask me to do so. A small number of students who use word processors incompatible with Intermedia retype their work on the system or have it scanned (using OmniPage) to produce documents in Microsoft Word, which are then transferred to Intermedia. What I find most interesting about the various paths that students take to place their work on Intermedia is that although one might expect everyone to write directly on the system, for a variety of reasons they do not—and yet they still manage to work collaboratively with instructors and fellow students within a hypertext environment!

Our experience with Intermedia, then, shows that readers and writers who share the same interface do not always take full advantage of this feature of hypertext systems. Our experience also suggests, however, that one can gain most of the advantages of hypertext as a collaborative working and writing environment without an advanced, high-end system like Intermedia. As our students have shown me, one can use the anthology or encyclopedia model, which combines two technologies and two eras of information technology. In this mode student (and other) contributors provide a person or persons who function as gateways to the multi-authored document. This person places—or approves the place-ment of—individual documents on the particular hypertext system and thereby oversees the direction of its growth.

This approach to combining print and hypertext anthologies (or group-created) documents itself takes various forms, each of which depends upon the relative power and control of authors and editor in relation to each other. The editor, for example, can retain complete power over which documents become part the metadocument, or that decision can be dispersed so that the editor shares it with an editorial board, the individual contributor, or the sum of all contributors. In addition, the gatekeeper function can also include linking. Thus, the student contributors can have complete control over linking, they can share it with an editor—either by having the ability to create links electronically or simply by indicating desired links, which may take the form of specific instructions ("Link words 'Benjamin Disraeli' in line 10 of present document to discussion of

Disraeli in first two paragraphs of document entitled "Queen Victoria becomes the Empress of India"), or more general ones ("Link phrase 'Benjamin Disraeli' in line 10 of present document to any discussions of Disraeli" or "We need a biography of Disraeli. Who wants to write one?").

Conclusions

I would like to conclude by emphasizing two points. First, given the proper assignments, students, even beginning ones, can produce useful materials and provide benefits for themselves and others by producing these materials. Second, although a high-end, fully networked read-write system like IRIS Intermedia obviously makes this kind of student-generated metatext easiest to accomplish, one can work with simpler forms of hypertext as well and one can effectively even include typed or word-processed materials, thereby creating a widely usable model of transition from print to electronic learning systems.

Appendices

Appendix 1. Reading List for English 34, *Fiction in English Since 1980: Post-Colonial, African, and Minority Literature*

Weeks 1 & 2 (24 January, Thursday, through 31 January, Thursday). History and His Story—Fictional Autobiography : Graham Swift, *Waterland* (1983)

Week 3 (5 February, Tuesday, through 7 February, Thursday). History as His Story—Fictional Autobiography: Salman Rushdie, *Shame* (1983)

Week 4 (12 February, Tuesday, through 14 February, Thursday) History and His Story—Fictional Autobiography: Kazuo Ishiguro, *The Remains of the Day* (1989)

Week 5 (21 February, Thursday). History and His Story—Autobiography: Wole Soyinka's *Aké: The Years of Childhood* (1981)

Week 6 (26 February, Tuesday, through 28 February, Thursday). History as Her Story—Autobiography and Fiction: Sara Suleri, *Meatless Days* (1989)

Week 7 (5 March, Tuesday, through 7 March, Thursday). History and Her Story—Fictional Autobiography: Jane Gardam, *Crusoe's Daughter* (1985)

Week 8 (12 March, Tuesday, through 14 March, Thursday). History as Her Story—Fictional Autobiography: Penelope Lively, *Moon Tiger* (1987)

Week 9 (19 March, Tuesday, through 21 March, Thursday). Post-imperial Travellers & Immigrants: Bruce Chatwin, *In Patagonia.* (1977)

Week 10 (2 April, Tuesday, through 4 April, Thursday). Post-imperial Travellers: Jan Morris, *Last Letter from Hav* (1985)

Week 11 (9 April, Tuesday, through 11 April, Thursday). Post-imperial Travellers & Immigrants: Peter Carey, *Oscar and Lucinda*

Week 12 (16 April, Tuesday, through 18 April, Thursday). Post-imperial Immigrants: Timothy Mo, *Sour Sweet.* (1985)

Week 13 (23 April, Tuesday, through 25 April, Thursday). After Independence: Chinua Achebe, *Anthills of the Savannah* (1987)

Week 14 (30 April, Tuesday, through 2 May, Thursday). After Independence: Anita Desai, *In Custody* (1984)

Appendix 2. Student Author Permission Form

[Note: Since placing your documents on the Intermedia system and linking them to others constitutes a form of publication, I would like to have your written permission (1) to retain your materials on the present Intermedia system or any other hypertext environment that might parallel or replace it; and (2) to include your documents in any hypermedia materials the university or I might publish or distribute in the future. We realized the importance of getting permission to publish in advance of any specific plans to do so when IRIS issued the prize-winning *Dickens Web,* which has a selection of student-created essays: at the last minute, we had to remove 4-5 excellent documents by students who turned out difficult to locate because they had graduated or were spending their junior years abroad. At the moment (December 1990), IRIS has no plans to publish any document sets like the *Dickens Web,* but it might in the future, and other colleges and universities that use Intermedia (or other hypertext systems) might wish to swap materials so all can benefit.

I hereby grant Professor George P. Landow, the Institute for Research in Information and Scholarship (IRIS), or Brown University, Providence, Rhode Island, permission to include materials I have written in any sets of hypermedia materials they publish or distribute. I understand that I shall receive a credit line on each document that I have contributed.

Signed_____

Date

Notes

1. During the academic year 1985–1986, the Annenberg/CPB Project, which partially funded this aspect of the Intermedia Project, provided the salaries of two graduate students, David Cody and Glenn Everett, who worked twenty hours a week, and of a postdoctoral student, Robert Sullivan, who worked half that amount. The Annenberg contract funded the cost of a third graduate student, Kathyrin Stockton, who worked twenty hours a week the following year when the system was first used.

2. For Intermedia, see Nicole Yankelovich, Stephen Drucker, and Norman Meyrowitz, "Intermedia: The Concept and the Construction of a Seamless Information Environment," *IEEE Computer* 21 (1988): 81–96, and Mark Walter, "IRIS Intermedia: Pushing the Boundaries of Hypertext," *Seybold Report on Publishing Systems* 18 (August 7, 1989), 21–32.

3. Other webs are smaller. *The Dickens Web,* a selection from *Context32* concentrating on the *Great Expectations,* contains 250 documents and almost

700 links, *Nuclear Arms* contains 79 documents and 361 links, and the *Apollo Missions* web 166 and 236.

4. George P. Landow, "Hypertext in Literary Education, Criticism, and Scholarship." *Computers and the Humanities* 23 (1989): 173–98.

5. For a list of faculty members from other institutions who contributed to *The Dickens Web*, a sample subset of *Context32* that IRIS published in 1989, see George P. Landow, *Hypertext: The Convergence of Contemporary Critical Theory and Technology* (Baltimore: Johns Hopkins University Press, 1992), 97–98. Similarly, Charles Ess, Professor of Philosophy and Religion, Drury College, who has used Intermedia in his teaching, contributed importantly to the section on Indian thought in *Context34*.

6. Apple Computer's introduction of A/UX 2.0 effectively ended the project, since Intermedia requires A/UX 1.1.

7. See Landow, "Hypertext in Literary Education."

8. See Landow, "Course Assignments in Hypertext: The Example of Intermedia." *Journal of Research on Computing in Education* 21 (1989): 349–65, and "Hypertext and Collaborative Work: The Example of Intermedia." In *Intellectual Teamwork*, 407–28, edited by Jolene Galegher, Carmen Egido, and Robert Kraut. Hillsdale, N.J.: Lawrence Erlbaum, 1990.

9. See Landow, *Hypertext*, 145–46.

10. The final assignment for the course appears below, and for the sake of completeness I include the second (the first being an introduction to Intermedia): "Part 1. Choose a passage approximately a paragraph or two in length from both *The Remains of the Day* and *Shame,* and use them to compare some aspect of technique (imagery, setting, characterization, style, and so on) in an essay of 3–4 double-spaced typed pages. (You can substitute *Waterland* for either novel in the pair.)

"Part 2. Pick a brief passage from the author read in the first three you have not discussed in part 1 and relate it to some aspect of context in a brief essay of 1–2 pages. One might for example, relate *The Remains of the Day* and *Waterland* to World War II, *Shame* to the history of Pakistan or Rushdie's own life, and any of the works to contemporary political events, say, what took place during the year Ishiguro's novel is set. Make sure you understand the difference between theme and context. You might find contextual information on Intermedia, both within the *Context34* Web and others, or you might wish to draw upon material you find in the library or in other courses."

11. Given that student-directed discussions took place during the greater part of almost every class meeting of English 34, this comment appears particularly interesting on two grounds: first, as other observers have reported, some members of groups find it easier to express their opinions in electronic forums (conferences systems, bulletin boards, or hypertext document sets) than in face-to-face conversation. Second, this student, who according to his or her own statement on the form attended most class meetings, still believes that written comments by other students conveys their views in ways that their ad hoc remarks in discussion do not. This student's observation, in other words, has interesting implications for anyone considering the social construction of knowledge.

12. For "virtual presence," see Landow, *Hypertext*, 129.

13. T. S. Eliot, "Tradition and the Individual Talent," in *The Norton Anthology of English Literature,* eds. M. H. Abrams, 2 vols., 5th ed. (New York: Norton, 1986), II, 2207–8.

14. Nicole Yankelovich, Norman Meyrowitz, and Andries van Damm, "Reading and Writing the Electronic Book," *IEEE Computer* 18 (October 1985): 15–30.

References

Eliot, T. S. "Tradition and the Individual Talent," in *The Norton Anthology of English Literature,* eds. M. H. Abrams, 2 vols., 5th ed. (New York: Norton, 1986), II, 2207-8.

Landow, George P. "Course Assignments in Hypertext: The Example of Intermedia." *Journal of Research on Computing in Education* 21 (1989): 349–365.

_____. "Hypertext and Collaborative Work: The Example of Intermedia." In *Intellectual Teamwork,* 407–428, edited by Jolene Galegher, Carmen Egido, and Robert Kraut. Hillsdale, N. J.: Lawrence Erlbaum, 1990.

_____. "Hypertext in Literary Education, Criticism, and Scholarship." *Computers and the Humanities* 23 (1989): 173–198.

_____. *Hypertext: The Convergence of Contemporary Critical Theory and Technology.* Baltimore: Johns Hopkins UP, 1992.

Yankelovich, Nicole, Norman Meyrowitz, and Andries van Damm. "Reading and Writing the Electronic Book," *IEEE Computer* 18 (October 1985): 15–30.

Yankelovich, Nicole, Stephen Drucker, and Norman Meyrowitz, "Intermedia: The Concept and the Construction of a Seamless Information Environment," *IEEE Computer* 21 (1988): 81–96.

Walter, Mark. "IRIS Intermedia: Pushing the Boundaries of Hypertext," *Seybold Report on Publishing Systems* 18 (August 7, 1989), 21–32.

12

The CUPLE Project: A Hyper- and Multimedia Approach to Restructuring Physics Education

E. F. Redish, Jack M. Wilson, and Chad McDaniel

1. Introduction

The computer is an information processing tool with revolutionary capabilities. Because education is about the structure and transfer of information, the computer has important implications for colleges and universities. With the computer as an integral part of the student's learning environment, previously unimagined possibilities open up, both for the number and kinds of students we can reach, for what they can learn, and for how we can help them learn it.

The Comprehensive Unified Physics Learning Environment (CUPLE)[1] is a project that is bringing together innovative uses of the computer for physics teaching into a single multipurpose learning environment. It integrates these with sets of powerful tools that can make the learning process much more active and enriching. It is a highly modularized environment whose structure could have significant implications for how the teaching of physics evolves.

In this chapter we first review the status of college level introductory physics teaching. In these courses we have typically been forced to be satisfied with only the best of our students achieving significant learning. Even those students often have to wait until later in their training to begin to learn many of the tools that are fundamental to the activities of the professional physicist. We then discuss how educational computer technology might be used to change this situation. Finally, we discuss the CUPLE environment as an example of a way to deliver the requisite computer tools.

How many of our students do we reach?
We teach physics in order to help the next generation of learners build their understanding of the basic ideas of physics. Our current techniques have been successful in continuing to produce new high quality research physicists, but it takes time. Physics majors learn the material through a spiral process that covers the same material a number of times at increasing levels of sophistication over six years of training. If the students don't "get it" the first time through, they can get it later.

However, fewer than 2% of the students who take introductory college physics will go on to be physicists and take the full spiral of physics courses. Most are taking physics as part of their training for other professions—chemistry, engineering, biology, medicine. Some are taking it as part of a liberal education. Most will never take another course in physics.

There is mounting evidence that for most of the students taking introductory physics, the classes are massive failures. After introductory physics, the student's basic view of the world remains decidedly non-Newtonian. Although most students achieve some fluency with the vocabulary and can reproduce on exams the solutions of problems whose near analog they have seen before, when tests are devised to probe their understanding of the basic ideas, their grades fall precipitously [6][25][26].

Many physics teachers are satisfied with this state of affairs (perhaps in the sense of making the best of an unsatisfactory situation). They feel that as long as physicists produce more physicists, they don't have to worry about the rest of their students. But economic and social changes associated with the development of technology and the information age result in increased pressure on the education system to deliver a larger fraction of technically literate graduates. We can no longer be satisfied if most of our students fail to get the point. In section 2, we discuss in some detail the problems the bulk of students in introductory physics classes have and the skills we would like them to learn.

Where do we need to do better?
Educational and cognitive studies suggest that some of the problems in the introductory course arise from two causes:

1. We do not focus enough on what it is we want them to know how to do.

2. We do not pay sufficient attention to our student's underlying mental models: neither to the ones they come in with nor to the ones they go out with.

First, our courses tend to focus too much on content and not enough on process. We do not want our students to just memorize a list of definitions and equations. We want them to build a robust mental model. We want them to structure their knowledge into a scientific framework that allows them to

• understand what evidence leads us to believe the elements in the structure,
• see the relation of the parts,
• use those relations in problem solving, and
• use the structure to solve problems they have not seen before.

Second, we often consider our students as tabulae rasae—blank slates—and assume we can "write knowledge" directly into their heads. We fail to realize that they come with "naive preconceptions" which can block them from understanding what we are trying to teach them. As a result, few of them rebuild their mental models to resemble the scientific, Newtonian structure we are trying to convey.

We discuss what educational and cognitive researchers have learned about the nature of mental models and how to change them in section 3.

Can the computer help?

The immense growth and availability of computer technology in the past decade has put a number of new and powerful tools into the hands of educators. Some of these are highly appropriate for addressing some of the problems discussed above. In particular, a number of developments, both in hardware and in software, have powerful implications for the development of new tools for learning:

On the hardware side, the development of fast 32 bit microcomputers puts the power of a 1970s mainframe on a student's desk for a cost of less than $2000. This power permits quick access to lots of material and quick response times. The recent incorporation of multi-media tools—sound and video—increases the richness and the texture of the materials available. And CD storage permits making immense quantities of material easily available.[2]

On the software side, the development of graphical user interfaces (GUIs) has made the computer much easier to use. Multitasking software allows the user to run many programs at the same time in different windows on the GUI screen. Modern software development methods strongly encourage building highly modularized materials. This permits effective cumulation of software developments so that we don't have to continually reinvent the wheel.

These technologies have important consequences for the teaching of introductory physics.

1. Multitasking, multimedia, and the availability of powerful tools allow students to work more like professionals.
2. The integration of materials, particularly those using computer based laboratories can help students develop better mental models.
3. Modularization of computer materials leads to flexibility and opens the possibility for the system to evolve continuously.

The success of various projects in physics education that use the computer demonstrates these principles. We discuss the results of these projects in section 4.

The CUPLE project

CUPLE is a project to bring together in a single unified computer environment some of the successful attempts to reach more introductory physics students and to train them more effectively and professionally. CUPLE is bringing together sophisticated tools for handling graphing, calculations, laboratories, and video with modularized text materials and a database of information. This unification opens up many exciting possibilities both for the student and the teacher. A prototype of the project has recently been completed and is described in section 5.

The long-term evolution of the curriculum

One difficulty facing any attempt to change the physics curriculum is the fact that it has a large inertia. Over much of this century, the curriculum has changed very little, despite momentous changes in almost all relevant factors:

- the numbers and types of students taking the course
- their background and the quality of their training

• the content of physics itself, and
• the tools and approaches used by the professional.

In section 6, we discuss the impact CUPLE can have on what can be learned in an introductory physics course and by whom.

In section 7 we discuss the inertia opposing curriculum reform, consider some of the factors responsible for this inertia, and suggest how these could be profoundly influenced by an environment such as CUPLE.

2. Two Problems with Introductory College Physics

In this section we elaborate on two basic problems in teaching introductory physics: (1) most students fail to build a coherent, scientific mental model of the material presented, and (2) the processes taught in the introductory course represent only a pale shadow of the activity of the professional scientist.

Most students in an introductory physics course do not build a coherent mental model of the subject
When we teach introductory physics, we want our students to build a well-structured, scientific mental model for how the world works. They should not only know how to solve basic physics problems, they should also understand why these problems are solved in the way they are. They should understand why we believe the results we present and under what conditions they can be applied.

There is, however, mounting evidence that our courses are not being effective in changing most students' views of the world into more scientific ones. When we probe the mental model underlying the student's problem solving skills, we learn that many students use tricks, memorization, and key words to solve problems, and that their underlying concepts may be severely deficient.

Lillian McDermott [15], David Hestenes [6], Ronald Thornton [25], and others, have documented the lack of effectiveness of traditional approaches to introductory physics in changing students' underlying concepts. These studies have been done across a wide range of schools and student populations. In a particularly revealing study, Eric Mazur, at Harvard, has demonstrated that even Harvard physics students exhibit the same difficulties [14]. Alan van Heuvelen at Las Cruces, New Mexico, found only 5 of 100 students shifting from a pre-Newtonian to a Newtonian view of motion after a year-long calculus-based class [28].

The situation may to deteriorate further as the crisis in education is producing students who are less well prepared than in the past. Fewer students are expressing an interest in science and math, and American students fare poorly against their analogous cohorts in Europe and Asia [29]. Furthermore, the demographics indicate that the student population is shifting. We must begin reaching a more diverse population of students than ever before.

Students in an introductory course often do not learn appropriate professional skills

The skills learned in a university environment are often not an appropriate preparation for the workplace environment in which our students will eventually find themselves. This problem is a general one in university training and has been highlighted by a group of cognitive scientists who encourage the replacement of traditional teaching by an "apprenticeship" type of activity. They note that in many fields, introductory students are not trained in activities that well represent what they will do as professionals [3][10].

These observations are true in physics as well. This can be a particularly serious problem for physics majors, as it distorts their early view of the profession. Students may need significant remedial activities (sometimes as late as after their candidacy exams) when they may be getting their first real taste of research. Even worse, many students who might do very well as research physicists can lose interest if the material seems dry or poorly motivated. We may select against students who are excellent researchers, but who do not do well on timed exams where speed is a factor. For the non-majors, inappropriate training can make it especially difficult to understand the ideas behind physics.

Some characteristics of the differences in approach between the way the beginning student is taught and the way the professional physicist works are listed in table 12.1.

Many of these differences flow from the common strategy of presenting introductory physics in the model of mathematics. Mathematics is an abstract science in which one can define one's own axioms and conditions. Consequently, her results can be both exact and precise. Physics, on the

Table 12.1
Comparison of students' activities with those of a professional physicist[3]

Students:	Professionals:
Solve narrow, pre-defined problems of no personal interest.	Solve broad, open-ended and often self-discovered problems.
Work with laws presented by experts. Do not "discover" them on their own or learn why we believe them. Do not see them as hypotheses for testing.	Work with models to be tested and modified. Know "laws" are constructs.
Use analytic tools to get "exact" answers to inexact models.	Use analytic and numerical tools to get approximate answers to inexact models.
Rarely use a computer.	Use computers often.

other hand, is an experimental science. Nothing in physics is "true" in the sense of mathematics. Physics is not an "exact science" constrained only by internal, self-defined relations. It's a science constrained by our observations of the real world and one in which we believe we know the accuracy of our approximations.

The primary reason for the distortion in the introductory course is the fact that, for most circumstances, obtaining approximate results without numerical methods requires a high level of mathematical sophistication not possessed by most students (even physics majors) at the introductory level.[4] The presence of the computer allows a fundamental change in this situation.

What skills do we expect physics students to acquire? An analysis will help us understand better what it is that is and is not taught in a traditional introductory physics course.

An outline of the general process skills required is given in table 12.2. We define two basic skills: having a scientific framework and number awareness. By *a scientific framework* we mean that the student must understand the "storyline" of science—that science means observation, hypothesis, analysis, and testing against observation. By number aware-

Table 12.2
Skill analysis for physics students

1. Basic skills
   A scientific framework
   Number awareness

2. Theoretical skills
   Analytic skills
   Estimation and natural scales
   Approximation skills
   Numerical skills

3. Experimental skills
   Error analysis
   Mechanical skills
   Device experience
   Empathy for the apparatus

4. General skills
   Intuition
   Large-problem skills
   Communication skills

ness, we mean that the student must understand the idea that aspects of the real world may be quantified by measurement and that the results of analysis have implications for observation in the real world. These two are a sine qua non of doing physics. It is often assumed by the introductory physics teacher (incorrectly!) that the first is present. The second is stressed in most introductory courses.

To these two basic skills, we try to add a set of theoretical or modeling skills. The first of these are analytic skills: students should be able to write equations from word problems, to solve a variety of equations, and to interpret their results in terms of the physical world. Some aspects of this skill are stressed in the traditional introductory course. Other theoretical skills needed by physicists tend to be shortchanged in an introductory course, even one restricted to majors. These include estimation, approximation, and numerical skills.

These three skills are essential in learning how to model physical systems and understand the implications of models built by other. Since physics is not an exact science, the "art" in the science is knowing what physical laws to apply under what circumstances and what additional complicating factors can be safely neglected. We call this "getting the physics right." It involves being able to estimate the size of an effect, and to calculate corrections by understanding approximations. Today, it often involves putting physical insight into and getting it out of a complex numerical calculation. Yet these skills—critical for the professional physicist and essential for the engineer—are almost completely ignored in traditional introductory courses.

Since physics is a science whose results are continually tested and evaluated against the real world, a physicist needs experimental skills as well as theoretical ones. Majors are often trained in error analysis, mechanical skills, and given experience with a variety of devices. A fourth component, empathy for the apparatus, is something which one hopes that students develop as a concomitant part of their experimental experience. Yet this skill is primary to their understanding of what even basic physics means and how the equations we write down relate to the behavior of the real world.

Finally, there are a number of general skills that all professionals must develop. They must build an intuition for their field—the ability to understand which tools apply in which circumstances and to have the complex network of internal checks that let them look at a wrong answer and have it not "feel" right. They must learn large-problem skills; the ability to take a significant problem and break it down into component, solvable parts in an appropriate manner while keeping track of the overall goal. Finally, they must build communication skills. In physics, as in any field, it does not suffice to do brilliant work in a notebook or in your head. Physics, as is any field, is a social agreement of what it is we know. To interact with the community one needs to be able to present one's results both in oral and written form in a clear and compelling fashion. This cluster of general skills is largely neglected in our professional training of physicists until they begin research in the second or third year of graduate school!

3. Can Educational Research Help?

To understand the implications of the problems that students have building appropriate mental models of the physical world, and to see what might produce effective solutions, we turn to some of the basic results of cognitive science as applied to learning theory. We briefly summarize a few of these results.

The problem of mental models

Students do not come to us as tabulae rasae. They have both knowledge of the world and patterns of expectation for how they should learn. These patterns are often referred to as mental models[5] (or schemas). Observations that have been made about mental models include:

1. Each individual must build his or her own mental models. They cannot be "transferred" from teacher to student.
2. Mental models can contain contradictory elements.
3. It is reasonably easy to learn something that fits in well with your existing mental model.
4. It is very difficult to change a well established mental model.
5. Individuals develop a variety of preferred approaches or learning styles.

Item 1 is the fundamental element in the modern constructivist credo. Listening to a lecture or reading a book is not an effective way of learning if one does it passively. Item 2 implies that as teachers we can be fooled about how much our students know if we are not careful in probing their mental models. They can learn to do problems without realizing the implications of their answers. Item 3 can be summarized with the observation that much of our reasoning is done by analogy. Item 4 says that it can be very difficult to learn something you don't almost know already. This can be an especially severe problem if "what you know ain't so." Item 5 reminds us that anecdotal evidence from a small number of students (those who think like their teacher) is not necessarily generalizable to all students. It also helps to raise our consciousness to the kinds of wrong paths our students can follow.

In line with these general observations, experimental evidence in specific cases now shows convincingly that most students in introductory physics courses do not develop good physical mental models, even when they know how to solve traditional problems reasonably well [2][6][24][28]. Why does this happen? Some specific findings regarding physics learning are:

- Introductory physics students come in with naive preconceptions about the world that don't get changed in the course.
- Students have trouble understanding what's important and how a part relates to the whole.
- Students have difficulty with the multiple-representation structure of physics.
- The thinking and learning styles of most students differ from that of most physicists (a highly selected and trained group).

Having lived in the physical world all their lives, our students necessarily come to us with preconceptions about it. We use the phrase "naive preconceptions" rather than the more commonly found "misconceptions" to stress that the ideas and models the students bring to a physics course are often adequate and sufficiently accurate for normal life in the everyday world. They are, however, not productive as a base for scientific generalizations and do not extrapolate correctly to situations less commonly encountered (where they can be dangerous).[6] These views can lead students to build a shell around what they learn in physics class and only apply it to their physics homework and exams. Success in that venue does not necessarily imply that they have integrated these views into their everyday conceptions of nature. Their naive preconceptions can even cause them to reinterpret what we tell them incorrectly, in order to make the results agree with their existing mental model [1].

If we want to overcome these scientifically unproductive mental models, we have to change our students' ways of thinking. Changing someone's mental model requires that the proposed change have these characteristics:

- It should be understandable.
- It should be plausible.
- There should be a strong conflict with the existing model.
- The new model should be seen as useful.

The judgment that a new model satisfies these conditions must be made by the students themselves. It rarely suffices to tell them, for example, that their view of the world contradicts an experiment shown as a demonstration in class. They must understand what is happening in the experiment, make their own clear prediction, and see clearly that it is controverted. Active engagement is crucial.

The problem of learning processes

"Doing physics" is not the same as "knowing physics." Many students satisfactorily learn to memorize and replay definitions and equations, but cannot use or put these together in any but trivial ways. Learning to do physics means learning to run the machinery, not just be able to name the moving parts. And physics, like most sciences, is a tightly linked and overlapping structure. Most problems are highly overdetermined: they can be viewed and solved in many different ways. One of the characteristics of physics that convinces us that it is "right" is the fact that all these different approaches fit together and give a consistent set of answers. Students learn this as they develop process skills to go with the content they have learned.

One particular difficulty that introductory students often have is that physics is highly multi-representational. Physics begins by selecting a phenomenon to analyze—a narrow slice of the real world. This slice is then modeled by an idealization—a "schematic" or "cartoon." In creating this, we decide what in our slice of the real world matters and what is irrelevant for the problem at hand. Then, that cartoon is translated into a variety of forms: words, equations, tables of numbers, graphs, diagrams, and so on. Each of these representations tells us something about our model. We are continually having to create these different representations and translate them, both one into the other, and into their implications as to what they say about the real world. This process is illustrated in figure 12.1.

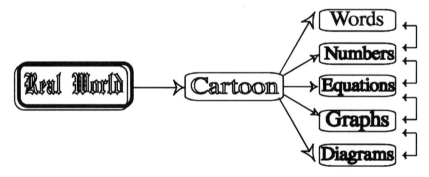

Figure 12.1
Physics describes the world with models that have multiple representations.

Students often have trouble with the multi-representational character of physics. Some students have trouble with geometry, some with algebra. Others can draw a graph but not explain what it means in words. The professional physicist has worked with these representations for so long, that he or she tends to see them as identical and not appreciate the difficulty a student may have in getting from one to the other.

A second problem we often encounter is that students rarely see the relations among the parts. Few students in an introductory class know what scientific mental models are like. Many students leave our pre-college educational system with the model that science consists of memorizing a large number of rules, principles, and equations, and learning tricks to spin obscure and meaningless words ("physics problems") into numbers ("correct answers").

When students see physics as a collection of independent equations to memorize, they lose the structure of the material. They do not realize why they are studying a particular equation or what implications it might have for their future studies. The process used and expected by physicists includes a continual calibration of the model against the real world and a dense interdependence of principles that provide numerous ways of looking at and checking each result. Introductory students often fail to gain the ability to apply the complex and tightly interwoven network of cross-checks that physics offers. (The professional would say: "Well, I got a solution. Is it right? Let's check that I used the right equation by deriving it from first principles. Let's check my units. Let's see if energy is conserved. What if I take limiting values? Does it make physical sense when I imagine what's happening in the real world. . . .")

We refer to the "independent-equations" way of thinking about physics as the *dead-leaves model*. Each equation is written on a leaf (or file card) and is inappropriately considered equal in importance and relevance. This is illustrated in figure 12.2.[7] We would much prefer our students to see physics as a living tree.

4. Can the Computer Help?

The immense growth of computer power in the past decade has made possible a number of innovative approaches to the problems discussed

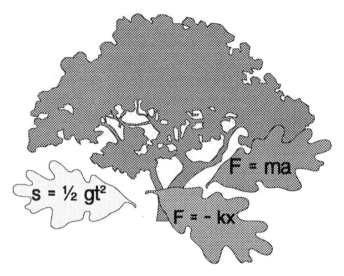

Figure 12.2
The "dead-leaves model" of physics

above. In this section, we consider a few of the approaches that have been tried and proven successful in attacking some of the fundamental issues.

Using the computer to build better mental models
A number of the developments in computer technology can help solve the problem of building good mental models. Microcomputer based laboratories (MBL) have already proven to be powerful and effective. Combining hypermedia with concept mapping should also prove to be a powerful technique.

MBL   The microcomputer can be used in the laboratory to collect and analyze data from measurements in real experiments. Microcomputer based labs (MBL) have been demonstrated to significantly help students break down their naive preconceptions and build up a strong set of underlying physical concepts [24][25]. It is the following characteristics of these laboratories that seem to be important:

• The instruments have short response times.
• Students can become the test objects, a get a strong kinesthetic interaction.
• It is easy to collect high quality-data.

• The equipment is highly modularized into easy-to-comprehend and manipulate chunks.

Modern data-collection systems for educational applications consist of an analog-to-digital converter (ADC)—a device that converts an analog signal from a measuring device (a *probe*) into a digital signal that can be analyzed by the computer. A variety of probes (distance, temperature, voltage, current, force, magnetic field . . .) can be plugged into the ADC which is in turn plugged into the computer. Students can learn to set up this equipment easily and to take excellent data in a few minutes. They can then quantify a wide variety of physical phenomena and see the result on the computer screen immediately.

One group that has been developing and using these tools in introductory physics teaching in especially effective ways are Ron Thornton in his project *Tools for Scientific Thinking* at Tufts University [25] and Priscilla Laws in her project *Workshop Physics* at Dickinson College [10]. Thornton has developed a series of labs that use the ADC plus computer to help students build the fundamental concepts of the physicist's world view. Laws has used these tools to develop a complete introductory physics course based on discovery labs and without traditional lectures.

When they use these systems to explore the real world, students can see the translation of their real world observations into graphs and numbers quickly and easily. Thornton, Laws, and their collaborators have shown that these methods produce the strong conflicts with a student's naive preconceptions needed to motivate change and help them develop good experimental skills, including an empathy for the apparatus.

Hypermedia   One of the problems students have in building up a good mental model of the content of the physics course is their inability to integrate the material into a coherent whole. The individual lecture and the "chapter a week" in the textbook may play a role in this difficulty. Certainly the tendency of textbook authors to summarize the material at the end of a chapter by a list of equations facilitates problem solving without thinking.

A textbook has a built-in tendency to linearity: the pages are numbered successively. The "space" in which a computer presents information is not so constrained. Any structure, any connection between parts can be displayed in effective and compelling ways. This has an important implication.

The structure of the material presented on the computer is not restricted to a single form. It can be organized in many different fashions and can emphasize non-linear links.[9] Hypermedia makes it possible to structure a student's access to materials and his or her view of the relation of the parts.

PhysNet is Peter Signell's project at Michigan State that modularizes the physics curriculum into more than 600 units and focuses on developing student learning skills. The PhysNet project has used a hypermedia-like approach (on paper!) with considerable success. Signell reports that the students understand the relations of units throughout the course better than with the traditional presentation [22]. Although this approach has proved successful at Michigan State and has been adopted at a few other institutions, the difficulty of administering and managing the system has limited the use of this approach. It's much easier to order a single textbook for all students than to provide each student access to hundreds of pigeonholes, each containing a unit, and to design an individualized content for each student. The advent of large data storage capabilities and hypermedia controlled access promises to free this interesting approach of its managerial chains.

Using the computer to develop appropriate skills

The computer can help substantially in introducing more professional skills in an introductory physics course. On the theoretical side, the traditional approach suppresses the fundamental idea of approximation since that requires too much mathematical skill. On the experimental side, the laboratory is frequently used to "demonstrate the truth of the equations taught in lecture." Labs are pre–set up, since there is too little time to have the students assemble and learn complex equipment. The result in both cases is a severe distortion of what the professional does. The general skills in table 12.2 are rarely included in an introductory course.

Professional productivity tools and theoretical skills   The introduction of more powerful and professional tools, such as programming languages, graphers, data accumulators, and symbolic manipulators gives even the introductory student the power to address more realistic problems than are possible with analytic hand calculations. In order to produce analytically solvable problems, introductory physics classes occasionally simplify the life out of a real world problem until it loses all interest. Einstein has been quoted as saying: "Physics should be as simple as possible—but not more simple than possible." The inclusion of professional productivity tools gives even the introductory student a much wider field to play on [13].

By putting programming tools in the hands of the physics major in the introductory class, the Maryland University Project in Physics and Educational Technology (M.U.P.P.E.T.) [19] demonstrated that introductory students could learn to solve complex physics problems using numerical methods. This resulted in a good first introduction to estimation, approximation, and numerical methods.

In fact, in one semester, the students learned (some came in with) enough programming skills to be able to design and carry out successful and interesting independent research projects in the second and third semesters of the class.

Modular laboratory tools and experimental skills   In her project, Workshop Physics, at Dickinson College [10], Priscilla Laws demonstrated that students could learn to assemble their equipment and take high quality data very quickly by using modular computerized data gatherers. This allows them to get a clearer picture of the experiment and to use the apparatus to think about and build an intuition for the physical system.

In her laboratory-based introductory class, Laws's students develop good experimental skills. By the end of the class, many are comfortably designing and assembling equipment to answer generally posed physics questions.

Developing generalized skills   In Signell's PhysNet project, much emphasis is placed on generalized skills. Students are evaluated on their ability to use resource materials. Their problem solutions are graded for quality and clarity of presentation as well as for content. (The grades are multiplied together so no credit is obtained for doing a problem wrong, but clearly.) Students develop self-pacing skills and are encouraged to carry out self-evaluations.

In M.U.P.P.E.T., students carrying out project work begin to learn how to work with large problems and they have the opportunity to learn communication skills by presenting their work both in written and oral form.

5. The CUPLE Project

The Comprehensive Unified Physics Learning Environment (CUPLE) is a multi-university project to develop an open-ended learning environment that incorporates and integrates the approaches discussed above. The idea of CUPLE is to build a working environment for the student that contains a rich set of materials that can present physics in a variety of ways. The resulting product should be able to address both the need to do research on student responses to different environments and to deal with the problem of diverse learning styles. Prototypes and developer tools have been produced and went into beta test in the fall of 1991. A full course in the CUPLE environment is expected to be available in the summer of 1993.

The basic CUPLE hardware environment requires:

- an IBM compatible microcomputer, preferably 80386 or 80486
- 4 Megabytes of random access memory
- VGA or super-VGA graphics
- a fixed disk with at least 40 Megabytes of storage
- at least one floppy disk (1.2 Megabyte or greater)

The CUPLE software environment requires:

- DOS (version 3.3 or later)
- Microsoft Windows (version 3.0 or later)
- Asymetrix ToolBook (version, 1.5 or later)
- a spreadsheet (preferably Microsoft Excel for Windows)
- a word processor (preferably Microsoft Word for Windows)
- Borland's Turbo Pascal (preferably for Windows)
- a symbolic math package (preferably MathCad or Mathematica)

A full CUPLE station also includes:

- an analog to digital converter (ADC)[10]
- a videodisc player and video overlay card.[11]

Eventually, we expect CUPLE to be distributed on CD rather than on floppy disk. As a result, the hardware will eventually need access to

• a CD reader.

Structure

CUPLE includes a variety of tools for both users and developers. The basic materials included are:

• Instructional text
• Microcomputer based labs (MBL)
• Computer simulation tools
• Text describing home labs and demos
• Interactive videodisc laboratories
• Extensive reference material (including video)

The contents of CUPLE will be based on materials from the projects in physics education mentioned above: M.U.P.P.E.T. (Maryland and RPI), PhysNet (Michigan State) , Workshop Physics (Dickinson), and Tools for Scientific Thinking (Tufts). In addition, CUPLE will also take advantage of recent innovative uses of videodiscs (particularly those of Dean Zollman at Kansas State). It will include videodisc hooks to *The Encyclopedia of Physics Demonstrations*, *The Mechanical Universe*, and the set of *Physics Cinema Classics* developed by the AAPT National Interactive Media Project. A variety of physics databases will also be included, such as the periodic table and chart of the fundamental particles, and collections of educational resources from the AAPT.[12]

Tools for the user

The heart of the CUPLE innovation is not only to bring together a number of diverse projects and their approaches to physics education, but to provide the student from the beginning with a working environment analogous to that of a professional. The emphasis is on tools that permit easy manipulation of the different representations so critical to understanding physics: graphs, numbers, data, and pictures. In addition to these tools for the user, the environment provides tools for developers that facilitate producing new modules and linking them into the full system. The prototype system contains several tools for dealing with a variety of modalities. Most of the basic tools and the system management structure is being built by the Academic Software Development Group at the University of Maryland.

Tools for exploring text Text materials are presented as units or "books" in ToolBook from Asymetrix. This hypertext product forms the backbone of the CUPLE environment. A standard frame has been developed with a variety of navigation, help, and annotation tools. (See figure 12.3.)

The buttons and icons in the toolbar on the right of the frame let the student access a glossary of physics terms, various forms of help text, or attach a "NoteMark" with his or her own annotations anywhere on the page. Each page may also contain one or more specialized icons. When the student clicks on one of these icons, additional information may be presented or a new activity launched, including graphs, video, animations, reference material and so on.

In addition to whatever links have been built in by the author, the user can bring up palettes of tools shown in figure 12.4 by clicking on the toolbox icon. Included are standard tools, such as a word processor, a calculator, and a spreadsheet, and our specially developed tools described below. Although the student's first use of a tool may be through an icon introduced in the text for a specific purpose, the same tool is available through the toolbox at any time for independent exploration.

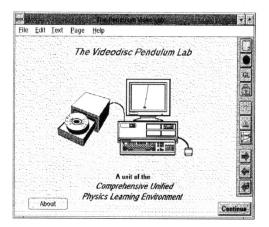

Figure 12.3
Title page and frame from a CUPLE unit

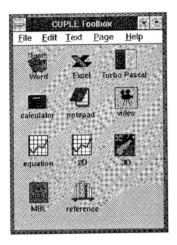

Figure 12.4
The CUPLE toolbox

Graphing tools   The CUPLE prototype includes a number of graphing tools: a three-function grapher, a three-dimensional graph display, and a set of tools for use in student programming. In figure 12.5 we show a sample screen from the three-function grapher. With this tool, the student can display up to three different functions, vary parameters, and change limits.

Calculational tools and simulations   A Windows version of the original M.U.P.P.E.T. toolkit (called *Window on Physics* or *WinPhys* for short) has been created for CUPLE by one of us (JMW at RPI). WinPhys is an object-oriented extension to Turbo Pascal that allows faculty and students to create their own programs for problem solving in physics with little more than a rudimentary knowledge of Pascal. Figure 12.6 illustrates the WinPhys pendulum program. With this program the student can study the damped driven pendulum, resonance, or the onset of chaos. The student can even modify the computer model in figure 12.6 through the use of the WinPhys system.

The Window on Physics materials allow students to include significant and powerful programming in their toolkit and thereby expand the activities they perform as part of their physics learning experience within CUPLE. The environment includes the WinPhys tools and a large number

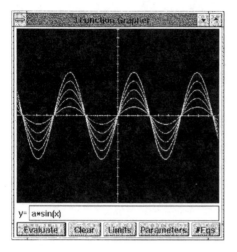

Figure 12.5
The three-function grapher

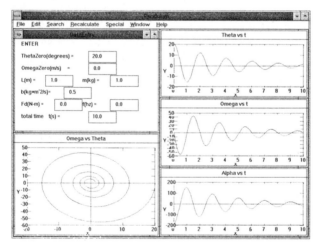

Figure 12.6
The WinPhys pendulum program

of sample programs. The tools let students and faculty develop programs easily and efficiently. The sample programs have their own intrinsic use at specific places in the curriculum. Because of their highly modular structure, they also serve as templates for cutting and pasting pieces of code into new programs. This structure greatly facilitates the development of new software.

The M.U.P.P.E.T. group has developed a number of simulation programs that can be used both to train the student's intuition and as productivity tools for student projects. These will be ported to CUPLE and integrated with the text materials.

Data-taking tools   The CUPLE project gets a powerful and important window on the real world through analog-to-digital converters. These devices come with a "shoebox of probes" that permit the user to take a wide variety of real world data directly into the computer. Figure 12.7 shows a sample screen from the program MOTION, which is designed to display data collected by a distance probe. The example shown is data taken from a sonic ranger positioned below a mass oscillating on a hanging spring. The data displayed includes the position, velocity, and

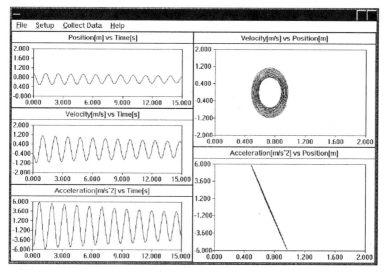

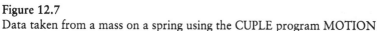

Figure 12.7
Data taken from a mass on a spring using the CUPLE program MOTION

acceleration of the mass. Two other plots that facilitate understanding of the theory, position vs. velocity and position vs. acceleration, are also shown.

Video display and measurement tools   Another CUPLE window on the real world is provided by the video display and measurement tools. These allow the user to display the output of video devices on a window in the computer screen. With the proper video equipment, the student can view and control from the computer the output of videodisc, VCR, or even a CCD device to display live output from a microscope.[13]

In addition to display, our video window provides graphing, measurement, and annotation tools that let students collect quantitative data from the video image on the computer screen. This data can then be exported directly to a spreadsheet for analysis and modeling. Figure 12.8 shows the video tool with data points obtained by following a video of a large amplitude pendulum.

This tool offers a new element of possible great signifigance. The "world in the frame" that is the fundamental starting point of a physics analysis gets a visual representation right on the screen. This video data does not need to be "canned" from a pre-existing videodisc. Students can use a hand-held video camera in the lab (and out in the world!) to take data which they can then analyze quantitatively. With multitasking, they may have one window open where the real-world video-camera data is displayed, another where the graph of the data from that video is

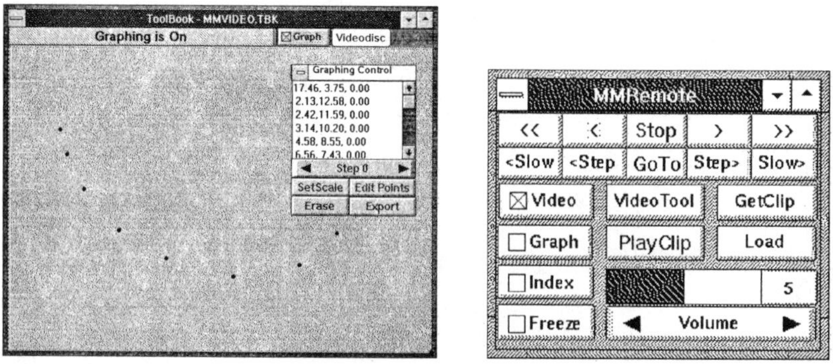

Figure 12.8
The CUPLE video window and remote control panel

displayed, and a third where a mathematical model is built. The linking and translation of the elements from the world to the various representations of physics can take on a new reality.

The browser One essential element of the full CUPLE system will be the Browser. This will be a graphical display that will allow the user to explore the systems and to understand the relation of the parts at a variety of levels of chunking. The next stage of CUPLE development will involve building the Browser software.

One way to help students build a structured model is to give them access to the course material via a structured hierarchical map. At the coarsest level, this map displays the universe of scientific thought as divided into broad areas of study—physics, chemistry, mathematics . . . This is represented by a series of nodes or bubbles on the computer screen. The student begins by "entering physics country"[14] by clicking on the "physics node." The node then opens up to show the next level of the hierarchy, a series of main topics or "states"—classical mechanics, electricity and magnetism, thermodynamics . . . Clicking on a state opens the hierarchy one more level to display the structure of basic units or "towns." These units are approximately equivalent to the material usually presented in one lecture. The relation between these parts is shown in a Signell or prerequisite map. The elements are linked to show which units should be mastered before starting any particular unit. A piece of this map is shown schematically in figure 12.9.

Once the student selects a particular unit, the screen will open up to yield a "town guide." The unit will contain a variety of activities—readings, labs, home experiments, demonstrations, programming, etc. It is at this level that detailed guidance will be provided by the CUPLE system. The path through the town will be selected by the teacher, just as he or she now selects readings and homework problems from a text.[15] The town guide will provide the student with a floating view of the structure of the unit and where he or she is in the unit. Students will also be able to mark parts of a unit as complete when they are satisfied they understand it.

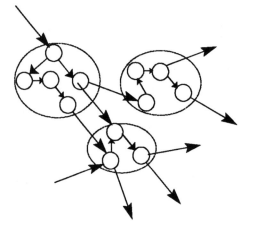

Figure 12.9
A piece of a Signell map (schematic)

Can CUPLE Help?

We believe CUPLE can provide an environment and tools that can help solve many of our basic problems with physics education.

CUPLE can be used to help build better mental models

Let's consider two examples of how the CUPLE system could be used: an introduction to projectile motion for underprepared students and a study of the pendulum by honors physics majors.

Enhancing a lecture   CUPLE provides a number of powerful tools that can enhance a lecture demonstration in ways that should facilitate a student's understanding of the underlying concepts and of the multi-representational character of physics. Some of these uses include: as an electronic blackboard for presenting high quality graphs, for quick and accurate collection and display of data, and for the use of video, from videodisc to videotape to a live camera.

The graphing tools can be used in a compelling way to deliver graphs that can be a significant improvement over hand-drawn graphs. One specific example is to consider a demonstration of the meaning of the derivative. Using the WinPhys function display, one can enter any function and show a graph of that function. By clicking with the mouse cursor on any point on the curve, the tangent to the curve is also drawn. Then one can "zoom in" on the neighborhood of that point, magnifying the view of the curve more and more. This displays in a clear and compelling fashion that when one looks at the curve in smaller and smaller regions, the curve and its tangent become indistinguishable.

The display of data associated with a lecture demonstration can also become more accurate and convincing. The PSL and ULI data accumulation tools together with the CUPLE data display programs allow the teacher to collect and display data in lecture in real time without the need to take large amounts of time or use pre-cooked data. The data can then be analyzed in class using a spreadsheet. The power of the tools is sufficient that the time required is not excessive for a lecture demonstration and the quality of both the data and the fits can be excellent.

Video can add an important component to the student's understanding of the relation of the real world and physical laws. For example, since their mental models of motion are strongly dominated by the concept of position, students often have difficulty accepting the idea that both position and velocity are needed to specify an object's state of motion at any given time. A frame-by-frame video display of two children throwing a ball back and forth can provide a compelling demonstration for this requirement. From a single frame, the student cannot tell which way the ball is travelling and where it will be in the next frame. At least two successive frames are needed to decide what the ball will do. As in the live-data demonstration, the CUPLE video tool can be used to extract data from the videodisc and fit it with a model using a spreadsheet. And it can be done in a sufficiently short time to permit it to be done as a lecture demonstration.

Training the underprepared student   Underprepared students often come to a physics class with many problems that make learning physics difficult. Among these are a lack of fluency with algebraic manipulations, difficulty reading and interpreting graphs, and an inability to relate these subjects to the real world. The result is often "encapsulation"—the student breaks the course materials up into small pieces suitable for memorizing but does not build the relations between the parts that constitute a good understanding of physics.

One can begin to address these difficulties early in the semester with a three hour CUPLE lab on projectile motion. The students begin in a lab where stations are available with MBLs and videodiscs. They perform an experiment with objects rolling up and down an inclined plane, accumulating and displaying data as the object moves. Their data is saved to a file. They then can move to the videodisc and take data both from a thrown projectile and a falling diver. Again, their data is saved to a file.

The students then move to a computer for a one hour session in which they first use the three-function grapher to see how the coefficients in the equation of a parabola effect the shape of its graph. They then work with a previously prepared spreadsheet to see how the formula for the motion of an object can be fit with parabolas and produce both tables of numbers and graphs. They then load the file with their data from the MBL into the same spreadsheet and fit the parameters to match (and incidentally extract the angle of inclination of the plane—which can be checked against a physical measurement). The data from the video can then be recalled and the data put into the same spreadsheet and the parameters extracted. Both the path of the projectile motion (x-y plot) and the height of the diver (y-t) are modeled with parabolas.

These activities provide a number of different ways of looking at the same subject: a parabola provides a good fit to many aspects of projectile motion. The student has the power to carry out many different activities, both in a guided and independent fashion. The multirepresentational character of physics as a description of the real world is dramatically illustrated.

How CUPLE can be used to expand student activities
Enabling the physics major   More advanced students can use the CUPLE materials to enrich their activities and extend the course materials into modern subjects. As an example, near the end of the first semester, students in a class for physics majors can use the pendulum program to explore the motion of the large-amplitude pendulum. This is a nonlinear system with highly complex behavior.

Students can study the qualitative behavior of the damped and driven system and explore the phenomena of resonance and chaos. They can then use the WinPhys system in programming mode and explore the numerical methods used to solve the equation and learn how to determine their accuracy and validate their correctness.

Finally, students can use the pendulum program as the jumping-off point for studying the pendulum and the nonlinear harmonic oscillator. This technique has been used in the M.U.P.P.E.T. project and we find that, given the power of the computer, many students can pursue interesting independent scientific research topics for term papers. When they do this, they both get early training in how to do research and develop a better idea of what professional physicists actually do.

Enabling the general student   The CUPLE environment offers the general student in calculus-based introductory physics a number of enhancements over the traditional textbook + problems + lecture + lab. It provides the students with additional power for investigation and exploration through a number of added tools and modalities. CUPLE should have a number of advantages for student learning.

• CUPLE encourages active learning by putting more power to explore in the hands of the student.
• CUPLE has an unprecedented flexibility to permit a variety of uses.
• By bringing the various modes of learning together in a single interactive environment, CUPLE enables a synergy to take place. Whichever mode the student is most comfortable with can help bring along their understanding of other modes.
• By linking a large data base of materials, CUPLE will improve accessibility of tools and information for the student.
• By controlling the student's access to material through a well-structured browser, CUPLE will encourage appropriate chunking and hierarchical thinking.

CUPLE as a research environment

Although the computer has been used in physics education for more than a decade, the wide availability of 32 bit, hypermedia, multitasking, multimedia materials is new. We believe that this power is bound to have an important impact on the way students learn physics. Nonetheless, it is essential to see what works and what doesn't and to understand the reasons why. CUPLE, because of its flexibility, can be used to test a number of important hypotheses in educational physics. Many important questions can be addressed in this environment, including: how students respond to hypermedia, how they learn to understand and translate multiple representations, and how to best classify and handle the variety of learning styles present in an introductory class.

The use of hypermedia has been studied extensively by workers in the field of Human-Computer Interaction. A number of workers have pointed out the dangers of giving a user free access to a large body of unstructured material. The result is often referred to as the user getting "lost in hyperspace." But the traditional lecture + text + lab course is also hypermedia. Even the material contained in a text by itself has substantial cross-linking. When the student fails to see the relation of the parts in different chapters of a text, or when the link between the lecture and lab is not made (a common complaint), the student could also be justifiably described as "lost in hyperspace." The CUPLE Browser is being designed to have a flexibility that will permit research on how the structure of the material presented affects learning.

Although it has often been observed that physics as a discipline depends heavily on multiple representations, there has been very little study on how the mode of presentation affects the student's ability to build the skills of understanding and translating these representations. CUPLE is an almost ideal environment for testing this, since it permits different representations on the screen at the same time.

Work with MBL tools has shown that its success is dependent on promptness. The graph must be displayed at essentially the same time as the event is occurring. How will this work when video measurement is used? In this case the event is "frozen"—recorded. It can be shown many times or in "instant replay" slow motion. Can the video serve a similar purpose as the MBL in helping students to learn to translate between the physical world and graphical representations? And if it can, does the timing of the link between the event and the graph remain and important factor?

CUPLE will also be useful for studying how a student's preferred learning style affects his or her learning. Is it best to work with a student's strength at first in order to establish the basic concepts firmly? Or is it better to work on their weaknesses so they develop a more balanced approach? It is very difficult to address questions like these with significant numbers of students in a paper and pencil environment. In the CUPLE environment students could be given a variety of choices for emphasizing different approaches: solve this algebraically, work with a graph, use video or real world data. . . . If tracking were added, we could follow the students' choices and see the impact on their learning.

The Evolution of the Curriculum

Even though significant changes in how physics can be taught are beginning to be possible, and evidence regarding their effectiveness is beginning to accumulate, there will still be major barriers to getting widespread adoption of new teaching ideas. Physics has changed significantly since the modern introductory physics course was set up at the beginning of this century (see for example Millikan's work, [14]), but the teaching of physics has changed very little.[16]

A particularly stark contrast exists between the drastic changes in physics as practiced and the nearly stagnant way physics is taught. This contrast exists both with regard to content and tools. Modern professional approaches, such as numerical calculations, symbolic manipulation, and the use of off-the-shelf modular experimental apparatus, are rarely introduced at the introductory level. Since most of our students never take courses beyond that level, they are never exposed to them. This severely distorts the way the students view what physics is and isolates them from many powerful ideas and methods[17] that could positively affect the way they think about their own profession and broaden their skills significantly.

Why is it so difficult to change the way we teach?

If we want to make a change in the way physics is taught, we encounter what appears to be a structural problem. The content and method of physics teaching, especially at the introductory level, has been too slow to change. Those changes that have occurred in our teaching have been primarily along the lines of emphasis.

Two observations on the evolution of physics teaching are important.

• Changes in physics education appear to occur via a "stick-slip" or "punctuated equilibrium" mode. That is, they happen in sudden jumps with long periods of stability.

• Only a very small fraction of physics teachers contributes to the development of educational innovations.

These contrast strongly with the evolution of physics content by researchers. Although sudden changes ("paradigm shifts" [9]) occasionally appear to occur in physics, most of the time the system evolves in a reasonably steady manner, with new physics being continually learned and adopted by the community [18]. Furthermore, a much larger number of physicists produce cumulative contributions to the research effort than to the educational system.

Why does this happen? One might conjecture that there is no problem in physics education and that therefore nobody needs to work on it. But there is increasing evidence of dissatisfaction with the traditional approach [7]. One might conjecture that few people are interested in innovative teaching. But our personal experience shows that although many physics faculty teach innovatively, very few publish their results, methods, and materials, and the accumulation of innovations among teachers is rare, even within a single college or university.

We believe that part of the problem is in the mechanisms present in the system for accumulating knowledge. In the research arena, the traditional method of presenting results is by publishing papers in a research journal. Dozens of such journals exist and more than ten thousand physics research papers are published every year. In the educational arena, the critical products are materials, not research papers of educational methods.[18] Essentially all of the materials used in physics teaching are in the form of textbooks. The number of new physics textbooks (not updated editions of old books) per year is on the order of ten. Furthermore, innovative textbooks appear rarely, and when they do, they usually have short lifetimes.

Part of the problem appears to be the difference in modularity. Physics research papers rarely create an entire field in one fell swoop. They do so a step at a time. Researchers can adopt new approaches in small bites. Furthermore, the effort to produce a research paper is an order of magnitude smaller than the effort to produce a textbook. A typical active physics researcher may produce two papers per person per year. A typical physics text may take two people five years to produce, or 0.1 papers per person per year. This represents a difference in effort ratios of a factor of 20. Although other important issues (such as the relative difference in prestige or reward for the two activities) cannot be addressed by using a computer, the issue of modularity can be.

Tools for the developer

CUPLE is set up to be a modular environment that can be modified or extended by the teacher. In addition to the materials produced for students, the CUPLE prototype includes a basic set of developer's tools. These include the CUPLE linking engine and a set of tools to simplify the construction of linked books.

The CUPLE engine Producing an open-ended hypermedia system is a substantial challenge. Each unit links to many others, so replacing or adding a new unit can have a "ripple effect" that could produce bugs in many other units. To prevent this from happening, we have developed a management tool for the CUPLE system that keeps track of and manages all calls between files. This is the heart of the system and is responsible for its flexibility and power. The developer can link new units to the system in a simple way.

Linking tools The authoring environment might be referred to as a "physics processor." The author simply brings up the CUPLE template under the ToolBook hypermedia system, selects author mode, and begins to type. The author can use the standard ToolBook palettes to add new text fields, graphics, colors, or buttons to the page. The CUPLE extensions to the standard menu allow the author to select Video, WinPhys, Laboratory, MBL (data acquisition), Demos, or String-and-Stickytape and the appropriate icon and code is added to the book. The author is prompted to enter the name of the specific video clip or program and the functionality necessary to do this is automatically added to the page.

The implications of an open system

We refer to the difficulty of producing educational materials in the current publishing environment as "the textbook lock." Educational materials are most conveniently delivered today as textbooks. This causes two problems. Firstly, the effort to produce a textbook is very large, reducing the number of individuals who might contribute innovations. Secondly, in a highly competitive publishing environment, there is great pressure on publishers and from publishers to produce texts which will capture a significant fraction of the market. This leads to pressure from publishers on textbook writers to imitate the most successful books. The result is a large number of books which differ little in content, arrangement, point of view, or types of problems included.

From the point of view of the social construction of knowledge, perhaps the most important innovation of the CUPLE system is that it is designed to be open. CUPLE is an environment that lets a teacher easily modify existing material or add additional material of his or her own. The CUPLE engine is a database that contains tools for linking and finding links. By following the modularized idea inspired by object-oriented programming, we have built a structure in which the interactions of the parts are tightly controlled and monitored by the CUPLE engine.

This tight control opens the system for growth and cumulation. Once the first CUPLE course is complete, we hope to establish CUPLE as a publishing environment—one in which teachers using it could develop and submit modules for peer review, testing, and incorporation into the full system.

The open structure of the system and the unprecedented modularization of the learning environment should permit many more teachers to add their contributions to an ever-growing and evolving structure, one that can embody a vision of the future that uses computer technology to put new power into the hands of both student and teacher.

References

1. A. Champagne, L. Klopfer, and J. H. Anderson, "Factors influencing the learning of classical mechanics," *American Journal of Physics*, 48 (1980) p. 1074.

2. Arnold Arons, *A Guide to Introductory Physics Teaching* (Wiley, 1990).

3. J. S. Brown, A. Collins, and P. Duguid, "Situated cognition and the culture of learning", *Educational Researcher*, (Jan-Feb 1989) p. 32.

4. R. D. Edge, *String and Sticky Tape Experiments* (Am. Assoc. of Phys. Teachers, 1981).

5. G. D. Freier and F. J. Anderson, *The Demonstration Handbook for Physics* (Am. Assoc. of Phys. Teachers, 1981).

6. I. A. Halloun and D. Hestenes, "The initial knowledge state of college physics students," *American Journal of Physics*, 53 (1986) p. 1043.

7. David Hestenes, "Toward a modeling theory of physics instruction," *American Journal of Physics*, 55 (1987) p. 440.

8. The Introductory University Physics Project, NSF project 1987-90, John Rigden (AIP) and Don Holcomb (Cornell), project directors.

9. T. S. Kuhn, *The Structure of Scientific Revolutions, 2nd Ed.* (U. of Chicago, 1970).

10. J. Lave, "Tailor-made experiments and evaluating the intellectual consequences of apprenticeship training," *The Quarterly Newsletter of the Institute for Comparative Human Development*, 1 (1977) p. 1.

11. Priscilla Laws, "Workshop physics: Replacing lectures with real experience," in CPI Conference ([12]), p. 22.

13. W. M. MacDonald, E. F. Redish, and J. M. Wilson, "The M.U.P.P.E.T. Manifesto," *Computers in Physics*, July/Aug. 1988.

14. Eric Mazur, "A hypermedia approach towards teaching physics," *The AAPT Announcer*, 21 (May 1991) p. 61.

15. L. C. McDermott, "Research on conceptual understanding in mechanics," *Physics Today* 37 (1984) p. 24.

16. Robert A. Millikan, *Mechanics, Molecular Physics, and Heat* (Ginn and Co., 1902).

17. Donald Norman, "Some observations on mental models," in *Mental Models*, D. Gentner and A. L. Stevens, eds. (Lawrence Erlbaum Associates, 1983) p. 7.

18. A. Pais, *Inward Bound* (Oxford, 1986).

19. *Proceedings of the Conference on Computers in Physics Instruction*, E. F. Redish and J. Risley, eds. (Addison-Wesley, 1990).

20. E. F. Redish, "The impact of the computer on the physics curriculum," in CPI Conference ([21]), p. 15.

22. Peter Signell, "Computers and the broad spectrum of educational goals," in in CPI Conference ([23]), p. 54.

24. Ronald K. Thornton and David R. Sokoloff, "Learning motion concepts using real-time microcomputer-based laboratory tools," *American Journal of Physics*, 58 (1990) p. 858.

25. Ronald K. Thornton, "Tools for scientific thinking: Learning physical concepts with real-time laboratory measurements," in CPI Conference ([26]), p. 177.

26. Alan van Heuvelen, "Learning to think like a physicist: A review of research-based instructional strategies," *American Journal of Physics*, 59 (1991) p. 891.

27. J. M. Wilson and E. F. Redish, "Using computers in teaching physics," *Physics Today* (Jan. 1989) p. 34.

28. *Science Achievement in Seventeen Countries*, International Association for the Evaluation of Educational Achievement (Pergamon Press, 1988).

Notes

1. The CUPLE project is supported in part by grants from IBM and the Annenberg/CPB Project.

2. A five-inch CD can hold up to 650 Megabytes of data. This is equivalent to a stack of more than a thousand standard 5.25 "floppy disks"—a stack more than 12 feet high. This can hold more than a hundred thousand pages of typewritten text.

3. Adapted from Brown, Collins, and Duguid, ref. [3].

Chapter 12

4. For example, solving for the corrections due to a small air resistance force on a projectile would require substantial experience with differential equations, a skill not usually possessed by the introductory student. This subject is often considered by physics majors at the junior level and there the problem is simplified (a linear or viscous force law is used rather than the more correct quadratic drag force) to permit the use of analytic methods. However, with the computer and a simple numerical solution using the Euler and half-step methods, the problem (with the correct force law) can be easily solved by the introductory student.

5. We use the term "mental model" here to stand for the set of propositions, rules, and ideas that an individual has about a particular phenomenon. This is the sense discussed by Donald Norman and others in their articles in the collection *Mental Models* [12]. The term has been used by others in the cognitive literature to have other more specialized meanings.

6. An individual whose intuition about motion is based on walking may get into trouble when driving on a highway at high speeds. Inadequate understanding of the concepts of linear and angular momentum can lead to tailgating (which produces "chain reaction" collisions on highways) and rollovers.

7. The three equations represented here, F = ma (Newton's second law of motion), F = –kx (Hooke's law for springs), and s = 1/2 gt² (distance a particle falls in time t under the influence of flat-earth gravity) are de riguer in any beginning physics course. Yet they have widely different structures and ranges of validity. Newton's second law is the general principle of classical dynamics. It determines the response of any particle to forces and holds for all systems from the scale of molecules to galactic clusters. Hooke's law is a phenomenological principle that describes how some systems deform in response to (small) forces. The projectile equation is a very special case, useful only for describing the motion of projectiles as long as the earth is approximated as flat and air resistance effects can be ignored.

8. Two excellent examples of such systems are the Personal Science Laboratory (PSL) from IBM and the Universal Laboratory Interface (ULI) from Vernier Software.

9. This is not to imply that material should always be presented in a non-linear fashion. Some material is inherently linear; and while people are learning to work in more flexible environments, linear approaches will continue to be valuable.

10. CUPLE software has been prepared for the PSL and ULI.

11. CUPLE software support has been developed for the VideoLogic card and IBM's M-Motion card. This software will work with any videodisc players supported by these cards.

12. Some of the materials to be included will be from String and Sticky Tape Experiments [3] and the Handbook of Physics Demonstrations [4].

13. In future versions we also plan to accomodate compressed digital video delivered over high speed networks.

14. We have chosen the map metaphor to explicitly invoke what is perhaps most people's most common experience with non-linear structured information.

15. The teacher will do this with "course-design software" associated with the Browser. The main outline of the selections will be chosen by the software in response to the teacher's selection of style and orientation. After this selection, the teacher will be able to modify the choices recommended by the system.

16. There have been changes since then, but Robert Millikan's 1902 course [seq reference Millikan10] is remarkably similar to what is taught today. The overlap in content (excluding electromagnetism which is not covered in Millikan's text) is approximately 75%.

17. Some of the important developments that are not included in the introductory physics course are: the discovery that the basic laws of the universe are not classical but quantal in character; the understanding of the microscopic structure of matter and how that structure determines the properties of materials; the way phase transitions occur; the fact that "classical" does not mean "predictable"; and many others.

18. Very few research papers on physics education are produced in a year and they are read by a very small fraction of the physics community.

13

Collaborative Virtual Communities: Using *Learning Constellations*, A Multimedia Ethnographic Research Tool

Ricki Goldman-Segall

Introduction

Multimedia ethnographic tools help build collaborative virtual communities among researchers, the researched, and the multiple users of the research by sharing not only the video and the text data, but also the interpretations. Described in this chapter is the rationale for and use of a specific multimedia environment called *Learning Constellations*—originally designed to explore the plurality of children's thinking styles (Goldman-Segall, 1990b, 1991a). Not only is *Learning Constellations* an example of a multimedia environment which promotes the making of connections and building of links among ethnographic video and text segments, but it is also an example of an environment for children or adults to become social creators of meaning. One young girl's relational style of thinking illustrates the importance of our continuing to design and use multimedia tools which have the potential to help us create meaning by making sense of the world through making connections and building links among discrete elements. The case study about this pre-teenager, Mindy, is particularly compelling when one closely examines the need for young women to weave their personal experiences into appreciated narratives. Projections for this method of multimedia ethnographic investigation will be directed at laying a foundation for future video studies concerning learners' needs for environments which foster connectedness, interdependence, intimacy, cooperation, and multiple points of view.

Why Use Multimedia for Ethnographic Investigation?

Many theorists and practitioners of ethnography and epistemology are beginning to ask themselves how to use emerging technologies as tools for their investigations. Increasingly, ethnographers are contemplating the use of computer-based systems to analyze text and video data, a method referred to in this chapter as "multimedia ethnography." Epistemologists are also unwrapping the layers hidden by conventional methodological tools. This section addresses three reasons for ethnographers and epistemologists to use multimedia tools. These reasons became clear to me as the three-year video ethnography I conducted of grade four and five children at a computer-rich elementary school in Boston, Massachusetts evolved. However, the crystallization of these ideas occurred in the final phases of building and using the tool, *Learning Constellations* (hereafter, often referred to as LC). Using LC to analyze and to share both the data and the analyses were instrumental in making sense of the video I had selected and placed on six videodiscs.

   These three reasons for conducting multimedia ethnography are: that the process of making discoveries and the process of communicating those discoveries are both enhanced as a recursive reaction, within the data and among the users; that the meaning of an event, action, or situation can be negotiated as "thick descriptions" as layered and contextualized narratives are created (Geertz, 1973; Bruner, 1986; Mishler, 1986; Etter-Lewis, 1991; Sacks, 1989); and that using multimedia ethnographic tools, such as *Learning Constellations,* presents a possible alternative paradigm to the current "instructionist" approach within the educational system.

Multimedia for Integrating Discovery and Communication
To situate this discussion of multimedia technology as an ethnographic tool for epistemological exploration, one needs to consider two strong currents within the educational community: collaboration on group projects and reflection upon the processes of creating, discovering, and inventing (Schon, 1991; Salomon, Perkins & Globerson, 1991; Granott, 1991). This movement tends to run in concert with the historical foundations of constructionist or constructivist learning which proposes that learning occurs best as a result of doing, creating, and building (e.g., Piaget, 1927; Montessori, 1967; Dewey, 1938; Papert, 1986). Theories of

concrete learning promote the manipulation of real or virtual objects. Proponents of constructionism point to the intrinsic motivational effects of building, designing, and playing (Malone, Lepper, Miyake & Cohen, 1987; Bruner, 1966, 1986). According to recent constructionist literature, we are able to construct our knowledge and also represent meaning concretely with our tools (Harel & Papert, 1991; Wilensky, 1991). Moreover, we engage in social learning through interacting with each other using our tools. Tools, in this epistemological sense, can be our language, our culture, or any vehicle for construction of meaning. Ivan Illich defines "convivial" tools as those being simple to use, accessible to all, and beneficial for humankind (Illich, 1973). Indeed, for Illich, a condom and a toothbrush are two examples of convivial tools. In this chapter, I use the term "convivial tool" to mean a device for social construction of meaning, with the potential to enhance communication and/or discovery.

Multimedia tools promote both the making of discoveries about the subject one is studying as well as the communicating of the discoveries. Each process is enriched and deepened. By using these tools to communicate one's discoveries, a recursive process is started which feeds back into the original data—"thickening" (Geertz, 1973) or layering the original video documentation so that new discoveries are made (Goldman-Segall, 1988, 1989c). As the multimedia system is used, people interact with the data, leaving their ideas printed in the documents with annotations and text footnotes. Moreover, they leave records of their travels by building Video Footnotes and Video Constellations—clusters of video segments which have been selected by an individual user and attached to documents and transcripts for themselves and others to view (see figures 13.2, 13.3, 13.4, 13.5, and 13.6 starting on p. 282). As users comment on comments, annotate annotations, and slice the video segments more closely, a virtual community of users is created. Users communicate with the travels of other users; they return to a place once visited to find that others have added new levels of understanding to what they had selected as significant. This process of being able to enter into the significant segments of others and to create meaning for oneself based on the meaning assigned by other users creates a communal construction of meaning.

In the summer of 1990, Maureen Hansen, a teacher from San Jose, California worked with *Learning Constellations*. She wrote about her experiences using *Learning Constellations* and the videodiscs in the following way:

From the notes of Maureen Hansen: As I viewed the material on the laserdiscs, in a non-sequential way, I was guided by topics at first, then I "hooked into" a particular child, and followed that child. I found myself reacting and analyzing quite independently from any of the suggested cues of the producer of the program. Then I thought, "Hot damn, this *is* a valuable tool." Yes, it has been structured with the premises, biases, and foci of one observer, but I am not limited or controlled by the structure inherent in *Learning Constellations*. I can choose my own non-orbital course, looping back, making lunar landings on many moons, and speeding light years beyond where the "mission command center" thought I was going! The analogy works because the ability of each viewer to pilot the craft is made possible by the branching nature of HyperCard. Layered on top of this are *Learning Constellation's* interactive aspects of adding observations through the notebook and suggesting alternative routes by developing a constellation. The material, the hours of film, has been edited. Yet, it seems that the individual chunks maintain their integrity. They are whole bites. This dedication to "purity" is essential if video is to be a valid research method. Also, the entire raw material must be preserved and made accessible to other serious researchers who might, someday, find meaningful segments from the tape on the figurative "cutting room floor." (1990)

This citation provides me with the understanding that my multimedia video-based ethnographic research environment can be appropriated by others to make their own discoveries. What I understand from this comment (and from the comments of many others who have used LC) is that users have an opportunity to "get close to" the selected video data and to build upon other's points of view. Users become researchers themselves, making new discoveries as they "pilot" their own "crafts," as Ms. Hansen would say. They leave their annotations and video footnotes, thereby communicating with the next user. Discovery and communication become much less distinct pursuits. They build upon each other, deepening, layering, and thickening the interpretation of the original documentation.

Multimedia for Integrating "Instructional" Paradigms

According to the venerated Harvard scholar Israel Scheffler, the traditional school curriculum is based on the tenets of empiricism, rationalism, and pragmatism (Scheffler, 1965). A colleague of Scheffler's, Zvi Lamm, describes the history of conflicting theories of instruction by naming three broad categories: Acculturation, Socialization, and Individuation. Only

Individuation addresses of the role of the individual learner as the focus of the learning process. As Lamm laments, schools are not guided by individuation. Schools are shaped around the notion that the learner is the proverbial empty vessel waiting to be filled by the knowledge existing in the world—mind as tabula rasa. Socializing the learner into accepting the standards of the dominant culture or acculturating the learner into taking on the values of that culture have originated from what Lamm calls a "monistic logic of imitation and molding" (1976, p. 15.) According to Lamm, Piaget refers to this method of instruction as:

the "receptive method" or the "method of transmission by the teacher." For Piaget, who developed the idea of activity as a means of learning and provided it with a scientific basis, there was no more negative method of teaching than that based on "reception" or "transmission."(1976, p. 15)

Paulo Friere, a radical educational thinker, calls this patter of instruction "the act of depositing" derived from the "banking concept of education" (Lamm, 1976, p. 15). The educator deposits knowledge into the learner like money is deposited into a bank. Other metaphors used to describe this method of instruction are what Postman and Weingartner call "vaccination" theory and Sartre calls "digestion" metaphor (Lamm, 1976, p. 16). The role of the educator is to find the right fix and to get that stuff taken into the system!

Over the past decade, opportunities to change not only our thinking about instruction, but also to change the act of instruction have become a possibility. The introduction of constructionist computer software such as Seymour Papert's Logo is a response to this change. Papert has proposed that individuals can take charge of their own learning using Logo, an object-oriented programming language. However, it seems that Papert has reconsidered his original vision of one computer for each child in America by the year 2000, given the current economic constraints. What he has not conceded, however, is that there are underlying constructionist themes in Logo that help the individual learners learn about their own solving of problems. These theories can make an impact on changing the way we think about "instruction."

Multimedia tools can expand our way of thinking about our own thinking more profoundly than computer software that does not incorporate video with text. Browsing through video and text, searching, annotating, linking text with video, and clustering discrete segments into meaningful chunks are ways to think about linking our various thinking processes. In fact, we link visual images, visual text, and verbal language and sounds in the real, not virtual, world quite regularly. Unfortunately, we do not see these connecting activities as being significant because they are associated with commonsense type functions that traditionally have been defined as women's work or women's ways of talking (Tannen, 1990). We seem to respect these activities only when they are conducted in the artistic realms of composing, writing, and painting—especially in works of collage and montage. In spite of the fact that these connecting activities are also the stuff of social relationships, conversations, and negotiations, they have only recently become 'accepted' as interesting: noted scholars are now investigating the making of connections (Gilligan, 1990; Fox Keller, 1983, 1985), and the linking of neural networks as ways to think how to build intelligent machines and robots (Fodor & Pylyshyn, 1988; Bereiter, 1991). What Brian Appleyard points out as needing to be changed is the fact that, throughout the centuries, the ability to connect and build webs of meaning have not been rewarded. Instead, we have been taught how to detach ourselves from our observations for the purpose of repeatability, testability and objectivity.

Most scientists still hold to the central element of the classical faith—that what they are doing is learning real things about a real world. And, if you do cling to that faith, then the subjectivity of which [Barbara] McClintock speaks is a serious form of heresy. It mixes the human with the inhuman, masculine mind with feminine nature. It is witchcraft. (1991, p. 6)

(Appleyard also makes the claim that there should be a Nobel Prize for witchcraft in order to celebrate the intuitive voice in understanding the total spectrum of human inquiry.)

The question is how can constructionist ethnographic multimedia tools in the educational system be used to open, extend, and even change the traditional instructional paradigms? Children, teachers, and researchers are beginning to think about themselves as "partners in cognition" (Salomon, Perkins, & Globerson, 1991). The belief in reflective collaboration has begun to spread in many domains (e.g., Diaute, 1988; Erickson, 1991). Teachers, children, and researchers see themselves as learners united in an interactive process where meaning is created through sharing narratives gleaned from real life experiences (e.g., Cole, 1989; Bar-On, 1991; Sacks, 1989; Schon, 1991). Using multimedia tools, communities share their research perspectives with each other and with other communities of users, creating what Geertz calls "commensureability" (1983).

In a talk at Harvard in the fall of 1990, the erudite Jerome Bruner spoke about how an individual reader can have multiple readings of a text (Bruner, 1990); each user interpreting a text by "recreating the virtual text in his mind as he reads." He noted that the interpretive processes become "loosened by the text in the reader's mind." What I would like to add to Bruner's notion of *the reader in the text* is that in a multimedia environment "texts" are text and video which are shared—multiple readings are loosened in the multiple readers' minds as they share the content from multiple perspectives. Readers are not separate islands but interwoven communities. As we share our multiple perspectives, we reflect more deeply upon our interpretations. We leave records of our communication, layering our descriptions in order to negotiate our conclusions.

The aim is not to reach complete agreement, but to find a negotiated agreement wherein our conclusions will tend to fall within the same broad categories. Geertz might say that our descriptions of our understanding of a culture or subject are "imprisoned in their own detail" and defensible generalizations are difficult to make (Geertz, 1973, p. 24). Nonetheless, we try to establish a conceptual framework for validating interpretive work. The task of building such a conceptual framework is to generalize within the particular event. In other words, within each event, we start with a set of signifiers or symbolic acts (Keywords or Themes in Hypermedia). Then, we analyze how they fit into a framework. As each new interpretive research topic yields its theoretical frameworks, layers are added. As interpretations continue to be used, revised, and elaborated upon, they become more and more reliable. When they stop being used, they are reformulated or discarded.

In short, the search to define "symbolic acts" or *grains* of discrete elements may help build a less gender-biased, and a more connectionist, rooted conceptual framework. This search could bring about postmodernist discussions about how works being "loosened in the mind" of the learner can support an alternative educational model. This, in turn, could feed into current educational theories, provoking educators to think of themselves as researchers and more importantly, for educators to encourage the learners they work with to become researchers.

How could multimedia ethnographic tools contribute to building a recording the world. Students could use video and other tools to collect their observations of their families, of waves in a puddle, of insects—of processes, states, and events. Adults and children could work in teams to design or use pre-existing multimedia tools, such as LC, to analyze their observations. Themes (or signifiers) can form the building blocks for joining video, sound, and text data into clusters or constellations. Annotations and videonotes in an on-going data-base could be used, revised, and elaborated upon as new discoveries are made in different domains. Interdisciplinary cross-referencing would probably occur simultaneously as users find new paths through their networks.

To summarize, the learner in the multimedia environment is a unique member of a virtual community. S/he is an active not a passive learner, a participant observer, a participant recorder and participant theory-maker. Lamm's three categories become unified and integrated within this way of learning. The learner is social, part of the culture, and has the potential to fulfill her or his needs for individuation.

Multimedia for Negotiating Meaning

A related reason for using multimedia ethnographic tools is that meaning through multiple readings of texts is negotiated. As we reflect upon our theories about learning and teaching, we address such issues as whether knowledge is out there to be transmitted or inside the brain "to be loosened."

Although many of us might like to think that there is consensus about the social creation of knowledge, especially those participating in the writing of this volume, the majority of epistemologists and educators still support the notion that Knowledge exists out there—in books and libraries, records, movies, and archives of all sorts. The role of the educator, then, is to find some way of getting what is out there into the head of the learner. (Methods courses in teacher education programs throughout the US and Canada still spend a great deal of their time in teaching new teachers how to present a body of facts, rather than helping prospective teachers to understand that one version of a subject is not sufficient if we want learners to become social constructors of knowledge.) This is not to say that we do not know we need to question what is written. We all need to have opportunities to substantiate what we read by cross–referencing. A rich culture exists of checking out what is written by exploring other sources such as film documentation and oral histories. This needs to be emphasized if we embark on a road of constructing theories from negotiated understandings.

For example, consider the recent revival of Nazi or Neo-Nazi propaganda material in the Southern States of America and in Austria. Neo-Nazis say that the Holocaust is a figment of Jewish manipulation. Fortunately, these claims can be counteracted with oral histories, visual and text documentation, cross-referencing, and checking who documented "what," "where," and "why." In other words, events have occurred in the history of humankind which are to be understood as close as possible to how they happened. Documents and films contribute to the building of thick contextual understandings. Nevertheless, the building or construction of knowledge is done in the mind of the reader/viewer even if it is shaped and influenced by the writer of the text or the filmmaker of the visual documentation. There may not be one best answer; but there *may* be one best negotiated answer based on mutual agreement. Individuals who report the events they witness cannot know the whole picture. However, when many observations are pulled together over a period of time, we can begin to speak with certainty about what happened "out there" and to us, even if we do not know everything that happened from every person's point of view.

This issue is also illustrated by several current events in the legal and political arena. Over the closing months of 1991, television viewers became consumers of two media events, both related to gender harassment. The first was the claim by Professor Anita Hill that Judge Clarence Thomas had harassed her ten years ago. Those of us who watched the hearings on the nomination of Thomas for the US Supreme Court seemed to have privy to the same information as did those deciding. A related media event occurred two months later with the court case against William Smith, Senator Edward Kennedy's nephew. Patricia Bowman testified that Smith had raped her. In both situations, it was as if we were there on the bench with the jury. But were we? Did we see what the jury saw? Did we really have access to every perspective possible? How was our interpretation assisted by where the cameras were situated? Did eyes meet and "speak" to each other "off camera"? What was the substance of the discussions taking place behind the scenes? Most importantly, how does a continuous coverage of an event aid our understanding and how does it thwart our understanding? As Gilbert Ryle, an Oxford scholar, once asked, how do we distinguish the thinker of thoughts, *le Penseur*, from the person sitting with his chin resting on his hand (Ryle, 1971)? How do we really know the intent and the meaning of an event for those to whom something has happened? If we cannot know this, how do we judge it?

Some journalists believe that continuous video coverage alleviates the bias to some extent. Does it really? Can the total coverage become so saturated in itself and so overwhelming in its mediocrity that the viewer is numbed and left incapable of sifting through the salient parts of the trial? From my experience, I found that I prefer continuous coverage of the events to the reporters' "spinning" on a subject. My focus in these video-marathons is not only on what is said, but on the gestural language. I want to try to understand what is meant when a person moves his eyes to the right and then to the left repeatedly and quickly. I want to make sense of what I can see (through the cameraperson's eye) and then listen to the reporters' interpretations. However, this does not mean that I have the good understanding of what really happened to Professor Hill, Judge Clarence Thomas, Ms. Bowman, or to William Smith. Furthermore, my analysis is not of the cases, but of the video of the cases.

The problem, however, is much deeper than one of point of view in video recording—although I have previously stated (Goldman-Segall, 1989c; 1990a; 1991b) that the issue of point of view and the eye of the camera must always be taken into account, even in the most "objective" video data collecting. The problem is *how* we construct meaning and even truth from what we see or experience. For example, we know that Mr. Smith was acquitted and is therefore innocent according to the legal system. We know that Judge Thomas is now a member of the US Supreme Court. We also know that Professor Hill and Ms. Bowman have not changed their versions of what happened to them. Is everyone simply 'lying'? Or, are these issues so gender-related that we have no method of having one person's experiences validated in a public forum? Or, is it possible that the legal system is facing the same kind of problem that the educational one is facing—that of not knowing how to come to terms with what is experienced by an individual and what can be proved (beyond a shadow of a doubt) as scientific truth. What seems to be missing in these and other cases is a platform for negotiated agreements reached through mediation.

Negotiating meaning through mediation theory and using multimedia have already been linked by Rosiland Gerstein in her doctoral dissertation called "Interpreting the Female Voice: an Application of Art and Media Technology" (1986). Gerstein discusses a multimedia interface and videodisc environment called *Marital Fractures* which she and Russell Sassnet built at MIT (1986). *Marital Fractures* gives a user access to documentary video on a couple's divorce. Gerstein interviewed and documented with video many encounters with this couple over several years. In fact, she was a good friend of the couple. Gerstein also intervened as a mediator in helping the couple deal with the practicalities of the divorce. What Gerstein accomplished with her work was not only to contribute to the designing of media technology as a tool for interpreting the female voice, but also to a possible future direction for multimedia design proposing that knowledge is linked to negotiated meanings. These negotiated meanings are not only happening on the level of the informants, the couple themselves, but on the level of the users.

Video Ethnography as Social Encounter with Self and Others

Historical Precedents for Using Video/Film for Research

What does it mean when we researchers refer to our video as *data?* Continually challenged by the emergence of video and computer technologies for recording, retrieval, selection, interpretation, analysis, and dissemination, researchers and practitioners alike have begun to reflect upon previous definitions that research data is text-driven. The historical roots of video as data are still quite tender. Video recording is a relatively new medium which first became accessible to those outside the broadcast studios in the late 1950s and early 1960s. However, film has been used for almost a century for fine-grained observations. (Around the turn of the century, photographer Edward Muybridge showed dancers, horses, and a host of people and animals "in motion" by shooting one picture close to another, creating the illusion of movement.) Margaret Mead and Gregory Bateson were using film as data as early as 1926. In a visionary article written in 1975, she spoke of the possible use and development of finer instruments for ethnographic investigation, in this way.

[W]ith properly collected, annotated and preserved visual and sound materials, we can replicate over and over again and can painstakingly analyze the same materials. As finer instruments have taught us more about the cosmos, so finer recording of these precious [anthropological] materials can illuminate our growing knowledge and appreciation of mankind. (1975, p. 10)

In fact, Mead also wrote how emerging visual technologies would be used in the educating students about observational methods.

The emerging technologies of film, tape, video, and, we hope, the 360 degree camera, will make it possible to preserve materials (of a few selected cultures, at least) for training students long after the last isolated valley in the world is receiving images by satellite. (1975, p. 9)

What strikes me as interesting is that Mead comments on how people will continue to study foreign cultures long after everyone is connected through some shared medium. For Mead, video transmission is a receptive or passive tool. The image that comes to mind is one of student ethnographers using film, tape, and video to understand exotic cultures while, simultaneously, these cultures are sitting in their tents watching *Dynasty* and *Wheel of Fortune*. In other words, what she did not foresee, or at least did not write about, in 1973, is that members of a given culture would have their own video tools to communicate from within their own culture to members of other cultures: penpals and friends sending each other video letters; business persons in Japan video-conferencing with their North American colleagues; or researchers, in geographically dispersed locations, calling up the same video clip from a common databank and collaborating with a shared desktop text and video editing tool. What we see happening down the road, not so far from where we are today, is that future ethnographers will not only be out in the field collecting data but be observing and recording the electronic intersection of cultures—or, what could be called the meeting place of virtual communities. This may sound far away from where we are today. It is not.

Television companies have already invested dearly in creating popular programs for members within the culture to show moments, often their most embarrassing moments, of their personal lives on television to members of the larger culture. Although this is a far cry from Geertz's notion of commensurability, the ability of one culture to communicate with another (or even to communicate within their culture) to the broader culture, something dramatic has changed in our thinking of the use of media. For example, in the 1960s, programs such as "Candid Camera," which showed moments of peoples' lives on network television, were filmed by a professional film crew consisting of directors, a team of writers, and camera persons. What the current programs do is to use videotapes filmed by oneself, or a friend, or a member of the family. The "other" or what we in ethnography often refer to as the "stranger" has come closer to home.

The camera has changed hands. This changing of hands, the filmmaker as the informant, is a relatively new phenomenon with only a few precedents in the past. There have been instances of ethnographic film-makers giving cameras to members of the culture they were studying to see how these individuals represented their societies. Some experimental documentary filmmakers and videographers address the fine line separating "who is filming" from "what or who is being filmed." An example is Fred Wiseman"s account of the lives of high school students in his film, *High School*. Wiseman followed a group of students as they roamed in and around their classes, the gym, and their home economics class to capture the disparity between what they were being taught and where they "were at." Wiseman gets involved in the lives of these students in order to comment on how unrelated to their lives the school system is. However close Wiseman comes to the point of view of the students, he is still "the outsider," describing the school culture from the stranger's perspective.

An example of how the camera changed hands is the way in which video was used as a democratization tool in the late 1960s; video became one of the important tools used in grass-roots interpersonal group therapy sessions. Members of the "me" generation turned the video-camera on themselves as part of a self-discovery process. This novelty faded by the late 1970s, and as times became more conservative—the camera turned away from self to a description of "me" in relation to others. The questions of the early eighties were: How does the individual fit into society (McElwee's *Backyard* or *Sherman's March*)? How are community or urban decisions made (Davenport's *New Orleans: A City in Transition*)?

The recent phenomenon of educators using video as a tool to study school cultures is relatively new. A breakthrough work is the study of preschools in Japan, China, and the United States conducted by Joseph

Tobin, Dana Davidson, and David Wu (1989). Interestingly, they mark their inspiration to conduct a multivocal ethnography from watching film ethnographer Linda Connor first show an informant, Jero, a movie she was filmed in and then interview her. Jero is a Balinese female shaman or medium who is the main character of Conner, Timothy Asch, and Patsey Ash's film, *Balinese Trance Seance* (1986). In the documentary, Jero enters into a trance to help grieving parents make contact with their dead child. Conners engages Jero in her reactions to the film, using the footage as a stimulant to probe Jero's memories of what she was thinking or feeling during the seance. Tobin, Davidson, and Wu pinpoint this event as the turning point in their own video research. They describe their own study as

... a telling and a retelling of the same event from different perspectives—an ongoing dialogue between Americans and Chinese, Americans and Japanese, and Chinese and Japanese.... [W]e introduce the voices of preschool teachers, parents, and administrators, who tell their own stories, creating their own texts that discuss, deconstruct, and criticize our account of their schools. Each of these texts reacts to earlier texts while never entirely replacing, subsuming, or negating them. (1989, p. 5)

Conceptually, their approach to conducting video ethnography was remarkably similar to my own study which began in the fall of 1985. My inspiration also occurred as a result of experiences with a documentary filmmaker. Richard Leacock, often called the father of the documentary, was then the head of the Film and Video Section of the MIT Media Lab (Leacock, 1975, 1986). Leacock's work demonstrates his uncanny sixth sense of knowing where to position the camera before an event occurs. *Canary Bananas*—a short black and white film Leacock made as a teenager about his life on the Canary Islands—greatly influenced my own filmmaking. *Canary Bananas* is a simple account about local people planting, harvesting, and packaging banana crops, surprisingly similar to early documentary films made in the Soviet Union about peasant life with the advent of technology. What influenced me was not the picture of life on the Canary Islands, but what a young teenager was able to understand about this life.

Watching *Canary Islands* gave me the idea that, under the right conditions, children would tell their best stories as "Directors" of the research project. What I envisioned was the growth of a video culture where filmmaking would become part of the daily culture of the school and children would not only tell the video ethnographer what they wanted to be filmed, but eventually *design and film their own narrative video "texts."* The role of the video ethnographers would be to analyze both their own video and the combined video of teachers and children from within the culture, thereby encouraging multiple points of view.

In practice, what I was able to accomplish over the years from 1985 to 1990 was to lay the foundations for creating video cultures. My goal was that researchers, teachers, and students would share their own video observations of themselves, of each other, and of their surroundings. In the following pages, I will describe the process of building an overall framework for building video cultures.

The Growth of Video Cultures

Video cultures begin when both the process and products of videotaping are shared among a group. Over the past seven years, I have been involved with the transmission of videotaping and video–analyzing skills to teachers, researchers, and to children. While working with Papert and our team of MIT researchers and teachers at *Project Headlight* in the Hennigan School in Boston over a five year period, I was also visiting a related community of teachers and children using Logo at the Gardiner Academy in San Jose, California. In both those Logo-based cultures, I had an opportunity to initiate the first steps in establishing video cultures.

In the early phase of my Hennigan study, both teachers and researchers watched footage I had been collecting. Discussions—about the nature of ethnographic footage, about what a child seemed to mean when he told a certain story, or about the way in which this footage could be accessed in a multimedia environment—were held periodically with teachers, researchers and cinematographer, Glorianna Davenport. Quite soon afterwards, fellow researchers began collecting video data in their studies—Idit Harel, Nira Granott, and Yasmin Kafai eventually integrating this activity in their own research paradigms (Harel, 1991; Granott, 1991; Kafai & Harel, 1991). In the second year of Project Headlight, with the help of Davenport and Leacock, I ran several video workshops for the incoming doctoral students focusing on both the technical aspects of working with video and with the conceptual issues in using video as data.

During the annual two-week summer Logo workshops for teachers, mini-courses for researchers and teachers in our group were given by both myself and Nira Granott. These workshops dealt with skills in using the camera and skills in viewing what what filmed. Meanwhile, throughout those years, I was visiting the teachers in San Jose, filming what was happening there and sharing what I was filming at the Hennigan School. My most coveted memories are the faces of young children in California watching the video of children in Boston. Of the two cultures, the teachers from the Gardiner Academy appropriated these ideas with the greater vigor. To date, they have purchased cameras, monitors, and are preparing for multimedia workstations. They are interested in encouraging children to explore a subject using their own videotaped observations and to use a software, such as *Learning Constellations*, for accessing the video on videodiscs.

In short, these skills in shooting, viewing and editing occurred over a slow but steady period. At *Project Headlight* in Massachusetts, these skills have developed gradually as Harel and Kafai continue to use video in their work, to explore the use of *Learning Constellations* as a multimedia model, and to adapt Logo into a software that can also access video. The Gardiner Academy's *Project Mindstorm* in California also continues to grow as teachers encourage students to use the camera and become aware of how they communicate to others what they see.

My own interest in creating video cultures also continues in my new location at the University of British Columbia, Canada. I teach courses on Multimedia Ethnography and am currently involved in research in a small middle school in a Vancouver suburb where students have used *Learning Constellations* to build their own constellations or clusters of video in order to build narratives about the video. The teachers and the school librarian are actively engaged in providing students with video skills and the beginnings of "a video culture."

Role of Video Ethnographer in Establishing a Video Culture
Four main roles seem to stick out in my mind as being the most significant in becoming a video ethnographer in the particular video cultures I have studied. They are: *becoming a friend* with a camera by encouraging children, teachers, and fellow researchers to share the direction; *becoming a facilitating participant recorder* by training fellow researchers, teachers

and children how to use video for observation; *becoming a storyteller* by selecting chunks of video sequences for juxtapositions of narratives; *becoming a navigator* by exploring and spreading the use of video technologies into new intellectual, territories. The questions I dealt with in each of these roles were: What does it mean to videotape as a friend? What do we learn about the person being videotaped and what do we learn about the video ethnographer in the process of videotaping? Whose story is being told in the videotape? How significant is it that we introduce the notion of intimacy into our research paradigms? None of these roles occurred linearly or without overlap, but they do provide the spectrum of my own experience.

However, the question most asked of video ethnographers is not focused on the role of the video ethnographer but on how we can rely on our video as data given the personal nature of the medium? What I came to realize was that one could not make video data objective, but one could change one's attitude toward the need for objective depersonalized data (Goldman-Segall, 1990b, 1991b). The assumption that video data needs to be "objective" in order to draw conclusions is challenged at each step in my study because video researchers must make subjective decisions about: whether to hold the camera or place it on a tripod; when to turn the camera on and when to turn it off; whether to record the entire event or to select parts of the event such as significant conversations, interviews, or presentations; and whether to share with informants and fellow researchers what is filmed or to screen out controversial moments. The issue is not how to make video research acceptable to empirical method-ological approaches, but how to rethink the way in which the video of the video ethnographer and the informants enters into the lives of those who are members of the culture and changes their way of viewing and expressing what they are trying to understand. As Mary Bateson points out, what we need to understand is the

. . . resonances between the personal and the professional. . . . You avoid mis-takes and distortions not so much by trying to build a wall between the observer and the observed as by observing the observer—observing yourself—as well, and bringing the personal issues into consciousness. . . . Then you look at the record to understand the way in which observation and interpretation have been affected by personal factors, to know the characteristics of any instrument of observation that make it possible to look through it but that also introduced a degree of distortion in that looking. (1984)

The following subsections describe the way in which the personal need to resonate with the professional in this approach to video research. This description will also show that using the video data with multimedia tools contributes to the building of a community of researchers and informants sharing their perspectives, their data and their analyses to build convivial ethnographic research environments.

Overcoming obstacles to become a friend with a camera   I cannot say that my first video ethnography at the Hennigan School started with a feeling of conviviality. It took one school term before I started looking forward to going to the school. My original reaction to the overall institutional atmosphere prevented me from willingly spending my time at the Hennigan School. In fact, while I was still only writing field notes, I found myself drowning in my frustration at hearing children being yelled at and punished. The camera gave me a tool to express what I saw; it gave me the ability to not only describe, but to create. As my early field notes reflect, the combination of the physical structure and the emotional atmosphere sent shivers down my back:

The Hennigan School is not a model school environment. The lasting impression is one of gray concrete covered with graffiti—and the graffiti seems a fitting response to the intransigence of the rigid physical structure. The building is low and sprawling, with no lawns except for a huge empty field in the back of the school. In a far corner of the field a few climbing structures are available to the children at recess. The girls, mostly of African-American, Hispanic descent, play skip rope while talking, braiding hair, and watching each other on the black asphalt of the parking lot. Smaller groups of girls and boys, in smaller gender-based groups, often hang out by the climbing apparatus, climbing or playing games. The boys tend to use the open field for kicking a few balls around, and running in all directions.

At recess, playground supervisors monitor the children. (I rarely see a teacher outdoors supervising or playing with the children.) The concern of the playground supervisors is to maintain a sense of order and to ensure the children's safety. In the name of protecting the children from harm, adults involve themselves in the interactions among the children. Often they are involved in resolving conflicts. The method most commonly used is one of singling out certain children to monitor an individual's behavior. One of the children in my study named Josh says that, when yelling at a group of children, certain adults will make up a name, such as Jill, on the likelihood that one of the children's name's will be Jill. Or if no one's name is Jill, the children will still be brought to attention for fear of their name being used next.

At the end of recess, an old-fashioned hand bell is rung by the head supervisor; the children return to their classrooms either when their teachers come to fetch them or when the supervisor leads them in lines to their classroom. They walk in rather scraggly lines through large grey concrete hallways and through the open area pods into their classrooms.

Adding to my initial reaction to the school was the nagging thought that our research efforts would be undermined by the fact that we were such a large group of researchers working with one section of the school consisting of twelve to fifteen teachers and approximately three hundred children. Some of my colleagues decided to conduct research of an empirical nature. Part of my search for an alternative method was a reaction to these two factors. In a sense, I wanted to be the proverbial "fly on the wall" so as not to add to the testing or questioning of children by teachers and researchers. I decided to watch, listen (with the camera), and become friends with children who wanted or needed a friend with whom to talk.

Given my desire to listen, children quickly related to me me as someone to talk to, to play with, and someone who cared about their own image of themselves. While videotaping in the computer pods, a child named James got upset with me because I did not go to him when he asked me to play. I said, "James, I have to work now." He looked at me with total confusion and said, "I thought you came here to play!"

To become a member of the community of children, I had to be able both to play while I worked and to work while I played. I had to be perceived as someone who was not going to evaluate them or to exercise any form of control over their behavior or their learning. If I was to be told authentic and personal thoughts, I could share my ideas with them but not instruct or supervise.

In the process of becoming a participating member of hundreds of videotaped conversations with children, I inadvertently fell upon things that I now believe would have remained behind closed doors if I had tried to ply them open (or only look for what we call in ethnography, shared meanings). In other words, I did not ask all children the same questions to compare answers. Instead, I tried to illicit stories which were meaningful for them. For several children, those stories reflect personal trials; for some, they illustrate part of a webbing of personal and social challenges; and for others, they resemble philosophical treatises.

Let me tell you, the reader, a short story about Andrew, a ten-year-old boy who invented stories on the spot. These stories showed as much about his personal life as it did his storymaking skills. In fact, he had never written a word of what he told me; he was a storyteller, working out serious crises occurring in his family. He tells me about an ugly duckling who has to prove to his family that he is brave.

Andrew: So another time when they were about to get shot by a hunter, flying in the air; the hunter was shooting bullets; the Ugly Duckling didn't [fly], he always wanted to play; he didn't want to learn how to fly, so he didn't. So he had to stay on the ground. He sees the hunter; he goes over and bites the hunter and his family gets away safely. And now they're starting to be convinced that the ugly duckling is brave, and it doesn't matter if he's ugly or not. It just matters how he acts, how he acts, what's his personality. And "THE END." (May, 1987)

The outstanding feature of this excerpt from his story is its autobiographical theme that the hero's saving others will win him the approval he is so anxiously awaiting. Andrew's main character is put in the position where he must first fight a shark and then a hunter. Fighting off the bad guys provides a way for Andrew's duckling to overcome his rejection. His family no longer sees him as being ugly; they begin to understand his brave personality through the way he acts. One is reminded of what another child once told me. He said that "ideas come from things that you experience. If you see people fighting, that's what you put in your picture." One can only speculate about Andrew's experiences as an inner-city child which make him feel that he has to win the admiration of others by fighting. As Andrew's teacher, Linda Moriarty said when she had just finished watching this video chunk:

Moriarty: That is so autobiographical to me, Ricki.
Ricki: How is it autobiographical?
Moriarty: I just feel a little bit now; you know, this could be very carried away or something, but I just feel that he is, trying to be important and, special. I don't know if it's brave or whatever; and he has such a reputation with his mother and with people of not being credible—you know, making up stories, doing all this stuff and he is bit by bit changing. But it's being accepted by his family; like, doing something special for the family and saving them or helping them and I think that's important. But getting recognized for that. He doesn't feel he's recognized for anything. He is talented, he is special, but his environment is not, it's not . . . He's not getting re-enforced at all. He's not fitting into the standard school environment because his writing skills and his behavior kinds of stuff are not the norm.

The fact that Andrew had family problems was no secret to Moriarty or to the school counsellor. His mother and father were no longer living together. His mother was young (from what Moriarty told me) and quite conscientious about appearance and language abilities but seemingly more concerned with her new relationship and than with Andrew. She regularly came to parent-teacher evenings asking how Andrew was doing—parents of the other children had been complaining about Andrew's influence on their children. Moriarty made me aware of the mother's feeling that Andrew was a bit too much for her to deal with. Therefore, it did not surprize Moriarty, the school counsellor, or myself to find out that Andrew was moved to a foster home later that year.

Finding the many pieces of Andrew's story took a long time. It took longer to get a handle on what these pieces meant. However, I am quite certain that the complete case study (as told in my dissertation) and the video portraits (on videodisc) would not be as rich and informative if Andrew and I had not been friends at that time. Moreover, I think that I might not have told my story about him with the care that he deserves had I not personally been involved in his life.

Becoming a participant recorder   Another role for the video ethnographer in creating video cultures is to facilitate others in the community who are interested in becoming participant recorders by viewing video with them, demonstrating video recording and editing skills for their own purposes, and sharing video observations.

My own style of shooting is what I call "affectionate" because I am always in eye contact with those I have conversations. The camera is held on my hip or lap (with the viewfinder pointed up and the microphone in my left hand or on a table.) The camera is held close to the center of the action to recreate the feeling of intimacy for the viewer. With the camera pointed up to the child, the viewer has to look up to the child. Another technique is to videotape an interaction for as long as the interaction lasts giving the informant the knowledge that she or he can take time to explain. From time to time, I step back from the activity to pan the overall atmosphere to provide context for a given scene.

Papert used to speak of my style of using video for eliciting responses by saying:

She hangs around the school and tries to get pictures, unobtrusively, of what the children are doing and sometimes tries to use her presence as a way of evoking discussion. By interviewing the children and letting the children interview her, they talk about things in different ways, and this is part of the "picture-making" becoming part of the culture of the school. (Goldman-Segall, 1991b)

Papert's point is not only about my style of doing video ethnography, but also about how emerging technologies are appropriated by the members of the culture exposed to the technologies. Papert believes that when we think about new technologies such as computers, we need to think about how technologies extend our natural cultures so that new kinds of things can happen to people.

Similarly, when we think about how the participant recorder—the researcher—who uses video technology as a tool affects the culture of children and teachers, we need to address how informants appropriate the video into their own lives, and how the introduction of video technology extends and enriches the existing culture. It is my experience that, when permitted, those being researched, the informants, do begin to appropriate the technology by "directing" the research. The participant recorder becomes the camera person following the direction of the informants. It is at this turning point that the informant shows the researcher what paths to follow.

In short, one becomes less a researcher in the eyes of informants and more a transitional friend with whom to share thoughts and have good talks. In the Hennigan School *Project Headlight* ethnography as well as in my current one, close attention is paid to using the camera as a vehicle not only to observe conversations, but to assist in becoming transitional friends. Children informants often refer to the camera in the interviews or conversations; adults do the same. They bring the camera into our conversations by waving at the camera and saying things like,

Josh: And like when they made video cameras, like you're shooting me now. When they made them, they probably thought about cameras. You take a picture, each second, if you put them together, you make a video, a scene happening. That's how somebody discovered it!

Trust, in these situations, is built over time as those filmed see themselves in the video footage, see each other, and have some opportunity to use the camera themselves, often to turn it on me, becoming participant recorders themselves.

Becoming a storyteller and a navigator   The third and fourth thematic roles in establishing these particular video cultures occurred in two extended phases of learning to be a video storyteller and a multimedia navigator. To tell my story of the children in this culture, I edited several short movies and then six videodiscs over a period of approximately five years. Two short documentaries called *The Growth of a Culture* (1987) and *Children are the Future* (1989a) were shared not only with teachers and researchers of the Hennigan School project, with a myriad of visitors to the Media Lab, with the children and teachers of *Project Mindstorm* in California, and with the children of the Hugh Boyd Elementary School in Richmond, British Columbia, but they were also shown internationally at several conferences and tens of presentations by Papert and myself. Reactions to *The Growth of a Culture* are usually focused on either Mindy, Andrew, or John. Children are especially curious about who these videotaped children are and what they like to do when they are not using Logo. Adults seem genuinely amazed that ten year olds can speak of the way electrons moves in a microchip with such clarity. This Hennigan culture was seen through my particular point of view extending the Logo culture far beyond those grey graffiti filled walls I initially felt imprisoned by.

The question is: how does this kind of video storytelling and navigating (or exploring) affect the creation of a video a culture or the creation of a virtual community with video? My best answer to this question is that video is shared by the community and multiple interpretations are encouraged (MacKay & Davenport, 1989; Davenport, Smith, & Pincever, 1991). This sets a precedent for a different kind of interaction among the informants and the researchers. Researcher as storyteller and (explorer or) navigator is not as formidable a role as researcher as pillar of truth and justice. From my perspective, it is also more honest.

Early in my own video storytelling phase, I realized that only linear editing would not yield interesting material to analyze. As visual ethnographers say, linear editing is a re-creation of reality, another kind of telling. In editing for linear presentation, the editor tries to communicate the essence of the experience by juxtaposing images that fit together to build meaning. What I wanted was to share the actual recorded moments, as closely as I could, to viewers who could build their narratives and their interpretations. (Or, at least, build upon my own.) I wanted to put together a non-linear story where users could navigate through new epistemological territory. I wanted to give the user the sense that she or he was moving through intellectual domains, or thematic thinking spaces.

To do this, I first needed to find a way to organize and categorize the extensive video data I had collected. My colleagues and I designed a HyperCard tool called *Star Notes*. Within *Star Notes* (see figure 13.1) I could log the video, find recurring themes and create stacks of those themes. Each chunk of video would be described on each card in *Star Notes*. There were spaces for the following information: Name (of scene), Description (of scene), Source (which tape number it came from), Date (that the video was shot), and most important, Keywords, (which later became the themes).

Each card contained a list of categories, or Keywords—stacks of cards in the same category which were instantly accessible by clicking on the name of the Keyword. The main themes underlying the observations emerged using *Star Notes*, and this guided the real estate of the six videodiscs (see Goldman-Segall, 1990b).

Star Notes is an efficient tool to thematize the video and organize the real estate of the videodiscs but it is not a navigational tool. It did not access the video. To do this, my colleagues and I built another tool. We called this navigational tool *Learning Constellations* (Goldman-Segall, Orni Mester, & Greschler, 1989b).

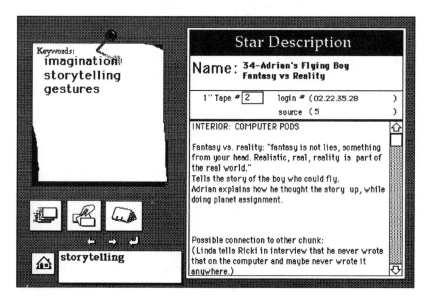

Figure 13.1
HyperCard Tool called Star *Notes* for logging video chunks

This last phase in creating a video culture was the phase of becoming a multimedia navigator. Now that the videodiscs were being pressed and the (linear) story was assembled, I needed a way to navigate through the video to analyze, to share my stories, and encourage others to build their own. For three years I had been developing a mental model of what the system should be able to do. Collaborating with filmmaker Vivian Orni Mester, and HyperCard builder David Greschler led to the building of the storytelling tool *Learning Constellation*—a HyperCard application for browsing, searching, and juxtaposing video and text segments. Using *Learning Constellations*, the user travels through domains or *galaxies*.

The first galaxy of LC is the Videodisc Table of Star Chunks where there is a complete listing of the chunks of video (see figure 13.2). In this galaxy each Video Star Chunk has the complete text transcripts. There are also tools available for searching through the database and for annotating individual chunks (figure 13.3). The text annotations are stored and can be retrieved in the Personal Notebook (see figure 13.4). All notes are grouped chronologically and thematically at the time they are created.

The second galaxy is the text of what I once called The Dissertation. Its current generic name is the Text Star Chunks. Each Text Star Chunk has video footnote tools and text footnote tools which enable the user to attach video or text to the written document (see figure 13.5). This function makes the document a growing collaborative archive.

The third galaxy is the The Linear Presentation—a short linear video presentation of the video for those users who want to see the sequential story. (Presently, the documentary video called *The Growth of a Culture* is available on my videodisc presentation. However, I envision that other users would just as easy be able to put their short linear presentations in this galaxy.)

The fourth galaxy is The Constellation Galaxy where users can either select a cluster of video chunks from an existing list of clusters built by other users, or build one of their own (see figure 13.6).

In short, LC allows: the manipulation of video observations and text; access to transcripts of the video, textual annotations, video annotations; and an interactive text document. It is possible to browse, search, annotate, define chunks, cluster or group chunks, and to write one's analyses from within a document domain. Integral to the system are navigational tools through the units of *star* chunks of video and text—

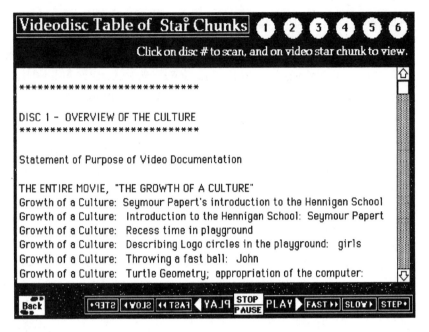

Figure 13.2
Videodisc Table of Star Chunks for access to video chunks on discs

tools for searching through the different domains or *galaxies,* for clustering *stars* chunks into *constellations,* and tools for assisting interpreting the data and building theories. (For a more detailed description of how *Learning Constellations* works, see Goldman-Segall, 1990a, 1990b, 1991a.)

All these functions were part of the video ethnographer building the video culture in the community.

Conclusion: Using LC to Create Virtual Communities

Women's lives have always been grounded in the physical by the rhythms of their bodies and the giving and receiving of tokens of love.

—Mary Catherine Bateson, *Composing a Life*

What I have claimed in this chapter is that a multimedia ethnographic research tool helped me to make discoveries about my data as well as to contribute to the building of a video culture in the schools and universities within which I have had the opportunity to learn. I would like to

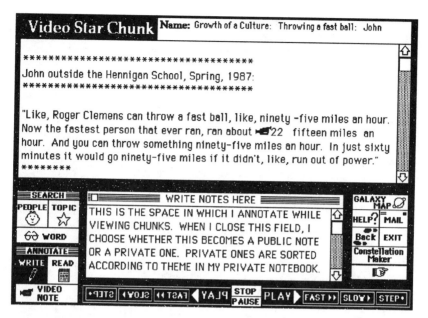

Figure 13.3
Video Star Chunk with transcripts: Access to Searching Tools, Annotations Tools, and Video Footnote Tools

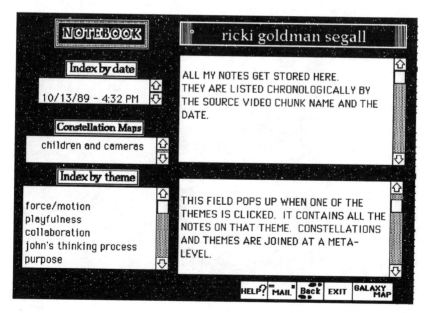

Figure 13.4
The Private Notebook: with indexing chronologically and thematically

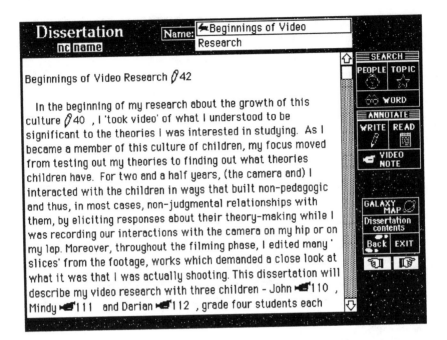

Figure 13.5
Dissertation Chunk (now called Text Star Chunk): with Video and Text
Footnote Tools represented as icons in the text

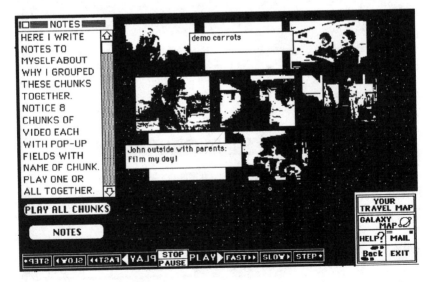

Figure 13.6
An existing "Constellation" or cluster of video chunks: "Children and Camera"
with digitized images and notepad

substantiate this claim in this last section by describing how my experiences with a ten-year-old girl named Mindy became meaningful while using *Learning Constellations*. I would also like to show how working with the data of Mindy enabled me to rethink the nature of the learning experience, that is, that it should address issues to do with making connections and building links.

Video data becomes "more interesting" through multiple perspectives
For a researcher who believes herself to be somewhat of the feminist persuasion, I initially reacted to my own data of Mindy with great reluctance. I will explain why this was so, and then describe how my attitude changed through working collaboratively on LC.

Mindy seemed to be the antithesis of someone I would find "interesting." When I decided to study with Papert, I hoped to show that girls, and especially girls from the non-mainstream non-White culture, could do as well as or better than White middle-class boys on the computer.

What I did not understand about my own objective was that I was applying the white male standard of what doing well in computers, science, mathematics or history means. Imagine my initial delight when I started videotaping Kathy, a very quick-minded mathematically inclined ten-year-old African-American girl who was a "dynamite" programmer! Kathy worked intensely and competently at the computer. Often, as I videotaped her, she would be so engaged in working out a computer bug, that she did not notice my sitting beside her.

The problem I was struggling with was how to get a handle on the development of a girl with excellent social skills like Mindy who was mostly interested in thinking about boys (and drawing girls) and who, as a result, was not doing very well in her course work. In fact, I believe that I did not focus my attention and the attention of the camera on Mindy as much as I did on Kathy and two boys named Josh and Andrew because I was still evaluating success in the traditionally male way. Only after spending two years in data selection and analysis while working with LC and the videodiscs did I begin to realize that what was happening to Mindy and what has been happening for generations to many young girls who approach puberty is that they "drop out" of being smart—they lose in sports to make the boys look better and they feign behavior which will help them achieve male and older female approval, at the expense of their intellectual needs.

Working with the videodisc data of Mindy (through searches, links, and making connections *randomly*) flooded my memory of the girls of my childhood, who had to come to terms with not having interpersonal skills recognized as being very interesting, even by women teachers. Working on the video data of Mindy has taught me compassion instead of anger, which was my earlier response to female subjugation through gender role stereotyping. Instead of trying to remake Mindy into a male scientist or to prove that Mindy and other girls could be as good as boys in the sciences, I began to see the value of the female voice in working out very complicated human dramas. Some may contend that these dramas are not the stuff of scientific investigation. It will be my contention, that until we begin to accept the interpersonal skills of persons whose main focus is the lives of human beings, we will never begin to reach below the tip of the iceberg at solving the fundamental balance between humankind and science. As Bateson so elegantly states:

For all of us, continuing development depends upon nurture and guidance long after the years of formal education, just as it depends on seeing others ahead on the road with whom it is possible to identify. A special effort is needed when doubts have been deeply implanted during the years of growing up or when some fact of difference raises barriers or undermines those identifications, but all of us are at risk, not only through childhood but through all the unfolding experiences of life that present new problems and require new learning. (1984, p. 202)

When thinking about Mindy's dreams—her aspirations and her fantasies, the nature of our biases about home and family are put into question. Let me describe Mindy to you from notes I have made while using LC:

Mindy often had her nails painted red and wore frilly clothes to school. On regular school days, it was not unusual to see Mindy wearing an off-white satin dress, white lace stockings, and white dress shoes. I often asked myself whether or not Mindy chose to wear this dress to school, whether it was hers or an older cousin's old "going out" clothes (which needed to be worn before she grew out of them), or, whether she was expected to look like a pretty little girl to please her family.

When I asked Mindy what she liked doing on the computer, she first mentioned how she liked "discoverin' stuff" and playing. However, as she caught herself saying the word "playing," she nodded her head from side to side wistfully. Watching this gesture and hearing her say the word "playing" gave me the clue to pursue her notion of play a bit further. For Mindy, playing on the computer meant making, or programming, girls:

Ricki: What do you like doing on the computer?
Mindy: I like discoverin' stuff. And I like playing.
Ricki: You like playing?
Mindy: Yeah! That should be the first thing I should say.
Ricki: What kind of things do you play on the computer?
Mindy: I play games, and I make, like, girls. I love making girls—on paper, on computer, on cardboard, on chalk, on anything, chalkboard!

Indeed, one of Mindy's favorite Logo projects was a graphic illustration of a girl in a dress with a bright yellow triangle as the skirt.

As I mentioned, my initial reaction to her obsession with making girls was that this was not particularly interesting. Even though I spent many hours with her over the years, I did not think my data would be very interesting to others. In retrospect, I must have known, intuitively, that Mindy held a clue for many of the issues I hoped to explore. What I did not know was how to pull it together to make sense of it, or to describe it to others, or to communicate something significant about gender and computers or gender and science.

What happened to change my perspective? If my notes had been fieldnotes, I think I could not have "seen" what was in front of my eyes. However, because my data was on video and then on videodisc, I could share selected observations with others. I could leave myself vulnerable to the scrutiny of others, in some sense. We would watch Mindy together and talk about my questions, my assumptions about marriage and monogamy. We could try to get below the surface of what Mindy was saying to what Mindy was hoping would happen in her life. Sometimes, these hopes and aspirations seemed totally mainstream gender-biased, from my perspective. But, I was not seeing the forest from the trees. Mindy was making her best shot at finding a role for herself within the culture. She was taking on these roles and working out scenarios for how to maintain her personal integrity in a world which she probably perceived as being filled with coercion.

Watching, in the presence of my colleagues, the following conversation I once had with Mindy about marriage provided me with a deeper understanding of how Mindy tries to work out: how to be who she is; what she needs to do; and how to come to terms with others.

Ricki: So, how will you know who to marry?
Mindy: I'll try a couple of dates. Until I see how he really; until I really know him. Yeah, like, if I ask him to baby-sit, see how he reacts on the children; say if he's going to be coming back. See, if he's O.K. when he comes back.

Ricki: If he keeps his word?
Mindy: Yeah. Honesty.
Ricki: So, that is the most important thing [for you]?
Mindy: (She nods her head.)
Ricki: How do you deal with it when people you love are not always honest all the time?
Mindy: Well, I try to make them understand that, like, if you're not honest, you go to stealing and if you go to stealing you'll go to drugs, and if you go to drugs, you'll die. If you lie, you'll steal, if you steal, you'll go to jail and if you go into drugs, or commit suicide, then you die.   /
Ricki: So, how could you help someone who is a thief, or who . . .
Mindy: Lies?
Ricki: Or who lies! Everybody lies a little bit, right?
Mindy: Yeah! Not big lies! Like a whole pack of lies, just one little bit.
Ricki: Sometimes, one lie leads to another???
Mindy: And then the other leads to another and then it becomes a pack of lies! *(She nods.)*
Ricki: It's hard to be honest.
Mindy: I know, like if you get into trouble, you're thinking of a way to get out of this; and then the next time you get in trouble, like, every day and then you have to come up with another lies.

Mindy has four brothers, two older, and two younger. The oldest one, Jamaal, was eighteen at that time and was in trouble with the law. What concerned Mindy more was the fact that he was dating a girl who was older than he was. The young woman wanted to marry Jamaal. Mindy thought that Jamaal shouldn't really marry a girl who is older than the boy. She strongly believed that the husband should be older than the wife. When I told her that my husband was younger than me, she giggled her self-conscious Mindy-giggle and went on to tell me about the room she was going to have in the new house of her father and his bride, mistakenly referred to by Mindy as her mother-in-law!

Mindy: And my father's gonna buy us a new house; I'm having my own room; my brother's gonna have his own room and my father and my, uhmm, mother-in-law are gonna have their room.
Ricki: And who do you share a room with now?
Mindy: My brother. I'm getting my own room within my house too.

I mention these issues because, as a female who, for many years, has tried to help young children extend their repertoire of things to think with and expectations to fantasize about, it was often difficult for me to become engaged in Mindy's conventional notions of marriage, home, family and happiness. Especially when I knew that Mindy was failing school, getting punished regularly at school and at home, and was often "lying" to teachers, friends, and family. (I use the word "lying" reluctantly.)

Working with *Learning Constellations* gave me the opportunity of seeing Mindy closer to how Mindy sees Mindy and not only as I might like to see Mindy.

Nuances and Gestures of Video Data Assist Writing Case Studies

Working with the video data also helped me to describe Mindy more carefully to others while writing my case studies. In fact, even now as I write this chapter, I refer to the actual video footage to check out the accuracy with which I describe these moments. Often, each viewing leads to a new rendering, in much the same way as a painter might decide to subtly change what to focus on while creating a given portraiture.

What I am suggesting is that delicate nuances shape the way the case studies are written when using a multimedia tool. The writer has immediate access to the video data: she or he can review it instantly; she or he can juxtapose it with other significant chunks; and she or he can examine it in slow motion, in pause, or in step-by-step motion to capture the range of nuances within a given gesture. More significant to the theme of this chapter, the writer can do this with the informant, with co-participants of that culture, or with strangers to the culture. All these readings of the video-text are loosened in the mind of the writer.

Let me give you an example of the kind of writing I think happens with multimedia tools to analyze the data:

Mindy had a way of engaging me in conversation. Maybe it was how her big round eyes would grab my glance and then diagonally look up to the right or left. Maybe her exaggerated gestures—her winks, her shrugging shoulders with her upturned face, or her hand resting on her hip—signalled her wondrous range of emotional responses which included intrigue, joy, desire, anger, frustration, sadness and embarrassment. Or maybe it was simply her warm responsive nature which made it so easy to spend time with her. Whatever the combination of interpersonal skills, Mindy was a joy to listen to. More than Josh or Andrew, Mindy could and would share intimacies with me about how she understood herself and those around her. Mindy was the only child in my study who did not need stories or objects to reflect upon the nature of life. Her own life and fantasies were the stuff of her inventions.

Mindy was notorious for not getting her homework done. Often I would observe Mindy sitting very distractedly in an empty classroom while the other children were in the computer pods. Mindy was stoic about her punishment and never complained to me. She would tell me that she had not done her homework, so she had to stay in the classroom and finish it. Knowing that these were the consequences of her actions did not deter Mindy from going to parties or watching television when she had homework to do.

Even when she told me about her trip to Haiti for her father's wedding, she seemed to know that there was a price to pay for not following the rules. As she told me, "I went to Haiti for twenty–one days, and my teacher got maaaaad!" Her eyes rolled and her whole face moved softly with her eyes, emphatically expressing how Ronkin got angry with her. When I asked her why Ronkin "got mad," she told me, "'Cause, I missed out on all my work. She told me to start working on this term, the third term; so, I'll be caught up on that; and I don't want to be kept back." Never having heard the phrase "kept back" and knowing Mindy was a very alert and bright young girl, I must have seemed very shocked:

Ricki: What would being "kept back" mean?
Mindy: You have to stay in the same grade.
Ricki: Oh, that would be, you mean . . . fail?
Mindy: Yeah.
Ricki: That would be a drag!
Mindy: Yeah, I know! So, I have two report cards more to improve and I'm going to improve.

At this point, Mindy's eyes opened very wide and her face became very resolute. Although we were both sitting on the floor and she was not much shorter than me, her eyes looked up at me sincerely. This is not to say that the gesture convinced me that Mindy would in fact change her ways, but it did show me how upset Mindy was that she might not pass into grade five.

I pursued the issue: "So, what are the chances of your failing?" She paused and said in a singing voice, "Well—ummmm, sort of." And then, her tone of voice began to change. A curtain came down between us. She tried to lighten the issue by using a humorous singing voice so that I would not really know how upset she was. Unfortunately, I didn't pick up the clues at the time and I continued to ask her how she felt and if she was upset. She smirked a tiny almost naughty smirk and very rhythmically said/sang to me:

Mindy: Let's put it this way, I had seven F's and seven D's, and three A's, the rest B's and S's.
Ricki: What were your A's in?
Mindy: I forgot. I just took a glance at it. And my mother got it and she signed it and gave it to my teacher. And my mother's gonna be here on Open Night, I mean, Open House and they're gonna talk!

Several things stand out. First, the gestural description is tied directly to the action: "Her eyes rolled and her whole face moved softly with her eyes." Second, voice intonation is easily analyzed when it can be seen in the context of the video: "And then, her tone of voice began to change. A curtain came down between us." Third, the gesture is reflected upon by the writer of the text: "Although we were both sitting on the floor and she was not much shorter than me, her eyes looked up at me sincerely. This is not to say that the gesture convinced me that Mindy would in fact change her ways, but it did show me how upset Mindy was that she might not pass into grade five."

Nevertheless, the most salient characteristic of written case studies based on video data is that they are usually written after the video has been viewed by a community of persons interested in the video. What I am saying goes back to my first reason for doing multimedia ethnography: the process of making discoveries in the data and the process of communication those discoveries become less distinct research pursuits. Moreover, multimedia ethnography builds a sense of community, not only virtual community, but real community.

The Real Community Builds the Virtual Community and Vice Versa
The final issue I would like to address in this chapter is how working in a collaborative community builds a virtual community for other users and how this continually feeds back into the real community. (Although I find the words *real* and *virtual* problematic for many reasons, I will not address why in this chapter. Instead, I will simply define the real community as working with other persons and the virtual community as working with computer simulations or videodisc recordings of people.)

The main point I would like to make is that working with LC and the video data has opened me up to other people's points of view in ways that I could not have foreseen. Obviously, each of us writes from her or his own point of view, but making these biases open to others has been a painful experience. When I first met Mindy, I saw only the stereotypical responses to what girls and boys should be. However, underneath Mindy's frilly clothes and white lace stockings was a strong young woman with a very determined sense of herself. It was not Mindy who was conventional in her views of marriage; it was me:

One cold February morning, Mindy and I were sitting on the floor near a muraled wall outside her classroom. She sat leaning to one side, her head tilted towards me and resting on her shoulder. The substitute teacher was not particularly concerned about what Mindy was doing, so we had the rare opportunity of just letting the conversation move to where it moved. The mood between us was very casual and the pace very slow in spite of the fact that, all around us, the room was filled with the movement and excitement of twenty or more children at the computers. The moment which stands out as being most characteristic of Mindy's approach to life was when she said the following:

Mindy: Well, when I grow up, if I get married, this is what I want my husband to be: I want him to be helpful, loving, and I want him to be understanding. Like, if I date someone else, he won't get all huffy and puffy. And, if he dates someone else, it's O.K. by me.

Mindy's father had just remarried a woman from Haiti. At the time of this interview, Mindy had just returned from a three week trip in Haiti where she had attended the wedding and celebrations. Her father's bride and a brother remained in Haiti; Mindy, her other brothers and her father returned. The bride and brother would be joining the family soon.

Needless to say, when Mindy told me that she doesn't want a husband who would get all "huffy and puffy" when if she decided to date someone else, I nearly fell over! Here was my conventional girl whose TV idol was Christie from *Three's Company* supporting extramarital affairs! Mindy's life was obviously filled with multiple ways of understanding human relationships. I was tied to my middle-class "Western" background in spite of the fact that I have always seen myself as anything but conventional! This brought about a complete questioning about my notions about "the other." I began to think that maybe a member of one culture should never attempt to study another culture. Certainly, we should be careful to not only select members of another culture who tend to be poor or undereducated according to social western norms because that is misrepresenting a whole group, by typecasting a given ethnic group. On the other hand, if we only represent our own culture to others, don't we simply reinforce the egocentricity involved in most research. Surely we cannot only reflect upon ourselves and the culture from which we come.

As Hammersley and Atkinson so aptly put it, we need to understand that we are part of the world we study (1983) and that our larger cultural membership is determined by being a part of the family of persons who are members of the life on this planet, in this galaxy, in this time. . . .

In using multimedia environments, such as LC, some of this problem is dealt with in a coherent way. Many persons begin to reflect upon the data and add their perspectives of "the other." The interpretation of the researcher is broadened by the layering of other people's points of view.

Furthermore, the informants themselves have an opportunity to comment upon and to reflect upon their own intentions of their actions. Both the interviewer/researcher and the informant have the potential for making adjustments to their original perspectives. They negotiate their understanding of what happened as collaborators. In this way, the virtual community feeds back into the real community. The net result is that we deepen our understandings by listening to and participating with others. By sharing our video observations, not only within a given research team, but also within a larger community, we develop multiple interpretations and new ways of looking at what we thought we knew.

Acknowledgments

I would like to thank Mindy for teaching how to understand the range of adult human relationships. For the countless hours of joy, while either being with her in person or working with the video data, I thank her and all the children of the Hennigan School and the Gardiner Academy. To the children's parents and teachers, especially to Maureen Hansen, I send my gratitude for giving me the permission to enter through doors which are usually locked. Many of them welcomed me (and my camera) into spaces without setting rules. This took courage and confidence.

I would also like to acknowledge individual persons and agencies: my current graduate students in my Multimedia Ethnography course at UBC, for their sensitivity to "the other"; Seymour Papert, for sharing his thinking with me on this subject over many years; Glorianna Davenport, for her constant encouragement and support; Idit Harel, for collaborating on the naming of this chapter; Mary Bryson, for her critical postmodernist interpretation of my work; Andrew Molnar of the National Science Foundation; and the National Science Foundation: grant #851031-0195, #MDR-8751190, #TPE-8850449; The McArthur Foundation: grant #874304; IBM Corporation: grant # SP95952; LEGO Systems A/S, Apple Computer Inc., and Fukatake. Although the ideas expressed in this work do not necessarily reflect the positions of the supporting agencies or individuals, I am very grateful for their support.

To those I share my day-to-day life with, I thank you for helping me continue to learn to see life from a multitude of perspectives. I am truly grateful.

References

Appleyard, B. December 7, 1991. The theory of inequality. *The Times Saturday Review*. London, England: The Times, 4–6.

Bar-On, D. 1991. Trying to understand what one is afraid to learn about. In *The Reflective Turn*, edited by Donald A. Shon. New York and London: Teachers College, Columbia University.

Bateson, M. C. 1984. *With A Daughter's Eye*. New York: Pocket Books.

Bateson, M. C. 1989. *Composing a Life.* New York: Atlantic Monthly Press.

Bereiter, C. 1991. Implications of connectivism for thinking about rules. *Educational Researcher* 20, no. 3:10–16.

Bruner, J. 1966. *Towards a Theory of Instruction.* Cambridge: Harvard University Press.

Bruner, J. 1986. *Actual Minds, Possible Worlds.* Cambridge, Mass., and London, England: Harvard University Press.

Bruner, J. 1990. *Acts of Meaning.* Cambridge, Mass., and London, England: Harvard University Press.

Cole, R. 1989. *The Call of Stories, Teaching and the Moral Imagination.* Boston: Houghton Mifflin Co.

Davenport, G. & R. Leacock. 1987. *New Orleans: A City in Transition.* 1983–1986 [Film and Videodiscs].

Davenport, G. 1987. New Orleans in transition, 1983–1986: The interactive delivery of a cinematic case study. Unpublished paper, Cambridge, Mass.: MIT Media Laboratory.

Davenport, G. T. A. Smith, & N. Pincever. July, 1991. Cinematic primitives for multimedia. *IEEE Computer Graphics and Application.* 67–74.

Dewey, J. 1938. *Experience and Education.* New York: Macmillan.

Diaute, C. 1988. Let's brighten it up: Collaboration and cognition in writing. In *The Social Foundation of Writing,* edited by B. Rafoth & D. Rubin. New York: Ablex Publishers.

Doland, V. M. 1989. Hypermedia as an interpretive act. *Hypermedia: Cognitive Issues* 1, no. 1.

Erickson, G. 1991. Seeing classrooms in new ways: On becoming a science teacher. In *The Reflective Turn,* edited by Donald A. Shon. New York and London: Teachers College, Columbia University.

Etter-Lewis, G. 1991. Black Women's Life Stories: Reclaiming self in narrative texts. In *Women's Words: The Feminist Practice of Oral History,* edited by Sherna Berger Cluck & Daphne Patai. New York: Routledge.

Fodor, J. A. & Pylyshyn, Z. 1988. Connectivism and cognitive architecture: A critical analysis. *Connections and Symbols,* edited by S. Pinker & J. Mehler. Cambridge, Mass.: MIT Press/Bradford Books.

Fox Keller, E. 1985. *Reflections on Gender and Science.* New Haven and London: Yale University Press.

Fox Keller, E. 1983. *A Feeling for the Organism: The Life and Work of Barbara McClintock.* San Francisco: W. H. Freeman.

Gerstein, R. G. 1986. Interpreting the female voice: An application of art and media technology. Ph.D. dissertation, Cambridge, Mass.: Massachusetts Institute of Technology.

Gerstein, R . 1986. *Marital Fracture: a Moral Tale* [Videodisc and Interface]. Cambridge, Mass.: MIT.

Geertz, C. 1973. *The Interpretation of Cultures.* New York: Basic Books.

Geertz, C. 1983. *Local Knowledge.* New York: Basic Books.

Gilligan, C. 1990. *Making Connections.* Cambridge, Mass. and London, England: Harvard University Press.

Goldman-Segall, R. 1987. *The Growth of a Culture.* A video portrait of Project Headlight at the Hennigan School. Cambridge, Mass.: MIT Council for the Arts.

Goldman-Segall, R. 1988. Thick descriptions: A language for articulating ethnographic media technology. Unpublished paper. Cambridge, Mass.: MIT Media Laboratory.

Goldman-Segall, R. 1989a. *Children are the Future.* A video portrait of children in Project Mindstorms in San Jose, CA.

Goldman-Segall, R. and V. Orni Mester and D. Greschler. 1989b. *Learning Constellations* [Six Videodiscs and Interface].

Goldman-Segall, R. 1989c. Thick Descriptions: A tool for designing ethnographic interactive videodiscs. *SIGCHI Bulletin* (Special Interest Group on Computer an Human Interaction) 21, no. 2.

Goldman-Segall, R. 1990a. Learning constellations: A multimedia research environment for exploring children's theory-making. In *Constructionist Learning,* edited by I. Harel. Cambridge, Mass.: MIT Media Laboratory.

Goldman-Segall, R. 1990b. Learning Constellations: A multimedia ethnographic research environment using video technology to explore children's thinking. Ph.D. dissertation, Massachusetts Institute of Technology.

Goldman-Segall, R. 1991a. Three children, three styles: A call for opening the curriculum. In Constructionism, edited by Idit Harel and Seymour Papert. Norwood, N.J.: Ablex Publishers.

Goldman-Segall, R. 1991b. A multimedia research tool for ethnographic investigation. In *Constructionism,* edited by Idit Harel and Seymour Papert. Norwood, N.J.: Ablex Publishers.

Granott, N. 1991. Puzzled minds and weird creatures: Phases in the spontaneous process of knowledge construction. In *Constructionism,* edited by Idit Harel and Seymour Papert. Norwood, N.J.: Ablex Publishers.

Hammersley, M. & P. Atkinson. 1983. Ethnography: Principles in Practice. London and New York: Routledge Publishers.

Harel, I. 1991. The silent observer and holistic note taker: Using video to document a research project. In *Constructionism,* edited by Idit Harel and Seymour Papert. Norwood, N.J.: Ablex Publishers.

Harel, I. and S. Papert. eds. 1991. *Constructionism.* Norwood, N.J.: Ablex Publishers.

Illich, I. 1973. *Tools for Conviviality* London and New York: Marion Boyars.

Kafai, Y. & I. Harel. 1991. Children Learning Through Consulting. In *Constructionism,* edited by Idit Harel and Seymour Papert. Norwood, N.J.: Ablex Publishers.

Lamm, Z. 1976. *Conflicting Theories of Instruction.* Berkeley, Calif.: McCutcham Publishers.

Leacock, R. 1975. Ethnographic observation and the super-8 millimeter camera. In *Principles of Visual Anthropology,* edited by Paul Hockings. The Hague, Paris: Mouton Publishers.

Leacock, R. 1986. Personal thoughts and prejudices about the documentary. Unpublished paper. Cambridge, MA: MIT Media Laboratory.

MacKay & G. Davenport. July, 1989. Virtual video editing in interactive multimedia applications. *CACM* 32, no. 7.

Malone, T.W., M. Lepper, N. Miyake, & M. Cohen. 1987. Making learning fun: A taxonomy of intrinsic motivations for learning. *Aptitude, Learning, and Instruction: III. Conative and Affective Process Analyses,* edited by R. E. Snow & M. J. Farr. (pp. 223–253). Hillsdale, N.J.: Erlbaum.

McElwee, R. 1984. *Backyard* [Film].

McElwee, R. 1987. *Sherman's March* [Film].

Mead, M. 1975. Visual anthropology in a discipline of words. In *Principles of Visual Anthropology,* edited by Paul Hockings. The Hague, Paris: Mouton Publishers.

Montessori, M. 1967. *The Absorbent Mind* trans. C. A. Claremont. New York: Dell Publishing.

Mishler, E. 1986. *Research Interviewing: Context and Narrative.* Cambridge, Mass.: Harvard University Press.

Papert, S. 1986. Constructionism: A new opportunity for elementary science education. Proposal to the National Science Foundation. Cambridge, Mass.: MIT Media Laboratory.

Piaget, J. 1927 [1969]. *The Child's Conception of Time.* New York: Ballatine Books.

Ryle, G. 1971. *Collected Papers.* New York: Barnes and Noble.

Sacks, K.B. 1989. What's a life story got to do with it? In *Interpreting Women's Lives: Feminist Theory and Personal Narratives,* edited by the Personal Narratives Group. Bloomingdale: Indiana University Press.

Salomon, G., Perkins, D. N., & Globerson, T. 1991. Partners in cognition: Extending human intelligences with intelligent technologies. *Educational Researcher* 20, no. 3.

Sassnet, R. 1986. *Reconfigurable Video.* Masters in Visual Science Thesis, Cambridge, Mass.: MIT.

Scheffler, I. 1965. *Conditions of Knowledge.* Chicago, Atlanta, Dallas, Palo Alto, Fair Lawn: Scott, Foresman and Company.

Schon, D. 1991. *The Reflective Turn.* New York and London: Teachers College, Columbia University.

Tannen, D. 1990. *You Just Don't Understand: Women and Men in Conversation.* New York: William Morrrow & Company, Inc.

Tobin, J. J., Wu, D. Y. H & Davidson, D. H. 1989. *Preschool in Three Cultures.* New Haven and London: Yale University Press.

Wiseman, F. *High School* [Film].

Wilensky, U. 1991. Abstract meditations on the concrete and concrete implications for mathematics education. In *Constructionism,* edited by Idit Harel and Seymour Papert. Norwood, N.J.: Ablex Publishers.

14

The Crisis Management Game of Three Mile Island: Using Multimedia Simulation in Management Education

Thomas M. Fletcher

One doesn't have to search very far to encounter enthusiastic proponents of multimedia. Apple's John Sculley was singing its praises in 1989 at MacWorld in Boston; IBM's general manager of Educational Systems, Jim Dezell, was espousing its potential in 1990 interviews; John Donovan, Senior Editor of BYTE magazine, labeled it "the next revolution in computing" in his December 1991 edition.

But the success of multimedia is not assured. It will depend on the industry's ability to address issues of cost, standards, storage technologies, copyright and licensing, the creativity and design of good applications, and, eventually, transmission and distribution capacities once compression/decompression of full motion video is resolved (Marsh and Vanston 1991). Discussion of these obstacles to widespread use of multimedia platforms that include desktop computers can be found elsewhere. The subject of this paper is to describe one attempt to provide creative designs for new multimedia applications.

From a design standpoint, the secret to effective multimedia is in weaving a coherent and engaging fabric of multi-sensory mediums into a seamless interactive experience. If the program stimulates one's curiosity, is challenging and is credible, it will be attractive and compelling enough that people will want to play it and use it to learn.

There are many designers and producers of multimedia educational products actively developing software titles in the hopes of encouraging the establishment of a significant installed base of hardware. Many of them are directed toward the K-12 educational market in math, science, language arts and other subjects; many toward military or civilian job training skills; some are titles in medical, legal, or financial planning programs. But little of the effort has focused on the teaching of management skills; the role of careful planning and open communication in a successful enterprise; the nonquantifiable skills of sensitive, reasoned, sound judgment under fire.

The Strategic Computing and Telecommunications in the Public Sector program at Harvard's John F. Kennedy School of Government has embarked on that effort: to marry multimedia technologies to subjects central to graduate and executive education in business and government.

The Call for Multimedia in Business and Government Education

The introduction to the demonstration of the Strategic Computing Program's first multimedia interactive case study contains this call for a new application:

With the dawn comes a new day. For some it may be their moment of opportunity and triumph. For others, the challenge of crisis and tragedy.

The success of our nation, of business, and of government, often depends on the ability of our leaders to cope with the unexpected . . . when a crisis is at hand; when an issue has been joined; when the news media want a story; when the public needs to know.

These are the times when the fortunes of our institutions are made or broken. Some people will be ready and succeed. The unprepared will fail.

One of Harvard University's professional schools, The Kennedy School of Government is dedicated through its teaching and research to the creation of excellence in public service. The School's Program on Strategic Computing and Telecommunications is combining multimedia interactive technologies, the university's case method of teaching, and direct feedback from renowned experts and Harvard faculty, to offer an innovative, powerful, and personalized tool for education.

The Harvard Interactive Series will consist of simulations in the form of instructional games. The student sits in the seat of a decision maker in government, politics, business, or the news media and navigates through a myriad of decision points. The choices made determine the course of history which is rewritten through the simulation.

The subjects of the first Harvard Interactive Series are crisis management and the public's right to know. There are few tasks more daunting, more challenging, than participating in the process of crisis management. Preparing for that moment is what the first interactive program is about.

All of us have looked on during a crisis situation wondering what was really happening? Who was in control? What would we be doing differently? If we had been in charge at Union Carbide before the crisis and its aftermath, what would we have done about the tragic, deadly gas leak at Bhopal, India in 1984? How would we have handled the Tylenol scare of 1982? Could we have done a better job in handling the Exxon Valdez oil spill?

Harvard Interactive Series simulations will be designed to give a student the chance to find out.

The Case Method of Teaching

Reliving stories can be a powerful teaching tool. Case studies used in teaching are stories that spell out facts relevant to an actual event, emphasizing the personalities of both the people and the organizations involved (Goldsmith and Boo 1989). The stories provide a framework for the discussion of management principles, policy alternatives, or philosophical issues related to the basic story. Magnus Communications Design in Toronto has won several awards for its two multimedia educational products that teach teenagers about the dangers of drugs, drinking, and AIDS. Their approach with these tools is to tell stories. Michael-john Morgan, President of Magnus says, "The most basic premise is that people haven't changed much since they sat around the campfire. What we've got to do is tell people stories. That's the way humans understand things. In a ten-second commercial, for example, regardless of what is being sold, there is some thread of a story there" (Caruso 1991).

A teacher of crisis management or crisis communications faces an enormous challenge in conveying to students the horror, the physical dimensions, the human emotions, the immediacy of the issues to be addressed. If what that teacher wants students to learn is sensitivity, concentration, sound judgment, leadership—and all while under extreme pressure—the challenge is great, indeed. Since with these subjects the stakes are so high that the future of a company and its labor force, or a political administration and its public support, or perhaps the health and actual lives of people are being held in the balance, it becomes imperative that the learning process be as effective as it can be.

Traditionally, instruction at Harvard University, especially the graduate professional schools like the Kennedy School of Government or the Harvard Business School, has been based on the Socratic method of teaching and the use of case studies. The typical case study is a hard copy document that is 10 to 20 pages in length with some appendices in the back. To prepare for class, students read through the case and spend a few hours thinking about the issues that surface through the telling of the story. Students then come to class and debate the issues for about ninety minutes.

What we are doing at the Kennedy School's Program on Strategic Computing and Telecommunications is merging the School's case method of teaching with available technologies to create a series of multimedia, interactive case studies. Our program was established in 1987 by Dr. Jerry Mechling as a collaborative, applied research effort to enable public managers and policy makers to understand and utilize the strategic impacts of information technologies. We conduct traditional, problem solving research, and produce publications and senior level executive training programs on the management, political, and organizational issues behind the emergence of new technologies in government.

Through the design of multimedia interactive cases we are identifying a strategic application for new technologies in the academic environment; strategic because it significantly enhances the way we educate current or prospective leaders and managers in government.

Using well-known, historical stories as the cases for the multimedia interactive simulations allows students of varying backgrounds and abilities to experience events that are benchmarks in national and international history—events that taught the professional world lessons in proper organization, sound management, and responsible leadership. These cases utilize the principles of intrinsic motivation addressed below and maximize the efficiency of learning by not risking the well-being, or the careers of any real people.

The Design of Instructional Multimedia

If multimedia is going to succeed, "it cannot be 'sold' on the merits (or flash) of the technology alone, but rather as the delivery system of solid instructional designs. A solid instructional design is one that reflects the best current knowledge of how people learn" (Brandt 1990).

Kosslyn, Chabris, and Hamilton (1990) believe cognitive science will provide the solution. They see multimedia and other new technologies of information delivery as "cognitive prostheses." "Just as a good prosthetic feels and works similar to the natural limb it replaces, an external source of information should behave like our own internal information processes." Cognitive psychologists believe three basic mechanisms for learning are: accretion (accumulation of new information), restructuring (processes whereby concepts are combined), and tuning (processes whereby concepts are differentiated). These processes are used to build a new model for the world—a model that is reexamined and adjusted as new information is received (Brandt 1990).

The pedagogic process of our multimedia crisis management simulation requires a student to use her accumulated knowledge and personal value structure to make decisions and commitments on behalf of her organization in response to new stimuli (information provided through the developing scenario). As a result of responses to the stimuli, the student discovers the dimensions of her value structure—a value structure that comes under ongoing challenge and scrutiny from characters in the simulation, evaluative response from the institutional perspectives in the simulation, and from substantive experts who offer feedback to decisions made. By the end of the simulation the student has experienced discovery, evaluation, and restructuring of her value system which she relied upon in making many managerial judgments.

This process captures the essence of "interactivity" as G.J. Gery has articulated it: a cycle that in its most generic sense is composed of a stimulus, a response, a response analysis, and feedback (Marlino 1990).

Human factors have been found to be critical in the success of computer-assisted instructional tools (Steinberg 1991). Among the most important in the design of the Three Mile Island (TMI) crisis management simulation were those of motivation—particularly the intrinsic motivations that come from within a student. Malone and Lepper (1987) give three classes: challenge, curiosity, and control; Malone's earlier (1981) studies suggested a fourth: fantasy.

One task facing a student navigating his way through the TMI scenario is the challenge of problem solving; the challenge of bringing to bear one's own instincts and accumulated knowledge to avoid the monumental crisis that TMI became. Conflicting institutional perspectives on what is the best course of action in a communications crisis like TMI make it difficult to identify the "correct" answers in a game of judgment. The challenge of finding a "better" way through the TMI scenario remains a significant motivational factor.

Curiosity, or novelty, is a second intrinsic motivator captured in the design of TMI. In this case we are mostly interested in cognitive curiosity.

Students become highly curious to explore in depth the story line of well-known historical events, putting themselves into the drama, and experiencing the surprises that unexpected information, sudden alarms or warnings, impending doom, or their own decision point choices produce.

The third source of intrinsic motivation is that of control. It is a basic feature and attraction of a player-controlled simulation exercise. In TMI there is considerable self-determination as much of the progression of the game and the learner's score is a direct result of choices he or she makes. There is even anecdotal evidence in the literature to suggest that learning is also more enjoyable when the student has control (Steinberg 1991).

Finally, there is the intrinsic motivator of fantasy. "Fantasy helps to satisfy emotional needs and enables students to vicariously experience power, success, fame, and fortune" (Steinberg 1991). Each of us can acknowledge that there have been times while watching a real crisis unfold on the evening news that we have imagined what we would do if we were in the position of power or control in that situation. The TMI multimedia simulation allows the student to sit in the seat of a decision maker and try his or her instincts and judgment—to live out the fantasy of saving the world from a crisis.

A Multi-sensory Approach to Learning

What makes multimedia educational tools so dramatic and exciting is the multi-sensory nature of them. Dr. Bernard Luskin of American Interactive Media uses the term "synesthetics" to describe the emerging revolution personified in the uniting of audio, visual, and computer power. It is a discipline that "recognizes that the combined use of all senses offers an experience that is greater than one based on an individual sense" (Luskin 1991). The greater number of senses brought to bear in building a model of reality in our minds, "the better the 'quality' of discussion we can have with ourselves, and the better our thinking" (Brandt 1991). (Since our sense of smell is the most powerful magnet for memory, the multimedia designers who come up with a way of incorporating fragrances in their programs will have a truly complete and powerful multimedia experience.)

Research has demonstrated that people recall about 25% of what they hear; higher than retention from reading (Seger 1990). Sound effects can heighten the reality of an occurrence; music can underscore the drama and emotion of the moment; and the spoken word can convey greater emotion, a sense of urgency, or a clue to the personality of individuals.

The Use of Imagery

Of particular value to the multimedia learning experience is imagery—the pictures, both still and full motion. There are at least two good reasons to insist on high quality images in a multimedia educational tool: they work as educational enhancers, and they are a fundamental part of our culture.

If a person recalls 25% of what he or she hears, that student's recall level goes up to about 45% if he or she both hears and sees the information (Seger 1990). It has been said that the band-width of the eye is a thousand times greater than the band-width of the ear (Taylor 1990). And because the brain is a very effective visual processor, learning is greatly enhanced by the integration of a visual medium — by expanding the multi-sensory experience to include imagery.

For White (1990) we are recapturing a dominant tool of education with the reintegration of imagery. She points out: "Both the Dark Ages and the Middle Ages were predominantly visual and oral ages, when authors such as Chaucer and Bocaccio wrote their stories to read aloud to others. . . . Print and reading played no major role as a learning tool for the average person in the West during those times." But the printing press made the reading of text the key to learning, and imagery was largely abandoned as an avenue for learning.

White (1990) points out that imagery encompasses two forms of visualization that can empower human learning: the external forms (paintings, sculpture, film, graphics, television, video, etc.) and the internal forms of mental pictures employed in imagination, in thinking, and in memory. In the TMI simulation, the video images are intended to represent some of both forms of visualization. We compensate for the possible lack of familiarity of the student with the physical images of the nuclear industry and TMI per se, by offering external, videodisc images in lieu of internal images which would have been prevalent in the minds of the characters in the real drama. Examples are the video images projected on the monitor during a telephone conversation with a simulation character. These images are props to the player's imagination to help "see" what a person on the phone is describing. One might think of them as "color commentary."

Another example of the use of imagery in the TMI simulation is the introduction to the game. It features video in a more conventional, linear presentation. The five-minute collection of dramatic news footage is intended to set the emotional stage for the simulation by stimulating anticipation of the crisis game and challenging the player to action.

One clip of full-motion video in the introduction is of the Love Canal, New York tragedy. It is difficult to avoid being affected by the compelling cries of sorrow and anger voiced by the mother of a young victim of chemical poisoning at the Love Canal as she pleads with the local Mayor to stop his inaction and "do something—do something decent, for a change!"

And one gets a much greater appreciation for the devastation of the Exxon Valdez oil spill in Alaska, when seeing the spectacular ABC News footage in the introduction showing the pristine beauty of Prince William Sound, its beaches and the surrounding mountains, and then viewing scenes of destruction caused by the oil spill.

The news clips underscore the power of the visual medium to convey the drama, the emotion, and the urgency of the moment that is inherent in crisis management and crisis communications. If the task is teaching a person what it's like to be under fire, or encounter the pressures of a rapidly developing crisis, a multimedia approach seems essential.

Given the educational potential and the rich resources of the ABC News archives, it is understandable that Bill Lord, Vice-President of ABC News, formed ABC News Interactive, a division of ABC News, and began producing multimedia educational products built on the backbone of their news footage. David Bohrman, executive producer of the company, has underscored the power of the visual medium in education: "Some images and events in history need to be seen as what they are, images and events, not just stories. This capability has never been available to people wanting to learn before" (Caruso 1991).

If, as the ancient Chinese proverb says, a picture is worth a thousand words, surely full-motion video coupled with the added impact of an audio tract is worth countless words in creating an environment for the student in which he or she will be largely consumed, completing the process of engagement in a simulation.

Television, itself, is a type of multimedia present in virtually everyone's home. It is the ubiquitous, visual technology that entertains and informs, often setting the social and political agenda. Some suggest America's younger generations are getting their values and culture from television. By the time an average young person graduates from high school today, he will have watched 20,000 hours of television, while having spent only about 12,500 hours in the classroom (Taylor 1990). But it is not the toy of only the young. Television news is omnipresent: covering war and peace negotiations; royal weddings and divorce cases in court; personal tragedies and moments of triumph; natural disasters and staged media events. CNN and Headline News are available "Any time; All the time." Our expectation, as viewers, is that television will be there to bring us a visual account of any reasonably significant event around the world.

Television is the great communicator and the standard setter. And therein lies the opportunity, the challenge, and the most significant cost, for multimedia tools. With the sophisticated look of network and cable television and the discriminating viewer television has trained, the credibility of visual images in multimedia education is waiting to be exploited, but is contingent on high production values in the video. Without them, the product suffers and the credibility of the program itself can fall into question.

Interactive Videodisc Technology

Another essential technology in the successful integration of images and sound with computers is the interactive videodisc. Its storage capacity, integration of still images with full motion video, multiple audio tracts, and rapid random access of visual images are invaluable assets in maximizing the necessary seamlessness of a multimedia simulation.

Perhaps the largest study about the cost and effectiveness of interactive videodisc applications has been conducted by J. D. Fletcher at the direction of the Department of Defense (DoD). It reviewed forty-seven studies in military training, industrial training, and higher education. The following is a partial listing of findings related to instructional capabilities of interactive videodisc systems (Fletcher 1991):

1. Interactive videodisc (IVD) instruction was used successfully to teach.
2. Overall IVD was more effective than conventional instruction.

3. IVD was equally effective for both knowledge and performance outcomes.

4. Within-group variability was smaller in IVD than in conventional instruction.

5. There was little in the reviewed studies to indicate how IVD instruction achieves its success.

6. IVD was less costly than conventional instruction.

The orders of magnitude in the above IVD advantages are significant enough to give a strong endorsement of IVD instruction. But many designers are already anticipating the abandonment of IVD for digital video. Estimates vary as to how long it will be before compression/decompression technical impediments to digitized full motion video are removed. Whatever the reliable estimate, it will be longer still before that new generation of multimedia tools are affordable enough for there to be an installed base sufficient to drive the design decisions of multimedia simulations.

So while videodiscs and analog images may not remain the technology of choice in the next iteration of multimedia tools, IVD remains a reliable, relatively inexpensive technology that can be incorporated into the multimedia platform today.

Participating in the Game: Discovery by Engagement

In order to properly design a vehicle that teaches intangibles and illuminates the art of management, as opposed to only the quantifiable, we have found it desirable to design greater complexity into the structure of the case studies by making them situational simulations. In the situational simulation the student "becomes" the protagonist in the story, and the significant pedagogical advantages of discovery through engagement are captured in the educational process. The student is caused to participate in the case study; to participate in the managerial dilemma that confronts him or her.

George Sarton called movable type "the greatest invention of the Renaissance" and the "savior of Western science" because it allowed for the mass distribution of information—exact copies of images and text, enabling every scientist to work from the same "database" (White, 1990). Multimedia case studies also allow us to disseminate exact copies of text and images, but, in addition, introduce them in the context of a simulation that begins to standardize the intangible forces that have a bearing on managerial judgment. If we succeed in these design subtleties, the independent variables isolated in the simulation will be those values brought to the exercise by the player. The result will be a successful exercise in self-discovery by the student.

Roger C. Shank, the director of Northwestern University's Institute for the Learning Sciences and an artificial intelligence researcher, believes the best computerized teaching tool, to date, is the flight simulator. He believes simulations can be used for other kinds of learning. Instead of learning from books in the traditional linear fashion, he believes students can learn on multimedia "discovery learning stations" (*Computerworld*, August 7, 1989).

Palenque is an example of a multimedia prototype that utilizes this concept of discovery-based learning. It is designed as a surrogate travel experience through an ancient Maya site. It is a highly realistic, yet simulated exploratory environment presenting the student with many options that can be pursued at will. The student experiences the Mayan ruins with the same sense of adventure and exploration as when taking a real trip to this unknown place (Wilson 1990).

If people recall 45% of what they hear and see, they recall 70% or more of what they do (Seger 1990). And so to maximize the effectiveness of the learning process, we want our student managers and executives to experience and participate in something that captures the intellectual and emotional tension of a real crisis.

The Palenque prototype offers a student discovery of a place; the Perseus Project of Harvard's Classics Department offers a journey through the Greek classics (Lambert 1990); and the ABC Interactive series offers discovery of important public affairs issues. The Three Mile Island crisis management game and others to follow will offer a person a participatory walk back through an important moment in history. It will be offered as a dress rehearsal for crisis complete with the time pressures, the emotional issues, the political environment, the confusion of the moment; and it will test a student's ability to respond to the challenges with decisions that don't put other people, their organizations, or themselves at risk.

Early Experiences with Three Mile Island: The Game

While the completed portion of the Three Mile Island multimedia simulation represents a demonstration tool covering the first few hours of the communications crisis from the perspective of one central role, the tool has been sufficient to use for its content in a number of forums.

Three times I have used the TMI case study at Department of Energy-sponsored workshops held to train public and private sector energy executives on the issues of energy emergency preparedness. At each regional session I used the TMI case to surface issues in crisis communications and media relations from the perspective of the utility company. The participants in each workshop numbered between 60 and 90.

To focus discussion and enhance the sense of participation among these relatively large groups of participants, I added an additional facilitating technology to the standard platform of the TMI program. A system of computerized, instant tallying handsets was used by each participant to register their individual opinions on what course of action to take at each of the decision points in the simulation. The tallying system, constituting a third screen of projected information in the classrooms, indicated in real-time the number of votes cast for each alternative at each decision point.

In these large classes, the focal point of the exercise was the group interaction centering around each decision by the protagonist in the unfolding crisis. As the group would vote on a course of action, there would be animated debate about the advisability of certain decisions. Significant differences surfaced on virtually every question, underscoring the validity of the exercise, the credibility of the answer sets offered students, and dismissing any question that a situational simulation based on a well known historical event would be predictable and, therefore, less engaging and effective.

Allowing for the group discussions at each decision point required that the time-sensitive feature of the exercise be disabled. While doing so eliminated a certain realism of the unfolding crisis, the dynamic of experiencing the TMI case in a large group offered its own pedagogical advantages.

One forum at which I used the TMI Crisis Management Game was a nuclear energy emergency preparedness workshop which Harvard's Graduate School of Public Health sponsors in the summers. The participants in the session were about 65 nuclear industry officials—mostly, nuclear engineers. In this case, the TMI program was used more as a multimedia case study, without some of the interactive advantages. As we proceeded through the scenario, participants were asked to consider options available to the case's protagonist. The multimedia case was used to seed discussion about crisis communications and news media relations in the nuclear industry. While there appeared to be more consensus of opinion in this discussion, it was impossible to quantify because no anonymous, instant tallying system was available for use. It was gratifying to note that this collection of nuclear industry experts overwhelmingly graded the multimedia exercise an excellent educational experience in their forum evaluations.

Only anecdotal evidence is available from the hundreds of people who have witnessed the demonstration as a one-on-one simulation experience. It has been very interesting to note how widely divergent people's opinions have been in responding to the decision point options. There is certainly no obvious course of action that players of the simulation elect to take. As with real life crises played out in an environment of cross-institutional pressures, the TMI crisis management simulation appears to be successful in subjecting the decision maker to the conflicting forces that make decisions complicated and difficult.

Markets for Multimedia Management Education

One of the exciting prospects for an interactive series, like this one, is the size of the potential market and the importance of addressing that market. While the home multimedia market holds great potential, especially in home video games and "edutainment" products, it is the business market that is expected to drive the initial success of multimedia (Marsh and Vanston 1991). The rationale for the argument is the same used by Willie Sutton when asked why he robbed banks: that's where the money is. Our interactive simulations should be well positioned to appeal to that market, both in terms of substance and process.

The training and retraining of mid-career managers, executives, and the labor force is becoming a reality and a necessity. Careers are being measured, not in lifetimes, but in decades or even years. The Conference Board's Human Resources Outlook Panel projected in 1990 that employers would have to develop entirely new hiring and training programs in order to staff effectively. Madelyn Jennings, Gannett Company's senior VP for personnel and a panel member, agreed that "training will probably be one of the big growth industries of the 1990s" (*Human Capital*, April 1990).

Workforce 2000, a study of the U.S. Department of Labor, found that the largest number of new jobs between now and the end of the century would be white-collar jobs, requiring entirely new categories of learning. Traditional forms of learning are becoming irrelevant, if not harmful to the modern knowledge worker (Perelman 1990).

The Harvard Interactive Series will address both the business and government education markets from post-secondary level to senior executive training. The TMI simulation is an example of a case with lessons for several markets: while the initial accident developed within the confines of a private utility company, the story line underscores the reality that a crisis in the private sector rarely is resolved in a vacuum. It often bleeds into the realm of the news media, government regulatory and oversight institutions, the political leadership, and the public's attention. The case study books are full of public and private entities who failed to acknowledge that their communities were interrelated and affected by each other's accidents and failures.

Three Mile Island: A Crisis Management Game

Having shared much about the underpinnings of the Three Mile Island crisis management simulation, I offer a textual walk through some of the demonstration. Some comments related to design objectives have been included to give game features some context.

The player of the Three Mile Island crisis management game can experience the crisis through the eyes of a company executive, a political aide, a government bureaucrat or a member of the news media. This demonstration focuses on the institution in which the crisis first developed, the utility company. I, as the player, participate in the simulation as the new Communications Services Director at Three Mile Island.

I enter my name to start the game and the Mac begins to generate a press release on the screen, complete with the sound of a teletype machine. The release, dated March 27, 1979, announces my appointment as the new

Communications Services director at Metropolitan Edison, the parent company of the Three Mile Island nuclear plant. The press release is an example of a card with textual information that places a player at a particular point in time and introduces some of the main characters of the simulation. It is also a visual device calculated to enhance the sense of engagement of the player by including sound effects, the structure of a press release, and the inclusion of the player's name in the body of the document.

Once the game proceeds past the opening press release and into March 28, 1979, an internal clock begins to control the pace of the simulation. Events and interruptions will take place in the simulation whether or not I, as the player, am prepared for them. As play begins on March 28 I find myself at my Reading, Pennsylvania office early in the morning. The Mac screen displays the "daily planner" card, which is the platform from which I navigate through the simulation. A video clip automatically plays giving us additional visual context for this exercise. The clip is of a peaceful, unsuspecting, residential neighborhood with the cooling towers at TMI on the horizon. This image heightens ones appreciation for the proximity of the accident site to a large population base and the potential problems inherent in that fact.

On the Mac screen, the daily planner indicates the time of day of the simulation, a brief textual description of that point in time, and the physical location of the player. At the bottom of the screen are a series of icons which are accessible to me throughout the course of the simulation.

In addition to the daily planner icon, which I click at any time to return to the unfolding scenario, are three icons: one representing my office files, an icon for a glossary of terms, and an icon of a series of rolodex cards on which are found the names and information of the main characters in the simulation. By clicking on the files icon, I see examples of the files I might consult at my discretion during the simulation to gain additional background information.

For instance, I can click on the "nuclear reactor schematic" file and see a diagram of the nuclear reactor process, or click on the "phone transcripts" file to access transcripts of any telephone conversations I have experienced during the course of the simulation. A number of technical terms in the body of these transcripts will be in bold hypertext. By clicking on them I can reference the glossary of terms for a brief definition of that word. As in the case of the card defining "reactor," a video icon might appear on the glossary card, and by clicking it I can access a small piece of video that helps me to physically define the location of a reactor at a nuclear plant.

The rolodex icon is my contact point with the outside world. On the rolodex are the names of all the main characters in the Three Mile Island drama. By clicking on the rolodex and then clicking the desired name on the index, I can access a card giving me a brief background on that individual. By clicking the telephone icon on any rolodex card I am able to place a call to that individual. Because the simulation is time-sensitive, the responses I receive, if any, to my telephonic inquiries will vary depending on the time at which I place my call. In some cases I will get no answer or busy signals. In others, if the party I am calling has no information to share at that specific time in the crisis, or worse, incorrect information based on rumor, I will be given that appropriate message. Part of my challenge will be to make judgments about what to believe and what to discount as I hear it from other parties.

There will be times during the course of the crisis when I will be interrupted in whatever I am doing by events that took place. In many cases I have the option of ignoring the interruption.

Because of space limitations, I am skipping ahead in the Three Mile Island scenario to a point in time approximately 4 hours after the accident. By this time in the simulation I have been a part of a 6:15 a.m. conference call with superiors informing me of the developing incident at the TMI plant; I have had some time to search the files for background information and memos outlining the political and organizational dynamics of my position; and, I have participated in the writing of a press statement describing the incident at the TMI nuclear plant. During these critical initial events I have been asked for my opinions and judgment on language characterizing the incident and suggested methods for disseminating information which may be inconclusive, but may also be threatening to various parties in the crisis.

I have just completed a phone conversation with the Associated Press, which I agreed to handle, responding to information that the AP had heard about an alleged general emergency at Three Mile Island. Now I go to my files to find an agenda for a staff meeting that I have called to brief my staff people who have just arrived for work at 8:00 a.m. On my Mac screen is a brief agenda of some questions that I need to answer for my staff. As I begin answering the questions for my staff regarding this incident my intercom buzzes with an interruption from my secretary:

Secretary: "Sorry to interrupt, it's Mike Pintek, News Director of WKBO radio, on Line 1. Will you take the call?"

The Mac screen asks me whether I want to take the phone call from Mike Pintek of a local radio station. I click on the button that say "No, I am in a meeting," and I am returned to the agenda of issues that I am discussing with my staff. As I offer a second explanation to my staff about the accident the buzzer sounds again:

Secretary: "I'm sorry but Mr. Pintek said to get you out of the damn meeting."

It seems that the news director on the telephone is rather persistent. This time on the Mac screen, I choose the option to take the call and push the "yes" button. Off the audio track I hear:

Mike Pintek: "Hello, Mike Pintek, News Director of WKBO radio, in Harrisburg. I have a newscast in about 15 minutes and I need information on the problem at TMI. The control room people say there is a problem and to call you. What's the situation there?"

Somehow, this news director has gotten through to the control room and wants to know what the situation is at TMI. While Pintek is speaking, the video monitor plays a brief video clip of the TMI site as it appears to the news media and any on-site observers at that time in the crisis. On my Mac screen is a decision card giving me three response alternatives of how to label the incident underway at TMI. I click my choice on the screen, indicating that the "site emergency" in progress is an NRC formality when "certain conditions" exist at the plant. I am hoping to nonchalantly dismiss the Pintek question, but Mike Pintek has a follow-up:

Mike Pintek: "What conditions?"

Again, the Mac screen gives me three response alternatives, each with a more detailed description of how to characterize the situation at the TMI plant. After I select an answer of "clarification" for Pintek, he is satisfied and the program refers me back to where I was prior to the interruption in the scenario: I am looking at the third question on a brief agenda from a staff meeting that I began a few minutes ago. I click on the explanation that I wish to give my staff. As this brief background meeting with staff ends, I find myself back at the daily planner, free to exercise any initiative in my efforts to handle the communications response to the emergency at hand.

Had we been following the simulation from the beginning of the scenario, you would know that already there has been a series of decisions I have been required to make that evaluates my initial attitudes about methods of communication to external organizations and the way I have chosen to characterize the status of the accident at this time. Appearing for the first time on the Mac screen is an icon that we call "evaluation." This icon appears at specific intervals during the simulation giving me the opportunity to get feedback from a number of sources. By clicking the evaluation icon the Mac screen displays the evaluation card listing six possible sources of feedback.

The first button on this card represents a key component in the educational value of this multimedia tool. Clicking on it will get me direct, personalized feedback on my decisions from real, substantive experts in business, government, politics, and the news media. The specific video clip that will be played for me at each juncture in the simulation is dependent on which expert I wish to consult and on the pattern of responses I have made to the decision points that have just been passed in the simulation.

In the case I am describing, I have just completed a briefing for my staff, most of whom are very inexperienced people and, therefore, are of marginal value to me as I attempt to handle the sensitivity of the TMI accident. The expert commentary I choose to receive is from Martin Linsky, a Harvard lecturer, who is a lawyer, a former elected official, a former publisher and editor of a newspaper, and an expert in the use of media in government. The following transcript of Mr. Linsky's reaction to the set of decisions I have been making during the past few minutes of the simulation gives an example of feedback I will be receiving during the simulation.

Martin Linsky: "Look, from what you tell me you're in a real bind because you got some people who are going to deal with the press who aren't prepared to deal with the press. They don't understand it; they haven't thought about it; they aren't experienced at it. Ordinarily, I'd say, look, you've got to tell the people who are going to deal with the press everything that you know so they can manage the situation and they can deal with the reporters on their (the reporters) own terms. But you are dealing with inexperienced people and they're liable to treat a conversation with a reporter as an ordinary conversation, or they're liable to be too defensive trying to control the information. So I think this is a situation, unfortunately, where you've got to manage what you tell your own people and assume and encourage them to tell the press everything that they know. Don't let this happen again."

We believe the educational importance of immediate, personalized, direct feedback from experts to whom I would not normally have access cannot be overstated. The power of the message is heightened in this case by having Linsky deliver his message to me "eye to eye" on full motion video. I sense his concern; I hear his urgency; I am impressed with the passion of his admonishment. This feature of our multimedia simulation is illustrative of the power and richness inherent in the integration of mediums and the storage capacity of the computer and videodisc.

In addition to the expert commentary, I can gain an "historical perspective" on the real Three Mile Island accident at this precise time in the scenario by clicking on the second button on the evaluation card.

Similarly, I can click on any of the four remaining evaluation buttons to get a quantified evaluation of my recent decisions from the perspective of any one of the four institutional entities that are represented in this crisis management simulation. For purposes of the demonstration, my decisions during the run-through of the simulation have been generally supportive of the utility company's interest in containing the dissemination of information until the extent of the incident is better identified. In my role as the Communications Director, I have chosen to down play the potential severity of the incident in any public statements or conversations. So when I click on the evaluation button marked "Company," I can view a graph that illustrates the general upward trend of support by the company for the decisions that I have been making in this scenario. If I return to the evaluation card and press the button for the "Press" or news media, I see that my performance on the very same decisions is not rated so charitably by them. While my decisions have been courting favor with company executives, there is growing suspicion among the news people and I am rapidly losing credibility with the news organizations—not good news for me, since "credibility" is the currency of this crisis management exercise.

One of the most difficult design challenges in this type of educational software is to build a credible mathematical model of evaluation that fairly reflects the conflicting priorities of the institutional interests represented in the real world crisis. A designer must be sensitive to the differing agendas of competing interests and give credit where and with whom it is due, as well as demerits with others. Rarely in a crisis game like this is a course of action clearly a win-win solution. It is more likely that the objective in a crisis is to minimize loss, stabilize a situation, and attempt throughout to maintain credibility for oneself and one's organization. Without credibility in crisis, one will no longer be allowed to play in the game.

To return to our scenario, I find myself at the daily planner, a few minutes after 8 o'clock in the morning when I am interrupted again.

Secretary: "Excuse me, it's Jack Herbein on the line."

Once again, on the Mac screen is a small decision card asking me whether I want to take this call from Jack Herbein, the company's vice-president for generation and my superior. I click on the "yes" button to hear the message.

Jack Herbein: "Hello, I've had a heck of a time getting through on the phone. The press must be catching up with this story. Before I left Philadelphia, I wanted you to know that this thing at TMI is more extensive than I thought. I don't know any details, but I'm about to leave for Three Mile Island by helicopter to find out. I'll try to keep you informed. Good-bye."

On the video monitor during this call are images of a developing crisis at the plant. For the first time there are visible signs at the gates to the site that suggest utility personnel are concerned about radiation levels around the site: workers are being evacuated and Geiger counters are measuring radiation in cars and on people.

Throughout the course of the simulation exercise, I, as the player, have had unlimited opportunity to be proactive as well as reactive to interruptions and information presented to me. As stated previously, a principal way of gathering information and interacting with several dozen of the main characters in the scenario is the rolodex icon which represents the player's telephonic access to the outside world.

As a result of the incoming call just received from Jack Herbein, I may, for example, be moved to attempt to call directly to the Control Room at the TMI nuclear plant and speak with the engineers in charge of handling the accident. I click on the name "Gary Miller" on the rolodex who is identified as the station manager for Three Mile Island. Then, by clicking the telephone button, I attempt to access him in the Control Room. As soon as the dialing tones conclude the call, the video monitor signals a successful call by showing me a video clip of engineers handling an emergency in the control room. An obviously harried, panicky voice delivers to me a message over the loud background noise of system alarms:

George Kunder: "Hello. Control Room. George Kunder speaking. Unfortunately, Miller is completely tied up handling the emergency right now. But I can tell you the story's not a good one. The accident is extensive enough that there's a real possibility of core damage, which, of course, means extremely high radiation on sight. Plus there have already been external radiation releases. How much? We aren't sure. We're trying to get things under control. Maybe Gary can call you later when things calm down. That's it for now though. Good-bye."

Shortly after receiving this latest status report from the Control Room, I receive a distressed interruption from my secretary:

Secretary: "Excuse me, but the phones are ringing off the hook. People are saying there's an accident at Three Mile Island. Civil defense is on alert. What's going on. What are you going to do?"

* * * * *

In playing the first Harvard interactive simulation, you get your chance to live one of the key roles in the drama that was Three Mile Island. You're no longer an observer; you're a participant and a decision maker. The simulation lets you test your theories, your knowledge, your instincts, your nerve, and rewrite history at Three Mile Island. As you begin the Crisis Management Game, you are now in control.

References

Brandt, Richard H. "Paradigms, Multimedia, and Tutoring, or, is Multimedia Going to Survive in the School?" *The Journal of Multimedia Computing* 1, no. 3:9–13.

Brandt, Richard. 1990. "Multimedia and Reality." *The Journal of Multimedia Computing* 2, no. 1:28–32.

Caruso, Denise. 1991. "Interactive Learning." *Publish* 6, no. 4:75–80.

Donovan, John W. "Multimedia: Solutions Anticipating a Market." *BYTE* 16, no. 13:151.

Fink, Steven. 1986. *Crisis Management: Planning for the Inevitable.* New York: AMACOM.

Fletcher, J. D. 1991. "Excerpts from "Effectiveness and Cost of Interactive Videodisc Instruction in Defense Training and Education." *The Journal of Multimedia Computing* 2, no. 1:33–42.

Goldsmith, Suzanne, and Katherine Boo. "The Case for the Case Study." *The Washington Monthly*, June, 1989, 18–25.

Heyer, Mark. "Tech 2000—A Focus for the 1990's." *The Journal of Multimedia Computing* 1, no. 1:44–46.

Kim, Yongmin. "Chips Deliver Multimedia." *BYTE* 16, no. 13:163–173.

Kosslyn, Stephen M., Christopher F. Chabris, Sania E. Hamilton. 1990. "Designing for the Mind." *The Journal of Multimedia Computing* 1, no. 3:23–29.

Lambert, Craig. 1990. "The Electronic Tutor." *Harvard Magazine* 93, no. 2:43–51.

Lillie, David L., Wallace H. Hannum, and Gary B. Stuck. 1989. *Computers and Effective Instruction: Using Computers and Software in the Classroom.* New York: Longman, Inc.

Luskin, Dr. Bernard J. "Synesthetics at 'The Laser's Edge,'" *The Journal of Multimedia Computing* 2, no. 1:43–46.

Malone, T. W. & M. R. Lepper. 1987. "Making Learning Fun: A Taxonomy of Intrinsic Motivations in Learning." In *Aptitude, Learning, and Instruction: III. Conative and Affective Processes,* edited by R. E. Snow & M. J. Farr. Hillsdale, N.J.: Lawrence Erlbaum Associates.

Malone, T. W. 1981. "Toward a Theory of Intrinsically Motivating Instruction." *Cognitive Science* 4, 333–369.

Marlino, Mary R. 1990. "Evaluating Multimedia: Lessons Learned from the Past." *The Journal of Multimedia Computing* 1, no. 3:14–18.

Marsh, Julia, and Lawrence Vanston. 1991. *Interactive Multimedia and Telecommunications: Forecasts of Markets and Technologies.* Telecommunications Technology Forecasting Group.

Martorella, Peter H. 1989. *Interactive Video and Instruction.* Washington, D.C.: National Education Association.

"New AI Lab for Learning." *Human Capital* 1, no. 1:11. From *Computer World,* August 7, 1989.

Perelman, Lewis J. 1990. "Learning as Work." *The Journal of Multimedia Computing* 1, no. 2:11–16.

Perelman, Lewis J. 1989. "The Learning Revolution." *Human Capital* 1, no. 1:28–33.

Perlmutter, Martin. 1991. *Producer's Guide to Interactive Videodiscs.* New York: Knowledge Industry Publications, Inc.

Robertson, Barbara. "IBM Goes to Hollywood." *The Journal of Multimedia Computing* 1, no. 2:36–42.

Seger, Randall. 1990. D I: "The New Standard for Education." *The Journal of Multimedia Computing* 1, no. 2:51–52.

Steinberg, Esther R. 1991. "Computer-Assisted Instruction: A Synthesis of Theory, Practice, and Technology." Hillsdale, N.J.: Lawrence Erlbaum Associates.

Taylor, Bruce A. 1990. "An Agent for Education Change: Interview." *The Journal of Multimedia Computing* 1, no. 2:24–27.

White, Mary Alice. 1990. "Imagery in Multimedia." *The Journal of Multimedia Computing* 1, no. 3:5–8.

Wilson, Kathleen S. 1990. "The Palenque Prototype: A Multimedia Design Example." *The Journal of Multimedia Computing* 1, no. 1:34–38.

"Workforce Challenges for the 1990's." *Human Capital* 1, no. 2:8–9.

15

Restructuring Space, Time, Story, and Text in Advanced Multimedia Learning Environments

Janet H. Murray

Building Structure in a New Learning Medium

As humanities education reflects increasing concern with cultural diversity and with fostering an understanding of multiple perspectives on the world, educators are drawn to multimedia environments. This is true across the disciplines. In *language learning* the new communicative methodologies strive to prepare students not only to study the literature of a foreign culture, but also to interact with contemporary speakers of the language in a culturally appropriate manner. Such an approach necessitates the use of film and video materials as well as print examples of "realia" (real objects from everyday life, such as train tickets and newspaper ads) as a source of the language as it is actually used by native speakers in their natural environment. It fosters a sense that the French spoken by a priest and a plumber, by friends and strangers, in public and in private, differ from one another in ways that reveal much that is important to know about the culture. *Literature* has long incorporated the study of narrative art in film, and along with *history* is moving toward cultural studies in which visual material and examples of popular culture, as well as art produced in film and video, are as important as print sources as objects of analysis.

As the objects of study have become more various the technology for accessing them has become more capable. In particular, interactive video, delivered for now on videodisc but eventually available in mammoth digital archives, offer an accessibility to visual material undreamed of only a decade ago. By combining the computer with the videodisc player (and eventually with digital sources of moving video) we have created a new medium in which text, still, and moving video can be synchronized, displayed, annotated, and recombined in ways that we are only beginning to discover.

The emergence of this new medium carries with it a need for the invention of new structures to exploit both the greater quantity of materials and the multiplicity of access that computers can offer. This chapter explores the structures we have invented at MIT for advanced multimedia learning projects in the humanities. These structures were developed for particular applications but also can be seen as multi-purpose building blocks of the new medium.[1]

Spacial Structures

The language learning videodiscs produced at MIT explore two genres, *interactive fiction* and *interactive documentary*.[2] In both of these forms we have found it useful to give students mobility in a simulated world, to locate them psychologically by giving them a strong sense of place and an ability to move through specific spaces. Both our documentary and our fictional discs, therefore, exploit spacial metaphors as important organiz-ing devices.[3] The two most important metaphors are the **map** and the **footpath**. The footpath is used in a technique known as **surrogate travel**, which can be used for exterior public spaces or for interior private (and even fictional) spaces.

In the disc *Dans le quartier St. Gervais*, the student is allowed to explore a neighborhood of Paris. Access is in several modalities. One key modality is the **map**.

In this mode the student can select a video clip from a menu that represents the actual geographic location of the store or church or streetcorner where the video was shot. Maps are embedded in one another, starting with an overview and moving to increasingly fine levels of detail. This allows the student to get a notion of the general geography of the area before choosing specific segments (figures 15.1 and 15.2). The advantage of the map as an organizing principle is that it is immediately grasped and provides the student with a navigational system familiar from everyday life. It is therefore useful in minimizing the disorientation problems that plague hypermedia design, while still preserving freedom of exploration. A map allows the designer to suggest pre-determined paths (such as progress down a particular street) without prescribing them. As

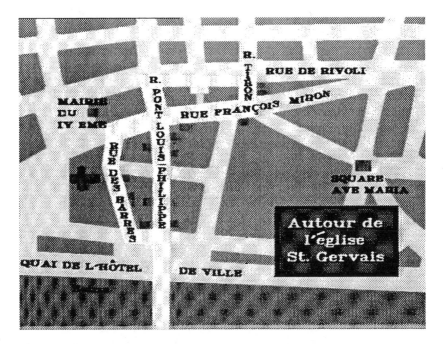

Figure 15.1

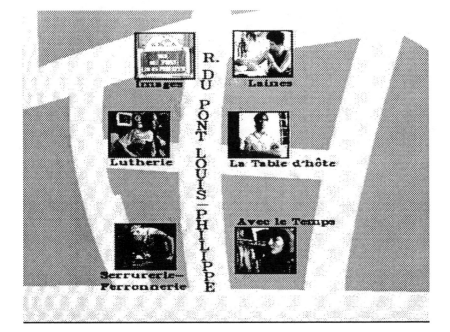

Figure 15.2

a result the student is free to progress in a straight line, systematically exploring one small area and then another, or to jump around from place to place. In either case, the student is provided with a picture of the whole and can place their individual explorations in the larger context.[4]

The same St. Gervais neighborhood can be explored "on foot" rather than by map, using a **surrogate travel** method (also referred to as a "movie map") based on the pioneering work of MIT's Aspen Disc, made by the Architecture Machine Group, a forerunner of the Media Lab.[5] In this modality, the user is placed in the position of a pedestrian, and moves step by step down a footpath by clicking on arrows on the computer screen. The arrows are displayed as part of a street map, thereby allowing the user to form a concept of their geographic position. The video screen shows what would appear to a person standing in that location. The student is given the illusion of moving through a space by the successive display of a sequence of still images that mimic a walk through the area (figures 15.3, 15.4, 15.5). The user can always move backwards as well as forwards and at some places has the choice of moving left or right (figures 15.6 and 15.7).

Figure 15.3

Figure 15.4

Figure 15.5

Figure 15.6

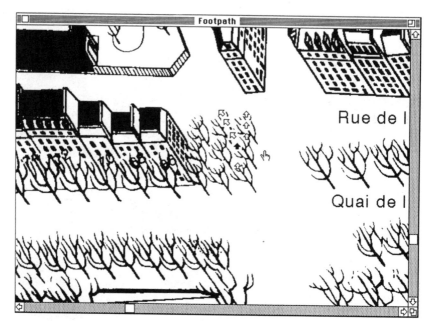

Figure 15.7

The advantage of surrogate travel is the feeling of psychological immersion in a simulated reality, in this case, the helpful illusion of actually visiting the country where the studied language is spoken. The detail of the movie map is also an advantage in teaching culture. Its disadvantage is its "pedestrian" point of view, in the metaphoric as well as the literal sense of the term. It is too constricting and uninvolving to move step by step through a place that has been recorded in such a rote, uninterpreted fashion. Therefore we have supplemented the footpath with *short video essays* in which the camera moves freely, focusing in on such details as a gargoyle on a cathedral or a teapot-shaped shop sign that convey the subjective feel of a place as interpreted by the video filmmaker. Video essays can also provide ambient sound which is difficult to link up to the still images of the movie map. These essays are available from the map menus and are described as "Son et Images" (sound and images of the place).

Since the interviews, footpath images, and video essays are all anchored in map-based representations of the neighborhood, the user may not distinguish among these modes of exploring the space. Ideally all of them would blend (along with the historic slides described later) into one integrated sense of the neighborhood which would include its geography, subjective feel, and its inhabitants.

The sense of psychological immersion created by giving the student control over a physical space is especially valuable in the context of fiction. In the interactive fiction *A la rencontre de Philippe,* a **map** is also used at certain times in the story in which the student is expected to visit different places in Paris in an attempt to help the protagonist find a new apartment. The map we are using is similar to one that Parisians use except that it has been made interactive and expanded for pedagogical purposes. As in Paris, the students are asked to first to determine the arrondissement of the street they wish to visit. They then choose the arrondissement by clicking on its number on an interactive map (figure 15.8), and receive a description of the character of the chosen neighborhood with an interactive list of those streets that play a part in our story (figure 15.9).

One of the most important story locales is the apartment Philippe has been sharing with his girlfriend Elizabeth. This apartment is presented in a manner similar to the **surrogate travel** of *St. Gervais.* The rooms of the apartment have been photographed so that the students can step through

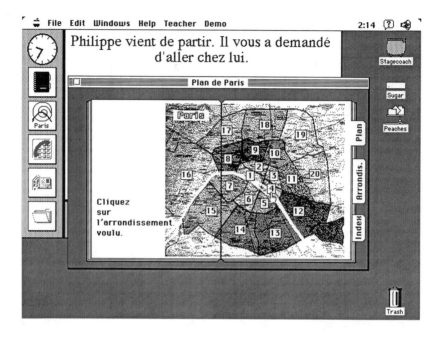

Figure 15.8

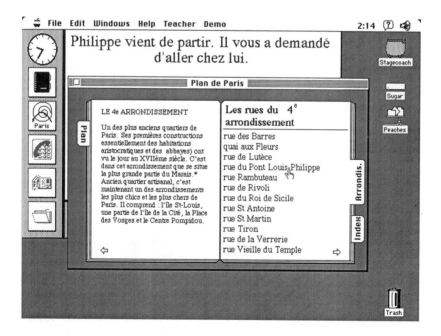

Figure 15.9

them and experience the illusion of walking around an authentic Parisian apartment. We have also made it possible to jump from room to room in order to move more purposefully. Again the method is to represent the space schematically on the computer with interactive arrows that indicate your position and allow you to move, and to provide on the video screen the view that you would see if you were standing in the position indicated by the currently blackened arrow (figure 15.10).

Another way in which we have sought to enhance the students' sense of immersion in a concrete world is by creating **simulated, interactive objects**. These objects can be seen on the video as photographed real objects (which are sometimes used by the protagonist, increasing the viewer's sense of their reality). They also exist in scanned-in reproduction on the computer screen where the can be used interactively by the student. In the study on the desktop are several such objects: a copy of the Figaro newspaper that can be opened to examine simulated apartment ads, a message machine that can be operated by clicking on its familiar buttons, and a telephone on which one can dial numbers within the story (which will lead to simulated answering machine messages and a text box of the

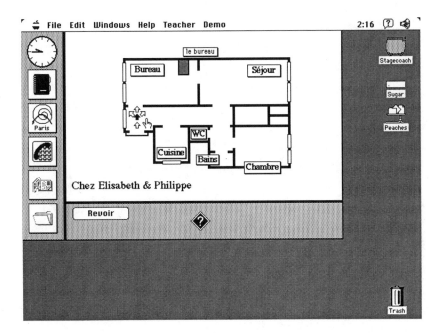

Figure 15.10

computer screen in which one can type in a message) and numbers outside
the story (in which case one will hear the "not in service" message used
in Paris) (figures 15.11 and 15.12). In *No recuerdo* a fax machine serves
a similar purpose. These simulated objects add to the verisimilitude of the
story and provide an element of surprise, while facilitating tasks that
require language comprehension.

Of course there are clear learning tasks involved in moving through the
space provided in the documentary and fictional environments, including
accessing information in answer to teacher's assigned tasks, listening to
authentic speech in a clear context and coming to an understanding of
the gist of what has been said. But the student's experience is not of
using a reference tool or taking a quiz or even of completing an exercise. The experience is framed as a **visit** because the spacial rather than
the pedagogical structure dominates the presentation. Although more
research needs to be done to identify the student's relationship to the
materials, anecdotal evidence gleaned from student evaluation forms
and comments to instructors and developers supports the notion that

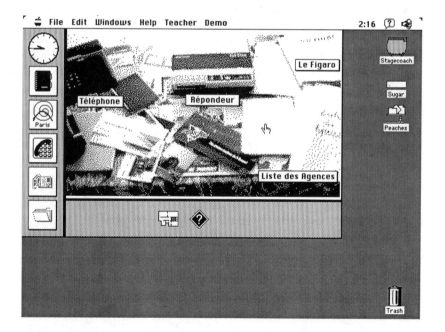

Figure 15.11

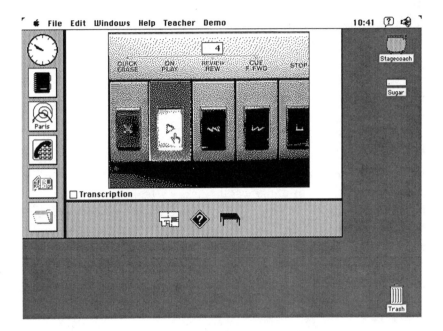

Figure 15.12

they feel as if they have been somewhere, that they have taken an imaginary journey. This assumption increases our responsibility to make the simulated environments as diverse, authentic, and non-stereotypical as possible.

Temporal Structures

Along with space the other great organizer of human consciousness is of course time, and so it not surprising that in establishing landmarks in a confusingly unstructured new medium we have relied on time as one of our principal coordinates.

In *St. Gervais* we make wide use of historical time. In addition to interviews and video and still renderings of the life of the contemporary neighborhood, we have over 600 still images of historical significance, recording the life of the neighborhood from the seventeenth century to the present. These historical slides have text files associated with them that are written in intermediate level French describing everything from life in the literary salons to the daily life of artisans. The student accesses this information by a kind of time travel that parallels the spacial travel. Because this is a hypermedia system, there are several ways to discover and explore the historical material. First of all, a student using the foot path would be alerted to historical material by a special sign that appears on the map. The student could click on this historical sign and move back and forth between annotated contemporary and historical views of the same location. Either through the map or through the lattice of cultural topics the students are given access to a navigational window that lets them change either time or place as they move around in the collection of historical slides (figure 15.13). This allows access that bypasses the map and footpath, subordinating the schematization of space to questions of temporal change in a variety of locations.

In the fictional world of *Philippe* and *No recuerdo* time is at least equally important, but it is *storytime* rather than historical time that the student is aware of. In both simulations a clock is provided (seen on the upper lefthand of the *Philippe* screens reproduced here) and certain activities—appointments, interviews, visits to particular locations—can

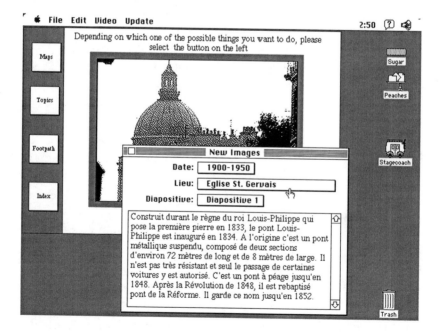

Figure 15.13

only take place during certain hours. The story clock controls the plot and keeps the story progressing in a predictable way toward a conclusion which in *No recuerdo* is set for a particular hour. The clock provides a structure within which the various permutations of the story can be contained.

But time in a fictional world is not governed by the sun. In the case of *Philippe*, in which all the action takes place within a single day, time is measured in two ways, corresponding to the two modes in which the story is presented. For the parts of the story presented as video segments (interrupted by questions posed to the student) the time is predetermined. A particular scene always takes place at the same time of day and runs for the same amount of fictional time. But Philippe also includes two periods of time in which the student is left "alone" to explore Philippe's apartment and to move around Paris. These time periods are bounded by appointments, and the student is given a fixed amount of time in which to explore. How is this time counted? Each possible action—making phone call, looking around Philippe's apartment, visiting a realtor or another apartment, etc.—is given a certain number of minutes, and the displayed clock advances accordingly until the student is reminded that it is time for their next appointment. In this way the fictional world is made more concrete, and the teacher can ensure that the student performs a certain number of desirable activities, while leaving open the choice of activities performed by any individual student.

In addition to the clock in the corner of the screen, the student has available an "agenda" or diary which records everything that happens during the day. This tool allows the student to review video segments from previous scenes, while still remaining within the sequence of events that marks his or her individual experience of the story. Any event listed in the sequence can be clicked on for reviewing. Afterwards the student is returned to the "current" story time—the time from which he or she began the review (figure 15.14).

Taken together the spacial and temporal structures, both taken from familiar objects, provide powerful organizers of the students' experiences. Although it will require more intensive study to fully understand how simulated space and time are understood by individual students and how they affect the learning process it seems likely that the psychological

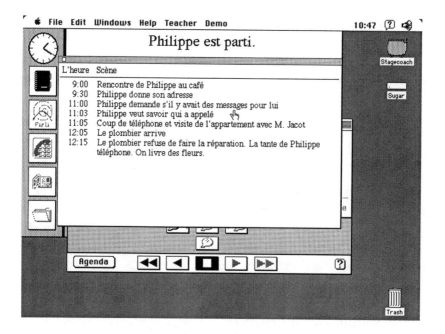

Figure 15.14

experience of immersion which these structures create also contributes significantly to students' motivation.

Story Structure

Narrative form is in itself an important organizing structure. Interactive fiction combines the expectations of conventional narratives (e.g., character, conflict, resolution) with innovative structures that allow viewers to affect the progress and outcome of the story.

Philippe and *No recuerdo* are both interactive stories (although *No recuerdo* also has some documentary elements based upon brief explorations of Bogota). *Philippe* is designed in an exploratory style. Although the student is asked to help the protagonist solve his problems there is no single right solution. Choices that the student makes all have consequences but there are many satisfying ways to end the story. In *No recuerdo* the student is under more pressure to find out a particular piece of information, but lack of success provides as much narrative interest as success. In either case it is involvement with the story that is rewarded, and the rewards are intrinsic. The more you understand and respond, the rich the fictional world revealed to you.

In any interactive fiction, the big question for the designer is how to build in the student's interventions. One method is to give the student a role in the story, preferably one that includes problem solving of some kind. The camera then represents the student and the actors address the student by looking into the camera (figure 15.15).[6] Both Philippe and Gonzalo (the protagonist of *No recuerdo*) look in the camera at times and directly address the student, who has a definite role to play in the drama. In *Philippe,* the student represents a visiting friend, in *No recuerdo* an investigative reporter.

First person video (as this approach is called) can be limited as a language learning technique because we want to show interactions between two or more authentic speakers, including speakers in intimate situations, which would be awkward to portray if the camera is meant to be a person rather than an observer (figure 15.16). For this reason we have

Figure 15.15

Figure 15.16

filmed some scenes in third-person point of view, with the student a proverbial fly on the wall, observing the scene but not really in it.

In cases where characters address the viewer directly the interaction begins to take on the form of a conversation. *Conversational form* is one of the emerging subgenres of interactive fiction, and it offers great promise to language teachers because the discourse features of conversation are often the focus of language instruction.[7] In *Philippe* we limit conversations to one or two interchanges, all of them answers to questions that Philippe directly poses such as "Where is the check for the plumber?" (figure 15.17). But in *No recuerdo* we are attempting to structure the story around several conversational interviews between the reporter and Gonzalo in which the student will be given the task of actively eliciting information. Although *No recuerdo* was originally designed for use with a natural language processing system that could parse and to some degree "understand" students' questions, both interactive stories are currently being implemented on the Macintosh with interfaces in which the student's part of the conversation will be chosen from a menu of possible remarks.

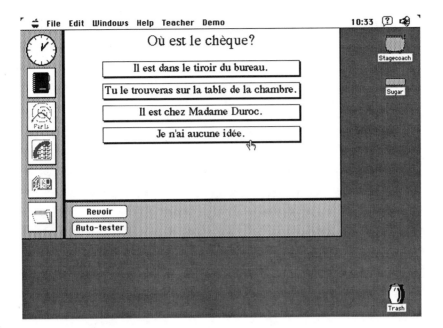

Figure 15.17

Another way of having the student affect the story is by creating an exploratory environment, a *microworld* to use Papert's term,[8] in which the student is free to try out a number of things, all of which have interesting effects. In *Philippe* the period in which the student can explore the desktop and can visit realtors and rental apartments provides such a microworld. If the student call a particular realtor, opportunities will arise later in the story. If the student listens to the answering machine, then he or she will gain information that will affect later developments. If the student calls a mutual friend of Philippe and Elizabeth after learning some key information, then the friend will help them make up. None of these are moments of obvious branching, yet all are changes in the configuration of the story resulting from the student's choices and actions.

Of course our effort is to combine the pedagogical task with narrative function, making the student's interactive participation in the story overlap with the learning task. In *No recuerdo* the student is a newspaper reporter and has to communicate with a demanding editor who exchanges faxes with the student-reporter. The student must compose faxes that are acceptable paraphrases of interviews with important characters, and must direct interviews so that informants answer the questions that the editor has posed. These tasks require the use of basic language skills, but they also make sense in terms of the story. When the student has trouble with one of these tasks the story is held up and the student is given pedagogical help in the form of fictionally appropriate communications from the editor. It is hoped that the overlap between the pedagogical and the fictional will aid in motivation and in focusing the student on the communicative nature of the task.

When dealing with fiction with a pedagogical purpose it is important to ally the pedagogical tasks with the imaginative realm of the story. What the student does to demonstrate or practice comprehension should be an intrinsic part of the fictional world and have a clear effect on the story. It should also be borne in mind that users like to play through the fiction several times, exploring different branches, and to compare their experiences of the story with other users (which can be useful for establishing communicative tasks across an intriguing knowledge gap in language classes). Student participation should therefore be designed so that successive plays provide additional information.[9]

Textual Structure

The question of textual structure in a hypermedia environment is worthy of a book of its own. I include it here in order to highlight some useful organizational tools that I think have significance beyond the particular projects in which they are currently employed.

Interactive Indexing and Topical Navigation

A documentary videodisc like *St. Gervais* can be thought of as a databank. Students are sent to such a disc with particular exercises, adapted to their level and learning task. The databank itself need contain no exercises, only supple means of access that will facilitate the learning tasks various teachers assign.

In thinking about ways to make the material of *St. Gervais* available to students we can look to analogies in structures designed for books The most obvious kind of information we would want to retrieve are topics and themes discussed in the interviews. Here it is useful to think about textbook readers for use in composition or introductory literature courses which are printed with more than one table of contents, such as one by author or chronology and one by topic or genre. A hypermedia data base also needs multiple contents and also multiple indices, and these structures must be available to the user from many points of access.

St. Gervais has an *index by topics* that is available at the top level, but also from any interview. One can review all the topics and who speaks to each one, or one can see just the topics list that deals with what the current interviewee is discussing, presumably in order to choose another interviewee who speaks to the same theme. For the historical information the topics are arranged like a *lattice* (figure 15.18) since subtopics like "the Family in the 17th century" belong under two general topics, "The Family," and "Daily Life in the 17th Century." Both of these arrangements would be difficult to duplicate in a linear form like the book. They are meant to take advantage of the webbing of information that hypermedia systems allow.

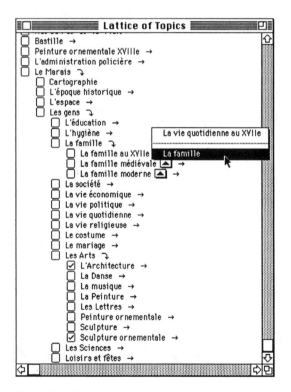

Figure 15.18

In fact from a language learning point of view even a fictional videodisc like *Philippe* (or *No recuerdo*) is to some extent a database. It is a repository of authentic language use that can be indexed and cross-indexed according to a multitude of language-teaching categories: grammatically, functionally, communicatively. The *Multiple Functions Index* of *Philippe*, for instance, includes grouped examples of greetings, leave-takings, requests for help, hesitations, and use of tricky idioms or colloquial expressions. In this way the disc has a usefulness beyond its structure as a story, and in an environment with easier access to multiple videos than we currently can sustain, could be part of an extensive reference library of the spoken language. (figure 15.19). More ambitiously, as these discs increase one could create cross-cultural indices that would show the same functional situation (e.g., greeting a friend) in several cultures and subcultures.

Moving in Both Directions between Words and Images
One of the key capabilities of an advanced educational hypermedia system is that you must be able to go from text to video and from video to text.

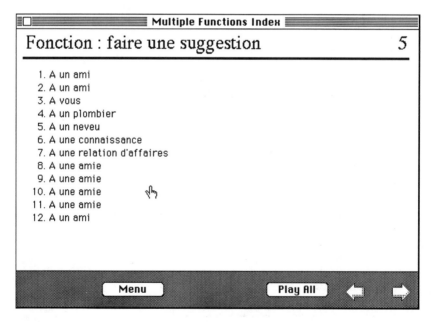

Figure 15.19

This is so little the norm that some hardware and software systems do not even allow for the possibility of the video to text move. Yet there are several situations in which this is utterly essential and which point to the centrality of this functionality for humanities applications in the future.

In language learning, for instance, it is desirable to present the student with the text of a film or video linked like subtitles to the running video. The linking must include alternate versions of the text, including key words, full transcript, and in some cases, translation or representation in alternate alphabets. The text itself must be hyperlinked to glossary and it is desirable to link the glossary back again into the video, so that multiple examples of the same word or phrase can be shown (figure 15.20). In working with this material, watching the film, stopping it, looking at the transcripts, backing up through the transcript to watch an earlier scene, using the glossary, students will not be aware of when they are using the text as a pointer to the video and when they are using the video frame number as a pointer to the text. Both are necessary functions of the medium.

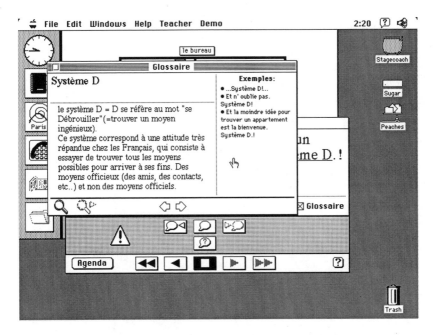

Figure 15.20

Another example of a teaching application in which one must be able to move in both directions is an interface under development at MIT for the display of text and videodisc versions of Shakespeare's plays which we hope to one day assemble into a massive interactive multimedia annotated Archive. An application like this models the kinds of functionality humanists will increasingly demand from computer-based environments. In such an Archive scholars or students will want to start from a great performance and refer back to the folio, quarto, and standard performance texts, as well as to start from the text and see versions of the same scene done in a variety of productions. In addition, text and video clips should be capable of being annotated, rearranged, and stored for retrieval in selected form. One should be able to write multimedia essays, incorporating video clips into text (figure 15.21). The interconnections in such a system would be dense (figure 15.22), and the key to making it workable would be to ensure that users could start with any piece of it—texts, films, or commentary—and access the appropriate parts of any other piece, without having to encounter a cumbersome apparatus or to follow rigid

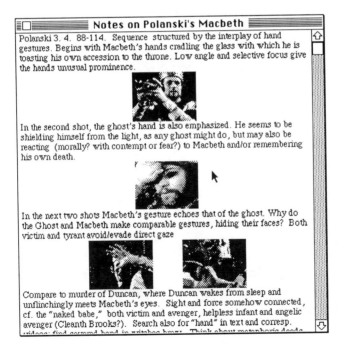

Figure 15.21

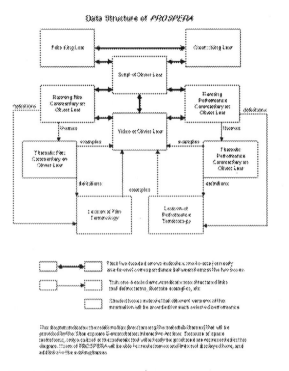

Figure 15.22

pre-formed paths. The invention of a medium to support such explorations is an important task in supporting the development of the next
generation of applications in the humanities.

Incorporating Sophisticated Search Mechanisms

At a less ambitious level, it is important to remember that the commercial
market is beginning to deliver to us the tools that will help us to take
advantage of the growing number of electronic texts and videodiscs
representing works of importance to humanistic study. Hypercard and its
imitators have been a tremendous help, despite the limitations of the
notecard metaphor, particularly for handling large bodies of text. The
next big improvement will be the integrated systems (like System 7 on the
Macintosh) in which we can see one application passing data to another.

For textual study, this is extremely promising as the following simple
example demonstrates. Using an off-the-shelf word processor (Nisus)
which has an exceptionally powerful macro and search capability, as an

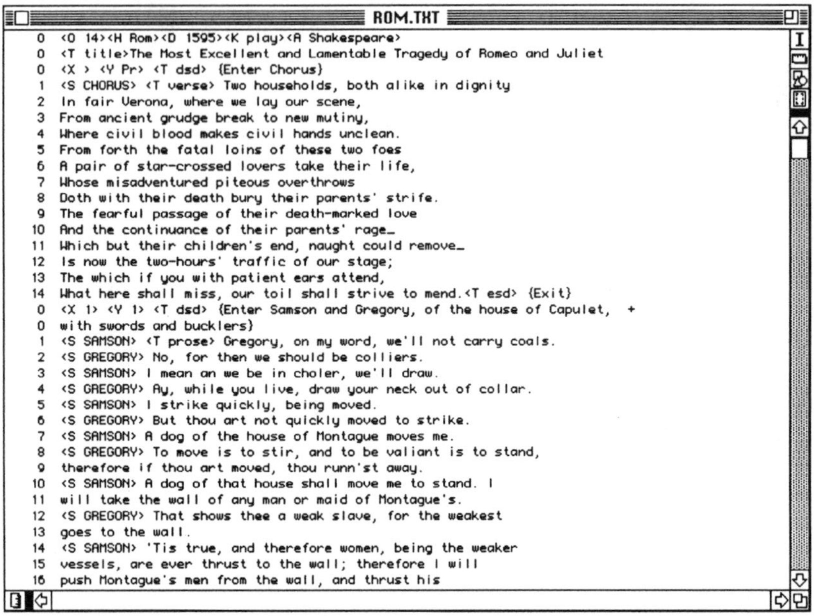

```
┌──────────────────────────── ROM.TXT ──────────────────────────────┐
│  0  <O 14><H Rom><D 1595><K play><A Shakespeare>                    │
│  0  <T title>The Most Excellent and Lamentable Tragedy of Romeo and Juliet│
│  0  <X > <Y Pr> <T dsd> {Enter Chorus}                              │
│  1  <S CHORUS> <T verse> Two households, both alike in dignity      │
│  2  In fair Verona, where we lay our scene,                         │
│  3  From ancient grudge break to new mutiny,                        │
│  4  Where civil blood makes civil hands unclean.                    │
│  5  From forth the fatal loins of these two foes                    │
│  6  A pair of star-crossed lovers take their life,                  │
│  7  Whose misadventured piteous overthrows                          │
│  8  Doth with their death bury their parents' strife.               │
│  9  The fearful passage of their death-marked love                  │
│ 10  And the continuance of their parents' rage_                     │
│ 11  Which but their children's end, naught could remove_            │
│ 12  Is now the two-hours' traffic of our stage;                     │
│ 13  The which if you with patient ears attend,                      │
│ 14  What here shall miss, our toil shall strive to mend.<T esd> {Exit}│
│  0  <X 1> <Y 1> <T dsd> {Enter Samson and Gregory, of the house of Capulet, +│
│  0  with swords and bucklers}                                       │
│  1  <S SAMSON> <T prose> Gregory, on my word, we'll not carry coals.│
│  2  <S GREGORY> No, for then we should be colliers.                 │
│  3  <S SAMSON> I mean an we be in choler, we'll draw.               │
│  4  <S GREGORY> Ay, while you live, draw your neck out of collar.   │
│  5  <S SAMSON> I strike quickly, being moved.                       │
│  6  <S GREGORY> But thou art not quickly moved to strike.           │
│  7  <S SAMSON> A dog of the house of Montague moves me.             │
│  8  <S GREGORY> To move is to stir, and to be valiant is to stand,  │
│  9  therefore if thou art moved, thou runn'st away.                 │
│ 10  <S SAMSON> A dog of that house shall move me to stand. I        │
│ 11  will take the wall of any man or maid of Montague's.            │
│ 12  <S GREGORY> That shows thee a weak slave, for the weakest       │
│ 13  goes to the wall.                                               │
│ 14  <S SAMSON> 'Tis true, and therefore women, being the weaker     │
│ 15  vessels, are ever thrust to the wall; therefore I will          │
│ 16  push Montague's men from the wall, and thrust his               │
└────────────────────────────────────────────────────────────────────┘
```

Figure 15.23

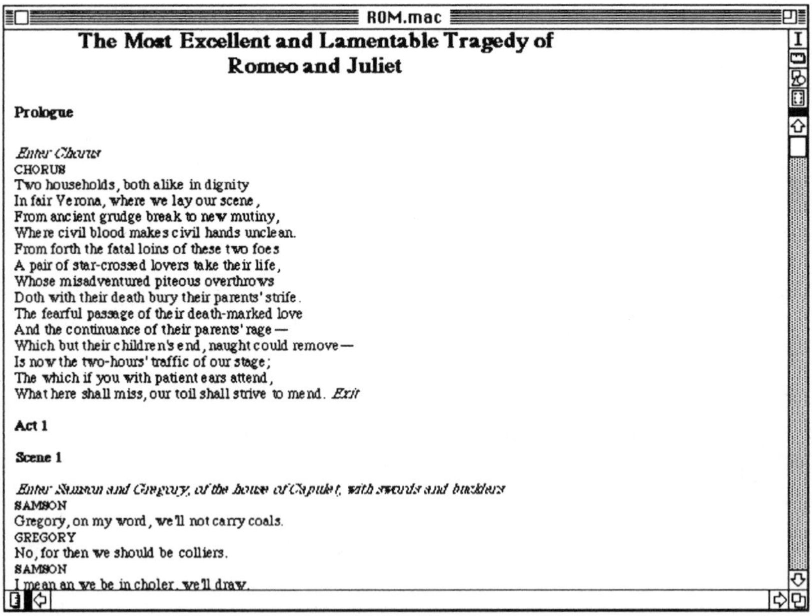

```
┌──────────────────────────── ROM.mac ──────────────────────────────┐
│         The Most Excellent and Lamentable Tragedy of               │
│                        Romeo and Juliet                            │
│                                                                    │
│  Prologue                                                          │
│                                                                    │
│  Enter Chorus                                                      │
│  CHORUS                                                            │
│  Two households, both alike in dignity                             │
│  In fair Verona, where we lay our scene,                           │
│  From ancient grudge break to new mutiny,                          │
│  Where civil blood makes civil hands unclean.                      │
│  From forth the fatal loins of these two foes                      │
│  A pair of star-crossed lovers take their life,                    │
│  Whose misadventured piteous overthrows                            │
│  Doth with their death bury their parents' strife.                 │
│  The fearful passage of their death-marked love                    │
│  And the continuance of their parents' rage —                      │
│  Which but their children's end, naught could remove —             │
│  Is now the two-hours' traffic of our stage;                       │
│  The which if you with patient ears attend,                        │
│  What here shall miss, our toil shall strive to mend. Exit         │
│                                                                    │
│  Act 1                                                             │
│                                                                    │
│  Scene 1                                                           │
│                                                                    │
│  Enter Samson and Gregory, of the house of Capulet, with swords and bucklers│
│  SAMSON                                                            │
│  Gregory, on my word, we'll not carry coals.                      │
│  GREGORY                                                           │
│  No, for then we should be colliers.                              │
│  SAMSON                                                            │
│  I mean an we be in choler, we'll draw.                           │
└────────────────────────────────────────────────────────────────────┘
```

Figure 15.24

interface we can make a recent database like the Oxford Electronic Shakespeare tremendously pliable. In its raw state the tagged text of the OES is very difficult to read (figure 15.23). The tags of course serve to mark off speakers, to set off stage directions from dialogue, and to indicate Act, Scene, and Line divisions. By teaching Nisus to decode these tags and setting up a style for displaying each category we can create text that is conventionally readable (figure 15.24), but that also retains the knowledge encoded in its tags, and can therefore be searched in boolean queries that take structural elements into consideration. For instance, using the Nisus search routines, one could ask for all the places where the word "honest" is said by the Nurse (figure 15.25). Furthermore, under System 7, one could feed the result of such a search to a program capable of controlling a videodisc and consulting a table that linked line numbers with frame numbers. Assuming that the videodisc had already been indexed, one could easily move in this way from a complex text-centered search of the play to a display of appropriate video clips.

This is a multifunctional multimedia environment that is potentially obtainable with little more than off-the-shelf products. It does not deliver

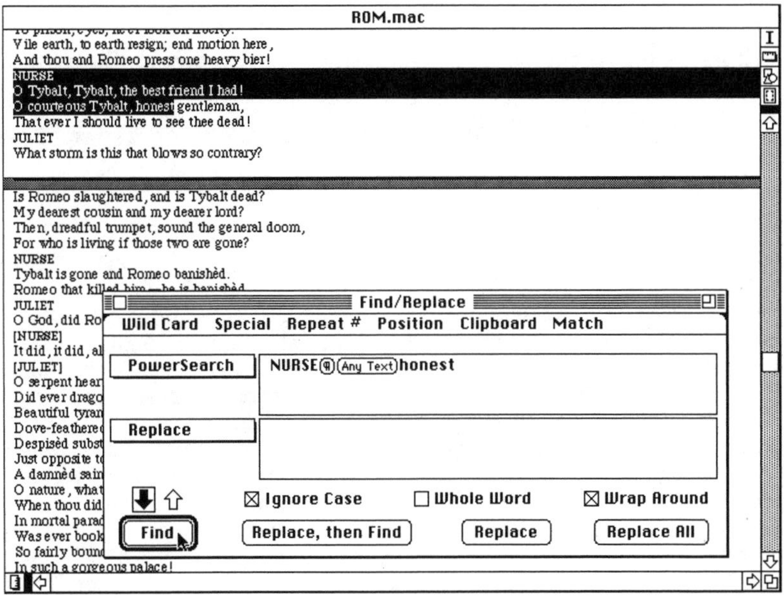

Figure 15.25

all the functionality humanities teachers and scholars will demand. But like Hypercard, it should help us to define a new standard of expectation.

Conclusion

The emerging structures of advanced multimedia teaching environments in the humanities are following key trends in the profession: the move to communicative language-teaching using authentic language spoken by native speakers; the interest in culture as a totality incorporating visual as well as textual material; the emphasis on interdisciplinary collaboration; the need to think in global terms and to reinforce awareness of multiple perspectives. One challenge posed by these new modes of inquiry is how to maintain such broad perspectives without becoming disoriented. Part of the solution to that problem will be the definition of structures of hypermedia that will facilitate a rich engagement with varied and dense materials without overwhelming ourselves. We must establish conventions by which we can feel in possession of clear landmarks without being forced through the same pre-marked paths. Only further use and sophisticated testing of hypermedia materials will reveal to us the best way to facilitate this exploratory yet oriented approach to learning. The joy of working with hypermedia can make us feel as if we are at liberty in an enchanted forest. The success of the medium as a long-lasting learning environment will depend upon inventing the right sort of road signs and compasses.

Notes

1. All of the structures described in this chapter are the result of collaborative work. Gilberte Furstenberg and Douglas Morgenstern are the language teachers who have been the primary shapers of the French and Spanish videodiscs, respectively. Ayshe Farman-Farmaian was the producer and co-designer of *A la rencontre de Philippe*; Michael Roper was the co-producer and director of *Dans le quartier St. Gervais;* Rus Gant was the producer of *No recuerdo*. Stuart Malone is the primary programmer-designer for all the projects in their Macintosh versions. Benjamin Davis of the MUSE Consortium at MIT also played a role in shaping these projects, particularly in their workstation versions. Charles Kerns, formerly of Stanford, currently with Apple Computer played a key role in developing the first Macintosh version of Philippe. My collaborators on the Shakespeare Interactive Archive Project are Peter Donaldson and Larry Friedlander, with Stuart Malone as principal programmer. As Director of the Athena Language Learning Project, under whose auspices all these projects are developed, I

have served as executive producer and co-designer, but the designs described in this article are to be taken as the result of this rich collaboration. The Athena Language Learning Project has for its principle sponsor the Annenberg/CPB Project. It is also received significant support from Apple Computer, Digital Equipment Corporation, International Business Machines Corporation, the Consortium for Language Teaching and Learning, the Florence Gould Foundation, and the National Endowment for the Humanities. My particular thanks to Stuart Malone for his help in preparing the visuals for this chapter and for the presentation upon which this chapter is based.

2. See Gilberte Furstenberg, Douglas Morgenstern, and Janet H. Murray, "The Athena Language Learning Project: Design Issues for the Next Generation of Computer-Based Language Learning Tools," in *Modern Technology in Foreign Language Education* ACTFL/NTC (1988); Janet H. Murray "Emerging Genres of Interactive Videodiscs for Language Instruction, *Multimedia and Language Learning*, published by the Institute for Academic Technology, University of North Carolina at Chapel Hill, 1990.

3. Visuals are drawn from the Macintosh versions of *Philippe* and *St. Gervais*. These applications were designed for a two-screen system in which the video images appear on a separate monitor. All interactivity is focused on the computer screen. Illustrations included here which show excerpts from the video are drawn from the video monitor; those that show interactive screens are drawn from the computer monitor.

4. Apple Computer's guidebook, *Human Interface Guidelines : the Apple Desktop Interface* (Addison-Wesley, 1987) recommends using visual metaphors drawn from everyday objects and actions. For the need for orienting cues in hypertext see George P. Landow, "The Rhetoric of Hypermedia: Some Rules for Authors," in Paul Delany and George P. Landow, *Hypermedia and Literary Studies*, MIT Press, 1990.

5. Andrew Lippman, "Movie-Maps: An Application of the Optical Videodisc to Computer Graphics," ACM, April, 1980.

6. This method poses some problems in languages which distinguish gender, since we would like to allow male and female students to be appropriately addressed. This problem can be addressed by recording two versions of statements made in direct address and by limiting the situations in which the student is addressed in is way.

7. See Janet H. Murray, "Anatomy of a New Medium: Literary and Pedagogic Uses of Advanced Linguistic Computer Structures" *Computers and the Humanities*, XXV, 1, 1991.

8. See Seymour Papert, *Mindstorms: Children, Computers, and Powerful Ideas* (New York: Basic Books, 1980).

9. A good example of this kind of educational application is the early history application *The Wouldbe Gentleman*, designed by Caroline Lougee and Michael Carter at Stanford University, which allows a student to try to succeed economically and socially in ancien régime France.

16

The Virtual Classroom: Software for Collaborative Learning

Starr Roxanne Hiltz

Introduction

Colleges and universities in the United States face tremendous challenges in the 1990's. The majority of students will not be 18–21 year olds who can afford to devote their full time to living on a campus and taking courses. The majority will have families and jobs, and will be either commuters or distance education students. The need to provide access to higher education for working adults is also widely recognized in Europe, where institutions such as the British and Danish Open Universities have provided opportunities for tens of thousands of distance learners.

Computer-mediated communication systems (CMCS), especially when enhanced to create what we refer to as a "Virtual Classroom," [TM] can make significant improvements in both access to and the quality of education. Currently over 80 programs worldwide are known to be offering courses partially or completely via computer-mediated communication. (See Harasim [1989], Mason and Kaye [1989], for short descriptions of many of these programs.)

The sophistication and flexibility of software structures for supporting distance education vary widely, from simple electronic mail systems to conferencing systems that have been specially enhanced to support classroom-like experiences, particularly group discussions and joint projects. This chapter presents an overview of case studies which were part of the largest project to date in creating, using, and evaluating such systems for education. It presents excerpts from a forthcoming book on the project (Hiltz, 1992).

The objectives of a Virtual Classroom are:

• To improve access to advanced educational experiences by allowing students and instructors to participate in remote learning communities at times and places convenient to them, using personal computers at home, on a campus, or at work; and,
• To improve the quality and effectiveness of education by using the computer to support a collaborative learning process.

Collaborative learning is defined as a learning process that emphasizes group or cooperative efforts among faculty and students. It stresses active participation and interaction on the part of both students and instructors. Knowledge is viewed as a social construct, and therefore the educational process is facilitated by social interaction in an environment which facilitates peer interaction, evaluation, and cooperation (Bruffee, 1986).

Major funding from the Annenberg/CPB Project enabled NJIT to develop the "Tools for the Enhancement and Evaluation of a Virtual Classroom." Software development and field testing, and evaluation of educational outcomes in the Virtual Classroom have been co-equal activities of the project. The first project focused on comparing the process and outcome of learning in a Virtual Classroom vs. a traditional classroom, for a variety of courses offered during a single year. Subsequent years focused on more intensive studies of three specific courses.

One way to understand the software which comprises the Virtual Classroom is with an architectural analogy. Think of all the different kinds of learning tools and spaces and ritualized forms of interaction that take place within a traditional classroom, and within an entire college campus or high school. All of these things exist within a Virtual Classroom, too, except that all of the activities and interactions are mediated by computer software, rather than by face-to-face interaction. Figure 16.1 summarizes some of the software facilities in the Virtual Classroom in terms of their counterparts in the traditional (physical) classroom. It is a "snapshot" of the set of facilities that existed at one point in time, Spring 1987, when the most extensive set of field trials and evaluations was conducted. This was a prototype constructed on EIES (the Electronic Information Exchange System) operated by New Jersey Institute of Technology since 1976 as a laboratory without walls for the design and evaluation of new CMCS structures. Subsequently, the software tools were incorporated into a new generation of CMCS, EIES 2, which is a

Virtual Classroom Software Feature	Functions	Traditional Classroom
Conferences	Class discussions & lectures	Classroom
Messages	"Private" student-student & student-teacher discussions	Office hours "Hallway" conversations Telephone Calls
Notebooks	Individual & working groups composition & storage of	Paper & ring binders word processor documents & diskette
Document read activity	Scan & read "published" material	Books & Journals
"Personal TEIES"	Create, modify & share diagrams	Blackboards
Exam	Timed student-teacher feedback with no other communication permitted during test taking	Exam
Gradebook (paper)	Teacher may record & change grades and averages; student may access only his/her grades	Gradebook
Pen-names & Anonymity	Encourage self-disclosure and experimentation	
Response Activity	Force independent thinking & active participation	
Selection Activity	Manage distribution of unique assignments	Circulate signup sheets
Directory	Self-supplied description of status and interest; telephone & mailing contact information; last time online; online groups the member belongs to.	

Figure 16.1
Some Communication Structures in the Virtual and Traditional Classrooms

distributed system that operates on many UNIX™ machines, and is available to other organizations for purchase. Many of the prototype Virtual Classroom features were incorporated in the EIES 2 version, but many new features have been added each semester, based on feedback from continuing field trials with online courses.

However, the analogy to a physical classroom may be misleading. Whenever one tries to emulate and support non-computerized processes within a software environment, fundamental changes occur in both the processes and the outcomes. Some things are lost and some are gained.

One difference between the two learning environments is that in the Traditional Classroom (TC), most interaction takes place by speaking and listening (though it may be supplemented by writing and reading from a blackboard or from "handouts"). In the Virtual Classroom (VC), interaction takes place almost entirely by typing and reading from a computer terminal (though it includes the use of print materials such as textbooks, and may be supplemented by an occasional face-to-face meeting or telephone call, or perhaps videotapes). Because it is located within a CMCS, interaction among teachers and students in the Virtual Classroom is also asynchronous, with the computer storing waiting communications for each participant. This means that the members of the class typically are not present at the same time or at the same place. They may be, by chance or by plan, but usually the interaction is spread out in both space and time. The Virtual Class is a "rolling present" that goes on around the clock, seven days a week. Each student types and reads at the pace and time that is most convenient. Students generally do not receive a response to questions or comments immediately, but rather the next time they sign online, someone will probably have responded. This different rhythm of interaction takes some time to get used to.

Some things that are simple in the TC, like smiling at or hugging a student, are greatly diminished in the virtual environment. Words and symbols for SMILE (-: and <<HUGS>> just don't feel the same, for instance! On the other hand, some kinds of interaction and learning suddenly become possible and "natural" in the VC. For example, simulations and role-playing exercises can move faster and allow more variations than traditional "laboratory" exercises.

Using the analogy of software structures to emulate interactional forms in the traditional classroom gives the unfortunate impression that the VC can never be more than a second-best simulation of a TC. On the contrary, a collaborative learning environment that is computer-mediated can support some types of activities that are difficult or impossible to conduct in face-to-face environments, particularly if there is a large class. Discussion and communication about the course becomes a continuous activity, rather than being limited to a short scheduled time once or twice a week. Whenever a student has an idea or a question, it can be communicated, while it is "fresh."

The initial pilot studies with online courses during the early 1980s used the existing EIES conference and message facilities to supplement traditional courses or to deliver non-credit continuing education courses. Though the results were promising (Hiltz, 1986), it was evident that there were many limitations to be overcome, particularly for standard college-level courses that required numerous assignments and examinations as part of the course work. Conceptually, we divided these into a set of structures called Branch Activities which could be attached to a class conference in order to support special types of assignments or delivery of material for activities that were to involve the whole class; a set of teaching support tools to help the instructor manage assignments and grading and quizzes for individual students; and micro-computer based software for the integration of graphical information with text information.

In this brief summary, only one of the special VC software features shown in figure 16.1 will be explained in detail, the "Response Activity," which has been the most frequently used. It allows the instructor a great deal of control over student participation.

"Activities" are executable programs that are attached to an ordinary conference comment. All of the responses related to that activity are gathered together there, instead of being scattered throughout a conference as many separate comments. Rather than automatically receiving everything that has been entered by any participant, as with comments, participants choose to undertake the activities in a branch only when they are ready to do so, and explicitly give a command. A record is kept of DONE and UNDONE activities, and a review choice helps users to keep track. While students may access only their own records of done and undone activities, the instructor can review the Branch Activities status of any of the students. Thus, activities are usually used for graded assignments.

In a Question/Response Activity, one or more questions for response by other conference members is contained in the main conference comment. The author of a Question/Response Activity has many parameters that can be set to tailor the interaction. Responses may show the full name of the student, be entered anonymously, or allow the respondent to decide whether or not to reveal his or her identity. Each person MUST ANSWER BEFORE SEEING THE RESPONSES OF OTHERS. This is very important for making sure that each person can independently think through and enter his or her own ideas, without being influenced by responses made by others. Alternatively the author may set it up so that participants cannot see other responses even after they answer, until the author "opens" the responses for viewing. This might be done for an essay-type quiz, for example.

An example of a collaborative learning strategy applied in the VC which is included in most courses is the "seminar" type of interchange in which the students become the teachers. Individuals or small groups of students are responsible for making a selection of a topic (usually from a list provided by the instructor as a Selection Activity); reading material not assigned to the rest of the class; preparing a written summary for the class of the most important ideas in the material; and leading a discussion on the topic or material for which they are responsible (usually via a Response Activity).

Seminar format is generally restricted to small classes of very advanced students in the face-to-face situation, because it is too time-consuming to have more than about 15 students doing major presentations. Second, less advanced students may feel very embarrassed and do not present material well in an oral report to their peers, and are even worse at trying to play the role of teacher in conducting a discussion. In the written mode, they can take as long as they need to polish their presentations, and the quality of their work and ideas is what comes through, not their public speaking skills. Other students can read material in a much shorter time than it would take to listen to oral presentations. If the material is poorly presented, they may hit the "break" key, or stop choosing sections to display from a reading activity, whereas etiquette dictates that they must sit and suffer through a poor student presentation in the face-to-face situation. Finally, it is easier for students to "play the role" of teacher in this medium, which is more equalitarian than face-to-face communication.

Seminar-style presentations and discussions are thus an example of a collaborative learning activity which is often difficult in the Traditional Classroom (TC), but which tends to work very well in the Virtual Classroom environment, even with fairly large classes of undergraduates. Other examples of collaborative learning strategy in the VC include debates, group projects, simulation and role-playing exercises, sharing of solutions to homework problems and/or answers to review questions for exams; and collaborative composition of essays, stories, or research plans.

Evaluation

The initial set of field trials explored how the process and outcome of teaching and learning in the VC differs from the traditional classroom. For this purpose, a wide variety of courses and settings were studied. Subsequent studies consisted of more intensive experimentation with and analysis of three specific courses using the technology: a writing course, a Computers and Society course, and a virtual management laboratory.

Design of the Quasi-experimental Field Trials

Institutions vary a great deal in the computing facilities which they provide for students, and in the characteristics of their students. Three types of learning environments were included in this study. NJIT is a comprehensive technological university enrolling about 8,000 students, which provides a microcomputer to each of its full time undergraduates. Upsala College is a small, liberal arts–oriented college with about 1000 students, which at the time of this project possessed only a single microcomputer laboratory, a total of seven machines with modems. We also included students enrolled in online distance education courses with two other institutions ("Connect-Ed," an online Master's degree program offered through the New School in New York, and Ontario Institute in Toronto).

For each of five undergraduate courses, we matched the same course with the same teacher, texts, and tests in Traditional Classroom mode with a mode employing the Virtual Classroom. Examination scores and other outcomes can then be compared for the two sections. In other words, at the core of the evaluation design is a 2 x 5 factorial design. Introduction to Sociology (SOC 150), was offered through Upsala. It is taken primarily by freshmen. Introduction to Computer Science (CIS 213) is a second-level course at NJIT, with a course in Fortran as the prerequisite. A statistics course was offered in two versions: a freshman-level course at Upsala with no mathematical prerequisites except acceptable scores on a Math Basic Skills test; and an NJIT upper-level first course in statistics for engineers, with a calculus prerequisite. Each of these courses had one section delivered traditionally, and a matched section delivered totally online. The fifth course was an introductory course in management offered to upper-class engineers at NJIT. For this course, the experimental section conducted all of its "laboratory" activities online, based on an organizational simulation, while still meeting face-to-face for lectures and exams.

A quasi-experimental design of matching face-to-face and online sections of these courses, all offered during the fall of 1986, was selected. The design is quasi-experimental rather than a fully controlled experiment for two major reasons: students self-selected mode of delivery, and the nature of assignments differed between matched sections. Efforts were made to encourage students to register in the experimental sections, but only with full information about the nature of this "unproven" method of delivery.

Initially, it had been intended to use exactly the same assignments in the matched online and Virtual Classroom sections of courses. However, the faculty members pointed out that this would be totally inappropriate, and would fail to take advantage of the unique opportunity offered by the VC for collaborative activities. So, the faculty members were freed to devise whatever assignments they thought most appropriate for this medium, provided the text books and the midterm and final exams were the same.

Each instructor incorporated collaborative activities in the online section which were different from the individual assignments given in the traditional section. This varied widely depending on the nature of the course. For example, in the upper-level statistics course, students could see one another's homework assignments after they had done their own, in order to compare approaches. In some assignments, each student chose one problem to work on instead of doing them all; the rest of the class could see their solution. In Introductory Sociology, many assignments made use of pen names and required students to enter analyses of how general concepts, such as role conflict, applied to their own lives. The use of pen names prevented embarrassment in using examples from their own experiences to share with the class. In Computer Science, the VC section had a final assignment requiring a group to complete a complex program by breaking it into subroutines, and then making sure that all the subroutines worked together to produce the correct overall result. Such an assignment was possible only for a group able to work together constantly, and to have an integrated facility online for showing programs to one another, compiling, and executing them. The traditional section had only individual programming assignments.

However, these introductory courses are not representative of the range of possible applications of the Virtual Classroom, or for exploring variations in process and outcome in such an environment. For these purposes, the sample was expanded to include many other courses which used the VC mode of delivery. For example, whereas all the instructors had extensive experience delivering courses in the traditional mode, this was a "first time" experience teaching an entire course in a Virtual Classroom. On the basis of this experience, they might change their minds about effective procedures in this new mode. It was possible to schedule online sections of the computer science, management, and the two statistics courses to repeat in the spring semester; but not possible, given teaching load limits, to also schedule a second "control" course in the spring of 1987. Therefore, the sample was expanded to include a repeat of these four courses online.

Second, four additional courses using the mixed mode approach were included in the study, but without "control" sections. These were a writing course, organizational communication, anthropology, and business French.

The third expansion of the sample and study design was based on the fact that there are many ongoing sets of courses which are currently being offered by other institutions online, but for which there is no traditional equivalent. These include graduate level courses in media studies, offered through Connected Education on EIES, with registration and credit at the New School, and a graduate level course offered by the Ontario Institute of Education. The distance education students in these courses are spread out over a wide geographic area, and never meet their instructor face-to-face, not even for training.

The purpose of including these additional courses in the study was to increase the overall sample size, and thus the chances of obtaining statistically significant results. The expanded sample of courses also increases the generalizability of the findings to a wider range of online offerings, and facilitates exploration of variations among online courses.

Evaluation Instruments and Procedures

Data collection and analysis was conducted under "protection of human subjects" guidelines, whereby all participating students were informed of the goals and procedures followed in the project and confidentiality of the data was protected. Data collection methods included:

- Pre- and post-course questionnaires for students
- Automatic monitoring of online activity

Participant observation (in all online conferences, in the microcomputer laboratories where students were directly observed interacting with the system, and as an instructor in one of the courses which used the VC)

- Use of available data such as grade point averages and SAT scores for participating students
- Descriptive case reports by the instructor for each course
- A small number of personal interviews with some of the most negative and most positive students who used the VC

Pre- and post-course questionnaires completed by students were the most important data source. The pre-course questionnaire measured student characteristics and expectations. The post-course questionnaire focused on detailed evaluations of the effectiveness of the online course or course segments, and on student perceptions of the ways in which the Virtual Classroom was better or worse than the Traditional Classroom.

One of the courses included in the data (Organizational Communication) was taught by the project director and author. The number of students involved (10) was not so large as to significantly "contaminate" the statistical results. In a demonstration project which is centered on iterative development (of software functionality and interface, and of group processes), it is essential for the designer to have such direct, "hands on" experience in using the groupware in the context of the application for which it is intended. Such participant observation of the interaction of software design and group processes is a vital source of qualitative insights and design ideas.

Hypotheses and Findings

Despite many implementation problems, including active resistance from many faculty members to allowing this experiment to proceed on their campus, the results of this field trial were generally positive. They support the conclusion that the Virtual Classroom mode of delivery is a viable alternative for college-level learning.

The following is a summary of the some of the major hypotheses and findings (see Hiltz, 1988a, for complete methodology and results).

H1: There will be no significant differences in scores measuring MASTERY of material taught in the virtual and traditional classrooms.

Finding: No consistent differences. In one of five courses (Computer Science), VC final grades were significantly better.

H2: Students will report that the VC, as compared to the TC, improves the overall quality of the learning experience.

Finding: On the average, students rated the VC as qualitatively superior to the TC. Some of the key comparisons are shown in figure 16.2.

Though the "average" results supported the above predictions, there was a great deal of variation, particularly among courses. Generally, whether or not the above outcomes occur is dependent on a large number of interrelated variables, including variations among institutional settings, variations among courses, and differences in student characteristics, as well as mode of delivery (totally online or mixed mode). The totally online upper-level courses at NJIT, the courses offered to remote students, and the mixed mode courses were most likely to result in student perceptions of the Virtual Classroom being "better." The totally online freshman-level courses at Upsala, where students did not have their own PC's, tended to have the least satisfactory results.

H3: Those students who experience "group learning" in the Virtual Classroom are most likely to judge the outcomes of online courses to be superior to the outcomes of traditional courses.

Finding: Supported by both correlational analysis of survey data and qualitative data from individual interviews. Those students who experienced high levels of communication with other students and with their professor (who participated in a "group learning" approach to their coursework) were most likely to judge the outcomes of VC courses to be superior to those of traditionally delivered courses.

Please compare online "classes" to your previous experiences with "face-to-face" college-level courses. To what extent do you agree with the following statements about the comparative process and value of the EIES online course or portion of a course in which you participated? (Circle a number on the scales.)

ACCESS PROFESSOR
Having the computerized conferencing system available provided better access to the professor(s).

	18%	21%	19%	15%	10%	9%	8%	
Strongly	1 :	2 :	3 :	4 :	5 :	6 :	7	Strongly
Agree								Disagree

N = 185 Mean = 3.4 SD = 1.9

CONVENIENT
Taking online courses is more convenient.

	26%	23%	16%	11%	9%	8%	7%	
Strongly	1 :	2 :	3 :	4 :	5 :	6 :	7	Strongly
Agree								Disagree

N = 185 Mean = 3.1 SD = 1.9

COMMUNICATED MORE
I communicated more with other students in the class as a result of the computerized conference.

	14%	21%	14%	18%	11%	11%	11%	
Strongly	1 :	2 :	3 :	4 :	5 :	6 :	7	Strongly
Agree								Disagree

N = 185 Mean = 3.7 SD = 1.9

INCREASED MOTIVATION
The fact that my assignments would be read by the other students increased my motivation to do a thorough job.

	16%	25%	14%	20%	6%	11%	8%	
Strongly	1 :	2 :	3 :	4 :	5 :	6 :	7	Strongly
Agree								Disagree

N = 185 Mean = 3.4 SD = 1.8

MORE BORING
The online or virtual classroom mode is more boring than traditional classes.

	8%	6%	8%	16%	16%	24%	22%	
Strongly	1 :	2 :	3 :	4 :	5 :	6 :	7	Strongly
Agree								Disagree

N = 183 Mean = 4.8 SD = 1.8

Figure 16.2
Comparison to Traditional Classrooms: Items from the Post-Course Questionnaire

MORE INVOLVED
I felt more "involved" in taking an active part in the course.

	17%	22%	18%	19%	13%	6%	6%	
Strongly	1 :	2 :	3 :	4 :	5 :	6 :	7	Strongly
Agree								Disagree

N = 183 Mean = 3.3 SD = 1.7

ASSIGNMENTS USEFUL
I found reading the reviews or assignments of other students to be useful to me.

	13%	23%	27%	20%	6%	7%	5%	
Strongly	1 :	2 :	3 :	4 :	5 :	6 :	7	Strongly
Agree								Disagree

N = 182 Mean = 3.2 SD = 1.6

NOT CHOOSE ANOTHER
I would NOT choose to take another online course.

	11%	9%	6%	10%	10%	19%	35%	
Strongly	1 :	2 :	3 :	4 :	5 :	6 :	7	Strongly
Agree								Disagree

N = 182 Mean = 5.0 SD = 2.1

BETTER LEARNING
I found the course to be a better learning experience than normal face-to-face courses.

	17%	15%	14%	25%	10%	9%	10%	
Strongly	1 :	2 :	3 :	4 :	5 :	6 :	7	Strongly
Agree								Disagree

N = 183 Mean = 3.6 SD = 1.9

LEARNED MORE
I learned a great deal more because of the use of EIES.

	10%	20%	15%	27%	9%	11%	8%	
Strongly	1 :	2 :	3 :	4 :	5 :	6 :	7	Strongly
Agree								Disagree

N = 182 Mean = 3.7 SD = 1.8

INCREASE QUALITY
Did the use of the system increase the quality of your education?

	12%	22%	22%	22%	8%	6%	7%	
Definitely	1 :	2 :	3 :	4 :	5 :	6 :	7	Definitely
yes								not

A Qualitative Study of an Online Writing Workshop
Since communication via CMC is entirely in the written form, it seems "natural" to use it in writing courses. The application of CMC to writing in higher education is a recent innovation. Its application to writing instruction is in the developmental stage and little is known about how students and instructors use the technology in the process of learning and teaching writing effectively. As her dissertation research at NYU, Beverly Rosenthal (1991) undertook a qualitative study of a Connect-Ed writing workshop conducted entirely synchronously through the EIES computer-mediated conferencing system. She used exploratory, systematic, and descriptive procedures to examine the archival record of the written transcript of all the discourse content and written drafts generated by six graduate students and the instructor in the eight week writing workshop.

Rosenthal concludes that there was a "match" among the participants, the task, and the technology which allowed successful collaborative writing to occur. She describes the roles and responsibilities delegated and assumed; strategies employed; and the conditions, efforts, skills, and technical resources which appeared to aid in creating a successful interactive writing environment within the CMC context. These include:

1. Equipment Access: Participants had access to the technology in their homes; were competent using it; and had a positive attitude toward it as a means of educational delivery.

2. Instructional Style: The instructor, a professional writer and experienced in the electronic classroom, established a workshop context. She explicitly employed a number of strategies to implement a student-centered, collaborative composing approach. She exploited communications opportunities available through the CMC medium to support this approach.

3. Mutual Feedback among Students: Students' activity in the workshop focused largely on feedback exchange on their drafts and related rhetorical and process problems. They used the communications opportunities to negotiate meanings in their drafts, which evolved through collaborative effort as collaborative products. In this process they also shared in knowledge building in the workshop.

4. Communications Style: Participants employed explicit and implicit strategies to encourage participation and interaction. They adopted informal, congenial, and humorous discourse norms that contributed to a rich social environment and friendly, interpersonal exchanges.

Collaborative Teaching: The Computers and Society Course
For seven semesters so far, we have been experimenting with teaching this
NJIT intermediate-level computer science course in a mixed modes
approach which combines once a week lectures or videotapes with the use
of the VC for all discussions, assignments, and some lecture-type material.
As a required course for all Computer Science majors, two or three
sections are offered every semester. Thus, the course serves as a research
site for exploring the use of CMC technology to integrate several sections,
taught by different instructors. So far, four different instructors have been
involved.

The class conference (or conferences) are the heart of the Virtual
Classroom, since they are a presentation and discussion space shared by
the entire class. An instructor may use more than one conference.

In Computers and Society, with 96 students one semester, we chose to
use one conference for most activities, but a second conference for two
student-led activities (reviews of research articles made by each student,
and the independent research report contributed by each student). By
setting up separate conferences, not only are activities ordered by being
conducted in different places, but students can be given different privileges
in the different conferences.

A necessary (but not sufficient) characteristic of a successful class
conference is that the students are motivated to participate actively, to
think about the material, and to respond to one another. One mechanism
used to elicit this participation is the "debate." If there are two sections,
they are assigned opposing sides, and there is a "prize" for the winning
semester. Students seem to generally enjoy getting into the spirit of the
debate format, referring to each other in the formalized manner of the
debate as "Mr." or "Ms." so-and-so. "The debate" has been retained as
an assignment which always involves all sections of the course each
semester. Many students contribute much more than the "minimum." In
the Spring 1990 debate, for instance, one student made about 25 entries.
Even after the debate was declared "over," the entries continued to come
in.

During 1988–89, Murray Turoff combined his "day" and "evening"
sections of Computers and Society with a semester for which Roxanne
Hiltz was responsible, to offer a joint online "triple semester" of the
course with a total enrollment of 96 students. We were attempting to

explore the limits of the present technology in terms of class size. There was a main class conference for all three sections combined, secondary conferences for special activities such as a debate and student reviews of articles, and also separate conferences for "Turoff's students" and "Hiltz's students." However, even this attempt to segment the activities did not create enough organization to allow the course to run smoothly. Most of the students constantly complained of "information overload" (such as 100 or more new comments waiting if they had not signed on for several days). Since each student was given assignments which required entering a minimum of one comment a week, and since the instructors were entering perhaps 40 comments a week between them, most of them responding to student contributions, it is not hard to understand how the amount of material generated might have seemed overwhelming.

There were so many students that the participants had trouble getting a "personal feeling" for each other. About the middle of the semester, we had a "student revolt" on our hands, with about a dozen complaining comments suddenly entered, demanding that one of the upcoming assignments be cancelled to allow everybody a chance to catch up. This was puzzling until we discovered that one of the students had chosen a very unusual topic for his project. The research project was based on the hypothesis that large online communities would be easy places in which to foment "rebellion against authority." The project took the form of an experiment. He sent personal messages to all classmates, urging them to follow his lead in the class conference and to complain and demand a reduction in work. Enough of his classmates complied so that his experiment can be considered a "success." The real subjects of the experiment, the instructors, gave a week's extension on an assignment in the face of what seemed to be overwhelming student opinion. This decision was based partially on their feelings that they were also having trouble keeping up with and responding to the barrage of comments, which was stimulating but exhausting.

However, phase two of the student's diabolical (from the point of view of the instructors) experiment "failed." The second phase was to try to prove the hypothesis that the technology could be used to foment ethnic or subcultural conflict. The student entered nasty ethnic attacks in the class conference, which made disparaging remarks about just about every ethnic group represented in the class except for his own. The other students did NOT follow this lead, but rather expressed feelings of strong disagreement and censure. So, there are some limits to anomie, even in a large Virtual Classroom.

Our tentative conclusions on the basis of this experience are that additional software and organizational strategies might make it possible to teach large online sections successfully, but that it will be difficult. Too many hours sitting in front of the CRT can strain anybody's eyes. We hope to try a large joint semester again, but with mixed media, delivering most of the "lecture" type material via videotape rather than via online texts.

In the Spring 1990 sections, taught by Roxanne Hiltz and Donna Dufner, there was a total of less that 50 students. All activities except the debate and one experiment were run in separate class conferences rather than jointly. This made the amount of material generated more manageable for the students. However, it was not as interesting for the instructors. Until a really good "hypertext" PC front-end is available to students, however, it seems necessary to limit the amount of material with which students must deal by setting up separate conferences for various activities, and limiting the number of students who actually participate in each conference.

"The right size" will differ according to the nature of the online activity and the volume of material it generates, and the experience of the students in using CMC. In an online writing course, for instance, Mary Swigonski required collaborative writing groups to read one another's drafts and comment on them. She used six or seven students in each group, and found that this was too much for the students to be able to cope with. She recommends writing groups of three or four, with final drafts presented back to the entire class for comment and reactions. By contrast, the six students in the Connect-Ed writing workshop who were experienced in taking online courses, managed the volume of communication very well.

Iterative Experimentation with an Online Management Laboratory

Though the findings of the original field experiment were promising, they left many questions unanswered, including:

• So much of the variance was due to differences among courses. Would the favorable findings for VC hold up if the experiment were repeated in the form of multiple replications in various modes for a single course, with the same instructor and basic syllabus?

• The tendency for instructors to curve final course grades within a section may have created the general finding of "no difference" in grades among sections of a course using different communication modes. The students told us that they learned more and that the Virtual Classroom is a "better" mode of communication than the traditional classroom. Couldn't we find an objective measure of student skills and knowledge acquired during a course, which would show definite differences in mastery associated with different modes of course delivery?

• Are the "advanced features" of a fully developed Virtual Classroom truly beneficial, or could you obtain similar results using less special features, and thus use almost any conferencing system? Moreover, how much of the results are due to "collaborative learning?" Couldn't you obtain the same results without any technology at all, by having teams of students engage in collaborative learning assignments without a conferencing system to support them?

The course selected for this further experimentation was Management Practices, a one-semester introduction to management. A total of fourteen sections of this course were taught by the same instructor, Enrico Hsu, over a period of four years, as part of his dissertation research (Hsu, 1991). All sections had the same basic syllabus and teaching technique, an "organizational simulation" in which groups of students form a simulated "start up" company and plan and market a "product." They learn how to be managers by practicing all of the steps necessary to organize a company and compete in the marketplace. Some sections undertook the organizational simulation in a traditional classroom. Some had the Virtual Classroom to support the communication and decision making among the organizational members. Then a second innovation was introduced: the integration of a PC-based management game, Business Simulator, which produces objective "results" in the form of indices of the performance of the simulated organizations, such as profitability and return on investment.

In addition to the comparability of game scores across sections, a second standard measure of the acquisition of business-related skills was instituted. This was a final group "game report," which was graded on a standard basis. The game report tested the students' ability to cooperate and coordinate their inputs to produce a well-organized, well-presented report on the activities and status of their simulated organization.

As part of the software evolution of the Virtual Classroom, the second version of the system, on EIES 2, allowed the attachment of "binary files" to any item. This means that if students have the same PC-based programs, they can pass around the files produced by these programs, even though they are only "machine readable" and would look like nonsense if you tried to print them out as straight text. This made it easy to integrate the use of the Business Simulator game into the online sections of the course.

In addition, some more advanced features, such as "forms" and "filters," were added to the EIES 2 version of the software. As a final experimental version of the management course, two sections were taught using all available "productivity enhancing" tools available through a combination of the central software and PC software used by all students. The latter included a common word processing program, spreadsheet, and data base.

Thus, there were a total of five conditions: TC alone, TC plus the Business Simulator, VC alone, VC plus the Business Simulator, and VC plus Business Simulator plus productivity enhancement tools. The results included:

• Game scores for sections with the Virtual Classroom were significantly better than those for the control sections offered totally in a traditional classroom setting. The same was true for grades on the group reports.
• Sections with Virtual Classroom integrated with the PC-based game were more active online and produced better reports.
• Sections with the most advanced set of productivity-enhancing tools and features performed best of all.

Thus, the breadth of the original field trials is methodologically balanced by the greater rigor of the management laboratory experiment. Both studies, in different ways, support the advantages of the Virtual Classroom as a mode of course delivery.

Modes of Use of the Virtual Classroom

There are several modes of employment of the Virtual Classroom. It can be used in a "mixed modes" manner on a local campus, to support a quarter to three quarters of the coursework for classes which also have some face-to-face meetings. This "adjunct" or "mixed" mode seems appropriate for a wide range of courses, including lower level courses. It can be used to deliver totally online courses, to remote or distance education students and/or students who are taking other courses at a campus in a traditional classroom. For totally online courses, it is recommended that the material be at a sophomore or higher level, or else that students be screened very carefully, to advise those with poor study skills against an introductory course offered online.

In addition, VC can be used in a "mixed media" distance education course, combined with video and/or audio graphical conferencing. For example, at the current time, it is being used in several courses at NJIT that are offered either via broadcast television or satellite. The broadcast courses use standard public television courses, such as "Discovering Psychology," produced by PBS, in conjunction with VC for interaction among the dispersed class members. The satellite-delivered courses are offered via the National Technological University. One "section" meets at NJIT, in the "candid classroom," where it is being broadcast to students enrolled in a remote "section," either through NTU, or carried to small groups of students on remote campuses of NJIT, through special lines. Thus, the whole class watches the real-time lecture at once, though some are on-campus and some are remote. The Virtual Classroom is used for all assignments and additional discussions, among the remote and on-campus students.

VC can also be used, very fruitfully, for remote education at the pre-college or graduate levels, or for continuing professional education of employees within organizations. Though not the purview of our project, the application area of continuing professional education may be the biggest "market" for Virtual Classroom in the long run. Such courses typically enroll mature, motivated students; focus on a few related topics; and have students for whom convenience of access would be very important.

Discussion of Findings

Having established through these demonstration projects that the Virtual Classroom is a viable mode for delivery of college-level courses, there is much to be learned about the software, teaching techniques, and contingencies which optimize outcomes for this use of interactive computer systems. For example, though most students and teachers found the special software developed to be useful, there are many improvements to be made in its functionality and usability. We have continued the process of iterative changes in the software, based on user feedback, while implementing the Virtual Classroom features as part of a new EIES2.

Informally, we have experimented with the limits on class size and the relationship between class size and the need for special software. The medium is a "natural" for small (10–15 students) online seminars which involve discussion and one or two long "papers" or "presentations" by students. For this liberal-arts small-group type of application, software such as the branch activities and the gradebook are not necessary: everything can be handled "manually" by the instructor. However, as class size and number of assignments and the technical nature of the material being taught increase, the special software enhancements such as the branch activities and the integration of graphics become necessary in order for the instructor and students to be able to handle the communications load.

With the existing software, we have successfully handled joint sections with approximately 50 students, in the Virtual Classroom environment. However, when we offered a "triple section" with 96 students online, the communication overload became unmanageable, even with the software enhancements we have thus far designed and implemented.

Another area for further research is "mixed media" courses which combine Virtual Classroom with modes other than face-to-face meetings, such as videotapes, audio elements, or PC-based software. It may be that an optimal mode of delivery for many distance-education courses is the use of videotapes or video disks for "lecture" type material, with the VC for discussion and assignments and the building of a supportive learning community.

The VC is not without its disadvantages, and it is not the preferred mode for all students (let alone all faculty). Students (and faculty) report that they have to spend more time on a course taught in this mode than they do on traditional courses. Students also find it more demanding in general, since they are asked to play an active part in the work of the class on a daily basis, rather than just passively taking notes once or twice a week. For students who want to do as little work as possible for a course, this mode of learning may be considered a burden, rather than an opportunity. The VC is also not recommended for students who are deficient in basic reading, writing, and computational skills.

We have noted that increased interaction with the professor and with other students is the key to superior results in the Virtual Classroom. Thus, the selection and orientation of instructors who can orchestrate such collaborative learning environments becomes the key to success.

Acknowledgments

Major funding for this project was contributed by the Annenberg/CPB Project, and the New Jersey Department of Higher Education. Current work on "Distributed Group Support Systems" is partially supported by the National Science Foundation. This chapter is based on excerpts from The Virtual Classroom: A New Option for Learning" (Ablex, in press).

References

Bruffee, K.A. 1984. Background and history to collaborative learning in American colleges. *College English* 46 (7), 635–652.

Harasim, Linda, ed. 1989. *Online Education: Perspectives on a New Medium.* New York, Prager/Greenwood.

Hiltz, Starr Roxanne. 1986. The Virtual Classroom: Using computer-mediated communication for university teaching. *Journal of Communication* 36:2, 95–104.

Hiltz, Starr Roxanne 1988a. *Learning in a Virtual Classroom*, Volume 1 of A Virtual Classroom on EIES, Research Report 25, Center for Computerized Conferencing and Communications, NJIT, Newark, N. J.

Hiltz, S. R. 1988b. *Teaching in a Virtual Classroom*, Research Report 26, Center for Computerized Conferencing and Communications, NJIT, Newark, N.J.

Hiltz, S. R. 1992. *The Virtual Classroom: A New Option for Learning.* In press.

Hsu, E. 1991. "Management Games for Management Education: A Case Study." Dissertation Proposal submitted to the Graduate School of Business, Rutgers University, Newark, N.J., written under the direction of Starr Roxanne Hiltz.

Mason, R., and Kaye, A. 1989. *Mindweave: Communication, Computers and Distance Education.* Oxford, England, Pergamon Press.

Rosenthal, B. 1991. "Computer-Mediated Discourse in a Writing Workshop: A Case Study in Higher Education." Doctoral Dissertation, New York University.

17

Medical Center: A Modular Hypermedia Approach to Program Design

Nels Anderson

Introduction

The current shift in medical education reform toward problem-based curricula is driven by two dominant forces: First, the sheer volume of medical knowledge is threatening to overwhelm the traditional delivery system which has focused on instructional outcomes in the information domain of learning. Second, the need to "decompress" curriculum information density has shifted the focus to instructional design models which provide increased opportunities for learners to acquire skills for independent knowledge acquisition and the coupling of this knowledge to the intellectual skills domain of clinical problem solving (Barrows, 1983).

Case studies are well recognized as powerful tools for focusing problem solving instruction and prompting learners to build schema for more efficient and systematic knowledge acquisition. Case study–based problem solving is also expected to promote development of meta-cognitive skills; i.e., "a person's awareness of how he or she learns or knows, as well as the strategies that make learning and remembering more efficient and secure" (Anderson, 1987). The building and linking of related basic science knowledge structures and the application of this knowledge in the strategic planning of clinical problem solving are the products of case study–based curricula.

Expertise in medicine is recognized by the efficiency of physicians to prune the problem search space and make accurate decisions based on a few critical cues or findings (Elstein et al., 1978). Clinical expertise is characterized by rapid recall from long term-memory of situation models or problem representations which serve to guide questioning, hypothesis testing, and the iterative process of cue acquisition and interpretation (Elstein et al., 1978, and Patel, Evans, and Groen, 1984).

Analysis of an expert performance in medical problem solving is expected to yield a body of heuristic knowledge and links (implicit and explicit) to the scientific knowledge structures upon which this expert behavior depends. A major goal of case study–based curricula is to guide novice learners in acquiring understanding of these relationships. This chapter introduces a modular, hypermedia program design model which addresses this goal by supporting learner access to indepth analysis of expert clinical problem-solving protocols.[1]

Medical Center Design Model

Medical Center programs are distinguished by their modular structure: (1) the Patient Simulation Module, (2) Hypermedia Database Modules, and (3) the Meta-Database Module which functions as a centralized resource for linking problem solving-protocols of the Patient Module to relevant content information in the program's Hypermedia databases. The user interface exploits the Medical Center spatial metaphor to provide orientation and navigational aids which decrease cognitive task scheduling demands on novice learners in navigating the complex information space of Medical Center programs (see User Interface below).

Specific clinical case studies provide the basis of Patient Modules and establish the clinical domain and dimensions of the program's problem-solving search space and guide the compiling of hypermedia database content. The Patient Module represents a major pathway for learner access to the expert performance of clinical problem solving.

Tools for protocol analysis are key to the successful design and development of Medical Center programs. We have adopted a top-down performance engineering design model (Harmon, 1982) for protocol analysis. This model focuses on the elaboration of basic science knowledge structures from links to the intellectual skills domain of expert clinical problem solving. The goals of this design effort can be summarized as follows:

1. To develop a complete set of design and production tools appropriate and effective across medical specialties.

2. To establish the foundation of program design on modern principles of cognitive science and models of human information processing and expertise.

3. To create an environment in which learning in the intellectual skills domain of problem solving is a major instructional outcome.

4. To couple progress in understanding the process of clinical problem solving with the development of meta-cognitive and strategic planning skills through exploration of expert clinical reasoning and linked knowledge structures.

5. To exploit the isomorphic relationship between domain knowledge structures and program hypertext/hypermedia structures (Tsai, 1988) to create opportunities for learners to build schemas of the relationships between content knowledge and its application in clinical problem solving.

The clinical specialty of Obstetrics and Gynecology was selected as the clinical domain for prototype program design and development. The complexity of reproductive dysfunctions, diagnosis, and treatment satisfies the need for a problem space sufficiently large for rigorous testing of design objectives. Furthermore, the enormous body of clinical and basic science knowledge relevant to problem solving in this domain is representative of the information density in other clinical specialties. Successful efforts to develop tools for compiling and structuring access to this information form the context of specific clinical problems would be expected to satisfy program design needs in other clinical specialties.

An important instructional objective in Medical Center programs is to assist learners in building schema for better understanding of the clinical problem-solving process. The design challenge to satisfy this goal is to develop a program environment in which webs (Carlson, 1990) of basic science knowledge are linked to the heuristics of expert clinical problem solving (See MetaDatabase below).

The Medical Center program design outlined in detail below is based on the knowledge that clinical problem solving is dominated by the informal reasoning process of clinical judgment in which expertise is commonly expressed as algorithmic (heuristic) or procedural knowledge (Elstein, 1988). On the other hand the facts, concepts, and basic science principles which establish the scientific basis of clinical reasoning are part of the information domain of learning or declarative knowledge. The Medical Center program design characteristic which separates content information (hypermedia databases) from its application (patient module) rests on this fundamental distinction between instructional outcomes in the intellectual skills and information domains of learning. The interface between content knowledge, its various transformations and application in clinical problem solving are functions assigned the meta-database module.

In summary, this integrated, modular design model consists of three basic components: (1) a patient module, (2) hypermedia database modules, and (3) a meta-database module which contains detailed knowledge of both the clinical case and links to relevant content information in the program's hypermedia databases. The user interface in this design model is based on the spatial metaphor of a Medical Center. Navigation is cued by data-type specific icons for the Library, Clinical Lab, Patient Record, Patient Module, and Computer Support (simulations and decision analysis).

The Patient Module is based on actual patient records and consists of a patient interview by an expert clinician. Analysis of protocols resulting from these unscripted problem-solving sessions followed Elstein's hypothetico-deductive model of clinical problem solving (Elstein et al., 1978). This analysis provides the basis to support learner access to expert clinical reasoning and associated webs of basic science knowledge. The meta-database module functions as the interface between learner exploration of the Patient Module and the program's Hypermedia Databases. The modular structure for this design provides a generic set of authoring tools for creating programs which support both direct access to content knowledge in the hypermedia databases and structured access to content knowledge through its application in expert clinical problem solving.

The User Interface
The user interface in our modular hypermedia program design is based on the spatial metaphor of a Medical Center (figure 17.1). This design exploits the well-developed Medical Center schema shared by our user population—medical students. Learner access to knowledge of Medical Center structural and functional units decreases the cognitive demands associated with navigation (Conklin, 1987) and promotes understanding of the relationships among data types.

Figure 17.1
The User Interface: Medical Center programs have adopted the spacial metaphor of a medical center to support navigation within the information space of
expert clinical problem solving. This initial program screen prompts the user to
choose between entering the Medical Center (click on Door Icon button) or
Help in the form of a guided tour of the program resources. Navigation within
Medical Center choice screens is based on pointing and clicking with the mouse
driven cursor.

Navigation Menu: The navigation menu is global, i.e., available at all times
and from all places in the program. Four of the six icon menu choices trigger
elaboration of the Medical Center metaphor into specific content data types:
library, clinical lab, patient record, and computer support. Each data type is
rendered as a separate hypermedia database.

The meta-database icon provides centralized access to the program's clinical
expertise and links to relevant content in the program's typed hypermedia
databases. The patient interview icon triggers access to the patient simulation
module.

In contrast to the global function of the Navigation Menu, screen-specific
icon buttons are content sensitive and support local navigational decisions. For
example, local navigation buttons in the initial user interface screen, ENTER
door button and HELP button provide access to the Medical Center Navigational Menu and Program Guided Tour, respectively.

The spatial environment is represented in the interface by specific Medical Center data-types including: Library, Clinical Lab, Patient Record, Computer Support, and Patient Module. Access to hypermedia databases is cued by data-type specific icons presented in the Navigation menu (figure 17.1). The Medical Center metaphor is elaborated by pointing and clicking on the selected icon. An important and powerful feature of this spatial metaphor design is the ability to present an appropriate level of abstraction to accommodate individual learner needs. For advanced user navigation the interface supports direct access to a centralized symbolic representation of program content (Meta-Database). Progress from novice, icon-supported navigation, to expert mode of navigation is designed to be an intuitive and seamless process reflecting the building and elaboration of individual learner knowledge structures.

The Patient Module

An important design goal and characteristic of Medical Center programs is to support multiple learner pathways to content knowledge. The Patient Module represents a major pathway for navigation from the domain of expert clinical problem solving (figure 17.3).

The Patient Module provides access to a real-time, high fidelity (video) patient interview in which the physician's performance is a natural reflection of his/her approach to clinical problem solving. Actual patient records provided the documentation for establishing the clinical problem as well as the specific clinical findings upon which the original diagnosis and treatment were founded. Based on this documentation a team of 4 or 5 experts in this field of clinical specialization construct a reference matrix of cues (clinical findings) and hypotheses which reflects their clinical judgment of the total clinical problem-solving search space (figure 17.2). Furthermore, cells within the matrix are assigned clinical weight on a 7-point scale (-3 -2 -1 (0) +1 +2 +3) in which + 2 and 3 are considered critical findings. This matrix of clinically weighted cues is the symbolic representation of the program's clinical expertise and provides the foundation for guiding exploration of the clinical reasoning and linked basic science knowledge structures upon which these assigned clinical weights depend.

The "patient" in our simulated clinical problem-solving session was a resident fellow in OB-GYN. Her detailed knowledge of both the specific case and patient behaviors under these conditions provided a very "rich"

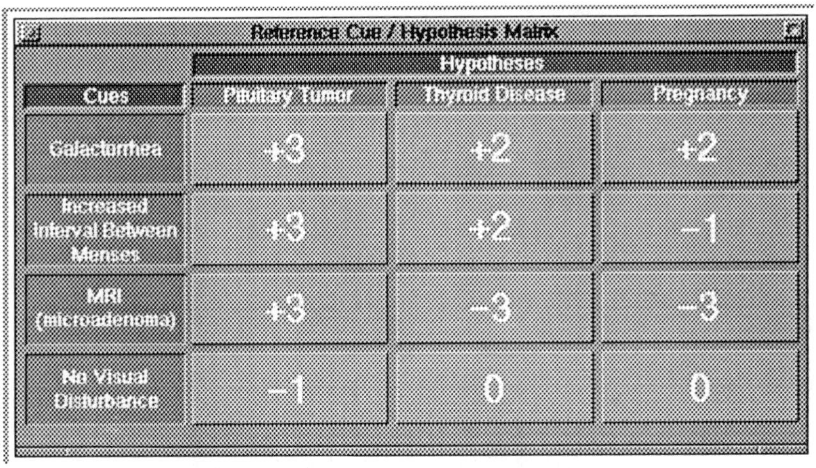

Reference Cue / Hypothesis Matrix			
	Hypotheses		
Cues	Pituitary Tumor	Thyroid Disease	Pregnancy
Galactorrhea	+3	+2	+2
Increased Interval Between Menses	+3	+2	−1
MRI (microadenoma)	+3	−3	−3
No Visual Disturbance	−1	0	0

Figure 17.2
Reference Cue-Hypothesis Matrix: The total Clinical problem solving search space of the program's Patient Module is symbolically rendered as a matrix of cues (or findings) and hypotheses. Documentation from the actual patient record and the clinical judgment of a team of experts in this field of clinical specialization established the dimensions of the reference matrix. The reference matrix generated for this case study, secondary amenorrhea in a reproductive aged woman presenting with a chief complaint of infertility, consisted of 57 cues, including lab tests and physical exam results and 9 hypotheses. Cells within the matrix are assigned weight by the team of clinical experts reflecting their judgment of the relevance and importance of the cue to a particular hypothesis. A seven-point scale (−3, −2, −1, 0, +1, +2, +3) was used where + 2 and 3 were considered critical findings for (+) or against (−) a particular hypothesis. The cue-hypothesis reference matrix is the symbolic representation of Medical Center program clinical expertise.

Matrix cells function as "buttons" with links to webs of relevant content information in the program's hypermedia databases.

Figure 17.3
Patient Simulation Module: The patient simulation module provides user access to an expert clinical problem solving protocol. Exploring these realtime problem solving sessions represents a major pathway for navigation of the programs hypermedia databases. Video browser gadgets at the bottom of the screen provide random access to protocol content and toggles overlay of doctor-patient dialogue on video freeze frames. Highlighted Information Search Units (ISUs) and Clinical finding or Cues, function as hypertext buttons for elaboration of clinical reasoning and relevant basic science content.

dialogue for analysis. In the clinical interview she provided an initial statement of chief complaint (infertility). Her responses to the physician's questions were unscripted and based on detailed knowledge of the clinical case. The physician conducting the interview was a recognized expert in this clinical specialty. He had no prior knowledge of this particular case. He was advised that he was the first physician to see this patient and that he should proceed in a manner following his normal and usual procedures for solving clinical problems.

These interviews were carried out in a clinical setting familiar to the physician. Two video cameras recorded all patient and physician behavior and dialogue. Upon request by the physician, physical exam and laboratory test data were provided from a "Data Bank," according to Elstein's protocol (Elstein et al., 1978), without comment or interpretation. These data are available in the program's Patient Record and Clinical Lab Modules, respectively.

Protocol transcripts were analyzed based on Elstein's hypothetico-deductive model of clinical problem solving (Elstein et al., 1978). Initial coding of the protocols identified information search units (ISUs) employed by the physician to elicit clinical findings or cues. This dynamic, real-time patient interview provides direct learner access to an expert performance in clinical problem solving. (See Discussion for summary of competing models of expert clinical problem solving.) Results from protocol analysis were in agreement with the findings from Elstein et al. (1978) including: early hypothesis generation based on a few critical findings; the application of powerful strategies to prune and focus the diagnostic search space; the application of strategies to protect against incomplete or misdiagnosis based on both positive and negative critical findings.

It is recognized that the problem-solving protocols generated in Medical Center Patient Simulation Modules, as in real world clinical medicine, represent the unique application of medical knowledge by an individual clinical expert. The primary purpose of patient simulations is, therefore, not to establish algorithmic protocols to be memorized but rather to provide the basis for in-depth analysis of the clinical reasoning process and linked medical knowledge structures which supported this expert performance of clinical problem solving.

User access to the patient interview protocol is supported by a random access video browser gadget (figure 17.3). The full text of doctor-patient dialogue, coded for information search units and cues, is presented as a graphic overlay on freeze-frames of the video segment (figure 17.3).

Information search units and cues function as hypertext "buttons." Exploration of the clinical reasoning and links to relevant basic science knowledge is initiated by "clicking" on the highlighted Cue or ISU. System response to specific, user interactions are mediated by the meta-database module. Meta-database support of user navigation from the patient module is acknowledged by presenting the Meta-Database screen (figure 17.4) configured for: (1) appropriate reference cue-hypothesis matrix cell, (2) its clinical weighing, and (3) prethreaded links to program resources which elaborate the clinical reasoning (WHY screens) and present relevant content information in the program's hypermedia databases. In

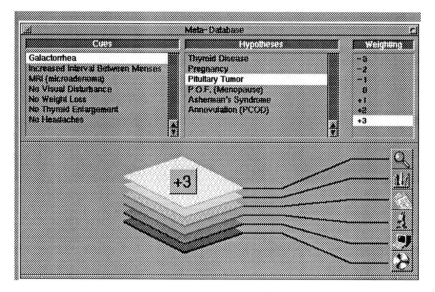

Figure 17.4
Meta-Database: The meta-database is a centralized symbolic representation of
the clinical problem-solving search space (reference cue-hypothesis matrix)
with links to relevant content information in the program's hypermedia
databases. Cue and Hypothesis field gadgets support browsing the entire search
space. Clicking on the value assigned specific matrix cells provides access to
elaboration of the clinical reasoning and prethreaded webs of related content
information.

summary, the Patient Module supports both in-depth analysis of the
expert clinical problem solving protocol as mapped onto the reference
cue-hypothesis matrix and access to the total clinical problem-solving
search space as represented by the meta-database reference cue-hypothesis matrix. Activation of cells in the matrix provides elaboration of the
clinical reasoning as well as links to prethreaded webs of relevant content
in the programs typed hypermedia databases.

Hypermedia Databases

The concept of unconstrained freedom to navigate through the total
information space of a program's hypermedia database has a powerful
attraction to authors and users alike (Conklin, 1987, and Jonassen, 1986).
However, in the absence of content schema or knowledge structures to
guide browsing, the demands of cognitive task scheduling, disorientation,
and general cognitive overload can greatly diminish the usefulness of

hypermedia databases to novice users (Conklin, 1987, and Jonassen, 1986).

A major challenge in Interactive Hypermedia program design is to create a spatial information environment populated with advance organizers (Armbruster, 1986), guided tours and navigational aids (Anderson, 1987) sufficient to prevent disorientation and cognitive overload while preserving the capacity to freely explore the program's information content. We have developed the concept of a Medical Center spatial metaphor (see The User Interface) to support navigation within the domain of clinical problem solving and to guide the organization of medical knowledge into data type specific hypermedia databases. Navigation within Medical Center hypermedia databases is cued by data-type specific icons (figure 17.1). In addition to providing a familiar context for exploring Medical Center knowledge, this structure encourages and facilitates content driven navigation in which the linking of related information promotes the development of knowledge structures or webs of semantically related information within the domain of clinical problem solving.

The separation of content knowledge from its application has many benefits both in terms of the modular structure which facilitates program development and in terms of accommodating user and local application needs (Thursh and Mabry, 1980). The list of benefits may be summarized as follows:

(1) ease of database maintenance including local control of program content.

(2) freedom to structure hypermedia databases which reflect the intrinsic characteristics of the data-type (Jonassen, 1986).

(3) provides data type specific Icon tools for navigating and browsing content (Conklin, 1987).

(4) makes development of an authoring shell for complex interactive multimedia programs possible.

The organization and structure of content in Medical Center typed hypermedia databases is outlined below.

The Library The graphic browser tool in the Library user interface (figure 17.5) supports access to books, journals, on-line databases (Med-Line), and a knowledge dictionary. Clicking on the selected knowledge

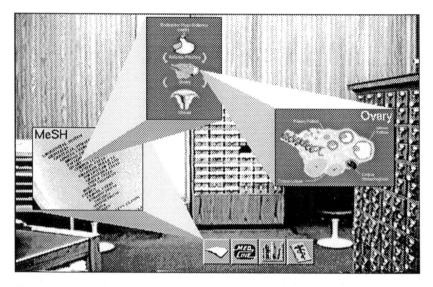

Figure 17.5
The Library: Clicking on the Library icon in the Navigation menu triggers
elaboration of the Medical Center spatial metaphor to the Library screen.
Library content is organized into four categories: Books, Journals, OnLine
Databases, and Knowledge Dictionary; each represented by an icon "button."
Access to Library resources from the Navigation menu provides a direct
pathway for content browsing and independent knowledge acquisition. On the
other hand, content driven links from the Patient Simulation or Patient Record
modules, for example, represent indirect prethreaded pathways to library
resource information. Support of multiple learner pathways to content knowledge, much of which is represented in the library module, is a major design goal
of Medical Center programs.

We have adopted a modified version of the National Library of Medicine
MeSH (Medical Subject Headings) indexing scheme for organizing and cross-
referencing library information. Keyword content entries under major headings
(including Anatomy, Physiology, Diseases, and Diagnosis) function as "buttons" with links to text and graphic elaborations which in turn have embedded
hypertext links to further related content in the library and/or other program
modules.

Access to "pools" of literature with embedded links to related content
expands the information space to create an environment in which learners have
opportunities to couple their elaboration of content knowledge structures with
deeper understanding of relationships among content data types.

acquisition tool triggers choice screens based on the National Library of Medicine's standardized nomenclature of Medical Subject Headings (MeSH) (figure 17.5). Journal references associated with MeSH headings may be cross-referenced to other journal references or other library documents. Abstracts or more lengthy discussion of reference content including data, and graphs are available. Textbook references include: author(s), title, chapters, and content descriptions. They are organized under MeSH headings and are cross-referenced to relevant journal references and other library data.

The Med-Line button provides direct access to all the on-line bibliographic search tools available through the National Library of Medicine. The Knowledge Dictionary is a special resource for in-depth information relevant to the program's problem-solving search space. The standardized MeSH indexing system also applies to knowledge dictionary content. Specific entries are often populated with hypertext buttons for elaboration of information webs within and between data types (figure 17.5).

The library module provides direct access to content knowledge and thus supports in-depth, content-driven knowledge acquisition without reference to the specific clinical case study. However, as discussed below, evaluation of the clinical weighing of cells in the cue-hypothesis matrix depends on elaboration of the clinical reasoning through links to relevant content in the programs hypermedia databases, including Library knowledge.

Patient Record Module   The patient record module contains complete documentation of the actual patient problem including: interview notes, physical exam results, clinical lab test results, diagnosis and treatment. This modular, highly structured and data-rich environment greatly facilitates navigation and provides opportunities to explore relationships among clinical findings and content data types.

The user interface to the patient record hypermedia database is illustrated in figure 17.6. Patient data are rendered as hypertext buttons linked to nodes in the reference cue-hypothesis matrix of the meta-database.

The Clinical Lab Module   Navigation within the clinical laboratory environment is cued by icons for diagnostic algorithms, imaging technolo-

382   Chapter 17

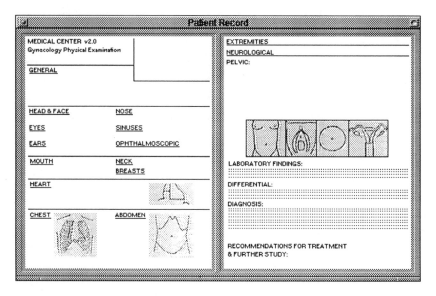

Figure 17.6
Patient Record Module: The Patient Record Module provides access to complete documentation of the original case study. This information is presented on four separate screens (two shown) which summarize findings from the clinical interview and workup protocol. The Patient Record Module is a very rich environment for browsing and building clinical problem-solving schema. Expert clinical findings from the patient interview, physical exam results, and laboratory tests are rendered as hypertext buttons for elaboration.

gies, reference value databases, and a complete record of tests results from the clinical case study.

The heuristic knowledge of clinical expertise can be represented in the form of flowcharts or diagnostic algorithms (Gold, 1985). Rule-based expert systems operate on this heuristic knowledge to simulate expert clinical problem solving (Clancy and Shortliffe, 1984). Decision nodes in diagnostic algorithms support hypermedia elaboration of the clinical reasoning and basic science knowledge relevant to specific procedures and diagnostic tests.

High resolution, non-invasive imaging techniques, e.g., MRI provide access to high-fidelity diagnostic and anatomical knowledge. Navigation through the MRI image archive is cued by an anatomical graphic browser tool. Detailed interpretation of images and links to relevant program content are available through an elaboration gadget.

Laboratory test results collected in the course of this case study are presented on standardized forms. Data on these forms function as active buttons with links to both elaboration of value interpretation and related content in the program's other hypermedia databases.

Computer Support The Computer Support Module provide access to physiological simulations and decision analysis programs. The human ovulatory cycle simulation supports user access to the full parameter space of the model for experimentation and testing of specific hypotheses (Kohn and Anderson, 1991).

In contrast to the informal reasoning of clinical judgment, decision analysis programs provide a formal analytical process for decision making. Specific protocols for decision analysis and their application in clinical decision making have been discussed in detail elsewhere (Kassirer, 1976). Although the general application of decision analysis in clinical decision making continues to be debated (Ransohoff and Feinstein, 1976) there is agreement that exposure to the process of decision analysis may improve clinical judgment through: (1) complete rendering of the decision tree, i.e., explicitly considering all possible outcomes, (2) probing the limits of clinical and basic science literature relevant to the assignment of probabilities at chance nodes, and (3) clear recognition of individual differences in the assignment of utility values. The simple decision tree supported in Medical Center programs is focused on analysis of the decision to carry out a diagnostic test (Pauker and Kassirer, 1980).

The Meta-Database Module

The modular structure of Medical Center programs in which content databases are developed and maintained separately from the application of this knowledge in solving clinical problems, highlights the need for an interface which links relevant database information to the intellectual skills domain of clinical reasoning and problem solving. The meta-database module serves this critical function and in a very real sense represents the uniqueness and power of Medical Center programs.

The concept of exploiting the medical center spatial metaphor to facilitate navigation within the information space of clinical problem solving has encouraged the assignment of content information to data type specific hypermedia databases as reviewed above.

The meta-database module has detailed knowledge of:

(1) the clinical expertise which defines the total problem-solving search space for the clinical case presented in the patient record module. This knowledge is symbolically represented in the form of a reference cue-hypothesis matrix (figure 17.2).

(2) the clinical problem-solving protocol generated in the Patient Simulation module (a subset of the reference cue-hypothesis matrix).

(3) links from the clinical domain (cells in the reference cue-hypothesis matrix) to WHY screens, which elaborate the clinical reasoning, and relevant content information in the program's typed hypermedia databases (figure 17.4).

The meta-database module represents a centralized resource for cue or hypothesis driven navigation of the program's databases (Fig. 4). Elaboration of the clinical weighing assigned to cells in the matrix in terms of clinical heuristic reasoning and the webs of linked basic science content information is initiated by "clicking" on matrix cells (figure 17.4).

Matrix rendering of clinical problem solving expertise provides the structure for guiding navigation. Coupling of clinical problem-solving heuristic knowledge with webs of basic science content information is the most distinguishing characteristic of the Medical Center program design. Novice model-tracing of clinical expertise coupled with content-driven navigation of hypermedia databases provides opportunities for the development of meta-cognitive and strategic planning intellectual skills as well as domain knowledge structures.

Discussion

This chapter outlines a modular, multimedia program design model in which specific clinical case studies, based on actual patient records, establish the program's clinical domain and guide the organization of database content. Implementation of this Top-Down design rests on strategies and tools for detailed analysis and representation of expert problem solving protocols. We have employed a general scientific problem solving method for protocol analysis modeled after Elstein's hypothetico-deductive model of clinical problem solving.

Rendering of the clinical problem-solving search space as a matrix of cues and hypotheses provides a very simple yet powerful tool for the symbolic representation of clinical expertise. The power of the matrix in our program design can be understood in terms of coupling a general scientific problem solving method with the heuristic knowledge associated with the clinical weights assigned to matrix cells. We have exploited this unique feature in the creation of the program's meta-database module which supports in-depth exploration of relationships between basic science knowledge and the expert practice of clinical medicine.

Heuristic knowledge acquired from experience and mentors appears to have a powerful transforming effect on the basic science knowledge structures compiled during the early years of medical study (Balla, Biggs, Gibson and Chang, 1990; Patel, Evans, and Groen, 1984; Patel, Groen, and Scott, 1988). The search for basic science principles from the context of expert clinical problem solving protocols has been termed a "frustrated" process and has led to the stunning conclusion that science is not basic in expert clinical problem solving (Patel, Evans, and Groen, 1984; Balla, Biggs, Gibson, and Chang, 1990). "The possibility that the basic biomedical sciences and clinical sciences might constitute essentially two different worlds" was suggested by this result (Patel, Evans, and Groen, 1984).

Critical review of competing models or theories of clinical expertise and medical problem solving is beyond the scope of this paper. However, the fundamental issues of problem representation and strategies for reducing the problem search space raised by research in medical problem solving clearly impact on our program design decisions. The following brief discussion will, therefore, focus on those issues which most directly affect Medical Center program design.

Models of expert clinical problem solving are distinguished by their relative weighing of indexed situation models (pattern recognition) recalled from long-term memory vs. application of more general problem solving strategies.

Patel, Evans, and Groen (1984) have argued that expert clinical problem solving is best described as a forward reasoning process in which physicians draw upon their large body of highly indexed knowledge of clinical problems and apply a small set of if—then production rules to arrive at a diagnosis without ever generating a hypothesis. Elstein, on the other hand, argues that although in simple or familiar cases forward chaining may be applied, the hypothetico-deductive model of hypothesis testing is applied when the problem cannot be readily identified as an instance of a larger class (Elstein et al., 1978; Elstein, 1988). The coding of clinical problem-solving protocols in terms of Information Search Units (ISUs) and clinical finding or CUES establishes the body of information upon which competing models or theories of clinical expertise and problem solving depend. The user interface to patient simulations in Medical Center programs is first of all designed to provide real time, high fidelity access to an expert clinical problem-solving performance, without preference to models for analysis or explanation of these behaviors. Program support for learner interaction with the protocol is based on the reference cue-hypothesis matrix as presented in the meta-database module. The ability to freely navigate within the problem space, as defined by the reference matrix, guards against imposing structure on the case study. Our expert protocol is offered not so much as a clinical problem-solving algorithm as a high-fidelity source of real-world expert clinical behaviors. As recognized by Elstein and emphasized by Patel expert performance in clinical problem solving is highly dependent on domain specific knowledge. The performance of our expert clearly reflects domain specific expertise in terms of: (1) rapid pruning of the search space, (2) focusing on a few critical findings, and (3) achieving an accurate differential diagnosis without unnecessary testing.

The need for major qualitative change in the goals and design of medical education is widely reorganized (Barrows and Tamblyn, 1980; Tosteson, 1981). The concept of exploiting case studies to establish clinical relevance and to provide opportunities for novice learners to acquire content knowledge and to develop general scientific problem-solving skills seems well founded (Barrows, 1983; Barrows and Tamblyn, 1980, 1979, 1976).

Medical Center programs are designed to support novice learner navigation through the information space of clinical problem solving and to provide links to basic science facts, concepts, and principles upon which these clinical decisions and judgments depend. User interaction with Medical Center programs is expected to support learning in both the intellectual skills domain of problem solving and information domain of building content knowledge structures.

Together, the modular structure of Medical Center programs, the separation of content data from its application in clinical problem solving and the centralized mechanisms for representing and linking relevant content to clinical problem solving provide a generic set of design and production tools for case study–based, interactive, multimedia instructional programs.[2]

Anecdotal Assessment

Although a formal evaluation has not been carried out, a brief summary of faculty and student reactions to the Medical Center program design is provided. Observations fall into three areas: (1) user responses to the Medical Center spatial metaphor interface, (2) linking of clinical problem solving protocols to basic science information, and (3) content navigation: structured vs. browsing.

New users are able to quickly enter the program (figure 17.1) and make purposeful navigational decisions from the choice screen (figure 17.2). Both novice and experienced users were able to access program modules with confidence they were navigating within a familiar schema. The program design goals of lowering the cognitive demands for navigation and promoting elaboration of user content schema seems well demonstrated. Novice users are particularly interested in probing the clinical reasoning of expert problem solving protocols. The meta-database concept and representation of the clinical problem solving search space as a matrix of cues and hypotheses, was quickly (intuitively) recognized as a tool for structuring access to knowledge which supports clinical decision making. The ability to freely browse program content through the Library MeSH structure, independent of the structured access to content from the meta-database was quickly recognized as an important navigational pathway for satisfying individual user interests. Freedom to edit the meta-database structure and to elaborate Library content information to an arbitrary level of detail were recognized by faculty as powerful tools to adapt program structure to local views and needs and to update program context.

Notes

1. Development System: This program was developed on an Amiga-based multimedia platform (Commodore Business Machines). Amiga-Vision (CBM) and Can-Do (Inovatronics) multimedia authoring systems were used.

2. Acknowledgment: I would like to recognize the contributions of Dr. Roger Young, Dr. Mina Selub, Mrs. Kathryn Nelms, and Mr. James Mooring to this project. A special thanks to Dr. Nancy Anderson, President of Interactive Learning Systems, Inc. for her support which made this work possible.

References

Anderson, N.C. 1985. Medical Education in Transition. *Medical Disc Reporter*, May/June 1(3) 3.

Anderson, T.G. 1987. Beyond Einstein. In Learning Tomorrow. Sueann Ambron and Cristina Hooper (eds.), *Journal of the Apple Education Advisory Council.* Spring, 3:194–213.

Armbruster, B.B. 1986. Schema Theory and the Design of Content-Area Textbooks. *Educational Psychologist* 21 (4):253–267.

Balla, J. I., Biggs, J. B., Gibson, M., and Chang, A. M. 1990. The Application of Basic Science Concepts to Clinical Problem-Solving. *Medical Education* 24:137–147.

Barrows, H.S. 1983. Problem-Based, Self-Directed Learning. *Journal of the American Medical Association* 250:3077–3080.

Barrows, H.S., and Tamblyn, R.M. 1980. *Problem-Based Learning: An Approach to Medical Education.* New York: Springer.

Barrows, H.S., and Tamblyn, R.M. 1979. *Problem-Based Learning in Health Sciences Education.* A Monograph from the National Medical Audiovisual Center, National Institutes of Health.

Barrows, H.S., and Tamblyn, R.M. 1976. An Evaluation of Problem-Based Learning in Small Groups Utilizing a Simulated Patient. *Journal of Medical Education* 51:42–54.

Carlson, P.A. 1990. Square Books and Round Books: Cognitive Implications of Hypertext. *Academic Computing*, April, 16–31.

Clancy, B.C., and Shortliffe, E.H. 1984. *Readings in Medical Artificial Intelligence: The First Decade.* Reading, MA: Addison-Wesley Publishing Company.

Conklin, J. 1987. Hypertext: An Introduction and Survey. *IEEE Computer* September:17–41.

Elstein, A.S. 1988. Cognitive Processes in Clinical Inference and Decision Making. In *Reasoning, Inference and Judgement in Clinical Psychology*, edited by D. C. Turk and P. Salovey: New York: Freepress/Macmillan.

Elstein, A.S., Shulman, L.S., Sprafka, S.A., et. al. 1978. Medical Problem Solving: *An Analysis of Clinical Reasoning.* Cambridge, MA: Harvard University Press.

Gold, J.J. 1985. Disorders of Sexual Differentiation and Development. In Robert Metz and Eric B. Larson (eds.), *Blue Book of Endocrinology*, pp. 124–150. Philadelphia: W. B. Saunders Company.

Harmon, P. 1982. The Design of Instructional Materials: A Top-Down Approach. *Journal of Instructional Development* 6 (1):6–14.

Jonassen, D.H. 1986. Hypertext Principles for Text and Courseware Design. *Educational Psychologist* 21 (4):269–292.

Kassirer, J.P. 1976. The Principles of Clinical Decision Making: An Introduction to Decision Analysis. *Yale Journal of Biology and Medicine* 49:149–164.

Kohn, M., and Anderson, N.C. 1991. Human Ovulation Cycle Simulation: Application of the National Biomedical Simulation Resource (NBSR) Simulation Control Program (SCOP) unpublished.

Patel, V.L., Evans, D.A., and Groen, G.J. 1984. Biomedical Knowledge and Clinical Reasoning. In David A. Evans and Vimla L. Patel (eds.), *Cognitive Science in Medicine*, pp. 53–108. Cambridge, MA: The MIT Press.

Patel, V.L., Groen, G.J., and Scott, H.M. 1988. Biomedical Knowledge in Explanations of Clinical Problems by Medical Students. *Medical Education* 22:398–406.

Pauker, S.G., and Kassirer, J.P. 1980. The Threshold Approach to Clinical Decision Making. *New England Journal of Medicine* 302:1109–1117.

Ransohoff, D.F., and Feinstein, A.R. 1976. Is Decision Analysis Useful in Clinical Medicine? *Yale Journal of Biology and Medicine* 49:165–168.

Thursh, D., and Mabry, F. 1980. An Interactive Hyper-Text of Pathology. *Proceedings of Computer Applications in Medical Care* 4:1820–1825.

Tosteson, D.C. 1981. Science, Medicine, and Education. *Journal of Medical Education* 56:8–15.

Tsai, C.J. 1988. Hypertext: Technology, Applications, and Research Issues. *J. Educational Technology Systems* 17 (1):3–14.

18

Prototyping Multimedia: Lessons from the Visual Computing Group at Project Athena Center for Educational Computing Initiative

Ben Davis

The question which asks how to use the computer in the enterprise is, in short, the wrong question. A better formulation is to ask how the enterprise should be run given that computers exist. The best version of all is the question asking what, given computers, the enterprise now is. The underlying problems of good practice in the modern age are the problems of control and underlying these in turn is the problem of control to what end.[1]

Looking through Computers

The educational implication of distributed multimedia is an important cultural index. The information age is multidimensional. We are confronted with an enormous amount of usable information if only we have a way to grasp it. The concept of multimedia is not new. A day in the life of the average person is complicated by telephones, print media, radio, TV, films, and copy machines.

Visual problem solving is nothing new. Cave painting was a means of explaining humanity's relationship to nature. Early mapmaking was the first measure of faith in graphically representing a future destination. Early cunieform was recorded language on portable clay tablets that made the bearer a transmitter.

Tom McArthur in *Worlds of Reference* describes this quite precisely:

The evidence is scant but compelling. It suggests that our remote ancestors had two crude modes of recording and reference: the "place of reference" and the "object of reference." The place was large and awesome and its displays could be gazed upon in more or less serial fashion, and in a way that is markedly like wandering inside a medieval cathedral or a modern museum. The object, however, was small and relatively homely, and was conveniently portable; its displays were also serial, whether scratched on wood or cut in bone, strung as beads on thread, knotted in rope or arranged with paint. Interested people had to travel to the place, but the object could travel to them or move around with them as part of their luggage. In this it markedly resembled a medieval scroll or a modern book.²

"Virtualizing" this condition of place and object of reference with a computer creates a completely flexible, transmissive model of information. As we add channels of hybrid information like sound, moving imagery, solid modeling, and alternative routes of approach to subject matter, we encounter the problems of the complex design of information conditions. The convergence of technologies is a natural phenomenon. Distributed computing power makes a new structure for understanding and makes natural and cultural history the best entertainment.

The term "scientific visualization" in computer science has commonly come to mean complex computational models which produce simulation data that require geometrically based algorithms for interpretation. Radio telescopes scanning the heavens produce more numerical data than can ever be examined point by point. What this means is that numbers become pictures.

The term "multimedia visualization" is used to indicate a context for combining graphic, textual, audio, and video representation (still and moving). This context not only includes scientific visualization information but allows scientific modeling (or any modeling for that matter) to be cross-referenced with audio/visual and textual information from other disciplines.

The distance learner today is served by broadcast, cable TV, radio, limited computer networks, libraries, and video cassettes. These media are the components of multimedia computing. The term "distributed multimedia visualization" is the future of the networked learner.

The use of communications technologies and distributed computer networks will be the vehicles that will bring interactive multimedia education to the distant learner. Increased data rates and higher bandwidth will be the technical innovations of the 1990s. Software development for this type of network is already being prototyped in anticipation of new information markets at MIT, IBM, Digital Equipment, GTE, NTT, and many other global computing/communications corporations.

In order to understand and take full advantage of "distributed multimedia visualization," it is critical to begin addressing issues of course design, user interface, conceptual framework, and audience impact now.

The sweeping technological advances in learning technologies now in prototype phase will be the substantive achievements of the twenty-first century. The educational equity and access to knowledge this represents is much like the invention of the printing press. In a sense, current multimedia applications are almost folk art in comparison to what they will feel like in ten years.

Ways of Seeing

"The purpose of computing is insight, not numbers."[3]

Visualization is a current buzzword. The number of journals and conferences on the subject multiplies annually. The basic questions of whether the user of electronic visualization can effectively distinguish between model and reality and whether the "mediated experience" actually diminishes the sense of real discovery will never be resolved.

These questions are attended by others: How does spatialization of information relate to visualization? How does image perception work? How do we conceptualize with vision? What elements of vision affect the other senses? What is the role of the illustration? What is a visual simulation? Is seeing believing/learning? A good deal of contemporary psychological research is leaving the verbal behavior tradition to investigate the questions of how video and imagery works.

This ability to model with whatever sense is in highest definition for the investigator is key to visualization as a concept. The sightless person uses sound as the visualization sense. The blind and deaf use touch as the primary instrument of visualization. Because we have used sight as our basic tool of survival it has become the prejudiced sense for visualization. We discuss visualization but what we really mean is whatever triggers imagination, whatever renders understanding. The clarity of understanding is dependent on the rendering of pattern that can be dissected and reassembled according to need.

This inclusive sensory definition of visualization is corroborated by interesting research in visual learning behaviors:

The first learning experience of a child is through tactile awareness. In addition to this "hands-on knowledge," recognition includes smelling, hearing, and tasting in a rich contact with the environment. These senses are quickly augmented and superseded by the iconic—the ability to see, to recognize and understand environmental and emotional forces visually. . . . We accept it (vision) without realizing that it can be improved just in the basic process of observation or extended into an incomparable tool of human communication. We accept seeing as we experience it—effortlessly.[4]

The cross-referenced nature of vision as described by I. L. Gregory anticipated the computational modeling called "hypermedia":

The seeing of objects involves many sources of information beyond those meeting the eye when we look at an object. It generally involves knowledge of the object derived from previous experience, and this experience is not limited to vision but may include the other senses; touch taste, smell, hearing, and perhaps also temperature and pain. Objects are far more than patterns of stimulation: objects have pasts and futures; when we know its past or can guess its future, an object transcends experience and becomes an embodiment of knowledge and expectation without which life of even the simplest kind is impossible.[5]

The historical research on memory and vision is especially important to grounding visualization as an academic subject. Cultural historian Robert O. McClintock at Teachers College Columbia University expressed this in a preliminary description for a joint proposal with the Visual Computing Group for a curriculum in understanding visualization:

Intellectual innovation in modern history has been closely associated with changes in the capacity to visualize and represent things. For example, the Renaissance is linked to the introduction of perspectival representation. The rise of early modern science depended in part on the ability to reproduce and disseminate conceptual drawings representing new theoretical perspectives accurately, and it was engendered by the telescope and microscope. The break with the traditional medicine of Galen coincided with the development of much more realistic anatomical drawings. The age of exploration is also the start of modern cartography. In premodern culture, pictures aided memory. In modern culture understanding of DNA has much to do with three dimensional computer modeling and holography. Pictures come to be ways of significantly representing and extending knowledge about the phenomenal world to the thinking mind. A digital image carries encoded information about the structure it represents rather than simple metaphor.

Yet, despite the evident linkage between the progress of culture and the power to visualize phenomena, and despite a rich literature that documents it, visualization has not been well used as a tool of advanced education. In the eighteenth century the well-educated person studied drawing not as a prelude to an artistic career, but in recognition that a person needed not only to speak, read, and write well, but also to effectively represent the world visually. The practice of including visual training in general education has died out. Only in art history and art appreciation courses does the educational system now recognize that the development of visual powers is important or anyone except the prospective artist or film critic.[6]

The reasons for visualizing information are to remember it and to be able to use what is remembered. The human memory and its need for pattern recognition is evident in our constructions for "getting there and back."

We moderns who have no memories at all, like the professor, employ from time to time some private mnemotechnic not of vital importance to us in our lives and professions. But in the ancient world, devoid of printing, without paper for note taking or on which to type lectures, the trained memory was of vital importance. And the ancient memories were trained by an art which reflected the art and achitecture of the ancient world, which could depend on faculties of intense visual memorisation which we have lost. [7]

Constellations are the invention of human imagination, not of nature. They are an expression of the human desire to impress its own order upon the apparent chaos of the night sky. For navigators beyond sight of land or for travellers in the trackless desert who wanted signposts, for farmers who wanted a calendar, and for shepherds who wanted a nightly clock, the division of the sky into recognizable star groupings had practical purposes. But perhaps the earliest motivation was to humanize the forbidding blackness of night.[8]

The origin of the map is lost to history. No one knows when or where or for what purpose someone got the idea to draw a sketch to communicate a sense of place, a sense of *here* in relation to *there*. It must have been many millenia ago, probably before written language. It certainly was long before the human mind could conceive of the worlds beyond shore and horizon, beyond Earth itself, that would be embraced through mapping.[9]

We now have tools of amazing grace that can render not only an image but the space the image behaves in. Consider the use of computational imagery for modern entertainment:

One of the group's (Lucasfilm) first computer graphics projects completed for a movie was the Genesis scene in Paramount's *Star Trek II: The Wrath of Kahn*, in which an experimental "Genesis bomb" is exploded on a lifeless planet with a cleansing wall of fire and then causing the planet to come to life. . . . Bill Reeves used a technique he developed for representing phenomena such as clouds, fire, smoke, and other objects that are not sharply defined by means of a particle field—a collection of randomly generated particles, the density, speed, shape, color are given as properties in a world coordinate system. As the sequence moves from one frame to the next, the algorithm randomly introduces new particles into the system according to density defined in the world- coordinate model, removes particles whose predetermined lifetime has expired, and moves the remaining particles at random. The illusion is that the cloud or smoke—or, in the case of Genesis, the wall of fire is actually moving and behaving as if it were made up of particles of matter being scattered by Brownian motion. . . . In all there were some 200 different particle systems containing some 75,000 particles. The initial explosion did not create the individual particles, but particle systems that moved in concentric circles away from the point of impact by generating more particle systems. This meant that, although the impact of the original bomb was created by one large explosion and about 20 smaller ones, generating some 25K particles, by the time the planet was engulfed in fire there were some 400 particle systems and some 750K particles.[10]

The Distributed Network

Andre Malraux, in his essays on art, suggested that the proliferation of technologies for distributing art ideas was creating a condition of "knowing" works of art the way one "knows" a familiar song from the radio or a personality from television:

Hitherto the connoisseur duly visited the Louvre and some subsidiary galleries, and memorized what he saw, as best he could. We, however, have far more great works available to refresh our memories than those which even the greatest museums could bring together. For a "Museum Without Walls" is coming into being, and (now that the plastic arts have invented their own printing press) it will carry infinitely farther that revelation of the world of art, limited perforce, which "real" museums offer us within their walls.[11]

The linking of powerful computation resources creates a web of intelligence. The injection of a high-powered computing system into what is essentially a much older intelligence system, the traditional physical-plant university, has changed forever the way education is done. It is the beginnings of the "University Without Walls."

The experience of designing and implementing such a structure is a grand experiment. There is no going back once the system is in place. The linking of student to student, student to faculty, student to library and archive, student to laboratory, student to external universities and museums is a revolution in cultural history. The technical history of Project Athena and the Visual Computing Group is instructive as such a pattern of change. The Visual Computing Group is now the MUSE Software Consortium, a part of the newly formed Center for Educational Computing Initiatives at MIT.

Currently there are only some twenty-five multimedia workstations on the Athena network that begin to approach visualization technology. The network itself, however, has been designed as a *scalable* system, fully capable of becoming a multimedia distributed network.

Project Athena was an eight-year (begun in 1983) research and development program sponsored primarily by Digital Equipment Corporation and IBM. (MIT, DEC, and IBM have spent one hundred million dollars on the project to date. Recently Apple Computer has made a quarter million dollar contribution as well.) Project Athena's goal was to explore new, innovative uses of computing in the MIT curriculum. The project was highly successful in developing a coherent computing environment of networked workstations.

The following is an excerpt from "Project Athena as a Distributed Computer System" by George Champine, former Associate Director for the Digital Equipment at Project Athena, Daniel Geer, former Manager of Systems Development at Athena, and William Ruh, former visiting scientist from IBM at Athena. The lengthy description of Athena is useful in understanding the complexity and thoroughness of system design that went into the project:

The Athena network consists of 1000 workstations in 40 clusters of 10 to 120 workstations each for use by students 24 hours a day. One of the clusters is an electronic classroom. In addition to the student clusters there are nine instruction development cluster and two facilities equipped to project images from workstation display screens. Workstation clusters have been installed in five student housing facilities, some with workstations in bedrooms and other with workstations in common areas.

Currently the system provides 10 Network File System Servers, 24 Remote Virtual Disk file servers, 79 Postscript printers, three name servers, there post office servers, and two authentication servers. Its supports the Digital Vaxstation and the IBM RT/PC. Plans are underway to employ the IBM PS/2 running AIX and the MacIntosh using AUX as network platforms. The system has 40 gigabytes of disk storage in the workstations and an additional 50 gigabytes of disk storage in the network file servers. Each workstation has from 50 to 100 megabytes of disk storage.

The network serves about 10,000 active user accounts which generate about 4000 logins and 9000 mail messages per day. The average student uses the system eight hours a week. In aggregate, users generate 12,000 questions per semester for the on-line consulting system and print three million pages per year. About 90 percent of the undergraduate students and 50 percent of the graduate students use the system. Usage is increasing about 15 percent a year as more students use the system and use it for more hours a day.

A major benefit of Athena is that students need learn only one system for educational computing. Athena presents a coherent model of computing in which all applications run on all supported workstations, independent of architecture. Because of the strong level of coherence, the human interface to the system is independent of the type of workstation being used. Thus, only one training program and one set of documentation are needed.

The initial time sharing environment installed for Athena in 1983 utilized about 63 VAX 11/750 mainframes and associated ASCII terminals running

Berkeley Unix. About 160 PC's were also used but did not run Unix. By 1987 this system was phased out entirely in favor of a uniform workstation environment and the time share computers were converted to file servers. Currently plans are being presented to broaden the reach of Athena into a diversity of vendor supported operating systems and licensed software.

The requirements for a distributed academic computing environment are predicated on a number of considerations. The system had to be *scalable* to support at least 10,000 workstations. It had to function 24 hours even though equipment failures might frequently occur in a system this large. Any user must be able to use any workstation. System services had to be secure even though the workstations are not. The system had to support a variety of hardware platforms. All systems application software should run on all workstations. And finally, the cost to own and operate must not exceed 10 percent of tuition on a sustaining basis. System support of public workstations is necessary because workstations are presently too expensive to be purchased by individuals. The plan has been to allow (but not require) individuals to purchase workstations when they become affordable.

The distributed system network relies on its three components: workstations, network, and servers. The user sees only the workstation, the network and servers are invisible. All services appear to be local and are available to the user with only a single submission of a password at login time. The actual delivery of the services is physically distributed over the system and communicated to the user transparently over the network. In concept, any operating system can be used workstations or servers in Athena. To achieve interoperability with other system components (and to gain access to the distributed services), the workstations need only support the Athena protocols for authentication, name service, file access, and print service.

One of the main attributes of the Athena system is its scalable design. By minimizing demands on scarce resources in network bandwidth, mass storage, and implementation labor, scalability becomes a key factor distinguishing this network from others that have a less opportunity for a sustainable future expansion. The campus network was designed with a backbone using optical fiber and a token ring protocol running 10 megabits per second. Network routers are attached to the backbone with each router supporting one Ethernet configured as an Internet Protocol subset. Because of the routers, traffic local to a subnet does not load the backbone. This approach gives a good measure of growth capability because as more workstations are added, more Ethernet subnets can be added to the backbone.[12]

The Visual Workstation

As part of this effort, the Visual Computing Group (VCG) was started in 1986 to experiment with the use of still and full-motion hypermedia. The VCG supported faculty members in the design of educational software involving audio and video materials as part of the content. The group offered expertise in both production of the audio-visual materials and in development of the controlling software applications.

As an experimental delivery system, the group modified a standard Athena workstation to support 256 color graphics as well as full-motion digitized video and audio. The visual workstation uses either an IBM PC-RT or DEC MicroVax II workstation as a base with a Parallax Graphics board added as the display subsystem. The IBM PS/2 is now under development under AIX and utilizes the IBM M-Motion video card. Apple has also become a research partner at Athena and the MacIntosh series of machines running under A/UX will also become 'Athenized' and should be equipped with a forthcoming video adaptor from Apple.

The Parallax Graphics board digitizes a standard NTSC video signal at 30 frames per second. The video images are presented on the display under the control of the X Window System, also developed at Project Athena. They can be moved, scaled and clipped as any other X Window. The system currently allows one window of full motion video. At the same time, though, it will allow hundreds of windows containing still images grabbed from the video source.

Distributed Authoring

After developing the multimedia workstation with its basic capacities for handling text, graphics, video, and audio, we realized the system was not easy to use. Without any high level information processing tools, the only access to the machine's potential was through Unix, C, X Windows, and the X Toolkit programmer's support package.

The system had been designed for MIT faculty to develop complex (language, architecture,engineering, neuroscience, biology, and reference) educational software. It was quickly apparent that no suitable application development tools were available for this purpose, and so in June 1987 we began to design a "construction set" for multimedia applications that would make it easy to implement the software proposed by the MIT faculty.

Over the course of the following year we developed a prototype system called MUSE. MUSE is an object-oriented system that provides information processing support for text, graphics, video, and audio. It allows one to create structured documents that combine all of these different kinds of information. Further, one can build these documents into complex fabrics of information, using the dynamic configurations found in hypermedia or other "low structure" systems, and also draw on more highly structured information found in conventional databases.

In essence, the aim of the prototype was to reduce the time and skill needed to produce interactive multimedia software. The approach we adopted was to extend the programming paradigms available to the application developer. This involved first understanding the structures of information that our target users wanted to produce, then finding efficient ways for them to articulate these structures. We arrived at a mixed-paradigm model, following the principle that people use a variety of expressive tools, and that no single approach will be efficient in all cases. The MUSE architecture provides two general and powerful models for representing the structural organization of information, and two for describing processes of change.

In MUSE, display materials are grouped into "information packages," which can include text, video, graphics, interactive manipulators, and dynamic indicators. When a package becomes activated, the display elements that make up its contents are presented on the screen. Any number of packages can be activated and displayed at the same time.

Packages are the "document units" in MUSE. They can be linked together in directed graph structures to form a network. Directed graphs are the basis for both "hypermedia" cross-referencing and applications based on state transitions. Within each package in a directed graph, Muse provides an internal multidimensional spatial framework that lays the foundation for dynamic system modeling.

Each package contains a set of "N" dimensions, which constrain the display of its elements. Each dimension has a valid range of values, and a current position. The attributes and behavior of package elements can be constrained to the position of one or more dimensions. These constraints are automatically maintained by Muse.

Package dimensions can represent physical time and space, or degrees of freedom in a dynamic system. A simple example is a package with one dimension called "time." The Muse author could describe a video window element within this package, which is constrained to the current position of the time dimension. Muse takes care of mapping the range of frames in a video segment into the range established by the time dimension.

Whenever the time dimension's position is changed, the video window is constrained to show the correct frame for that moment. A dimension's current position is changed by a "set-position" signal, which can be generated by timers or by user-interface elements like scrollbars.

Suppose that you wanted to attach synchronized subtitles to the video segment. This is accomplished by constraining both the video element and subtitle text elements to the same time dimension. Each subtitle is assigned to ranges of time on the dimension during which it is "active."

The MUSE dimension functions as a timeline, with video and two streams of subtitles extending over time. Within each stream the subtitles are shown in white. The current position determines what subtitles and video are shown at any time.

A scrollbar can now be constrained to the time dimension, so that it both indicates the current position and allows it to be changed. The user can then drag the scrollbar through time, and the video and subtitle streams maintain their synchronization. For normal motion video display, a timer is set to update the position of the time dimension at the appropriate rate.

Multimedia Editing

MUSE offers a wide range of possibilities in terms of application design. These possibilities are being made available to users through a set of dynamic, graphic-oriented editors. In MUSE, the editors are constructed in a modular way. The basic philosophy is that editors themselves should be modifiable. For any given application, the requirements for creating, deleting, or modifying materials will vary; better to tailor the editing capabilities to meet the needs of the application than try to meet all possible requirements in a static set of editors.

In MUSE, the editing capabilities are grouped in three layers. The first will treat basic data entities—individual objects of text, graphics, video, and so on. The second will provide facilities for compounding these individual data elements into coherent packages. These compounded information packages are the fundamental units in Muse. The third level will provide mechanisms for connecting the packages themselves into complex systems.

We are currently focusing on the first and second of these levels. At the base level, the editors include a video editor which provides fundamental capabilities for defining video objects, and "MuseAlbum," an electronic photo album for storing the video objects. Related to these are "Hot Spots," used to define scalable, polygonal cross-reference regions within the images, "XDither," used to reduce the full color images to bitonal bitmaps, and "Micon Maker," used to create sequences of X11 pixmap objects that can be used as motion icons (micons), a term coined by Russell Sasnett).

At the second level, the base editors are being integrated into compounding editors. At present we have "VideoAnnotator," used to synchronize text objects with graphic or video. This is used, for example, to add subtitles or annotations to motion video. Work is also under way on "MuseEd," a general purpose editor for creating and modifying Muse packages.

The approach we are taking is to provide the base editing functions as compiled modules that can be accessed directly from Muse. This means that the editors themselves, such as "Video Clipper" and "Muse Album," can be implemented as Muse packages. This makes it relatively easy to connect them together, drawing on the internal communication facilities built into Muse. So, for example, the level 2 editors such as "MuseEd" can draw in the level 1 editors as sub-packages, simply providing the additional communication needed to connect them. In addition, the Muse editors can be copied and re-edited in the same way as any other Muse package; this makes it possible to customize editors for particular applications.

The ability to edit the editors themselves will be one of the most valuable features of a general multimedia system. The Muse prototype has been developed to meet the needs of MIT faculty, and students will begin to use the system in the coming fall semester. Already, with the first materials, we can see the beginning of a change. In the past, teachers prepared materials and students reviewed them. Now, students are asked to create. With a broad array of expressive media, the ability to create complex visual images combined with text and numbers, students will be allowed to articulate their own perceptions.

In this context, the tools of expression within the system take on a greater significance, not only enabling expression to occur, but in subtle ways shaping the user's understanding of the domain of inquiry. Our effort has been to create a toolmaking tool; to understand the range of expressions that people want to create, to see how they conceptualize the structure of their objectives, and then to find ways that tools can be created allowing the expression of these structures.[13]

From an educational standpoint, the purpose of the system was to provide support for three principal types of software—interactive presentations, simulations, and reference materials. Presentations, either linear or branching, form the basis of expository teaching materials. Simulations give students control over dynamic system models based on graphic or video images, which is the most popular use of the workstations among MIT faculty. Reference materials are used to make large bodies of information accessible to student researchers, with tools to build such materials into their own notes and presentations. In the Muse architecture, all of these capabilities are integrated into a coherent environment, so that an author can freely mix the different kinds of materials in a single application.[14]

Ways of Learning

MUSE's application-driven development has been a unique opportunity to allow real subject matter to dictate the evolution of tools. MIT in this case has become a laboratory of possiblities for multimedia development. Each application, either intended for completion and delivery to students or prototyped for study and/or fund raising, has provided the opportunity to better understand what this new medium can reveal about "ways of learning."

Currently, the design of MUSE is being shaped by some thirty applications already utilizing its basic tools. These can roughly be divided into courses, reference materials, and telecommunications projects.

What is to be sought in designs for the display of information is the clear portrayl of complexity. Not the complications of the simple; rather the task of the designer is to give visual access to the subtle and the difficult—that is, the revelation of the complex.[15]

The concept of the possibility of a "multimedia language" has had a great deal to do with the group's interest in Janet H. Murray's Athena Language Learning Project that has produced two foreign language teaching projects in French (Gilberte Furstenberg's "Direction Paris") and Spanish (Douglas Morgentstern's "No Recuerdo"). Language is an environmental condition. It is best to live in the culture that speaks a language in order to be immersed in it. Simulating that experience is an excellent reason for using a visualization technology.

The French project, "Direction Paris," is divided into two parts. "A la rencontre de Philippe" is an interactive fictional story of a young writer in Paris who must make up with his girlfriend or else find a new apartment. The interactive model is a basic "choice tree" structure that allows the student to react to Philippe's problems and travel down different paths. They also use his answer phone as an audio device for getting clues to who he's going to have a problem with next. Filmed on location in Paris by Ayshe Farman-Farmarian, the scenes are elegant and very filmic. The second two sides of the French videodisc are a documentary called "Dans le Quartier St. Gervais" and are video footage shot in the neighborhood where the fictional character Philippe is searching for a new apartment. The student can ramble around the neighborhood and talk to "old timers" and newcomers to the area getting their mixed reactions to people like Philippe moving into the neighborhood. The mixture of fact and fiction is especially compeling.

In "No Recuerdo," the Spanish student is confronted with the mystery of Gonzalo, a Colombian scientist who has lost his memory. By accessing interviews with his friends and relatives, visiting sites in Colombia, and looking through his "visual memories," the student either unravels the story, helps Gonzalo get his memory back, or fails and lets the world fall into a memory plague where characters on the disc respond to questions with blank stares and "no recuerdo" ("I don't remember").

The Mechanical Engineering Project on bearings (produced by David Wilson of the Mechanical Engineering Department) utilizes interactive videodisc, computer graphics, and expert system software to provide students with a reference system that allows them to see how bearings are used in real applications (motion video) as well as how to design simple machines and evaluate their bearing choices.

"New Orleans: A City in Transition" (produced by Gloriana Davenport of the Film/Video Department at the MIT Media Lab) has a visual database of more than five hours of moving video concerned with urban planning, design, and the implementation of cultural change. The visual computing system for this project allows a student to respond to prepared questions by selecting information from libraries of maps, documents, moving interviews, documentary footage, still photographs, and graphics and actually uses the system to edit and present the information on the workstation.

The Geology Engineering Educator (by Herbert Einstein of the Civil Engineering Department) is an electronic book consisting of five hundred photographs of geologic formations that the student can outline using a graphics package and query for text and graphic information about their structure and composition.

Visual reference projects include the Boston Architecture Collection from the Rotch Visual Collection (produced by Merrill W. Smith, Associate Rotch Librarian). This videodisc and text database provide an in depth study of city planning, architecture, and transitional images from 1620 to the present.

The Neuroanatomy Learning Environment (Steven Wertheim, Department of Health Science and Technology) combines an illustrated videodisc glossary, 3-D computer graphics, a slide browser, and dissection film for exploration of the human brain. This project also plans to employ image processing to enhance areas of the brain for identification.

Introduction to Biology (Sheldon Penman of the Department of Biology) is a set of basic learning modules written around existing videodiscs of Cell Biology that employ narrated audio tracks and still frame/motion video of molecular materials.

The Image Delivery System (Patrick Purcell, MIT Media Lab) is designed to use telecommuncation technology to remotely serve the workstation visual images from the Boston Architecture videodisc. A student can call for still video images from the Rotch Library by using the MIT cable TV system connected to each workstation and associate the image with an on-line text database.

Understanding Imagery is a project of the Visual Arts Program (Edward Levine, Ben Davis) that allows students to explore the history of rendering technologies and the images they create from cave painting to electronic simulation.

The Visual Computing Group is also involved in a joint proposal to create a *Collection Image System* for the Native American Collections at the National Museum of Natural History at the Smithsonian Insititution in Washington, D.C. This project (MITSI) will initially provide Visual Workstation support for curators and researchers using the Southwest Collections.

Other prototypes involving curatorial and exhibition support include *Man Ray's Paris, 1921–39*, an electronic book extending the portraits of some thirty artists, writers, and musicians from the twenties and thirties into archives of painting, photography, and music. *Seeds of Change* is a prototype for the National Museum of Natural History on the effects of the discovery of the New World. The *Flight of the Daedalus* is an electronic catalog of the design, implementation, and history of the flight of the MIT-designed human powered aircraft. The *Film Anatomy Prototypes* are electronic tools for studying the anatomy of the films of Hitchcock, Ridley Scott, and Orson Welles.

The Visual Computing Group also worked with MIT's Center for Space Research Man Vehicle Laboratory "telescience" experiments. By adapting the multimedia workstation to receive digital data, voice, and live satellite video links to the Kennedy Space Center, faculty and students can monitor real-time experiments anticipating the use of the multimedia workstation as a NASA system link to the Spacelab and Space Shuttle.

New Initiatives

Since the end of Project Athena in July 1991, MIT has formed a new Center for Educational Computing Initiatives (CECI) that involves a number of efforts in leading edge technology for education including the MUSE Software Consortium for multimedia development. The MUSE Software Consortium (MSC) will carry forward the work of Project Athena's Visual Computing Group.

After five years (1986–1991) of systems and software research and development on multimedia, the strategy for development of authoring tools has become much clearer. The rationale for creating a multimedia authoring consortium like the MUSE Software Consortium at MIT has evolved from some serious revelations. The first concerns the fact that multimedia is not a peripheral technology. Multimedia is a *field*. The complexity of factors associated with the sychronization and distribution of an ever increasing and converging variety of media technologies is a reality. The production and organization of applications in this field will grow exponentially. The creation of standards in computing, communications, and media types will be a fluid situation that will follow a path of "updates." Control software for multimedia will be a consistent research problem that will require international cooperation and collaboration and will rely on a "version" strategy to meet the needs of ever changing communications technologies. The markets for this field will shift and focus on new objectives in relation to technical breakthroughs and innovations. The MUSE Consortium was created to participate in and give credence to this situation. Corporations and academic research partners will collaborate on a common software strategy that will serve both the immediate needs and long-term vision of an emerging *medium*, a medium that is only in its earliest stages of conscious design.

The consortium targets near-term, pre-competitive technologies that will enable the delivery of multimedia software. The MSC will use existing standards when possible and establish new standards when necessary. Working prototypes will be developed that can be widely used and evaluated by MIT and industrial participants rather than a software product in the sense of commercial quality assurance and documentation.

Multimedia addresses a broad spectrum of markets and will make use of many near-term technologies. In this regard, we expect the following technologies widely available to workstations within the next five years:

- 100+ MIP CPUs
- Flat panel megapixel 24 bit color displays
- Enormously extended memory
- Compatibility with gigabit networks

The research to be undertaken by the consortium will center around three major areas:

- The creation of platform-independent, multimedia authoring environments including tools for the C and C++ languages consistent with the X Window System. The X Window System is a trademark of the Massachusetts Institute of Technology. This software platform will be portable across diverse hardware architectures subject to the reasonable constraints of the hardware's functionality.
- The development of multimedia network services, including the transmission of digital video, the manipulation of remote multimedia databases, and collaborative software editors are of primary interest. The MSC envisions designing and creating both the server and client software for such network services.
- The creation of a range of exemplar multimedia applications in diverse areas spanning education and industry, and incorporating both reference resources and visualization tools. These applications will enable the

consortium to set priorities on enhancements to the multimedia platform that are closely linked to the actual needs of multimedia application developers.

This effort will ensure that the production of multimedia enabling software will be oriented towards open systems standards, will be available to MIT computing initiatives both present and future, and will have sufficiently diverse industrial support to have an impact on international multimedia engineering. The MSC plans to create and maintain connections to other institutions and universities pursuing initiatives that are focused on near-term solutions to multimedia development. The combination of multivendor, industrial sponsorship, and ties to major institutions that use multimedia computing as well as our ongoing relationships with other universities offer the prospect that the merged effort will create a de facto standard for multimedia computing.

A variety of projects are now underway underway with the Center for Educational Computing Initiatives (CECI) and the MUSE Software Consortium (MSC):

CECI/MSC is collaborating with the new national library of France, the Bibliotheque de France, to open in 1995 to explore software for structured access to multimedia materials and to develop multimedia extraction tools for users doing research with the libraries text, visual, and audio collections. This collaboration includes proposed software development and ongoing discussion projects to bring experts together to analyze the impact and importance of electronic multimedia access to libraries for education and research.

Prototyping is underway for developing an interactive multimedia catalog for portions of the Harvard Collection of Historic Scientific Instruments. The catalog is intended to serve the needs of the curator, scholars, students, and the general public by providing multiple interfaces to and views of the same underlying visual and catalogoue data.

The MIT Museum and CECI/MSC are producing a multimedia catalog of its collection of historic instruments, architectural renderings, photographic collections, and MIT related documents and memorabilia. The first collection to be prototyped will be the works of *Harold Edgerton* including the films, photographs, and stroboscopic equipment used by Edgerton to invent and explore stop-action photography.

Prototyping has begun with the Musee d'Orsay in Paris on a visual interface for the current text-based system the museum uses to allow visitors to recall selected digital images of the impressionist collections. This interface research is concerned with how museum visitors recall images in the actual collection in order to obtain more information about the works, the artists, and the time period in which objects were created.

In collaboration with the American University of Beirut, CECI/MSC is developing a project to build a multimedia atlas on the geography of Lebanon. The project includes an evaluation of authoring systems for low cost platforms. The finished application will be delivered to students at all educational levels in Lebanon.

A collaborative effort with the Boston Latin School is underway to transfer knowledge on multimedia technologies and applications. Work includes adapting capabilities of a high-end multimedia network system (university research setting) to a moderately low-end system (high school setting); designing classroom environments in which distributed computer applications are an integral part of the teaching process and analyzing its effects on students and teachers; gaining practical experience in the uses of distributed multimedia applications and collaborative work in a non-technical setting.

CECI/MSC is collaborating with the Rene Dubos Center for Human Environments in New York City on the design and development of a series of multimedia computer applications to teach environmental literacy. The series will span all major areas of the environment and will be targeted to secondary and elementary students. Each application in the series will incorporate a multimedia version of the Encyclopedia of the Environment being written by the Dubos Center. Staff of the Dubos Center have primary responsibility for the application content, while CECI has responsibility for the multimedia implementation.

CECI/MSC is also collaborating with the Groupment des Chambres Commerce et Industrie Hainaut-Cambresis (GHC), a center for the production of corporate training materials in Valenciennes, France, in order to better understand the international implications of multimedia materials for corporate training. This project focuses on the use of the MUSE system for creating multilingual electronic training materials for understanding pollution and waste management in corporate settings. The global nature of environmental education necessitates the understanding of how software not only crosses different industrial boundaries but cultural divisions as well. The project also extends to educational centers in Spain and the United Kingdom through connection to the GHC in France as well as content links to the MSC/Rene Dubos Project.

Dimensional Imagination

As all media move toward the digital state they present new promises and new problems. As video, sound, graphics, and text become equal partners in computer transmission, their collusion will cause difficulties in everything from technical issues of movement and storage to copyright and freedom of expression. As the computer relentlessly continues to integrate technologies and media, creating a condition of continuous hybridization of information, utilities for managing shifting conditions will be paramount.

The portent of mechanisms like MUSE lie in their extention into not only multimedia organizers and hypermedia linking tools but into collaborative network tools for group design, decision making, and idea formulation that employ media in thought provoking combinations. The old expression "to see what I mean" takes on a profound literal meaning.

Mass media communication could become less of a strategy for self-perpetuation and increasingly become a substantive reference system that can popularize in the most positive sense without trivializing. Communications will become less of a "thing" fragmented by market constraints and more of a process for understanding global change.

Reading "distributed multimedia visualization" as "networked dimensional imagination" suggests that the linking of the electronic classroom to the electronic laboratory to the electronic library and museum creates a world of possible new inventions, both literally and figuratively. The social, economic, and political implications of such a construction is bewildering in light of current structures for moving and storing information.

The notion of education merging with entertainment media is not new but in the digital realm it becomes a given. What is behind an image will become equally as important as what the next image will be. The linking of images will not only be sequential but will become "nodal." The prospect of "hyper-visualization" is daunting. Interconnected by future "virtual reality" display systems, global multimedia networks create a new dimension of natural and cultural immersion.

Notes

1. Beer, Stafford, *Brain of the Firm: The Managerial Cybernetics of Organization* (London: The Penguin Press, 1972), p. 31.

2. Tom McArthur, *Worlds of Reference* (New York: McGraw Hill, 1988), p. 9.

3. R. W. Hamming, *Numerical Methods for Scientists and Engineers* (New York: McGraw-Hill, 1962).

4. Donis A. Dondis, *A Primer of Visual Literacy* (Cambridge, MA.: MIT Press, 1973), p. 1.

5. I. L. Gregory, *Eye and Brain* (New York: World University Library, 1966), p. 8.

6. Robert O. McClintock, from an unpublished position paper on multimedia, Teachers College, Columbia University, Department of Computing, Communications, and Technology, New York, 1989.

7. Francis Yates, *The Art of Memory* (Chicago: University of Chicago Press, 1966), p. 7.

8. Ian Ridpath, *Star Tales* (New York: Universe Books, 1988), p. 1.

9. J. N. Wilford, *The MapMakers* (New York: Vintage Books, 1982), p. 7.

10. Robert Rivlin, *The Algorithmic Image* (Redmond, Washington: Microsoft Press, 1986), p. 238.

11. Andre Malraux, *The Voices of Silence* (Princeton: Princeton University Press, 1978), p. 16.

12. George Champine, Daniel Geer, and William Ruh, "Project Athena as a Distributed Computer System," *Computer Magazine*, IEEE Computer Society, September, 1990, p. 40–51.

13. Ben Davis, Matthew Hodges, and Russell Sasnett, "Educational Multimedia at MIT" *Advanced Imaging Magazine*, July, 1989, p. 32–36.

14. Ben Davis, Matthew Hodges, and Russell Sasnett, "Multimedia Design Documentation," in *Society of Text*, ed. Edward Barrett (Cambridge: The MIT Press, 1989), p. 20–30.

15. E.R. Tufte, *The Visual Display of Quantitative Information* (Cheshire, Connecticut: Graphics Press, 1983), p. 191.

19

Engineering-Design Instructional Computer System (EDICS)

David Gordon Wilson

Introduction

Background to the problem
The current difficulty in effectively teaching mechanical-engineering design in a modern university can be ascribed to three trends:

1. the range of disciplines that design has to cover, or at least to give students some acquaintance with, is continually expanding;

2. the share of the curriculum that is devoted to teaching design has been significantly reduced over the last fifty years, with an increased emphasis on engineering physics, so that the background of the younger design instructors often includes little real design; and

3. the range of preparation of undergraduate students entering mechanical engineering is much more varied now, and the mechanical experience is generally less, than in the past.

Students have been led to believe from high school on that a good background in the basic disciplines is all that is needed to be a well-prepared engineer. The recovery of our technological leadership requires design, and design requires the mastery of real-world details and what is known as "good engineering practice."

To put the overall problem into more personal terms, when the author was an undergraduate in the late forties, studying among others of very similar backgrounds, we were introduced to designs using principally ferrous and nonferrous materials formed on rather simple production equipment. We took courses that stretched over three years, in company with fellow students who, like us, enjoyed building "gadgets" and tuning up motorcycles and automobiles. As teachers in the 1990s we must make our students at least aware of an enormously wider range of technology and of materials that can be formed in a huge variety of ways. At MIT, we teach only two required mechanical-engineering-design courses each having two lecture hours per week for one semester. More than a third of our bright, eager and intelligent students do not know what is meant by such everyday engineering terms as washer, flange, set screw or keyway.

Another third of the students have good mechanical-engineering shop and drawing experience from either their high schools or their home environments or both. Pitching the level of a lecture to them leaves the less-experienced students floundering. But the experienced students become bored if the instructors spend too much time explaining the differences between screws, bolts and studs, for instance.

The results of these dilemmas have been dissatisfying to all. At MIT we have tried various solutions, without outstanding success. We have searched for texts to try to specify a course of self-study for those whose background is lacking, but so far have not found any single book that is particularly helpful. We have tried dividing classes into two groups, and giving parallel lectures on fundamental and more advanced topics, a situation that leads to unfairness in treatment and grading. With the enormous expansion of the world of engineering, and therefore of the range of knowledge to which, we all agree, students must be exposed, it is inevitable that the level of skill in individual areas cannot be as high as when the curriculum was less demanding. However, we are in danger of not advancing the capabilities of some inexperienced students in the direction of synthesis, because we may be actually lessening their self-confidence in design. They become afraid to put their ideas down on paper because they don't know how to handle details. We are graduating students who do not know any traditional methods for fastening a wheel to a shaft, for instance. What we propose here is aimed, in particular, at giving self-study resources to students who perceive that their preparation for design courses is inadequate in some respects. The same resources can give information in-depth to more advanced engineers. They have been used by some instructors in the workshop or laboratory as the only resource available to groups of students who have been given specific quiz-type questions on engineering hardware.

The teaching of mechanical-engineering design is the subject of an on-going vigorous debate. The debate usually concerns rather high-level design concepts. Students cannot attain the level at which these concepts have relevance if they have no idea how to fit a rotor to a shaft, or put the shaft in bearings, or to put the whole assembly into a casing. We know that children go through phases in their drawings of people: first, limbs come directly out of faces, and only later are bodies added and limbs attached to them. Likewise, many students seem to start with design sketches of the type shown in figure 19.1. We need to educate them past this early stage before they can become productive.

Analogy between designing and writing

An analogy may further illustrate the goals of EDICS. Engineering design is similar to writing a novel. An author may choose from an enormous range of possibilities of plot, structure and style. There is no formula or algorithm for success. Many renowned authors maintain that they re-write and revise their material dozens of times before they are happy with the overall result. Intuition and feeling will play large roles. If a novel is warmly received, the author's creativity will be applauded. But, except for rare, iconoclastic writers, their creativity will be based on using the accepted words, grammar, and rules of the language. If they do not know how to use the language, their creativity will have very little scope for expression.

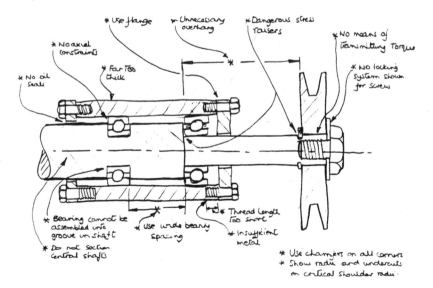

Figure 19.1
Typical sophomore design sketch

This is a very close analogy to engineering design. A large proportion of students do not know the equivalent in design of the words, grammar, and rules of language. Their attempts at creativity are similar to those of an adult trying to write a novel in a foreign language. The results in both cases are usually pathetic.

We find that it is continually necessary to advise students as follows. "Do not try to be creative in designing fastenings for traditional materials (for instance)—you are following several hundred years of development. It is likely that there are small improvements still to be made in fasteners for particular applications. But if you want to change the world, use "good-practice" methods for all the small details, like the words and the grammar in writing, in your design, and give full rein to your creativity in the big picture, the overall design."

The purpose of this development is, then, to convey information on the words and the grammar of engineering design as part of our effort at MIT to retn to hands-on engineering education. We chose to start with three areas of design at a rather fundamental level:

1. the choice of bearings and bearing systems;
2. the choice of methods of mounting rotors to shafts; and
3. the choice of methods of joining and capping cylinders (figure 19.2).

These three areas appear in most mechanical-engineering designs, so long as "cylinders" are broadly interpreted to include many forms of machine housings. They are areas in which most students seem to have perpetual difficulty.

In each area the nine divisions or chapters shown in figure 19.3 were set up.

Alternative Approaches

The great amount of work required to develop a system of the type discussed has caused us to wonder if this is the most cost-effective way of achieving our goals. If we could have found all the information in a book we should certainly have specified it. Should we have spent our time writing one or more books? Written matter has the enormous advantage over film, video, and computer-based presentation in its availability at any time and at any place to which one wishes to take it. However, for the present topic areas, books have some disadvantages.

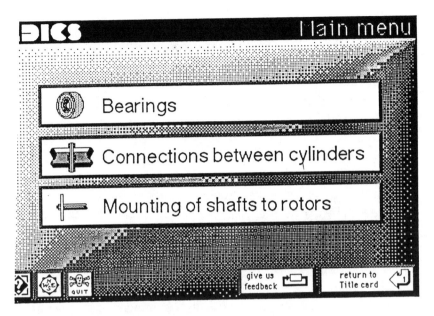

Figure 19.2
The three topics in EDICS's main menu

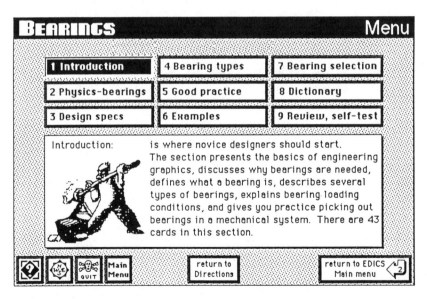

Figure 19.3
The nine subsections in each main topic

The first is that the very large range of possibilities inherent in engineering design, being multidimensional, is difficult to convey, especially to inexperienced students, on two-dimensional and mostly monochromatic pages.

The second is that design is extremely broad. A personal library of many large handbooks is required by experienced design engineers for the practice of their craft. Many more would be needed to bring some of their learned experience to students. The quantity of text would become unmanageable. The interrelationships between and among various sections of the many handbooks would be impossible to highlight dynamically. (At MIT we tried specifying that incoming design students buy just one handbook—Marks' *Standard Handbook for Mechanical Engineers*—but the large quantity of available information in that one text appeared to produce a kind of panic revulsion. Students were scathing in their denunciation of this excellent book. The experiment was a failure.)

A third is that books involve, normally, less interaction than computer tutorial systems. This interaction appears to increase the effectiveness of instruction.

Videotapes and videodisks can overcome the first disadvantage, giving multidimensional still and moving images in color of actual and simulated hardware. Videotapes in particular are being used widely for simple instruction. When one buys an "internal" hard disk for a computer, for instance, it is likely to be accompanied by a videotape showing how it should be installed. There is no doubt that a videotape is an enormous improvement over the printed word in conveying how something specific should be done by someone relatively inexperienced.

Therefore we might ask ourselves whether we would not be more effective had we expended the same effort into producing a large number of short videotapes, or one or two longer videotapes, combining lecture and demonstration material in imaginative ways.

We believe that these would not solve the problem. There is a great difference between having a short videotape for one specific need, and a long video dealing with many broad topics to do with a given area such as "bearing selection." The producers of the long video will have a prototype user in mind, one who will have only the bare minimum of preparation. This user may enjoy the video in toto. Anyone else will feel trapped, rather as a visitor to a museum feels trapped when told that he/

she can see the exhibits only in a guided tour. There are areas that the visitor will know well. There will be others that are of little interest that the visitor will want to skip. The essence of computer control of videodisks is that skipping over, from, or to areas of little or of great interest can be carried out virtually instantly. More of the student's time can be devoted to gathering new knowledge and associating it with existing knowledge than will be the case with one-dimensional media.

While we believe that interactive video has advantages over these alternatives in introducing unfamiliar topics, we do not subscribe to the philosophy that holds that the printed word is doomed. At the present stage of multimedia technology and techniques, it seems possible to treat only rather simple concepts. We expect that the use of EDICS will lead to more knowledgeable study of texts, rather than to the abandonment of reading.

Other interactive-video work

Many developers of electronic educational materials have espoused the virtues of interactive media. Authoring systems such as Claris's Hyper-Card that allow direct "point-and-click" connection to other files or "screens" or segments of other media such as videodisks simply through directing a mouse or tracking ball to on-screen "buttons" give users a heightened sense of control. The production of interactive programs has been rising, particularly of programs produced on rather specific and narrow topics, such as on the collection in the National Gallery of Art, and for instruction on manufacturing, maintenance, and overhaul procedures in automobile companies and the armed forces. There have also been pioneering programs on undergraduate chemistry and physics instruction. However, we know of no educational programs using interactive video in the field of engineering design.

The Development of EDICS

Low-level work funded by MIT's Project ATHENA started in 1983–84, but the major part of EDICS development was funded by a grant from the National Science Foundation starting in 1988. A rather pioneering approach to the program structure and content was taken.

1. A broad definition of bearings was devised that was felt to be more useful and more comprehensive than that used by all texts that were consulted (figure 19.4).

2. Bearings were characterized by the degrees of freedom that they permitted, and by the "physics" of the form of constraint that they employed. This also seemed to be a new and useful approach (figure 19.5).

3. All bearings were shown to fall into four categories of forms of constraint, which could be produced by:

sliding elements;

rolling elements;

flexing elements; and

noncontact forces such as those produced by hydrostatic or hydrodynamic fluids or magnetic fields (figure 19.6).

4. Shaft-rotor couplings were characterized by the torque-capability ratio, TCR, being the ratio of the ultimate torque of the coupling with the ultimate torque of the shaft alone.

5. Cylinders were defined very broadly to include engine blocks and gear casings as well as tubes and pipes. The selection system involved the possible uses of cylinders—simple enclosures, means of enclosing fluids, and structural elements—and their shape and size. For instance, screwed connections cannot be used for noncircular cylinders, and are not used for cylinders over a certain diameter (about 100 mm).

6. We encouraged users, through on-screen animations, to estimate values such as shaft speeds and loads, and other forms of periodic feedback and testing (figure 19.7).

7. We devised simple forms of expert system to try to transfer to a novice user an expert's rapid selection-and-exclusion approach to the selection of the various alternatives.

8. We set up "good-practice" sections of the program.

9. We arranged a common dictionary that could be accessed by clicking on italicized words.

10. About forty minutes of video on a wide range of aspects of the three topics were produced.

Hardware selected

The year 1988, in which we started our major effort to develop EDICS, was propitious because of the many alternative "platforms" that were becoming available. We chose to use the Apple Macintosh computer for several reasons.

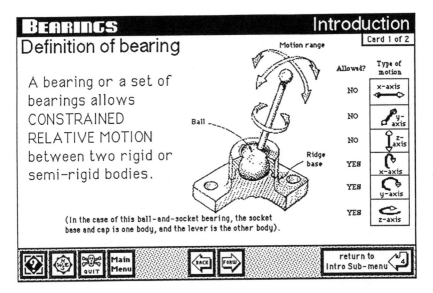

Figure 19.4
Definition of a bearing

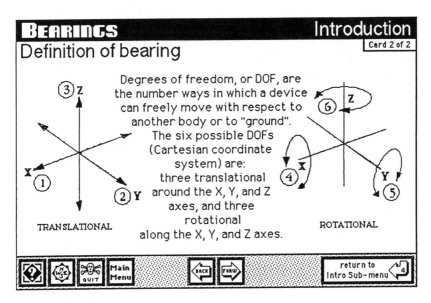

Figure 19.5
Degrees of freedom of a bearing

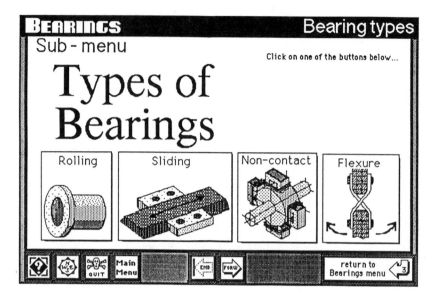

Figure 19.6
Four categories of bearing constraints

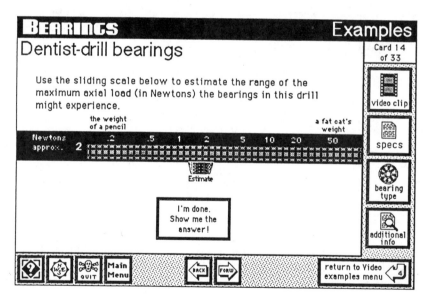

Figure 19.7
Incorporation of user self-evaluation

1. It is very popular among students. Besides easing eventual adoption and use, this enabled us to hire skilled undergraduates ("hackers") to help with program development.

2. The Macintosh was then being shipped with HyperCard software included, providing an easily available route to interactive-video applications.

3. The very vigorous state of development of hardware and software for the "Mac" promised continual improvements in capability and performance.

The choice involved one possible disadvantage: we could not then have the video output on the monitor, and accordingly we developed a two-screen system consisting of the Apple monitor and a standard (NTSC) color TV. The MIT Athena Visual Computing Group with whom we have been working throughout is developing the Muse multimedia interface and is transferring EDICS to its single-screen system. New software coupled with hardware boards is also becoming available that could enable us to show the video output on the Mac screen. However, the two-screen system has, at present, considerable advantages in clarity and impact.

We developed EDICS on a Macintosh II with 5 Mb RAM and a 140-Mb external hard-disk drive. Apple now makes considerably faster computers, but EDICS works well on mid-range machines.

We also chose to use the Pioneer LD-V4200 videodisk player, the Farallon MacRecorder with SoundEdit, and the ProViz Video Digitizer with HyperVision.

Software

The software used for EDICS development included the Apple Claris HyperCard authoring system; Claris MacDraw II, MacPaint II, Studio 1 for drawings; Electronic Arts Studio 1 with Animation Driver XCMD for animation and painting; MacroMind Director and Player as animation tools; the Farallon ScreenRecorder recording utility; Individual Software's 101 Scripts and Buttons; MacUser HyperCard Toolbox; Apple ResEdit as an editing utility; and Altsys Fontastic Plus for font animation.

Program Structure and Route Guidance

Any complex program must, in general, follow a structure similar to that of a molecule: it is either a branched tree or a ring. The tree structure is natural in instruction because a hierarchy of information is to be expected, and is used here (figure 19.8).

A small tree presents few problems to the user or to the developer. A large, complex tree with many branches and twigs can cause almost insurmountable problems of consistency in many aspects to the developer, and can seem somewhat frightening to a user. For the user of a simple branched program is less an observer of the tree but more a blind crawler, taking one branch after another, not knowing what has been missed in the neglected branches and unsure of how to get back to either the branch points or to the beginning.

We put strong emphasis on equipping the user of EDICS with maps, parachutes for quick exit, and other aids to give the user the ability to hop from branch to branch with as much preview as possible about what to expect, and to highlight a once-used path with an evanescent "scent" to allow previous tracks to be identified (see next paragraph).

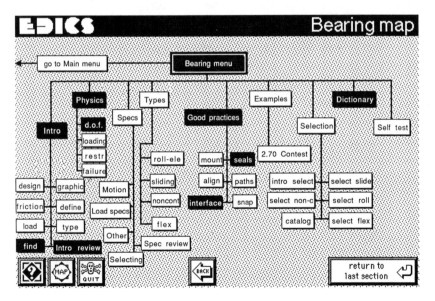

Figure 19.8
Navigation map

The user-friendly mouse, with a button that can be "clicked" when an on-screen arrow points to a "button" area on the screen, was used for almost all control. Once EDICS is on screen, six "guidance" buttons are standardized in position and configuration along the bottom of the frame (figure 19.4). Two with arrows simply indicate that the user can go one step forward or one back. A long button with a bent-backwards arrow gives access to the last section covered. A query button is for general help. A "points-of-the-compass" button brings up a map of the program tree, with black-on-white labels on the various branches. As these branches are entered, the video on the labels is reversed, white-on-black. The user can quickly see what has and what has not been covered, and can go directly to another point on the tree by clicking on that branch. The last "guidance" button is a skull-and-crossbones, for an immediate exit.

The language of engineering drawing

All present-day teachers of engineering design know that it is difficult to convey information about hardware to students when engineering drawing is no longer a required course. We found that it was essential that EDICS users be given some rudimentary acquaintanceship with isometric and orthogonal drawing because we had to use drawings to explain design concepts. Interactive video is a particularly powerful method of demonstrating the relationship between a photographic view of an object, an isometric view, and a multiview drawing with orthogonal projections. We carried this out with a video shot of a pillow-block plain bearing, coupled on the computer screen with an isometric sketch, which was animated. First the isometric was cut by planes, and then it was rotated to show cross-sectional views (figure 19.9).

We have tried in EDICS to make extensive use of graphical representations and drawing techniques, including freehand sketching, blended with similar-sized real images and animations. The intent is to foster the mental imagery and visualization so important to the practice of creative engineering design.

Music and animation

Animation is used to produce moving images on the Mac monitor. The purpose of these animations is sometimes just to enliven the program, and

The Social Creation of Knowledge: EDICS, cont.   14

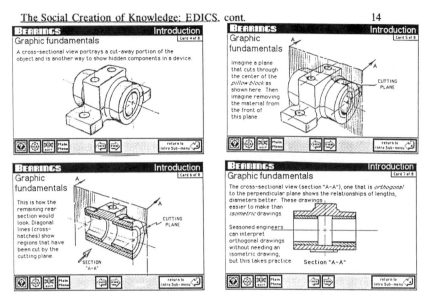

Figure 19.9
Isometric and orthogonal drawing

sometimes to illustrate engineering principles or good practice (figure 19.10).

Music and other sounds are also used to make the presentation more interesting and to convey information from the computer program—for instance, on whether or not the user has given the correct response to a question in a moving cartoon section called "Find the bearings" (figure 19.11). The videodisk provides a track of coordinated sound, when needed, for the video portions.

Organization
Decisions on overall pedagogical strategy were made by the faculty (Ernesto Blanco and Woodie Flowers in addition to the author) and on video and sound taping by the video producer, Seichi Tsutsumi. Virtually all other decisions were made by the graduate research assistants, Douglas Marsden and David Crismond. Much of the actual programming was carried out by a cadre, reaching a maximum of about ten, of enthusiastic undergraduates working under the MIT UROP (undergraduate research-opportunities program), or as part of their bachelor theses. Their imaginative inputs had a great deal to do with EDIC's acceptance by undergraduates.

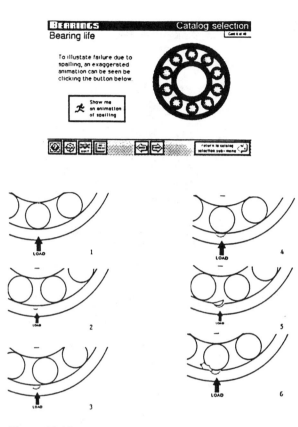

Figure 19.10
Animation in EDICS

Professional crews were used to take all video and sound pieces under the producer's direction, ensuring a very high standard to be reached. Undergraduates were again employed to present many of the artifacts and devices that were assembled, principally by the faculty, for illustration. Most of the textual and illustrative materials were generated by the faculty and were typed and digitized for transfer into EDICS.

Industrial inputs
Considerable help was received from a collaboration with the research department of The Timken Company. We also received helpful inputs from TRW on bearing-failure modes and from SKF on rolling-element theory.

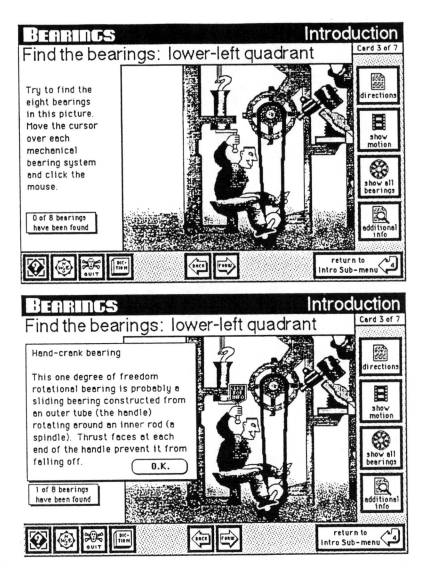

Figure 19.11
Find the (nonhuman) bearings

Alternative Methods of Using EDICS

These are alternative ways in which EDICS can be, and has been, used.

1. The EDICS "station" has been set up in a "cluster" of computer terminals available for student use. The instructor in a class in which any of the three EDICS topics is to be discussed in a forthcoming class suggests that any students who feel that their previous experience is below some defined norm for the class should look through the relevant section(s), individually or in groups.

2. An EDICS station is located in a laboratory or workshop where students are to disassemble a series of devices—for example, a powered lawnmower—and they are asked to describe the components with reference to their treatment in EDICS.

3. EDICS is used by an instructor in a classroom. The ideal arrangement is for the room to be equipped with two projectors that can produce simultaneous large-screen images of the computer screen and the TV monitor. The instructor can call up examples, stills, videos, animations, and so forth, as required to illustrate the lecture.

Student Reactions

Initial student reactions have been predominantly highly favorable. When used in the laboratory, many students have been strongly complimentary, and have asked if they could come back after class to work on EDICS in their own time. These comments are anecdotal. A careful and thorough attempt at evaluating EDICS as an alternative to the best available textual material has been carried out by Crismond.[1] This has shown that students generally prefer using EDICS over the best available text. There are three aspects in which EDICS has advantages over texts.

1. Videos of artifacts being used, disassembled, manufactured, and so forth convey much more about them than is possible in the still images in a book. Moreover, many more "stills" can be economically provided than is possible in a book.

2. Hypertext-like connections enable the EDICS user to move rapidly to various aspects of a concept or artifact. S/he does not have to look in an index and then search among many pages for a related aspect. Usually it can be accessed by simple "point-and-click" operations. The advantages of EDICS grows rapidly as the coverage increases to the point where many separate handbooks would be required in a text version of the material.

The user then has to look in several indices, whereas the multimedia approach seems capable of including a large amount of data in one easily accessed collection.

3. EDICS incorporates many ways in which the user is asked to give feedback, usually by estimating some quantitative or qualitative aspects. (For instance, "guess the speed of the dental drill".) This type of engagement of the user reinforces learning and keeps the user alert.

Future Work

Future versions of EDICS and future trials should incorporate the following changes, which will be tested to measure their effectiveness.

Instructor inputs

We wish to provide means by which an instructor could make a short (eg ten-minute) videotape on a special topic and for it to be accessed by students from within EDICS. Software is becoming available for storage of such sequences on the hard disk and for consequent rapid retrieval from it.

Collaborative learning

Although we had intended to arrange that EDICS be used by individual students, it seems likely that groups of three or possibly four learn faster on account of their interaction and comments. We will test this hypothesis.

Authoring and user-printing

We want to test the effects of encouraging users to write or type notes on the EDICS material. We may also allow users to print out a small quantity of EDICS screens and will test the effects on retention.

Human factors in education

We will measure some human factors, including the time to learn the interface; the error rate; the speed of navigational performance; and knowledge retention over time.

New topics
We are developing "modules" on fasteners, drafting and graphics, estimating, and power transmission. Other schools trying EDICS will, we hope, develop other modules fitting the same overall framework.

Conclusions and Recommendations

1. A resource has been developed that makes available to students who may lack experience in some aspects of mechanical-engineering design a means of finding more information on acceptable design approaches in, initially, three pervasive areas: the selection of bearing systems, the mounting of rotors on shafts, and the joining and capping of cylinders.
2. The system developed employs text, line illustrations, animations, and still and moving videos, in an interactive environment. Design has been presented in the same manner in which it is practised. Users learn the rudiments of orthogonal drafting; and many technical terms (e.g., "gasket") that are not well explained in a text dictionary are shown with great clarity, and with fast, easy access simply by "clicking" on the word.
3. The time and resources required to produce an interactive-video program are far greater than those to produce an equivalent text, but the added dimensions of the discovery and learning experience indicate that it should be a more effective teaching device.

Acknowledgments

This work was supported in part initially by a grant from Project Athena, MIT, and latterly by a grant from the National Science Foundation. The grants officer was Dr. Edward W. Ernst. Among the many others who contributed greatly to the development of EDICS were Seichi Tsutsumi, Ernesto Blanco, Woodie Flowers, Douglas Marsden, David Crismond, Benjamin H. Davis, Hans Peter Bradmo, Pascal Chesnais, Glorianna Davenport, Megan J. Smith, Peter S. Orvos, Ravi R. Bhatia, Jon Demerly, Rob Flemming, Bob Kupbens, Brian Lasher, Jong Lee, Rick Olegario, Russ Stevens, Tim Tuttle, Evren Unver, Lauralee Grizzaffi, Michael Hess, Mark Housman, Rob Kim, and Joe DiMare. This article was based on the project final report to the National Science Foundation and on an article written for *Mechanical Engineering* (ASME).

References

Crismond, David P. Initial Draft of MSME Thesis. To be published at MIT, Cambridge, MA, June 1992.

Dixon, John R. The State of Education. Two articles on engineering design science, and subsequent reader correspondence, in *Mechanical Engineering*, ASME, New York, February–May, 1991.

Dyrud, Marilyn A. *Engineering Technology Education: Bibliography 1990.* Engineering Education, ASEE, Washington DC, May/June 1991.

Kerr, A. D., and R. B. Pipes. Why We Need Hands-on Engineering Education. *Technology Review* 90, pp. 34–42, M.I.T., Cambridge, MA, 1987.

Marsden, Douglas W. Development of the Engineering-Design Instructional Computer System (EDICS. MSME thesis, MIT, Cambridge, MA, June 1990.

What is Multimedia? a special issue of *PC Today*, Peed Corp., Lincoln, NE, June 1991.

20

Computers and Design Activities: Their Mediating Role in Engineering Education

Shahaf Gal

Introduction

Expectations of educational technology to improve teaching and learning are probably as old as the introduction of the blackboard and chalk into education. Years ago, radios, motion pictures, and television generated hopes similar to the ones now raised by the introduction of computers. Seemingly, these technologies added to the teacher repertoire, but none has made the anticipated "Great Leap Forward" of education. Instead, technologies prior to computers seemed to have followed a familiar cycle: exhilaration—scientific credibility—disappointment—blame (Cuban 1986, 1989).

Perhaps more than many of the educational technologies introduced before it, the computer has generated hopes of transforming the content and the context of education. Recently, however, concerns about the quality of the computer as learning environment have been echoed in the discipline of computer science, especially regarding the design of new interactive computer tools for education and the workplace (Winograd and Flores 1986; Dreyfus and Dreyfus 1986; Wenger 1990; Clancey 1989; Brown and Duguid 1990a, 1990b; Brown 1991). Voices expressing dismay are being heard in the educational community as well (Scheffler 1990; Cuban 1986, 1989). Is now the stage of disenchantment with computers? Can we expect the computer to follow the path of prior educational technologies that tried to transform teaching and learning? Possibly, as long as the focus is on the computer and not on the educational experiences within which computers could play a role.

As a case in point, this chapter focuses on the Bridge Design Contest which took place at the Civil Engineering Department at Massachusetts

Institute of Technology in the winter of 1988. From a detailed examination of students' use of a computer expert system to design their models of bridges the chapter asks, how do design activities, supported by a computer, enhance students' learning of engineering?

The chapter suggests that multimedia design activities, enriched by computers, can play an important intermediatory function between education and work.

Computers and Engineering Education at MIT

Civil engineering was the first engineering curriculum at MIT. Since then, it has undergone a series of transformations, which reflects the trends in engineering overall and the transformation of engineering as a profession. These changes have been influenced by advances made in computer science and computer technology.

Until the end of the World War II, structural engineering was considered an "elevated craft" at the center of the field. After the war, engineering evolved to become a discipline of academic study. The theory of structural behavior became a special case of Newtonian physics. And, by the end of the 1950s, advanced mathematics were intrinsic to structural analysis. Exercises in structural analysis, which were always an integral part of teaching students about structural behavior, reflected the change in the profession. Students were given problems of structural engineering that were represented by complex, multiple differential equations. Analytic exercises consisted of a graphic display of a structure. The students' task was to calculate its behavior by using the appropriate equations. In the engineering laboratory, students learned the underlying structural properties of materials (like steel) used in construction.

Computers that were introduced in the sixties to support engineering education aligned with the hard-core scientific spirit of the time. The computers were used for automation of equation solving. Digital computers were considered a substitute for the graphic methods. Programs like STRUDL had a computational model, and an analytic power of finite-element analysis, which saved students from doing the tedious number crunching and the iterations of structural design.

A dramatic shift took place in the early eighties. Personal computers started to become popular, and new computational models emerged from the rival disciplines of computer sciences and artificial intelligence (AI). The first computer-aided design programs were introduced for structural and electrical engineering. Their effect was widely felt in engineering.

The Department of Civil Engineering responded by attempts to re-define itself. In its Constructed Facilities Division a shift was proposed from "traditional structural components" to computer-aided design of "engineering systems." The division proposed to develop a *Computer Aided Teaching System* (CATS): a multi-purpose intelligent tutoring system for graduate and undergraduate engineering education.

The educational intentions of CATS initiators were to transform the educational process of engineering. The teachers envisioned a role for a computer-based tutor to provide a learning environment that could enable students to focus on design. Their idea was to build an "expert system" that captures the knowledge of professional structural engineers. The system would provide students with a way to correct their "causal reasoning," free them from the tedious computations involved in design, and offer them a database of "design knowledge." It would also enable students to shift to iterative preliminary design in which large chunks of detailed design were automated.

With the expert system, believed the teachers, students would move from "passive learning" to "interactive learning." In an interactive learning environment, students would deal with more realistic, complex, and larger structural design problems. The computer would serve the students like an expert engineer, enabling them to create and test designs and provide feedback on their work.

Growltiger

The software package *Growltiger* (GT), which was used by the students in this study, was the second program developed at the Constructed Facilities Division. The program draws its name from one of T. S. Eliot's poems in the *Practical Cats* collection. It was taken to represent a practical CATS in engineering and was developed as an alternative to STRUDL. The software, explained its developer, set out to recapture what had been lost in the sixties–the interactive graphic analysis of the old-fashioned methods–while retaining the analytic power of finite-element analysis.

Growltiger was planned to serve students as a *design tool* and as a *virtual laboratory* for experimentation in structural engineering. Both purposes fit the approaches mentioned above. As a virtual laboratory, GT is programmed as a channel of guided-discovery, whereas the dialogue, its content, and the process lead toward known results. The system guides students to enter the necessary data for the structural analysis, to manipulate the appropriate computational components, and to evaluate the results against known parameters of structural engineering. However, its capability to function as a design tool fits with the fermentative approach toward self-discovery. In this mode, GT provides basic structural elements (like beams) and analytic formulas with which students can design and test their own structures and proceed to evolve their structures through iterations until they are satisfied with the outcome.

The program provides structural analysis for two-dimensional structures. It is an object-oriented program written in the C language. The program is used on a monochrome megapixel display workstation which supports the X Window System and Xlib Version 1.0. The underlying behavioral simulation uses established procedures from structural engineering expressed by matrix algebra algorithms.

Growltiger has two basic options which serve as an educational tool for design. The program assists the designer by creating indeterminate structures that cannot be designed without analysis and cannot produce an analysis without a design. A default setting deals with this issue, offering standard-sized beams and standard material and four types of structures. This way, students test how their designs behave in accordance with a range of standardized degrees of tolerance. The test can serve as a starting point from which students try to optimize the structure. They can change the shape of their structure, the loading, and stiffness. Within seconds the new structure can be analyzed.

Students can also choose to build their own structures. Aside from curves, they can design the structure, decide on the kind of material, and choose the loading system. To help students gain a feel for the deflection, the program can display the deflection moving from zero deflection to the full range (see Appendix).

The bridge design contest

Although some of the teachers have used GT in their classes, the educational approach which the program developer envisioned, (namely, in the context of design exercises that challenge students with real-life problems) has been practiced only to a very limited extent. The Bridge Design Contest was one of the few options in which, potentially, GT could be used, as conceived by its developer.

The contest took place at MIT in the winter of 1988, during one month of independent activities. It was the fourth competition. Seventeen MIT students from several different departments within the School of Engineering participated in the contest. Enrollment in the contest was voluntary and no academic credit was given. Some of the students worked in teams while others worked alone. There were both experienced and inexperienced students of engineering, from first-year undergraduate to graduate levels.

The students' task was to build, within three weeks, models of bridges that could withstand real load. Participants were given a kit of materials containing strings, wire, glue, and a variety of wood blocks—basswood, balsa, and pine. The kit of materials weighed approximately 1.5 pounds. Students were encouraged to use *Growltiger* (GT)—an expert system engineering program—and the engineering lab to build their models. In preparation students also received an article about bridge design, listened to two lectures on bridges, and observed a demonstration of GT.

The use of materials and some rules for design were set in advance by the instructor. Some of the rules were that pine blocks could only be used for the construction of towers, that the bridges were to be a minimum of 36 inches long, and that the bridges could have a maximum of three supporting towers or piers. Students were also penalized for excessive use of materials.

By "loading-day" twelve bridges were ready to be tested. The bridges' strength was tested by a loading mechanism. Two "gangplank" third-class levers were connected to a reaction frame and bridge-decks to apply load to the bridges at eight loading points.

The contest took place in two phases. In the first phase, the bridges had to withstand a slowly applied load of 1000 pounds on either side. Some bridges were eliminated at that stage. A few bridges lasted to the second stage. In the second phase, a 1/2-inch support settlement was introduced to one of the towers, randomly selected. The students decided the fate of their bridge by "walking the plank" away from their bridge models.

Making Sense of the Students' Bridge Building Activities

Research on the use of computers in education often relies on existing perspectives to provide analytic frameworks. However, the intended use of the computer says nothing about its actual use. To make sense of the actual use, the predefined purpose of the computer, as set by the perspectives, needs to be set aside. Such a research approach creates room for alternative interpretations and could serve to gain new understanding of computer use (Lepper 1985; Scheffler 1990). To achieve this goal, the study follows the broadly defined perspective of interpretive research.

The interpretive research approach focuses on the ways community members manage their activities. This methodological approach, explains Geertz (1973), is an effort

. . . to describe and analyze "the meaningful structure of experience . . . as it is apprehended by representative members of a particular society at a particular point in time—in a word, a scientific phenomenology of culture. (p. 364)

The research, therefore, will construct the context of the students' work and their experiences over time with the computer program.

Interpretive research focuses on learning about the symbol systems in the informants' terms rather than arranging "abstracted [theoretical] entities into unified patterns" (Geertz 1973:17). It assumes that while there might be ideal, and perhaps desired modes of actions in culture, actual experience rarely lives up to them. People construct their living experience in ways that are meaningful to them and then hold on to them (Geertz 1973, 1983; Clifford 1988). Therefore, the focus is on the actors' *skills* to shape their experiences. Skill is the capacity and proneness to apply knowledge in the specific situation. Actors use *reflective thought* to construct meanings, to make sense of their activities, and to direct them toward new discoveries of ways of acting (Geertz 1973:59–78; Bartlett 1954:197–238; Ryle 1949). The cyclical dynamics of applying knowledge to situations, based on what is learned and known to the person, is what one attempts to account for and to interpret.

Studies in this mode were carried out in various settings; for example, research on design activities (Bamberger and Schön 1983; Schön 1990b), computer strategies (Turkle and Papert 1990), teacher development (Bamberger, Duckworth, and Lampert 1981; Bamberger et al. 1982), mathematical skills (Lave 1986), cultural patterns (Geertz, 1973, 1983), and cognitive skills (Martin and Scribner 1988; Martin 1990).

Design as learning

The perspective used to make sense of the students' activities views educational learning as a process of design. In the "design professions" the process of design has been to plan new things, such as buildings or products. Traditionally, in engineering education, design has been an exercise for teaching students to carry out structural analysis. Viewing the bridge building as a design activity, in which students interact with the materials and available technology, alters traditional design exercises and their purpose. When a broader definition is applied to design activities ". . . all of us do [design]," writes Schön, "insofar as we make things out of the materials of a situation under conditions of complexity and uncertainty" (1990b:18). Thus, educational and design environments have much in common. In both, learning occurs under complex and uncertain conditions, and knowledge is generated, enacted, and reflected upon (Schön 1990b).

The study of the design activity as a computer-based educational environment focuses on the students' ongoing process of sense making—generating meanings of their work. The learning situation is perceived as a dynamic environment where "conversations" occur between the materials and the participants' knowledge, intentions, and attached meanings (Bamberger and Schön 1977, 1983). Using the metaphor of "computer as sandcastle," Bamberger (1983) describes the process of conversational learning with computers:

By "conversation" I mean the conversations we have with materials as we build or fix or invent. As we perturb these materials, arranging and rearranging them, watching them take shape even as we shape them, we learn. The stuff talks back to us remaking our ideas of what is possible. The back-talk leads to new actions on our material objects in a spiral of inner and outer activity: inner intention gives way to reflection on and responsiveness to the back-talk of the materials, leading to new outer actions on objects and thence once more to changed intention. It's a kind of "research"—one that is as familiar to the scientist designing a theory as to the painter or composer designing an artifact. (p. 2)

It is similar to the process of making art, in which meanings and values "are anchored [and] are realized by way of *expressions*" which get shaped and at the same time molded by the materials at hand (Dewey 1934:273–74).

Perceiving the learning environment as both a place to design learning and where learning is a design activity makes room for questions regarding the nature of the interaction and the learning involved (Bamberger, Duckworth, and Lampert 1981; Schön 1983, 1987, 1990a, 1990b; Winograd and Flores 1986). In this context, the focus is how personal knowing evolves because of interaction with technology (Bamberger and Schön 1978, 1983; Suchman 1987; Schön 1990b).

Building Bridges and the Role of *Growltiger*

Students' interviews and design notebooks and observations of their work provide the data for the study. All the students were invited to be interviewed. However, 10 of the 17 students completed the set of three one-hour interviews—before, during, and after the contest. All the interviews were audiotaped and fully transcribed.

The first interviews were conducted before the student started to work. The questioning probed the students' work plan, their initial design for the bridge, the anticipated problems and ways to resolve them. During the second week of the competition the students were interviewed again. In the semi-structured interview students were asked about their progress based on observations of their work, their design notebooks, and their personal accounts. Students shared their design dilemmas. They reflected on their progress, their use of the expert system, and their future plans. Immediately following the contest, after the bridges were tested for their ability to sustain load, students were interviewed for the third time. The focus then shifted to students' reflection on experiences, what they learned from the exercise, mistakes they made, and strategies they wished to use in the future.

In the first stage of the analysis, based on interviews and design notebooks, vignettes were created that captured the students' experiences. The vignettes described the students' process of work, their use of media, and learning experiences, as they progressed in building the bridges. Four of the 10 cases were then selected to represent the range of students' interactions with the expert system (table 20.1).

The selection of the cases took into consideration: the students' experience with computers, and specifically with GT; their experience in

Table 20.1
Students' background

Name	Department	Year	Design Experience	Computer programming	Design Contest	Place
Warren	Elec. Engin.	5	much	experienced	4th entry	1st
Ray	Mech. Engin.	4	moderate	experienced	1st entry	4th
Sten	Aero. Engin.	2	much	experienced	1st entry	last
Mark	Physics	1	none	experienced	1st entry	3rd to last

structural engineering; building experience; their actual use of the GT and other media in the process; their success in the bridge design contest. It also took into consideration the cases where the process of design was more elaborated.

A detailed description of the students' use of the computer emerged from this process of analysis.

Growltiger in-action

Within the design learning environment, the students used GT for a variety of tasks. These roles emerged in the context of the problems they faced over the course of their work, and which they believed the computer could resolve. Among the factors influencing the changes were the problem at hand, their trust of GT, its perceived usefulness in solving prior problems, their competency of use, the availability of other tools, and time constraints. Hence, their intentions and use, and their learning from using the computer varied.

Figures 20.1 and 20.2 map the progress of the four students' work. The arrow points to the tool (listed in the four columns) which most influenced their decisions at each moment. The focus of the decision is written on the left side of the chart.

Analysis of the cases shows that Mark and Sten used a similar approach to design, yet they integrated GT into their work in different ways. Ray and Warren shared a perspective of design, which was very different from Mark's and Sten's, and they made different applications of GT. The following analysis therefore uses the similarities as background to highlight the differences in the use of the computer.

Mark	GT Lab Kit Readings	Sten	GT Lab Kit Readings

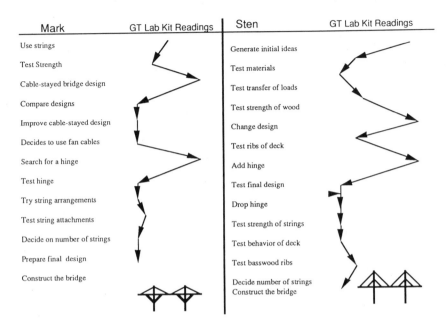

Mark:
Use strings
Test Strength
Cable-stayed bridge design
Compare designs
Improve cable-stayed design
Decides to use fan cables
Search for a hinge
Test hinge
Try string arrangements
Test string attachments
Decide on number of strings
Prepare final design
Construct the bridge

Sten:
Generate initial ideas
Test materials
Test transfer of loads
Test strength of wood
Change design
Test ribs of deck
Add hinge
Test final design
Drop hinge
Test strength of strings
Test behavior of deck
Test basswood ribs
Decide number of strings
Construct the bridge

Figure 20.1
A map of Mark and Sten's work progress and use of tools

Mark and Sten—GT: A blueprint provider   Much is identical about Mark's and Sten's process of building their bridges. They built cable-stayed bridges which were similar in design and relied on same materials —strings—as main load-carriers; they had similar approaches to design. Both saw the process of bridge design in the shape of an inverted funnel: one begins with an assortment of bridge designs with limited constraints and a low degree of specificity. Then, their ideas become subject of a test against known engineering concepts. The test was to be performed by a trusted mechanism, in both cases GT executed most of the testing. As a result, a ready-to-build bridge would be conceptualized.

Mark counted on GT from the beginning to do the analysis of the bridge design, and anticipated being able to channel the process of design through *Growltiger*:

That's fairly straightforward—the computer program itself has an option in which you can input your structural components and you just type the numbers for that and see what the computer gets with it . . . However, it may change fairly rapidly depending on the outcome of what the computer says.

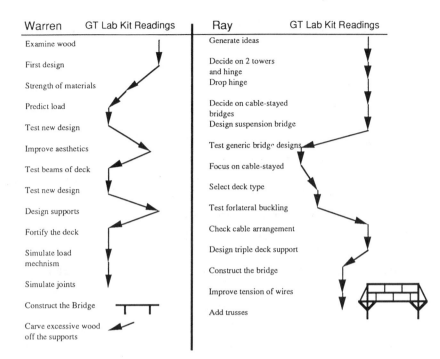

Figure 20.2
A map of Warren and Ray's work progress and use of tools

He started by feeding general bridge designs into GT. These designs were analyzed by the program, and Mark received a negative response on all the designs. At this stage, the computer was used to provide conceptual information about design the of bridges.

The rejection of the preliminary designs led Mark to change his strategy. He decided to feed GT with various designs of bridge elements:

I played around with cable-stayed bridges mostly, with radial versus harp, with tall and short towers, with different cable arrangements. This gave me several important points: decks are in tension between towers and in compression outside of them; cables take small amounts of load.

Mark said that a result of this experience with GT gave him "a feel of bridges so I could better predict their behavior." The things he learned, which gave him the feel for bridges, came about when he *changed* his strategy of work with GT. He saw that the computer could provide him with specific details about the behavior of elements of bridges, and their behavior in relation with other elements, for example, that decks were in tension between towers.

In this process, GT's role was altered from a system that provided overall information about "Bridges" to one which *conceptually* designed "a bridge"—his bridge. Reflecting on his work, Mark commented on this transition in his use of GT: "I worked in two phases. A basic design, which I worked on in GT, I narrowed down the basic design . . . I worked on GT just for the basic concept."

As a result of this experience, Mark implicitly made a third shift in his use of GT. The computer had become a mode to provide and produce *exact* construction plans for his bridge. For example, in one session Mark changed the height of the bridge and the shape of the deck until he received an exact design. In another session he decided on the number of strings. Moreover, the computer was trusted to provide the necessary information for his bridge design. Thus, for Mark, GT changed over time from an engineering tool to a *prescriptive blueprint provider.*

Sten started with a design process which at first drew on readings, the lab, and thinking on his own. He mistrusted GT and began to use it only once he had a design he thought was final and even named, *Stormbridge.* After testing the idea of a hinge on the computer, Sten felt that he could use GT to test other specific components of the bridge, such as the locations to attach the strings and the connection of the ribs to the towers:

Growltiger helps visualize and actually will help me build the model because I'll know where I can make certain attachments. And that was a big problem, I had to figure out where I'm going to put the struts in relation to the load points and concerns such as, "Will this be symmetrical? Am I putting too much tensile stress around this point and not enough between the points?"

At this point Sten used GT like the second stage in Mark's use of it, to gain a conceptual view of his bridge. But soon afterward, Sten relied on GT for specific construction plans: "Because it has a grid, it has a very detailed drawing for representation. It let me decide finally on what my exact measurements were going to be." Following his use of the computer to decide on the location and number of strings Sten empowered it to give him a "green light" to move on to the construction of the bridge: "[After testing the design] I thought I guess it works, it should work the way I want it to. *Growltiger* gave me a green light to go ahead with the construction."

Sten and Mark had different points of departure to their work with GT. Mark first used the tool to gain conceptual understanding; while Sten started to use it when he had already made up his mind about the bridge design and wanted to gather a detailed conceptual acquaintance with it. Both students searched and found in the computer an environment they believed could provide a reliable visualized feel for bridges and a strong sense of predictability. This is where their approaches converged. The next step for both was to use GT as a provider of a blueprint for construction.

Ray and Warren—GT: An image footholder Ray and Warren worked in very different ways. The starting point for Warren was the kit with a specific design in mind. Ray, however, began by deciding on preliminary conceptual constraints, as part of his belief in a "classical top-down approach." Common to both was a perception of the design of the bridge, as a process where their ideas, materials, and tools interacted. In this context, GT was one tool among others; its usefulness was tested by whether it can contribute a unique perspective on the problem at hand.

From the demonstration of GT, Ray discounted and mistrusted it as "just too unreliable." Since the program's graphic imagery and computing relies on a linear model, GT cannot accurately predict the failure load nor the failure mode—which element will break first—of a structure. Neither is the system useful for manufacturing of the bridge because its design model is too simplistic. Finally, GT does not deal with the design in its actual environmental context.

He first attempted to work in his top-down approach. Time constraints and his inability to yield enough concrete constraints on his bridge design caused him to re-think his design approach. Feeling stuck, Ray used GT to try to come up with basic design ideas that could guide his work. Of the six bridges he brought to test, two performed well, a girder bridge and a cable-stayed bridge. Their performance surprised him, and he learned that they transferred loads by different mechanisms; the cable-stayed bridge by using cables to transfer the load, and the girder bridge by its rigid beam. He then tried various structural alterations on each to see the effect.

Although brief, this one-time session with GT turned out to be very important to his work. It placed the first concrete design reigns over his work—from there he worked within the conceptual frame of these two bridge designs. Following the session with GT, Ray decided to change his overall approach to design. He realized that he needed to start from "bottom-up," building a model from the components to a general design. Ray also shifted to work mainly in the lab, where in line with his bottom-up approach, he tested various elements of the bridge. Having concrete visual frames of complete structures of bridges most likely made him feel comfortable enough to make the transition.

The session with GT also influenced the conception of trying to merge the two load carrying-devices, a strong deck and strings, in his bridge design. Possibly the most critical learning for Ray was the conceptualization of the bridge. After holding on to so many constraints and pieces of the structure—it all came together:

> I didn't come up with that idea. You see, this is a result that came up together from the constraints propagation, from the top and from the bottom, it suddenly popped right up there . . . I stuck with it right away because, I just felt good about it because, all the problems I was worried about before, like materials, strings that I had, vertical alignment, vertical force performance, whatever, was solved by this design.

This moment culminated in one coherent image of a bridge. Not by intention, *Growltiger* served as a preliminary trigger to this moment. At the session with GT, Ray for the first time narrowed down his broad constraints to concrete visual structures. Although he had no idea yet of what his final design might be, he gathered images of the possible to play against or to fall back on if necessary. The load mechanism in his final design integrated the two load-carrying devices of the girder and the cable-stayed bridges. His system transferred the load by two decks that support the main deck and are connected to each other by strings serving as vertical tensiles. For Ray, GT provided a *mental foothold* in the fragmentary jigsaw puzzle that he was putting together.

Warren too was aware of the limitations of the computer system. But he thought that GT would be useful for "trying to get a feel for the model." From GT he could gain a "ballpark figure" for how the model should look "assuming that it's [design] ideal." He further believed that if one approached GT with questions, then the system could be used to find an answer, to "justify" the claim:

> I had some idea of what I wanted to do, I think it's going to work pretty good. And then I went to GT and tried to justify it, whether it does [work] or not . . .

I think with a simulator, you really do need to have an idea and know what you want to do—the simulator isn't going to give you new ideas. It isn't going to say, "yeah, do it this way instead." You have to really go in and know what you want to do, from previous experiences with other designs. And then with the simulator, you can verify that it's going to work. I think that's the most a simulator can do.

Warren used GT a number of times. In his first use, Warren tested the need for strings in his design. *Growltiger* showed that strings were useless, and he dropped them. When testing the deck, Warren realized to his surprise that one of the beams did not carry weight. Later, Warren used GT to try to simulate the loading mechanism, and the joints of the bridge. In all those cases he treated the data as ideal.

This approach served him for two purposes: it gave Warren a testing ground for his ideas; and, it served him to set a goal to build toward. For example, in the case of the joints, he commented:

I think with the gluing stuff in GT, it assumes an ideal joint, so the better you can make those joints, the closer it is going to come out to the way GT predicts, [the more] it's gonna help . . . You don't really care about a numerical value because GT assumes infinite strength.

In this sense, Warren perceived GT as a tool that can help in the design process. What made the computer useful, however, was that Warren constructed design problems for GT to solve and was successful in shaping the test on GT. Reflecting on his work, he explained:

I think GT gave me some ideas of what to look into and then the ideal was more like, "yeah, I want to do it this way," and just go with it, then try it out. I don't think GT said, "OK, you should put this here, put that there." I think the idea came from me, I want to put these spaces here, there, and so forth . . .

Shaping the use of the computer in the *service of* receiving answers to a specific question and the acceptance of the findings as relative to the tool's capabilities made Warren successful in using it. He was able to gain an awareness of "the aesthetics of what's going on" in the structure. *Growltiger* gave him ideal images of potential structural solutions.

Ray and Warren made similar use of GT. But while Ray made an unintentional use of the program to provide structural images, Warren constantly used it explicitly as a method of design. The structural images he gathered were more specific, informative, and elaborate.

Mark and Sten and Ray and Warren made different applications of GT (see table 20.2).

Table 20.2
Students use of GT

Purpose of *Growltiger*	Articulated Approach	Non-articulated Approach
Blueprint Provider	Sten	Mark
Mental Footholder	Warren	Ray

The first pair used GT toward the specific, particular, and concrete construction of bridges. The others used GT to create images of ideal structures and structural elements. Ray and Mark, although at opposite sides of this polarity between the imaginable and the real, shared the less-articulated use of the program. Sten and Warren shared clarity of purposeful method.

Generative design learning environment

As the cases show, each of the students was engaged in and created a *different* learning environment. They each carved a "personal design world" for the purpose of dealing with the same task (Schön 1990b; 1990c). These worlds were crafted, building on their conceptions of the task, their personal work repertoires, knowledge, and opportunities. In the process of their work, students' needs and perceptions and understanding of the tools evolved, along with their personal knowledge. The learning environment was consequently in constant change and served different purposes at different times. Within the environment, the relationships between the tools, the bridge, and the student shifted.

Each students' intention was to build a bridge that could withstand enough load to win the contest. To reach that end, available for the students' were four tools, the engineering lab, the kit, GT, and readings. Their use of the tools varied in its intensity, purpose, and timing. Schematically, their working environment consisted of the four components shown in figure 20.3.

Over time the bridge became an additional tool from and toward which the orientation to the other tools transformed. The bridge became an anchoring tool. It anchored their perceived needs for information on how to proceed with building their bridge. As the bridge was conceptualized and physically shaped, the students' used the tools to resolve design problems.

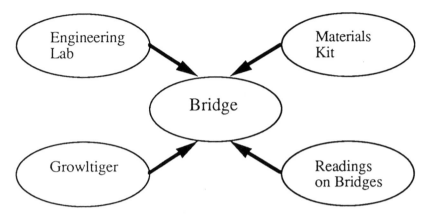

Figure 20.3
Design learning environment

The computer, in the context of a design learning environment, can be said to have *mediated* the students' knowledge of engineering. Broadly, the cycle of their computer use is shown in figure 20.4.

Students come to the design setting with some knowledge of engineering, experience, and personal strategies for work. They raise questions about their next steps in design, and use the tools to seek answers to their inquiries, which produce learning and new knowledge. And the cycle continues. This mediated activity is the main content of the design learning environment.

Placed back in the context of engineering education, how can the students' active role in coming up with work environments and use of the computer best inform the use of computers for engineering education?

Educating Students as Engineers and the Role of the Computer

The students were engaged in creating a bridge design they could trust to help them build a bridge. To achieve that goal their main activity was the *practice of knowing and verifying* their engineering knowledge about bridges. They *engineered* the building of a bridge model.

They found that the design environment constantly challenged their knowledge. They also realized that such an environment is full of uncertainties, a need for decisions to be made about tools, for a constant search for questions, and for answers to their questions. In this fluctuating

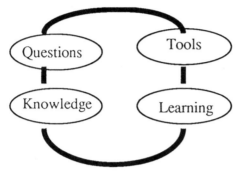

Figure 20.4
Cycle of mediated knowledge

design world, they came up with strategies to discover knowledge about the behavior of bridges. These strategies reflect the students' active search for ways to close the gaps between engineering theory and the making of bridges. These ways demonstrate their *practice* of making things and knowing about things. Their work environment resembled work situations engineers face in the real world. As such the students experienced engineering education that resembled *practical knowledge* (Schön 1983, 1987, 1990a, 1990b).

To engineer: Making things in theory or practice

The bridge design learning experiences are uncommon in engineering education. Educating students to become engineers is commonly separated from the practice of engineering. Students learn while an engineer works; students use theories while engineers practice engineering. The rationale behind the dichotomy is that students need to master a body of knowledge before they can practice engineering. That body of knowledge is better transmitted to them in an academic setting, away from real-life work situations. Supporters of this view claim that extracting essential engineering concepts from messy situations helps students recognize the important components of engineering. It prepares them *for* practice. Educational activities of engineering, therefore, often consist of structured activities built to highlight particular theoretical engineering concepts.

The dichotomy between theory and practice is well embedded in the social institutions, in the training of practitioners, and in research (Schön

1983, 1987; Scribner and Cole 1983; Lave 1986, 1988; Rogoff 1984). Nor is the gap between theory and practice new. Practitioners and educators recognized and felt it before. The Wright brothers, for example, described their failure to apply theory to their flight experiments:

Having set out with absolute faith in the existing scientific data we were driven to doubt one thing after another, till finally, after two years of experiments, we cast it all aside, and decided to rely entirely on our own investigations. (Baynes and Pugh 1981:183)

As engineering evolved from a pragmatic craft of building things to an academic discipline this gap between theory and practice emerged there as well. In the process, methods of building things became conventions which in turn evolved to theories of structural behavior. Structural behavior closely linked with Newtonian physics and advanced mathematics became an integral part of structural analysis. Teaching methods changed over time to correspond with this shift. Exercises in structural behavior evolved to consist of mathematical calculations of structural behavior.

Along with this transition, the mode of description became abstract and detached from the actual experience of building structures (Billington 1983). To handle the growing sophistication in analysis of structures, tools were introduced as aids for students. Computers and programs, such as STRUDL, are last in the line that can be traced back to the introduction of slide rules and calculators. Such tools assisted to express the theory and "translate" it to practice and vice versa (Petrosky 1982). In the process, the gap between the *education* of engineers and the *practice* of engineering grew.

The problem of educating for practice has become noticeable especially to those who tried to teach practical engineering applications to students. In 1902, Hawkins, an author of the manual *Mechanical Drawing*, gave a word of advice to engineering students:

A single word of advice before introducing the elementary work connected with mechanical drawing: if the student should experience difficulty in mastering the diagrams and curves abounding in this book, let him consult an experienced draughtsman or teacher, who, by a few strokes of a lead pencil, can easily make them plain; that knowledge—which cannot be printed or self-taught—termed *the Craftsman's Art*, is communicated largely by personal telling and showing, from man to man; in drawing, this help should be thankfully availed of, when necessity arises . . . (Baynes and Pugh 1981:179–180)

The problem of bridging theory and practice was also felt by the students in the bridge design contest. Before the contest, Sten sincerely believed that armed with theoretical knowledge of structural engineering he would be able to build a strong bridge: ". . . [W]hen I had seen [the bridge design contest] my first impression was, I had these [theories] for my structure [class], I can do anything and everything." Mark's comment after the contest resonates the dichotomy often found between learning the conceptual frame of engineering and the actual *making* of objects:

I only wish I could build another [bridge] from what I learned . . . I learned a great deal in this contest about bridges and perhaps a little engineering. Bridges will never be the same again.

His comment also suggests that he learned more about the practice of making bridges than about theoretical conventions used to represent the structural world.

The practice of engineering

The examples from the Wright brothers and Hawkins, as well as the students' experiences, suggest that the art of making things is different from conceptual explanations. Similarly, a growing body of research shows that practitioners often describe and practice their expertise differently, as for example, service representatives (Orr 1987), psychotherapists, architects and students (Schön 1983; 1991), doctors (Smith 1990), and engineers (Bucciarelli 1984). Their practice is often intuitive and tacit to an extent that it is hard for them to communicate it to others.

Such expertise is described by Sturt (1923), a wheelwagon craftsman, who knew what works with hind-wheels, but could not spell out the reasons:

The nature of this knowledge should be noted. It was set out in no book. It was not scientific. I never met a man who professed any other than empirical acquaintance with the wagon-builder's lore. My own case was typical. I knew that the hind-wheels had to be five feet two inches high and the fore-wheels four feet two; that the "sides" must be cut from the best four-inch heart of oak, and so on. This sort of thing I knew, and in vast detail in course of time; but I seldom knew why. And that is how most other men knew. The lore was a tangled network of country prejudices, whose reasons were known in some respects here, in others there, and so on. In farm-yard, in taproom, at market, the details were discussed over and over again; they were gathered together for remembrance in village workshop; carters, smiths, farmers, wheel-makers, in thousands handed on each his own little bit of understanding, passing it to his son or to the wheelwright of the day, linking up the centuries. But for the most part the details were but dimly understood; the whole body of knowledge was a mystery, a piece of folk knowledge, residing in the folk collectivity, but never wholly in any individual. (pp. 18–19)

This expertise is rarely captured by the schematic descriptions or get entered into professional textbooks (Schön 1983, 1987; Scribner 1984).

Preparing students to become engineers implies that they need opportunities to learn this kind of expertise, and they need to get exposed to ways to integrate theory and practice. But there is a problem: being tacit and often out of the realm of verbal communication, how could such practical knowledge become available to students?

In engineering, the answer to this problem touches upon the kinds of design activities students should be given to learn engineering. The discussion at MIT about the role of the computer in design activities reflects this dialogue. On the one hand there were teachers who wanted to use the computer to simplify the mathematics and ease the burden of calculations. They wanted to leave the focus of the design exercises on confirmation of theoretical concepts of structural behavior. Another group of teachers wanted to see the computer utilized to transform design activities for students to experience real-life engineering situations.

This debate reflects the ongoing educational dialogue about the appropriate methods to teach engineering and design. The writings of Christopher Jones, for example, an industrial designer and a teacher of design for over thirty years, display the shifting views about about design activities.

In 1970, in the first edition of *Design Methods: Seeds of Human Futures*, Jones compiled an array of approaches to design methods which can lead a designer to the "right" product. His attempt was to seize the essence of design as embedded in generic approaches that can be applied to any design situation. This suited the trend of the time when the design process was "captured" by models, flow charts, and procedures. Students and laymen, it was believed, learn and work by these approaches (Bucciarelli 1984, 1988; Hubel and Lessow 1984).

A decade later, in the second edition of *Design Methods* (1980), Jones criticized his earlier approach to design. In the new introduction he points out that designers need to be aware of their *process* of design. Every design project is unique and has its special specifications. Designers, he wrote, ought to expand their repertoire of relating their design to a specific context. This is where they fall short of answers in relation to craftsmen to whom, by the nature of their work, each case is unique. Still, Jones agreed with other designers such as Asimow (1962), in focusing on prescribed design processes as important to overcome the uncertainties of decision making embedded in product design.

In *Essays on Design* (1984), written four years later, Jones shifted his focus from design procedures to the practice of making things. Reflecting on his earlier approach he wrote:

> To me theories are safe but temporary stepping stones across the dangerous waters of life, the unknown. But it is the unknown, not theories or principles, that are the source of the new. The whole point of transformation, the central part of the design process, is to change what already exists, and this includes both theories and practices. Each should influence the other. To make theory the master of practice is surely a form of repression! (p. 7)

The approach to design should be "design the designing": making designers aware of their intuitive process of design and the constraints created by their rationale and the tools used for design. He conveyed his message by experimenting with designing new formats for writing about design. Jones wrote:

> when one gets into work on new problems: nobody knows how to do it. So you cannot use an existing process when you're in that kind of a problem with novelty and a need for innovation. Then you need to 'design the designing' let's say as well as design the output of the designing. And this designing the designing is really the whole thing. 'Designing designing' that gives the feeling of it its a rather poetic phrase rather than mechanical it sort of lifts you up a bit? (1984:43)

Caplan (1982) iterates this point by suggesting a process of "situation design" where design ought to be situation-specific and conceptually understood by all (see also Papanek 1985).

Students design the designing

As shown before, the design environment was fluctuating and ever-changing. The students' practice of building a bridge created an opportunity which embodies and transcends the distinction between theory and practice. As part of the bridge design contest their work integrated theoretical concepts and personal experience. They had to think about the pragmatics of a bridge structure that sustains load. At the same time they became aware of, learned about, and applied theoretical engineering concepts.

The computer played a unique role in this situation. It helped them test theoretical concepts and structural considerations, and connect and translate engineering concepts to concrete structural considerations. For example, many students told of the computer's power of visualization, how it gave them a "feel" for bridges and for some of the structural engineering concepts. Sten commented during his work, "*Growltiger* helps visualize and actually will help me build the model because I'll know where I can make certain attachments. And that was a big problem . . ." Ray, against his skepticism, felt that the visualization could be useful:

Looking at the bending and how it behaves, I think you get some ideas of how stable, about the overall performance.

Warren was able to see the dynamics of the beams of the deck:

If you really sit back and think about it, if you say "of course this bar is not going to load very much because the deck is going to bend more here and less there, so this bar will carry more weight and that bar less." But of course I didn't see it right off, but looking at GT I said "Wow, sure, of course."

The computer graphics helped them grasp the problem they faced.

During their interaction with GT, learning for the students often occurred when their models and productions on the computer were counter to their expectations. These moments often led to changes in strategies or new ideas for design. For example, Ray, who used the computer the least shifted from his "top-bottom" approach to a "bottom-up" approach in which he tested various structural elements without a definitive bridge model in mind. In that session, he also learned about the strength of the girder bridge. Its strength surprised him, and the concept of decks to spread the load was incorporated into his final design. *Growltiger*'s rejections of the first designs that Mark submitted brought him to try new designs. In the process he felt that he learned about bridges.

The students' experience of coming up with ways of making things aligns with situations engineers face: they too often encounter uncertainty and dilemmas about their design. And they too seek ways to verify their often incomplete knowledge. For example, Maillart, an engineer who pioneered the use of concrete for bridges, searched for ways to learn about the success of his bridges. Because of the new materials, Maillart found that he had to devise new techniques to graphically represent the bridge and possible failure modes. At the same time, he would go to the bridge to look for any signs of structural stress, such as cracks in the concrete (Billington 1979, 1983).

Engineering tools as a way of knowing about things
Tools are a way to express knowledge of a profession. Computers can offer a potential bridge between the practice of education and communities of practice. In engineering design, computers can link theoretical concepts with practical considerations, by creating learning opportunities for experimentation. They can translate professional language to expressions understood by practitioners.

The language of expert communication helps practitioners of the same trade understand one another. By the same token it makes it difficult for others to make sense of their knowledge. In a guide to his students, Otto Wagner, a known architect, criticized at the turn of the century the tendency of architects to display drawing in non-communicative ways for clients:

The main reason that the importance of the architect has not been fully appreciated lies in the store of forms employed by him up to now; that is, in the language he has directed to the public, which in most cases is completely unintelligible. (1902: 65)

In this sense, tools of the trade conceal at the same time that they present knowledge (Pugh and Bayne 1981; Latour 1986). Clients could probably recall the difficulty of deciphering the engineering or architectural drawings in order to "see" their house (Kidder 1985).

In structural engineering, draft drawing evolved into a language by which engineers communicate—display—their knowledge. Engineering drawing using the conventions of descriptive geometry on which theoretical aspects of modern engineering drawing are based, was first standardized by Gaspard Monge, a French military engineer in 1795 when he published *Geometrie descriptive* (Booker 1963). Since then, descriptive geometry has become the core language of engineering which students ought to master (cf. Adler 1912). Other tools of the trade vary in their abstraction, from surveying tools to charts with symbols. Still all are ways to organize expertise.

Computers for engineering design
While there are conventions, practitioners' use of their respective technology, from photocopying machines (Suchman 1987) to computers (e.g., Winograd and Flores 1986; Turkle and Papert 1990) is shaped by their work, *in-action*. The strategies and ways in which they use the technology

is often *not* captured by the technical manuals or work descriptions. It also does not necessarily match the vision of the designers of the toolmakers, especially in the case of computers (cf. Suchman 1987).

Knowledge and understanding of how tools get used in practice most often does not inform the design of (and is usually *left out* of) the knowledge base of expert systems (Brown 1991; Clancey 1991b; Wenger 1990). This has led computer scientists and educators to express concerns about the quality of the computer as a learning environment for education (cf. Scheffler 1990) and the workplace (Sachs 1990). Much of the discomfort with current applications is their limited capacity to integrate with communities of practice, and to link with the knowledge of practice (Winograd and Flores 1986; Dreyfus and Dreyfus 1986; Wenger 1990; Clancey 1989; Brown and Duguid 1990a, 1990b).

Expert systems are built based on the espoused expertise of professionals. They, therefore, miss much of the actual activities that practitioners do. This limitation could mean that those who use the computer will learn the theory of practice but will not experience it in actuality. For that reason, Dreyfus and Dreyfus (1986), for example, expressed concerns about expanding the use of expert systems. They warn medical students to limit their use of *Guidon*, an expert system designed to help teach doctors to diagnose and learn about meningitis and bacteremia (Clancey 1986):

One can only hope that someone has the sense to disconnect the doctor from the system as soon as he or she has reached the advanced beginner stage. Otherwise, such CAI [Computer-Aided Instruction] techniques could become a disastrous educational practice . . .

What knowledge an expert system should include is an ongoing debate among computer scientists. Opinions range from those who believe that all knowledge can and should be represented on the computer (e.g., Simon 1969; Moravec 1988). For example, Moravec (1988) writes about the coming of a "postbiological world" dominated by "self-improving, thinking machines" that will be "as complex as ourselves" (pp. 1–5). Being as complex as human beings, by default, these machines will include the tacit expertise. Others focus on the communication process with the machine (Wenger 1987; Winograd and Flores 1986). A recurring theme among this group is how to make computers that fit with their users' needs like a hammer's "readiness-at-hand" (e.g., Brown and Duguid 1990a; Winograd and Flores 1986).

Educators, however, writes Scheffler (1990), should not be blinded by the intentionality of making computers as convenient, predictable, and purposeful as a hammer to drive nails. Having an established implicit instrumentality of a hammer (or a computer), he explains, does not rule out that it will be used in other ways. Neither does it imply that the tool is useful for its intended purpose. The key question is whether the actual use of the computer serves an *educational purpose.*

Inscribing knowledge in design environments: An educational role for the computer

The computer was one medium by which the students conveyed, verified and predicted the behavior of their bridges. *Through* the use of GT, engineering concepts were represented to the students. Also, through GT the students expressed representations of their ideas for designing bridges. Students shaped their work environment and their strategies to design bridges to align with the computer system.

The students used GT similar to scientists' reliance on tools they believe appropriate to model and measure a phenomenon. In this sense, GT was enlisted by the students as an *inscription device* to inscribe knowledge. The term is borrowed from studies on the sociology of science that frame the scientific process as a practice of the construction of knowledge (Latour and Woolgar 1979; Latour 1986; Knorr, Krohn, and Whitley 1981; Knorr-Cetina 1981). An inscription device, wrote Latour and Woolgar (1979):

> . . . is any item or apparatus or particular configuration of such items which can transform a material substance into a figure or diagram which is directly usable by one of the members of the office space . . . An important consequence of this notion of inscription device is that inscriptions are regarded as having direct relationship to "the original substance." The final diagram or curve thus provides the focus of discussion about properties or the substance. (p. 51)

Inscription devices are made by an agreed-upon technique. They are also an agreed-upon mode to describe reality, by a community with shared practice (like scientists or engineers).

Computer representations are an inscription device of engineering. Two processes of inscriptions interact in the computer. As explained, GT is an "expert system" that captured the knowledge of professional structural engineers. *Growltiger*, then, is not a blackboard. Its representations utilize a method of structural analysis which interprets the incoming data.

The mode of feeding data to the computer is another kind of inscription. The student enters the appropriate data. The data are integrated into the programmed conceptual representation of engineering. To provide an image of a steel bridge, for example, GT is fed with numbers derived from a sample of pieces of steel. These are placed under the loading device which gives a reading of the load capacity at a specific point load. Over a number of experiments, by use of a statistical formula (Young Modulus) one derives a number that *represents* the loading strength of "all similar pieces of steel." This number is used by the computer to simulate the behavior of a class of "steel beams."

Computers for reflective practice

The students' activities show some of the risks and the potential of the role of the computer as an inscription device. Mark and Sten interacted with GT in a way that trusted the data to represent reality. They did not see their interaction with GT as a negotiation between two knowledge systems. The screen display did not reflect or express their models, nor did it prescribe a "right" approach to structural behavior of bridges. On the screen appeared inscriptions of their designs which they *trusted* to be the one and the right answer to the engineering problem they faced.

Taking the computer's response for granted is echoed by Latour and Woolgar (1979) as one of the features of inscription devices. Once they are formed:

. . . [I]nscriptions are seen as direct indicators of the substance under study . . . A second consequence, however, is the tendency to think of the inscriptions in terms of confirmation, or evidence for or against, particular ideas, concepts, or theories. There thus occurs a transformation of the simple end product of inscription into the terms of the mythology which informs participants' activities. (p. 63)

These two consequences are important especially for the use of computers. Users are not usually aware of or do not know the steps involved in programming the computer. They are also unaware of how their input is interpreted to graphic or textualized representations. Therefore, the computer's inscription tends to be taken for granted, as in the cases of Mark and Sten. These inscriptions often are used as a rigid barometer to test ideas.

Mark's and Sten's use of GT shows how a computer that guides students toward a *one right answer* espoused from a model that is unshared with the students can inhibit learning. Therefore, in a learning environment where the computer provides all the responses, students' learning of design could confine learning rather than expand it. But this does not have to be the case.

Warren and Ray used the system to provide them with images of potential application of structural designs to their specific tasks. They treated the data that GT presented to them as working ideas. To them, the inscriptions presented on the screen were one possible scenario. It is as if they asked GT, for example, "*What if* I want to build a deck with these specifications, tell us how you envision it." The distinction Warren and Ray made was not between reality and the realism of the computer simulation. *They were making a distinction between a theoretical model of structural engineering displayed in the graphic images of the computer and their personal practice of engineering as experienced in building the bridge.* The computer is useful to test personal representations and accepted models of structural behavior.

The potential of the computer can also be realized to create learning situations based on the *mismatch of knowledge*. All the students experienced moments of learning when the computer's inscriptions were *not* taken for granted, or when their images were in *conflict* with the simulation of the computer. These often surprising moments led students to reflect on their knowledge and practice, to question the computer's capability to represent knowledge, and to seek alternative ways to find solutions. Mark, for example, learned about bridges when his designs were rejected by the program. Ray shifted his approach to design and later integrated structural elements that he saw on the computer to his model. Sten tested the basswood ribs in the lab because the numbers provided by GT were "too close." Warren was surprised to see a beam that did not carry a load.

Students also learned as a result of their shifts between tools of inscription, namely, the lab and the computer. This shows the potential of placing computers in a multimedia environment for learning. Having tools available to cross-reference, to test structural problems off and on the computer, helped all the students. In the process they gained new insights. The learning was not restricted to engineering. They also learned about the effectiveness and the limitations of the tools to inscribe relevant engineering issues. For example, when Ray moved to the engineering lab, he realized its effectiveness to provide him with a "feel" for the materials. At the same time, he became aware that GT showed him a complex structural analysis of two models that he could not have experienced in the lab. Warren tried to harness GT to provide more real data on the impact of the loading mechanism on his bridge. Similarly, when Mark was unsatisfied with GT's ability to simulate the attachment of the strings to the ribs, he improvised a new way to test it at the lab.

These issues show the potential of computers to serve as inscription devices in a design learning environment with multimedia tools. The use of computers as inscription devices also shifts the focus of research on computers to the role constructed *for* the computer by various users in the course of their work. The role of the computer is then measured by its unique contributions and by its capabilities to complement work with other tools of the profession (cf. Schön 1991).

If reflective practice and learning are the focus of education, the computer can provide opportunities to enrich practical knowledge. The potential contributions of the computer are in its capabilities to provide new ways to verify and inquire about practical knowledge, and to inscribe images of workable solutions practitioners seek.

Appendix

Screen display of *Growltiger*
The three screen displays show a process of improved design by one of the participating students. Figure 20.5 shows the bridge design. In figure 20.6, the student hand-drew suggestions to improve the design following a test for deflection that showed main stress to appear around the middle support. The final design with the improvements drawn in is shown in figure 20.7.

Acknowledgments

Many thanks to Professors Donald Schon, Carol Weiss, and Sheldon White, and Dr. William Clancey for their comments on other versions of this paper, and to M. G. Wood for her rigorous editing.

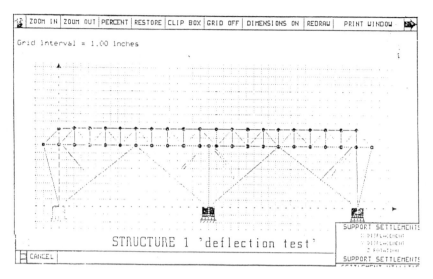

Figure 20.5
Bridge design under deflection test. Note middle support is lower than the outer supports.

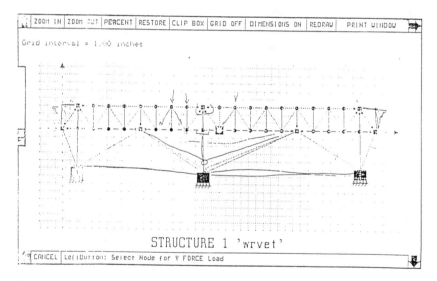

Figure 20.6
Handwritten improvements following the deflection test. The student's arrows point to places which are under the ribs of the deck.

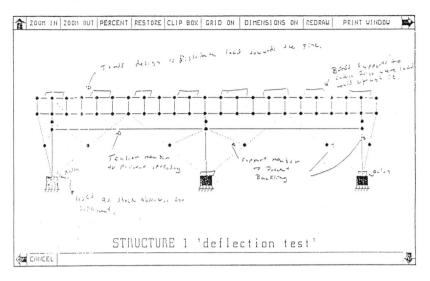

Figure 20.7
Final design

The educational changes in the Department of Civil Engineering at MIT described here are based on D. Schon and W. Overmeer, May 1988. "Project Athena at MIT: Computing in the Department of Civil Engineering." In S. Turkle et. al. (Eds.) *Project Athena at MIT*, MIT University, Internal Report.

References

Adler, A.A. 1912. *The Theory of Engineering Drawing.* New York: D. Van Nostrand Company.

Asimow, M. 1962. *Introduction to Design.* New York: Prentice-Hall.

Bamberger, J. 1983. *The Computer as Sandcastle.* Working Paper, Cambridge, MA: MIT.

Bamberger, J., Duckworth, E., and Lampert, M. 1981. *Final Report: An Experiment in Teacher Development.* Cambridge, MA: MIT, NIE Grant #G-78-0219.

Bamberger, J., Duckworth, E., Gray, J., and Lampert, M. 1982. *Analysis of Data From an Experiment in Teacher Development.* Cambridge, MA: MIT, NIE Grant #G-78-0219.

Bamberger, J., and Schön, D.A. February 1977. *The Figural Formal Transaction: A Parable of Generative Metaphor.* Working Paper, Cambridge, MA: MIT.

Bamberger, J., and Schön, D.A. March 1983. "Learning as Reflective Conversation with Materials: Notes from Work in Progress." *Art Education.* Vol. 36, 2: 68–73.

Bartlett, F. C. 1954. *Remembering: A Study in Experimental and Social Psychology*. London, UK: Cambridge University Press.

Baynes, Ken, and Pugh, Francis. 1981. *The Art of the Engineer*. London, UK: Lund Humphries Publishers.

Billington, D. P. 1979. *Robert Maillart's Bridges: The Art of Engineering*. Princeton: Princeton University Press.

Billington, D. P. 1983. *The Tower and the Bridge: The New Art of Structural Engineering*. New York: Basic Books.

Booker, Peter. 1963. *A History of Engineering Drawing*. London, UK: Chatto and Windus.

Bourdieu, Pierre. 1990. *The Logic of Practice*. Stanford, CA: Stanford University Press.

Bronfenbrenner, U. 1979. *The Ecology of Human Development: Experiments by Nature and Design*. Cambridge, MA: Harvard University Press.

Brown, J. S. January–February 1991. "Research that Reinvents the Corporation." *Harvard Business Review*, pp. 102–111.

Brown, J. S., and Duguid, P. March, 1990a. "Enacting Design for the Workplace." Presented at the conference *Technology and the Future of Work*. Palo Alto, CA: Stanford University.

Brown, J. S., and Duguid, P. 1990b. "Toward a Unified View of Working Learning and Innovating." To be published in *Organization Science*.

Bucciarelli, L. L. 1984. "Reflective Practice in Engineering Design." *Design Studies* 5,3:185-190.

Bucciarelli, L. L. 1987. "Engineering Design Thinking." Reno, NV: ASEE Annual Conference Proceedings.

Bucciarelli, L. L. 1988. "An Ethnographic Perspective on Engineering Design." *Design Studies* 9, 3:159-168.

Caplan, R. 1982. *By Design: Why There are No Locks on the Bathroom Doors in the Hotel Louis XIV, and Other Object Lessons*. New York: McGraw-Hill.

Clancey, W. J. 1986. *From Guidon to Neomycin and Heracles in Twenty Short Lessons: ONR Final Report 1979 - 1985*. Palo Alto, CA: Stanford Knowledge Systems Laboratory, Report No. 86-11.

Clancey, W. J. 1989. "The Knowledge Level Reinterpreted: Modeling How Systems Interact." *Machine Learning* 4: 287-293.

Clancey, W. J. 1991a. "The Frame of Reference Problem in the Design of Intelligent Machines." In K. VanLehn and A. Newell (Eds.) , *Architectures for Intelligence: The Twenty-Second Carnegie Symposium on Cognition*. Hillside, NJ: Lawrence Erlbaum Associates.

Clancey, W. 1991b. "Interactive Control Structures: Evidence for a Compositional Neural Architecture." Presented at the *NATO Workshop on Emergence, Situatedness, Subsumption, and Symbol Grounding*. Brussels, Belgium.

Clancey, W., and Rochelle, J. 1991. "Situated Cognition: How Representations are Created and Given Meaning." Presented at the *AERA Symposium, Implications of Cognitive Theories of How the Nervous System Functions for Research and Practice in Education*, Chicago, IL.

Clifford, J. 1988. *The Predicament of Culture: Twentieth-Century Ethnography, Literature, and Art*. Cambridge, MA: Harvard University Press.

Cuban, L. 1986. *Teachers and Machines: The Classroom Use of Technology Since 1920*. New York: Teachers College Press.

Cuban, L. 1989. "Neoprogressive Visions and Organizational Realities." *Harvard Educational Review* 59, 2:217–222.

Dede, C. 1986. "A Review and Synthesis of Recent Research in ICAI." *International Journal Man-Machine Studies* 24:329–353.

Dewey, J. 1934. *Art as Experience*. New York: Minton, Balch and Company.

Dreyfus, H. L., and Dreyfus, S. E. 1986. *Mind over Machine: The Power of Human Intuition and Expertise in the Era of the Computer*. New York: The Free Press.

Erickson, F. 1986. "Qualitative Methods in Research on Teaching." In M.C. Wittrock Ed. *Handbook of Research on Teaching*. New York: Macmillan Publishing. 3d ed.

Gal, S. March, 1990. "Knowledge-based Systems, and More: Toward a Multimedia Environment for Learning Structural Engineering." Presented at the Spring Symposium of the *American Association for Artificial Intelligence*. Palo Alto, CA: Stanford University.

Gal, S. July 1991. *Building Bridges: Design, Learning, and the Role of Computers*. Cambridge, MA: Qualifying Paper submitted to Harvard Graduate School of Education.

Guba, E. G. 1985. "The Context of Emergent Paradigm Research." In Y. S. Lincoln (Ed.), *Organizational Theory and Inquiry: The Paradigm Revolution*. Beverly Hills, CA: Sage Publications.

Geertz, C. 1973. *The Interpretation of Cultures*. New York: Basic Books.

Geertz, C. 1983. *Local Knowledge: Further Essays in Interpretive Anthropology*. New York: Basic Books.

Glaser, B. G., and Strauss A. L. 1980. *The Discovery of Grounded Theory: Strategies for Qualitative Research*. New York: Aldine Publishing.

Jones, J. C. 1970. *Design Methods: Seeds of Human Futures*. New York: Chichester.

Jones, J. C. 1980. *Design Methods: Seeds of Human Futures*. New York: Chichester. 2d ed.

Jones, J. C. 1984. *Essays in Design*. London, UK: John Wiley and Sons.

Kidder, T. 1985. *House*. Boston, MA: Houghton Mifflin.

Knorr, K., Krohn, R., and Whitley, R. 1981. *The Social Process of Scientific Investigation*. Boston, MA: Kluwer.

Knorr-Cetina, K. D. 1981. *The Manufacture of Knowledge: An Essay on the Constructivist and Contextual Nature of Science*. Elmsford, NY: Pergamon Press.

Latour, B. 1986. "Visualization and Cognition: Thinking with Eyes and Hands." *Knowledge and Society: Studies in the Sociology of Culture Past and Present* 6:1–40.

Latour, B. 1987. *Science in Action*. Cambridge, MA: Harvard University Press.

Latour, B., and Woolgar, S. 1979. *Laboratory Life: The Social Construction of Scientific Facts*. Beverly Hills, CA: Sage Publications.

Lave, J. 1986. "The values of Quantification." In J. Law (Ed.) *Power, Action and Belief: A new Sociology of Knowledge?* Boston, MA: Routledge and Kegan Paul.

Lave, J. 1988. *Cognition in Practice: Mind, Mathematics, and Culture in Everyday Life*. Cambridge University Press.

Lepper, M. R. January, 1985. "Microcomputers in Education: Motivational and Social Issues." *American Psychologist* 40, 1:1-18.

Martin, L. M. W. April 1990. "Learning to Use Computerized Machinery on the Job." Paper presented at the annual meeting of the *American Educational Research Association*. Boston, MA.

Martin, L. M. W., and Scribner, S. 1988. *An Introduction to CNC Systems: Background for Learning and Training Research*. Laboratory for Cognitive Studies of Work. New York: City University of New York.

Moravec, H. 1988. *Mind Children: The Future of Robot and Human Intelligence*. Cambridge, MA: Harvard University Press.

Orr, J. 1987. *Talking about Machines: Social Aspects of Expertise*. Report for the Intelligent Systems Laboratory. Palo Alto, CA: Xerox Palo Alto Research Center.

Papanek, V. J. 1985. *Design for the Real World: Human Ecology and Social Change*. Chicago, IL: Academy Chicago.

Petrosky, H. 1982. *To Engineer Is Human: The Role of Failure in Successful Design*. New York: St. Martin's Press.

Rogoff, B., and Lave, J. (Eds.) 1984. *Everyday Cognition: Its Development in Social Context*. Cambridge, MA: Harvard University Press.

Ryle, G. 1949. *The Concept of Mind*. New York: Barnes and Noble.

Scheffler, I. 1990. "Computers at School?" In V.A. Howard (Ed.) *Varieties of Thinking*. New York: Routledge.

Schön, D. A. 1982. "The Fear of Innovation." In Barnes, B., and D. Edge (Eds.) *Science in Context: Readings in the Sociology of Science*. Cambridge, MA: MIT Press.

Schön, D. A. 1983. *The Reflective Practitioner*. New York: Basic Books.

Schön, D. A. 1987. *Educating the Reflective Practitioner*. San Francisco, CA: Jossey-Bass.

Schön, D. A., and W. Overmeer 1988. "Project Athena at MIT: Computing in the Department of Civil Engineering," In S. Turkle *et al.* (Eds.) *Project Athena at MIT*. Cambridge, MA: MIT, Internal Report.

Schön, D. A. 1990a. "The Design Process." In V.A. Howard (Ed.) *Varieties of Thinking*. New York: Routledge.

Schön, D. 1990b. "The Theory of Inquiry: Dewey's legacy to education." Presented at the annual meeting of the *American Educational Research Association*. Boston, MA.

Schön, D. April, 1990c. "The Theory of Inquiry: Dewey's legacy to education." The second lecture. Keynote talk, Ben Gurion University, Beer-Sheva, Israel.

Schön, D. June, 1991. "Designing as Reflective Conversation with the Materials of a Design Situation." Edinburgh, UK: Keynote talk for the *Edinburgh Conference on Artificial Intelligence in Design*.

Schön, D. A., and Rein, M. 1977. "Problem Setting in Policy Research." In C. H. Weiss Ed. *Using Social Research in Public Policy Making.* Lexington, MA: Lexington Books, D. C. Heath.

Schön, D. A., Drake, W. D., and Miller, R. I. 1984. "Social Experimentation as Reflection-in-Action: Community-Level Nutrition Intervention Revisited." *Knowledge: Creation, Diffusion, Utilization* 6,1: 5-36.

Scribner, S. 1984. "Studying Working Intelligence." In B. Rogoff and J. Lave (Eds.) *Everyday Cognition: Its Development in Social Context.* Cambridge, MA: Harvard University Press.

Scribner, S., and Cole, M. 1983. *The Psychology of Literacy.* Cambridge, MA: Harvard University Press.

Simon, H. 1981. *The Sciences of the Artificial.* Cambridge, MA: MIT Press, 2d ed.

Skrtic, T. M. 1985. "Doing Naturalistic Research into Educational Organizations." In Y.S., Lincoln (Ed.) *Organizational Theory and Inquiry: The Paradigm Revolution.* Beverly Hills, CA: Sage Publications.

Sturt, G. 1923. *Wheelwright's Shop.* Cambridge, UK: Cambridge University Press.

Suchman, L. 1987. *Plans and Situated Actions: The Problem of Human-Machine Communication.* New York: Cambridge University Press.

Turkle, S., and Papert, S. 1990. "Epistemological Pluralism: Styles and Voices Within the Computer Culture." *Signs: Journal of Women in Culture and Society,* 16.

Wagner, O. 1988. *Modern Architecture.* Santa Monica, CA: The Getty Center for the History of Art and the Humanities. A translation and reprint of the 1902 Edition.

Wenger, E. 1987. *Artificial Intelligence and Tutoring Systems: Computational and Cognitive approaches to the Communication of Knowledge.* Los Altos, CA: Morgan Kaufmann Publishers.

Wenger, E. 1990. *Toward a Theory of Cultural Transparency: Elements of a Social Discourse of the Visible and the Invisible.* Doctoral thesis. Irvine, CA: University of California.

Winograd, T., and Flores, F. 1986. *Understanding Computers and Cognition: A New Foundation for Design.* Norwood, NJ: Ablex Publishing.

Additional references that informed this paper in the areas of bridge construction and design:
Bridges
Leonhardt, F. 1983. *Bridges: Aesthetics and Design.* London, UK.

Podolny, W. Jr., and Scalzi, J. B. 1986. *Construction and Design of Cable-Stayed Bridges.* 2d ed. New York: John Wiley and Sons.

Walther, R. et. al. 1988. *Cable Stayed Bridges.* London, UK: Thomas Telford.

Design and Engineering Design
Dreyfus, H. 1955. *Designing for People.* New York: Simon and Schuster.

Gordon, J. E. 1978. *Structures: Or, Why Things Don't Fall Down.* New York: Plenum Press.

21

The Need for Negotiation in Cooperative Work

Beth Adelson and Troy Jordan

In this chapter we make concrete some of the relationships between negotiation and the coordination necessary to cooperative work. Towards this end we describe a computer application NegotiationLens. This tool embodies a theory designed to help those engaged in coordinating complex tasks. The theory is appropriate for fostering cooperative work in that it moves negotiating parties out of adversarial positions and improves long term working relationships. It does so by having the parties make explicit their needs, resources, and the criteria underlying any positions they have taken. In this way it helps the parties to jointly develop mutually acceptable solutions.

We argue that the tool which embodies this theory can help with the selection, decomposition, and reformulation of goals; with the resolution of financial and time constraints; and with the negotiation of role interdependencies and conflicts. In this way we place negotiation theory within the context of emerging work on coordination theory.

1 Introduction

The growing body of literature on cooperative work describes a number of tasks in which, increasingly, multiple actors come together with multiple goals and complex sets of constraints. These tasks include collaborative engineering and design; writing; research; and strategic planning and decision-making (Malone & Crowston, 1991; Crowston, 1991; Grudin, 1988 & 1991; Tatar, 1988; Greif, 1988; Groenbaek, Grudin, Bodker, & Bannon, 1991; Lee, 1990; Lee & Malone, 1988 & 1990; Winograd & Flores, 1986; Stefik et al., 1987; Conklin & Begeman, 1988). However, as Malone and his colleagues have cogently argued in their work on coordination theory these tasks require that at a minimum goals, actors, and constraints all need to be coordinated (Malone & Crowston, 1991; Crowston, 1991; Lee, & Malone, 1988 & 1990). This generates the issue of what *coordination mechanisms will be successful*. In this chapter we focus on *negotiation* as one major mechanism for achieving coordination, and on NegotiationLens, a cooperative work tool that assists negotiating parties in accordance with the approach to negotiation that we set forth.

1.1 Performing Complex Tasks: Coordination through Negotiation

In a recent set of papers Malone and Crowston use their developing Coordination Theory as a framework to: analyze the effects of information technology; aid the development of cooperative work tools; and explore the implications of distributed computer architectures (Malone & Crowston, 1991; Crowston, 1991).

As a central part of this work, Malone and Crowston identify aspects of complex cooperative tasks which require coordination. These include: the selection, decomposition and reformulation of goals; the resolution of financial and time constraints; and the resolution of role interdependencies and conflicts. Below we describe, for each of these aspects of cooperative work, how coordination can take place via negotiation. In Sections 2 and 4 we provide a detailed account of how the negotiation techniques mentioned here can succeed both in principle and in practice.

Aspects of cooperative tasks requiring coordination:

1. Goal Selection: Goal selection problems can arise when two groups with complementary roles are assigned to work jointly on a project within an organization. Consider the following example. Management has given a multi-media and a curriculum development group the task of working together to develop a line of multi-media educational software. Although there is a clear and possibly explicitly acknowledged opportunity for mutual gain, there is also room for hidden conflict. Each group may, through unconscious habit, approach this new collaboration as an opportunity to create a breakthrough product, but only within their own sphere (Carroll, 1990). That is, the two groups may have *implicit* conflicting goals and the first place the goal conflict will become evident is when an attempt is made to produce an initial product design. If, in accord with our prescriptive theory of negotiation, each group now makes their goals

explicit, they have a chance to jointly formulate a *mutually acceptable* set of goals. This will increase the chance of developing a design which will, over the life of the project, better satisfy both groups (Susskind & Cruikshank, 1987; Brockner & Rubin, 1985; Raiffa, 1982; Fisher & Uri, 1981; Fisher & Brown, 1988).

Note that in this section we rely on the assumptions of our prescriptive theory of negotiation: that needs can be made explicit; that this will then allow parties to jointly develop mutually acceptable solutions; etc. In Sections 2 and 4 we present the arguments and evidence which support our theoretical assumptions.

The use of computer-based decision-making tools can also make clear the need for negotiation during the goal selection process (Lee, 1990; Conklin & Begeman, 1988; Adelson, 1991 & 1991a). For example, Lee's Sibyl is a system which has been used effectively in group decision-making (Lee, 1990). However, the tool presupposes the existence of a set of shared goals and as we saw above this may not always be the case. As a result we take the position that a negotiation tool like NegotiationLens (Section 4) and a decision-making tool like Sibyl may form a complementary set of group-ware tools (In Section 4.1 we discuss the integrated environment which would allow the use of NegotiationLens together with Sibyl).

Resolving the goal selection problem allows the following coordination issues to be resolved as well.

2. Goal Decomposition: There is a way in which the successful negotiation of a set of goals can aid in the goal decomposition which follows the task of goal selection. The goal decomposition process entails making decisions about the functional features of the to-be-designed system. What the functionality of the features should be, and therefore, how and by whom they should implemented is again likely to be a subject of debate in the kind of multidisciplinary effort described in the above example.

However, under our theory part of the goal selection process (point 1) involves an exploration of the criteria underlying the goals; and a discussion of the legitimacy of these criteria.This means that when the parties are now trying to make decisions about who should build what, they have criteria to turn to whose legitimacy they have previously decided upon.

3. Goal Reformulation: The role negotiation plays in this coordination problem is interesting. That is, negotiation both causes the problem and points out its value. Part of our negotiation process includes a detailed exploration of novel negotiated solutions. However, the process also includes exploration of alternatives which may suit the parties better than working together. For example, in situations where even initial goal conflicts cannot be resolved, working separately may turn out to be the best alternative for both sides. However, on reflection this can be a desirable outcome. If both parties can quickly identify a situation which does not allow a joint resolution they can retreat from the particular effort, thereby preserving the collaborative relationship for future ventures (Fisher & Uri, 1981; Fisher & Brown, 1988).

This means the parties may change their goals, sometimes quite radically, as a result of the negotiation process, but the radical change may be quite constructive in the longer term.

4. Allocation of Limited Resources: Here we present two examples. The first concerns limited financial resources the second concerns time constraints.

(a) Managing Monetary Constraints: The following example illustrates the need for, and the value of negotiation in situations concerning the coordination of monetary resources: An educational institution had, not unconventionally, divided its computer-based activities into two organizational entities; a Computer Science department and a Computer Services center (which provided data analysis and word processing facilities to the university as a whole). As background, both organizations were fairly new and needed to increase their facilities. Additionally, the university had, at the time, very limited resources for new projects. The Computer Science department had been approached by a computer company and been offered a "matching grant," an arrangement under which the company would sell the department $40,000 worth of equipment for $20,000. The Computer Science department got the administration to agree to this outlay of money and made arrangements with the computer company to proceed with the deal. At this point Computer Services heard about the arrangement and became concerned that the outlay would eat up the administration's entire computer budget for some time to come. Computer Services therefore persuaded the administration to cancel the arrangement (without notifying Computer Science). Shortly after this the computer company representative who had initiated the arrangement both with Computer Science and internally with his management called the Computer Science department to tell them that the administration had reneged on its half of the funding. He also told them the university had put the company to a lot of trouble and had in the process made him and his manager look bad. He informed computer science that, as a result, the company had decided that in the future they would not be willing to offer matching funds to any part of the university. Adding jealousy to frustration, he explained that another local university had instead been chosen for the matching fund program.

Clearly this was a situation in which computer science and computer services should have been working together. Had computer services entered into a negotiation with both computer science and the administration they would have been encouraged to look at the long term implications of cancelling the grant. Further, they would have been motivated to create more productive alternatives. For example, they could have settled on a solution in which they either shared the initial grant, or took turns benefitting from future grants offered by the computer company.

(b) Managing Time Constraints: Here we present a negotiation which successfully resolved an issue concerning time constraints. In this example a disagreement arose in a research group when a visiting researcher told her manager that she wanted to start up two new projects and the manager replied that she should not do so until she had completed the one project she had already started. At this point, the manager of the group, the researcher and her colleague on the existing project entered into a negotiation. Each side had already expressed what they had seen as the optimal scheduling, so they proceeded to make explicit both their constraints/needs and their resources. The group manager was worried that the researcher's desire to start new projects signaled a loss of interest on the part of the researcher and so he was worried that the current project would not be finished; the work done so far would be lost; and the time the colleague had invested in training the researcher on the lab's equipment would turn out to have been wasted. The researcher explained that she had committed to give a set of talks on works-in-progress and so her desire to start new projects, rather than signalling a loss of interest in the current project, simply represented a need to have three projects solidly underway in the next month. She also volunteered that once the talk was out of the way she would have sufficient time and resources to complete all three projects, which were of interest to the group, to the manager's satisfaction. She went on to outline a plan of work for herself and her research assistants which lent support to her claim. The negotiation resulted in a mutually agreeable timetable and a smoother group dynamic based on a better understanding of the general needs and expectations of the group members. Additionally, it strengthened the relationship between the researcher and her colleague in that they agreed to (and did) jointly write a paper on the first project upon its completion.

5. Role Interdependencies: Conflicts can arise when two organizational entities with different goals have occasion to deal with a third party. An aspect of the dispute between Computer Science and Computer Services (point 4a) serves as an example and can be used to illustrate the potential of negotiation in role interdependency issues. When the representative for Computer Science was informed that the department was no longer eligible for the matching grant program he responded adversarially rather than collaboratively to the situation. His goal was to try and get the computer company to separate its opinion of computer science from its opinion of computer services in order to regain computer science's eligibility. Basically he said that the ill-advised behavior of computer services was not to be taken as a predictor of the behavior of computer science. He further stated that now that he was aware of the type of behavior that might be expected from computer services he would in the future take action to prevent a situation like the current one from arising. In effect he was casting aspersions on another part of his organization in order to preserve the reputation of his own group.

However, had computer science and computer services entered into a goal-setting negotiation with the administration, the not unimportant goal of making the entire organization look good may very well have become a goal adopted by all the parties.

6. Role Conflicts: One situation in which role conflicts can arise occurs when two individuals in different groups each feel that they must individually complete a given piece of a joint project. The following example is provided by Grudin (1991). Typically on large software projects the functional design specifications are produced by the software engineers. Eventually these specs are turned over to a group who is also

responsible for producing the user interface. This can create a situation in which the software engineers and the user interface designers both feel a need to "own" the user interface. As Grudin points out there can be many reasons underlying this feeling. One, of course is professional pride, but others include "turf battle" sorts of motivations and questions concerning who actually is the person best qualified to do the work.

Here an aspect of the negotiation process which was touched upon in our discussion of goal selection can prove useful in resolving concerns about professional pride and task assignment according to qualification. If the parties enter into a discussion which allows them to develop objective criteria for judging who is actually is best qualified to do each piece of the work it becomes easier to amicably resolve the division of labor.

The turf battle issue is also susceptible to negotiation. Under our negotiation framework needs such as maintaining one's previously established areas of responsibility both become clear and are taken into account in constructing negotiated solutions.

In the following section we provide an account of the theory of negotiation whose elements we assumed in presenting the above negotiation scenarios. As we see it, each of the above aspects of cooperative work may call for a negotiation which uses some or all of the elements of our theory of negotiation.

2 Foundations of our Theory of Negotiation

In the last decade, research and practice in the field of negotiation has resulted in a body of work which we synthesize here into a framework for a prescriptive theory of negotiation (Susskind & Cruikshank, 1987; Brockner & Rubin, 1985; Pruitt & Rubin, 1986; Raiffa, 1982; Fisher & Uri, 1981; Fisher & Brown, 1988; Kolb, 1983; Adelson, 1991 & 1991a). The theory has three central features: (1) It is intended to move the negotiating parties into a *collaborative* rather than an adversarial stance. (2) The parties *jointly* construct mutually acceptable solutions. (3) The parties are hoped to solidify or improve existing working relationships. As a result, its application to cooperative work situations is highly appropriate.

In this section we discuss the elements of the theory and the way in which they foster successful negotiations whether they concern goal selection or decomposition; resource allocation; or role conflicts . In Section 4 we describe the system which embodies the theory and give an example of its use.

1. Making Needs Explicit: In Section 1.1 we saw the use for this negotiation element in looking at the resolution of goal selection and resource allocation issues. In this part of the negotiation the parties are asked to state what they need in order to reach a successful resolution of the situation. Part of this process includes:

(a) Making implicit desires explicit. This allows both sides to better understand both their own needs and the needs of the other party.

(b) Providing explanations as to the importance of each need. This allows each party to feel that the other has well-motivated rather than simply arbitrary needs.

(c) Developing objective criteria concerning the legitimacy of each need. This will aid both parties in deciding which of their positions are reasonable as the negotiation proceeds.

2. Making Resources Explicit: This element was discussed with regard to the resource allocation process. Here the parties state what they can offer each other in their collaborative endeavor. This stage makes clear the boundaries of the situation. Additionally, it can make each party feel that the other is making a good-faith effort.

3. Matching Interests to Resources: This is a process by which the parties look for opportunities for mutual gain. But, the discovery of these opportunities has in practice been markedly difficult. However, in the course of developing our software we have developed a way of increasing the likelihood of noticing these opportunities. That is, in our version of the theory the parties systematically compare a given need against the currently listed resources. This process was illustrated in the time allocation example (Section 1.1, point 4b), it allowed the manager and the researcher to establish that the researcher did in fact intend to complete the project in question to the manager's satisfaction.

4. Developing Joint Solutions: Here the parties are encouraged to: i. initially develop a variety of solutions which might accommodate the needs of both sides equally; and ii. iterate through this process by evaluating emerging solutions until a mutually agreeable one is found.

(See point 6 and Section 4, point 5 below.) In the time allocation negotiation we saw an example of the development of a joint solution.

5. Developing Alternatives: In addition to developing possible negotiated solutions the parties are asked to individually examine their alternatives to working together. This serves several functions. When good alternatives to working together do exist, knowing these alternatives can increase the parties confidence in their own resources, allowing them approach the negotiation with a mind-set which has been found, perhaps counter-intuitively, to foster flexibility. However, it can also allow the parties to quickly decide that the current collaboration should be abandoned. As mentioned above, the interesting point here is that this kind of determination, when made early on often preserves the collaborative relationship, allowing future joint efforts to succeed.

In the case where good alternatives are not found, it can increase the parties commitment to the negotiation process, thereby motivating the parties to construct a joint solution. For example, in the matching grant example (Section 1.1, point 4a), had the parties considered the difficulties which ensued from working against each other it might very well have increased their motivation to enter into a negotiation.

6. Respecting the Other Side: A central part of this theoretical framework is that it asks the parties to commit to respecting each. Part of this respect entails having the parties to make their needs, resources and rationales explicit. It also takes the form of having the parties treat the needs of the other side as seriously as if they were their own and so manifests itself in the development of mutually beneficial alternatives. Additionally it means the parties not only commit to the negotiation as a whole but also to the agreements which result.

The time allocation example is a good illustration of parties acting with commitment and respect.

3 Object Lens: An Environment for Developing Partially Automated Cooperative Work Applications

NegotiationLens is built upon Object Lens and designed to be used in conjunction with it. We begin with a description of Object Lens. Our goal here is to give the reader a feel for the user's experience of the Object Lens system.

Object Lens is an object oriented environment that integrates hypertext, object oriented databases, and electronic mail facilities in order to allow users to develop applications to support cooperative work (Lai, Malone & Yu, 1989; Lee & Malone, 1988 & 1990). Further, the system was designed to be used both by experienced and unsophisticated computer users. Object Lens has been referred to as a semi-formal system (Lai, Malone & Yu, 1989). That is, Object Lens users create applications in which objects can either be manipulated by user-created, formally specified "agents" (see Section 3.1, point 3 below) or by the users themselves. For example, a mail message can be forwarded either automatically by a user-created agent which has been defined to forward all messages containing a given key word in the subject field or by the user herself because of its potential interest to another user. The intention here was to allow users to automate tasks to the degree that they felt offered the most convenience, and also to allow users to increasingly automate tasks as the tasks became better understood. One Object Lens application, "Scheduler'sAide" illustrates this feature of user-determined levels of automation (Resnick & Jordan, 1990). Scheduler'sAide provides support for meeting scheduling, by generating and disseminating queries about possible meeting times and collating the responses. However, it was designed not to require fully maintained on-line calendars, but to permit and encourage each user to formalize the process, as she chose (Grudin, 1988). In a fully automated version, Scheduler'sAide becomes an automatic meeting scheduling application, where each user constructs agents to check their personal calendar and respond according to their specified method (i.e., always double book, allow 15 minutes between meetings, etc.).

3.1 Elements of Object Lens

1. *Objects* are the main currency in Object Lens. Each object is of a given type, and types are related to each other through an inheritance hierarchy displayed as a graph in the user's environment (figure 21.1 illustrates a hierarchy that includes types such as *MESSAGE*, used in Object Lens e-mail, and *FOLDER* described in point 2 below). Mouse-clicking on a type creates a new object of that type. An object of a given type will have pre-specified field names as well as pre-specified actions that can be performed

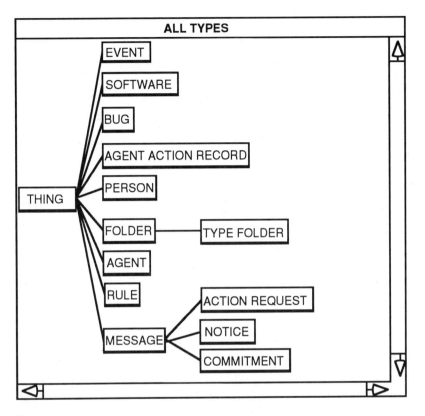

Figure 21.1

on it. For example, objects of type *MESSAGE* have fields such as *To*, *From*, *Cc* and *In-Reply-To*. The actions that can be performed on them include *Send*, *Reply* and *Forward*. Because the objects in the system have pre-specified fields and actions they have been termed semi-structured. This structuring is what supports the semi-formal nature of the system. That is, the formally defined fields and actions can be manipulated by the formally defined system agents, but additionally, the fields can include text that can be manipulated as the user wishes.

2. *Folders* are objects that contain collections of other objects. They serve to facilitate the viewing of related objects in that they present objects in a table format. Each object appears in a single row in a table, along with the contents of selected fields. (See figure 21.3 which illustrates a folder containing messages). Users can choose which fields to show in order to high-light essential information for the task at hand.

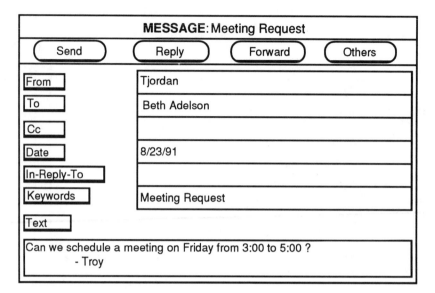

Figure 21.2

3. *Agents* are specialized objects. They have the ability to inspect the contents of a folder and manipulate the objects within in useful ways. *Agents* are defined as sets of condition-action rules that allow users to describe the conditions under which an object should be acted upon, along with the action that should be taken when those conditions obtain. In Object Lens an agent can cause and object to be moved, deleted, or copied. Other actions include changing a field's value or sending the object to another Object Lens user via e-mail. An *Agent* can be triggered directly by the user or it may be set to trigger at certain times or by events such as the addition of an object to a folder.

4. Object Lens's hypertext facility allows users to make *Links* to other objects in the environment. For example, in the *Text* field of a *DOCU-MENT* object, an author may place a link to an object of type *REFER-ENCE* to tell a co-author about an important citation that she has in her bibliography database. When the author receives the *DOCUMENT*, mouse-clicking on the link displays the *REFERENCE*. Object Lens users can share objects in two ways. The first is via the existing e-mail system. The second is by saving objects in a shared file space such as a fileserver. Other users can then load these objects into their own knowledge space.

```
┌─────────────────────────────────────────────────────────────────────┐
│                          FOLDER: Untitled                             │
│  ( Send )          ( Reply )          ( Forward )        ( Others )   │
│  ┌──────┐ ┌──────────────────────────────────────────────────┐  ┌─┐ │
│  │ Name │ │ Messages Re: O.L. database project meeeting       │  │△│ │
│  └──────┘ │         Name              From              Date  │  └─┘ │
│  ┌────────┐│ Let's meet Monday 10:00  Presnick@eagle.mit.edu  Fri, 31 May 91 12:40  △│
│  │Contents│├                                                    │  │ │
│  └────────┘│ Demo on Tuesday ?        Ackerman@athena.mit.edu  Fri, 31 May 91 16:39 │
│           │ Re: Demo on Tuesday?     jin@eagle.mit.edu        Mon, 3 June 91 12:40 │
│           │ A Hypervoice application presnick@eagle.mit.edu   Mon, 3 June 91 12:40 │
│           │ Ol Distribution          tjordan@eagle.mit.edu    6/4/91            ▽│
│           └──────────────────────────────────────────────────┘     │
│                                                                  ▽  │
└─────────────────────────────────────────────────────────────────────┘
```

Figure 21.3

3.2 LensWriter

Along with NegotiationLens we have implemented LensWriter to support collaborative writing efforts. An author begins the writing process by creating a new instance of type DOCUMENT and then entering the text (figure 21.4, upper left). An author can ask others to comment on the work by sending them a copy via E-mail or saving the object in a shared space.

To comment on the work, a co-author adds ANNOTATION objects. Annotation objects are created by mouse-clicking on the *Add Note* button on the top horizontal menu bar (figure 21.4, upper left). This gives the co-author an object with *Label, Creator,* and *Text* fields (figure 21.4, lower left). The co-author can then type her comments into the the *Text* field. When she is done she can click on the object to iconify it. Next she can use the mouse to place it in the appropriate spot in the margin of the text. If the co-author has filled in the *Label* field its contents will appear on the icon, serving as a quick reference to the icon's contents (fFigure 21.4, upper right).

When the first author wishes to view the comments she simply mouse-clicks on the icon (figure 21.4, bottom right). A comment can be deleted by clicking on the menu bar's *Delete Note* button. Both the original author of the DOCUMENT and the creator of the comment can delete the note, other co-authors cannot.

4 NegotiationLens

NegotiationLens, was designed to guide negotiations for parties involved in coordinating aspects of cooperative projects. Using the elements of the

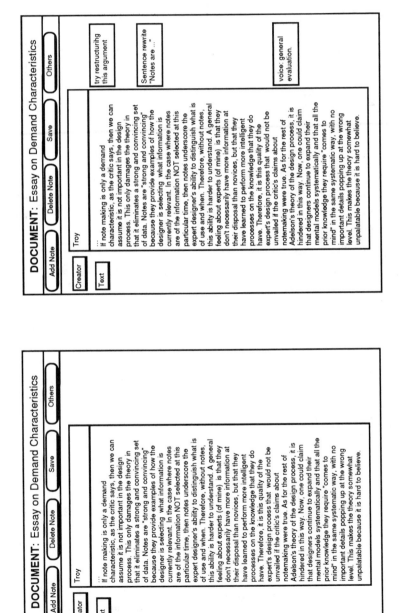

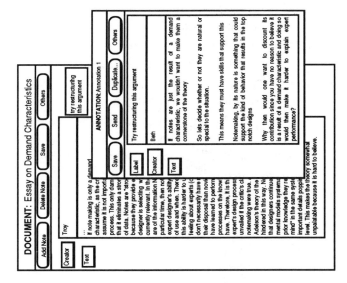

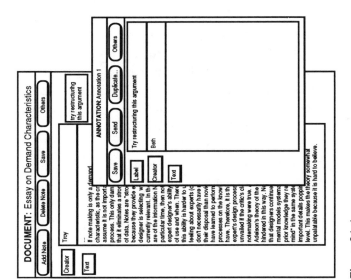

Figure 21.4

theory outlined in the previous section, the tool fosters collaborative as opposed to adversarial negotiation. In the process of guiding the parties it provides a sort of spread sheet for keeping track of the state of the negotiation. That is, at each stage in the process, the tool offers an a Object Lens style window which serves as a workspace designed to make it easy to enter and consider the needed information. The tool purposely does not make any decisions for the parties since one of the motivations of the work was to have the parties develop and internalize negotiation skill.

By way of an overview, in the process of using the tool, the two (or more) parties jointly build a solution by considering the needs as well as the resources which they bring to the table. Additionally, they are encouraged to move into collaborative positions because they are allowed to back off from any initial unilaterally proposed solutions as they are prompted through the stages listed below.

(Note: The examples in the figures come from the time allocation negotiation described in Section 1.1, point 4b)

1. Problem Statement: Both parties begin by separately stating the problem as they see it (figure 21.5).

Here and throughout the negotiation process users follow the simple Object Lens conventions for creating objects. The windows/objects in figure 21.5 for entering the problem statements were each created by mouse-clicking on the appropriately named button in a "root level" window which prompts the user to generate each of the objects needed for the negotiation.

2. Initial Solution: Both parties separately propose an initial solution which is satisfying to their side. It has been found that this step ultimately allows the parties to move out of inflexible starting positions (Brockner & Rubin, 1985; Pruitt & Rubin, 1986; Susskind & Cruikshank, 1987). A party strongly committed to an initial position frequently needs to be able to state a solution that accommodates that position in order to feel it has been heard and considered (Figure 21.6).

3. Underlying Needs and Resources: Based on their "Problem State-ment," rather than on their "Initial Solution," the parties now jointly construct a list of what they need from the situation and what resources they are willing to contribute (figure 21.7). Additionally each party can enter a weight indicating the importance of each of the needs they have

PROBLEM STATEMENT: Time Allocation: Manager&Colleague's

(Add Note)   (Add Resoource)   (Send)   (Others)

| Creator | Troy |

| For Negotiation | time allocation |

| Text | Ursula put a good deal of fher time into training Revecca to use out equiptment when she first came to the lab. This looked like it was going to pay off because Rebecca's first project was quite creative and in many ways it clearly had the potential to be a useful contribution to the work of the lab. But now Rebecca suddenly wants to stat up two more projects. While these projects are also potentially promising I am afraid that Rebecca will not complete what she has started. If ths happens, I will be faced with an unpleasant choice. I will either have to accept that Ursula's time was wasted or I will have to, unfairly ask Ursula to do all the work on what was supposed to be a joint project between her, Rebecca and the several assistants Rebecca brought to the lab.

I am concerned because our previous experiences with visiting researchers has been mixed. Some have made valuable contributions, but others have not had a sufficient sense of committment and have left things hanging. It is very hard to tell which category a visitor falls in. |

PROBLEM STATEMENT: Time Allocation: Researcher (Rebecca)'s

(Add Note)   (Add Resoource)   (Send)   (Others)

| Creator | Troy |

| For Negotiation | time allocation |

| Text | Based on the first project, which has been handed off to my research assistants for implementation and my ideas for the two other projects which I want to work on during my visit to the lab I committed to give some talks on my work-in-progress.

Given this committment, and the fact that I habitually start on new projects while my assistants finish their first pass on an implementation, I want to begin work on the next two projects.

If I follow this plan not only will I be able to meet my committment for the talks, but I'll be able to produce the most in my time at the lab.

While the first project is being implemented, I think I should go ahead with the design of the next two projects and then after the talks are done I can work on seeing all three projects through to completion.

My assessment is that I'll even have time to write a paper on the first project jointly with Ursula. I know she has been looking for someone to help her with her writing in order to build up her vita. I have lots of experience with this kind of mentoring and I would like to do this in return for all the help she has given me. |

Figure 21.5

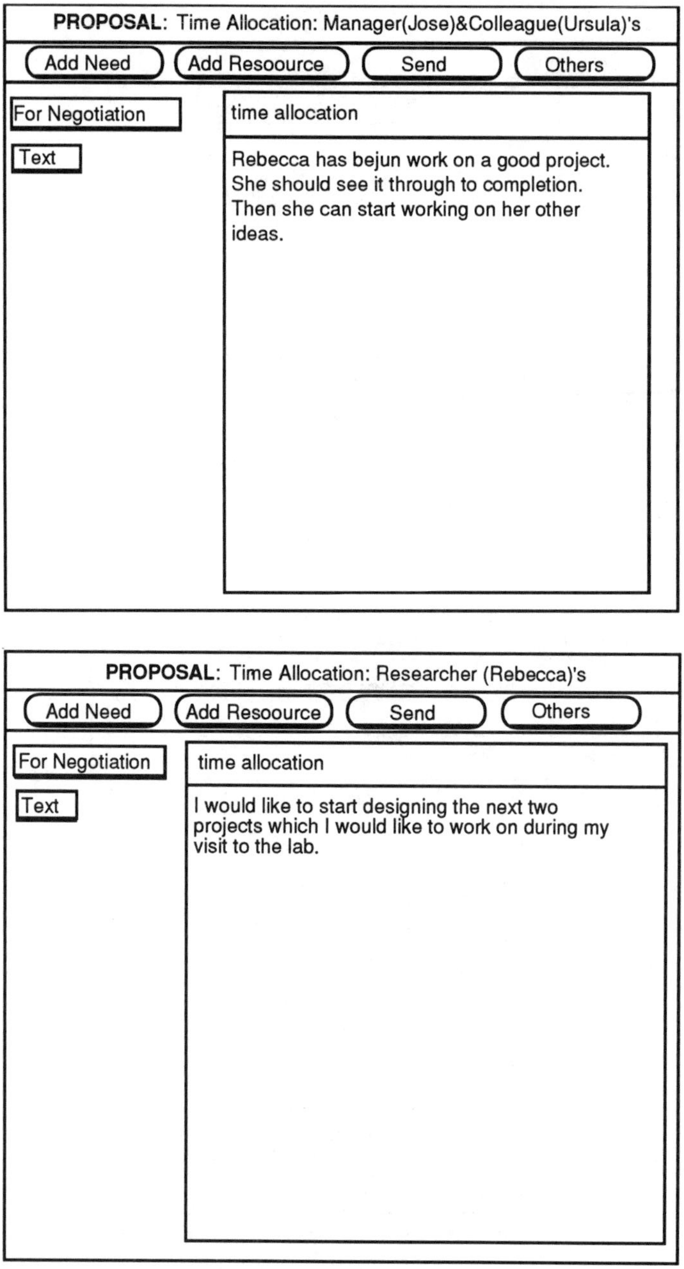

PROPOSAL: Time Allocation: Manager(Jose)&Colleague(Ursula)'s

(Add Need)   (Add Resoource)   (Send)   (Others)

| For Negotiation | time allocation |

| Text |

Rebecca has bejun work on a good project.
She should see it through to completion.
Then she can start working on her other
ideas.

PROPOSAL: Time Allocation: Researcher (Rebecca)'s

(Add Need)   (Add Resoource)   (Send)   (Others)

| For Negotiation | time allocation |

| Text |

I would like to start designing the next two
projects which I would like to work on during my
visit to the lab.

Figure 21.6

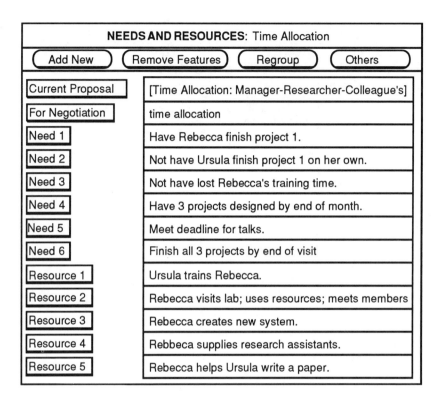

NEEDS AND RESOURCES: Time Allocation	
(Add New) (Remove Features) (Regroup) (Others)	
Current Proposal	[Time Allocation: Manager-Researcher-Colleague's]
For Negotiation	time allocation
Need 1	Have Rebecca finish project 1.
Need 2	Not have Ursula finish project 1 on her own.
Need 3	Not have lost Rebecca's training time.
Need 4	Have 3 projects designed by end of month.
Need 5	Meet deadline for talks.
Need 6	Finish all 3 projects by end of visit
Resource 1	Ursula trains Rebecca.
Resource 2	Rebecca visits lab; uses resources; meets members
Resource 3	Rebecca creates new system.
Resource 4	Rebbeca supplies research assistants.
Resource 5	Rebecca helps Ursula write a paper.

Figure 21.7

listed. (The weights are shown and discussed in conjunction with point 5 below.)

4. Collaborative Solution, Matching Needs to Resources: The parties then jointly construct a new solution by considering how the "Resources" match the "Needs." In figure 21.9 we see the system has grouped the needs separately from the resources. As mentioned above, systematic matching is critical both in discovering a successful solution and in increasing a sense of collaboration between the parties. It is this stage that uncovers the previously non-obvious ways in which the parties can help each other. Sometimes these matches, although previously unnoticed, are easy to recognize when the parties systematically go through each need and compare it to each resource. However, we have also found that this careful comparison process has turned up matches which were both surprising and useful to the parties (Adelson & Jordan, in press). Figure 21.8 illustrates the window containing the joint solution.

PROPOSAL: Time Allocation: Manager-Researcher-Colleague's

Add Need	Add Resoource	Send	Others

For Negotiation	time allocation
Text	Rebecca can begin designing the two new projects and then work on her talk while the implementation of her first project is being completed. She and her research assistants will then complete all three projects and write up the results of her first project with Ursula.

Figure 21.8

NEEDS AND RESOURCES: Time Allocation

Add New	Remove Features	Regroup	Others

Current Proposal	[Time Allocation: Manager-Researcher-Colleague's]			
For Negotiation	time allocation	Sat/Util	Owner	Weight
Need 1	Have Rebecca finish project 1.	10	m&c	10
Need 2	Not have Ursula finish project 1 on her own.	10	m&c	8
Need 3	Not have lost Rebecca's training time.	10	m&c	7
Need 4	Have 3 projects designed by end of month.	10	rbca	10
Need 5	Meet deadline for talks.	10	rbca	10
Need 6	Finish all 3 projects by end of visit	10	rbca	10
Resource 1	Ursula trains Rebecca.	10	m&c	
Resource 2	Rebecca visits lab; uses resources; meets members	10	m&c	
Resource 3	Rebecca creates new system.	10	rbca	
Resource 4	Rebbeca supplies research assistants.	10	rbca	
Resource 5	Rebecca helps Ursula write a paper.	10	rbca	

Figure 21.9

5. Iterating: If the parties feel dissatisfied with the newly developed solution, NegotiationLens provides them with a means for understanding the source(s) of their dissatisfaction. The parties can now select the *See Features* button (figure 21.7, second button from left in top horizontal menu bar) allowing them to look back at how important they believed each need was to them at the time it was listed. (The two rightmost columns in figure 21.9 show the current list along with who entered each need and how important it seemed at the time.) The parties can also now enter a number in the "satisfied/utilized" column (figure 21.9, third column from right) to indicate how well each need is being satisfied by the current proposal and how well each resource is being taken advantage of. Additionally, selecting the *Regroup* option on the menu bar in figure 21.9 allows the parties to request that the needs and resources list be sorted by weight, by weight for each owner, by satisfaction/utilization or by satisfaction/utilization for each owner.

Several things can happen as a result of sorting and inspecting the weights and satisfaction values. The parties can decide that the current proposal is not satisfactory because the initial list of needs and resources was inaccurate or incomplete. As a result, they can revise the list. They can decide that the list was accurate but that the weights were not and so they can revise the weights. Additionally, they can see which needs are not being met and look for resources to fill them. All of these alternatives can result in the generation of a new proposed solution.

Because the solution process involves making both sides' resources explicit, it can result in the construction of solutions which are more satisfying than unilaterally proposed solutions. Additionally, because the needs and resources of both sides are brought into the open, the process can move the parties towards a better long-term relationship.

4.1 Using NegotiationLens in the Context of the Object Lens Environment

In the last section we described the way in which NegotiationLens leads parties who desire to work together through a collaborative negotiation having its roots in the theory described in Section 2. In isolation, NegotiationLens gives the parties a mechanism for capitalizing on most but not all aspects of the theory. On the other hand, as we mentioned in

Section 3, NegotiationLens was designed to be used within the broader Object Lens environment and so negotiators who take advantage of two additional features of Object Lens in conjunction with the features of NegotiationLens can carry out a full version of the negotiation described in our theory.

In the theory the parties are encouraged throughout the negotiation both to develop joint solutions and alternatives to working together. Object Lens facilitates this process in that it (1) allows the members of a party to provide extensive comments to existing proposals, either through the use of LensWriter or by adding comment fields; and (2) then allows these comments to be shared through the Object Lens mail system, Information Lens.

Additionally, as users become increasingly skilled, Object Lens will allow users to create agents to automatically facilitate parts of the negotiation. For example, consider the case in which one member of a party finds that she is regularly mailing out proposed solutions to other members of her party for comment. Object Lens will allow her to create agents which both add comment fields to proposals and then cause them to automatically be mailed to her co-workers.

5 Concluding Remark

In this chapter we have described a tool which embodies a theory of negotiation designed to help those engaged in coordinating complex tasks. We believe that the tool can help with the selection, decomposition and reformulation of goals; with the resolution of financial and time constraints; and with the negotiation of role interdependencies and conflicts. In this way the work deals both with issues relevant to theories of negotiation and coordinated work.

References

Adelson, B. Educational tools for what you wanted to do anyway. *Proceedings of the Fourteenth Annual Meeting of the Cognitive Science Society*, 1991.

Adelson, B. A collaborative negotiation tool. *SIGCHI Bulletin*. October, 1991a.

Adelson, B. and Jordan, T. Uncovering Design Rationale through the Negotiation Process. In Moran, T. and Carroll, J. (eds.). *Design Rationale*. In press.

Brockner, J. and Rubin, J. *Entrapment in Escalating Conflicts.* New York: Springer-Verlag. 1985.

Carrol, J. *The Nurnberg funnel: Designing Minimalist instruction for practical computer skill.* Cambridge, MA.: MIT Press. 1990.

Conklin, J. and Begeman, M. gIBIS: A hypertext tool for exploratory policy discussion. In Tatar, D. (ed.) *Proceedings of the Second Conference on Computer-Supported Cooperative Work.* ACM press. 1988.

Crowston, K. *Towards a Coordination Cookbook: Recipes for Multi-Agent Action* Doctoral Dissertation, MIT Sloan School. 1990.

Crowston, K. Malone, T. and Lin, F. *Cognitive science and organizational design.* HCI, 3, 59-85. 1985.

Fisher, R. and Brown, S. *Getting Together.* New York: Penguin. 1988.

Fisher, R. and Uri, W. *Getting to Yes.* New York: Penguin. 1981.

Greif, I. *Computer Supported Cooperative Work.* I. Greif (ed.). San Mateo, CA: Morgan Kaufmann. 1988.

Groenbaek, K. Grudin, J. Bodker, S. and Bannon, L. Cooperative System Design. In *Participatory Design.* Schuler & Namioka (eds.) Hillsdale, NJ.: Erlbaum. 1991.

Grudin, J. Why CSCW applications fail. In Tatar, D. (ed.) *Proceedings of the Second Conference on Computer-Supported Cooperative Work.* ACM press. 1988.

Grudin, J. Systematic sources of suboptimal interface design in large product development organization. *HCI.* June, 1991.

Kolb, D. The *Mediators.* Cambridge, MA.: MIT Press. 1983.

Lai, K., Malone, T. and Yu, K. "Object Lens: A 'Spreadsheet' for Cooperative Work." *ACM Transaction on Office Information Systems,* 6(4) pp. 332-353. 1989.

Lee, J. Sibyl: A qualitative decision management system. In P. Winston (ed.). *AI at MIT* Vol. 1. Cambridge, MA.: MIT Press. 1990.

Lee, J. and Malone, T. How can groups communicate when they use different languages? In R. Allen (ed.) *Proceedings of the ACM Conference on Office Information Systems.* Palo Alto, CA. 1988.

Lee, J. and Malone, T. Partially shared views. *ACM Transactions on Information Systems.* 1990.

Malone, T. and Crowston, K. *Toward an Interdisciplinary Theory of Coordination.* MIT Center for Coordination Science Tech. Report CCS TR 120. 1991.

Pruitt, D. and Rubin, J. *Social Conflict: Escalation, stalemate and settlement.* New York: Random House. 1986.

Resnick, P. and Jordan, T. Scheduler'sAide: an Application in Object Lens to Support Meeting Scheduling. Internal Memo, Center For Coordination Science, Massachusetts Institute of Technology. 1990.

Stefik, M., Foster, G., Bobrow, D., Kahn, K., Lanning, S. and Suchman, L. Beyond the Chalkboard. *CACM,* 1987.

Susskind, L. and Cruikshank, J. *Breaking the Impasse: Consensual Approaches to Resolving Public Disputes.* New York: Basic Books. 1987.

Tatar, D. (ed.) *Proceedings of the Second Conference on Computer-Supported Cooperative Work.* ACM Press. 1988.

Winograd, T. and Flores, F. *Understanding computers and cognition.* Norwood, NJ: Ablex. 1986.

22

Teaching Hypermedia Concepts Using Hypermedia Techniques

Peter A. Gloor

Introduction

Multimedia aids can greatly improve the quality of presentations. The combination of the computer with an adequate projection gives additional capabilities for presenting facts and algorithms that would be hard to explain with static aids such as blackboard or slides. It was possible in the pre-computer-age to present animations and movies with film or video, but the use of the computer allows a level of interactivity that could not have been achieved with traditional means.[1]

The hypertext concept is not only well suited for computer-aided instruction programs, on-line manuals and tutorials, technical documentations and sales presentations, but also for basic presentations in classroom teaching. Anybody who has ever tried to find a particular slide in a stack of unsorted slides in the middle of a presentation can appreciate the capability of direct access to any part of information at every point of the presentation.

For a one-semester course about hypermedia taught to about 30 graduate students majoring in computer science at the University of Zurich I decided to use hypermedia itself as the basic *technology* of presentation. I used the hypermedia course as a testbed for the use of hypermedia presentation techniques. For the hypermedia authoring system I chose Apple's HyperCard because

• Macintoshes are very popular at the university of Zurich. Every student could read the HyperCard stacks individually in parallel with the course.
• It is very easy to integrate simple animations directly into HyperCard[2] and the possibility always exists of launching other applications directly from within HyperCard.

• There are a lot of examples of hypermedia applications written in HyperCard, including computer aided instruction programs, on-line manuals and tutorials, technical documentations and sales presentations.

I had the students fill out a questionnaire about the use of hypermedia for presentations and improved my presentation system in the course of the lecture based on the students' reactions.

In the rest of the chapter I will discuss briefly the advantages and disadvantages of using hypermedia techniques for presentations. I will then present my experiences with the hypermedia technology for classroom presentations. I will point out the original environment I used for the presentations and also mention the modifications I did on the original system as a reaction to the student's suggestions.

Use of Hypermedia for Classroom Presentations

In this chapter I will compare the respective advantages of hypermedia and traditional classroom presentation techniques. The advantages offered by using hypermedia are twofold: the hypertext concept offers easy linking and nonsequential access to related ideas, multimedia techniques allow the easy integration of simulations and animations into the presentations.

Advantages of hypermedia for presentations
Multimedia aspects:

• *Integration of text, graphics and images:* Hypermedia allows for fast switching between different presentation media as text, graphics and images.

• *Integration of simulations and animations:* Hypermedia is well suited for the explanation of dynamic actions and processes. It is easy to integrate short animations and simulations directly into the normal presentation flow. It is not the aim of this paper to discuss, for example, algorithm animation for educational purposes (for an overview of this domain see e.g., Brown 1988 and for the use of HyperCard for algorithm animation see Gloor 1989).

• *Direct modification, adaptation and reuse:*
In contrast to slides and overhead transparencies it is easy to modify a hypermedia based course:
-In the middle of the presentation a screen can be modified by using the editing tools of the hypermedia authoring system.

-The whole presentation or parts of it can be reused easily for the construction of new presentations.

Hypertext aspects:

• *Clear structure of the whole course:* By using outlining techniques (as in MORE for the Macintosh) a clear and concise structure of the whole content of the course can be achieved. Ideally the whole course is organized hierarchically.

• *Direct access to every part of the course:* Every part of the whole course can be accessed directly. If the presentation is organized logically, and navigation in the hyperspace is supported by a clear structure of the document, every node of the hypertext document can be reached (in at most a few mouse clicks) by following the correct links.

• *Attractive medium:* The bare fact of using hypermedia as a presentation means makes the presentation more attractive for a technically interested audience.

Disadvantages of hypermedia for presentations

• *Labor intensive preparation:* Contrary to a blackboard-based lecture a hypermedia presentation needs the same amount of preparation as a slide- or overhead transparency-based lecture.

• *Expensive and even immature hardware:* Hypermedia presentations need adequate hardware. This means that in addition to the computer some projection facilities, such as a video projector or LCD display (to be put on an overhead projector) have to be available. Prices for LCD displays have declined considerably in the last few years, but overhead projectors for transparencies or a simple blackboard are much cheaper. However, there are technical problems concerning the projection quality:

-Video projectors often whistle in operation and it is sometimes difficult to get an image which is free of flickering.

-The refresh rate of LCD displays often is not fast enough for quickly running animations. Only today the first LCD displays with color capabilities are appearing.

• *Difficulties of producing hardcopy manuscript:* Hardcopy production is a general problem for hypermedia documents. The non-sequential structure can only partially be brought to a sequential medium like paper. For my course I used the easiest approach by offering a printed manuscript as a sequence of screen copies and by restricting the use of scrolling fields for the presentation (about the use of scrolling fields vs. fixed pages see below).

• *Presentation speed:* Hypermedia offers the same possibilities and dangers of information overload as overhead transparencies, i.e., it is possible to present to the audience too much material in a short period of time. The elimination of this problem demands a lot of discipline and self restriction from the speaker.

Description of the Hypermedia Presentation System

For the purpose of the hypermedia course, I designed a simple authoring environment in HyperCard that is described below.

To ease the navigational task and to solve the problem of being lost in hyperspace I used a strictly hierarchical structure (figure 22.1) for the organization of the information contained in the course. The hierarchical structure has been directly transferred to the HyperCard implementation.

To keep the presentations as simple as possible and to avoid cluttering up the screen, I declined using unnecessary graphical elements on the screen. For example the main presentation screen did not have an aesthetically appealing border. This decision was criticized by the students and has been revised in the current version of the hypermedia presentation system.

There is a node[3] at the top, from which every chapter can be reached. Each chapter is implemented as a HyperCard stack. For practical reasons,

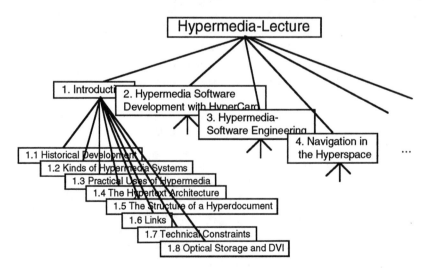

Figure 22.1

the node at the top is integrated in the HyperCard Home stack. Every text card has four navigational buttons (figure 22.2).

The navigation buttons allow the direct jump to the topmost card in the home stack (table of contents), to the subtitle card of the particular chapter, to the previous card inside the chapter and to the next card inside the chapter (figure 22.3).

If the user jumps back to the table of contents or to the subtitle card, the entry in the table of contents or the arrow in the subtitle card belonging to the original text card will be highlighted. This mechanism works like an overview map (Trigg 1988) and gives the reader the necessary information about where he has been in the document before jumping to the table of contents.

Evaluation of the User Interface

In the course of the lecture I modified various components of the user interface. The focal points of my experience are summarized in the following paragraphs:

"Typewriter" presentation vs. "screen for screen" presentation

For the presentation of text with the computer I used two methods:

• *Typewriter like presentation* "Typewriter" text cards presented line after line of text with the same speed as the speaker talked. The text appeared on the screen character by character as if it had been typed with a typewriter. This method was appreciated because it offered a quick orientation to an easily distracted auditor.

• *Presentation card by card* For the most part ordinary text cards were used where all text contained in a card could be seen by the audience the whole time. This method offered a greater degree of freedom to the auditor to read ahead and to find contextual information. It was also easier for the auditor to get a global impression and to see logical connections. In addition the (small) card size forced the teacher to structure all the information into logically-connected chunks, thus fitting well to the hypertext metaphor.

In a survey the audience was asked which of the two methods would be preferred if only one were available. The audience voted clearly (9:6) for the presentation of whole text cards because it felt that the additional freedom to have contextual information available the whole time was

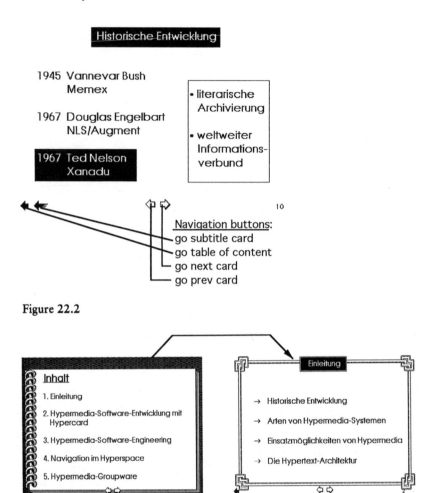

Figure 22.2

Figure 22.3

worth the effort to find the actual keyword themselves. The audience (advanced students) felt themselves unnecessarily lead by the nose by the typewriter like type of presentation. They also found it boring to be forced to read at the same speed as the teacher talked.

Text size limited to cards vs. unlimited text in scrolling fields
Sometimes the teacher finds it impossible to shrink or to divide logically coherent information. As a quick solution to this problem scrolling fields were used to present bigger chunks of text which could not be placed on one card. The use of scrolling fields offers the possibility of demonstrating the unity of text. But the audience soon voted against the presentation of text in scrolling fields (10:6). Text on scrolling fields proved to be hardly readable on the projection screen. In addition it was hard to maintain orientation in the scrolling text. It was found that by additional effort by the teacher, every one of those scrolling text fields could have been subdivided further in card sized text chunks, a process which would have added considerably to the readability and understandability of the content.

Nonbordered text vs. bordered text
As can be seen in (figure 22.2) and (figure 22.3) only the subtitle cards were bordered in the original presentation system, while for the sake of simplicity and so as not to distract the reader, the ordinary text card was not bordered. I made this decision thinking that the screen border would be frame enough. But in the survey the audience clearly opted (11:6) for borders around the text on the grounds that the frame aided in concentrating on the text and improved the structure of the card.

Black text on white background vs. white text on black background
The audience clearly preferred (15:1) black text on white background. As McKnight, Dillon, and Richardson 1990 have noted, human reading habits have been formed by printed books and newspapers which usually have the same arrangement. Knowing this I first wanted to present all text "black on white," but some people in the audience voted for a better readability of "white on black." With video projector and LCD display it is very easy to switch between the two formats (all one has to do is to press

the button "invert") so I tested both variants on the auditorium, which indeed voted clearly (as expected) for the "black on white" variant.

Use of visual effects for the navigation

To ease the navigational task, buttons with different icons were used as principal navigational aids, the different shapes of the icons indicating the position of a text card in the chapter: e.g., the "go table of contents" button of the last card in a subchapter has a different shape than on the other text cards ("" instead of " ⬅ "). In addition to different shaped buttons, visual effects were used as navigational aids

• to go back to the subtitle card ("visual effect checkerboard to black")
• to go to the first card of a subchapter ("visual effect iris close to grey")
• to go to the table of content ("visual effect iris open to black")
• to go from the previous card to the next card and inverse ("visual effect scroll right/left")
• to jump across chapters ("visual effect zoom open").

In the first version of the hypermedia presentation system every time a subchapter was finished and a new one started the screen flashed in order to elucidate the change.

As can be seen in figure 22.4 one half of the audience was satisfied by just using buttons for navigation and were able to dispense with visual effects for the navigation. The bigger part of the audience found the visual effects more confusing than helpful, but the controversy mainly originated from the flash at the change between two subchapters. The other visual effects were found helpful and thus will be used also in future presentation systems.

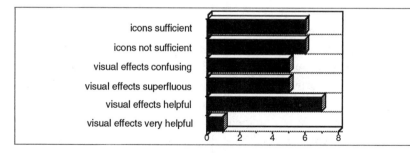

Figure 22.4

The Improved Hypermedia Presentation System

After evaluating the student feedback and my own experiences I decided to integrate the following changes in the current version of my hypermedia instruction program. These changes are in a wide range consistent with the stack design guidelines for HyperCard stacks as suggested by Apple (Apple 1989).[4]

Present text in card-sized textual chunks
In the current version of the hypermedia course text is presented primarily on window-sized cards. This presentation style forces the hypertextual organization into small chunks of information and results in a well structured organization of the whole text.

Use typewriter cards sparingly
This technique is only advantageous if a sequence of essential keywords has to be presented where the speaker whishes to emphasize every word. I did not dispense with typewriter cards totally, but I am using this technique even more sparingly.

Eliminate scrolling fields
Because of disorientation problems and reading difficulties, this presentation style has been eliminated.

Border screens with a simple border
The improved text card includes a plain border for better readability (figure 22.5).

Use sounds sparingly
In the first version the typewriter cards used a typewriter sound, but this sound disturbed more than it helped in the orientation. Repeated use of the same piece of music in every introduction belongs to a radio or TV show, but not to a speaker-based presentation!

Use visual effects for navigation economically and carefully
Consistent use of visual effects for the transition to a predetermined part of the presentation seems to support the navigational task. It has therefore been used even more in the current version.

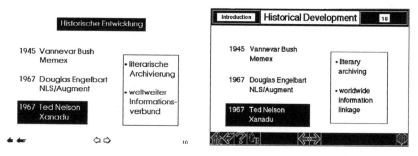

Figure 22.5

Add the capability to add hypertext notes to the hypermedia manuscript

The first version of the hyperdocument had no built in capability to add notes. Every student had to program this extension herself in HyperCard. The current version of the hypermedia manuscript includes this useful feature (figure 22.6).

Extent of the presentation cards with annotation fields

A speaker often needs more information for her talk than just the keywords she presents to the audience. In the first version of the hypermedia course, notes written on paper were used; but there should be a capability to add notes to the hyperdocument that are invisible to the auditorium. On the Macintosh this means the use of an auxiliary monitor that is not projected on the wall. On this auxiliary screen the notes for the speaker can appear. This is not a hardware problem (it is possible to connect several monitors to a Macintosh), but it was impossible in bare Hyper-Card version 1.2, because in HyperCard 1.2 the window size is restricted to one small sized rectangle. This extension is implemented easily in newer versions of HyperCard (greater and equal version 2.0) and other products (e.g., SuperCard) capable of using multiple freely sizable and locatable windows.

Added bilinguality

To make the course more flexible to use and to broaden the possible audience the current version of the hypermedia course is completely German/English bilingual. The reader has a button on each card to switch between languages.

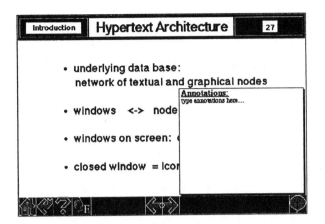

Figure 22.6

Desequentialization of the whole course structure

To make the single chapters of the course more easily accessible the strict ordering sequence of the course has been resolved. This manifests mainly in the table of contents that has been changed from a sequential listing of chapters to a more adequate graphical representation of the course contents (figure 22.7).

Conclusion

The primary disadvantage of hypermedia today is the immaturity of the technology. The multimedia presentation aids of today (LCD display and video projector) are usable, but improvable. Their reliability is good,[5] but the projection quality is sometimes poor and does not achieve the quality of transparencies on an overhead projector. It has to be added that the situation has improved considerably since I taught this course for the first time (1989) and can be expected to become even better in the next few years. When I was teaching the latest version of this course at MIT (Fall 1991) I decided to do away with the overhead transparency backup; a decision I had not to regret.

Hypermedia offers good capabilities as a presentation aid in classroom presentations. For the presentation of plain text, slides or overhead transparencies are almost always sufficient. However, in special cases, in particular, if the presentation flow is dynamic and the sequence of the text

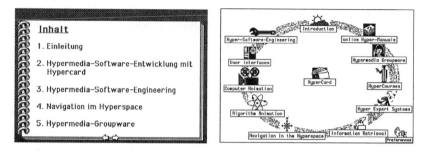

Figure 22.7

cannot completely be prepared in advance, the use of hypermedia technologies offers clear advantages.

The real strength of hypermedia for presentation becomes apparent if
graphics, sounds or animations need to be integrated in the presentation.
It is natural that algorithm animations and simulations are used at first in
courses and presentations in the computer science domain, but there are
numerous other application fields (e.g., geography, biology, etc.) where
the hypermedia technology will be extremely helpful in explaining ideas
and concepts.

Acknowledgments

I would like to thank Kurt Bauknecht and the other faculty members in the
Computer Science Department of the University of Zurich as well as
Charles Leiserson and David Tennenhouse at MIT for giving me the
possibility to test my ideas in practice. I would also like to thank Chris
Lindblad and Chris Sawyer-Lauçanno for the thoughtful proofreading of
an earlier version of this paper.

References

Apple. 1989. *HyperCard Stack Design Guidelines.* Reading, MA: Addison-
Wesley.

Brown, M. H. 1988. *Algorithm Animation.* Cambridge, MA: MIT Press.

Gloor, P. 1989. Algorithmen-Animation mit Hypercard. *Proc. GI-Jahrestagung
89*, München, Informatik Fachberichte 222, Berlin: Springer.

Gloor, P. 1991. Presenting Hypermedia Concepts Using Hypermedia Techniques. *Hypertext/Hypermedia '91*, Tagung der GI, SI und OCG Graz, Informatik
Fachberichte 276, Berlin: Springer.

McKnight, C.; Dillon. A.; and Richardson, J. Problems in Hyperland? A Human Factors Perspective. *Hypermedia*, vol.1., no. 2. Autumn 1990.

Trigg, R. H. Guided Tours and Tabletops: Tools for Communicating in a Hypertext Environment. *ACM Trans. on Office Information Systems.* vol. 6., no. 4. October 1988.

Notes

1. This paper is an extended and revised version of a paper that has been presented at the Austrian/German/Swiss Hypertext/Hypermedia '91 in Graz, Austria (Gloor 1991).

2. As well as in the algorithm and data structure course as in the operating system course at the university of Zurich, HyperCard animations of most of the basic algorithms have been successfully used (Gloor 1989). These animations were developed by students at the university of Zurich.

3. In HyperCard a node is called "card."

4. Apple applies the guidelines only to HyperCard stacks, but I claim that most of the findings mentioned in this paragraph are valid for any hypertext system used for presentation purposes.

5. I had an overhead transparencies backup of the whole lecture that I never used.

23

Computer Integrated Documentation

Guy Boy

Introduction

Text and graphics are common media for transmission of knowledge between people. In large organizations, such as NASA, an enormous number of documents are produced to transfer knowledge from designers to manufacturers, or from manufacturers to operations people, for instance. These documents are generally paper-based.

Documentation is very labor-intensive, requiring a great deal of expertise and development time. One significant problem that interests us is that expert developers may no longer be available by the time a very large documentation project is nearing completion. If a user needs help from documentation developers,they may have been assigned to a different project or changed employment. In the former case, they have to carry out a tremendous amount of problem solving activity to understand and retrieve the information needed by the user. In the latter case, the user usually does not try to go further in the documentation. An important question is: how can we capture knowledge in a way that it will be useful for users in the future? Part of the answer to the question is provided by the use of hypertext (Conklin, 1987) that provides a technology for incremental annotation. Hypermedia is an extension of hypertext that incorporates other media than text, such as graphics, animations and sound (Yankelovich et al., 1988).

With current documentation systems, it is difficult to integrate different sources of knowledge in a problem solving task. Integration can be done during the problem solving process (as is done now), i.e., users construct on-line dynamic bindings between various available sources of knowledge. However, it can be facilitated if the knowledge is prepared in an appropriate form and the connections between the various chunks of knowledge are already pre-programmed, as in a hypermedia framework.

It is well known that the technical paper documentation for an aircraft, for instance, weighs approximately the same as the aircraft. Obviously, such documentation cannot be available on-board. Often, most of this technical information is not necessary. In very specific cases which generally lead to incidents and accidents, "good," complete, and active technical information may be very useful for avoiding a catastrophe. Thus, computer-based documentation must be designed to be useful for the user. In aeronautics, for instance, most flight manuals have been recently computerized and are available on on-board CRT displays (Airbus A320 and Boeing 757 and 767). However, they include only shallow knowledge sufficient for most operations. They do not provide assistance for lower levels of detail, which may be useful in complex and unexpected situations, or in the maintenance of faulty devices. For example, on the Space Station Freedom, it will be necessary to get answers inferred from more detailed levels of information. Shallow knowledge will not be sufficient.

The Computer Integrated Documentation (CID) project began in 1989 to propose a computer-based alternative to the current practice. Three aerospace applications are serving as real-world problem domains for the development of CID: the Space Station Freedom Requirements documents, Space Shuttle mission control procedures manuals, and F-18 emergency procedures. These applications offer a wide variety of problems in technical documentation for both design and operations issues.

This chapter discusses many issues associated with building modern electronic documentation. First, it describes navigation in hypertext space. It also gives a sample session of CID use. From the outset, indexing has been identified as a key issue in CID. A special section is devoted to the description of semantic indexing in context where the major features of CID such as the acquisition, storage and use of contextual knowledge are presented. Some lessons learned from CID development and use are presented as well as related work. Finally, some of the problems associated with CID are discussed and further research issues are described.

Navigation in Hypertext Space

Descriptors and Referents

Indexing is the process of building descriptors {d} (descriptions) from referents {r} and linking them together in a given context (r->d). A descriptor is any piece of text (word, sentence, or paragraph) or image (marked area or label on part of an image) that describes objectively or subjectively any other piece of documentation. Descriptors can be single-term or multiple-terms. A referent is any piece of documentation (word, line of text, paragraph, picture, moving video or animated sequence, program, volume, library) that is described by at least one descriptor. Referents are always characterized by an objective identifier, but they also can have subjective identifiers. Let r be a referent, $\{d_1, d_2, ..., d_n\}$ a set of descriptors each of them independently describing r. There must be at least one d_i that uniquely describe r. For instance, the address of this referent is such a descriptor. Generally, the other descriptors (other than d_i) are added because they are more convenient for users, even if they do not uniquely describe r. Descriptors are not necessarily included explicitly in the content (text or graphics) of a referent. A referent can be any part of the documentation including the table of contents and the index. Tables of contents or indexes are usually found more convenient because of their well known structure (hierarchical and alphabetical).

Information retrieval is the process of retrieving referents from available descriptors in a given context (d->r). Information retrieval is a process of *abduction* using indexing knowledge, i.e., knowing r->d and d, r becomes a valid hypothesis. We say that indexing defines a set of semantic relations that are used in information retrieval. Figure 23.1 shows an example of semantic relations between referents via descriptors.

In a conventional book, the table of contents is a list of descriptors that have a one-to-one mapping into a corresponding list of referents. As a matter of fact, the table of contents is directly a list of referents. These descriptors/referents are presented hierarchically to help the user browse the book. By observing the fact that people like to use this hierarchical feature, one of the basic assumptions in CID is that its referent space is hierarchically structured. In other words, we deliberately take the metaphor of conventional books for the design of electronic documentation, i.e., books are structured hierarchically as shown in figure 23.2. In CID,

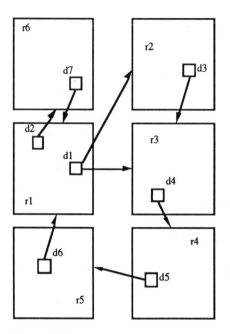

Figure 23.1

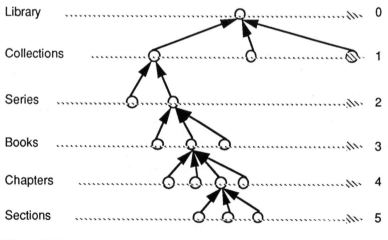

Figure 23.2

such a hierarchical structure is kept as the backbone of the documentation. However, transverse links can be built. In a conventional book, you also get a list of descriptors, called an index, that is presented alphabetically. We preserve this metaphor in CID, i.e., each referent has its own index entry.

Hypertext and Knowledge

Whenever people want to express their knowledge, they write it or draw it on the available media. When paper became available, people learned how to use it to express their own knowledge to transmit it to others, e.g., letters, reports, books. They learned how to organize their ideas to transcribe them onto paper. They generally used hierarchies for structuring. At the other end, readers learned to understand what writers wrote. Readers wanted to extract knowledge from text. Text analysis methods have been developed to accomplish this goal.

In the early 1960s, Theodor Nelson coined the word "hypertext." Hypertext offers a new dimension in writing and reading. It allows the user to easily branch to pieces of text that are not directly in a hierarchy. Until recently, hypertext was reserved to a small group of people. In 1987, Apple Computer, Inc. started to commercialize HyperCard™.

Separating the knowledge-base indexing and information retrieval mechanism from the actual hypertext provides modularity in CID, i.e., both can be edited and maintained separately. However, this is not the only important consideration in this issue. Generally, indexing and information retrieval knowledge is not explicit and constitutes human expertise. If the goal is to help a user browse and retrieve appropriate information, such knowledge should be made explicit and implemented in an intelligent assistant system, as described in Boy, 1991a, built on top of the hypertext. It is indeed the *hypertext metalevel.* A major advantage of this architecture is that this metalevel is easily programmable and allows the inclusion of knowledge on the links of the hypertext.

The block representation has been developed to represent procedures in flight and robotics operations (Boy & Caminel, 1989). Furthermore, we have shown (Boy, 1990) that the block representation maps well into the hypertext representation. In particular, knowledge blocks adapt well for representing procedures used in document browsing. They are used to represent links between descriptors and referents. A knowledge block contains goals, a set of conditions, and a set of actions to achieve the goals. Conditions are decomposed into triggering conditions, abnormal conditions, and contextual conditions. In CID, triggering conditions are represented by descriptors that the user selects. Contextual conditions may describe the external environment, e.g., type of user, type of task when consulting the documentation, time period, etc., or internal history of the current documentation use, e.g., the last visited referents, the last selected descriptors, etc. Actions are represented by referents where the user wants to go. A goal is reached when the user selects the success postcondition corresponding to the chosen referent. Conversely, an abnormal condition corresponds to a failure postcondition.

Users browsing and formulating their descriptions of the referents content contribute to the augmentation of the knowledge base by acknowledging success (or failure) postconditions after a successful (or unsuccessful) search. The more the block base grows, the more it becomes an ontology of the knowledge included in the documentation as perceived by users. The CID can then be considered as a knowledge acquisition tool for users to build their own ontology of the documentation. This overall process has been called: *index management and maintenance*.

The Block Representation as a Navigation Aid

In the documentation domain, blocks are used to represent *contextual links* between descriptors and referents. This aspect has been developed in Boy, 1991c. In this view, documentation can be represented by two entities: referents and contextual links. As each referent r is described by a set of descriptors $D(r)$, a contextual link between two referents r_1 and r_2 implicitly assume that r_1 and r_2 share at least one common descriptor.

In CID, referents are represented by a database (text or graphics), and contextual links are represented by a knowledge base (contextual links) as shown in figure 23.3. Each descriptor represents a *semantic direction* linking a set of referents. For instance, let us assume that the referent r1 has two semantic directions (descriptors d_1 and d_2) corresponding to the following contextual links:

$$\{d_1; (r_2 \mid C_{12}), (r_3 \mid C_{13})\} \text{ and}$$
$$\{d_2; (r_4 \mid C_{14}), (r_5 \mid C_{15})\}$$

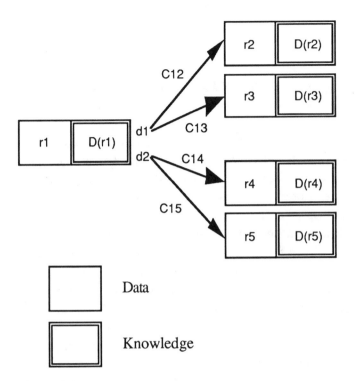

Data

Knowledge

Figure 23.3

where $\{d_1; (r_2 \mid C_{12}), (r_3 \mid C_{13})\}$ must be read: the contextual link between the descriptor d_1 and the referent r_2, in the context C_{12}, and the referent r_3, in the context C_{13}.

If the current context is properly identified and the system knowledge is stabilized (i.e., sufficient contextual links have been built), then contextual links help the user to decide the current most appropriate action to take. For instance, if the user is facing the referent r1, then the system proposes two possible semantic directions d_1 and d_2, if the user selects d_1 the system proposes to go to r_2 or r_3 according to the current context. In this sense, a referent and its associated knowledge base could be called an *active document*, i.e., a *documentation agent* capable of helping the user for his next move. The first major issue in this approach is the acquisition of general contextual conditions. A second important issue is to help the user quickly finding his way in the documentation.

Indexing Hypertext Documents in Context

Introduction
Retrieving specific information from large amounts of documentation is not an easy task. It can be facilitated if information relevant in the current problem solving context can be supplied automatically to the user, in understandable terms and in a flexible manner (e.g., allowing the user to ask questions). This is a long-term goal of Computer Integrated Documentation (CID). As a first step towards this goal, we are developing an intelligent hypertext interface to help users browse through large documents in search of specific information.

A typical screen of CID windows is shown in figure 23.4. It includes a control panel that allows the user to control the entire library. Among its various capabilities, it also converts flat text documents into hypertext, indexes them, and records users' traces in the documentation. Both text and graphics capabilities are available within CID.

This section provides an approach for information access based on the actual use of the hypertext system itself. First, it presents a new approach to incremental context acquisition in information retrieval that modifies existing relations between descriptors and referents by using on-line user feedback to either reinforce or correct the system's knowledge in case of success or failure. This feature allows the system to tailor itself to the user. Second, CID includes a mechanism that allows presentation of referents that are most likely to be useful, thus providing focus for the search in a hypertext database. (The user can, however, access all the descriptors and referents at any time). This model consequently improves the performance of the system.

The Problem
From analyses we have conducted during the design (and redesign) of CID, and from the current users' feedback, the following issues have been identified. When looking for specific information, people usually employ both the table of contents (hierarchical browsing) and the index of the available documents to guide their search. Even then, however, the search is not very focused, and it is common for users to examine several places in the documentation before finding the information needed. For example, when the index is used and a descriptor is looked at for the first

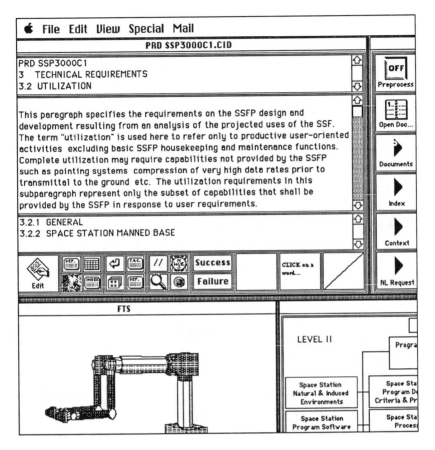

Figure 23.4

time, the first page indicated is usually chosen. If the corresponding information turns out to be relevant for the user's purposes, the user is satisfied, and the retrieval process is finished. If, on the other hand, the corresponding information is not relevant, the user will normally go back to the index and try the second page proposed, and so on. This leads to a sequential trial-and-error decision process, which can be tedious and slow. To avoid repeating this lengthy process each time, people tend to build context around the descriptors already used. For instance, they tend to remember that a particular referent was successful in a specific situation. This memory however does not generally last very long unless the same context occurs often.

CID has been designed to assist in this process by attempting to immediately provide the user with the information that is likely to be relevant to him/her *in context*. This chapter presents an approach *to indexing in context*, in which indices are particular procedures that are modified incrementally *by experimentation*, remembering what the user found useful in a specific context. Using this approach, CID provides tailored guidance to users browsing a document, by watching the users perform their browsing tasks. As Chen and Dhar (1987) mention, to make large information banks more accessible by computer, it is best first to try and understand how reference librarians actually help users, and then to try to include these capabilities in on-line systems. The major problem in incorporating a model of user-librarian interactions into the system is the difficulty of acquiring the information for this model. CID's on-line knowledge acquisition approach allows semi-automatic acquisition of a librarian model.

Organization of Technical Documentations   In existing technical documentations, such as those common at NASA, information is structured hierarchically. Designing a complex system like the Space Station Freedom is an iterative process. Its documentation system is designed to handle a huge amount of information. It is organized around the Program Requirement Document (PRD), which establishes the highest level requirements associated with the Space Station Program. Generally, the other documents expand upon the topics expressed in the PRD. Each document includes the following major nodes: a description of the document, a preface, a table of contents, a body of text segmented into sections and subsections, an abbreviations table, a definitions table, and appendices. Each major node may contain a hierarchy of nodes. For instance, in the body of text, there is a hierarchy of sections. There are links between sections which are linear (section to next section) and nonlinear (reference to a section other than the next one). There are references to other major nodes within a document and sometimes to other documents. In the current implementation, a referent is typically the name of a HyperCard card in a given stack. In this chapter, a referent will also represent its content. In a regular book, the table of contents provides a list of descriptors (section titles). In this case, each descriptor corresponds to only one referent (a page number). The index also provides a list of descriptors, each of which usually has several referents, i.e., a sequence of page numbers. As a result, the user may need to look at several referents before finding the information needed.

Browsing through Large Texts   It takes years of training to be a flight controller in the Space Shuttle Mission Control Center. As part of this training, people learn to use a large corpus of documentation to solve problems. They acquire a deep knowledge of the organization of these manuals in order to access the proper sections as quickly as possible. Currently the operational documentation used by flight controllers is paper-based. In the short term, the goal of CID is to help people access documentation on a computer more efficiently. One thing CID attempts to do is to help narrow the search through documents while allowing the full browsing freedom to which people are accustomed.

People typically use descriptors to retrieve information. As they start looking for information, they normally employ the *explicit* descriptors provided in the documents, e.g., table of contents or index. Unfortunately the descriptors provided are *context-free*, and, generally each descriptor can describe many referents, the problem of decidability introduces a major problem of backtracking that the user may not accept, especially when dealing with real-time operations. As a result, people usually build implicit descriptors as they browse through documents, that is they build a cognitive representation of the documentation that provides relations between pieces of information and their approximate locations in the documentation. They remember that this particular piece of information was (or was not) very interesting in a special context. These cognitive maps are later used to guide their browsing task. They are thus situation- and user-dependent.

Hypertext provides good support for browsing in documentation and for naturally building associative links between descriptors and referents. To automatically help the user, the problem thus becomes to "contextify" the links between documentation nodes, that is to provide relations between descriptors and referents that are valid in a given context. These relations will vary depending on the situation and the user. In the current work, context has been limited to user profile. Providing a context for the referents reduces the number of possible referents for a descriptor that a user has to look at and thus narrows the search. In this chapter, we present a technique to acquire context for these relations automatically. We define the context acquisition problem as discovery of "abnormal conditions" and generation of recovery actions, as well as reinforcement of current actions. Our system observes the user's actions during the browsing tasks, and, by noting whether a specific referent was considered a success or failure by the user in a particular context, it is able to refine the indices to reflect their context of use. In this way, our system automatically acquires the knowledge necessary to operationalize a user model: which indices are appropriate when, and for which user. This is a significant departure from current work in user modeling, where systems are able to obtain and refine user models (Kass, 1987; Kobsa, 1989). The way these models are exploited is *hardcoded* in the systems and thus inflexible (Paris, 1987). We are currently working on an extension of context that allows inclusion of immediate past user actions.

An Adaptive Documentation Browsing System

A browsing facility has been developed to help users search for specific information in the available documentation. CID, like the printed documentation, includes a table of contents and an index. When the user selects a descriptor, a menu of ordered actions pops up. Selecting an action may lead to the display of referents presented in sequence or in parallel. In this paper, an action will be associated with a single referent. These referents have been found successfully in the *same context* in past retrievals. The user specifies success or failure with a single mouse click. The order of referents is based on the past success rate of each referent in this context. These menus can be very different among users and in various contexts.

CID has two major components: a hypertext system and a knowledge-based system. One of the major goals of this project is to keep documentation independent from the knowledge of how to use it. This latter knowledge is represented in the system in the form of *contextual links* (or blocks) containing preconditions (*triggering conditions* and *contextual conditions*) and a list of referents together with an indication of how often each referent was successful (a *reinforcement slot*), and a description of the situations in which the referent was *not* successful (called an *abnormal condition).* The reinforcement slot and the abnormal condition can be seen as an indication of whether or not the user's *goal* for finding specific information was achieved. An example of a contextual link is shown in figure 23.5.

Typically, in CID, a triggering condition is characterized by a descriptor. The selection of a descriptor by the user thus triggers a list of actions to be considered. When there are several descriptors in a contextual link, these descriptors are aliases or synonyms. The contextual conditions then indicate under which conditions the actions presented to the user are actually appropriate. Contextual conditions characterize the environment in which the retrieval has been made successfully. For instance, let us assume that one wants to retrieve some very specific information on the air conditioning in the main cabin of the Space Station. The first thing one may try is to browse the documentation with the descriptor "air conditioning." If the retrieval context can be specified, e.g., "you are a designer, you are interested in the connection of the air conditioning system, and you have very little information about the electrical circuitry in the cabin," then a more efficient search can be accomplished. The search will not be the same under another context, e.g., "you are an astronaut, you are in the Space Station, and you are freezing." Importantly, in our system, contextual conditions for a particular contextual link are learned *through experimentation.* Contextual conditions allow clustering of contextual links, and, when the system is operational, pruning of inappropriate contextual links.

```
(TRIGG. COND.      (Descriptor-1))
(CONTEXT           (C1 C2 C3))
(ACTIONS           (R1 +5 ((AC1 1) (AC2 3)))
                   (R2 +3)
                                   (R3 +2)
                                   (R4 +1))
```

Figure 23.5
Example of a contextual link. Descriptor-1 is valid if the context conditions (C1, C2, C3) are satisfied. The referent R1 has a *reinforcement slot* of +5, indicating that it has been successful 5 times and has been not found useful in two abnormal conditions AC1 — with its reinforcement slot of 1 — and AC2 — with its reinforcement slot of 3. The referent R4 has been successful once.

The current context is set up at the beginning of the session. It can be a default profile attached to the user name and automatically set by the system after login. It can be changed at any time by the user, or modified by the system following changes of sensor values if the documentation system is connected to a real-time system (e.g., in the case of documentation used in process control). In a given context, the user generally selects a descriptor to get a list of potential referents. When the user selects a referent R from this list, the system automatically activates the link between the selected descriptor and the referent R. This activation leads to the presentation of the referent R.

CID has two modes of operation, which correspond to the two modes of activity in documentation use: (a) *experimental browsing*: a casual approach, often seen in activities such as exploratory learning, in which the computer can take an active role by suggesting interesting information to be examined; (b) *intentional search*: a deliberate search for information to fill a particular need, e.g., to prepare a report or answer a specific question. Experimental browsing allows augmentation of the initial set of links between descriptors and referents. Initial links can be built automatically assuming that descriptors are explicitly included in referents. Our system scans the hypertext database and extracts each descriptor together with a list of referents that corresponds to all the locations where this descriptor has been found. The corresponding contextual links generated this way are context-free. However, this automatic approach is generally not sufficient because some referents can be implicitly described by a descriptor included in the text. In this case, human intervention is necessary, i.e., the user can describe referents during experimental search. Intentional search is used to refine existing contextual links of knowledge, by acquiring more contextual conditions or refining the existing ones. In the next section, we focus on this mode.

Acquiring Indices by Experimentation

We will use the above example, with the descriptor Descriptor-1 (triggering precondition) "air conditioning" and the current context (C1, C2, C3) "you are a designer, you are interested in the connection of the air conditioning system, and you have very little information about the electrical circuitry in the cabin." A contextual link is first triggered by the descriptor. As there are four possible referents in the documentation, the four referents, (R1, R2, R3, R4), are presented: "a list of the vendors of air conditioning systems," "a description of the air conditioning system," "a checklist of what to do when the air conditioning fails," and "a diagram of the electrical circuitry in the main cabin of the Space Station." The first one is not satisfactory in the current context: it is a failure. This is indicated by a keystroke from the user. The second and the third are also failures. Failure cases will be presented in the third paragraph of this section. Fortunately, the fourth one will give the information that is needed: it is a success. The system thus learns that R4 is successful in this context. If this is repeated frequently, R4 will be presented automatically from Descriptor-1 and the contextual conditions (C1, C2, C3).

To observe the user, inputs to CID include user judgments on the success of actual retrievals. After a referent has been found, the user can select either "success" or "failure." The system automatically records this selection by adding +1 or −1 to the reinforcement slot attached to the original contextual link referent inferred by the descriptor used.

Suppose now that, using the same contextual link, a particular situation is observed in which the user indicates R1 as a failure. It would now be inappropriate to repeat this experience again and again. Instead, CID notes that an *abnormal condition* has been encountered, and this knowledge is added to the contextual link. Like actions, reinforcement values are also associated with abnormal conditions. Abnormal conditions can be seen as exceptions to the "normal" use of the contextual link. When a failure occurs, the system attempts to obtain from the user the reason for this failure. A list of previously acquired abnormal conditions is automatically presented to the user when he/she indicates his/her willingness to provide an explanation. The user may select one of the explanations provided or generate a new one. The selection is then processed automatically and kept in the corresponding contextual link as an abnormal condition. If the user also provides a solution for recovery, this solution is recorded and used for implementing a recovery contextual link. A new contextual link is created and implicitly attached to the original one through the abnormal condition.

If the abnormal condition is observed many times, its negation will automatically be added into the appropriate context for the contextual link, as the situation which used to be considered "abnormal" can be considered as "normal." A rote learning algorithm used to augment the system's knowledge has been presented elsewhere (Boy, 1990) and will not be repeated here.

Sample Session

The user double clicks on the CID application. A window called "CID Control Panel" appears on the screen, and a control box pops up asking the user to identifies himself or herself. Here, I gave my name. The system acknowledged it by providing my default profile considered as the current context (figure 23.6). The CID Control Panel includes a "Preprocess" button that allows preprocessing any text file that could be edited on a variety of text processors. Preprocessed files can be converted into CID stacks using the "Convert" button. "Open Doc..." and "Close Doc..." allow one to open and close any CID document. "Overview" and "Network" permit displaying global or zoomed graphical representations of any CID document. By selecting "Indexer," the user gets a new window allowing extraction of descriptors of any CID document. If "Navigator" is selected, then a small tool window appears. It can be used

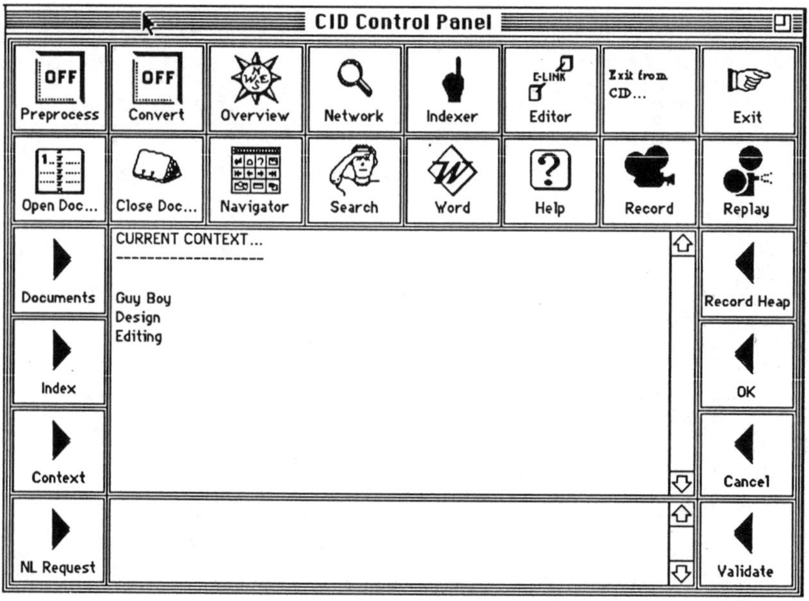

Figure 23.6

to browse more efficiently in the CID documentation. The "Record" and "Replay" buttons are used to record sequences of user's actions on CID, and eventually analyze and replay them. On-line "Help" is available at any time.

When the user selects the "Open Doc..." button, CID asks for a file name and a new window appears on the screen showing the open CID document for example (figure 23.4). Each generic CID card includes a set of buttons for editing, displaying abbreviations, figures, definitions, the table of contents of the document, the overview and the network, user's satisfaction (success) or dissatisfaction (failure), displaying descriptors and related referents.

If the user selects the "Index", then a list of descriptors appears (figure 23.7). He or she may select one of them, e.g., the first one in the list "Assembly Complete." If the button "E.B." (experimental browsing) is selected, then the system will search all the contextual links including the selected descriptor. If the button "I.S." (intentional search) is selected, then, if the button "P." (possible context attributes) is selected, the system will search all the contextual links including the selected descriptor that

```
┌─────────────────────── PRD SSP3000C1.CID ───────────────────────┐
│  A  B  C  D  E  F  G  H  I  J  K  L  M    1st  +                  │
│  N  O  P  Q  R  S  T  U  V  W  X  Y  Z                            │
│ ┌──────────────────────────────────────────────────────────┐ ▲  │
│ │ AC,Assembly Complete                                      │ ▢  │
│ │ AIS,Automated Information Security                        │    │
│ │ A&R,Automation and Robotics                              │    │
│ │ ATAC,Advanced Technology Advisory Committee              │    │
│ │ APM,Attached Pressurized Module                          │    │
│ │ C&T,Communication and Tracking                           │    │
│ │ CCSDS,Consultive Committee for Space Data Systems        │    │
│ │ CDR,Critical Design Review                               │    │
│ │ DMS,Distributed Management System                        │    │
│ │ ECLSS,Environmental Control and Life Support System     │ ▼  │
│ ├──────────────────────────────────────────────────────────┤ ▲  │
│ │ There are 2 referents linked to this descriptor. You may select one... │
│ │ 1.3 PROGRAM SUMMARY                                      │    │
│ │ 3.1.1 MISSION                                            │ ▼  │
│ │ Edit   I.S. P.    E.B. N.                                │    │
└──────────────────────────────────────────────────────────────────┘
```

Figure 23.7

share at least one attribute of the current context, i.e., "Guy Boy, Design, Editing." If the button "N." (necessary context attributes) is selected, then the system will search all the contextual links including the selected descriptor that share all the attributes of the current context. The corresponding referent titles are displayed, and the user may select one of them. The user can retrieve a descriptor using the alphabetical search buttons, or scroll the list. He or she can edit new descriptors.

If the user selects "1.3 PROGRAM SUMMARY," then the system will display a new window of that referent, showing the first occurrence of "Assembly Complete" in the text field (figure 23.8). The user may then click on "Success" to acknowledge his/her satisfaction. In this case, the system will reinforce the contextual link between "Assembly Complete" and "1.3 PROGRAM SUMMARY" in the current context "Guy Boy, Design, Editing." If the user clicks on "Failure," the system provides a list of possible explanations of failure. The user may select one of them or create a new one. Then, the system adds this abnormal condition to the contextual link.

The current context may be changed at any time by the user or by any means, e.g., output of a sensor monitoring and diagnosis system. The

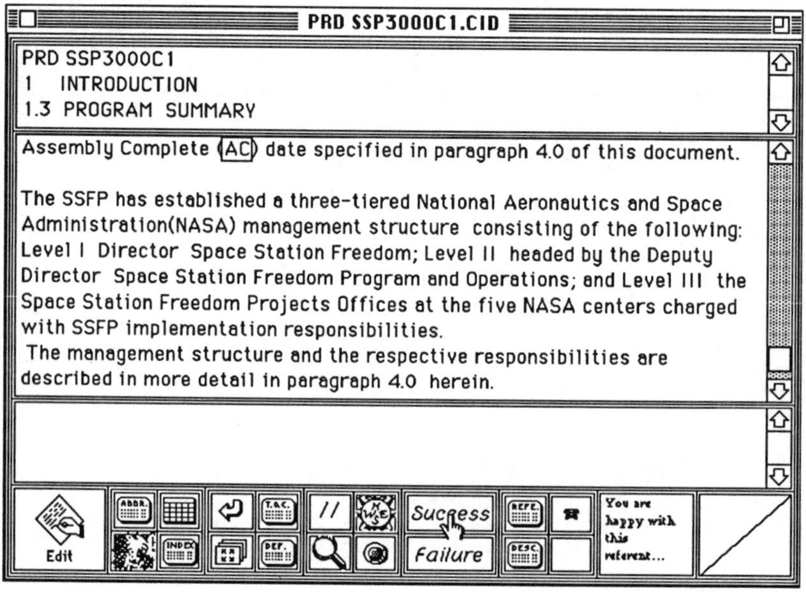

Figure 23.8

overview and network of a CID document increase graphical navigation capabilities (figure 23.9).

Lessons Learned and Relation to Other Work

Use of CID
We have analyzed (Boy, 1991c) various uses of documentation systems available at NASA including Space Station Freedom (SSF) program requirements documents, and Space Shuttle operations procedures manuals. The former type of documentation has been called design documentation, and the latter operational documentation.

Design documentation is generally handled using keyword search. People find this very difficult in practice because keywords are used in a

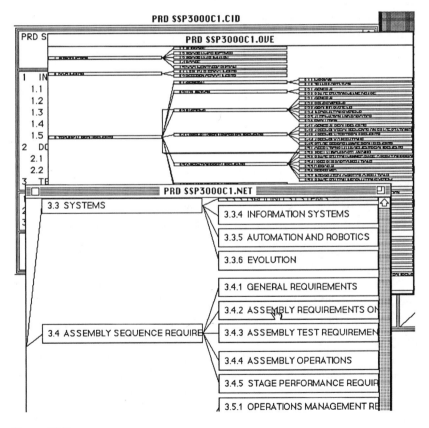

Figure 23.9

full-text search mode. Consequently, people using such systems come up with either hundreds of references or nothing, according to the recall/precision criterion (Salton, 1989). We have found that CID's approach introducing the experimental browsing mode, allows the user to index referents with concepts that are not necessarily words or term-phrases included in the text. Another aspect is that current systems used at NASA have poor navigation capabilities (often none at all). People tend to construct their own cognitive maps of the documentation even if nothing is provided to make explicit the documentation topography. We have found that explicit maps of the documentation are very useful. These maps can be local ("where to go next?"), or global ("where am I?"). They can also present either the hierarchical structure of the documentation (local or global tables of contents), or the conceptual relationships between referents via descriptors (local or global conceptual indexes).

Operational documentation systems (usually paper-based) are generally handled using tables of contents. Furthermore, expert users tend to develop robust search strategies based on experience and context. We have observed that, unlike the design documentation users, operational documentation users have very integrated cognitive representations of the documentation they use, i.e., they know its hierarchical structure and an extensive set of conceptual links. The reason is that operations people, in a Mission Control room for instance, are highly trained to solve problems using operational manuals. Furthermore, they update such documentation from their own experience (not only its indexing but also its content). CID will facilitate this painful and expensive process.

Initial results indicates that CID is very useful both for indexing documents in context, and for improving the revision process of the documentation itself. Context-sensitive information retrieval gives extended possibilities such as providing search expertise from other users, e.g., "what would John Smith do in this situation?" We are currently testing CID with SSF and Space Shuttle specialists in order to get more information on the level of acceptance of CID learning capabilities and behaviors by both design and operations people. First results have shown that, not surprisingly, the expansion of the contextual link base has to be controlled carefully. Currently, this expansion is controlled by a threshold on transformed reinforcement coefficients that are computed from the cumulative number of feedbacks (successes and failures) and the cumulative time between user's feedbacks. We have introduced a coefficient of seriousness that overrides the transformed reinforcement coefficient in the case of critical links, especially when the time between feedbacks is large.

The first version of CID is implemented on a Macintosh II Cx in Allegro Common LISP, HyperTalk and C. The current version uses HyperCard (version 2.0) and several external functions in C. HyperCard is a good prototyping tool that is easily disseminated at NASA because of its widespread availability. This allows CID to be tested on a very large scale. Although we do not have quantitative results yet, our experience with CID to-date is very encouraging. The Space Station Freedom documentation application currently contains approximately 160 descriptors linked to the documentation. It includes IARC (Index Acquisition and Refinement according to Context), a system that implements the context acquisition technique described above.

Relation to Other Work

Semantic indexing has been investigated by several authors. Dumais et al. (1988) propose a method for organizing nodes into a semantic structure on the basis of the overlap of the descriptors used in the referents. Stotts and Furuta (1988) proposed a model of hypertext based on Petri nets. Their system enforces browsing restrictions, for instance, deactivates some links. Like CID, a medical handbook system described by Frisse and Cousins (1989) separates the "index space" from the "document space." They have shown how some index architectures can be exploited for enhanced information retrieval, query refinement, and automated reasoning. Their index space model is based on inference using belief networks of descriptors. The I³R system (Croft & Turtle, 1989) uses a Bayesian inference network to acquire information about user's needs and domain knowledge. Crouch, Crouch, & Andreas 1989 have used cluster hierarchies to help navigate in hypertext structure. All these contributions to information retrieval developed methods for refining links between descriptors and referents. However, the concept of context has not been presented explicitly in any of them.

Weyer (1988) advocates the fact that information should be adaptable to the learner's preferences, and links should depend on the user's previous actions and current goals. This point of view supports our knowledge-based approach to hypertext. Other approaches have been developed to acquire and refine links on-line. For instance, Kibby and Mayes (1989), in their StrathTutor hypertext system try to eliminate the need for exclusively manual methods for creating links between hypertext nodes by generating links based on knowledge acquired when the user browses through the system. Also, Monk presents a method for constructing a personal browser (Monk, 1987). In this approach, the system monitors the user's navigation behavior and interrupts the user to ask whether it should add a node to the browser when it has been accessed frequently.

CID uses the concepts of context and abnormal conditions to learn from users. The work done on exceptions by Winston (1983) and Williamson (1986) is similar to our use of abnormal conditions. We have extended this approach with the use of dynamic reinforcement, and have incorporated these theoretical considerations in an actual implementation.

Finally, this work is a departure from current work on user modeling research, in which user models (possibly acquired automatically) are exploited by the system in predefined ways. As a result, these systems cannot update their user models based on experience. In contrast, our system can perform this updating automatically. In other words, our systems learns to *operationalize* user models automatically, based on experience.

Conclusions and Future Research

Current results have shown that hypertext is a good programming tool for the development of such systems. While hypertext systems increase accessibility, they do not provide any built-in selectivity mechanism. In other words, while non-linear or hypertext systems may dramatically increase the accessibility of information, this increased accessibility may magnify an already severe problem of selection (Jones, 1987). For these reasons, our knowledge-based system technology can be very helpful in alleviating the selection problem and cognitive overhead of the user. Our approach to retrieval is unique because the design of contextual links to retrieve information is based not only on the way the documentation has been built, but also on user's information requirements and suggestions when they are operating systems. Thus, the user continually augments and refines the intelligence of the retrieval system.

Besides providing an intelligent interface for browsing large documents, the ability of our system to automatically acquire the context in which strategies are appropriate is significant. First, it allows the system to provide a *tailorable* browsing facility. Indeed, the system will learn which referents are to be presented for which user. Second, it shows that it is feasible to immediately incorporate the user's feedback into the system's knowledge, with the possibility of improving the system's performance. In this way, there is no need to collect and analyze large amounts of information about how users interact with the system because the system performs this task itself. Third, with CID we are explicitly specifying a *systematic domain* (Winograd and Flores, 1987), i.e., development and use of technical documentation. To paraphrase Winograd and Flores, the impact of CID comes not because the programs it includes are "smart" but because it allows people to operate effectively in a systematic domain that is relevant to human work.

This work could be extended easily to university documentation. Indeed, science, humanities, and engineering students for instance use documents extensively to support their education and training. This documentation is usually available in libraries. As computers become increasingly available in universities, electronic documentation will also be used. Students could increase their knowledge more easily by contextualizing their search strategies in the documentation. Furthermore, contextual knowledge can be built over the years and serve new students as a good librarian would do. Finally, maintenance of such bodies of knowledge would increase understanding of the main topics of concern to students when they use university documentation.

In conclusion, our system automatically learns how to exploit available user models and descriptions of context. This provides more flexibility than is possible in other systems, and allows our system to adapt itself to the user. Of course, many issues remain to be addressed. First, formalization of the contextual conditions is still problematic. On one hand, the contextual conditions should be minimal to avoid excessive calculations. On the other hand, they must include as much information as possible to characterize the current situation. Second, we are still trying to define by experimentation the "ideal" threshold on abnormal condition reinforcement coefficients (Boy, 1990), for deciding when to create a new contextual link, delete an "unused" one, include an action in a contextual link, or generalize two similar contextual links. To solve both problems, future work here will include the development of a context clustering mechanism.

Acknowledgments

I would like to thank Cécile Paris, Nathalie Mathé, and Catherine Baudin for very pertinent comments on the block representation that support the contextual links. Philippa Gander, Monte Zweben, and Peter Friedland also provided astute advice towards improving the quality of this paper. I am grateful to Bharathi Raghavan, Fabian Garcia Pastor, and Joshua Rabinowitz for their contributions to the CID system.

References

Boy, G.A. & Caminel, T. (1989). Situation Pattern Acquisition Improves the Control of Complex Dynamic Systems. *Third European Workshop on Knowledge Acquisition for Knowledge-Based Systems*, Paris, July.

Boy, G.A. (1990). Acquiring and refining indices according to context. In *Proceedings of the Fifth AAAI-Sponsored Knowledge Acquisition for Knowledge-Based Systems Workshop*. Banff, Canada, November.

Boy, G.A. (1991a). *Intelligent Assistant Systems*. Academic Press, London.

Boy, G.A. (1991b). Indexing Hypertext Documents in Context, *Proceedings of Hypertext'91*. San Antonio, Texas, December.

Boy, G.A. (1991c). Computer Integrated Documentation. Technical Memorandum, NASA Ames Research Center, Moffett Field, CA, to be published.

Chen, H. and Dhar, V. (1987). Reducing indeterminism in consultation: A cognitive model of user/librarian interactions. In *Proceedings of the Sixth National Conference on Artificial Intelligence*, Seattle, Washington, July.

Conklin, J. (1987). Hypertext: An Introduction and Survey. *Computer*, September.

Croft, W.B. and Turtle, H. (1989). A Retrieval Model for Incorporating Hypertext Links. *Hypertext'89 Proceedings*, pp. 213-224, ACM press, New York.

Crouch, D.B., Crouch, C.J. & Andreas, G. (1989). The Use of Cluster Hierarchies in Hypertext Information Retrieval. *Hypertext'89 Proceedings*, pp. 225-237, ACM press, New York.

Dumais, S.T., Furnas, G.W., Landauer, T.K., Deerwester, S. and Harshman, R. (1988). Using Latent Semantic Indexing to Improve Access to Textual Information. *Proceedings of the ACM CHI'88*, pp. 281-285, Washington D.C., May 15-

19.
Frisse, M.E. and Cousins, S.E. (1989). Information Retrieval from Hypertext: Update on the Dynamic Medical Handbook Project. *Hypertext'89 Proceedings*, pp. 199-212, ACM press, New York.

Jones, W.P. (1987). How do we distinguish the hyper from the hype in non-linear text ? In *Human-Computer Interaction - INTERACT'87*, Holland. Elsevier Science Publisher.

Kass, R. and Finin, T. (1987). Rules for the implicit acquisition of knowledge about the user. In *Proceedings of the Sixth National Conference on Artificial Intelligence*, pp. 295-300, Seattle, Washington, July.

Kibby, M.R. & Mayes, J.T. (1989). Towards Intelligent Hypertext. In McAleese, R. (Ed.) *Hypertext Theory into Practice*, Albex, pp. 164-172.

Kobsa, A. (1989). A taxonomy of beliefs and goals for user models in dialog systems. In Alfred Kobsa and Wolfgang Wahlster, editors, *User Models in Dialog Systems*. Springer Verlag, Symbolic Computation Series, Berlin Heidelberg New York Tokyo.

Monk, A. (1989). The personal browser: A tool for directed navigation in hypertext systems. *Interacting with Computers*, 1, 2, pp. 190-196.

Paris, C.L. (1987). The Use of Explicit User Models in Text Generation: Tailoring to a User's Level of Expertise. PhD thesis, Columbia University Department of Computer Science, 1987. To be published in the "Communication in Artificial Intelligence" series, Steiner and Fawcett (eds), Frances Pinter, 1991.

Salton, G. (1989). *Automatic Text Processing: the transformation analysis, and retrieval of information by computers*. Addison Wesley, Redding, Ma.

Stotts, P.D. and Furuta, R. (1988). Adding Browsing Semantics to the Hypertext Model. *Proceedings of the ACM Conference on Document Processing Systems*, pp. 43-50, Santa Fe, NM, December 5-9.

Weyer, S.A. (1988). As we May Learn. In Aubron, S. & Hooper, K. *Interactive Multimedia: Visions of Multimedia for Developers, Educators, & Information Providers*. pp. 87-103, Microsoft Press.

Williamson, K.E. (1986). Learning from exceptions in databases. In T.M. Mitchell, J.G. Carbonell, and R.S. Michalski, editors, *Machine Learning: A Guide to Current Research*. Kluwer Academic Publishers.

Winograd, T. and Flores, F. (1987). *Understanding Computer and Cognition*. Addison Wesley, Reading, MA.

Winston, P.H. (1983). Learning by augmenting rules and accumulating sensors. In *Proceedings of the International Machine Learning Workshop*, pp. 22-24, Monticello, Illinois, June.

Yankelovich, N., Smith, K.E., Garrett, L.N. and Meyrowitz, N. (1988). Issues in Designing a Hypermedia Document System. In Aubron, S. & Hooper, K. *Interactive Multimedia: Visions of Multimedia for Developers, Educators, & Information Providers*. pp. 33-85, Microsoft Press.

Zimmerman, M. (1988). TEX version 0.5. Technical report, Silver Spring, MD.

24

The Worcester State College "Elder Connection": Using Multimedia and Information Technology to Promote Intergenerational Education

Virginia Z. Ogozalek, Maureen E. Power, Mary Ann Hebhardt, Donald F. Bullens, and Judith A. Perrolle

Introduction

In 1984, Delphis Bibeau took his first computer class and wrote a BASIC program—"How to Shoot Craps"—that may well have driven Las Vegas into bankruptcy, had Del's proposed field trip ever taken place. Since then, he's mastered SPSS, a graphics cartography package, and is now learning to write Lotus 1-2-3 macros. All in all, a typical computer student—except that Delphis Bibeau is 76 years old.

Students like Delphis are not uncommon at Worcester State College. Given the law of the Commonwealth that allows persons aged 60 and over to attend college tuition-free, Worcester State has promoted a vital intergenerational educational environment in which older and younger students learn together in the classroom, discuss politics in the hallways, and socialize over lunch.

Many of these elders take computer courses, learning programming, word processing, and other software applications alongside traditional college-aged students who cannot remember a time before computers. In a society where computers are a cultural icon of the youth generation, the classroom dynamic of young and old students meeting technology together is unique and exciting.

This chapter will describe the role of information technology in facilitating the intergenerational education process at Worcester State. The first section will provide a general overview of research involving information technology, multimedia, and the elderly. The second section will explain the concept of "intergenerational education" and describe the implementation of such a program at Worcester State College. The third and fourth sections will focus on the role of information technology and multimedia in this intergenerational setting, followed by a final discussion of the broader social implications of combining technology with an intergenerational approach to education. We hope that by sharing some of our experiences we will encourage similar experimentation in other academic communities.

Information Technology and the Elderly

The computer revolution is converging with yet another unprecedented trend—the graying of America. The present elderly population of 29 million is expected to grow to over 65 million, or more than 1/5 of the population, by the year 2030 (Office of Technology Assessment, 1985). Since so many Americans are now living the full complement of their years, with some spending as much as a third of their life span in retirement, there is an increasing need to tap the resources of the well, mobile elders, and to expand new options for mature adults. Computer technology can be a remarkable tool for empowering older people not only to bridge the age gap, but also to "retool" in order to pursue meaningful roles in modern day society, whether in the world of work— paid or unpaid—or leisure time activities.

As elders begin to use computers, increasing attention is being paid to the special needs of this age group. Potential computer applications which may enhance elders' lives include telemedicine and computerized health care kiosks (Holmes, Holmes, and Teresi 1988; Greenberger and Puffer 1989; Katzowitz 1989), "smarthouse" technology (LaBuda, 1988), and computerized retirement and estate planning (Bollier 1989). The success of such systems will depend upon their accessibility to elders. Older people tend to have slower reaction times, poorer vision, and are more likely to have other disabilities which may require special computer designs (Perrolle 1987).

Elders' attitudes toward technology were once thought to have a major effect on how they use computers. Early studies of "hands-on" computing by elders focused mainly on playing computer games (Danowski and Sacks 1980; Weisman 1982); however, elders soon began to explore a wider range of computer activities. Kearsley and Furlong (1984) conducted programming workshops for senior citizens, described in their book *Computers for Kids Over 60*. This program later evolved into a nationwide networking program called "SeniorNet" (Furlong 1989; Rice 1988), which allows seniors to access bulletin boards and electronic conferences on topics ranging from the politics of health care to household hints and recipes. Eilers (1989) describes similar computer classes at the Little House Aging Center in Menlo Park, California, where seniors initiated their own programming courses. Currently, elders are involved in a wide range of computer activities, ranging from desktop publishing (Sanner 1986) to electronic mail (Hahm and Bikson 1989) to memory enhancement (Finkel and Yesavage 1989) to computerized decision making (Johnson 1990).[1] Surveys conducted by the AARP (Edwards and Englehardt 1989; Kerschner and Hart 1984), the Aspen Institute (Tingay 1988), and other researchers (Gilly and Zeithmal 1985; Krauss and Hoyer 1983) all suggest that elderly people have generally positive attitudes toward computer technology. Controlled experiments that have been done also indicate that elders are potentially capable computer users (Ansley and Erber 1988; Czaja, Hammond, Blascovich, and Swede 1989; Finkel and Yesavage 1989; Zandri and Charness 1989; Johnson 1990; Ogozalek and VanPraag 1986).

Recent experience in the world of work also provides new evidence that older workers are not only competent computer users, but also that the employment of these older workers can increase productivity and stability while lowering company costs. For example, Days Inn of America, the nation's third largest hotel chain, operates a sophisticated 24-hour telecommunications systems to provide reservations for over one thousand hotels and inns. Younger workers have been difficult to find, and, when hired, their turnover rate is quite high—almost one hundred percent. In 1986, the company began recruiting older workers to work at its two reservations centers in Atlanta and Knoxville. They found that older workers could be trained to operate the sophisticated computer software in the same two week period as younger workers required; in addition, the older workers stayed on the job longer and were more successful at sales (Teltsch 1991; Commonwealth Fund Study of Older Workers 1991).

The combination of computers with other forms of media such as video holds promise for use by the elderly as well. One of the best known experiments is the Berks Community Television Project in Reading, Pennsylvania, which recently celebrated its tenth anniversary. In this project, elders develop their own programming for an interactive television system which allows face-to-face teleconferencing at various sites in the city. Unlike the computer, the television is familiar and friendly to elders, with a number of studies suggesting that television viewing is the most frequently reported daily activity for elderly Americans (Nussbaum, Thompson, and Robinson 1989) at an average level of over five hours of viewing per day (Neilsen Estimates 1975).

A common thread which runs through all of these examples is the elders' hope that by learning to use computers and interactive video, they will bridge the technology gap between older and younger generations. For example, one of the most successful Berks Community Television projects involved interactive television conferences between elders in an age center and students at a nearby high school. In most cases, however, elders are segregated into their own "electronic communities." Computer classes may be held in age centers (Eilers 1989) and computer networks may be open mainly to senior citizens (Furlong 1989) or contain information of particular interest only to elders, such as the Rand Corporation retirement planning project (Hahm and Bikson 1989).

Unlike these programs which are designed specifically for seniors, the computing environment at Worcester State College is intergenerational— a 70-year-old grandmother is likely to find herself pondering a computer problem alongside a 35-year-old businesswoman and an 18-year-old football player. The next section describes this "Elder Connection" program at Worcester State.

Intergenerational Education at Worcester State College

Our growing elder population may be viewed as an asset or liability, as a social problem or a societal resource. This is a policy issue of crucial importance and one that may be impacted by institutions of higher education, both public and private, in Massachusetts and across the country. The elder education program at Worcester State is based on the philosophy that elders have the capacity to transform society and that an intergenerational approach to solving social problems will tap unused resources of young and old alike (Power 1988). The experience at Worcester State supports earlier findings that the graying of the college classroom enhances learning for all age groups, because of heightened levels of discussion, questioning, and, in general, a more interactive learning environment (Kay 1983).

The program began in the fall of 1982 when Dr. Maureen Power and a group of Gerontology Certificate students formed the Elder Connection Club. Many of the students had done fieldwork with elders in the community; since the experience had proven valuable, a proposal was made: Can we get the elders to come to us? Out of that discussion, the idea of Elder Week was born. In the spring of 1983, two hundred elders a day came to the campus to participate in a wide array of workshops, classes, and forums. The following fall semester, 126 elderly students officially enrolled in classes. Since then, the number of elders registered each semester varies from an original high of 126 to 80 to 149 in the Fall 1990 semester. Through the efforts of "Elder Outreach" coordinator Julia Mack, an 83-year-old graduate of the program, collaborative links are being established with the business community. The emphasis, in Julia's words, is to "get to elders before they sit down," with the result being that some older students are registering into the program even before they retire.

The "elder program" at Worcester State is, quite simply, the college. Elders are integrated into the regular programs of the college. They attend classes, campus functions, join clubs, sing in the choir, enter their poetry in the campus newspaper, eat with the students in the cafeteria, hustle for parking spaces. Some are A+ students, while others struggle to pass. In short, they have become part and parcel of campus life. Like the younger students, they too ponder where their new education will lead them. Some who begin to take classes merely for enrichment suddenly find they can "cut it with the kids" and begin exploring new options for themselves. For example, Joann Strandberg, a recent retiree, decided at the end of a class in career planning to move in the direction of becoming computer proficient and setting up a small home business training elders to use personal computer usage.

It is probably not by chance that the college is located in Worcester, Massachusetts, which, according to the 1987 Statistical Abstract of the United States, has the fifth largest proportional elderly population in the United States, with 16.3 percent of its residents aged 65 or older (Zuckerman 1990). As the American population ages, more and more cities will have a similar demographic mix, making Worcester a representative city of the future. If Dychtwald and Flower (1989) are correct in saying that as the population ages, more and more elders will return to school seeking lifelong learning experiences, then the Worcester State College intergenerational mix may be highly typical of the college population of the future.

Information Technology and Elders at Worcester State

Given the desire of many elders to be current and to keep up with their grandchildren, it is not surprising that Computer Science is especially popular with this age group. To date, over 100 elders have taken computer courses at Worcester State. At first there was no explicit agenda to have a program involving seniors and computers; interested elders simply began showing up in computer classes. Most take beginning courses such as introductory programming or word processing and spreadsheeting; a few like Delphis Bibeau move on to advanced courses involving data bases and graphics. Reasons for taking the courses range from developing new skills for the job market to improving communication with computer-literate grandchildren. Goals may be modest; for example, Eva Johnson, using a computer for the first time at age 67, expressed a great sense of accomplishment at being able to word process a letter to a friend. On the other hand, after classes in programming and Lotus 1-2-3, John Powers, aged 81, is writing advanced mathematical procedures to develop a new calendar for the coming millennium.

Intergenerational computing is not without problems; when elders first use computers, they often have problems with the new technology—for example, seeing the screen or using the keyboard. One such student was Selma Gotlieb, aged 73. During her Lotus 1-2-3 class, she would constantly move her head trying to focus on the small screen. When asked to type in the number "145," she used the small "L" key for the number one (remember—old typewriters did not have a number one key). She was constantly asking the younger students sitting beside her for help and they seemed to be annoyed at her interruptions. At one point, she announced to the class that she couldn't see much use for the computer. Two attributes Selma did have, however, were a strong mathematical background—she had been a math teacher—and patience. Within a month, Selma became the unofficial class tutor. Younger students were constantly asking her for help with their projects, both mathematical and technical. Today, she runs her synagogue's "coupon campaign" with the help of her Lotus 1-2-3 package and PC.

This type of learning pattern—a slow start followed by a high level of success after some extra practice—is often displayed by other elder computer students at Worcester State, and has been documented elsewhere as well (Zandri and Charness 1989). Likewise, it is common for younger students to initially express skepticism about an elder class member's ability to use a computer. However, when younger students see older people who are enthusiastic and capable computer users, negative stereotypes are quickly dispelled. A typical reaction is that of Jill, aged 19, who sat next to Rose, aged 69, in a beginning computer course: "I was surprised to see someone my grandmother's age learning to use a computer, but now that the course is over, I can say that I wouldn't have passed the course without her help." Younger students also become aware of age-related differences which may affect the use of computers by the elderly and are more likely to design computer systems with features that may be helpful to the elderly or handicapped. For example, in an upper-level computer course which involved a class project to create a graphics-based advising system, many students came up with design specifications which included larger-than-normal fonts, so that users with visual problems could read the screen easily.

Research Involving Computer Use by the Elderly

This unique educational environment has stimulated research involving computer use by the elderly based on the observation of needs and capabilities of older computer students; all studies have directly depended on the participation of the elder students at Worcester State. The research has involved innovative computer interfaces with the potential to make information technology more accessible to elders, thus giving both older and younger students the opportunity to try new technologies such as speech recognition systems, natural language interfaces, and multimedia computers.

A common problem for elders seemed to be typing; many elders expressed the wish that they could "talk to the computer." This possibility was tested in the first research project, a human factors experiment conducted at Digital's Software Human Engineering Laboratory which compared the performance of older and younger users on keyboard and voice input computer-based composition tasks (Ogozalek and VanPraag 1986). Worcester State students of all ages used a simulated "listening typewriter" to compose letters and gave their opinions as to how speech recognition systems should be designed in the future. Results of the study showed that elderly and younger users were comparable in both their performance and attitudes toward computers, with both groups having a significantly greater preference for speech recognition systems as compared to keyboard input—in other words, users of all ages would rather talk to the computer than type.

With the abolition of mandatory retirement by federal statute in 1987, an increasing number of workers have chosen to remain on the job well past the age of 70 (Levine 1988), and many elder students at Worcester State are now learning computer skills with the goal of improving their marketability in the workforce. In 1989, Professor Mary Ann Hebhardt conducted a study in which elders learned to use Lotus 1-2-3, one of the most popular software packages in the business place. Hebhardt compared the performance and attitudes of elder adults using a restricted natural language interface (Lotus HAL) with that of elders using a more traditional menu interface (Lotus 1-2-3). While Lotus 1-2-3 requires the user to repeatedly select technical-sounding commands from a menu of hierarchical choices, Lotus HAL allows the user to enter commands in familiar English-like phrases and interprets, to a limited degree, the corresponding computer commands. After elders used both programs for a two-day training period, results showed a statistically significant advantage to using the natural language interface for both ease of computer use and performance level on a problem solving task. All elders participating in the experiment experienced an increase in confidence in their ability to use computers and enthusiasm ran high—attendance for the sessions was perfect, even on a day when the rest of the college was closed down because of snow!

Currently, Worcester State College computer students of all ages are joining the multimedia revolution; interestingly, the opportunity to do so was directly a result of the work being done with elderly computer users at the college. As part of her Ph.D. dissertation project, Dr. Virginia Ogozalek applied for an equipment grant from IBM and the United States

Pharmacopeial Convention (USPC) to test the "Visualized USP DI" system, a multimedia prototype of the USPC's influential reference book United States Pharmacopeia Drug Information for the Consumer Volume II (Advice for the Patient). The proposed experiment would compare the "Visualized USP DI" with a text-based computer, as well as a traditional printed leaflet (Ogozalek 1991a). The system's designer, Dr. Bill Felkey of the Auburn University School of Pharmacy, was interested to see how older patients would use the multimedia interface, and so the USP DI system was sent to Worcester State for the duration of the experiment.

Initially, the multimedia system was used solely by the elderly students who were participants in the study. However, since a diminishing budget has drastically reduced the availability of state-of-the-art computer equipment on campus, it was not long before all computer students, including those under age sixty, were clamoring for the opportunity to try out the multimedia equipment. Thus, there was a "technology transfer" with a unique twist; this time, it was the older students who were showing off to their younger counterparts. Almost immediately, older and younger students began working together to explore other multimedia applications which could be useful to seniors, including travel information systems and financial planning applications.

The students' work culminated in the "Intergenerational Multimedia Fair," which was attended by over 300 participants, including at least 100 elders, and given coverage by both the local newspaper and TV station. Although many of the elders were WSC students, others came from nursing homes and senior centers. The fair consisted of over 30 exhibits, including multimedia and hypermedia systems on special loan from IBM, as well as a special "building blocks" exhibit designed by the students to educate participants about the individual components of multimedia systems.[2]

In a follow-up survey of the fair conducted by students Carl Bush, James Lockwood, and Elaine Hayeck, nearly one-hundred percent of respondents aged 60 and over agreed with statements such as "I think that multimedia technology can appeal even to those people with no previous computer experience" and "Multimedia technology can be used to help motivate students at all levels in the education system." For the most part, respondents found the systems physically accessible and were not excessively bothered by visual, audio, or reaction time problems, although less than one-third of the respondents felt that they could use a multimedia system without help from others. Nevertheless, a majority of elders felt that senior citizens can become as proficient with computers as younger users and expressed interest in taking computer classes that involve multimedia. Figure 24.1 provides a partial summary of survey results.

The success of the Multimedia Fair has given new energy to the intergenerational computing program at Worcester State. Currently, students are working on a project to study how elders use touchscreens. Proposed research includes studies involving computer use by older workers, as well as additional exploration into the potential of multimedia technology for tapping the resources and knowledge of the community's elders. The college is moving forward with plans to establish an Intergenerational Institute, which will incorporate a vision of creative new learning options for young and old together, including an intergenerational computing center with ongoing workshops, labs, and student-assisted learning.

Conclusions

The Worcester State "Elder Connection" program is an educational initiative which allows older and younger students to exchange knowledge and information in a unique intergenerational setting. Although elderly students are still a small minority in the university environment, their numbers will grow with the aging of the baby boom. As colleges and universities face a shrinking pool of the traditional college-aged student and begin to seek other markets, more programs will open up for mature students. Morris and Caro (1991) suggest that, given the projections of declining numbers of young people entering the labor force, colleges and universities ought to take on the role of strengthening the employment skills of mature adults. Whether one is seeking leisure time activity or retooling for the workplace in today's technological society, computer literacy is essential, enhancing opportunities, employment and otherwise, for people of all ages. The role for computer education has become ageless.

It is instructive to note that today's traditional college-aged students (18–23 years old) will eventually be "old" for more years than they have already been alive. Hopefully they will be tomorrow's able elders. How are they being prepared for their own personal careers in aging? What can

Agree	Disagree	Neither Agree Nor Disagree	No Response

1. I think that multimedia technology can appeal even to those people with no previous computer experience.

| 31 | 0 | 0 | 4 |

2. Multimedia technology can be used to help motivate students at all levels in the education system.

| 30 | 0 | 1 | 4 |

3. The combination of graphics, still photos, motion video, and audio narration in these computer systems is a powerful communication method.

| 29 | 0 | 0 | 6 |

4. It was easy to understand the language and images used by the multimedia demonstrations.

| 20 | 4 | 4 | 7 |

5. I found the computer screens difficult to read.

| 2 | 22 | 5 | 6 |

6. The audio portions of these systems were difficult to hear.

| 8 | 19 | 4 | 4 |

7. I find using the touchscreen less cumbersome than a keyboard.

| 22 | 4 | 4 | 5 |

8. The computer systems went too fast for me.

| 8 | 14 | 7 | 6 |

9. It was difficult to select options from the computer menus.

| 6 | 16 | 7 | 6 |

10. I am more at ease dealing with computers after my experiences today.

| 19 | 6 | 7 | 3 |

11. I could run a multimedia system without help from others.

| 11 | 17 | 3 | 4 |

12. I would consider myself an experienced computer user.

| 1 | 23 | 9 | 2 |

13. I found it easy to meet and talk with new people at this gathering.

| 30 | 0 | 2 | 3 |

14. I would be interested in taking classes related to today's presentation.

| 23 | 3 | 3 | 6 |

15. Senior citizens can become as proficient with computers as the younger generation of computer users.

| 31 | 1 | 2 | 1 |

Figure 24.1

colleges and universities do to channel the talents and resources of the ever growing elder populations? Can higher education have a role in fostering intergenerational interdependence?

It is the authors' opinion that colleges and universities are in an enviable position to make a significant impact on these issues, by "intergenerating" their campuses and equipping students of all ages with the tools of the culture. As a society, we cannot afford to cast aside the talents and skills of the elder population. The Worcester State College experience challenges the myths of aging and demonstrates that the intergenerational approach to education stimulates learning, provides new models of successful aging for younger students, and broadens horizons for the wider academic community. The integration of information technology into such educational environments heightens the learning potential across the age span. On the convergence of this technological wave and the age wave we create the new options for our future together.

Notes

1. See Ogozalek (1991b) for a review of the literature on computing and the elderly.
2. For a detailed description, including the results of a survey of over forty elder participants, see Ogozalek, Bush, Lockwood, and Hayeck (forthcoming).

References

Ansley, Jane and Joan T. Erber. 1988. Computer interaction: Effect on attitudes and performance in older adults. *Educational Gerontology* 14: 107–119.

Burns, Red. 1988. A two-way TV system operated by senior citizens. *American Behavioral Scientist* 31: 576–587.

Bollier, David. 1989. Review Conference on New Electronic Technologies for the Elderly: Issues and Projects. *Aspen Forum Report #11*. Truro, Mass: Aspen Institute.

Commonwealth Fund. 1991. Americans over 55 at work program. Paper presented at the annual conference of the National Council on Aging, Atlanta.

Czaja, Sara J., Katka Hammond, James J. Blascovich, and Helen Swede. 1989. Age-related differences in learning to use a text-editing system. *Behaviour and Information Technology* 8: 309–319.

Danowski, James and William Sacks. 1980. Computer communication and the elderly. *Experimental Aging Research* 6, no.2: 125–135.

Dychtwald, Ken and Joe Flower. 1989. *Age Wave: The Challenges and Opportunities of an Aging America*. Los Angeles: Jeremy P. Tarcher.

Edwards, Roger and K.G. Englehardt. 1989. Microprocessor-based innovations and older Americans: AARP survey results and their implications for service robotics. *International Journal of Technology and Aging* 2: 43–55.

Eilers, Merry Lee. 1989. Older adults and computer education: "Not to have a closed door." *International Journal of Technology and Aging* 2: 57–76.

Finkel, Sanford I. and Jerome A. Yesavage. 1989. Learning mnemonics: A preliminary evaluation of a computer-aided instruction package for the elderly. *Experimental Aging Research* 15, no. 4, 199–201.

Furlong, Mary S. 1989. Crafting an electronic community: The SeniorNet story. *International Journal of Technology and Aging*, 2: 125–134.

Gilly, Mary and Valerie Zeithmal. 1985. The elderly consumer and adoption of technologies. *Journal of Consumer Research* 12: 353–358.

Greenberger, Martin and James C. Puffer. 1989. Facilitating health communication for the older person. *International Journal of Technology and Aging* 2: 153–170.

Hahm, Wendell and Tora Bikson. 1989. Retirees using E-Mail and networked computers. *International Journal of Technology and Aging* 2: 113–124.

Holmes, Douglas, Monica Holmes, and Jeanne Teresi. 1988. Routine collection of medication side-effect data using computer terminals located in a senior center. *The Gerontologist* 28: 105–107.

Johnson, Mitzi. 1990. Age differences in decision-making: A process methodology for examining strategic information processing. *Journal of Gerontology* 45, no. 2: 75–78.

Katzowitz, Lauren. 1989. Adapting New Electronic Technologies to Serve the Frail Elderly Living at Home. *Aspen Forum Report #10*. Truro, Mass.: Aspen Institute.

Kay, Edwin and Barbara Jensen-Osinski. 1983. The graying of the college classroom. *The Gerontologist* 23, no. 2: 196–199.

Kearsley, Greg and Mary Furlong. 1984. *Computers for Kids over 60*. Reading, MA: Addison-Wesley.

Kerschner, Paul A. and Kathleen C. Hart. 1984. The aging user and technology. In *Communication technology and the elderly: Issues and forecasts* (135–144), edited by Ruth Dunkle, Marie Haug, and Marvin Rosenberg. New York: Springer.

Krauss, Iseli and William Hoyer. 1983. Technology and the older person: Age, sex, and experience as moderators of attitudes toward computers. In *Aging and Technological Advances* (93–111), edited by P. Robinson, J. Livingston, and J. Birren. New York: Plenum Press.

LaBuda, Dennis. 1987. Potential of computer technology is on the rise. *Perspectives on Aging* 16, no.1: 14–16.

Levine, Martin L. 1988. *Age Discrimination and the Mandatory Retirement Controversy*. Baltimore: Johns Hopkins University Press.

Morris, Robert and Francis Caro. 1991. *Employment Training for Mature Adults: An Important New Direction for Higher Education*. Boston: Gerontology Institute, University of Massachusetts.

Neilsen Estimates. 1981. National audience demographics report, November 1981. In *Nielsen '81*. Chicago: A.C. Nielsen.

Nussbaum, Jon F., Teresa Thompson, and James D. Robinson. 1989. *Communication and Aging*. New York: Harper and Row.

Office of Technology Assessment. 1985. Technology and Aging in America. Washington, D.C.: U.S. Congress.

Ogozalek, Virginia Z. 1991a. The "Automated Pharmacist": A Comparison of the Use of Leaflets, Text-Based Computers, and Video-Based Computers to Provide Medication Information to the Elderly. Ph.D. dissertation, Northeastern University, Boston, Mass.

Ogozalek, Virginia Z. 1991b. The social impacts of computing: Computer technology and the graying of America. *Social Science Computing Review*, Winter.

Ogozalek, Virginia Z., Carl Bush, James Lockwood, and Elaine Hayeck. (Forthcoming). Introducing elders to hypermedia: A "Deconstructionist" approach.

Ogozalek, Virginia Z., and John Van Praag. 1986. Comparison of elderly and younger users on keyboard and voice input computer-based composition tasks. In *Proceedings CHI'86 Human Factors in Computing Systems* (Boston, April 13–17). New York: ACM.

Perrolle, Judith A. 1987. *Computers and Social Change: Information, Property, and Power*. Belmont, CA: Wadsworth Publishing.

Power, Maureen E. 1988. Intergenerational education: The time is now. *Commonwealth Review* 1, no.1: 16–19.

Rice, Michael. 1988. Case by Case: Examining Applications of New Electronic Technologies to Meet the Needs of Elderly People. *Aspen Forum Report #4*. New York: Aspen Institute.

Sanner, Richard. 1986. Computerized communications. In *Computer Technology and the Aged* (pp. 37–47), edited by Francis McGuire. New York: Haworth Press.

Teltsch, Kathleen. 1991. New study of older workers finds they can become good investments. *New York Times*, May 21, 1991, A10.

Tingay, Michael. 1988. Attitudes and Technologies—Striving to Match New Electronic Information Products and Services to the Needs and Interests of Elderly People. *Aspen Forum Report #7*. New York: Aspen Institute.

Weisman, Shulamith. 1983. Computer games for the frail elderly. *The Gerontologist* 23: 361–363.

Zandri, Elaine and Neil Charness. 1989. Training older and younger adults to use software. *Educational Gerontology* 15: 615–631.

Zuckerman, Amy. The Graying of Worcester. *Worcester Magazine*, February 1990, 6–8.

25

Paradoxical Reactions and Powerful Ideas: Educational Computing in a Department of Physics

Sherry Turkle

Prologue: The Athena Aesthetic

Massachusetts Institute of Technology has been known for its contributions to computer science for over forty years. MIT scientists were central to the early development of cybernetics; its graduates founded computer companies that made Boston's Route 128 an internationally recognized center of research and development. However, even by 1980, MIT had not yet confronted the challenge of using computers to do its own job: the use of computers in university education.

In some ways this was surprising. MIT had made an early commitment to research on the use of the computer as a cognitive tool. In the early 1960s, its "Project Mac" developed time-sharing as a technical means for personal use of the computer for intellectual expression long before personal computers existed as physically independent objects. By the mid-1960s, the community in and around Project Mac, including undergraduate and graduate students who had easy access to time-sharing terminals, was using computers to write, communicate, and explore ideas.

But the Project Mac community was a minority, a computer elite within the School of Engineering. The idea that all students, all studies, and all teaching would take on new forms in a computer-rich environment had its first implementation at other universities. It was only in 1983 that MIT embarked on "Project Athena," a large-scale experiment in the use of computers in the undergraduate curriculum.[1] At MIT something like this could never be small: Athena was built around a $50 million gift of equipment from International Business Machines and Digital Equipment Corporation and an institutional commitment to raise an additional $20 million to support faculty development of educational applications.

The ideas for what Athena should be grew out of priorities that had developed over many years within the School of Engineering.[2] The engineering faculty believed that for MIT to take a leadership position in educational computing it was necessary to establish a new, networked, uniform, and graphically sophisticated computer utility. In their view, this computer utility—the engineers referred to it as the "system of pipes"—would be the sufficient condition for innovations in education because MIT faculty would develop educational software once the computer system was in place. There would be "a thousand flowers." And MIT being MIT, with its entrepreneurial, even "Darwinian" spirit, it was expected that these flowers would not simply bloom; they would compete, and the best would thrive.

The School of Engineering originally tried to raise the money to make this vision a reality within its own domain. However, when IBM and Digital made their very large offers, the MIT administration insisted that the resources be spread throughout the institution. In an undertaking of this scale, it was not acceptable for there to be "haves" and "have-nots." And so a vision of an experiment in educational computing drawn up by and for the School of Engineering became a program for all of MIT.

The computer is an exemplary, culturally constructed object, an object that different people and groups of people apprehend with different descriptions and invest with different attributes. In their guidelines for Athena its engineer-architects inscribed their image of the ideal MIT computer culture, a culture that was modern and state of the art, built around a networked community not of simple "users" but of highly fluent computer professionals. To this community MS-DOS would be unacceptably low-tech and the Apple lower still, truly a computer for the "rest of them."

Thus Athena was first of all characterized by its emphasis on high technology. Athena began as an educational experiment without any specific "educational" thinking or philosophy beyond the idea of creating a technology garden and letting a thousand flowers bloom. Every educational application of technology is a marriage of idea and tool. The architects of Athena were engineers and computer scientists. They believed that the idea would be the easy (and inexpensive) part; with the right tools in the hands of the right people, the ideas would come. This meant that the heavy investment of time and money was targeted for the development of the technical infrastructure; MIT faculty were expected to create the educational applications as something of "an exercise for the left hand." From the earliest days of Athena, this "materialist" perspective, corresponding to a toolmaker's view of innovation, clashed with a more "idealist" one—that it was the idea behind the educational application that needed the infusion of new resources. Despite the language of "a thousand flowers," the engineers' desire for technical leadership and system coherency placed severe constraints on the kind of educational proposals that Athena would entertain. For one thing, there were constraints on the computer languages that Athena projects could use. Four languages were allowed, with the notable absence of BASIC, the language in which most currently available educational software was written and Logo, a language at the center of a long tradition of MIT research in computers, education, and learning epistemology. And there were constraints on the computer operating system: it had to be UNIX, deemed by the engineers to be state of the art, although MS-DOS and the Apple Macintosh systems were already on their way to becoming the common coin of rapidly and spontaneously growing MIT personal computer cultures.

When a professor of music who had used the Logo language on personal computers to teach composition and analysis for over a decade was denied Athena funding she was told by Athena's director that her work was not in an acceptable language and her insistence on continuing with Logo was technically indefensible: "All computer languages are equal in the sense that a program to accomplish a given task can be written in any of them," he said. From an engineering point of view, he was right. But she was not an engineer. From her point of view, from the perspective of her research on the epistemology of learning, it was more important that different computer languages encouraged different kinds of thinking and concept formation. Similarly, when proposals came in from historians in the School of Humanities and Social Sciences to use Athena funds to create data bases and bibliographical resources, Athena found such applications too mundane, too far from the technological cutting edge.

So a second and related characteristic of the Athena vision was a necessarily narrowed view of computational and educational diversity. The much-vaunted image of a thousand flowers reinforced its architects' belief that Athena was about freedom and decentralization, but there was another reality. Over many years, the School of Engineering had developed a computer culture with its own intellectual aesthetic, with its own ideas about what was important and what was trivial. What was important was cutting-edge technology and "big," high-profile, technology-driven ideas. What was important was making a big difference in the teaching of the core undergraduate subjects. When this vision was projected onto MIT as a whole it translated into guidelines for "acceptable" diversity in Athena proposals. For example, to keep the project focused on undergraduates, Athena resources would not be made available to graduate students. To keep the project focused on instruction, Athena would not support research, not even for undergraduate theses. To keep the project focused on the technological future, Athena would not support word processing. Athena tried to encourage faculty initiative by offering small development grants, but was best designed to identify, encourage, and reward large flagship projects that used advanced technology to develop software for large lecture courses.

The Athena architects talked about a thousand flowers, but from the point of view of many MIT faculty members, they wanted all the flowers to be roses. Behind the mandate for diversity were assumptions about what kind of diversity would be acceptable. And even a call for every species of flowers in a garden will be perceived as constraining if you are talking to constituencies who want to plant shrubs.

Athena was announced as a five-year experiment. During that time, it did not meet the expectations of its architects. Although there were significant, even stunning achievements in individual departments, the dream of a coherent network was thwarted by technical difficulties. And the dream of intellectual diversity within the constraints of technical coherency met with an even more profound challenge. Since computers extend the power of the mind and affect how people think and work, the machines become intimate intellectual partners. Experiences with computers naturally become woven into the social fabric and creative styles of individuals and groups. In the context of scholarly disciplines, what might seem like a technical preference (for a computer language or programming style or operating system) often expresses deeper intellectual values. It soon became clear that disciplines and subdisciplines within the Institute wanted to build their own computer cultures with their favored languages, machines, operating systems, and styles of educational innovation. Computers became enmeshed in cultural forces that refused to be easily denied or sidestepped.

A centralized and technology-centered approach to change simplifies such issues of context to open a window for decisive action, but such simplification brings with it a special vulnerability: an underestimation of the influence of psychology, history, tradition, and culture. In the case of the introduction of computers in education, the vulnerability is costly. It meant that Athena was able to recognize and claim as successes those achievements that took place within its intended framework, for example, intelligent tutors in Civil Engineering and interactive, multimedia foreign language environments, whose educational ideas were embedded in advanced technical applications. However, other significant effects of the Athena experience could not be recognized as successes. In the 1980s, Athena was a major context for the further development and growth of rich and diverse computer cultures at MIT, including and especially those that grew up around the officially "Athena outlawed" Macintosh and DOS systems. And Athena was the context for the disciplines to grapple with a technology that raised fundamental questions about styles of learning even about their objects of study. One of the ironies of the Athena experience was that the project, by defining itself in terms of specific technologies and a narrow view of diversity, could not recognize, nurture, or indeed, claim credit either for the development of an increasingly pluralistic computer culture or for these intense and productive intellectual debates.

Thus, Athena deserves close study not only for what we can learn from its technological successes and failures in its *intended* direction, but also and especially as an environment that spawned a range of unintended cultural developments. It presents a cautionary tale about the limits of technocentrism and centralized planning in educational computing that has implications for thinking about the introduction of computation in a wide variety of organizational environments. Central to this story is the problematic nature of mandating diversity. Notions of diversity tend to express cultural values. One person's or one group's diversity is another's constraint.

Athena provides a place to study the tension between the diversity of computational practice and a procrustean computer ideology that has a hard time recognizing diversity outside of its toolmaker's framework.

This chapter begins to explore this tension as it was played out in an MIT academic department with a strong history of commitment to educational innovation, the Department of Physics. The case of Athena in Physics is noteworthy because it so clearly illustrates how computational ideologies can blind potential innovators to powerful educational effects. From the point of view of Athena's architects, the Department of Physics was a reticent, indeed resistant, partner. However, when we step outside that frame, we can see success rather than resistance: in Physics, the Athena experience raised old theoretical issues in new and more concrete forms and led to a clash of intellectual cultures whose sparks raised fundamental epistemological issues.[3] Part One describes the historical reticence of this department towards educational computing and how Athena provided an impetus for several of its members to move beyond it. Part Two examines the institutional paradoxes: Athena could not properly see the physicists' achievements and although funded with Athena money, most of the physicists were left feeling that they achieved their successes in spite of rather than because of the project.

Computers in Physics: Beyond the Data Processing Culture

For the past thirty years, computers have been an essential element in physics research. Because of physicists' need to process large amounts of data, FORTRAN was the language of choice and became deeply embedded in the physics culture. Thus most physicists' ideas about computers grew out of experiences in a particular and very limited kind of computer culture: the data processing culture.

Although in recent years, the speed and interactivity of personal, dedicated computers have provided possibilities in data collection and analysis that have little to do with the "number crunching" of the FORTRAN culture, its domination was resonant with a general reticence about computers among physicists. In the data processing world, the researcher stands at a considerable distance from the tool. At MIT a number of distinguished members of the Physics Department felt that this kind of distance was appropriate for keeping computers in their proper place. Indeed, some actually saw computers as posing a threat to serious work in physics. Professor emeritus Victor Weisskopf, who had been chairman of the department for many years, feared that computers would take physicists too far away from the steps between problem and solution. When colleagues would show him their computer print-outs, he was fond of saying, "When you show me that result, the computer understands the answer, but I don't think *you* understand the answer." Professor Herman Feshbach, who followed Weisskopf as department chair, had co-authored a classic text on methods in mathematical physics with MIT colleague Phil Morse. Within the department its implicit message about a hierarchy of methods was summarized in a way that made it clear that computers were for second class minds, or as one MIT physicist put it: "If you are really gifted at solving problems in mathematical physics, you might have as a corollary that somebody who has to resort to a computer to solve problems is not as clever as somebody who can solve them with mathematical techniques."

But the story of computers in the discipline of physics cannot be so simple because only a small subset of "real world" physics problems are soluble by purely mathematical, analytical techniques. Most require experimentation where you do trials, evaluate forces, and fit data to a curve. Not only does the computer make such numerical solutions easier, but in a practical sense, it makes many of them possible for the first time. Professor Anthony French, whose own work in science education went back to the 1960s when he collaborated at MIT with Jerrold Zacharias on a new physics curriculum for high schools, stressed that computers could put even beginning students in touch with a physics that they would otherwise only be able to read about.

The chief difficulty of teaching elementary physics is that it tends to be presented as a set of absolute truths. Students don't see the things that go outside these oversimplified models; they are simply not things you can handle in simple terms. But the computer makes that possible.

Here French acknowledged that computers undermine certain oversimplifications, but he feared they have the opposite effect as well, encouraging subsitutes for direct experience:

In general, students come here innocent of any particular acquaintance with the real world, the physical world. . . . So, if there is anything at all that can be achieved by direct experience, I would want to go for that rather than for the substitute.

This theme of the computer's "dual effects" as a tool that both masks and reveals nature ran through the feelings physicists brought to the opportunities presented by Athena. This was true for both faculty and students. Like their professors, physics students talk both of the new possibilities for numerical solutions and the dangers of reality "substitutes" that mask nature. One says, "Using computers as a black box isn't right. For scientists who are interested in understanding phenomena and theorizing, it's important to know what a program is doing. You can't just use them to measure everything." For another, computers speed things up too much: "When you plot data with the computer, you just see it go 'ZUK' and there it is."

For both faculty and students, computers are good when they make it clear that the world is characterized by irregularities that demand a respect for measurement and its limitations. And computers are bad when they interfere with the most direct possible experience of that world. The faculty teaches that it is always better to get your hands dirty and speak reverentially of the power of direct, physical experiences in their own introductions to science, of "learning Newton's laws by playing baseball." Demonstrations, although seductive, are dangerous when they take you away from direct experience. And the faculty fears that if simulation becomes too easy, students will turn away from the messy reality to which they owe a first allegiance. In this context, simulation is only acceptable when there is nothing else to work with.

For although baseball may be a medium for learning Newton's laws, there is no such direct access to quantum physics and special relativity. This is where technology is grudgingly granted its necessary role. French described the "amazed" reaction of the "technologically skeptical" senior theorists when presented with a film that represented wave packets propagating as a function of time and fragmenting on collision.

You see this thing moving along and doing remarkable things. That's something the likes of which had never been seen. It is difficult to calculate that count without a computer. Seeing it as a moving picture is also wonderful. There's been published recently a handbook, a picture book of quantum mechanics which includes, among other things, some of these wave packet collision things, but to see them just static doesn't begin to give the effect of watching a screen and seeing these things actually happen.

Edwin Taylor, a researcher in the MIT Physics Department, had like French, collaborated with Zacharias in the 1960s. When Athena resources became available, Taylor proposed a computer project in the spirit of that film on wave packets. But now, Taylor argued, the computer's interactivity would make it possible to go beyond the passive experience of *watching* a film to an experience of actually *living* in the quantum world. Taylor's goal was to create a computer environment where students could develop intuitions about the world of "invisible" physics in the same sense that they develop intuitions about the world of classical physics: by manipulating its materials. Metaphorically speaking, computers would make it possible for students to "play baseball" in the quantum world.

One of Taylor's relativity programs simulates what it looks like to travel down a road at nearly the speed of light. Shapes are distorted; they twist and writhe. Objects change color and intensity. All of this can be described mathematically, but without the computer they cannot be experienced. Taylor shares his colleagues' reticence about "demonstrations," so his students are required to use his programmed worlds as utilities for problem solving. But for many of his colleagues, this safeguard did not go far enough.

Professor Martin Deutsch exemplifies the opposition to Taylor's Athena work. Deutsch's feelings about simulation are negative and impassioned. Deutsch feels that simulations always function as black boxes. As such, they run counter to his style and to what he considers most important in physics education: "I like physical objects that I touch, smell, bite into. . . . The idea of making a simulation . . . excuse me, but that's like masturbation." Deutsch characterizes his views as extreme and characterizes Taylor's work as good—but dislikes the genre. Indeed, he laughingly accepts a characterization of it as a "good thing of the bad kind." Deutsch fears that students watch "as they would a movie" and come to believe that something will happen in the real world because they have seen it in the computer model. When such opposition mounted, the Physics Department refused to make a commitment to use Taylor's programs in its large introductory courses, a decision that led Athena to cancel Taylor's funding because of its emphasis on developing software for large lecture courses.

From the official Athena perspective, the resources given to Taylor was money not well spent because it did not lead to a "big" change in undergraduate teaching. But within the Physics Department, the long debate about whether to use Taylor's programs in introductory courses became an important forum for discussion of whether the "culture of simulation" poses a threat to science. An engineer is satisfied with a simulation, went the dominant view, and a physicist wants to be in touch with the real. Some faculty likened all "canned" or prepackaged programs to viruses that could inject the scientific culture with engineering values. Others grudgingly accepted that in the case of quantum physics simulation may be a necessary evil, but the talk inevitably turned to "how one thing might lead to another," and computers might be used to demonstrate something that could be done in a traditional laboratory setting. And here, the consensus was that computers had to be kept in their place. Demonstrations would always be anathema, "the stuff of engineering education."

An interchange between physicists John Negele and Robert Ledoux spoke eloquently to this issue. Negele described how a physicist must come to grips with how light behaves both like a particle and like a wave.

Negele: If you have a dike, and two little openings, the waves of water will propagate through those two little openings. They'll form little rings, which will then interfere with one another, and you'll see the results of these two wave fronts coming out, interfering with one another. That's a very clear wave front. If you think about shooting bullets through these two holes, you know the bullet goes through one or through the other. Now, you're being told as a student of quantum mechanics that sometimes you're supposed to think about light in one way and sometimes you're supposed to think about it the other way. And so a very important experiment comes to mind. You take this case of two slits and decrease the level of illumination so you're very sure photons are only going through one at a time. You would be tempted to say, "Well, by gosh, this is going through one at a time, they are managing to diffuse. It's a fantastic experience for a physicist who is beginning to think about quantum mechanics. And I think many of us have the same reactions, that to simulate that on the computer . . .

Ledoux: It's a cheat.

Negele: It's almost sacrilege.

In the Physics Department, work on computer-resident quantum microworlds continues as does the debate about the proper role for simulation. The debate is increasingly impassioned and interesting as the available programs become more sophisticated and force new distinctions among demonstrations, simulations, and models. What is the epistemic status of an interactive simulation? Is it unfair to reduce a microworld to the status of a simulation? Not so long ago such questions were only philosophical. The computer presence makes it possible to address them empirically and to study the educational effects of different styles of computer use.

Such study was the idea behind a Freshman Seminar proposed to Athena in its earliest days by Professor Robert Hulsizer. Hulsizer's original proposal was ambitious: to use the seminar to rethink the freshman physics curriculum in light of what computers had to offer. When Athena's rules for funding proposals for the School of Science made it impossible for Hulsizer to receive salary support that would release him from other teaching duties and give him the time to develop such a curriculum, he scaled down his project.[4] The seminar took on a more modest goal: to teach students to use computers for numerical problem solving. Hulsizer ran the seminar for two years. When he retired in 1985, two junior faculty members, Robert Ledoux and Stephan Meyer, were asked to take it over. Ledoux's formulation of its continuing purpose: "to let students learn how to use the computer, show them the power of solving problems numerically, the power, you might say, of 'just plotting stuff.'"

For years MIT faculty have complained that their students' ability to deal with scale is deteriorating and that the microchip is at least partly to blame. The slide rule, goes the received wisdom, demanded that its user specify the placement of the decimal point in his or her answer; the calculator makes no such demand. Ledoux subscribes to this theory; he feels that his students "have gotten lazy; they don't want to do things by hand and they don't want to include units in their calculations."

Thus when Ledoux was asked to teach the Freshman Seminar, he redesigned it to emphasize scale and physical measurement. A return to the slide rule was not a practical option, but Ledoux wanted to use the computer to increase student awareness of the uncertainty and error involved in any experiment. He wanted to create a computational analog to "back of the envelope calculations" where "you need to understand the scale you are working in, the units you are using, the number of significant digits that make sense." He points out that when it comes to understanding scale and error, failure to get things straight while at MIT can translate into "a space shuttle blowing up." Since the stakes are so high, the faculty have to serve as "mind police."

In any model you have to state error. It's an unpopular but fundamental topic. I think it is something in which MIT education is very deficient . . . I've never heard a student say, "I took a course in error analysis." I've never seen that . . . There may be some in applied math, but for physical measurements, you have to learn it through a lab. So we try to provide that service. We're ideologues in this; we're preachers.

In one Freshman Seminar exercise, students interact with a computer program that simulates a ball dropping in space. Students may vary the ball's weight and the height from which it is dropped. Students learn about measurement and error when they are asked to account for the effects of forces that are factored out of "pure theory," for example, friction and wind drag. One student in the Freshman Seminar testifies to the success of this exercise when he says, "When you have to consider these forces that otherwise you ignore in dealing with plain [analytical] theory, it changes things radically. You really try to make the connection between theory and data. It's not someone else's experience. You have to make it work for yourself." Ledoux notes that when students are asked to measure the acceleration due to gravity and state the uncertainty, "this blows their minds totally."

People are used to textbooks. They are used to computers. They understand that the computer is marvelous to take data and reduce it, but what does it mean to have an error? If someone said, "g = + 9.81," that's totally meaningless. 9.81 plus or minus what? And so we try to drill into them the whole idea of error analysis.

In the Freshman Seminar, the computer is being used for a "paradoxical effect": a tool usually associated with rules and precision is used to bring students closer to the messiness and irregularity of the real world. "When students plot points for the first time, they literally understand what the physical screen is, what the graphics screen is, and how to actually put points on the screen," says Ledoux. "So, if a curve drawn on the screen and a theoretical curve don't look the same, students are in a position to investigate the screen's resolution. If the two things overlap, they may differ at the tenth of a pixel level, which you can't see." And yet, this tenth of a pixel level may be critical. "If the space shuttle blows up it may be the margin of error that makes all the difference." It is important to note that to use technology for this purpose, the physical computer must be made transparent—this intellectual aesthetic demands direct contact with the physics behind the machine.

Similar intellectual values stand behind computer use in Martin Deutsch's Athena-funded Junior Physics Laboratory. For this laboratory, Deutsch wrote computer programs which will not accept a data point without the specification of an error factor. To remove this feature, says Deutsch, students "have to take affirmative action. The default is always to put an error in." While some computer cultures celebrate the computer's opacity—you don't need to know what is going on inside the hardware or software to use a spread sheet or word processor—Deutsch uses the computer to argue the aesthetics of the transparent in the physical sciences. While some computer cultures celebrate abstraction and simulation, Deutsch uses computers to promote a revaluation of the concrete.

Deutsch became interested in computers in the 1960s when he "discovered" the PDP-1. For a few years he devoted himself to that machine, writing programs in machine language, getting involved in its internal architecture, "having a good time." Then for ten years he had nothing to do with computers until he met the Apple 2E: "I bought a 2E and I said, 'This is going to change my life.' And it did. For the first time in my life, I could write."

Deutsch does not work through problems by making a plan and following it through from top to bottom. He prefers to assemble the elements and "sculpt" a solution. The combination of this sculpting style of work and a perfectionistic nature had always made writing painful to the point of near impossibility. Deutsch found it too linear a process for his associative style. The computer presented a new opportunity.

A person like me can never write anything. By the time I had five sentences down, I'd start correcting them. And by the time I'm through correcting them, I've lost the train of thought. So I used to do things like use a tape recorder, put it at the far end of the room, hang up the microphone, walk over to the other end of the room so I couldn't get to the machine in time to stop it, you see, and start talking. Because once you have a draft, you can work on it. And of course, the word processor solves all that. You can just put it in any old way and then start working on it.

Deutsch uses the sculpting style, a concrete "playing with" the materials at hand not only for writing but for doing science. The abstract and formal have long been privileged in science, its canonical values have put a premium on "objectivity" defined as the observer's distanced relationship with the object of study.[5] But Deutsch describes his work in physics in terms that privilege the concrete and a closeness to the object.[6] Recent writing in scientific ethnography has gone far to reveal such concrete thinking in science-in-practice despite idealized, after-the-fact reconstructions of the discovery process.[7] Deutsch makes no such after-the-fact reconstructions. He admits to using a style reminiscent of what Claude Levi-Strauss called "bricolage" or tinkering, a "science of the concrete."[8]

The bricoleur scientist does not move abstractly and hierarchically from axiom to theorem to corollary. Bricoleur scientists construct theories by arranging and rearranging, by negotiating and renegotiating with a set of well-known concrete materials. While hierarchy and abstraction show up in how structured programmers use a "planner's aesthetic," bricoleurs rely on negotiation and rearrangement of their materials. The bricoleur resembles the painter who stands back between brushstrokes, looks at the canvas, and only from this contemplation, decides what to do next. Bricoleurs use a mastery of associations and interactions. Unlike the planner, where mistakes are missteps, theirs is a navigation of mid-course corrections. A paradigmatic bricoleur, Deutsch admits that he "never reads the literature first. I first try to solve the problem." Not surprisingly, Deutsch uses the concrete, sculpting style in computer programming as well.

In both the popular and the technical culture there has been a systematic construction of the computer as the ultimate embodiment of the abstract and formal. Deutsch illustrates another side to the computer's intellectual personality. It can support a bricoleur's style of concrete thinking that runs into conflict with standard ways of doing things within the established computer culture. Deutsch is not alone. A close look at programmers at work makes it clear that the practice of computing supports a pluralism that is denied by the social construction of the machine. Despite widespread stereotypes about computers encouraging or even enforcing one style of use (a "top-down," planned, and structured style) computers can become partners in a variety of intellectual approaches, including some which, like Deutsch's, deal with the world of formal systems by using objects rather than the rules of logic to think with.[9]

Unlike many of his colleagues whose experiences with computers had been limited to batch processing and FORTRAN, Deutsch's background led him to see them as personal tools that can flexibly enter the researcher's intellectual space and support a variety of intellectual styles. He had used them to get into a new relationship with words and saw little reason why they couldn't be used to get into a new relationship with scientific data.

But this would not follow from a model of computer use where the scientist fed data into a machine and used a FORTRAN program to get it out.

For Deutsch, the most valuable instrument in the laboratory is his Swiss army knife, a simple, understandable, and all-purpose tool. Other people want to use the most up-to-date tools. Deutsch wants to use the most transparent ones.[10] He has generalized his ideas about the knife's intellectual power and in the realm of computers, this translates into a preference for general-purpose computers that allow you to "look under the hood." Without transparency, Deutsch claims you lose a sense of your material and how it is being transformed by technology. And when you lose a sense of the "intermediate steps," then, he says "you are an engineer, not a scientist."

When Deutsch approached his colleagues about using personal computers as intellectual tools in the service of a more transparent physics, he felt misunderstood:

They didn't know what I was talking about. Everybody knew what a computer was. It was in a computer center where you submit your stuff in the evening and pick it up the next day. And I said, "Look, this is really going to change. We're really going to have new things."

In the early 1980s Deutsch created an ad hoc committee on computers within the Physics Department, to "stir the pot," to create an awareness of the new possibilities. And just at this point, Athena was announced. Deutsch thought that its preoccupation with networks were off the main point of what computers could do for education. What he saw as exciting was an opportunity to bring computers into students' lives as direct, personal, and transparent tools. Deutsch's idea was simple: introduce personal computers into the physics laboratory required of all majors in their junior year. His goal was to make computers the Swiss army knives of the Junior Laboratory.

Deutsch begins with the assumption that the most dangerous thing in a laboratory is a "black box," an incompletely understood procedure or piece of equipment. Ideally, "each apparatus should be simple enough so that the student can open it and see what's inside." For practical reasons, students can't design all of their instruments for themselves, but they should be able to feel that they *could* have. Deutsch's educational philosophy is based on his learning style: it emphasizes intellectual ownership through working in a transparent environment.

As Deutsch sees it, his lifelong battle against the black box is a "rearguard action" because "as techniques become established, they naturally become black boxes." But "it's worth fighting at every stage, because wherever you are there is a lot to be learned if you keep the box open that you will surely miss if you close it." Deutsch made the computer a new weapon in his battle by writing data collection and analysis programs that could be transparent to their users. One such program was for the Stern-Gerlach experiment on space quantization. When an electron travels around an atomic nucleus, a magnetic field is set up. Classical physics predicts that if influenced by another magnetic field, the orientation of the electron will be deflected. One expects a continuum of deflections depending on the strength of the external magnetic field and the magnetic momentum of the atom itself. But quantum physics predicts that only two positions occur and the Stern-Gerlach experiment demonstrates this space quantization. A beam of silver atoms is passed through a magnetic field and then onto a film plate. The atoms form smudges from which their orientation can be determined. Originally in a mixed state, once they enter the magnetic field the silver atoms are arranged into the two orientations predicted by quantum theory.

Before the computer was used to collect the data for this experiment, students had to move the magnets manually, read the meter, and record measurements with a painfully slow pen-recording device. The process was laborious. Deutsch says that "you could never quite figure out what was going on because it would take fifteen minutes to do any one thing." Now in the laboratory, the computer is attached to an apparatus that collects data from the film smear, and it does the calculations necessary to determine the shape of the orientations. Two peaks appear, indicating the two magnetic moments predicted by quantum mechanics. Because of the computer's speed, the peaks appear in a dramatic fashion. For Deutsch, this makes the experiment an illustration of what he thinks is most important about science.

It brings together something profound and something mundane — that combination, it's like love! The mundane part: something as simple as remembering to degauss the magnet in the experiment. The profound part: the space quantization. That the mundane and profound go together — like washing dishes and love — it's one of those things that is hard to learn.

Deutsch wrote all of his "transparent" Junior Laboratory software by himself; some of his students had trouble with its "homebrew" nature, finding the system truly transparent only to its author. But even the students who criticized the software's bugs and lack of documentation appreciated how Deutsch's efforts protected the immediacy of their contact with data. "The software was designed so you can still see the raw data. We're still doing our own data analysis. It's a tool that doesn't change the data fundamentally, just does the things you'd know how to do anyway." And students reported how powerful was the experience of using the computer to analyze data in the Junior Laboratory. For example, one recalled how before the computer, access to the data in an experiment in resonance fluorescence was through Polaroid photographs taken of an oscilloscope.

Before you could only get a qualitative understanding. There was less data on the photo than you have on the computer. Now, you can get an exact fit of the data to the function and see the deviations and how much of it doesn't fit an exact curve. Seeing that the data fits in spite of the variations is part of the allure of physics.

Here again, as in the case of the Freshman Seminar, we see a paradoxical effect. The tool so long associated with precision allowed an appreciation of the "messiness" of nature. And as in the case of the Freshman Seminar, the tool so many feared would force an alienation from the real brought students closer to it because they are able to get their hands dirty playing with data. Speaking of the resonance flourescence experiment, Deutsch commented that the computer enabled laboratory physics to "come alive"; students could get closer to underlying experience. With the computer "a student can take thousands of curves, and develop a feeling for the data. Before the computer, nobody did that because it was too much work. Now you can ask a question, and say, 'Let's try it.'"

In the Junior Laboratory, computers allowed a subject as abstract as quantum mechanics to be directly experienced through a hands-on exercise. Computers provided a window onto theory through glimpses of physical phenomena that opened science up to intuition. Some of Deutsch's students used this new point of contact as a supplement to traditional mathematical understanding. But other students, particularly those who like Deutsch himself are bricoleurs by intellectual temperament, said that they had a sense of "really understanding" for the first time.

Computers offer a great deal to bricoleurs. Computational objects belong to both the world of ideas and things and can offer concrete physical access to formal systems. Computers make it possible to manipulate the abstract as though it were concrete. When Deutsch talked about his writing, he was describing an intellectual style that puts a premium on the manipulation of the tangible. What is true of text can be true of a mathematical curve.

The Junior Laboratory was funded by Athena, but its intellectual aesthetic stoods in sharp context to Athena's ideas about the importance of "big ideas" and big technology in educational computing. Through that evaluative prism, Deutsch had a "small idea": relationships with modest, "transparent computers" could have positive pedagogical effects. Deutsch wanted to use the computer in a low-tech and unobtrusive way, as an extension of current laboratory practice. Deutsch had no technical "feats" to report; his students needed no special place or special machines. Athena hoped for courseware that could be used around the Institute and could become influential when shared with other universities and colleges. Deutsch produced no overarching abstractions, nothing easily exportable. His intellectual investment was in a different kind of process: helping students develop a personal relationship with a new tool. From the point of view of Athena, Deutsch's experiment was rendered almost invisible.

The quantum microworlds, the Freshman Seminar, and the Junior Laboratory were very different from each other; each experiment was marked by the intellectual personalities of the faculty who ran them. Their diversity suggests that educational innovation involving computers requires the widest latitutde for diverse intellectual styles. Taylor's computational aesthetic involves an opaque machine. For him, only the quantum processes need to be made more transparent. In contrast, Deutsch and Ledoux stress computational transparency. In the use of computers for simulation, Deutsch and Taylor find little to agree on. But each is committed to using computers in education. To be successful, the organizational framework in which such innovations are carried out must be able to accommodate, respect, and reward their differences. The architects of Athena took diversity as a goal, but they expected the diversity would be in the *content* of educational software written according to a certain abstract model of what would constitute an innovation. The experiences of intellectual disciplines with computers suggests something different: a diversity of diversity, a need for pluralism.

The positive side of the Athena experience in physics was that individuals used its resources to explore a range of issues within their own intellectual culture. The side of the story that reads as a cautionary tale raises the question of why each felt that his work was actually inhibited by the Athena organization, that he had done his work *in spite of* its constraints. How did the organization evolve in a way that gave faculty the sense that to exploit intellectual opportunity you had to use Athena resources but circumvent Athena culture?

The Institutional Paradox: Managing Innovation

The roots of this paradox lie first of all in Athena's history. Designed in the School of Engineering, it developed priorities appropriate to that School's disciplinary needs and the interests of its corporate sponsors, in particular, the emphasis on building an advanced computer utility that had system coherency at its heart. The decision to accept hardware gifts from two vendors and to make Athena Institute-wide intensified the engineers' focus on system coherency. They wanted equipment that had not been built for compatibility to run on the same network and to serve courses across all subject matters.[11] Of course, the ideal of "coherency" was given an educational as well as a technical rationale. With system coherency, a student's one-time investment in learning would provide access to the full range of Institute-developed educational software. Since it was the faculty who were to write the software and this required money, Gerald Wilson, Dean of the School of Engineering, made a commitment to raise an additional $20 million to support faculty proposals in all the schools.

The presence of money to spend set up a logic of its own. From the point of view of the engineering faculty at the center of Athena, you couldn't just give it away and you couldn't give it directly to departments because they didn't yet understand the technical system. The engineers turned to the model they knew best, a federal system along the lines of the National Science Foundation. There would be requests for proposals, faculty review committees within each of MIT's schools—Engineering, Science,

Humanities and Social Science, and Management. There would be a central Athena administration that would insure that all proposals conformed to technical rules that would insure "system coherency" and to administrative rules that would insure Athena's commitment to major change in undergraduate education. I have already discussed some of these rules. What is important to note here in this discussion of paradox is how many of them went counter to longstanding MIT customs and to MIT's own institutional sense of its greatest strengths. For example, despite a widespread feeling that computers were most valuable as productivity tools to be used in personal workspaces, the Athena machines would only be allowed in centralized public clusters; despite a MIT tradition of integrating research and teaching, Athena resources would not be available to students for research use, not even for senior theses; despite the close integration of undergraduate and graduate education, Athena would not be available for graduate courses or graduate students; despite the fact that most students and faculty relied on computers for word processing, Athena would not support such a mundane application. And of course, despite MIT's sense that decentralization and entrepreneurship had made for its historical strengths, Athena was built as a hierarchical structure. From the point of view of those at the center of Athena, none of these rules were "really" constraints. They were simply technical requirements for keeping the system maximally available to undergraduates and firmly pointed toward future developments in educational rather than research computing. From the point of view of one computer culture, its computational aesthetics always seem natural, like the simple expression of the computer's true nature. Put somewhat differently, for an engineer, constraints are empowering; they allow you to get things done. From outside of the engineering culture, constraints are inhibiting. In the history of Athena, things looked different from the center and the periphery.

The School of Engineering had raised the money for Athena. It had the understandable feeling that it should be somehow thanked for its efforts. Yet when the central administration decided to take that money and distribute it around MIT as a whole, the engineers became the "them" in a division between "us and them." From the center, hard work on the part of the engineering faculty had led to free resources for everyone. But other faculty complained that the project had been negotiated and finalized without any consultation with the Institute faculty as a whole. Athena was presented as a fait accompli. Faculty comments were disgruntled. Athena seemed an uninvited guest or an unwanted gift. "They are going to tie us to mainframes"; "They are going to give us terminals"; "They are going to commit us to a system which they know is the only right one to use"; "This gift reminds me of someone who brings two ex-smokers a crystal ashtray as a housewarming present." In the School of Science, and perhaps most particularly within the Department of Physics, Athena brought the added irritation of engineers telling scientists what to do.

As independent and successful scientists, the physicists were accustomed to setting their own educational priorities. Martin Deutsch spoke of their "instinctive negative reaction to anything that smells at all like something that will regulate or control our activities, because basically our success, when it comes, comes from the fact that we disregard such things." His colleague John Negele went further. He felt that Athena's rules and regulations did more than discourage independent-minded scientists: they actually insured that nothing important would happen at MIT.

Independent of Athena, Negele had been thinking about new ways to teach computational physics, but soon after Athena was announced he decided that "at MIT conditions were not right" for him to pursue this demanding intellectual job. In his view although Athena said that it wanted to encourage "big ideas," it tended to see such ideas as byproducts of powerful technologies. Thus, it would provide and support hardware but did see its job as providing the kinds of support traditionally considered necessary for "intellectual" advances, most significantly time and intellectual freedom. To make this point, Negele contrasted his Athena experience with that of a colleague who became involved with educational computing at California Institute of Technology. "At Cal Tech," said Negele, "conditions were right":[12]

At the same time as the first meetings were occurring here with Project Athena, his chairman at Cal Tech told him that they were interested in a serious effort to get some serious intellectual involvement of physicists using computers in undergraduate education. He didn't want menus which gave students a convenient way of doing repetitious exercises.

The Cal Tech chairman didn't ask for a proposal that followed a fixed set of technical rules and regulations, but provided two assistants, a computer office workstation, and a year off from regular teaching. Negele's colleague at Cal Tech used these resources to develop a textbook and computer exercises that Negele now uses in his MIT course on computational physics: "He could use whatever computer language he wished, and was told that whatever he created, he would own, hardware, software, a book, whatever." And he was guaranteed that when he was done, students would take the course he developed because it would be on a "short list" of courses that satisfied a new computational requirement.[13]

Negele's narrative directly criticizes Athena's model of how to manage innovation. In his view, careful work went into designing the system, but insufficient attention was paid to creating the personal and organizational conditions for the kind of intellectual work that interested Negele. Negele didn't need a sophisticated network; he needed time and intellectual freedom but at least as the Physics Department came to understand policy, Athena would not grant faculty released time from teaching by paying academic year salaries, the same constraint that had frustrated Robert Hulsizer's original plans to revamp the undergraduate curriculum.[14] Negele chafed at defending his proposal to a funding committee made up of people outside his field. He couldn't have an Athena machine in his office and of course would not own any marketable products that came out of his Athena work.

Negele's narrative also describes a clash of intellectual cultures. Within the MIT engineering culture, one becomes successful by getting grants to develop advanced technical systems with widespread applications. The architects of Athena had a "materialist" view of what was required to produce successful products. It was difficult for them to believe, as did Negele, that breakthroughs would come from time spent on educational research, on *thinking* rather than tool building. From Negele's "idealist" perspective, the Athena ideology of a "thousand flowers" was not so much a call for diversity as a vote of no confidence about educational research. If you don't believe that such research could lead to any consensus about its quality, it makes sense to simply let individual faculty members do their own thing.

Finally, Negele's narrative raises questions about the balance between centralization and decentralization in the management of educational innovation. In the intellectual climate of the Physics Department, Athena was experienced as disrespectful of the faculty's knowledge, autonomy, and right to be consulted on matters of intellectual substance. Negele recounts that when Athena was first presented, he and a group of colleagues asked the chairman of the MIT faculty why there was no real faculty participation in its planning. Negele reports that the reply to their question described a closed door: the chairman of the faculty "had asked about this and had been told that the negotiations with the vendors, with IBM and DEC, were too sensitive to allow the faculty to get involved." Negele began working with Athena as early as he could, but felt that the key decisions had already been made by an inner circle of engineers. "They created a huge number of committees and I was a real sap, and it took me about a year to figure out what these committees were about. These committees were to give the impression of involving faculty. But there was no substance. Nearly every major decision had already been taken."

For example, while he was serving as a member of a "technical issues" committee, the Athena restrictions on computer languages and operating systems were brought up for discussion. Negele insisted that the restrictions were not "technical issues," but a form of censorship inappropriate in a university. "It was as though they were saying, 'these are the approved books and these other ones have too much secular humanism in them or whatever.'"

If my department chairman told me what book I must use to teach a course, I would hand in my resignation. As a professor of physics, I believe I am the person who can make the best judgment as to what textbooks to use when I teach a course. Now who are these people at Project Athena? And who do they think they are that they should tell me what languages I'm allowed to use to teach a course and what languages I'm not allowed to use?

Negele says that the result of his objections was that he was asked to "cool it." He was made to understand that this question, for better or worse, was closed.

In fact, Athena would later soften many of its restrictive policies. The language restrictions were softened because of technical difficulties and increasing pressure to get things running. The ban on word processing was lifted in the face of massive violations and student protest. When surveys of how students actually used Athena showed that despite official discouragement, over 80 percent of all use was for word processing, the system relented.[15] The "policy-in-practice" about not granting faculty salaries was never Institute-wide, but a provisional decision on the part of the allocations committee in the School of Science and it, too, would change. But such relaxations of the rules were several years in coming. Certainly, in physics, the rules about salary, languages, and operating systems contributed to an environment openly hostile to Athena. As Negele saw it, they led his colleagues to a basic assumption that "Athena is something they don't even want to *hear* about. They think it's such a stupid, ridiculous, terrible mistake. They aren't even going to waste their time talking about it. In physics, Athena created conditions for things *not* to happen." In his view, the centralized Athena administration was insensitive to the educational needs of the departments, for example, when it prohibited use of the system for senior theses and undergraduate research.

There was a great resistance to using Athena machines for senior theses. They were supposed to be used for large courses. That was crazy. At that time, there was nothing of intellectual substance that had been developed for large courses, but yet there was a whole generation of students coming up with senior theses and UROP [undergraduate independent research] projects.

When Negele evaluated the Athena experience as a whole, he noted that no textbooks have been produced and that in his opinion, the majority of proposals, although "nice," "don't blaze the way." They don't put MIT in a position of intellectual leadership in a way that I would like to see." Negele believes that the straightforward acknowledgment of a missed opportunity would be a good first step towards doing things better. Not surprisingly, his ideas about doing things better are firmly opposed to where Athena began. He thinks one should "abolish all those silly rules." Indeed, one might look at the "Negele Plan" as a suggestion that MIT switch to what he has understood as the "Cal Tech Plan": identify faculty members who are willing to experiment, put a machine in their offices, give them each a machine to take home, give them a semester or a year off to work, and tell them that they own their products. In other words, give faculty incentives that will make it worth their while to be taken away from their major research interests. In addition, show confidence in the strength and integrity of intellectual communities by decentralizing funding decisions. That power should go to departments. "A chairman knows his faculty." In sum, take the emphasis off technology and put it into people and their ideas.

As things turned out, Athena projects in the Physics Department would have proceeded more smoothly if the emphasis had not been on cutting-edge technology.[16] Taylor fought for the right to use only the "bottom end" of Athena equipment because he wanted his relativity software to be easily exported to other universities which would not have such advanced machines. Ledoux and Meyer fought Athena for the right to use BASIC in the Freshman Seminar. Since its purpose was not to teach a new programming language but numerical problem solving, they wanted students to program in this familiar and Athena-disapproved language. Only after long negotiation did Athena grudgingly agree to support an IBM version of BASIC for the seminar. But the physicists wanted "Quick BASIC, Microsoft Version 2," arguing that it was better suited to their educational purposes. "We would have been fools not to use it," insisted Ledoux. In the end, the Physics Department purchased its own Quick BASIC for the Freshman Seminar, but this meant that Ledoux and Meyer had to update and maintain the software themselves. "It takes manpower to do something that Athena doesn't support," said Ledoux. "It is a manpower that Athena doesn't provide." Again and again the physicists' insisted that there was a high cost to using Athena: lost time, wasted energy, and the widespread sentiment that to make an Athena project work, you had to circumvent Athena.

Athena created a climate in which the choice to use BASIC or Logo or currently available technology was read as a sign of failure. Faculty felt like "second class citizens" if their innovations were not technical but "simply" educational. Athena was supposed to be about freedom and diversity but here again we meet the questions: "Diversity for whom?"; "Freedom for whom?"; "Freedom from whom?"

From the point of view of the engineers at the center of Athena, freedom meant escaping from the "confines" of IBM PCs and "impoverished" computer languages like BASIC. From the point of view of most Athena users on the periphery of power, such freedoms meant new constraints. From the perspective of the center, a funded Athena proposal provided money and undisturbed work. From the point of the periphery, Athena restrictions violated intellectual freedom. And as for the privilege of working undisturbed, Alan Lazarus, Chairman of the Physics Department's Education Committee, made it clear that for those who had worked on the

Freshman Seminar, the fact that Athena "left them alone" was read as a distressing lack of support.

Lazarus commented that Athena's concession to allow BASIC in the Freshman Seminar served to intensify rather than abate his faculty's hostility: "We finally got them [Athena] to agree that it was okay but then they disowned us. They said, 'Here are the terminals, but don't expect us to keep them up to date, or put new operating systems on them. You're on your own. This put people off rather severely."

Athena seemed not to care what we did with the terminals or what we had developed. Nobody came around and said, "What have you guys done, show us, give us a demonstration." We have invited people over, but nobody, as far as I know, came. We mentioned this to the people at Athena and they said, "We have no provision for that sort of thing." It was clearly "Here they are, good-bye." It was not the kind of mutual working together it should have been.

In the Physics Department, different faculty were disappointed with Athena for different reasons. From the physicists' perspective, the problem with Athena was not that it was "one-sided" but that its technological emphasis made it virtually "none-sided." Deutsch, Ledoux, and Meyer were working on a small scale, experimenting with technically mundane uses of the computer in the service of encouraging a new and more transparent relationship with tools of measurement. They felt undermined by Athena's distaste for the "small," the "homebrew," the "low-tech," and for BASIC. Negele's interest in computational physics, Hulsizer's in new curricula, and Taylor's in quantum microworlds fit better into Athena's "big ideas" category. But they also felt let down. Taylor could not meet Athena's demand that he get his materials into large courses. Decisions about changing the curriculum in large courses demands consensus within disciplines, yet the Physics Department case study demonstrates that computers are just as likely to sharpen debates within them. For Negele and Hulsizer the problem with Athena was its notion that educational ideas would follow from technical advances, that educational issues could be dealt with in one's spare time. Thus, despite the achievements of faculty working within it, in the Physics Department Athena suffered from its reputation of pleasing none of the people all of the time.

The story of Athena's first five years reflects tensions that characterize MIT as a whole: the tension between a powerful School of Engineering and a distinguished faculty in the arts, sciences, and humanities who often feel marginal to institutional priorities; the tension between a powerful, centralized Provost's office and its diverse, independent, and entrepreneurial constituencies; the tension between a faculty promoted for its research contributions and the demand for innovative teaching. Athena was a new stage on which these larger institutional tensions were played out. Thus it is not surprising that it brought to the surface a range of issues that must be addressed by the institution and not only in the context of computing. For example, the Athena experience dramatized that if educational innovation is to occur, junior faculty must be given greater incentives to participate in it. Martin Deutsch commented that he was free to throw himself into Athena work because as an older and very senior member of the department he could come to it "without ambition."

I don't have to write two papers a year, three papers a year, I don't have to write any papers a year if I don't feel like it. It's easy for me . . . in a funny way, and that goes into many things. It's easier when you're sort of pulled out a little bit, out of the struggle. I could afford to play.

In the Physics Department, major Athena commitments were made by people marginal to the department such as Taylor who holds a research appointment and must therefore survive on the kind of "soft money" Athena provided and by "elder statesmen," such as Deutsch and Hulsizer. The younger faculty who participated were assigned to their roles. "Elder statesmen" and "marginals" are naturally limited in their ability to effect lasting change, and the younger recruited faculty will "cycle out" when their assignments end. Not only is educational computing marginal to their research careers, but they can't afford to make it more central. The incentive system will ultimately punish them if they remain involved for too long.

Although Project Athena won a new visibility for educational innovation at MIT, that doesn't translate into promotion and tenure within a discipline. To sustain educational innovation in a research institution, either senior faculty have to commit to ongoing responsibility or the incentive system has to change to reward junior faculty who do educational research. At the very least, experiments in educational computing need support staff trained in the various disciplines who can take the burden off the faculty in the production and maintenance of software. What does not work is the Athena solution where it was assumed that a serious experiment in education could be done as an "exercise for the left hand," something for faculty to do on the side, something that junior faculty would have no problem fitting in alongside their disciplinary research programs. This model denied the difficulty of educational innovation, saw such innovation as possible without serious research, and allowed the incentive system to remain unquestioned and unmodified.

Epilogue: Powerful Ideas or Paradoxical Effects

Physicist Judah Schwartz holds a joint appointment at MIT and at the Harvard Graduate School of Education where he heads a program in educational technology. He was involved in an Athena-funded software development project for an experimental freshman curriculum and served as chair of a faculty subcommittee that examined the impact of Athena on the residence system. Schwartz began a conversation about Athena by recalling a lecture by Barbara Tuchman on "How I Write My Books." "The first sentence out of her mouth," said Schwartz, "was `First you have to have an idea.'" He continued:

You need to have an idea, a powerful idea, in order to do something that is conceptually interesting. Physicists have been using computers forever and will continue to use computers forever. It doesn't make a conceptual difference in what they do and so they are very casual about computer use, and I think properly so. The question of how to make a conceptual leap is much subtler, and with far fewer answers. It's something whose major intellectual impetus derives from trying to understand something about how people learn about abstraction and the building of quantitative models. MIT doesn't have such an enterprise.

Schwartz is correct when he says that the Athena experience in physics proceeded without what he would classify as "powerful ideas," for example, new models of how people learn about abstraction. But in fact, it ended up challenging the notion that for something interesting to happen you need to start with *that kind* of powerful idea just as it challenged its own starting assumption that the ideas that would matter in educational computing would grow out of advanced technical innovations. What we have seen in physics is that powerful effects could follow from relatively mundane uses of computers.

First, in the Freshman Seminar, numerical problem solving with the computer presented a challenge to the traditional "textbook physics," skewed towards those problems that can be solved analytically. As such experiences become widespread, there may be change in what is considered "high" or prestigious physics, a position currently occupied by the "pure" (i.e., mathematical) approach. And in this setting, the computer brought students closer to the "real" by forcing a new consideration of error and the limitations of measurement.

Second, in the Junior Laboratory, when computers relieved the tedium of data collection and data plotting, students were able to implement thought experiments which gave theory a concrete and more intuitive dimension. For some, these new possibilities were a supplement to traditional mathematical understandings. For others, they seemed to present a new and privileged path of access to science because they offered the ability to play with the abstract in a concrete, almost tangible form. In the Junior Laboratory as in the Freshman Seminar, students were put in a better position to honor the scientist's primary allegiance to nature's "messiness" because they were better equipped to handle uneven and anomalous data. Before the computer entered the laboratory, if a students' one round of an experiment yielded only anomalous data, the student could not bring his or her experimental result in relation to theory, but would have to rely on prepackaged, idealized data. The computer made it possible to generate a richer and more representative data set.

Finally, looking at the Athena experience in the Physics Department as a whole, it is clear that even with relatively mundane and "low-tech" uses of computers, different people made them their own in their own ways, using different intellectual approaches and different points of contact with what the technology has to offer. Martin Deutsch used a "different" computer than did John Negele or Edwin Taylor. The physical machines may have been the same; the machines in the mind were not. The fact that computers invite their personal appropriation suggests that the most productive uses of educational computing will demand an epistemological pluralism, an acceptance of the validity of multiple ways of knowing and thinking.

From the time that it was announced as an MIT-wide plan, Athena declared ambitious educational and epistemological goals, for example, to use computers to "help students learn more creatively and fully" by developing "new conceptual and intuitive understanding."[17] But in fact, many MIT faculty simply expected computers to help them do what they already did faster and better. According to this line of reasoning, the computer is "just a tool" that would help students do the old things more efficiently. Important educational effects would follow but it was expected that they would take place *away from* the machines. For example, when computers speeded things up in the laboratory, students would have more time to study underlying theory and mathematics outside of the laboratory. Thus despite its official rhetoric, as an educational experiment Athena proceeded with a widespread and conservative hypothesis that if things were going to change, it would not be by much, or at least not in significant qualitative ways.

The story of Athena in physics challenges this hypothesis because computers not only enabled students to do the old things more quickly, they opened up new ways of thinking. And even doing an experiment more quickly (in the Junior Lab the time for performing experiments was reduced by a factor of five to six) led to significant qualitative changes as students were able to run through many variations of the same experiment, developing a new feeling for what was going on. Students experienced a greater ownership of theory because they had the feeling that they were confirming it for themselves.

By being a magnificent tool, the computer became more than "just" a tool. Most surprising of all, this machine that is most commonly thought of as the ally and embodiment of the abstract showed its vocation as an actor in the revaluation of the concrete. The story of Athena in physics makes it clear that it is naive to launch experiments in educational computing that expect diversity in content but not in the form and feeling of computer use.

Notes

1. This study of the Physics Department was part of a larger project on the educational impact of Athena. In Spring 1986, the Project Athena Study Group, an MIT faculty committee chaired by Professor Jean de Monchaux, Dean of the School of Architecture and Planning, mandated a study of the impact of Athena on teaching and learning. Four departments were chosen as case studies: Architecture and Planning, Chemistry, Civil Engineering, and Physics, with Sherry Turkle and Donald Schon as principle investigators. The field studies began in April 1986, were completed in Fall 1987, and were reported in Sherry Turkle, Donald Schon, Brenda Nielsen, M. Stella Orsini, and Wym Overmeer, "Project Athena at MIT," May 1988. This essay draws on a chapter I authored in that report, "Athena in Physics," and is based on field research by myself and Brenda Nielsen (including observation and interviews with faculty and students)

and on a roundtable discussion with department members which served as a feedback session after they had read an early draft of this chapter. Early drafts profited from comments by all members of the research team and by Seymour Papert, Director of the Learning and Epistemology Group in MIT's Media Laboratory. All persons quoted have had an opportunity to review their quotations.

2. Two important MIT documents for tracing the developing vision of an Athena-like activity are *Report of the Ad Hoc Committee on Future Computational Needs and Resources,* April 1979 (committee co-chairs Weston Burton and Michael Dertouzos) and Joel Moses, *Report on Computers and Education for the School of Engineering,* October 1982. Other data on the growth of the Athena vision come from conversations with its central architects, among these Michael Dertouzos, Professor of Electrical Engineering and Director of the Laboratory of Computer Science, Robert Logcher, Professor of Civil Engineering, Joel Moses, Professor of Electrical Engineering, and Gerald Wilson, Dean of the School of Engineering which took place in the context of the larger study of Athena at MIT (see note 1).

3. This essay covers Athena activity in Physics from the beginning of the project until Fall 1987.

4. In faculty interviews, it became clear that many faculty saw a refusal to fund faculty salaries and to thus grant faculty "released time" to do Athena work as "Project Athena Policy," especially during the early years. They were interpreting decisions by one or more of the faculty review committees which gave this as a rationale for not funding proposals. Athena's Executive Committee, however, never officially adopted this policy which emerged nevertheless, as what Donald Schon refers to as a "policy-in-use."

5. For a discussion and critique of this position from a feminist perspective see Ruth Bleir, ed., *Feminist Approaches to Science* (New York: Pergamon, 1986), Sandra Harding and Merrill B. Hintikka, eds., *Discovering Reality: Feminist Perspectives on Epistemology, Metaphysics, Methodology, and Philosophy of Science* (London: Reidel, 1983) and Evelyn Fox Keller, *Reflections on Gender and Science* (New Haven: Yale University Press, 1985).

6. On the theme of closeness to the object as a style of doing science see Evelyn Fox Keller, *A Feeling for the Organism: The Life and Work of Barbara McClintock* (San Francisco: W. H. Freeman, 1983).

7. A sample of relevant studies is provided by Karin Knorr-Cetina and Michael Mulkay, eds., *Science Observed: Perspectives on the Social Studies of Science* (London: Sage Publications, 1983). See also Karin Knorr-Cetina, *The Manufacture of Knowledge: An Essay on the Constructivist and Contextual Nature of Science* (Oxford: Pergamon, 1981); Bruno Latour and Stephen Woolgar, *Laboratory Life: The Social Construction of Scientific Facts* (Beverly Hills, CA: Sage, 1979).

8. Claude Levi-Strauss, *The Savage Mind* (Chicago: University of Chicago Press, 1968). In his contrast of bricolage with Western science Levi-Strauss ignored the significant aspects of bricolage in the latter. Recent writers have written about Western science in a way that begins to redress this imbalance. See, for example, Paul Feyerabend, *Against Method: The Outline of an Anarchistic Theory of Knowledge* (London: NLB, 1975) and N. R. Hanson, *Patterns of Discovery* (Cambridge: Cambridge University Press, 1958). In a less formal vein, see

Richard Feynman, *Surely You're Joking, Mr. Feynman* (New York: Norton, 1985).

9. For a more explicit discussion of computer "style" and the issue of personal appropriation, see Sherry Turkle, *The Second Self: Computers and the Human Spirit* (New York: Simon and Schuster, 1984) and Sherry Turkle and Seymour Papert, "Epistemological Pluralism: Styles and Voices Within the Computer Culture," *Signs: Journal of Women in Culture and Society* 16, 1 (Autumn 1990).

10. For an explicit discussion of the relationship between bricolage as a style and a preference for transparent understanding, see Turkle and Papert, "Epistemological Pluralism."

11. Because of the gift from two vendors, MIT was divided into two camps. The Schools of Science and Humanities and Social Sciences would get IBM equipment; the engineers would get machines from Digital.

12. It is important to note that Negele is reporting a version of the situation at Cal Tech based on the experience of one colleague whose freedom he envied. But Cal Tech itself has been involved in serious battles over the rights to educational software produced using its resources. Negele's version of "the Cal Tech Plan" is most usefully read as a screen on which he can project his vision of the ideal institutional structure for innovation in educational computing.

13. Although 35 sophomores signed a petition asking Negele to teach computational physics, only ten of them were able to fit this elective into their schedules because the Physics Department had just added a new required subject for majors. Cal Tech required students to take courses that used educational computing, while at MIT, Athena courses are electives and with rare exceptions, electives are doomed to low enrollments. Negele suggests that subjects which use educational computing be made requirements for graduation. "Students could choose among what was available — the Architecture students might tend to go one way, the Physics students another." But as students "made one or more natural couplings," faculty who had put in the time and effort would know that there was a clientele for their work.

14. See note 4.

15. From 1985, Athena commissioned surveys of patterns of student use, done by Karen Cohen, Principal Research Associate. They appeared as "Project Athena Impact Study Reports."

16. This was not true in all departments. In Chemistry, for example, projects suffered because the most advanced equipment was late or never arrived. See Sherry Turkle and Brenda Nielsen, "Chemistry" in Turkle et al., "Project Athena at MIT."

17. "Project Athena Faculty-Student Projects," *MIT Bulletin*, March 1985.

Index of Key Terms

The MIT Press, with Peter Denning as general consulting editor, publishes computer science books in the following series:

ACL-MIT Press Series in Natural Language Processing
Aravind K. Joshi, Karen Sparck Jones, and Mark Y. Liberman, editors

ACM Doctoral Dissertation Award and Distinguished Dissertation Series

Artificial Intelligence
Patrick Winston, founding editor
J. Michael Brady, Daniel G. Bobrow, and Randall Davis, editors

Charles Babbage Institute Reprint Series for the History of Computing
Martin Campbell-Kelly, editor

Computer Systems
Herb Schwetman, editor

Explorations with Logo
E. Paul Goldenberg, editor

Foundations of Computing
Michael Garey and Albert Meyer, editors

History of Computing
I. Bernard Cohen and William Aspray, editors

Logic Programming
Ehud Shapiro, editor; Fernando Pereira, Koichi Furukawa, Jean-Louis Lassez, and David H. D. Warren, associate editors

The MIT Press Electrical Engineering and Computer Science Series

Research Monographs in Parallel and Distributed Processing
Christopher Jesshope and David Klappholz, editors

Scientific and Engineering Computation
Janusz Kowalik, editor

Technical Communication and Information Systems
Edward Barrett, editor